FOUNDAT ~~ION~~
ACCOUNTING

by Tony Hines

L

Re

2oP

© T. HINES 1986, 1987, 1990

First published in Great Britain 1986 by Checkmate Publications.
Reprinted in 1987.

Second edition published in Great Britain 1990
Checkmate Publications, PO Box 585, Deeside, Clwyd. CH5 2DE.

British Library Cataloguing in Publication Data
Hines, Tony
Foundation accounting.
1. Accounting
I. Title   II. Series
657   HS5635

ISBN 1 85313 059 1

Text set in 10/11 pt Univers
by Merseyside Graphics Ltd., 130 The Parade, Meols, Wirral L47 5AZ.
Printed by Alden Press Ltd., Osney Mead, Oxford OX2 OEF.

Cover design by Merseyside Graphics Ltd.

CONTENTS

Chapter	Page

PREFACE to the second edition

The purpose of this text is to provide a very thorough introduction to Financial and Cost Accounting for professional foundation examinations. It does not, however, assume any previous knowledge or level of competence and the earlier chapters in the text are designed to introduce newcomers to the basic concepts of accounting.

A major concern of most people studying accounting for the first time is the terminology. Accounting is the language of business. To assist students I have included a comprehensive glossary of terms such that space would allow in a text of this size.

The emphasis throughout the text has been to explain concepts in clear, precise terms and to illustrate the concepts where appropriate using examples which avoid unnecessary complications and inordinately large numbers. Neither does anything to help a student's understanding of the subject.

The second edition has been thoroughly revised and extended to reflect the emphasis in the professional foundation examinations and to include some additional topics that have been requested by professional tutors using the book for the Chartered Institute of Management Accountants foundation paper in accounting; The Chartered Association of Accountants level one papers and the Association of Accounting Technicians Final level.

There are many questions throughout the text some of which are self-check and some with answers in the text. There is also a bank of multiple choice questions with answers at the back of the book. Some questions are included which have previously appeared in the examination papers of the following professional bodies:-

> The Institute of Chartered Accountants in England & Wales (ICAEW)
> The Chartered Institute of Management Accountants (CIMA)
> The Chartered Association of Certified Accountants (ACCA)
> The Association of Accounting Technicians (AAT)
> The Chartered Institute of Bankers (IOB)
> The Chartered Institute of Secretaries and Administrators (ICSA)

all of whom gave permission for previous examination questions to be used. These bodies are not responsible for any of the solutions provided since these are the sole responsibility of the author.

Finally, I am pleased to see the book in its second edition, having firmly established itself on many reading lists for professional and academic courses world-wide.

Tony Hines 1990

HOW TO USE THE QUESTIONS IN THIS BOOK

This book contains four types of questions:-

1. Self-Check where appropriate to ensure that readers grasp important concepts before progressing to examination, numerical type questions.

2. Those marked with an X where the answer is excluded from the text are suitable to try when you are confident with the topic.

3. Those marked with a Q where once again answers are not provided in this text but are available in fully worked style in Questions and Answers in Accounting by the same author, published by Checkmate Publications.

4. Those not marked have answers provided either fully or in list format at the end of the text.

5. Multiple choice questions in Appendix ii. on page 555 with answers on page 567.

Although every effort has been made by the author to include as many and varied questions as is possible in the text it is essential that the student obtains up-to-date papers from the appropriate examining body together with the examiner's report, taking note of the comments.

This will ensure that a serious student intending to pass the examination is fully equipped to do so. You should remember that examiners are human and although they work within guidelines that the emphasis in examination papers may well reflect their interest or 'pet hobby horse' so by reading up-to-date papers and the journals of the relevant body you will be able to gain insight to current thinking.

ACCOUNTANCY AS A PROFESSION
– history and development

FROM BARTER TO MONEY

Although economic transactions have been recorded for many hundreds of years as evidenced by pre-christian documents about trade, biblical records and feudal accounts of trading; accountancy as a profession is a recent phenomenon. Man has always kept records of what he owns, owes and is owed by others even if it has not always been recorded in written form or in monetary terms. Barter was the original basis of exchanging one's goods or services in return for receiving someone else's goods or services at agreed units. For example, maybe two sheep would be exchanged for one cow or three hens for one sheep and so on. The problem with barter as a means of exchange is that measuring value was difficult and although you may wish to exchange your surplus of goods or services immediately you may not wish to accept in return what the other person has to offer. You may wish to defer your receipt to a future date. Thus early traders quickly devised a more satisfactory method of exchanging goods and services by using base metals such as gold or silver as a common medium of exchange and later such metals became the foundations for monetary units which we now have in coin and paper form. Maybe we are now witnessing a further change in the development of money from coins and paper to a series of electrical signals representing credits and debits to personal incomes and wealth with the advancement of new technology, the developments of plastic cards (Visa, Access, Master-charge, American Express, Diner's Club, various other bank cards etc.,); bar codes signalling values on goods and so on.

FUNCTIONS OF MONEY

The use of money in whatever form was a useful development to enable trade to be transacted more efficiently and more quickly. Money has the following advantages over barter: It is
a)   A medium of exchange that is commonly acceptable.
b)   A common measure of value; nearly everything can be measured in monetary terms.
c)   A means of deferring payment since you can agree to pay a specific sum of money at a future date.
d)   A store of wealth such that if you do not wish to make a purchase at the same time you sell you can store your wealth in money until such time that you do wish to buy.

RECORDING TRANSACTIONS

With the advent of money it was easier to record business transactions in units of currency. In the fifteenth century an Italian Monk, Luca Paciola, developed and refined a system for recording business transactions of the monastery in its wine trading which was to form the basis for recording all business transactions world-wide and became known as double-entry bookkeeping. The idea behind the system was quite simply that if you record the reality of any financial transaction one party receives something in exchange for something that is given and hence you record the transaction twice which should also prevent a transaction from being overlooked or forgotten about. For example, when a sale is made you give goods on which you have placed a value in exchange for money (or a claim to money – a debtor who will pay at some future date) and hence cash is received to that sale value. Double entry book-keeping would record the transaction thus:-

---

DEBIT   – CASH / BANK Account with the receipt of value
           — OR DEBTOR Account if credit has been allowed

CREDIT   — SALES REVENUE Account for the value of goods
             given.

So it was that all financial transactions could be recorded in this way using this system of debits and credits. Debit simply means the left hand side of the account and credit the right hand side of the account. Thus for every transaction there must be one debit entry and one credit entry and the sum of all debit and credit entries should always agree if the recording has been consistent. This is tested by extracting what accountants call the Trial Balance. As you will learn later in your studies this does not always mean that the debits and credits have been entered into the correct types of account.

THE FIRST PROFESSIONAL ACCOUNTANTS

Accountants were those people who became skilled in using the system of double entry book-keeping and could use their skill to collect, classify and record financial transactions to determine what the venture owned, was owed by others outside the venture and owed to others outside the venture. In drawing up financial statements they were able to compile:

a)   A list of what was owned; owed by the venture and owed to the venture at a point in time. This is what we now call THE BALANCE SHEET.

b)   A Statement showing revenue and expenses incurred in a period to show profits or losses incurred on the venture. This is what we now call the PROFIT AND LOSS ACCOUNT.

THE EARLY TRADERS

Originally most business ventures were set up for a specific time period with a specific purpose in mind. Once the venture was completed the profits would be distributed usually in cash to each of the adventurers in accordance with the agreed split which would usually be determined by the amount of capital contributed by each adventurer, the knowledge and skill contributed by each adventurer and the amount of work undertaken by each party to the venture. Sea voyages to acquire spices in the orient and sell them back home give a good example of the type and nature of such ventures. Ships could be purpose built for the one venture or series of ventures or they could be rented from owners – usually Captains prepared to buy ships on the off chance of them and their ships being hired for such ventures. At the conclusion of the voyage the ship if owned could be sold to other adventurers requiring ships, hired to other adventurers or retained for a future venture.

The structure of business organizations for such ventures would take one of the following forms:

a) Sole trader (for example the owner captain taking the business risk for a specific purpose).

b) Partnership (a group of individuals forming a partnership for a specific venture).

c) Joint Venture (similar to a partnership but this time rather than individuals forming one single partnership a joint venture might consist of a grouping of various other partnerships and/or sole traders to undertake a specific task).

There were no such things as limited companies prior to the nineteenth century and so if you entered a venture for profit you risked everything you owned in the venture. Not a problem if you were successful but one failure could be enough to remove all your personal wealth gained from a number of previous successes.

As international trade developed so too did the scale of the ventures they became more costly to mount and hence risks became higher for the individuals with enough wealth to mount the ventures. A series of financial disasters made adventurers reluctant to take such personal risks. To encourage both more risk taking by entrepreneurs and more venture capital to finance new ventures a new form of business ownership was devised to remove personal risk from business risk. It was called the JOINT STOCK COMPANY. The idea behind the joint stock company was that parties to the company called shareholders would take a stake in the company entitling them to a share of the profits of the company equivalent to the proportion of money they put in to the company in proportion to the total share capital of the business. For example, if the total share capital of the company was to be £100 and you decided to risk £10 in the venture you would receive a proportion of the profit equivalent to your risk which in this case is:- £10/£100 = 1/10. If the venture was unsuccessful the most the individual shareholder could lose in this case would be the £10 stake he agreed to subscribe to the company.

DEVELOPMENT OF TRADE

As the industrial revolution gathered momentum and the need for capital became greater and the strive for increased productivity and output developed so too, more and more businesses organized themselves as Joint-Stock (stock = share) Companies which we now refer to as LIMITED COMPANIES. Three important developments followed:

1)   Limited Companies tended to be used for more than one venture and hence this type of business organization lasted much longer than had any previous types of business venture with the exception of say individual sole traders.

2)   Not only were limited companies lasting much longer but they tended to be able to undertake much larger projects than previous forms of organization.

3)   Not only was liability of the members (the Shareholders') limited to the amount they had agreed to subscribe in the form of share capital to the venture but the members themselves were not necessarily the managers of the business. Owners they were; managers not necessarily although some could be if they wished. The concept of the Professional Manager was born with the creation of the Stock Exchange to facilitate the provision of venture capital from those people prepared to take a risk with their capital in return for a share of the profit in the venture but without necessarily being involved with managing the venture. The management was left to those with the knowledge and skills in the product, process or market place to run the business. The owners (shareholders) would appoint professional managers to manage the business on their behalf. Success or failure of their appointments would be judged by the return on their capital invested reported by managers in the form of Annual Financial Statements (Accounts) presented to the shareholders' at the annual general meeting of the company.

THE NEED FOR PROFESSIONAL ACCOUNTANTS

The need developed for more people having the necessary skills to prepare and present financial statements. With the development of joint-stock companies it was inevitable that a regulatory framework for controlling their activities should also develop. A system of Company Law developed placing restrictions on activities of companies in the light of experience with dealing with companies and to protect investors who had been misled and de-frauded by the unscrupulous managers of some limited companies. One such requirement important to the development of the Accounting Profession was that of the limited company subjecting itself to an annual audit (check as to the truth and fairness of the annual financial statements presented by the company) by an independent accountant, that is, one who did not prepare the accounts for the company.

A BRIEF HISTORY OF PROFESSIONAL BODIES

The first professional body of accountants was established in the 1860's in the U.K. It was the Institute of Chartered Accountants in Scotland and was later followed by The Institute of Chartered Accountants in England & Wales and The Institute of Chartered Accountants of Ireland. These bodies served the purpose of members who were now establishing themselves as individuals or partnerships concerned with auditing limited company accounts. Through the interchange of ideas professional standards of practice were being established. Training for membership of these bodies became established on a similar basis to the legal profession whereby students of practitioners served a period of articles for which they paid or were paid very little in return for acquiring the knowledge and skills of accountancy from their masters such that they would be able to undertake office as auditor to these newly established and growing number of limited companies.

Later the Association of Certified and Corporate Accountants (nowadays known as The Chartered Association of Certified Accountants) was formed to provide an opportunity for those people wishing to train as accountants who did not have sufficient personal wealth to undertake articles in practice or who wished to train not in public practice but rather in commerce or industry. This Association is an international body and has members from overseas as well as the U.K. mainly in the Commonwealth Countries. In 1919 The Institute of Cost and Works Accountants was formed to provide an institution exclusively devoted to the needs of those accountants working in industry and in particular in costing. Today the Chartered Institute of Management Accountants is the name of the institute and states as its main objectives:- 1) to promote and develop the science of cost and management accountancy and 2) to provide a professional organization for cost and management accountants. It too is an international body once again operating mainly in the old Commonwealth countries. Finally of the six chartered bodies which are part of the Consultative Committee for Accounting Bodies (CCAB) in the U.K. there is the Chartered Institute of Public Finance and Accounting originally the Institute of Municipal Treasurers. It is the smallest of the chartered bodies with about 12,000 members all of whose members work mainly in local government, national government or for public authorities or nationalized or public industries.

In addition to the six chartered bodies there are a number of smaller professional bodies of accountants which developed to fulfil the needs of their members. Some of these bodies are quite old and well established and one should not be misled into thinking that their membership is any less qualified than some of the chartered bodies. The largest of these non-chartered bodies is The Institute of Financial Accountants originally established as the Institute of Book-keepers in 1916. It was the first body of professional accountants to represent solely the interests of internal commercial and industrial accountants in the U.K. The institute is an international body once again operating mainly in the old Commonwealth countries. Today it has over 10,000 members. There is the Society of Company and Commercial Accountants formed in 1927 with over 7,000 members. There is the Association of International Accountants with some 2,000 members and the Association of Cost & Executive Accountants with a membership in excess of 2,000.

In addition to the chartered six and the non-chartered four there is the Association of Accounting Technicians which was set up by sponsorship from five of the chartered bodies (not the Irish body) Institute of Chartered Accountants in Scotland, England and Wales; the Chartered Association of Certified Accountants and the Chartered Institute of Management Accountants; the Chartered Institute of Public Finance & Accountancy to provide a second tier body of professional support staff in accounting and finance. There are currently over 12,000 members and some 30,000 students. Qualification for entry to this new professional grouping is by examination and experience. It is the only professional body to represent accounting technicians worldwide.

If you are now confused by the proliferation of professional accounting bodies in the U.K., it is worth noting that we are unique in our position of having such a large number of professional accountancy bodies. If you consider further that there are other professional bodies whose members are trained in accountancy (for example: The Institute of Chartered Secretaries and Administrators) and a large number of people qualified by experience who may not have any formal education or professional qualification but who nevertheless may as part of their job perform accounting duties then it becomes even more so.

AUDITING AND ACCOUNTANTS

The only bodies of professional accountants authorized by the Department of Trade to perform the audit of limited companies are: The Institute of Chartered Accountants in England & Wales (members use designatory letters ACA or FCA); The Institute of Chartered Accountants Scotland (CA); The Chartered Association of Certified Accountants (ACCA or FCCA).

From time to time the Department of Trade may authorize those accountants having similar overseas qualifications where reciprocation is usually a requirement for granting license. The name accountant is not restricted in its use to those who are members of professional bodies although there are and have been moves afoot to restrict the term especially in the light of changes taking place with regard to the European Economic Community's (EEC) eighth directive.

WHAT ACCOUNTANTS DO

The work that accountants tend to do regardless of how they qualified tends to be varied and could fall into one of the following categories:

1) Audit work (usually ACA/FCA; ACCA/FCCA; or CA)
2) Taxation
3) Insolvency
4) Treasurership
5) Financial Accounting
6) Management Accounting
7) Costing
8) Internal Audit
9) Company Secretarial
10) Financial Management
11) Other Management
12) Corporate Finance
13) Management Consultancy
14) Education & Training

THE FUTURE FOR PROFESSIONALS

It is interesting to note developments in the changing requirements of the institutes regarding training and experience and their attempts to obtain an ideal mix to equip recruits to the profession with the skills they will need in future. The emphasis has been placed for example upon information technology and continuing education for members to update their knowledge and skills, with the threat of competition from other professions and from new technologies performing traditional roles such as book-keeping and financial management more quickly and in providing opportunities for those without traditional skills in accountancy to use the tools and techniques which were once the sacrosanct province of the professional accountant. Major firms of chartered accountants now earn a high proportion of their total fee income from providing other services such as management consultancy and the share of incomes from this and other sources apart from traditional audit work appears to be growing. The language used to describe tomorrow's Chartered Accountants in the journal of the Institute of Chartered Accountants in England & Wales in December 1987 was "training the business professional"; words like multi-disciplinary and commercial awareness are used to describe the types of skill required by tomorrow's accountants. At the same time there is similar concern in other professions, for example law, where traditional markets have been eroded through more open competition and revised legislation. The British Institute of Management and its charter group have also been considering the training required by tomorrow's managers to create the Chartered Manager. So it can be seen that as the needs of business and commerce change so too must the professional bodies adapt and be flexible enough to provide the services required by the new structures. The new Financial Services Act; the Insolvency Act 1986; the Companies Act

1985; E.E.C. legislation; New Stock Exchange requirements; the changing structure of the U.K. Economy and the international economy (changes in world banking practices etc.); changes in the socio-political structure; changes in education; Financial scandals (insider dealing); investor protection and so on will all have an effect on the accounting profession. It may be time again for the professional bodies in the U.K. to consider merger or closer co-operation to protect all their interests in the face of external hostility. Are we witnessing the winds of change?

ACCOUNTING THEORY AND PRACTICE

One final point; although most professions have their roots in theory and the practice developed from the theory, with accounting the practice came first and now the profession is searching for its theoretical roots. University courses in Accounting and Finance have become more prevalent during the past twenty or thirty years in the U.K. following the patterns established by the U.S. universities. It is interesting to note that many of these courses developed within faculties or departments of economics and that is where you would expect accounting to have its roots. It is after all applied economics; it is the recording, classifying and recording of economic transactions for an organization which is then reported and communicated to those parties having an interest in the statements.

SUMMARY OF DESIGNATORY LETTERS OF ACCOUNTANCY BODIES

Membership of a professional body of accountants entitles the member to use designatory letters after his or her name to show their affiliation. There are usually two grades of membership which are: associateship and fellowship. Associates prefix membership with an A and Fellows with an F. Fellowship is the highest grade of membership and is intended to recognise greater experience. It is more expensive in terms of annual subscription but does not carry any extra benefits than that of associate apart from recognition.

The Institute of Chartered Accountants in England and Wales (ACA or FCA)
The Institute of Chartered Accountants in Scotland (CA)
The Institute of Chartered Accountants in Ireland (ACA or FCA)
The Chartered Association of Certified Accountants (ACCA or FCCA)
The Chartered Institute of Management Accountants (ACMA or FCMA)
The Chartered Institute of Public Finance and Accounting (IPFA)
(the above are members of the CCAB)
The Institute of Financial Accountants (AFA or FFA)
The Society of Company and Commercial Accountants (ASCA or FSCA)
The Association of International Accountants (AIAA or FAIA)
The Association of Cost and Executive Accountants (ACEA or FCEA)
Technician Grade
The Association of Accounting Technicians (MAAT or SAAT)
M = Member   S = Senior

THE BUSINESS ENVIRONMENT
– types of business activity

THE BUSINESS ENVIRONMENT

To understand the language of business which is accounting it is essential to understand the environment in which business is carried out. There are two aspects it is important to grasp which are:

a)   Types of business activity
b)   Types of organization structure

TYPES OF BUSINESS ACTIVITY

The type of business activity will and should determine the need for appropriate methods of recording financial transactions and in preparing financial statements which are useful and meaningful to the type of business concerned it is necessary for accountants to fully understand the nature and purpose of the organization upon whom the report is being made.

Businesses can be classified as falling into one or more of the following standard business groupings:

a)   Primary Producers. Farming and Agriculture together with fishing and mining excavation would fall into this category of primary producer. Natural resources are being exploited to provide an income. It is the most basic and most traditional of human economic activity.

b)   Manufacturing. A manufacturer be he a car maker; a tin can maker; paint producer; producer of clothes or whatever converts raw materials of steel, plastic, glass, tin, oil, fabrics etc., into finished goods for sale to wholesalers, retailers or directly to the public which may be for the home market or for export. You should note that what may be classified as raw material to one producer may well be classified as a finished manufactured good by another. For example: Flour is the finished product sold by a flour miller but to a baker it is the raw material from which bread is made.

c)   Service business. Services do not manufacture finished products for sale but rather provide a service to the customer which usually provide immediate benefits. A service is consumed as soon as it is provided. For example if you have your hair cut this is a service which brings immediate benefit to the consumer which may be style, smartness or simply a feeling of well-being. A travel agent offers the consumer the benefit of a holiday in return for money. A holiday is not manufactured; it does not have to be made from raw materials and it is normally taken in a particular resort that exists whether or not tourists call. The travel agent normally sells a package which has been put together by a tour operator to provide certain benefits perceived as desirable by the customer. For example: a hotel with swimming pool; shower, colour T.V., and sea view; first class service; sunshine; and various amenities within easy reach of the hotel. Theatres provide a service, a pleasurable evening's entertainment out of the home. Transport services provide people with seats, comfortable or functional, depending on what you are prepared to pay to wherever you want to go. In these last two cases where plays are scheduled or transportation is scheduled then of course if seats are not filled at scheduled times by paying customers then the service has failed to generate income for its providers. You can think of other services such as: insurance, banking, accountancy, taxation, auditing, management consultancy, training, education, legal, surveying, recruitment and job agencies, restaurants, hotels, cafes etc.

c) Non-Profit making Organizations. These exist to provide benefits to members and not to make a profit. They do however need to generate income to incur the expenditure in providing the range of services to members. Income for such societies, clubs and professional institutions or associations may be attracted from various sources such as: members' subscriptions, trading activities undertaken by the organization (bar trading, food services, publications, jumble sales etc.), Dances, Dinners, Social Functions and Donations.

d) Wholesalers. A wholesaler is a trader who will buy goods from manufacturers and primary producers at home or from abroad dealing direct or with import agencies in order to pass on those goods and services to retailers for re-sale by the retailer to the final consumer. The price paid by the wholesaler will be less than the price charged to the retailer and hence the wholesaler is able to make a profit ('a turn from the transaction'). The goods sold by the wholesaler do not change form when they are passed on and the important function of the wholesaler is essentially the ability to break bulk by buying large quantities and distributing in smaller quantities to retailers.

e) Retailers. The retailer is a trader in goods or services and most people are familiar with this form of business activity since it is the most likely contact group for the public at large. Retailers may trade in various goods and services; one only has to think of the high street shops and chains such as W.H. Smith where you might have bought this book or Marks & Spencer, Next, Principles, Travel Agents and so on. The retailer will normally buy from a wholesaler at a lower price than the price charged for the goods or services provided in the shop. The difference in price is often referred to as the retailer's "mark-up", a term with which you will become more familiar as you read later sections of the book. You should note that some retailers may well buy direct from the manufacturer or primary producer to cut out the wholesaler ("the middle man") in the hope to earn higher profits. Furthermore, some retailers are themselves wholesalers too, such as W.H. Smiths; the Co-op; ASDA etc.

EXPANSION AND GROWTH OF BUSINESS

A business may wish to earn higher profits from its business activities and as a result attempt to expand its areas of activity. For example, a retailer may decide to become a wholesaler in the goods it supplies since it has already a number of outlets for the products which form a substantial percentage of the total market. This change in structure is referred to as integration and in this case it is called vertical integration. If on the other hand the business decided to expand by entering a totally different area of retailing activity, say from clothes to perfumes, then it is referred to as horizontal integration. The business has integrated with another business at the same stage of activity — retailing.

In the case of vertical integration this may be forward or backward. Forward vertical integration would be the case of a business integrating from primary to manufacture to wholesale to retail.

INTEGRATION OF BUSINESS ACTIVITY

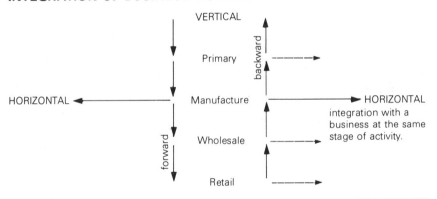

FORMS OF BUSINESS ORGANIZATION

The form a business organization adopts depends on its ownership, its purpose and its resources. The accounting requirements and the presentation of financial statements will take account of the form the business takes.

A business may be organized as:-

a)   Sole Trader
b)   Partnership
c)   Private Limited Company
d)   Public Limited Company
e)   Unincorporated Associations
f)   Public Ownership

The different types of financial statement necessary for the different forms of organization will be discussed in the relevant chapter.

SELF-CHECK QUESTIONS
1. Name the six types of business activity discussed in this chapter.
2. A business may achieve growth in a number of ways; name two ways.
3. A business which expands by merging with other businesses at the same stage of activity is said to have _____ integrated.
4. A business which merges with other businesses at different stages of business activity is said to have _____ integrated.
5. Describe briefly what is meant by forward integration and backward integration.
6. Briefly state three forms of business organization and ownership.

THE NATURE AND PURPOSE OF ACCOUNTING
– uses, users and information

THE ACCOUNTING FUNCTION

Definition: Accounting has been defined in different ways, below are the most commonly used definitions:-

"The accounting function is to record, classify and report financial information to satisfy users of financial information – e.g. managers, employee groups, shareholders, creditors and external agencies such as the Inland Revenue, H.M. Customs and Excise, the Department of Trade and Industry, etc".

The above definition essentially describes the stewardship function of FINANCIAL ACCOUNTING. Financial accounting is concerned with reporting financial data in order to meet the diverse requirements of the user groups described in the definition. It is also concerned with compliance; compliance with company law (The Companies Act 1985); compliance with Statements of Standard Accounting Practice; compliance with International Accounting Standards and the generally accepted principles upon which all financial statements should be prepared; compliance with stock exchange requirements, if applicable. Historically the major concern of FINANCIAL STEWARDSHIP was to safeguard the assets of the business.

"Accounting is to communicate the economic performance of the enterprise to those who wish to use financial information to plan control and take decisions to achieve stated goals".

This second definition is essentially concerned with using accounting information as the basis of managing the enterprise. It can be seen, therefore, that there are two major strands to the accounting function; one mainly concerned with financial stewardship and reporting to comply with various rules and regulations imposed upon the organisation and one mainly concerned with providing information to those whose function it is to manage the organisation. It should, however, be remembered that both these accounting functions may and do overlap. The base information although used for different purposes will be from the same source.

ACCOUNTING AS PART OF THE TOTAL INFORMATION SYSTEM

The accounting function should be considered as part of the total management information system for the organisation as a whole. Indeed the accounting function will have recorded a great deal of data which, if classified, allocated and applied to particular management problems could be used to help achieve a solution which is optimum (the best one). It should be noted that quantitative information may be only part of the solution, albeit a major part and that qualitative factors should also be considered.

OBJECTIVES OF FINANCIAL STATEMENTS

People usually want to know a number of things: how well they have done, how much money they owe and what is owed to them by others outside the business. Those are the fundamental things with which people are concerned with when using financial statements. It should be stressed at this stage that accounting is more than just bookkeeping, although bookkeeping is an essential part of the system. Bookkeeping was developed by Luca Pacioli, a Venetian monk, and his book on the subject was published in 1494. The double entry system is probably the most logical system that there could be for recording economic events, which after all is what we are concerned with as accountants. The definition given by the American Accounting Association (A.A.A.) in 1966 was "The process of identifying, measuring and communicating economic information to permit informed judgements and decisions by users of the information."

Who, then, are the users of financial information? The users may be defined in two categories. First of all, there are those people within an organisation, the managers of the organisation, who will want financial information so that they can plan and control the direction of the business. Secondly, there are users outside of the organisation who will wish to use published financial information in order to make their own decisions.

EXTERNAL USERS OF FINANCIAL INFORMATION

Let us first of all look at those users from outside the organisation. In 1975, a document called the Corporate Report was published by the English accounting bodies which identified a number of users of financial information. The categories which this report defined were as follows:

1. **The shareholders,** and this included not just those people who already held shares in the organisation, but potential shareholders of that particular organisation.

2. **The creditors** of the organisation, and this included potential holders of debentures and loan stock together with the actual holders of debentures and loan stock.

3. **The employees** of the organisation, which again included potential employees as well as past and existing employees.

4. **The analyst advisor group,** as the report called it, which included financial analysts, economists, journalists, researchers, trade unions, stockbrokers, statisticians, insurance and credit rating agencies and so on.

5. **The business contact group** which included customers, trade

creditors, competitors, business rivals and those interested in mergers and amalgamations or takeovers.

6. **The government,** who would be interested for a number of reasons: for example, the Inland Revenue for tax purposes, the Department of Trade and Industry for statistics, and Local Government, who would be interested in organisations operating within their locality.

7. **The public at large,** which included taxpayers, ratepayers, consumers, other interest groups such as political parties, ratepayers' associations, environmental protection groups and regional pressure groups.

It is generally accepted that all these people have an interest in the use of published financial information.

INTERNAL USE OF FINANCIAL INFORMATION

Management Accounting

Management accounting is defined by the Institute of Cost and Management Accountants in their official terminology as follows: The provision of information required by management for such purposes as

i)   formulation of policies
ii) planning and controlling the activities of the enterprise
iii) decision-taking on alternative courses of action
iv) disclosure to those external to the entity (shareholders and others)
v)   disclosure to employees
vi) safeguarding assets.

The above involves participation in management to ensure that there is effective:-

a) formulation of plans to meet objectives (long-term planning)
b) formulation of short-term operation plans (budgeting/profit planning)
c) recording of actual transactions (financial accounting and cost accounting)
d) corrective action to bring future actual transactions into line with long and short-term plans (financial control)
e) obtaining and controlling finance (treasurship)
f) reviewing and reporting on systems and operations (internal audit, management audit).

It can be seen from this definition that management accounting and financial accounting overlap and as such they should not be treated in total isolation from each other. Both published and unpublished sources of information are used in effective management accounting.

Accounting in its widest sense is the effective communication of economic information about the organisation's performance to user groups. In order therefore to achieve this objective, the statements need to be presented in a suitable format relevant to each user group. This is partly the reason why firms produce a separate report for employees about the organisation's economic performance. Pie charts and graphs are among the methods used to present significant financial information in simple terms in order to convey a measure of performance to the employees of the organisation. Performance, however, is not the only reason for wishing to convey information. Of course, published information is not wholly going to satisfy the needs of the users. However, since we live in an imperfect world and perfect information is not forthcoming then we have to make do with the best possible information we can obtain. The following list gives some of the reasons why users may wish to have information about an organisation, and these were identified in the Corporate Report. (Accounting Standards Committee 1975).

REASONS FOR WANTING FINANCIAL INFORMATION
— A CHECKLIST

Performance measures

To evaluate the performance of the entity.

To assess the effectiveness of the entity in achieving objectives which have been established by the management, the shareholders, the owners (if not shareholders) or by society.

To evaluate the management performance, for example, how effective and efficient has management been in achieving objectives which may affect employment, investment or profit distribution.

To obtain information about the experience of company directors and the officials in the organisation.

Financial position

To assess the financial and economic stability of the reporting organisation. How vulnerable is the organisation to merger or takeover bids, or indeed to closure?

To assess the liquidity of the enterprise, and to obtain a picture of the future requirements for additional fixed and working capital. How able is it to raise long and short term finance?

To assess the capacity of the enterprise to adapt to the external environmental demands placed upon it, either economic or social or political. For example, is the enterprise able to deal with and respond to economic, social or political pressures by re-allocating resources? For example, if an entity has branches overseas and an overseas country decides to expropriate (take over the assets of the company by nationalisation), then how flexible will the organisation be in re-structuring or re-allocating its resources in order to deal with such an event?

Future prospects

Some users will wish to analyse the future prospects of the entity; for example, shareholders will wish to know the capacity of the organization to pay a dividend, both presently and in the future. They may also wish to know if there is going to be any dividend growth. Employees will wish to know how remuneration is going to change in the future. Both shareholders and employees may wish to know how future cash flows will change in order to predict future levels of investment, output and employment.

Comparisons

Some users will wish to make economic comparisons either for the same entity over a given number of years or for the entity against other similar enterprises in the same or different industries.

Segmented information

Some users will wish to assess the performance of a particular unit within the organization as a whole. For this reason they may wish to focus on a particular subsidiary or associated company within a group.

Compliance with legal and social requirements

Some users of financial reports will wish to ensure that company law is adhered to or other legal requirements which the enterprise should observe are being followed. In addition the Inland Revenue, for example, would wish to ensure that tax regulations are being observed.

Certain pressure groups may wish to know whether the entity is acting in the interests of society as a whole. Other organizations such as the government and some of its departments, may wish to ensure that the organization is acting in the national interest. For example, a company producing weapons would not be acting in the national interest by selling those weapons to enemies during a period of war.

Some other reasons why users may wish to have financial information

In order to evaluate the user or the user group's interest in respect of the entity. For example, will the organization in question have a damaging or beneficial effect on the quality of life of the particular user?

Some people may wish to know who owns and who controls the organization in question, for a variety of reasons.

Some users will wish to know the nature of business that the enterprise undertakes, the types of products produced and the market in which it operates, for instance, certain countries may wish to know where else a particular company is trading, and might ask: is it trading with an enemy nation? Is it trading in countries which are hostile to the interests of the user?

It can be seen from the above that information needs of users are many and varied. The difficulty, of course, is to present financial statements which are meaningful to each of the user groups identified. The objective of the 'Corporate Report' was defined fundamentally to communicate economic measurements of, and information about the resources and performance of the reporting entity useful to those having reasonable rights to such information. This is a valid statement, but meeting this objective is more difficult than would at first appear. The major characteristic of corporate reports must therefore be relevance to the user.

CHARACTERISTICS OF DESIRABLE INFORMATION

1)   **It must be understood by the users.** This does not simply mean that the report must be simple, since that might not be consistent with the complexities of the economic situation being described. It does, however, mean that too much detail must not be disclosed which would obscure the real information content of that report. Too much detail would simply cause a corporate report to be data.

2)   The information contained in financial statements needs to be **reliable, and the users need to place confidence in that information.** Nowadays one of the major purposes of an audit is to provide user confidence in financial statements. Audits are not simply to detect fraud and error, which was their original fundamental purpose.

3)   **The reports need to be objective.** They should not be biased in any way towards or against a particular group.

4)   **They need to be up to date;** therefore the timeliness of a report is important. The more up-to-date the information, the more relevant it obviously is.

5)   **The report needs to be comparable** with other financial statements. In this sense there needs to be consistency in the application of accounting concepts and policies in order to achieve this comparability. Financial statements need to be comparable from one period to the next and from one organization to another.

All these measures were discussed in the Corporate Report published in 1975, and although the corporate report was never given full implementation by the English professional accounting bodies, it certainly still holds a pride of place within those bodies. Perhaps in many ways the ideas contained therein were ahead of their time. Nevertheless it gives us in this text a good starting point from which to consider the uses to which financial information may be put.

PROBLEMS IN PRODUCING DESIRED INFORMATION

There are many practical problems associated with producing the desired information for all the user groups we have identified.

1)   Information understood by one group of users, e.g. shareholders may not be suitable or relevant to another group, employees.

2)   Is the answer therefore to produce many different reports relevant to each user group? This may be the ideal situation, but what of the cost, not only in the preparation of reports but in terms of auditing? All statements would need to be audited to provide user confidence in the reliability of the information provided.

3)   We would need to identify all user groups and ensure that reports provided them with the information they required without bias to any

particular group. How do you achieve equal weighting in objectives of all the different reports which may be required in practice to give a true and fair view?

4) Information may become outdated since it takes so long to produce all the relevant information for each user group.

SELF-CHECK QUESTIONS

1. Give a brief definition of Accounting.
2. State six user groups of external financial accounting information.
3. Briefly distinguish between Financial Accounting and Management Accounting.
4. Give six reasons why people require financial information.
5. Briefly explain the characteristics of desirable information and problems in satisfying those desires.

ACCOUNTING CONCEPTS

– the fundamental principles

These are the rules of the game, and there are a number of concepts which are implicit in drawing up financial statements. For example, only those items which can be measured in monetary terms are recorded in financial statements. Therefore, when communicating economic performance of an organization, we measure its assets and liabilities at a point in time (the balance sheet) and we only record assets measured in terms of money. This may seem strange since some people would regard human resources as a major asset. Indeed, if you consider a football team or a firm of accountants, the footballers or accountants are the most important asset the organization has. Nevertheless, at present human resources are not given a monetary value and are not consequently recorded as such in financial statements. This is the **MONEY MEASUREMENT CONCEPT.**

Furthermore, most financial statements record past events, that is, the Profit and Loss Statement and the Balance Sheet. The value of sales, cost of sales, expenses and assets and liabilities are measured at their bought in (or sold out) value. This is the **HISTORIC COST CONVENTION.** In recent times, however, there have been attempts to take account of changing price levels (see Accounting for Changing Price Levels).

Statement of Standard Accounting Practice 2 (SSAP 2) mentions four major concepts which are considered important in drawing up financial statements. These concepts are:

1. **The Going Concern**
2. **Prudence — conservatism**
3. **Consistency**
4. **The Matching Principle or the Accrual Concept**

THE GOING CONCERN

The idea that the enterprise is a going concern is fundamental to the preparation of financial statements. It simply means that the enterprise will continue in operational existence for the foreseeable future, thus the business is not likely to go into liquidation. If the business were to go into liquidation, the assets on the balance sheet would need to be written down to the amount they would realise in a forced sale situation.

PRUDENCE OR CONSERVATISM

The idea of prudence is two-fold. First of all, any gains must not be included in the accounts until they have been realised or there is a high degree of certainty that they will be realised by receiving the actual cash. In other words, sales or profits must not be anticipated. This is the idea of not counting one's chickens before they are hatched. The second aspect is that of losses. For example, if we know that the enterprise has incurred an expense or we can foresee a loss with a high degree of certainty, then we should take steps immediately to ensure that the financial statements reflect this situation. In other words, we need to take account of the information we have to hand with regard to a particular situation. The way in which we would do so would be to debit the relevant expense account and once again credit a provision for the particular item and the provision would be shown on the balance sheet as a liability, so a provision is a liability account.

CONSISTENCY

There needs to be a consistency in the treatment of similar items from one financial period to the next. Obviously if we were not consistent from period to period then comparison of the financial statements becomes impossible and the economic performance of the firm cannot be assessed. There may be occasions when we break the consistency rule owing to a policy change. For example, a change in depreciation policy. If however we disclose this by way of note, then the two financial periods may still be compared. Therefore, we do to some extent follow the idea of consistency.

THE MATCHING PRINCIPLE OR THE ACCRUALS CONCEPT

This again has two aspects. Firstly, we try to match the using up of a particular asset over the particular life of the asset, as we described with depreciation. Hence, we try to match time, or for example if we rented property then we try to match the rent for the periods for which we rent the property with the accounting periods of the financial statement, so there is an idea of what accountants sometimes call periodicity. If we do try to match the time periods there will be occasions when we have either paid in advance or incurred the expense and not yet paid for it, hence we will have either a pre-payment or an accrual. A pre-payment is something we have paid in advance, an accrual is an expense we have incurred but not yet been invoiced or paid for. A pre-payment is classified as a current asset and would be shown immediately below debtors on the balance sheet. The relevant expense account in the profit and loss statement would be reduced by the amount the enterprise had pre-paid. The bookkeeping entry for pre-payment would therefore be as follows:

Debit the Pre-payments Account (Balance Sheet –
Current Assets)
Credit the relevant Expense Account (Profit & Loss)

The bookkeeping entry for an accrual would be:

> **Debit** the relevant Expense Account (Profit & Loss)
> **Credit** Accruals (Balance Sheet – Current Liabilities)

In addition to matching time we also try to match the costs of making a particular item or selling a particular item with the revenue, that is the sales income earned in a period or from the product. Thus we try to match cost and revenue. This then gives us a good idea of our profitability on a particular item that we sell.

Those, then, are the four major accounting concepts discussed in Statement of Standard Accounting Practice number 2. There are at least seven other items which are often thought of as important accounting concepts, which are dealt with below.

THE ENTITY CONCEPT

This simply means that the financial information reported in the accounting statements should be restricted to the particular entity in question. In other words, it should not record the owner's private transactions within the business accounts. This sounds obvious, but often students confuse private transactions made by the owner of the business with the transactions of the entity concerned. For example, the owner places money in the business at the start which as we know is called capital, and capital is shown on the liability side of our accounting equation. It is also recorded on the asset side as cash put in by the owner. I am often asked the question by students, "Why is capital shown on the liability side? Surely capital is an asset". This is because they do not understand the entity concept. The entity receives the asset of cash but incurs a liability to the owner, in other words the business entity needs to repay the owner in the event of closure.

PERIODICITY

Financial statements need to be prepared for a defined period of time. This is normally one year, the business financial year. For example, the government draws up its financial statements from April 6th to April 5th, i.e. the fiscal year. Other organizations may draw their accounts up from the 1st January to the 31st December in each calendar year, or for a full year ending on any other particular date which they choose.

MONEY MEASUREMENT

Accounting information can only really be recorded by translating economic performance of an enterprise into quantitative terms, in other words money. It can measure the money that comes into the business and the money that goes out of the business. We are unable to record in financial statements the current impetus of the sales force, or the goodwill earned through industrial relations. For example, if we think of certain types of business such as a football club where we have players worth millions of pounds, the players are not shown as an asset to the football club on its balance sheet, and yet the players are probably the biggest asset that most football clubs possess, since their success depends on their players. Another example might be a firm of professional accountants. The biggest asset they possess is their staff and the quality and knowledge that they have. However, once again this is not recorded in the balance sheet. So items in financial statements need to be measurable in monetary terms.

HISTORIC COST

Normally financial statements will be drawn up using the historic cost convention. This is because goods and services are purchased or sold at an invoice price and the agreed price paid is the price at which items coming into or going out of an organization can be recorded. It should be noted, however, that there have been attempts to take account of changing price levels and financial statements are now designed to achieve this objective in accord with Statement of Standard Accounting Practice number 16. This however has met with objections and is currently undergoing revision.

REALIZATION

A transaction is normally recorded when the legal title in a particular good or service is transferred. For example, if I am in the business of selling motor cars, the title in the motor car will pass to the buyer when the contract of sale has been completed. At this point the selling and buying organizations will record the transaction in their financial statements. There is a legal obligation on the seller to supply goods or services and on the buyer to pay for them.

THE DUAL ASPECT

Every transaction involves the giving and receiving of something. This is reflected in the bookkeeping, hence the double entry consists of a debit and a matching credit. Every credit must have a debit and every debit must have a credit.

MATERIALITY

The idea of materiality is simply one of common sense. It is a practical idea. It states that other rules may be ignored if the time and hence the cost involved in rigidly following the other rules outweighs the benefit of implementing the particular rule. For example, if we came to the end of a financial period and we found that we had stocks in our balance sheet of a particular class, say, raw materials stocks £2 million, and suddenly we realised that we had, say, £5 more in our stock rooms than we had on our balance sheet. In this case it is unlikely that the user of the financial statement would have interpreted the originally presented information any differently if it was amended. The change is therefore not material to the user's understanding of the financial statements, and the cost of amending the figures would outweigh any benefit gained by the user in his understanding of the financial statement. Therefore, the £5 stock is said not to be material. If on the other hand the raw material stock figure reported in the balance sheet was £2 million and according to the stock records the figure was understated by £500,000 (25%), then it could be regarded as material to the way in which the user of the financial statements would interpret the statement. The figure is so obviously understated that it may lead the user to reach incorrect decisions on the basis of the reported figures.

Furthermore, what may be considered not material to the financial statements as a whole could be regarded as material within a section or cost centre of the organization. For example: consumable stores may be valued at £500 in a balance sheet total for all stocks of £4 million and a total asset position of £12 million. Therefore, a reported difference of £250 in the consumable store total would seem to be not material to the financial statements as a whole. However, within the consumable stores valuation the difference represents 50% and is material to that section.

SUBSTANCE OVER FORM

Some transactions have a legal form which is different from the underlying commercial reality (substance). The accounting treatment would, however, reflect substance (reality) over form. Examples would include:-

1. Hire Purchase Transactions.
and
2. Goods sold with a retention to title (Romalpa clauses) would also be recorded as a normal credit sale since the reality is that it is just an ordinary sale unless the buyer becomes insolvent.

CHAPTER SUMMARY — ACCOUNTING CONCEPTS CHECKLIST

SSAP2 - GOING CONCERN
           PRUDENCE
           CONSISTENCY
           MATCHING PRINCIPLE OR ACCRUALS
           CONCEPT

OTHERS - THE ENTITY - BUSINESS ORGANIZATION
           PERIODICITY
           MONEY MEASUREMENT
           HISTORIC COST
           REALIZATION
           THE DUAL ASPECT
           MATERIALITY
           SUBSTANCE OVER FORM

SELF-CHECK QUESTIONS

1. Briefly explain the following concepts:
   - Historic cost convention
   - Money measurement
   - Periodicity
2. Briefly explain the four fundamental concepts stated in SSAP 2.
3. What is the concept which distinguishes the transactions of a personal nature from those of a business nature?
4. When is a sale a sale? - Briefly explain what you understand by this statement in relation to the concept of realization.
5. "Goods sold with a reservation of title clause should not be recorded as a sale until they are paid for." Do you agree with this statement? Briefly discuss with reference to the realization concept and substance over form concept.

THE BALANCE SHEET EXPLAINED
– Terminology and language of business

The Balance Sheet is a statement of a business's assets and liabilities at a point in time. It is as if business is suspended at that point and a snapshot taken of what the business owns, is owed and owes to others. The Balance Sheet comprises the following categories:

Fixed Assets Items which the business buys with the intention of keeping and using in the business to produce revenue. For example: land and buildings, machinery, motor vehicles. An asset will normally be regarded as fixed if it is to be kept for a period longer than one year. The charge for the use of the asset is called depreciation (more on this later).

Current Assets Items which the business buys for almost immediate use such as **stock;** the money owed to the business by **debtors** (people who have bought goods from it but not yet paid for them), and the **cash** a business has to use (BANK or CASH).

Long Term Liabilities What the business owes to others, normally where it has longer than one year to pay up. For example: loans, mortgages and debentures. Mortgages and debentures simply being special types of loan.

debentures

Current Liabilities What the business owes to others which it will have to settle in the short term (i.e. within 12 months). For example, amounts owed to trade creditors for stock items purchased for resale, on credit terms. Other creditors will include amounts owed for expenses incurred, income tax liabilities and money owed to the Customs and Excise for VAT.

Capital At the outset this is the money the owner or owners of the business put in at the start to finance the business. However, in an established business Capital is the excess of assets over liabilities.

Reserves which are undistributed profits and effectively increase the capital employed in the business.

THE BALANCE SHEET EQUATION

Assets are the resources a business needs to be in business and comprise one side of the traditional form of Balance Sheet. The other side of the Balance Sheet tells the story of how those assets have been provided. Thus the Balance Sheet equation is:

$$\text{ASSETS} = \text{CAPITAL} + \text{LIABILITIES}$$

Two things basically happen in a business, which are, money comes in and money goes out. You need to know where the money comes from. Similarly, money goes out, that is it is spent on the things you mean to keep and use in the business over a period of time, e.g. Fixed Assets (land and buildings, machinery, motor vehicles) or Current Assets (stock) or alternatively it is spent on running the day to day business, on expenses such as advertising, travel, wages and so on.

The money coming into a business will come from one of the following sources:-

1. Capital — what the owner puts in
2. Liability — what the business borrows
3. Sales — from the revenue earned by selling its goods and services. This will find itself on the balance sheet via profit added to Capital or in the case of companies retained within Reserves.

Retained equation

The easiest way to understand this Balance Sheet equation is to process a number of transactions. One further point that needs to be made is that the business transactions undertaken by a business need to be kept separate from those of the individual or partners who run the business, otherwise confusion will arise. This is **THE ENTITY CONCEPT.**

EXAMPLE

The following transactions are undertaken by Lewis, a sole trader in waffles.

1. He starts in business as a trader with £4,000 of his own money in cash.
2. He buys a machine to produce waffles for £1,000 cash.
3. He also buys a small secondhand van for £2,000 cash in order to make delivery to customers.
4. He buys stock for resale for £500 cash.
5. He pays expenses for advertising £100 cash.
6. He sells all of his stock for £1,000 cash.

Let us now deal with each of the above transactions, using the Balance Sheet equation.

1. Lewis commences with £4,000 in cash, thus the business is liable to the owner for £4,000 he introduces. In return the business has an asset of cash.

    ASSETS   =   CAPITAL + LIABILITIES
    CASH £4,000   =   OWNER £4,000 + zero liabilities

2. The next event used some of the asset of cash and exchanged this for a machine. Thus, the asset of £1,000 cash changed form into another asset worth £1,000.

ASSETS		=	**CAPITAL + LIABILITIES**
1. Cash	+ 4,000	=	OWNER + 4,000
2. Cash	– 1,000		
3. Machine	+ 1,000		
	4,000		4,000

You will see that the two sides of the Balance Sheet remain the same at £4,000.

3. Another asset is bought and paid for in cash. Just as in the second transaction, cash changes into another asset.

ASSETS		=	CAPITAL + LIABILITIES
1. Cash	+ 4,000		OWNER + 4,000
2. Cash	– 1,000		
3. Cash	– 2,000		
2. Machine	+ 1,000		
3. Van	+ 2,000		
	4,000		4,000

Cash has been reduced by £2,000 and replaced with a motor van worth £2,000.

4. Once again the asset of cash is reduced and replaced by stock worth the same amount, £500.

ASSETS		=	CAPITAL + LIABILITIES
1. Cash	+ 4,000		OWNER + 4,000
2. Cash	– 1,000		
3. Cash	– 2,000		
4. Cash	– 500		
2. Machine	+ 1,000		
3. Van	+ 2,000		
4. Stock	+ 500		
	4,000		4,000

BEFORE dealing with the next two transactions the concept of **PROFIT** needs some explanation. **PROFIT** in the accounting sense is the residue that is left for the owner from the sale of goods less the cost of those goods less any expenses incurred in making the sale.

Thus
> **Sales** (S)
> **–Less Cost of Sale** (COS)
> **=GROSS PROFIT** (GP)
> **–Less EXPENSES** (E)
> **=NET PROFIT** (NP)

Note it is the net profit which may be retained by the owner.

$$S - (COS + E) = NP$$

Gross Profit is sometimes referred to as Trading Profit.

Profit is a reward for risk and effort to the owner of the business (the

Entrepreneur, i.e. risk taker) and as such is added to the owner's funds when it is left in the business. Profit helps the business to grow. Not all businesses make a profit all of the time, sometimes losses are made. Losses are the opposite of profit and cause a reduction in the owner's wealth (just as profit adds to the owner's wealth). Therefore, if a net loss occurs it must be deducted from the owner's funds, that is, Capital.

To summarise then:-
Profits are added to Capital and increase it
Losses are subtracted from Capital and reduce it.

In order to deal with profits and losses our Balance Sheet equation needs to be expanded to deal with revenue (sales income) and expenses.

Thus:

ASSETS + EXPENSES = CAPITAL + LIABILITIES + REVENUE

Note: **Revenue – Expenses = Profit**

Let us now deal with the last two transactions for this period.

5.   Expenses of £100 have been paid using cash.

ASSETS + EXPENSES			=	CAPITAL + LIABILITIES + REVENUE
1. Cash	+4,000			OWNER + 4,000
2. Cash	–1,000			
3. Cash	–2,000			
4. Cash	– 500			
5. Cash	– 100			
2. Machine	+1,000			
3. Van	+2,000			
4. Stock	+ 500			
5. Advertising		+ 100		
	3,900	+ 100		4,000

6.   The final transaction involves four entries in the Balance Sheet equation. A sale is made which earns the business the asset of £1,000 cash.

Thus:
ASSETS + EXPENSES = CAPITAL + LIABILITIES + REVENUE
Cash + **1,000**   **Sale** + 1,000

But what event took place to earn that revenue? All the asset of stock was sold. Therefore, the asset of stock must be reduced by £500 and that is the cost of making the sale. The transaction may be recorded as follows:-

ASSETS + EXPENSES = CAPITAL + LIABILITIES + REVENUE

4.   Stock + 500

6.   Stock − 500 Cost of Sale + 500

This transaction is a tricky one so it may help to go through the steps again.

The full Balance Sheet equation now looks like this:-

	ASSETS + EXPENSES		= CAPITAL + LIABILITIES + REVENUE		
1. Cash	+4,000		OWNER 4,000		
2. Cash	−1,000				
3. Cash	−2,000				
4. Cash	− 500				
5. Cash	− 100				
6a Cash	+1,000				Sale + 1,000
2. Machine	+1,000				
3. Van	+2,000				
4. Stock	+ 500				
6b Stock	− 500	Cost of Sale + 500			
5. Advertising		+ 100			
	4,400	**+ 600**	= **4,000** + **0** +		**1,000**
	5,000		**5,000**		

You will have noticed that every transaction is recorded twice. For example, when the owner introduced money into the business, the asset of cash was increased (debited) and a liability by the business to repay the owner reflected under Capital. £4,000 was entered as a credit. You can see that two entries have been made to record the reality of the transaction. One a debit entry and the other a credit. This is known as the dual aspect of accounting.

You have in fact been introduced to the double-entry concept which was developed by an Italian monk named Luciano Pacioli in the 15th century. The system was developed which although simple, is very logical and quite ingenious. It ensures that if items are recorded correctly the two aspects of each transaction are arithmetically equivalent and the recorder is disciplined to make two entries. It does not however ensure that certain types of error will not occur, known as:

1.   Original entry — incorrect on both sides of the accounts.
2.   Omission — items missed out of the books.
3.   Commission — entries in an incorrect account.
4.   Error of principle — entries in the wrong type of account, e.g. a disposal of a Fixed Asset in a Sales Account.
5.   Compensating errors — an error on the debit side compensated coincidentally by an error for the same amount on the credit side.

6. Complete reversal — a debit entered as a credit and vice-versa. Nevertheless, it was an important development and continues to be a useful check on accuracy.

DEBITS AND CREDITS

You have probably heard of the terms debit and credit. However, if you think of them in the light of your experience, which may only be through your bank account, you will probably not be thinking in the framework of accountancy. If we refer back to our Balance Sheet equation, the assets and expense accounts are debit accounts. That is to say, when an asset is added or an expense incurred a debit entry is made (see the chapter on bookkeeping). The right hand side of the Balance Sheet equation are credit accounts. When a liability is incurred, a sale made or capital introduced the appropriate account is credited.

CASH OR CREDIT

Before we proceed any further, you have also probably noticed that all the transactions we have recorded so far deal in cash receipts and payments. However, in business many transactions are undertaken on credit terms. For example, if the business buys stock for resale it will most likely be allowed trade credit, which might mean something like 30 days before payment is due. No doubt some evidence of the business's creditworthiness will be required before credit is extended. Credit-worthiness is normally established by the business supplying two trade references to the new supplier (i.e. a statement from someone you already trade with, establishing a sound track record of payment). In the case of a new business a bank reference may suffice or you may have to wait until you have established yourself as a reliable customer before credit is allowed. Similarly, your business will probably have to allow a period of credit to customers, and their credit rating will also have to be established. The credit period allowed will normally be determined to some extent by what other people in your particular line of business allow. Obviously, if you step out of line with your competitors by not allowing credit terms which are as good as theirs, you will lose business.

SUMMARY — THE BALANCE SHEET EXPLAINED

The Balance Sheet is a statement of assets and liabilities at a point in time.
ASSETS = CAPITAL + LIABILITIES
The full equation to obtain a trial balance would be Assets + Expenses = Capital + Liabilities + Revenue.
The Balance Sheet terminology was explained: FIXED ASSETS, CURRENT ASSETS, CURRENT LIABILITIES, LONG TERM LIABILITIES, CAPITAL and RESERVES.

---

increase → reflected.

SELF-CHECK QUESTIONS

1. What is the Balance Sheet?
2. Give brief definitions of the following terms:-
    (a) Fixed Assets
    (b) Current Assets
    (c) Long Term Liabilities
    (d) Current Liabilities
    (e) Capital
3. Briefly explain the balance sheet equation.
4. Explain the following terms:-
    (a) Debit
    (b) Credit
5. Using the balance sheet equation complete the following:
    (a) Assets £5000, Capital?, Liabilities £2000
    (b) Assets?, Capital £3000, Liabilities £1000
    (c) Assets £6000, Expenses £1000, Capital £3000, Liabilities £2000, Revenue? 2000

SUMMARY OF THE BALANCE SHEET EQUATION

ASSETS + EXPENSES = CAPITAL +LIABILITIES + REVENUE			
INCREASE	**DR**		**CR**
REDUCE	**CR**		**DR**

FIXED ASSETS

Items of 'CAPITAL EXPENDITURE' which will generate income and be consumed over a number of financial periods (i.e. greater than one year).

e.g. Plant and Machinery
Land and Buildings
Motor Vehicles etc.

Their consumption is charged as an expense called DEPRECIATION.

CURRENT ASSETS

Items used in the present financial period to operate the business (consumed in less than one year).

e.g. STOCK
DEBTORS and PREPAYMENTS
BANK
CASH

EXPENSES

'Allocations' for non-trading goods and services consumed in the present financial period 'matched' with Revenue of the financial period.

e.g. Administration
Sales and Marketing
Factory Overheads
Finance Expenses (Bank Charges and Loan Interest etc.)

CAPITAL

The funds the owner puts into the business to finance it, i.e. Equity.

Sole Trader — Owner's Money
Partnership — Owners' Money
Private Ltd. —(Shareholders'
PLC   (Money
Cooperatives/Clubs —
Members' funds

N.B. DRAWINGS in the case of Sole Traders and Partnerships are the opposite of CAPITAL and treated as such. — Limited Companies, Private and Public both pay DIVIDENDS.

LIABILITIES

Purchases (from Suppliers for Trading Stock) bought on credit terms from CREDITORS not yet paid for. Or Expenses incurred but not yet paid. CURRENT (short term) Creditors which may be Trade or Expense. Accruals for expenses or goods. LONG TERM — Bank Loans, Mortgages, Debentures etc.

REVENUE

Trading Income from SALES or Non-Trading Income, e.g. Royalties, Discount Received, Commission Income, Patent Income or Income from the Disposal of Fixed Assets.

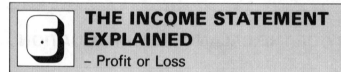

THE INCOME STATEMENT EXPLAINED
– Profit or Loss

A QUESTION OF PROFIT OR LOSS

We have in the previous chapter already summarised the Income Statement as follows:

Sales	**S**
Less Cost of Sales	**COS**
Gross Profit	**GP**
Less Expenses	**E**
Net Profit	**NP**

i.e. **S–COS = GP**
   GP–E   = NP

The Net Profit is then transferred to the Balance Sheet and added to Capital.

EXAMPLE: The following is the opening statement of affairs of Brown, a sole trader.

BROWN — Balance Sheet at 31.12.–4

FIXED ASSETS	Cost	Depreciation	NBV
	£	£	£
Motor vehicles	10,000	—	10,000
CURRENT ASSETS			
Stock	2,000		
Debtors	2,500		
Bank	1,000	5,500	
LESS CURRENT LIABILITIES			
Creditor		(1,500)	
Net Current Assets OR Working Capital			4,000
			14,000
Financed By			
Capital			14,000

During the year the following transactions took place:-

	£
Sales	30,000
Purchases	15,000
EXPENSES — Administration	2,500
— Rent & Rates	1,000
— Light & Heat	500
Debtors at 31.12.–5	2,000
Creditors at 31.12.–5	2,500
Stock at 31.12.–5	3,200
Bank at 31.12.–5	?

Brown's Income Statement would look as follows:-

BROWN — Trading and Profit & Loss Account
for the year ended 31.12.19–5

	£	£
Sales		30,000
Less Cost of Sales		
Opening stock (per opening b/s)	2,000	
Add Purchases	15,000	
	17,000	
Less Closing Stock	(3,200)	(13,800)
GROSS PROFIT		16,200
Less Expenses		
Administration	2,500	
Rent and Rates	1,000	
Light and Heat	500	(3,000)
Net Profit		12,200

The Net Profit appears to be retained within the business and is therefore added to the Capital held by Brown at 31.12.19–4, as shown in the Balance Sheet at 31.12.–5.

BROWN — Balance Sheet at 31.12.19-5

	£	£	£
FIXED ASSETS	Cost	Depreciation	NBV
Motor vehicles	10,000	—	10,000
CURRENT ASSETS			
Stock	3,200		
Debtors	2,000		
Bank	13,500	18,700	
Less CURRENT LIABILITIES			
Creditors		2,500	
Net Current Assets or Working Capital			16,200
Total Net Assets			26,200
Financed By			
Capital at 31.12.–4	14,000		
Add Net Profit Retained	12,200		
Capital Employed			26,200

Thus, the closing Balance Sheet for Brown based on the hypothesised 19-5 transaction is now complete.

However, we can now usefully consider further possible types of transactions. Several such items are therefore covered below. Journal references are given and shown in a summary at the end of the chapter.

CARRIAGE INWARDS *(Journal ref: 1)*

This is an extra charge placed on the buying firm for the delivery of goods to their premises. It will often be invoiced as a delivery charge or paid to British Rail or a private haulage company but is always termed as carriage inwards in the financial statements.

The accounting entry for Carriage Inwards is as follows:-

DEBIT   — CARRIAGE INWARDS ACCOUNT — Trading A/c
                Trading Expense

CREDIT — CASH ACCOUNT if paid in cash or
                CREDITOR if not yet paid   — B/S

How would a charge for carriage inwards have affected the Income Statement of Brown? Well, let us suppose that a charge for goods delivered to Brown had been made by the suppliers for carriage of £1,000. The Income Statement would now look like this:

BROWN — Trading and Profit & Loss Account
for the Year Ended 31.12.19–5

	£	£
Sales		30,000
Less Cost of Sales		
Opening Stock	2,000	
Add Purchases	15,000	
	17,000	
Add Carriage Inwards	1,000	
	18,000	
Less Closing Stock	(3,200)	14,800
GROSS PROFIT		15,200

Thus, trading expenses have increased by £1,000 which has the effect of reducing the Gross Profit by £1,000. Profit and Loss Expenses have not changed and therefore, the Net Profit will alter by the same amount as the Gross Profit, that is £1,000 to £11,200.

If Net Profit has reduced by £1,000 this means that the addition to CAPITAL will be £1,000 less and that the Financed By side of the Balance Sheet will only total £25,200. Where is the effect of this change shown on the other side of the Balance Sheet?

Look back to the Accounting Entries; so far we have only dealt with one side of this entry. The other side will depend on whether or not payment has been made. If payment has been made in cash then of course the cash account (i.e. Bank in this case) will be reduced by £1,000 to £12,500, which makes the two sides equal. Alternatively, if it has not yet been paid the money will be owed to a creditor and therefore, the creditors figure would increase by £1,000 making the two sides agree.

CARRIAGE OUTWARDS *(Journal ref: 2)*

This is an expense to the business for delivering goods sold, which is not recharged to customers buying the goods. For example, some goods are sold inclusive of delivery to the customer's premises and thus, the expense of delivery is suffered by the selling firm.

The Accounting Entry is:-

DEBIT — Carriage Outwards Expense Account — P/L

CREDIT — Cash or Bank Account when paid for — B/S
or Creditor if not yet paid for — B/S

If Brown had had to deliver his goods to customers then he would have incurred further expense of carriage outwards, which would need to be shown in the Profit and Loss Account. Let us assume that the expense incurred was £500, and building on our example so far, how would this be shown? As follows:-

		£
GROSS PROFIT		15,200
LESS EXPENSES		
Administration	2,500	
Rent & Rates	1,000	
Light & Heat	500	
Carriage Out	500	4,500
Net Profit		10,700

The effect on the Balance Sheet would be to reduce the Net Profit added to Capital down to (10,700 + 14,000) = £24,700. The Bank Account would be reduced by £500 on the other side if payment has been made. Alternatively, if the expense has not yet been paid for in cash, then the firm's liabilities would increase by £500, i.e. Creditors. Either way the result would be to balance the Total Net Assets at £24,700.

RETURNS INWARDS *(Journal ref: 3)*

These are goods which have been sold to a customer but for some reason they proved to be unsatisfactory and the customer returned them. The transaction can no longer be classified as a sale since this would have the effect of overstating the profit by the amount of the returns. However, in order that the business can control the goods returned, rather than simply deduct the returns directly from the Sales Account, a separate Returns Inward Account is opened. The Accounting Entry is:

DEBIT — RETURNS INWARDS TRADING ACCOUNT

CREDIT — DEBTOR — if not paid — B/S
or BANK — if cash refunded — B/S

Supposing Brown had £500 worth of goods returned to him by customers. How would this affect his Income Statement? Like this:-

	£	£
Sales		30,000
Less Returns Inwards		(500)
Net Sales		29,500
Less Cost of Sales		
Opening Stock	2,000	
Add Purchases	15,000	
	17,000	
Add Carriage Inwards	1,000	
	18,000	
Less Closing Stock	(3,200)	14,800
GROSS PROFIT		14,700
LESS EXPENSES (TOTAL)		4,500
Net Profit		10,200

The effect on the Balance Sheet would be to reduce the Financed By side to (14,000 + 10,200) = 24,200. The Total Net Assets would also be reduced by either lowering Debtors by £500 if the customer returning the goods had not yet paid or if the customer had paid by returning his money and hence reducing the Bank Account by £500.

RETURNS OUTWARDS *(Journal ref: 4)*

These are purchases of Stock which for one reason or another need to be returned to the supplier because they cannot be used by the business. They are, therefore, a reduction of goods purchased and must be deducted from purchases. For convenience and control purposes, a separate account called Returns Outwards is opened. The Accounting Entry is:-

> **DEBIT — CREDITOR — B/S**
>
> **CREDIT — RETURNS OUTWARD — Trading Account**

Suppose Brown had to return £100 worth of goods bought for resale, the effect on the Income Statement would be as follows:-

		£
Sales		30,000
Less Returns Inward		(500)
Net Sales		29,500
Less Cost of Sales		
Opening Stock	2,000	
Add Purchases	15,000	
	17,000	
Add Carriage Inward	1,000	
	18,000	
Less Returns Outward	100	
	17,900	
Less Closing Stock	3,200	14,700
GROSS PROFIT		14,800

DISCOUNT RECEIVED *(Journal ref: 5)*

This is a discount given by a supplier of goods. It may be given as a Trade Discount and simply by being in that particular line of business you are given a Trade Discount. The discount may be given as a result of buying large quantities, i.e. a purchasing (economy of scale) discount. Alternatively, the discount may be given as a result of prompt payment. Suppliers often grant 5% discount for payment received within 30 days. This is called a CASH DISCOUNT.

TRADE DISCOUNTS

Most businesses will deal with trade and purchasing discounts by entering the goods purchased in the stock account at the net figure. Thus, following the rule in SSAP9 that stock is valued at the lower of cost or market (net realisable) value.

CASH DISCOUNTS

In the case of a discount received for prompt payment, there is no way of knowing whether or not this will be obtained at the time of purchase. It is prudent therefore, to enter the cost of goods bought in full in the Purchase Ledger and to treat the DISCOUNT as a Non-Trading Income in the Income Statement.

Supposing Brown received £500 as a discount for prompt payment during the year. The Accounting Entry is:-

> **DEBIT — CREDITOR — B/S**
>
> **CREDIT — DISCOUNT RECEIVED — P/L**

Income Extract for Brown

	£
GROSS PROFIT	14,800
Add Non-Trading Income	
Discount Received	500
	15,300
LESS EXPENSES (TOTAL)	(4,500)
NET PROFIT	10,800

The effect on the Balance Sheet is to increase the Financed By side to (14,000 + 10,800) = 24,800 and to reduce liabilities, i.e. Creditors by £500, thus increasing Total Net Assets by £500 to £24,800.

Other types of non-trading income might be:-
- Investment Income
- Income from Royalties (although this depends on the source)
- Commission
- Patent Income

DISCOUNT ALLOWED *(Journal ref: 6)*

This is an expense to the business allowing its customers discount either for prompt payment or for some other reason, e.g. trade, or just to make a sale. If the discount is given as a trade discount it would more properly be reflected as a reduction in selling price. If it is given to make a sale which otherwise would not be gained, then it would be right and fair to charge the expense to Selling and Marketing Expenses. If, on the other hand, the discount was allowed in order to obtain prompt payment from a customer, then it would be right and fair to treat the expense as a Finance Expense when classifying expenses. The Accounting Entry is:-

> **DEBIT — DISCOUNT ALLOWED EXPENSE ACCOUNT P/L**
>
> **CREDIT — DEBTORS ACCOUNT — B/S**

Discount allowed increases expenses and reduces debtors who owe the business for goods.

Let us assume that discount is allowed of £100. This has the effect of increasing expenses by £100 and thus reducing profit by the same amount. The Debtors figure in the Balance Sheet would also be reduced by £100.

PROVISION FOR DOUBTFUL DEBTS *(Journal ref: 7)*

Doubtful debts are fully explained in Chapter 17. However, they deserve further brief mention here since students often have difficulty in dealing with provisions and write offs. A doubtful debt is a debtor about whom you have a measure of uncertainty in their ability to pay. It may be that you consider the whole debt as doubtful or merely part of the debt as doubtful.

When a debt is considered doubtful it is prudent to make provision for the part you consider might not be paid. Examination questions usually specify the amount of debt to be treated as doubtful.

The accounting entry is:-

> **DEBIT   — BAD AND DOUBTFUL DEBT EXPENSE ACCOUNT — P/L**
>
> **CREDIT — BAD AND DOUBTFUL DEBT PROVISION — B/S**

Sometimes a separate account is shown for doubtful debts only, and some firms combine the two as I have.

Be sure to understand that a doubtful debt may still be paid by the debtor, whereas a bad debt is definitely not going to be realised. If a doubtful debt is eventually realised then the provision for that doubtful debt is no longer required and the accounting entries can be reversed, that is:-

> **DEBIT   — BAD AND DOUBTFUL DEBT PROVISION — B/S**
>
> **CREDIT — BAD AND DOUBTFUL DEBT EXPENSE ACCOUNT — P/L**

EXAMPLE   In the case of Brown, supposed he considered that 5% of his closing debtors of £2,000 could turn out to be bad. That is, at the moment they are doubtful.

$$(5\% \times £2,000) = £100$$

A provision for £100 needs to be made just in case (prudence concept).

DEBIT — BAD AND DOUBTFUL DEBT EXPENSE A/C £100

CREDIT — PROVISION FOR BAD AND DOUBTFUL DEBT A/C — £100

What is the effect on the Income Statement? It increases expenses in the Profit and Loss Account as follows:

Income Statement Extract:

	£	£
GROSS PROFIT		14,800
Add Non-Trading Income		
Discount received		500
		15,300
LESS EXPENSES		
Administration	2,500	
Rent and Rates	1,000	
Light and Heat	500	
Carriage Out	500	
Bad and Doubtful Debts	100	4,600
Net Profit		10,700

The effect on the Balance Sheet is to make the Financed By side (14,000 + 10,700) = £24,700. Thus a reduction of £100 from the example at Journal Ref. 5. The total net assets are also reduced by £100 since Debtors £2,000 are now shown net of the provision for £100 at £1,900.

	£	£	£
Current Assets			
Stock		3,200	
Debtors	2,000		
Less Provision for Bad and Doubtful Debts	(100)	1,900	
Bank		13,500	
			18,600

BAD DEBTS *(Journal ref: 8)*

These are debtors about which there is certainty of non-payment, i.e. the debtors are definitely unrealisable. The accounting entry is:-

---

DEBIT   — BAD DEBT EXPENSE — P/L

CREDIT — DEBTOR — B/S

Where a business has already made a provision for a doubtful debt and the doubtful debt turns bad then the accounting entry is:-

---

DEBIT   — PROVISION FOR DOUBTFUL DEBTS — B/S

CREDIT — DEBTOR — B/S

Thereby avoiding a double charge for the one expense to the profit and loss account. You will note that the accounting entries do not affect the Income Statement, only the Balance Sheet.

EXAMPLE   Let us suppose that in the case of Brown £50 worth of the provision for doubtful debts already made at Journal Ref. 7, turned out to be definitely bad. Furthermore, a debtor owing £100 for whom no provision had been made also turned out to be bad. The remaining provision for £50 being held in case other debtors prove to be bad. We would deal with this situation as follows:-

---

DEBIT   — BAD DEBT EXPENSE ACCOUNT £100   P/L

CREDIT — DEBTORS   £100 B/S

DEBIT   — PROVISION FOR DOUBTFUL DEBTS £50   B/S

CREDIT — DEBTORS   £50 B/S

The effect on the Income Statement would be as follows from the one shown at Journal Ref. 7.

Income Statement Extract:

	£	£
		15,300
LESS EXPENSES		
Administration	2,500	
Rent and Rates	1,000	
Light and Heat	500	
Carriage Out	500	
Bad and Doubtful Debts	200	
		4,700
Net Profit		10,600

Note: Bad and Doubtful Debts are shown as one category. Bad Debts are in fact £150 and Doubtful Debts now only £50.

The effect on the Balance Sheet is to reduce debtors by £150, i.e. the amount of Bad Debts now written off, and to reduce the Provision for Doubtful Debts to £50.

Thus the Balance Sheet Extract is as follows:-

CURRENT ASSETS	£	£	£
Stock		3,200	
Debtors (2,000 – 150)	1,850		
Less Provision for Bad			
and Doubtful Debts	(50)	1,800	
Bank		13,500	
			18,500

ACCRUALS *(Journal ref: 9)*

These are amounts of monies owed by the business for goods and services which have been incurred but have not yet been paid in cash. They have a dual aspect like every other accounting transaction. Profit needs to be reduced by the amount of the accrual either by increasing purchases or the appropriate expense category. The Balance Sheet needs to show a liability equivalent to the accrual.

The accounting entry is:-

> **DEBIT — either PURCHASES ACCOUNT if the accrual is for goods — T/A**
>
> **or RELEVANT EXPENSE ACCOUNT — for service — P/L**
>
> **CREDIT — ACCRUALS ACCOUNT — B/S**

EXAMPLE In Brown's case supposing he had incurred further Administration Expenses of £100 which had not been paid at the year end. The transactions would be recorded as follows:-

> **DEBIT — ADMIN EXPENSE ACCOUNT £100**   **P/L**
>
> **CREDIT — ACCRUALS ACCOUNT**   **£100 B/S**

The effect on the Income Statement is to increase expenses by £100 and thus reduce profit by £100.

The effect on the Balance Sheet is to show a current liability called an Accrual for £100.

Balance Sheet Extract

CURRENT LIABILITIES	£	£
Creditors	2,500	
Accruals	100	2,600

PREPAYMENTS *(Journal ref: 10)*

Prepayments are payments which have been made in respect of a future accounting period and therefore, the amounts need to be removed from the expenses of a current accounting period.

For example, in Brown's case let us suppose that the Rent and Rates Expense had been paid for a period of 16 months. This means that four months rates have been paid in advance of the current accounting period and must therefore be removed from the Income Statement in accordance with the accrual concept or matching principle.

$$\frac{£1,000 \text{ Rent and Rates}}{16 \text{ months}} = £62.5 \text{ monthly charge}$$

therefore, only 12 months × £62.5 = £750

should be shown in the current Income Statement as an expense for rent and rates. £250 is therefore a prepayment.

The accounting entry is:-

DEBIT — PREPAYMENT ACCOUNT — CURRENT ASSET — B/S

CREDIT — RENT AND RATES EXPENSE A/C — P/L

Note: you could credit any relevant expense account where a payment in advance has been made.

The effect on the Income Statement is to reduce the rent and rates expense to £750 and show a current asset in the Balance Sheet, i.e. a prepayment of £250.

Let us now show the final Income Statement and complete Balance Sheet for Brown at 31.12.19–5 having taken into account all the adjustments made.

BROWN — Trading and Profit and Loss Account
for the year ended 31.12.19–5

	£	£	£
Sales			30,000
Less Returns Inward			(500)
Net Sales			29,500
LESS COST OF SALES			
Opening Stock		2,000	
Add Purchases	15,000		
Carriage Inward	1,000 ✓		
	16,000		
Less Returns Outward	(100)	15,900	
		17,900	
Less Closing Stock		(3,200)	(14,700)
GROSS PROFIT			14,800
Add Non-Trading Income			
Discount Received			500 ✓
			15,300
LESS EXPENSES			
Administration		2,600	
Rent and Rates		750	
Light and Heat		500	
Carriage Out		500 ٭	
Discount Allowed		100	
Bad and Doubtful Debts		200	4,650
Net Profit/(Loss)			10,650

To summarise the changes we have made, I have journalised the entries showing the effect on both the Income Statement and the Balance Sheet. *(ignoring narratives)*

	Journal Entries			
Ref.	*Account Name*		*£Dr*	*£Cr*
1	Carriage In	P/L	1,000	
	Bank A/c	B/S		1,000
2	Carriage Out	P/L	500	
	Bank A/c	B/S		500
3	Returns In	P/L	500	
	Debtors	B/S		500
4	Creditors	B/S	100	
	Returns Outward	P/L		100
5	Creditors	B/S	500	
	Discount Received	P/L		500
6	Discount Allowed	P/L	100	
	Debtors	B/S		100
7	Bad and Doubtful Debts	P/L	100	
	Provision for Bad and Doubtful Debts	B/S		100
8	Bad Debt Expense	P/L	100	
	Debtors	B/S		100
	Provision for Doubtful Debts	B/S	50	
	Debtors	B/S		50
9	Administration	P/L	100	
	Accrual	B/S		100
10	Prepayment	B/S	250	
	Rent and Rates	P/L		250

You may like to compare the Balance Sheet totalling £26,200 at 31.12.19–5 with the Balance Sheet given below which is after implementing the above journal entries.

Balance Sheet for Brown at 31.12.19–5

	£ Cost	£ Depn.	£ NBV
FIXED ASSETS			
Motor vehicles	10,000	–	10,000
CURRENT ASSETS			
Stock	3,200		
Debtors	1,250		
Less Provision	(50)	1,200	
for Bad and			
Doubtful Debts			
Prepayments	250		
Bank	12,000	16,650	
Less Current Liabilities			
Creditors	1,900		
Accruals	100	(2,000)	
Net Current Assets or Working Capital			14,650
Total Net Assets or Net Worth			24,650
Financed By			
Capital		14,000	
Add Net Profit Retained		10,650	
Capital Employed			24,650

TRADING ACCOUNT. This account shows sales (at selling prices) less the cost of making sales (i.e. sales at cost price) to give a GROSS PROFIT. Cost of Sales is usually arrived at by Opening Stock + Purchases + Carriage In less Returns Outwards and any closing stock to carry forward to a future period. PROFIT AND LOSS ACCOUNT. This account shows Gross Profit less all expenses (overheads or indirect expenses) to arrive at a NET PROFIT for the period.

NON-TRADING INCOME. A business could also receive income not in the course of normal trading activities. Such income should be treated as Non-Trading Income and may be added to Gross Profit before expenses are deducted or shown separately as non-operating income in operating statements.

Non-Trading Income may include:- Investment Income, Profit on Disposals, Discounts Received (Cash/Settlement only), Patents or Royalties Income.

		£
EXAMPLE:	Gross Profit	X
	Add Non-Trading Income	
	Discount Received	X
	Investment Income	X
		X
	Less Expenses	
	detail	

SELF-CHECK QUESTIONS

1. Briefly explain each of the following terms:
    (a) Carriage Inward
    (b) Carriage Outward
    (c) Returns Inward
    (d) Returns Outward
    (e) Discount Received
    (f) Discount Allowed
    (g) Bad Debts
    (h) Doubtful Debts
    (i) Accruals
    (j) Prepayments
2. State how the Net Profit is obtained using the symbols in the text.
3. Why is an Income Statement necessary?
4. Is there a difference between Income and Cash?
5. Show the effect on both the Income Statement and the Balance Sheet if Brown decides to depreciate motor vehicles at 20% per annum on a straight line basis as from 1.1.19–5. (Depreciation is described fully in Chapter 15.)

DAY BOOKS
– sometimes called Journals

WHAT ARE DAY BOOKS?

Businesses need to know who owes money to them and who they owe money to. When business is transacted using credit rather than immediate cash payment, the seller issues a Sales Invoice which is a record of the sale and the buyer will receive the sales invoice as a record of the purchase. To the buyer the sales invoice is a Purchase Invoice. The SALES DAY BOOK will list all the sales invoices issued on a particular day, showing: The customer's (Debtor) name; customer reference; total invoiced amount; any trade discount allowed may be recorded and any value added tax to be paid by the customer. On any particular day the totals of all invoices extracted from the day books would then be posted to the LEDGERS and it is only at this point that double entry bookkeeping is applied. Similarly the PURCHASE DAY BOOK will list all the Purchase Invoices received by the business. SO DAY BOOKS ARE JUST LISTINGS OF INVOICE DETAILS? YES!

ARE DAY BOOKS ONLY NEEDED FOR CREDIT TRANSACTIONS?

Well, for purchases and sales made in exchange for cash we can record the transaction in the CASH BOOK which in effect would act as the day book. So yes, only credit transactions need to be recorded in the SALES OR PURCHASE DAY BOOKS. These day books are sometimes referred to in other accounting texts as JOURNALS. In this text you will learn that the word JOURNAL has a special meaning and is not used to mean day book.

DO BUSINESSES ALWAYS HAVE CREDIT AND CASH TRANSACTIONS?

A business may have credit or cash transactions only or both but invoices are only necessary as a monetary record of credit transactions.

HOW ARE CASH PURCHASES RECORDED?

These are recorded on the credit side of the cash book as a payment and as a debit to the Purchase Account in the ledger. Whereas credit purchases are recorded initially in the PURCHASE DAY BOOK and transferred, or as we say in accounting, POSTED to the ledgers later as a debit to the Purchase Account and a credit to the Creditor Account.

HOW ARE CASH SALES RECORDED?

These are recorded as a debit in the CASH BOOK and a credit to the SALES

ACCOUNT in the ledgers. Whereas a credit sale will initially be recorded in the SALES DAY BOOK before posting to the relevant ledger accounts. See if you can think of what those ledger accounts would be?

WHAT ARE THE STAGES OF A CREDIT TRANSACTION?

STEPS	DOCUMENT TO RECORD STEPS
1 Place the order	PURCHASE ORDER or NOTE
2 Confirm the order	PURCHASE ORDER
3 Order accepted by supplier	ORDER ACKNOWLEDGEMENT
4 Goods Issued	DESPATCH or DELIVERY NOTE
5 Invoice despatched	INVOICE
6 Goods accepted	GOODS RECEIVED NOTE
7 Payment	REMITTANCE ADVICE

A transaction must always be supported by documents. The documents provide an audit trail and are a means of control for the business.

WHAT INFORMATION SHOULD AN INVOICE CONTAIN?

1 The name and registered address of the person supplying the goods or services.
2 V.A.T. registration number if the business is registered for Value Added Tax.
3 The date the goods are supplied.
4 An invoice number or reference.
5 Quantity supplied.
6 Description of goods or services supplied.
7 The customer order reference.
8 Unit Price
9 Any Discounts Allowed.
10 Value Added Tax.
11 Total Price to be paid.
12 Terms and Conditions of sale under which goods or services are supplied.
13 How Payment should be made and to whom and when.

CAN CUSTOMERS QUERY INVOICES?

Most certainly a customer may refuse to accept an invoice as a valid debt for the following reasons:

1 Goods supplied are faulty.
2 Prices charged are in excess of those agreed.
3 Quantity of goods received were less than the quantity shown on the invoice.

4 The calculations or casts on the invoice are checked and found to be incorrect. A cast is a term used to indicate adding up.

WHAT HAPPENS IN THESE CASES?

A CREDIT NOTE may be issued if goods are returned by a customer or there is an error on the invoice to take account of the overcharged amounts. Alternatively the original invoice may be withdrawn and a fresh invoice which is agreed as being correct is supplied.

CREDIT NOTE

S. LEE DEESIDE INDUSTRIAL ESTATE, CHESTER		**CREDIT NOTE** **No.123**	

VAT REG No: 340 3981 77

SHIP TO: BILL TO:

CUSTOMER ORDER NO.	DESPATCHED BY	INVOICE NO.	INVOICE DATE/TAX POINT

Cat. No.	Quantity	Description	Price	£

Gross Value of Goods
Less Trade Discount
Net Value of Goods
Plus VAT @ 15%

E & O E   **TOTAL CREDIT**

SELF-CHECK QUESTIONS

1. Briefly explain the purpose of Day Books.
2. Are day books only necessary to record credit transactions?
3. Explain how cash transactions are recorded.
4. What documents are necessary to record credit transactions?
5. What details should an invoice contain?

CREDIT SALES
– taking on debtors

CREDIT TRANSACTIONS

It is normal in most businesses to allow customers a period of credit before the sales income is paid in cash. The normal procedure is to agree the terms and conditions of sales, supply the goods or services and issue a sales invoice which will specify the date by which the customer (Debtor) should pay for the goods or services supplied. The customer (Debtor) will use the allowed credit period to get money in from his customers so that he can meet his obligation to pay the outstanding debt without recourse to any other means of credit such as a bank overdraft or loan. When his credit period has elapsed the customer (Debtor) should pay the invoiced amount by sending a cheque or paying in cash.

SALES INVOICES

An order will be received from a customer and after checking that the goods are available for supply in the right quantity at the right price the goods will be despatched with a delivery note the details of which will be used to raise a SALES INVOICE. The sales invoice will usually be sequentially numbered for reference, it will contain the date of despatch, date of invoice, tax date, customer name and address, delivery name and address if different, details of discount allowed for trade and/or any settlement discount, carriage or delivery charge, sales tax such as V.A.T., Total Amount Payable and the credit period allowed (for example: payment is due within thirty days of the date of this invoice). Often the invoice states E & O accepted which means that errors and omissions will be accepted.

DOUBLE ENTRY RECORDING FOR SALES

The sales invoice will first be recorded in the Sales Day Book which is simply a daily listing of all sales invoices issued. It is a diary of sales made by the business on credit. The day book is also called a Sales Journal by some people. The total of the sales day book columns for each day will be posted to the relevant ledger accounts. This usually means that total sales value will be posted to the Total Debtor Account often called The Debtor Control Account or the Sales Ledger Control Account. The figure is posted to the left hand side or left column marked Dr for Debit. The corresponding double entry is posted to the Sales Account in the Nominal Ledger as a Credit entry in the right hand side of the account marked Cr. Only the sales value net of any sales tax is posted to the sales account and any tax such as Value Added Tax will be posted to the Nominal Ledger V.A.T. account as a credit entry. The dual aspect of the transaction is now fully complete and total debit values are equal to total credit values.

EXAMPLE OF DOCUMENTS

A PURCHASE ORDER

ORDER			
		Order No.	
		.... 19	
		To:	

From:
S. LEE
....
DEESIDE INDUSTRIAL ESTATE
....
CHESTER
....
Tel.: 547 7143

Please supply as under, in strict conformity with the particulars given, any deviation from which will be at your own risk, unless referred to and authorised by us. The number of this Order must be quoted on the Invoice for the goods.

Ref.	Description	Qty.	Unit Price	TOTAL

INVOICE

S. LEE
DEESIDE INDUSTRIAL ESTATE, CHESTER

VAT REG No: 340 3981 77

SHIP TO:	BILL TO:

CUSTOMER ORDER NO.	DESPATCHED BY	INVOICE NO.	INVOICE DATE/TAX POINT

Cat. No.	Quantity	Description	Price	£

Gross Value of Goods		
Less Trade Discount		
Net Value of Goods		
Plus VAT @ 15%		
Invoice Total to be paid		

E & O E

30 DAYS NETT. SETTLEMENT DISCOUNT 2% for payment within 7 days of the Invoice date.

REMITTANCE ADVICE
Please tear off and return with your cheque.

Name_____   SALES INV/No.
Address_____
_____
Cheque enclosed £ _____

AN INVOICE WITH A REMITTANCE ADVICE

```
┌─────────────────────────────────────────────────────────────────────┐
│                                              │ NO              │
│  S. LEE        GOODS RECEIVED NOTE           ├─────────────────┤
│                                              │ DATE            │
│  ┌──────────────────────────────────┐       ├─────────────────┤
│  │ FROM                             │       │ PURCHASE        │
│  │                                  │       │ ORDER NO        │
│  ├──────┬──────────────────┬────────┼────┬──┴─────────────────┤
│  │ QTY  │  DESCRIPTION     │ No of  │ STORES REF             │
│  │      │                  │PACKAGES│ BLOCK    │    BIN       │
│  │      │                  │        │          │              │
│  │      │                  │        │          │              │
│  │      │                  │        │          │              │
│  ├──────┴───────┬──────────┴────┬───┴──────────┴──────────────┤
│  │  INSPECTION  │ ENT'D STOCK RECORDS │ RECEIVED BY          │
│  │ DATE │INITIALS│ DATE │INITIALS│                            │
│  │      │        │      │        │        STOREKEEPER        │
│  └──────┴────────┴──────┴────────┴───────────────────────────┘
└─────────────────────────────────────────────────────────────────────┘
```

EXAMPLE — SALES DAY BOOK ENTRIES

SALES DAY BOOK

Date	Name	Invoice Ref.	Folio	£
January 1	R. Smith	01/001	DL19	500.00
January 5	A. Jones	01/002	DL10	200.00
January 7	S. Adams	01/003	DL01	100.00
Transferred to Sales Account			NL60	900.00

The entries in the ledgers could be as follows:-

SALES LEDGER

	S. ADAMS	DL01
	£Dr	
January 7 Sales A/c NL60	100	

	A. JONES	DL10
	£Dr	
January 5 Sales A/c NL60	200	

	R. SMITH	DL19
	£Dr	
January 1 Sales A/c NL60	500	

Note the sales ledger is sometimes also referred to as the DEBTORS LEDGER.

NOMINAL LEDGER
Sales Account

		£Cr
January 7	Credit Sales for week SDB11	900

DEBIT   — DEBTOR CONTROL ACCOUNT (Sales Ledger Control)
          with the total amount of the invoice owed by the
          customer. (Asset Account Balance Sheet)

CREDIT — SALES ACCOUNT (Nominal Ledger — Revenue P & L)
          with the sale value of goods or services.

        — V.A.T. Account (Nominal Ledger – Balance Sheet
          Creditor owed to H.M. Customs – Liability – if
          applicable.) with any tax amount on sale.

Totals from the day books are posted for convenience to keep the number
of transactions entering the ledgers down to a minimum. It will still be
necessary to enter the customer's personal account with the individual
invoice amount for that particular customer to keep track of what the
customer (Debtor) owes to the business. Often these personal accounts are
referred to as 'Memorandum Accounts' and do not conform to the double
entry principle since it is the total account that has been treated as having
double entry for total sales and total debtors. Nevertheless, the entries in the
personal memoranda accounts will be posted to the same side (Dr. Debit)
as they are in the total Debtor Control Account.

WHEN CUSTOMER PAYS

When the Debtor pays either in cash or by cheque the double entry
recording would be as follows:

DEBIT   – CASH ACCOUNT if cash   – ASSET BALANCE SHEET (+)
          – BANK ACCOUNT if cheque – ASSET BALANCE SHEET (+)

CREDIT – DEBTOR ACCOUNT   – ASSET BALANCE SHEET (–)

Note: If Control Accounts are used for debtors then it is the total debtors
that would be credited as part of the double entry and the memorandum
(individual debtor) account would also need to be credited with the full
amount paid by the customer to keep track of what the customer owed at
that point in time after the payment was recorded.

SALES RETURNS (OR RETURNS INWARDS)

Sometimes customers will decide to return the goods they agreed to buy for
one reason or another. For example: unsatisfactory, not of the required
quality, faulty, defective, incorrect quantity supplied or untimely supply and
the goods are no longer required. For whatever reason the return is made
once it is accepted as a legitimate return the original sale needs to be
removed from the sales account and the indebtedness of the customer

needs to be removed from the debtor account. This is recorded as follows:

> DEBIT   – SALES RETURNS ACCOUNT – Nominal Ledger
>   Revenue (–) with the sale value of goods returned
>
> CREDIT – DEBTORS ACCOUNT – ASSET BALANCE SHEET
>   with the sale value of goods returned

It is usual to keep a separate account for returns rather than simply reduce the sales account so as to keep track of the number and value of goods returned in a period of time.

CREDIT NOTES

These are simply the reverse of an invoice for sales. They acknowledge the removal of debt by a customer formally for whatever reason. They are normally sequentially numbered and contain similar information to that on the invoice. A diary of credit notes issued is often maintained in day book format. A credit note would be raised for the return of goods previously thought to have been sold – to acknowledge Sales Returns. Credit notes would also be used to remove and record part of a debt no longer valid. For example, where the customer agrees to keep the goods supplied but expects not to pay full price for some reason such as a quality or quantity discrepancy.

RETURNED GOODS — WHAT HAPPENS?

If the goods returned are found to be resaleable they will be taken back into stock at cost value. If the goods are defective they may be treated as having some value and sold for scrap or treated as having no value and remain a cost to the business as waste. This of course depends on many factors not least the nature of the business, scope of damage and whether or not goods were purchased or made since it may be possible to claim against a supplier for a defective item that has been purchased rather than manufactured.

TRADE DISCOUNT

If you sell goods to a wholesaler or retailer they would not expect to pay the same price as customers comprising the general public. Traders will be selling your goods on to the general public and in return for increasing your market will expect to make a profit on the sales in order to achieve such profit they will need to buy the goods from you at a discounted price that is less than retail price. Wholesalers who will tend to buy goods in larger quantity than an individual retailer and will expect a higher trade discount for 'breaking bulk' and passing on your goods to other retailers. Individual retailers buying goods in smaller quantity will receive less trade discount and the general consumer buying direct from you would expect to pay the full retail price. Only wholesalers and retailers should be allowed trade discount.

Example:		Wholesaler		Retailer	Public
Selling Price		£100		£100	£100
Less Trade Discount	(40%)	40	(20%)	20	nil
Invoiced Price to be paid		60		80	100

It is the invoiced price of goods sold that is entered in the day book and subsequently into the Sales Account as a credit and in the Debtor or Sales Ledger Account as a debit.

CASH or SETTLEMENT DISCOUNTS may also be given to any type of customer for prompt payment. Since it will not be known whether or not a customer is likely to take advantage of such discounts until after the sale is made it does not affect entries in the sales day book or the ledgers at this stage. It will, however, be necessary to record such discount at the time the customer pays in cash or by cheque.

SELF-CHECK QUESTIONS

1. What is the purpose of the sales day book?
2. The sales day book is also called the sales
3. The total of the sales day book is entered into two ledger accounts – once as a debit and once as a credit. Name the accounts and state which is debited and which is credited.
4. The entry into the sales day book is made from what document?
5. Credit Notes are used for what purpose?
6. Returned goods will first be recorded in the sales
7. Goods may be returned for various reasons. Give three examples.
8. Enter the following invoice details into the sales day book and post the items to the relevant accounts in the sales ledger and the sales account in the nominal ledger.

19–8
January	1	Credit sale to F. Smith	£300
	5	Credit sale to J. Jones	£200
	7	Credit sale to M. Read	£100
	10	Credit sale to R. French	£600
	20	Credit sale to D. Bird	£500
	31	Credit sale to S. Snodden	£200

9. Enter the following transactions into the sales day book and then post to the relevant ledger accounts for Debtors; Sales and V.A.T.

19–7			Total Invoice £	V.A.T. £
May	1	Credit sale to J. Davis	115	15
	5	Credit sale to F. Smith	230	30
	8	Credit sale to D. French	460	60
	20	Credit sale to T. Taylor	345	45

10. Tommy Smith, a sole trader of 15 Pilgrim Walk, Chester is selling litre tins of paint at a recommended retail price of £5 per litre for any colour. During the month of June he makes the following sales:

June 1   To Sid Smith, 24 Frodsham Street, Chester, 10 litres of white gloss; 20 litres of red gloss and 5 litres of green gloss. 20% trade discount is allowed.

June 5   To Bromborough Building & Paint Supplies, The Rake, Eastham, 100 litres of rose white; 150 litres of cherry red; 200 litres of peach. 35% trade discount is allowed.

June 20   To Mary Rose, 15 Seaside Walk, Parkgate, 10 litres of yellow paint at full price.

June 30   To Francis Wood, Wellington Road, Stockport, 6 litres of red gloss and 10 litres of white, allowing 10% trade discount.

All paint supplied is subject to Value Added Tax at 15%.

You should:
(a) design an invoice to suit Tommy Smith's business needs.
(b) write up the invoice necessary for each of the above transactions.
(c) enter the invoices in the sales day book and code them for reference in some suitable manner.
(d) post the invoices to the debtors personal accounts and make the appropriate entry in the control or total debtors account.
(e) transfer the total to the Sales Account in the Nominal or General Ledger.

CREDIT PURCHASES
– using other people's money

We have just discussed what happens when a business makes a sale allowing credit. In this chapter we are concerned with what happens when purchases are made on credit terms. Remember one businesses sale is another businesses purchase. Therefore, the seller's sales invoice becomes the buyer's purchase invoice.

RECEIPT OF INVOICES

When a purchase invoice is received it should be stamped with the date it is received and details from the invoice should be entered into the Purchase Day Book which is simply a daily listing of all purchase invoices received. The day book will therefore be a chronological (date order) listing of all invoices received. Sufficient detail needs to be extracted from the invoice to answer any queries and to trace the correct invoice once it has been filed away. The following detail is normally noted: the date of receipt, the name of the supplier (Creditor), the total amount of the invoice, the goods or service value, the amount of Value Added Tax on the invoice if any, a reference and possibly in some systems there might be what are called day book analysis columns to state what type of purchase was made (e.g. raw materials tinplate or raw materials copper or work-in-progress components). In a computer system day book this analysis would be done by keying in an appropriate code number which would identify the type of purchase made.

ARE ANY CHECKS MADE BEFORE ENTRY TO THE DAY BOOK?

Yes, the purchase invoice should be checked by a responsible person to ensure that:

1)   The purchase was made by the company (an authorised officer thereof as evidenced by an Official Order).

2)   The prices quoted and any discounts allowed are calculated correctly and in accordance with what the purchasing officer agreed.

3)   The down-casts and cross-casts are arithmetically correct (i.e. the additions across and down is what accountants and those versed in accounting call casts).

4)   The amount of Value Added Tax has been charged at the appropriate rate in force and that the supply is a taxable supply or, if not, that V.A.T. has not been applied to the invoice.

5)   The total amount payable is arithmetically correct and that credit terms and any conditions attached to the invoice are in accordance with what has been agreed.

6)   The goods have been received (as evidenced by a goods received note GRN) in good condition and in the right quantity and of the right quality.

INTERNAL CONTROL

These checks are often referred to as Internal Checks; they form part of the 'Internal Control' procedures followed by the firm. In addition to the checks described Auditors like to see what they call the segregation of duties so that the person who places an order is not the same person who checks the invoice; checks the goods received and approves payment otherwise if this is the case it is easier for that person to defraud the company. For example, by authorising payments for goods never received to bogus or fictitious suppliers (himself by other names); or to a real supplier where the buyer and supplier have colluded to defraud the buyer's company by the supplier receiving cheques for goods never supplied but invoiced and authorised by the buyer so that the cheque sum can be split between the two fraudsters. Segregation of duties is easier for the large organization but not always possible in the smaller business for obvious reasons. However, small businesses will most often have the close control and direction of the owners which prevent fraud from taking place.

Having checked the above detail and found it to be correct the invoice can be accepted by the firm as a true record of its obligation to the supplier who is now called the CREDITOR (someone to whom the business owes money for goods or services supplied).

HOW WOULD THE ACCOUNTANT OR ACCOUNTS DEPARTMENT CHECK?

The invoice would be checked against a copy of the original order and copy of a goods received note which the accounts department would probably retain in a file as part of their system. The Authorised Purchasing Officer would also be expected to check the purchase invoice and sign or initial the invoice to evidence that prices, discounts, quantities, quality and terms and conditions are in accordance with the agreement made (the contract) and this signature would act as approval for payment too!

WHAT HAPPENS IF SOMETHING IS NOT RIGHT?

It depends upon the circumstances but if invoices are incorrect in any way the receiving firm can quite legitimately refuse to accept the invoice until it is right in every detail. In such a case the invoice would not be entered in the Purchase Day Book until it was right.

BUT ISN'T THIS CUMBERSOME?

Yes, but it is right! However, when a firm does regular business with the receiving firm often the incorrect purchase invoice is accepted and entered in the day book and corrections effected using credit notes to make adjustments to the original invoice, where appropriate but this is not always possible.

HOW ARE TRADE DISCOUNTS TREATED?

For the purpose of recording purchases it is the net (of trade discount) figure that is entered in the day book as the purchase total and later in the ledgers. Any settlement (cash) discounts will not be known until the firm makes a decision to accept or reject any discount for early settlement and therefore, such discount would be shown as a non-trading receipt in the form of income at a later stage but not taken into account at this point.

THE LEDGERS

The total of the Purchase Day Book for each period, (be it a day or week or some other time period) will be transferred (posted) to the ledgers as follows:

DEBIT — PURCHASE ACCOUNT (Nominal Ledger)

CREDIT — CREDITOR or PURCHASE LEDGER ACCOUNT

The purchase accounts will need to be entered individually since as described earlier there may be many different types of stock held by the firm. Similarly each creditor's personal account will need to contain detail about what is owed to that creditor. Note day book totals can only be posted in total to totals accounts or what accountants call CONTROL ACCOUNTS.

EXAMPLE OF DAY BOOK AND LEDGER ENTRIES

The following invoices have been noted in the Purchase Day Book:–

PURCHASE DAY BOOK

Date	Name	Invoice Ref.	Folio	£
August 1	J. Jones	08/01	PL 10	100
3	K. Astbury	08/02	PL 01	200
5	A. Davies	08/03	PL 05	500
Transferred to Purchases Account			NL 50	800

The entries made in the ledger accounts could be as follows:

PURCHASE LEDGER

A. Davies			Page	PL 05
				£ Cr
August 5	Purchase	PDB 81		500

K. Astbury			Page	PL 01
				£ Cr
August 3	Purchase	PDB 81		200

J. Jones			Page	PL 10
				£ Cr
August 1	Purchase	PDB 81		100

Note the purchase ledger is sometimes also referred to as the CREDITORS LEDGER.

NOMINAL LEDGER
Purchases Account

				£ Dr
August 5	Credit Purchases for week	PDB 81		800

RETURNS OUTWARDS (or PURCHASE RETURNS)

Sometimes it may be necessary for the receiving firm to send back the goods received because they are faulty or not of the right quality or specification required. Such returns are called returns outwards and are the exact opposite of returns inwards. A seller's returns inwards has of course been the buying firm's returns outwards.

The returning firm will issue a document called a 'DEBIT NOTE' to the supplier (seller) which gives details of the amount of allowance to which the firm returning the goods is entitled. The debit note is then listed in the Returns Outwards Day Book. The Purchase Day Book and the Returns Outwards Day Book taken together will give the total of net purchases made by the firm in a given period. For example, if the Purchase Day Book for the month totalled £2,000 and the Returns Outwards Day Book totalled £100 then the net purchases for that month would be £1,900.

The double entry for returns outwards is:

DEBIT — PURCHASE or CREDITORS LEDGER personal account	**(B.S.)**
CREDIT — RETURNS OUTWARDS ACCOUNT — Nominal Ledger	**(P&L)**

The debit note is called so because it is a note of a reduction in a liability (reduction of what is owed to the Creditor [supplier]) and hence the supplier's account in the Creditor's Ledger is debited with the amount on the note to record this. This entry effectively reduces the total creditors to be shown on the balance sheet by the same amount. The double entry recording is completed by crediting the Purchases Account to remove from the purchases for that period the goods that have been returned to suppliers. However, we do not credit the purchases account directly but rather have a separate account called Returns Outwards. This separation of purchases and returns enables the firm to keep track of total purchases and total returns and to identify problem suppliers or purchases in specific time periods and avoids confusion arising in the purchases account.

EXAMPLE

A firm issues a debit note for goods received from Swan; the amount of the goods returned is £100. This would be recorded in the Day Book and Ledgers as follows:

RETURNS OUTWARDS DAY BOOK

Date	Name of A/c	Debit Note	Folio	£ Amount
August 1st	Swan	08/01	PL 50	100.00
	Transferred to the Returns Outwards A/c		NL 90	100.00

Note if this was the only return noted in August the total for the month £100.00 would be posted as a credit to the Returns Outwards Account which is held on page 90 of the Nominal (General) Ledger in this case. The individual returns would be recorded as debits to the supplier's personal accounts in the Purchase (Creditors) Ledger. In this case Swan's account is held on page (folio) 50 and we have made note of that reference in the day book.

PURCHASE LEDGER
SWAN

Date	Account Name	folio	£ Dr
August 1st	Returns Outwards	RODB 08	100

NOMINAL LEDGER
RETURNS OUTWARDS

Date	Account Name	folio	£ Cr
August 1st	Returns for month	RODB 08	100

SELF-CHECK QUESTIONS

1. Give another name for the Purchase Day Book?
2. What detail is normally shown on a purchase invoice?
3. Where is the purchase invoice first recorded?
4. How is the double entry of a purchase transaction recorded?

Return Outwards

5. Is trade discount:
   (a) shown on the invoice?
   (b) shown in the day book?
   (c) recorded in the ledgers?
6. Is settlement or cash discount:
   (a) shown on the invoice?
   (b) shown in the day book?
   (c) recorded in the ledgers?
7. What checks should be made before an invoice is accepted as a true record of indebtedness?
8. Another name for the Purchase Ledger is?
9. Another name for the Nominal Ledger is?
10. Accounts held in the Purchase Ledger are often called Personal Accounts, do you know why?
11. What do you understand by the terms:
    (a) Internal Check?
    (b) Internal Control?
12. What is a debit note?
13. When and why is a debit note necessary?
14. Give another name for Purchase Returns?
15. Where are purchase returns first recorded?
16. How are purchase returns recorded in the ledgers, state the double entry?

QUESTIONS

1. Boyle makes the following purchases for May:
   May 1st. Buys goods from Davis on credit £500
   May 5th. Buys goods from Smith on credit for £1,000 list price less trade discount of 10% which has not yet been deducted from the list price.
   May 20th. Buys goods on credit £750 from Jones who allows 20% trade discount from the list price shown.

   Record the transactions shown above in:
   (a) The Purchase Day Book
   (b) The Purchase Ledger
   (c) The Nominal Ledger

2. Smith makes the following credit purchases in June:
   June 1st. Buys goods costing £1,000 on credit from Evans
   June 5th Buys goods costing £2,500 on credit from Davis
   June 12th. Buys goods at list price before discount £5,000 from Astbury who allows a trade discount of 25%
   June 20th. Buys goods at list price before discount £3,200 from Griffiths who allows 20% trade discount. Griffiths also allows a settlement discount of 2% if payment is received within seven days.
   June 30th. Buys goods from Clay at a cost of £6,600 before discount. Clay allows trade discount of 33.3%.

Note at the end of June no payments have been made to any of the above suppliers.

(a) Enter the Purchase Day Book for the month.
(b) Post the items to the supplier's personal accounts.
(c) Post the total purchases to the nominal ledger account.

3.   Zachary buys the following goods on credit during May:
     May 5th. Buys goods at cost £500 from Jones.
     May 10th. Buys goods at list price £1,000 from Wood who allows 25% trade discount on the list price.
     May 15th. Returns the goods bought from Jones on May 5th since they are unsuitable, a debit note has been raised for £500.
     May 20th. Buys goods at list price £3,300 and is allowed 33.33% trade discount of this price from Harris. Harris will also allow a cash discount of 1% if the account is settled in seven days.

     From the data above see if you can:
     (a) Write up the day books.
     (b) Post the relevant ledger accounts.

4.   Briefly explain how a settlement discount such as that in question three above should be dealt with in:
     (a) The Day Book.
     (b) The Ledger.

5.   Try question one again but this time assuming that all purchases have Value Added Tax applied to them at a rate of 15%.

THE LEDGER
– the books of account

The four essential parts to any accounting system are referred to as the LEDGERS and are:-

		Type of Account
1.	The Cash Ledger	Asset
2.	The Sales or Debtors Ledger	Asset
3.	The Purchases or Creditors Ledger	Liability
4.	The Nominal or General Ledger	Assets, Liabilities, Revenue, Expense or Capital

THE CASH BOOK (LEDGER)

All cash receipts and payments are recorded in this ledger. Cash is an asset.

> **DEBIT — DR. RECEIPTS**
>
> **CREDIT — CR. PAYMENTS**

THE SALES OR DEBTORS LEDGER

All sales made on credit terms are recorded in this ledger. It forms a record of what the business is owed by its customers. When the contractual sale is made and the title to the goods passes from the seller to the buyer, a legal claim to their cash price accrues to the Seller and is enforceable against the buyer who is the debtor. The title to the goods normally passes from seller to buyer when the goods are invoiced. There are exceptions to this rule which you may like to consider at a more advanced stage and there is the legal case of **ROMALPA** and clauses which are now referred to as **ROMALPA** or **Retention of Title** clauses. Thus, the accounting treatment will be determined by the circumstances.

The debtor is recorded (because it is an asset account) on the debit side of the Debtors Ledger and an entry made to the credit of the Sales Revenue Account in the Nominal or General Ledger. Note: there needs to be a Sales Revenue Account in the Nominal Ledger to record all sales, i.e. both cash sales and credit sales.

Thus a credit sale will be recorded as follows:-

> **DR — Debtor's Ledger Account — B/S**
>
> **CR — Sales Revenue Account — Nominal Ledger — P/L**

Note: a cash sale would be recorded simply missing out the Debtors Ledger Account. Thus:-

> **DR — Cash Book — B/S**
>
> **CR — Sales Revenue Account — Nominal Ledger — P/L**

When the debtor settles his account, the debtor balance needs to be cancelled in the Debtors Ledger by crediting the Debtor. The cash receipt is recorded as a debit in the Cash Book. Thus the asset of a debtor has now been replaced by the asset of cash.

> **DR — Cash Book — with the receipt — B/S**
>
> **CR — Debtors Ledger Account — payment — B/S**

THE PURCHASE OR CREDITORS LEDGER

Just as the Debtors Ledger records all credit sales, the Purchase or Creditors Ledger records all purchases made by the business on credit terms. Creditors are a liability, since at the end of the credit period allowed, amounts due to them are going to have to be settled by a cash payment.

CASH BOOK	
DEBIT	CREDIT
Receipts	Payments

CREDITORS LEDGER	
DEBIT	CREDIT
Cash Paid	Purchase made on credit

Note 1:
When the business buys an item from a supplier, the supplier becomes a creditor of the business. This fact is recorded by crediting the Liability Account (i.e. in the Creditors Ledger) which is in the name of that supplier. The debit is recorded in the Nominal Ledger in the appropriate expense account,

e.g. Advertising Expense Account or if the creditor is a Trade Creditor supplying the 'Stock in Trade' of the business, the debit entry is made in the PURCHASES ACCOUNT which is a sub-division of the STOCK ACCOUNT. Thus, the relevant asset or expense account contains the debit.

Note 2:
When the business pays the creditor (supplier) in cash, the creditor is discharged by debiting the Creditors Ledger. The corresponding entry for payment is recorded in the credit of the Cash Book.

Thus to summarise, when the business buys goods or services using credit, it is recorded as follows:-

---

DR — **Purchase Account** if stock bought

    — **Fixed Asset Account** — if machinery, land etc. bought

    — **Expense Account by type of expense**

CR — **CREDITORS LEDGER**

When payment is made to the creditor:-

DR — **CREDITORS LEDGER**

CR — **CASH ACCOUNT**

THE NOMINAL OR GENERAL LEDGER

Nominal in this sense means pertaining to a name. Thus, the Nominal Ledger contains within it a number of accounts by name. It is sometimes referred to as the General Ledger, general because it contains every account for which there is no place within any of the other ledgers.

We have discussed the other ledgers, and they only deal with 1) The Cash Account 2) The Debtors and 3) The Creditors. All the other accounts are held in the Nominal or as it is sometimes also called, the General Ledger.

SUMMARY — THE LEDGERS

The books of account are divided for convenience into four main ledgers, which are:-

        THE CASH BOOK
        THE SALES OR DEBTORS LEDGER
        THE PURCHASE OR CREDITORS LEDGER
        THE NOMINAL OR GENERAL

SELF-CHECK QUESTIONS

1. There are four main sub divisions of the financial accounting ledger, name them.
2. The cash book records cash receipts and payments but which is recorded on the left hand side and which on the right?
3. The nominal ledger records all transactions apart from those dealing in (a) Cash (b) Sales and (c) Purchases. TRUE OR FALSE?
4. Briefly explain the difference between the sales account in the nominal ledger and the sales ledger?
5. Briefly explain the difference between the purchase account in the nominal ledger and the purchase ledger.

THE FINANCIAL ACCOUNTING SYSTEM

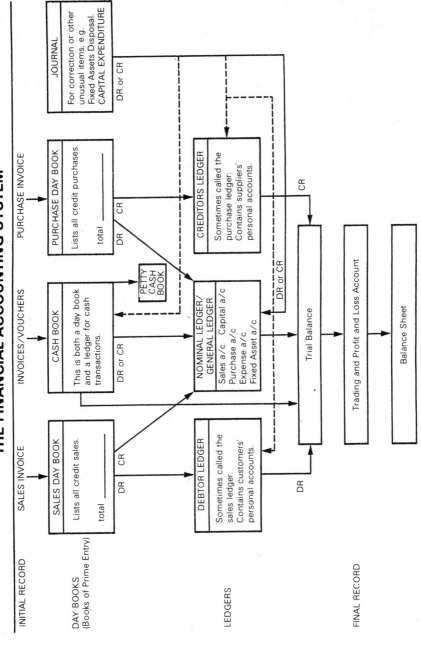

THE TRIAL BALANCE
– a means of control

DEFINITION

This is simply a listing of account balances extracted from the ledgers at a point in time. Remember the balance sheet equation:-
DEBIT balances are assets and expenses.
CREDIT balances are capital, liabilities and revenue accounts.
If you are in any doubt, revise the balance sheet equation.

PURPOSE OF THE TRIAL BALANCE

The double entry system means that every transaction recorded in the books of account has a **dual aspect. EVERY DEBIT HAS A CREDIT.** For example:-

If a business received £200 in cash for a sale, the dual aspect of this would be recorded as follows:-

---

DR — Cash Account — Cash Book — Balance Sheet

CR — Sales Account — Nominal Ledger — T, P & L

It can be seen that if this was the only transaction in the books of account for a period and we were to extract a trial balance, our list of balances would be as follows:-

TRIAL BALANCE AT . . . .

	£Dr	£Cr
Cash A/c	200	
Sales A/c		200
	200	200

Thus if we extend this to all ledger accounts we should be able to extract a list of balances for all transactions which have taken place during an accounting period where the debit balances will equal the credit balances.

A MEANS OF CONTROL

The trial balance is a means of quickly checking that we have a list of balances which agree before we proceed to the final financial statements (Trading and profit and loss account and balance sheet). It does, therefore, act as a control mechanism. If the trial balance does not agree it will be because one or more of the accounts within the ledgers is understated or overstated. This may be due to part of the dual entry being under or overstated, or a one sided entry having been made or an undercast or overcast of one or more of the accounts. In such cases a suspense account should be opened and the amount of the difference placed in suspense until the errors can be found and reallocated to the correct accounts using journal entries. Finding the errors may involve clerical staff in a time-consuming process of checking all the balances on the ledger accounts.

ERRORS WHICH WILL **NOT** BE DISCOVERED BY THE TRIAL BALANCE

The following types of error will not prevent the debit and credit entries from agreeing in a trial balance:-

1. **Errors of omission** – missed out completely, i.e. no debit or credit entry for a particular transaction.
2. **Errors of commission** – right type of account but wrong classification.
3. **Errors of principle** – an entry in the wrong type of account, e.g. Capital Expenditure shown as an expense (revenue).
4. **Reversed entries** – entered debit as credit or vice versa.
5. **Compensating errors** – an error of coincidence.
6. **Original entry** – error at original stage, i.e. in the day book. For example, £98 entered as £89 into the right accounts, but the wrong amount entered as debit and credit.

LEDGER ACCOUNTS — (sometimes called 'T' accounts because they are shaped like the letter T)

CASH A/C		SALES A/C	
£Dr	£Cr	£Dr	£Cr
SALES 200	Balance c/f 200	Balance c/f 200	CASH 200

If we go back to our original example of our two ledger accounts making up the trial balance, you will note that the closing balances are on the opposite sides to what they appear in the trial balance, thus the closing credit balance shown in the cash account appears on the debit side of the trial balance. This is because the closing credit balance in the cash book represents the amount of cash that the business has in hand at the end of the period. Carried forward balances in asset accounts are normally shown on the credit side. At the start of the new accounting period they will reappear as opening balances on the debit side. Closing balances on expense accounts are normally on the credit side. These balances are, however, normally closed off at the end of an accounting period and taken to the debit side of the profit and loss account. Liability accounts will normally have closing debit balances to carry forward at the end of an accounting period. At the start of the new accounting period the brought forward balance will be on the right hand side of the account, that is the CREDIT side. The capital account may be regarded as a liability of the business to the owners of that business. The revenue accounts will normally have closing debit balances to carry forward, they will be brought forward to the credit side of the trading and profit and loss account at the end of the accounting period.

DEBITS AND CREDITS

Debit simply means the left hand side of an account. Credit simply means the right hand side of an account. For accounting purposes you should not think of Debits or Credits as having any other meaning.

SUMMARY — THE TRIAL BALANCE

1. A trial balance is a list of balances at a point in time which is extracted from ledger accounts.

2. It acts as a control mechanism insofar as every debit has a corresponding credit entry.

3. It is quick and easy to extract from the ledgers before proceeding with final financial statements.

4. It will only reveal errors of understatement or overstatement.

5. A suspense account may be required until the detail of such errors described in 4. above are discovered and corrected using Journals.

6. There are a number of errors that will not be revealed by the trial balance — omission, commission, principle, compensating, reversal and original entry.

7. Closing carry forward balances in the ledger accounts are placed on the opposite side of the trial balance.
   See Chapter 21 for fuller explanation of errors.

EXAMPLE:

T. LEAF — ACCOUNT BALANCES AT 31.12.-5
extracted from the ledger are as follows:-

Fixed Assets	£
Land & Buildings	10,000
Motor Vehicles	5,000
Stock at 1.1.-5	3,500
Debtors	4,100
Bank	3,000
Cash	100
Purchases	15,000
Carriage In	100
Carriage Out	150
Discount Allowed	200
Returns In	150
Wages (to staff)	3,150
Bad debts	100
Post & Stationery	350
Light & Heat	650
Rent & Rates	1,400
Sales	20,000
Creditors	3,650
Discount Received	200

Provision for Depreciation	
Land & Buildings	3,000
Motor Vehicles	1,000
Capital	15,000
Loan	3,750
Provision for Bad Debts	250

Notes:
1. Stock at 31.12.-5 was £4,250.
2. The balance on the rent and rates account contains a payment of £200 in respect of 19–6 (pre-payment).
3. An invoice for £500 in respect of purchases made in December has been completely omitted from the books of account. It has not yet been paid.
4. A postage expense of £50 has been correctly entered in the postage account but no other entry has been made. The amount is still owed to a creditor.
5. Discount received of £50 has been correctly entered in the Debtors account but no other entry has been made.
6. Office equipment bought at a cost of £2,000 on the 1.1.–5 has been correctly entered in the bank account (for the payment) but wrongly

entered as a purchase. It is policy to depreciate office equipment at 10% per annum on cost.

7. A purchase for £500 made from R. Bowen has been correctly entered in the purchases account but wrongly entered in J. Bowen's account (Creditor).

8. An expense for light and heat of £152 has been entered into the correct accounts but at the wrong amount of £125. It has not yet been paid.

You are required to:-
(Note: you should only attempt part (1), (2) and (3) of this question at this stage. Try part (4) after reading Chapter 13.

1) Construct a trial balance from the list of balances before any adjustments are made.

2) Write down the necessary journal entries, to deal with the adjustments necessary to correct the accounts described in notes 2–8 above.

3) Construct an amended trial balance after the journal entries have made the necessary corrections.

4) From the amended trial balance construct a trading and profit and loss account for year ended 31.12.–5 and a balance sheet as at that date.

ANSWER:

T. LEAF — TRIAL BALANCE AT 31.12.-5 (before adjustment)

	£Dr	£Cr
Fixed Assets		
Land & Buildings	10,000	
Motor Vehicles	5,000	
Stock at 1.1.-5	3,500	
Debtors	4,100	
Bank	3,000	
Cash	100	
Purchases	15,000	
Carriage In	100	
Carriage Out	150	
Discount Allowed	200	
Returns In	150	
Wages (to staff)	3,150	
Bad Debts	100	
Post & Stationery	350	
Light & Heat	650	
Rent & Rates	1,400	
Sales		20,000
Creditors		3,650
Discount Received	200	
Provision for Depreciation		
Land & Buildings		3,000
Motor Vehicles		1,000
Capital		15,000
Loan		3,750
Provision for Bad Debts		250
Suspense Account		100
	46,950	46,950

JOURNAL

Reference to notes in question	Account Name — Narrative	£Dr	£Cr
2	Pre-payment A/c	200	
	Rent & Rates A/c		200
	Rent Prepaid		
3	Purchases A/c	500	
	Creditors A/c		500
	Error of Omission		
4	Suspense A/c	50	
	Creditors A/c		50
	(to correct)		
	One sided entry into Postage Expense		
5	Suspense A/c	50	
	Discount Received		50
	To correct one sided entry in Debtors only.		
6a.	Fixed Asset Office Equipment A/c	2,000	
	Purchases A/c		2,000
	To correct error of principle		
b.	Depreciation Expense —		
	Office Equipment A/c 10% per annum on cost.	200	
	Provision for Depreciation — Office Equipment A/c		200

7	R. Bowen — Creditor A/c	500	
	J. Bowen — Creditor A/c		500
	Error of Commission		
8	Light & Heat A/c	27	
	Creditors A/c		27
	Error of Original Entry		

SUSPENSE A/C

		£Dr		£Cr
4.	Creditors A/c	50	Balance b/f from	
5.	Discount received	50	original trial balance	100
		100		100

T. LEAF — AMENDED TRIAL BALANCE AT 31.12.-5

	£Dr	£Cr
Fixed Assets		
Land & Buildings	10,000	
Motor Vehicles	5,000	
Office Equipment	2,000	
Stock at 1.1.–5	3,500	
Debtors	4,100	
Bank	3,000	
Cash	100	
Purchases	13,500	
Carriage In	100	
Carriage Out	150	
Discount Allowed	200	
Returns In	150	
Wages (to staff)	3,150	
Bad Debts	100	
Post & Stationery	350	
Light & Heat	677	
Rent & Rates	1,200	
Sales		20,000
Creditors		4,227
Discount Received		250
Provision for Depreciation		
Land & Buildings		3,000
Motor Vehicles		1,000
Office Equipment		200
Capital		15,000
Loan		3,750
Provision for Bad Debts		250
Pre-payment	200	
Depreciation Expense	200	
	47,677	47,677

SELF-CHECK QUESTIONS

1. Briefly explain the purpose of a trial balance.
2. Debit and credit have a specific meaning in accounting, give a brief definition.
3. Why may the trial balance be regarded as a control mechanism?
4. Certain types of error will not be discovered by the trial balance. Name the errors and give concise explanations why this is so.
5. Define the term 'suspense account' and explain the purpose of such an account.

THE CASH BOOK
– receipts and payments

The Cash Book is referred to as a book of prime entry since it is the first place a cash transaction is recorded. It is also a part of the Ledger, that is the final record of the transaction. It is therefore unique in its role in the accounting system.

CONTENTS

It contains a record of all receipts and payments made by the business. Receipts are recorded on the left hand side (the debit side) and payments are recorded on the right hand side (the credit side).

For convenience, it contains separate columns for Bank and Cash transactions. Payments and Receipts made by cheque pass through the Bank Account and will be shown in the Bank column. Other transactions which are made in cash will be shown in the Cash column.

EXAMPLE

Jones undertakes the following transactions in the week ending 7.5.–5.

		£	
1.5	Balances b/f Bank	1,000	in hand
	Cash	500	in hand
3.5	Paid Plod – Creditor by cheque	250	
	Paid Green – Cash	200	
5.5	Received and immediately paid into the bank –		
	Cheques from Debtors	650	
6.5	Cash Sales	150	

Jones Cash Book would look like this:

Date	Account	£Dr Bank	£Dr Cash	Date	Account	£Cr Bank	£Cr Cash
1.5	Balances b/f	1,000	500	3.5	Plod — Creditor	250	
5.5	Debtors	650			Green		200
6.5	Cash Sales		150				
				7.5	Balances c/f	1,400	450
		1,650	650			1,650	650
8/5	Balances b/f	1,400	450				

Note how opening cash and bank balances are shown on the Receipt side, i.e. the debit side of the Cash Book. Closing balances in hand are shown on the right hand side, i.e. the credit side, and then brought forward on the left at the start of the next period.

BANK OVERDRAFT

A business may need to overdraw on its current account for short periods when cash usage is high. An overdraft would be shown as follows:-

		£Dr				£Cr	
Date	Account	Bank	Cash	Date	Account	Bank	Cash
31.5	Balance c/f	500		31.5			
		500				500	
				1.6	Balance b/f	500	

CONTRA ENTRIES

These are entries which are shown on both sides of the Cash Book and a symbol ¢ is shown alongside the entries to show that they are contra to each other.

EXAMPLE

Suppose Jones decides to withdraw cash by cheque from his Bank Account in order to use in the business, say, £500. It will be shown thus:-

		£Dr					£Cr	
Date	Account	Bank	Cash	Date	Account		Bank	Cash
8.5	Balances b/f	1,400	450	8.5	Cash	¢	500	
8.5	Bank ¢		500					

£500 has come out of the bank and is now ready cash to use in the business.

DISCOUNTS

A third column is normally shown in the Cash Book for discounts received and allowed. This column does not form part of the double entry system. It is merely shown by way of note for convenience. It is convenient to record discounts in the cash book since the discount forms part of the total payment or receipts.

EXAMPLE

A payment is made by cheque to Fred a Creditor for £300 after deducting 5% discount for prompt payment. Jed pays his debtor account of £500 after deducting a 10% discount.

The Cash Book would reflect these transactions as follows:-

Date	Account	Discount Allowed	Bank	Cash	Date	Account	Discount Received	Bank	Cash
X	Jed	50	450		X	Fred — Creditor	15	285	

You will notice that the discount entries could not possibly be part of the double entry system. They are only there by way of note. Furthermore, when the Cash Book is totalled the two **DISCOUNT COLUMNS** will contain different totals and **do not have to balance.**

RECEIPTS AND PAYMENTS ACCOUNT

The Cash Book is in effect a receipts and payments account, showing receipts on the left hand side and payments on the right hand side of the account.

Some small non-profit making organizations such as clubs or charities may present an annual financial summary in the form of receipts and payments account (i.e. a cash account), without taking account of debtors and creditors and without presenting a balance sheet.

OWNERS CAPITAL AND DRAWINGS

Capital put in by the owner will be shown as a Receipt in the Cash Book. Drawings, that is cash withdrawn from the business, will be shown as a payment to the owner.

The accounting entries are:
Capital Introduced

DEBIT — CASH BOOK

CREDIT — CAPITAL ACCOUNT

Drawings

> **DEBIT — DRAWINGS ACCOUNT**
>
> **CREDIT — CASH ACCOUNT**

Let us now look at a fully worked example.

EXAMPLE

Freddie Flippant undertakes the following transactions during the month of May. He does not, however, know how to record these in his Cash Book and therefore requires your help to write up his ledger. He does know that the balances brought forward on 1 May were £74 in cash and £1,120 in the bank:

May 2   Paid secretarial expenses in cash £50.
May 4   Withdrew £400 from the bank for business purposes.
May 5   Paid for office repairs in cash £250.
May 6   Made cash sales £110.
May 9   Terry Paylate paid his debtor account in full £255 by cheque.
May 10   The following payments are made to:
           Joe Truculent – Cleared the account of £120 but deduct 2% discount before paying by cheque.
           Sid Snodgrass £160 deducting 2% discount paid by cheque.
           Mike Mercury £200 less 2% discount paid by cheque.
May 12   Terry Paylate's cheque is returned by the bank as unpaid because it was not signed.
May 17   Cash sales £180.
May 18   Willie Wonker pays £300 by cheque after he has taken a 5% discount.
May 20   Wages paid in cash £150.
May 25   Freddie Flippant withdraws £500 for his own use by cheque.
May 27   Terry Paylate returns his cheque properly signed and dated.
May 31   All the cash is banked except for a £10 float.
May 31   Flippant buys a machine by cheque for £800.

F. FLIPPANT — Cash Book

Date	Account	Discount Allowed £Dr	Cash	Bank	Date	Account	Discount Received £Cr	Cash	Bank
1/5	Balance b/f		74	1,120					
					2/5	Sec. Exp.		50	
4/5	Drawing ¢		400		4/5	Drawing ¢			400
					5/5	Repairs		250	
6/5	Cash Sales		110						
9/5	T. Paylate			255					
					10/5	J. Truculent	3		117
						S. Snodgrass	4		156
						M. Mercury	5		195
					12/5	T. Paylate			255
17/5	Cash Sales		180						
18/5	W Wonker	15.78		300					
					20/5	Wages		150	
					25/5	Cash Drawing			500
27/5	T. Paylate			255					
31/5	Cash ¢			304	31/5	Bank ¢		304	
					31/5	Machine			800
31/5	Balance c/f			189	31/5	Balance c/f		10	
		15.78	764	2,423			12	764	2,423

ANALYSIS COLUMNS WITHIN THE CASH BOOK

RECEIPTS				£DR				PAYMENTS				£CR			
Date	Description or Account Name	Total	VAT	Discount Allowed	Bank	Cash	*	Date	Description or Account Name	Total	VAT	Discount Rec'd	Bank	Cash	*
1	2	3	4	5	6	7	8,9 etc	1	2	3	4	5	6	7	8,9 etc

The two-column cash book would show only the bank and cash columns (6,7). The three-column cash book would show columns 5,6 and 7 taking account of discount in addition to bank and cash.

It should be noted that the discount columns do not form part of the double-entry system, they actually contravene it. Nevertheless, it is convenient for discounts to be recorded in this book of prime entry in order that total payments or receipts may be reconciled with the relevant debtor or creditor accounts.

In practice, it is more convenient to have a cash book with analysis columns as shown above, in order that total receipts and payments may be classified into their appropriate account headings. The layout shown above would allow the following information to be recorded:-

Receipts
1. The date the transaction is entered.
2. The name of the account that the transaction affects, and any further information, e.g. invoice reference.
3. The total receipt.
4. The value added tax amount.
5. Any discount the business allowed, i.e. the amount in pounds.
6. If the payment was received by cheque, it would be entered in the bank column.
7. If payment was received in cash, it would be entered in the cash column.

Note: The remaining columns would be used to show an analysis as to the source of receipt, for example,
   8 - this column may show the amount received from debtors.
   9 - this column may show receipts in respect of royalties.

Further columns may be used to show receipts from other incomes, e.g. commission, patents, investments, and so on. There may also be a column in respect of capital.

Obviously the type and nature of the business will determine what these column headings are, and the number of column headings the business requires. It is normally not necessary to have more than 16 columns of analysis within the cash book. Where transactions are few, it is appropriate to have a sundries column to deal with miscellaneous receipts.

Payments
Columns 1 - 7 are the same as for receipts excepting, of course, that they are in respect of payments made by the business. The analysis columns may be detailed as follows:-
  8. Creditors i.e. payments made to suppliers in respect of stock purchases.
  9. Motor vehicle expenses.
 10. Travel and subsistence expenses.
 11. Sundries.

There might be other column headings which the business would find useful to have within the cash book where a large number of transactions for that particular type of payment occur. Once again this will depend on the type and nature of the business concerned. The sundries column would deal with miscellaneous expenses.

THE END OF AN ACCOUNTING PERIOD

At the end of an accounting period, say each month, (if monthly accounts are to be extracted) it would be necessary to total all columns in the cash book. In respect of columns 6 and 7, both on the receipts and payments side, the totals would be made to agree by placing a balancing figure in the column falling short of the higher total. This figure is called the balance to carry forward and is carried forward to the next accounting period. If the balance is on the right hand side, then it means that the business still has money in the bank and cash in hand. If the balance is on the left hand side, i.e. debit balance, this would need to be funded by overdrawing on the bank account.

THE PETTY CASH BOOK

Most organizations will operate a Petty Cash Book. This is a subsidiary of the main Cash Book. It is used for incidental expenses, for example, tea, coffee, sundry expenditure, incidental expenses for travel and subsistence.

THE IMPREST SYSTEM

Using an imprest system for Petty Cash is common. The system involves drawing a sum of money from the main Cash Book to use as a float and placing the sum, say, £100 to the debit side of the Petty Cash Book (i.e. left side). The cash will then be drawn and used for incidental expenses. Petty Cash Vouchers will be completed for each amount withdrawn, showing details of what the cash was used to obtain. As the cash is drawn down to zero, it will be replenished with a further sum to make the balance up to £100, drawn from the main Cash Book. The process will be repeated as the system enters another cash cycle.

CASH BOOK (Extract)

£ Dr   **£ Cr**

                              1.1.–6   To Petty Cash   100

PETTY CASH BOOK (with Analysis Columns)

Date	Description — Detail	Voucher No.	£ DR Receipts	Tea	Travel	Post	Stationery	Sundries
				PAYMENT ANALYSIS £ CR				
1.1.86	CASH BOOK	C1201	100.00					
2.1.86	Travel — Training Manchester	PC1201			10.00			
3.1.86	Tea & Coffee	PC1202		5.00				

The accounting entries necessary to effect the transfer of cash from the Cash Book to the Petty Cash Book are:

> **DR PETTY CASH BOOK — with the receipt**
>
> **CR CASH BOOK — with the payment to transfer**

In the main Cash Book, one of the payment analysis columns would be headed up Petty Cash. Just as described when we discussed the main Cash Book, the payment columns at the end of a period for each class of expense would be totalled and transferred to the relevant expense account within the General or Nominal Ledger. The accounting entries are:

> **DR Relevant Expense Account — Nominal Ledger — P/L**
>
> **CR Petty Cash Account — Nominal Ledger — B/S**

SUMMARY — THE CASH BOOK

The Cash Book is both a book of prime entry (the initial record) and a ledger. Receipts are recorded on the left hand side, i.e. the debit side, payments are recorded on the right hand side, i.e. the credit side. There are usually a number of columns on each side of the cash book giving an analysis of receipts and payments. The ledger part of the cash book may be thought of as the bank and cash columns, all other columns may be regarded as prime entry columns only.

The Petty cash book is a subsidiary of the Main cash book, dealing in small sums of money.

SELF-CHECK QUESTIONS

1. "The Cash Book has a dual purpose in the Financial Accounting system". Briefly explain what is meant by this statement.
2. Briefly explain the role of the petty cash book and give two examples of transactions that would be dealt with in this book.
3. The opening cash book balance b/f is £500 and petty cash b/f is £5. Record the following transactions in the cash book and petty cash book respectively:-
    (a) £100 drawn in cash for petty cash on January 1st;
    (b) £10 petty cash spent on tea and coffee on January 2nd;
    (c) £50 petty cash drawn for travel on January 3rd;
    (d) £10 of the £50 drawn for travel is returned on January 5th;
    (e) £40 petty cash used to buy stamps for postage on January 6th.
    Now rule off the cash book and petty cash book for the week ending January 7th.

FINAL FINANCIAL STATEMENTS FOR A SOLE-TRADER
– from initial record to final record

Let us take an example of a person who sets up a small business as a sole trader and observe the transactions which take place during the month of January. We will record the transaction in the Ledger Accounts and then extract a Trial Balance. Finally, we will construct the Trading and Profit and Loss Account for the month of January and a Balance Sheet at 31st January. A further two periods will then be examined to show the effect of transactions upon the Ledger and the final accounts.

KEY TO INITIALS USED THROUGHOUT THIS CHAPTER

NL	Nominal Ledger
₵	Entries shown on both sides of account = CONTRA
DR	DEBIT = Left hand side of an account
CR	CREDIT = Right hand side of an account
T/P&L	Trading and Profit and Loss Account
P/L	Profit and Loss Account
TB	Trial Balance
BS	Balance Sheet
CB	Cash Book
DL	Debtors Ledger
CL	Creditors Ledger
SDB	Sales Day Book
PDB	Purchase Day Book
VAT	Value Added Tax
PROV	Provision
CR	Are sometimes, if not always, indicated by being bracketed
A	Asset
E	Expense
C	Capital (may be regarded as a liability to the owner)
L	Liabilities
R	Revenue (Sales Income)

SUMMARIZED DETAIL

January

1st   S. Lee commences in business with £10,000 of his own money. He opens a business bank account and deposits the money in that account by cheque. Registers with HM Customs and Excise for VAT.

3rd   He buys shop premises for £20,000. Paying a deposit of £4,000 by cheque and obtaining a mortgage (loan) for the balance of £16,000 from a Building Society.

4th   Lee buys stock for resale from Smith a supplier at a cost of £4,000 plus VAT, payment to be made on 30th January by cheque. Only limited credit is allowed initially to Lee whilst Smith takes up references from the bank of Lee. VAT was chargeable at 15% (£600).

6th   Additional stock is purchased from Jones Ltd. at a cost of £2,000. No credit was allowed by Jones and payment was made immediately by cheque.

8th   The following expenses were paid by cheque:

— advertising to run for the month of January in the Local Gazette costing £300.

— wages to staff for one week £100.

10th   The following sales were made on credit terms to Atkinson Limited.

		£	VAT £	Total £
Invoice No.	100 Goods	500	75	575
	101 Goods	100	15	115

15th   Cash Sales were made amounting to £500 in total. There was no VAT charged on these sales as the goods were zero rated.

16th   Draws £200 by cheque from the bank and pays wages £100. The remaining £100 is left in the safe as a float.

20th   Sales were made to French Ltd. on credit terms

	£	VAT £	Total £
Invoice No. 102 Goods	300	45	345

21st   £500 cash is paid into the bank.

25th   Cash sales amounting to £345 all of which were subject to VAT, i.e. £300 goods, £45 VAT.

28th   Postage and stationery expenses are paid in cash £75. This was for letterheads, cards and mailing to customers.

30th   Cheque for £4,600 is made payable to Smith and posted to him. Atkinson paid by cheque £575 in respect of invoice 100.

31st   Wages paid by cheque £100.

Lee counted up the stock he had left and placed a value at cost of £5,000 on the stock.

SALES ACCOUNT

£ Dr			£ Cr
		10.1 Atkinson — Debtor	500
		Atkinson — Debtor	100
		15.1 Cash	500
		20.1 French Ltd. — Debtor	300
31.1 Balance c/f to P/L	1700	25.1 Cash	300
	1700		1700

VAT CONTROL ACCOUNT

Inputs	£ Dr	Outputs	£ Cr
4.1 Smith — Creditor	600	10.1 Atkinson — Debtor	75
		Atkinson — Debtor	15
		20.1 French — Debtor	45
		25.1 Cash Sales	45
		31.1 Balance c/f	420
	600		600

POST & STATIONERY

£ Dr			£ Cr
25.1 Cash	75	31.1 Balance c/f P/L	75

SMITH — CREDITOR ACCOUNT

£ Dr			£ Cr
30.1 Bank	4600	4.1 Purchases	4000
		VAT	600
	4600		4600

ATKINSON — DEBTOR ACCOUNT

£ Dr			£ Cr
10.1 100 Sales	500	30.1 Bank	575
VAT	75		
101 Sales	100		
VAT	15	31.1 Balance c/f	115
	690		690

FRENCH LTD. — DEBTOR ACCOUNT

	£ Dr		£ Cr
20.1 Sales a/c	300		
VAT	45	31.1 Balance c/f	345
	345		345

BANK AND CASH ACCOUNT

	£Dr RECEIPTS			£Cr PAYMENTS	
Account Name	Bank	Cash	Account Name	Bank	Cash
Jan 1st Capital A/c	10,000		Jan 3rd Shop Premises (F.A.) A/c	4,000	
Jan 3rd Mortgage A/c	16,000		Jan 3rd Shop Premises (F.A.) A/c	16,000	
Jan 15th Cash Sales A/c		500	Jan 30th Smith – Creditor A/c	4,600	
Jan 16th Bank A/c ¢		200	Jan 6th Purchases A/c – (Jones)	2,000	
Jan 21st Cash A/c ¢	500		Jan 8th Advertising Exp.	300	
Jan 25th Cash Sales A/c		300	Wages Exp.	100	
VAT A/c output		45	Jan 16th Cash ¢	200	
Jan 30th Debtors – Atkinson	575		Wages Exp.		100
(Inv. 100)			Jan 21st Bank A/c ¢		500
			Jan 28th Postage & Stationery A/c		75
			Jan 31st Wages Exp.	100	
Jan 31st Balance c/f	225		Jan 31st Balance c/f		370
	27,300	1,045		27,300	1,045
Feb 1st Balance b/f		370	Feb 1st Balance b/f	225	

CAPITAL ACCOUNT

	£ Dr			£ Cr
31.1 Balance c/f	10,000	1.1	Bank	10,000

FIXED ASSET AT COST — SHOP

	£ Dr		£ Cr
3.1 Bank			
Mortgage - B.Soc.	16,000		
Bank	4,000	31.1 Balance c/f	20,000
	20,000		20,000

MORTGAGE LOAN

	£ Dr			£ Cr
31.1 Balance c/f	16,000	3.1	Bank	16,000

PURCHASES A/C

		£ Dr			£ Cr
4.1	Smith — Creditor	4,000			
6.1	Jones Ltd — Bank	2,000	31.1	Balance c/f P/L	6,000
		6,000			6,000

ADVERTISING A/C (EXPENSES)

		£ Dr			£ Cr
8.1	Bank	300	31.1	Balance c/f P/L	300

WAGES A/C (EXPENSES)

		£ Dr			£ Cr
8.1	Bank	100			
16.1	Cash	100			
31.1	Cheque Bank	100	31.1	Balance c/f P/L	300
		300			300

S. LEE TRIAL BALANCE AT 31.1.–5

	£ Dr	£ Cr
Sales		1,700
VAT receivable	420	
Post & Stationery Expenses	75	
Creditors		NIL
Debtors (345 + 115)	460	
Bank)	45	
Cash)	100	
Capital		10,000
Fixed Assets — Shop at Cost	20,000	
Mortgage — Loan		16,000
Purchases	6,000	
Advertising	300	
Wages	300	
	27,700	27,700

S. LEE TRADING AND PROFIT AND LOSS ACCOUNT
FOR THE MONTH ENDED 31.1.–5

	£	£
Sales		1,700
Less Cost of Sales		
Opening Stock @ 1.1	NIL	
Add Purchases	6,000	
	6,000	
Less Closing Stock @ 31.1	(5,000)	
		(1,000)
Gross Profit		700
Less Expenses		
Post and Stationery	75	
Advertising	300	
Wages	300	
Total Expenses		(675)
Net Profit		25

S. LEE BALANCE SHEET AT 31.1.–5

Fixed Assets	**£ Cost**	**£ Prov. for Dep'n**	**£ Net Book Value**
Shop Premises	20,000	—	20,000
Current Assets			
Stock (@ valuation)	5,000		
Debtors	460		
VAT Receivable	420		
Bank	45		
Cash	100		
		6,025	
Less Current Liabilities			
Creditors	—	NIL	
Net Current Assets			6,025
Total Net Assets			26,025
Financed by			
Capital	10,000		
Add Net Profit Retained	25		
Total Equity		10,025	
Loan Capital			
Mortgages		16,000	
Capital Employed			26,025

PERIOD 2 — FEBRUARY — S. LEE

During period 2 the following transactions are completed. You are required to record these transactions in the books of account.

February

3rd   Cash Sales amounting to £345 inclusive of VAT.

5th   Sales made to Robertson on credit £1,000 = VAT   15%.

6th   Atkinson paid his outstanding account in full.

10th   Travelling Expenses in respect of visits to customers amount to £57.50 which have been paid in cash. VAT is included in this charge at 15%.

         Wages are paid by cheque £100.

         Sales made to Atkinson £500 for goods plus VAT at 15%.

15th   Cash Sales amounting to £500 plus VAT at 15%.

         Sales made to David £500 plus VAT at 15% on credit.

17th   Advertising expenses were paid by cheque in respect of advertisements placed in the local Gazette £300.

21st   French Ltd. paid his outstanding account by cheque.

         Further sales amounting to £1,150 inclusive of VAT were made to Atkinson.

         Wages £100 paid by cheque.

28th   Mortgage interest was paid amounting to £150 — by cheque. A further £30 was paid to the building society to reduce the capital outstanding on the loan.

         Sales for cash £500 plus VAT at 15%.

         Stock remaining at this date was valued at cost £2,500.

After all the entries have been made in the books of account, you should try and

1.   Extract a Trial Balance at 28/2.

2.   Construct a Trading and Profit and Loss Account for the two months ended 28/2 for Lee.

3.   Construct a Balance Sheet at 28/2.

You will see that I have recorded the transaction for S. Lee during the first period using traditional book-keeping techniques, with two columns showing debits (DR) on the left hand side of the account and credits (CR) on the right hand side of the account. Balances to carry forward are shown on that side of the account where the shortfall occurs. For example, a cash account showing the following entries has a shortfall on the right hand side. Thus, the balance to carry forward of £450 is shown on the right hand side (Credit).

DEBTORS LEDGER CONTROL ACCOUNT

Receipts		£ Dr	Payments		£ Cr
1.1	Balance b/f	1,000	10.1	R. Jones	100
			15.1	W. Smith	200
			20.1	T. Fry	50
			25.1	D. Peel	200
			31.1	Balance c/f	450
		1,000			1,000

You will, however, note that some systems have three columns showing DR CR Balance. Most mechanical or electronic data systems adopt this approach. The above entries would then be recorded as follows:

DEBTORS LEDGER CONTROL ACCOUNT

Date	Account Name	£ Dr	£ Cr	£ Balance
1.1	Balance b/f			1,000
10.1	R. Jones		100	900
15.1	W. Smith		200	700
20.1	T. Fry		50	650
25.1	D. Peel		200	450

Thus, a balance is easily extracted on any account at any time.

PERIOD 2 — S. LEE

SALES ACCOUNT — NOMINAL LEDGER

Date	Account	Ref	£ Dr	£ Cr	£ Balance
1.2	Balance b/f				1700.00
3.2	Cash			300.00	2000.00
5.2	Robertson — Debtor			1000.00	3000.00
10.2	Atkinson — Debtor			500.00	3500.00
15.2	Cash			500.00	4000.00
15.2	Davis — Debtor			500.00	4500.00
21.2	Atkinson — Debtor			1000.00	5500.00
28.2	Cash			500.00	6000.00

If no day book was used in a mechanical or electronic system the entries might go straight into the Sales Account in the Nominal Ledger as above. The Sales for the two months to 28.2 are £6000. This is the balance extracted for the Trial Balance which will subsequently enter the Trading Account.

Where a day book is used we could record the events as below:-

SALES ACCOUNT — NOMINAL LEDGER					
Date	Account	Ref	£ Dr	£ Cr	£ Balance
1.2	Balance b/f				1700.00
28.2	Sales Day Book Totals			4300.00	6000.00

Having made all the entries in the relevant accounts which are summarized below, you may extract the balances on the Ledger Accounts at 28.2 and place them in the Trial Balance at that date.

ATKINSON — DEBTOR DL

Date	Account	Ref	£ Dr	£ Cr	£ Balance
1.2	Balance b/f				115.00
6.2	Bank			115.00	NIL
10.2	Sales Account	SDB2 NL	500.00		500.00
	VAT Account	NL	75.00		575.00
21.2	Sales Account		1000.00		1575.00
	VAT Account		150.00		1725.00
28.2	Balance c/f				1725.00

ROBERTSON — DEBTOR DL

Date	Account	Ref	£ Dr	£ Cr	£ Balance
1.2	Balance b/f				NIL
5.2	Sales Account		1000.00		
	VAT Account		150.00		
28.2	Balance c/f				1150.00

DAVIS — DEBTOR DL

Date	Account	Ref	£ Dr	£ Cr	£ Balance
1.2	Balance b/f				NIL
15.2	Sales Account		500.00		
15.2	VAT Account		75.00		
28.2	Balance c/f				575.00

FRENCH LTD. — DEBTOR DL

Date	Account	Ref	£ Dr	£ Cr	£ Balance
1.2	Balance b/f				345.00
21.2	Bank		345.00		NIL

DEBTORS CONTROL ACCOUNT DL

Date	Account	Ref	£ Dr	£ Cr	£ Balance
1.2	Balance b/f				460.00
6.2	Bank			115.00	345.00
21.2	Bank			345.00	NIL
28.2	Day Book Totals				
	for Credit Sales		3000.00		3000.00
	for VAT		450.00		3450.00
	Balance c/f				3450.00

NOMINAL LEDGER ACCOUNTS

	TRAVELLING EXPENSES NL					
Date	Account Name	Ref	£ Dr	£ Cr	£ Balance	
1.2	Balance b/f				NIL	
10.2	Cash		50.00		50.00	
28.2	Balance c/f				50.00	

	WAGES EXPENSE ACCOUNT NL					
Date	Account Name	Ref	£ Dr	£ Cr	£ Balance	
1.2	Balance b/f				300.00	
10.2	Bank		100.00		400.00	
21.2	Bank		100.00		500.00	
28.2	Balance c/f				500.00	

	ADVERTISING EXPENSE ACCOUNT NL					
Date	Account Name	Ref	£ Dr	£ Cr	£ Balance	
1.2	Balance b/f				300.00	
17.2	Bank		300.00		600.00	
28.2	Balance c/f				600.00	

There were no entries in the Post and Stationery Expense Account for the month of February. This account would thus look as follows:-

POST AND STATIONERY ACCOUNT NL					
Date	Account Name	Ref	£ Dr	£ Cr	£ Balance
1.2	Balance b/f				75.00
28.2	Balance c/f				75.00

VAT CONTROL ACCOUNT NL					
Date	Account Name	Ref	£ Dr	£ Cr	£ Balance
1.2	Balance b/f				420.00
10.2	Travel Expenses		7.50		
28.2	Sales Day Book			645.00	(217.50)

MORTGAGE INTEREST EXPENSE ACCOUNT NL					
Date	Account Name	Ref	£ Dr	£ Cr	£ Balance
28.2	Bank			150.00	150.00

MORTGAGE LOAN ACCOUNT NL					
Date	Account Name	Ref	£ Dr	£ Cr	£ Balance
28.2	Balance b/f				16000 Cr
	Bank		30.00		15970 Cr

Note that during February more cheques have been paid out than received and the small balance £45 brought forward in the bank together with receipts in the month was insufficient to meet payments. Lee would need an overdraft for £175 from the Bank to cover his temporary cash shortage.

Thus, the closing debit balance at the bank indicates this. He still has cash in hand of £1537.50. If he wished he could use this £1537.50 cash to remove the overdraft. He would simply bank say £1437.50 and leave £100 cash in hand. You may like to try recording this transaction and changing the Trial Balance to reflect it.

SUMMARY OF ADJUSTMENT IN TRADITIONAL FORM
FOR PERIOD 2

BANK & CASH ACCOUNT

Date	Receipts	£ Dr Bank	£ Dr Cash	Date	Payments	£ Cr Bank	£ Cr Cash
	Balance b/f	45.00	100.00		Travel		50.00
	Cash Sales		345.00		VAT		7.50
	Debtor	115.00			Wages	100.00	
	Cash Sales		575.00		Advert	300.00	
	French Debtor	345.00			Wages	100.00	
	Cash Sale		575.00		Mortgage	180.00	
	Balance b/f	175.00			Balance c/f		1537.50
		680.00	1595.00			680.00	1595.00

SALES ACCOUNT NL

£ Dr		£ Cr	
		Balance b/f	1700
		Robertson	1000
		Atkinson	500
		Cash	300
		Cash	500
		Davis	500
		Atkinson	1000
Balance c/f	6000	Cash	500
	6000		6000

VAT ACCOUNT NL

Balance b/f	420.00	R	150.00
Travel Cash	7.50	A	75.00
		C	45.00
		C	75.00
		D	75.00
		A	150.00
Balance c/f	217.50	C	75.00
	645.00		645.00

DEBTOR CONTROL ACCOUNT DL

Balance b/f	460	A Bank	115
R	1150	F Bank	345
A	575		
D	575		
A	1150	Balance c/f	3450
	3910		3910

TRAVEL EXPENSE ACCOUNT NL

Bank	50		50

WAGES EXPENSE ACCOUNT NL

Balance b/f	300		
Bank	100		
Bank	100	Balance c/f	500
	500		500

ADVERTISING EXPENSE ACCOUNT NL

Balance b/f	300		
Bank	300	Balance c/f	600
	600		600

MORTGAGE INTEREST EXPENSE ACCOUNT NL

Bank	150	Balance c/f	150

MORTGAGE LOAN ACCOUNT NL

Bank	30		16000
	15970		
	16000		16000

S. LEE — TRIAL BALANCE AT 28/2

In this case		£ Dr	£ Cr
L	Bank — overdraft		175.00
A	Cash	1537.50	
R	Sales		6000.00
L	VAT payable		217.50
A	Debtors	3450.00	
E	Travel Expenses	50.00	
E	Wages Expenses	500.00	
E	Advertising	600.00	
E	Mortgage Interest Expenses	150.00	
L	Mortgage — Loan		15970.00
E	Post & Stationery	75.00	
L	Creditors		—
L	Capital		10000.00
A	F.A. Shop @ Cost	20000.00	
A	Stock Purchases	6000.00	
		32362.50	32362.50

FINANCIAL STATEMENTS — PERIOD 2

S. LEE TRADING AND PROFIT AND LOSS ACCOUNT
FOR 2 MONTHS TO 28.2

	£	£
Sales		6000
Less Cost of Sales		
Opening Stock @ 1.1	NIL	
Add Purchases	6000	
	6000	
Less Closing Stock @ 28.2	(2500)	
Cost of Goods Sold		(3500)
Gross Profit		2500
Less Expenses		
Travel	50	
Wages	500	
Advertising	600	
Mortgage Interest	150	
Post and Stationery	75	
Total Expenses		(1375)
Net Profit		1125

BALANCE SHEET AT 28.2

Fixed Assets	Cost £	Prov. for Dep'n. £	NBV £
Shop	20,000	—	20,000
Current Assets			
Stock	2500		
Debtors	3450		
Bank	—		
Cash	1537.50		
		7487.50	
Less Current Liabilities			
Creditors —Trade	NIL		
—VAT	217.50		
Bank Overdraft	175.00		
		(392.50)	
Net Current Assets			7095
Total Net Assets			27095
Financed by			
Capital	10000		
Add Profit	1125		
Total Equity		11125	
Mortgage Loan		15970	
Capital Employed			27095

PERIOD 3 — MARCH — S. LEE

Record the following transactions in Lee's books.

March — week ending

7.3   The following sales were made and invoices need making out and
       recording in the books.

		Invoice No.	£ Goods	£ VAT
	Jones	300	300	45
	Davis	301	400	60
	Atkinson	302	1000	150
14.3	Smith	303	300	45
	Jones	304	100	15
	Atkinson	305	500	75
	Brown	306	100	15
	Davis	307	100	15
21.3	Jones	308	400	60
	French Ltd.	309	500	75
	Atkinson	310	100	15
28.3	Jones	311	100	15
	Atkinson	312	400	60
	Smith	313	100	15
	Atkinson	314	200	30

March — week ending

7.3   The following purchases were made:-

		Invoice No.	£ Goods	£ VAT
	Smith — Creditor	P300	300	45
	Taylor — Creditor	P301	1000	150
14.3	Smith — Creditor	P302	500	75
	Brown — Creditor	P303	100	15
21.3	Smith — Creditor	P304	500	75
	Taylor — Creditor	P305	500	75
	Jones — Creditor	P306	100	15
28.3	Smith — Creditor	P307	100	15
	Jones — Creditor	P308	100	15

The following expenses were paid weekly by cheque:-

Secretarial Expenses	£25 per week
Wages	£100 per week
Advertising	£25 per week

Invoices were received in respect of Secretarial Expenses and Advertising.

A receipt was signed by employees for wages received (you may like to design such documentation and record the information in the books of account).

Other transactions:-

£1,200 cash was paid into the bank on 31.3.

All February Debtors paid by cheque on the last day of March. Similarly all creditors were paid by cheque on that day.

When all the entries have been made in the books of account you may like to try and complete the following financial statements.

1.   A Trial Balance at 31.1.

2.   A Trading and Profit and Loss Account for the 3 months to 31.3.

3.   A Balance Sheet at 31.3.

4.   A VAT Return for the 3 month period suitable to submit to HM Customs and Excise.

Note: Lee decided at the start of February to mark up stock purchases for resale by 50%.

$$\text{Mark Up} = \frac{\text{Profit}}{\text{Cost of Sales}} \times \frac{100}{1}$$

$$\text{Margin} = \frac{\text{Profit}}{\text{Sales}} \times \frac{100}{1}$$

Conversion

$$\text{Mark Up} = \frac{1}{2} \quad \therefore \quad \text{Margin} = \frac{1}{2+1} = \frac{1}{3}$$

Profit referred to here is GROSS PROFIT.

PERIOD 3 SUMMARIZED

Monthly Totals (4 weeks)	**Goods**	**VAT**	**Total**
Sales Day Book Totals	4600	690	5290
Purchase Day Book Total	3200	480	3680
Expenses Secretarial (4 × £25)	100		
Wages (4 × £100)	400		
Advertising (4 × £25)	100		

	£
Balance c/f in Sales Account for 3 months to 31.3	10600
Balance c/f in Purchases Account for 3 months to 31.3	9200
Balance c/f Expense A/c Secretarial (New A/c)	100
Wages	900
Advertising	700

Other Expenses A/c balances re Travel, Mortgage Interest and Post and Stationery would be as for February since transactions did not affect those accounts in March.

VAT CONTROL ACCOUNT

Creditors re Purchases	480.00	Balance b/f	217.50
Balance c/f	427.50	Debtors re Sales	690.00
	907.50		907.50

All other balances would be as for February apart from Bank and Cash shown below, and Debtors.

PERIOD 3

S. LEE — BANK AND CASH SUMMARY FOR MARCH

RECEIPTS		£ Dr		PAYMENTS		£ Cr	
Date	Account	Bank	Cash	Date	Account	Bank	Cash
1.3	Balance b/f		1537.50	1.3	Balance		
31.3	Debtors	3450.00			b/f	175.00	
	Cash ₵	1200.00			Secretarial	100.00	
					Wages	400.00	
					Advertising	100.00	
				31.3	Creditors	3680.50	
					Bank ₵		1200.00
					Balance c/f	195.00	337.50
		4650.00	1537.50			4650.00	1537.50

There were no cash payments apart from the transfer of cash to bank.

PERIOD 3 FINANCIAL STATEMENTS

S. LEE — TRADING AND PROFIT AND LOSS ACCOUNT
FOR 3 MONTHS TO 31.3

	£	£
Sales		10600
Less Cost of Sales		
Opening Stock @ 1.1	NIL	
Add Purchases	9200	
	9200	
Less Closing Stock @ 31.3	(2633)	
Cost of Goods Sold		(6567)
Gross Profit		4033
Less Expenses		
Secretarial	100	
Wages	900	
Advertising	700	
Travel	50	
Mortgage Interest	150	
Post and Stationery	75	
Total Expenses		(1975)
Net Profit		2058

S. LEE — BALANCE SHEET AT 31.3

	£ Cost	£ Prov. for Dep'n.	£ NBV
Fixed Assets			
Shop	20000	—	20000
Current Assets			
Stock	2633		
Debtors	5290		
Bank	195		
Cash	337.50		
		8455.50	
Less Current Liabilities			
Creditors	NIL		
VAT payable	427.50		
		(427.50)	
Net Current Assets			8028
Total Net Assets			28028
Financed by			
Capital	10000		
Add Profit	2058		
Total Equity		12058	
Add Mortgage Loan		15970	
Capital Employed			28028

DRAWINGS — Are a reduction of capital, they are not an expense.

If the owner withdrew any cash for himself during the first three months, you would need to show the amount as a cash payment (CREDIT) in the Cash Book and as a DEBIT in the Nominal Ledger Account for Drawings.

The accounting entries are:-

DR — Drawings Account — Nominal Ledger — B/S

CR — BANK or CASH Account — Nominal Ledger — B/S

The balance for either bank or cash in the Current Asset section of Balance Sheet would be lower by the drawings figure. The financed part of the balance sheet would detail drawings as follows:-

Financed by

Capital	X		
Add Profit	X		
	X		
Less Drawings	(X)		
Total Equity		X	
Add Loans		X	
Capital Employed			X

THE VAT RETURN for the period to 31.3

Outputs for the period Box 8   £10,600
i.e. the Sales Account Balance

Inputs for the period Box 9   £11,575
Includes Purchase A/c balances and
all Expense A/c balances
i.e. (9600 + 1975)

Note: the matching principle does not apply to the VAT Return. i.e. it is purchases not cost of sales which are included in the inputs.

VAT due on outputs from the
VAT Control A/c   £   907
should be placed in Box 1

VAT due on inputs — Box 4   £   480

The Box 1 figure will also be placed in Box 3, and Box 4 in Box 7. The differences between Box 3 and 6 will be the same as the balance c/f on the Control Account, i.e. £427.50. This is also the figure shown on the Balance Sheet as a creditor.

VAT RETURN

Return of Value Added Tax

For the period

to

For Official Use

H M Customs and Excise

To be returned not later than :

These dates must not be altered without the agreement of Customs and Excise.

Registration No   **Period**

Please complete the whole of this form. The note on the back and *Filling in your VAT return* will help you to do this. Return it, with any VAT due in the enclosed envelope to the Controller, VAT Central Unit, H M Customs and Excise, 21 Victoria Avenue, SOUTHEND-ON-SEA X

SS99 1AL

Complete all boxes (writing "none" where necessary). If an exact amount of pounds is to be entered write "00" in the pence column. Do not put a dash or leave the column blank.

FOR OFFICIAL USE

		£	p
VAT DUE in this period on OUTPUTS (sales. etc) certain postal imports and services received from abroad	1		
Underdeclarations of VAT made on previous returns (but not those notified in writing by Customs and Excise)	2		
TOTAL VAT DUE (box 1 - box 2)	3		
VAT DEDUCTIBLE in this period on INPUTS (purchases, etc)	4		
Overdeclarations of VAT made on previous returns (but not those notified in writing by Customs and Excise)	5		
TOTAL VAT DEDUCTIBLE (box 4 - box 5)	6		
NET VAT PAYABLE OR REPAYABLE (Difference between boxes 3 and 6)	7		

Please tick only ONE of these boxes:

box 3 greater than box 6   payment by credit transfer ☐   payment enclosed ☐

box 6 greater than box 3   repayment due ☐

			£	p
Value of Outputs (excluding any VAT)	8			00
Value of Inputs (excluding any VAT)	9			00

How to pay the VAT due

Cross all cheques and postal orders "A/C Payee only" and make them payable to "H M Customs and Excise". Make credit transfers through account 3078027 at National Girobank or 10-70-50 52055000 for Bank Giros You can get pre-printed booklets of credit transfer slips from your local VAT office In your own interest do not send notes, coins, or uncrossed postal orders through the post

Please write your VAT registration number on the back of all cheques and credit transfer slips.

Please tick box(es) if the statement(s) apply:

box 5 includes bad debt relief ☐   box 8 includes exempt outputs ☐   box 8 includes exports ☐

Retail schemes If you have used any of the schemes in the period covered by this return please tick the box(es) to show all the schemes used

☐ A ☐ B ☐ C ☐ D ☐ E ☐ F ☐ G ☐ H ☐ J

Failure to make a complete return or to pay the full amount of VAT payable by the due date is an offence.
DECLARATION by the signatory to be completed by or on behalf of the person named above.

I, ... declare that the
(full name of signatory in BLOCK LETTERS)

information given in this return is true and complete

Signed ....   Date .... 19 ......
(Proprietor, partner, director, secretary, responsible officer, member of club or association, duly authorised person)   *Delete as necessary*

FOR OFFICIAL USE

VAT 100   F 3740 (April 1985)

THE DISTINCTION BETWEEN CAPITAL and REVENUE EXPENDITURE – or how long will it last?

CAPITAL EXPENDITURE

Items which the firm buys with a view to increasing the earnings power of the business and which have a useful life, longer than 12 months, that is, the period of the current income statement are referred to as items of capital expenditure. Fixed assets are items of capital expenditure. The book-keeping entry is as follows:-

> **DR — Fixed Asset Account — B/S**
>
> **CR — Cash/Creditor (Loan Account) — B/S**

REVENUE EXPENDITURE

Revenue items of expenditure are charged to the current income statement. Such expenses are incurred in the day-to-day running of the business. Thus their usefulness is consumed within the income period, normally twelve months.

DISTINCTION

How do we distinguish between items of capital expenditure and items of revenue expenditure? The decision normally revolves around how long we intend to keep and use the item bought, and less importantly but nevertheless the practical problem regarding value. Normally if an item bought is expected to last longer than the period of one income statement, it would seem only right that we charge the relevant portion we consume during each income period, i.e. **the matching principle.**

This charge is, of course, depreciation. The practical problem regarding value is simply a question of cost and benefit, for example if a firm buys a new calculator for £15 which it estimates will remain in use for 5 years, strictly speaking the calculator should be capitalised and written down in value at £3 per annum. The £3 per annum being the depreciation charged to the income statement. In practice, many firms have a policy not to capitalise items below a certain value, e.g. £50, £100. Accountants refer to this concept concerning value as materiality. Does it, for example, affect the way in which the user of a financial statement will interpret the information if we decide to capitalise or not to capitalise a low value article such as a calculator?

ACQUISITION COSTS

Acquisition costs for items of capital expenditure should also be capitalised. For example, legal costs on buying premises or the cost of carriage inwards on capital items or installation costs of plant and machinery.

EXAMPLE

Sam and Ella run a small food shop. Classify the following transactions as either capital (C) or revenue expenditure (R).

		Answer
i.	Repairs to a meat slicer.	**R**
ii.	A new tyre for the van.	**R**
iii.	An additional shop counter.	**C**
iv.	Renewing the sign writing on the shop.	**R**
v.	Fitting partitions in the shop.	**C**
vi.	Roof repairs.	**R**
vii.	Installation of an alarm system.	**C**
viii.	Wages of a shop assistant.	**R**
ix.	Carriage on returns out.	**R**
x.	A new cash register.	**C**
xi.	Repairs to the office safe.	**R**
xii.	Installing an extra toilet.	**C**
xiii.	Legal cost of collecting debts.	**R**
xiv.	Legal charges on acquiring new premises.	**C**

R = Revenue, **C** = Capital

SUMMARY

It is important to distinguish between
1 Capital items which will be bought with a life expectancy greater than one year. These are placed in the balance sheet as fixed assets and their consumption is estimated as an expense called depreciation.
2 Revenue expenditure is applied to items which are consumed within one year. That is charged to the accounting period in which they are consumed. They are profit and loss account items.
3 The Matching Principle is the main concept to bear in mind. You need to match the expense against the revenue it has helped earn.

SELF-CHECK QUESTIONS

1. Mutt and Geoff Ltd. trade in audio equipment. The reported net profit for the year ended 31.12.–4 was £30,000. Upon investigation as internal auditor you suspect some transactions which you have discovered, will materially affect the financial statements.

    1. A microcomputer bought for the sales department at a cost of

£4,500 which includes £1,000 software has been charged to sales and marketing expenses.

2. A spondooly machine costing £2,000 has been charged to the servicing department as an expense.

3. A reconditioned engine costing £1,500 has been added to the motor vehicle account in the fixed asset register.

4. Legal expenses in respect of an insurance claim on repairing the shop front have been placed in the fixed asset account for buildings. Cost £1,000.

5. The cost of repair to the shop front £10,000 has also been placed in the fixed asset account of buildings.

6. The cost of installing new telephone equipment £1,000 has been charged to the telephone expense account. The equipment has, however, been purchased by the organization and only the line is rented from British Telecom.

7. A service contract on the new computer has been placed in the fixed asset account for office machinery £250.

Other information you have gleaned is as follows:-
Depreciation policy — buildings depreciated over their useful life on a straight line basis 50 years.
Plant and machinery is depreciated at 10% on a straight line basis.
Office machinery is depreciated at 10% on a straight line basis.
Fixtures and fittings are depreciated at 10% per annum on a straight line basis.
Motor vehicles are depreciated at 25% per annum on a reducing balance basis.

Note: It is the policy of the organization to charge a full year's depreciation in the year of acquisition. It is also policy not to capitalise items below £100.

Required:
1. The journal entries which you feel are necessary in respect of correcting the above transactions.
2. A brief explanation supporting your decision.
3. A financial statement suitable for presentation to management showing the corrected net profit figure to the year 31.12.-4.

2. Distinguish between capital and revenue expenditure, giving two examples.

3. A road haulage business have just purchased two new tractors costing £25,000. However, before bringing them into use they need to be painted in the company's livery at a cost of £1,000. Explain how you would treat the expenditures giving your reasons.

4. CAPITAL and REVENUE.

1. The estimated net profit for Dalglish Limited for the year ended 31st March 19-5 is £10,100 before the following items are taken account of:

(a) The cost of a new workshop built during the year and completed on 30th September 19-4 at a cost of £20,000.
(b) The cost of a new word processor bought on 1st January 19-5 for £2,500.
(c) Repairs to typewriters incurred on 1st January 19-5 — £500.
(d) The cost of installing a re-conditioned engine in a delivery van on 30th June 19-4 — £500.
(e) Legal expenses paid in respect of the new workshop — £500.

It is the policy of Dalglish Ltd. to charge depreciation as follows:-

(i) Buildings are written off in equal instalments over 20 years.
(ii) All plant, machinery and office equipment is written off over 10 years on a straight line basis.
(iii) Motor vehicles are written off at 25% p.a. on a reducing balance basis.

N.B. Depreciation is apportioned on a monthly basis.

Required:

1.(a) Distinguish between Capital and Revenue Expenditure.
Explain with reference to each of the items (a) to (e) above why you have chosen to classify each of them either as Capital or Revenue Expenditure.

2. Calculate a revised estimated profit after taking account of each of the items (a) to (e) and show your answer clearly in the form of a statement.

DEPRECIATION
– the reduction in the value of assets

DEFINITION

Depreciation is a charge (expense) for the use of a fixed asset, that is a proportion of capital expenditure charged to the revenue account via depreciation. It is an estimate of the using up of an asset over time (e.g. wear and tear).

Depreciation is a charge for
1)   Use of an asset (wearing out or wear and tear as a result of use)
2)   Time-ageing of an asset
3)   Obsolescence.

In other words, not only may a fixed asset be depreciated through use, but it may also lose value owing to age or by means of technological advancement causing the asset to become obsolete.

There are various methods for the calculation of depreciation. The most common of these methods are:-

1)   The Straight Line Method
2)   The Reducing Balance Method
3)   The Sum of the Year Digits (SYD)

The choice of method will depend upon the opinion of the professional accountant as to the most appropriate method, given the particular circumstances. Professional judgement based upon experience is called for in making the choice. Some guidance is given in the Statement of Standard Accounting Practice on the depreciation of fixed assets (SSAP 12).

Straight Line Depreciation — charges an equal proportion of the cost to the Profit and Loss account each year over the estimated life of the asset as an expense for using the asset.

$$\text{STRAIGHT LINE DEPRECIATION AMOUNT} = \frac{\text{COST less SCRAP or Residual Value}}{\text{Estimated Number of Years useful life}}$$

Thus, an asset costing £1,000 estimated to have a useful life of 5 years and a scrap value of nil would be depreciated using this method as follows:-

$$\frac{£1000 - NIL}{5 \text{ years}}$$

$$= £200 \text{ per annum}$$

Graphing this information we get:-

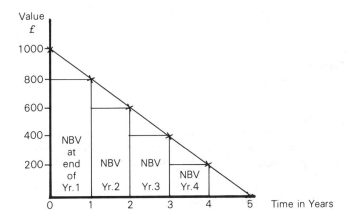

This graph of the function gives a straight line, hence the name straight line depreciation. You will note that the Net Book Value (NBV) at the end of the 1st year is £800 thus a fall in value (depreciation) has taken place of £200.

Reducing Balance Method — Using the information contained within our example above we can illustrate the reducing balance method. In order to calculate a rate of depreciation, use the following formulae:-

$$\text{Reducing Balance Rate} = 1 - \sqrt[n]{\frac{S}{C}}$$

where n = Estimated useful life
S = Scrap Value or Residual Value
C = Cost

thus $\quad 1 - \sqrt[5]{\frac{0}{1000}} \qquad = 75\% \qquad 1 - 0.25$

The approximate rate obtained is 75% per annum. However, unlike the straight line method, the rate 75% is applied to the Net Book Value or Reduced Balance.

	1 Net Book Value		2 Rate %	3 Amount of Depreciation
Start of Year 1	1000*	×	75%	750
2	250	×	75%	188
3	62	×	75%	47
4	15	×	75%	11
5	4	×	75%	3
				999

*Note: the Net Book Value = Cost at start
1–3 gives NBV for start of next year.

It can be seen that the rate we calculated (75%) would leave a residue value of £1 at the end of the 5th year. The formula is designed to leave a zero book value at the end of the estimated life. The residue in this case will be due to roundings. In practice, I would simply write off the residual £1 in the final year.

Graphing the information we get:-

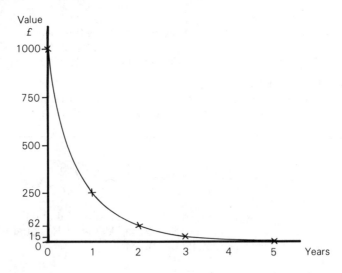

This time we obtain a curve. You can see that by choosing this method of depreciation the asset loses most value in the first year. Using the reducing balance method will always mean that an asset loses most of its value in the early years. Thus profit would be correspondingly lower in the early years.

Sum of the Year Digits (SYD) — Using the same information let us illustrate how depreciation is calculated using this method.

Year	Cost £	Rate of Depreciation	Amount £ p.a.	NBV £
1	1000	5/15	333	667
2	1000	4/15	267	400
3	1000	3/15	200	200
4	1000	2/15	133	67
5	1000	1/15	67	0
$\sum 15$			1000	in total for 5 years

The sum of the year's digits is 15
(i.e. 1 + 2 + 3 + 4 + 5 = 15)
The asset is then depreciated in proportion with the number of years it has left to be used. For example, in the 1st year it still has 5 years, therefore, 5/15; in the second year still 4 years, thus 4/15 and so on.

Once again the asset loses most value in the early years. In this case 60% of the value has been used in two years.

Graphing this information we get:-

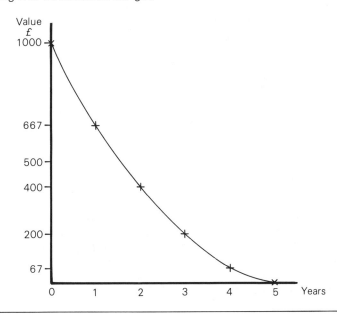

COMPARING THE METHODS (for an asset costing £1000 and lasting 5 years).

Net Book Values	Straight Line £	Reducing Balance £	SYD £
At the end of Year 1	800	250	667
2	600	62	400
3	400	15	200
4	200	4	67
5	0	0	0

The straight line method suggests that the asset wears out evenly through use or time over the 5 years.

The reducing balance method suggests that most of the fall in value takes place in the first year.

The SYD method would suggest also that most of the value is lost in the early years, but it gives a much smoother decline in value than the reduced balance method.

SSAP 12

In the Standard Statement of Accounting Practice depreciation is defined as "the measure of the wearing out, consumption or other loss of value of a fixed asset whether arising from use, effluxion of time or obsolescence through technology and market changes". The definition deliberately refers to the losing of value rather than the cost and this has been done so that it covers not only historic cost depreciation but depreciation based on changing price levels. In other words to cover any inflation accounting system that might be brought into operation. The Standard goes on to say that depreciation should be allocated to each accounting period in order to charge a fair proportion of the using up of the particular asset. Depreciation includes amortization of fixed assets whose useful life is pre-determined, for example, leases, and for the depreciation of wasting assets. A wasting asset of course is an asset like a mine where the land is only useful during the period when profitable extraction can be undertaken.

LAND AND BUILDINGS

Land and buildings deserve special mention. Prior to the Standard being introduced, freehold and long leasehold properties were very rarely charged depreciation. However, the Standard now says that the land should not be depreciated but the property which stands on the land needs to be depreciated and written off over the useful life of that particular property. Land, of course, does not depreciate; in fact you may ask yourself the question, "Does not land appreciate?" and we will turn our attention to appreciation below. Some land, of course, would depreciate, as we have already discussed in the case of a wasting asset, such as a mine, an oil well or a quarry, or that particular kind of item. The exception with regard to properties are those investment properties which are not really owned for use by the owner but simply owned as a means of creating a return on one's investment when used by a third party. In the case of those properties, they should be treated like other investments and shown at the market value of the investment. That's a special case.

APPRECIATION

Some assets, like land, may appreciate. Normal accounting procedure would tend to ignore appreciation since if appreciation were to be brought into the accounting concept it would contravene both the historic cost idea and also the concept of prudence. Current Cost Accounting does attempt to take account of appreciation — see SSAP 16.

THE RATE OF DEPRECIATION

The rate at which depreciation should be charged will depend on three factors:-

1) The cost or value of the asset, value particularly in the cases of changing price level statements.

2) The particular type of asset and the length of time which it is estimated to have as a useful life. Time, use and obsolescence will have to be taken into account here in the accountant's professional judgement.

3) The residual value which one estimates, that is to say the estimated value of the asset at the end of its useful life.

No particular method of depreciation is favoured over any other method in the Statement of Standard Accounting Practice number 12. This, once again, is left to professional judgement.

DISCLOSURE

In the financial statements where depreciable assets are shown, the following items should be disclosed:-

1) The depreciation method used, i.e. straight line or reducing balance, or some other method.

2) The useful lives of the assets, in other words the time period over which they are being written off.

3) The total depreciation allocated for the particular period of the financial statement.

4) The gross original cost (or later revaluation) of depreciable assets together with the accumulated depreciation charged to date.

If there is a change of accounting policy with regard to depreciation then this too needs to be stated in the notes to the financial statement. Such notes should state the revised depreciation policy, and quantify the effect of the change of policy. It should also state when the new policy came into operation.

ACCOUNTING TREATMENT

**DEBIT DEPRECIATION EXPENSE ACCOUNT
(PROFIT AND LOSS)**

**CREDIT PROVISION FOR DEPRECIATION ACCOUNT
(BALANCE SHEET)**

We have introduced a new item called a provision. We are already familiar with expense account items; now let us look to the definition of a provision. A provision is an amount set aside out of revenue to meet a liability or expense which, although recognised, cannot be determined with substantial accuracy at the balance sheet date. There are other provisions in addition to depreciation, e.g. one could have a provision for bad debts or a provision with regard to a contract.

OTHER IMPORTANT POINTS

In practice, items of capital expenditure may be incurred at any time during the financial period in question, that is to say they will not be incurred only at the start and finish of a particular period.

This raises a practical problem with regard to depreciation. Should we depreciate a full year's charge in the year of purchase, even if the fixed asset is bought during the last month or last few months of the particular year in question? Or should we, on the other hand, merely charge depreciation by month, or by day, or however? This is a matter of policy; different firms will have different policy decisions. Some firms will indeed charge a full year's depreciation for the year of purchase, regardless of when the purchase was made. Others will in fact take a proportion, normally based on months rather than days. Often it is a matter for practical convenience. Remember that depreciation is only an estimate of the wearing out of a particular asset, and as such is not as scientific as some texts would have one believe, or indeed as some accountants would have one believe. Similarly, in the year in which an asset is disposed of, some firms will charge a full year's depreciation for the disposing year, others will charge none for the year of disposal. The profit or loss on disposal is in effect an adjustment of previous estimates to reflect actual depreciation which has occurred between the purchase (or revaluation) date and the date of disposal. Where no depreciation is charged in the year of disposal, it does have the advantage of making the disposal accounts easier to calculate.

Other accounting concepts need to be taken into account with regard to depreciation. For example, once a business has decided on a particular method of depreciation for a particular class of asset, it should continue to apply the same method consistently over time, hence the concept of consistency. The concept of prudence should also be taken into account. This is a matter for professional judgement; for example, if one were to buy a micro computer, one should not estimate the useful life of that machine to be ten years if it is likely that technical innovation will make it obsolete in a shorter period of time.

Finally, it needs to be emphasised that the amount at which a particular fixed asset is shown in the balance sheet, that is the net book value of the asset or the written down value of that particular asset, is not the value of the asset. It merely represents the proportion of the original cost or value which has not yet been written off at the balance sheet date. Depreciation is **not** a means of ensuring that replacement of the asset will take place out of the provision. It is simply a charge to the business for the use of a particular asset over time.

SUMMARY

Depreciation is a charge (expense) for using a fixed asset (capital expenditure item).
It represents:- 1 Wear and tear of an asset through use
            2 Ageing
     or 3 Obsolescence

There are various methods for calculating depreciation, the most common of which are:-
            1 The Straight Line Method
            2 The Reducing Balance Method
            3 The Sum of the Years Digits

SELF-CHECK QUESTIONS

1. We buy a machine for £5,000 and estimate its useful life to be 5 years, after which time we expect it to be sold for £1,000 as scrap.

   Required: the annual charge for depreciation for each of the five years
   using   (a) The Straight Line Method
              (b) The Reducing Balance Method
              (c) Graph the Straight Line Method

2. C.J. buys a grott dispenser for £6,250. It is estimated to last 8 years, after which time it will be sold as scrap for £650. Advise C.J. on which method of depreciation to use in order to show the best profit by the end of the fifth year.

3. Jones buys a machine for £4,000 which he estimates will last 8 years and be worthless at the end of the eighth year.

Required:
1. Calculate the annual rate of depreciation to be applied to the cost.
2. Annual amount of depreciation to be charged each year.
3. Graph the information.
4. Show the balance sheet extract for each of the 8 years.

4. SUM OF YEAR DIGITS
    Fred buys a machine for £5,000 which he estimates will last 5 years and have a scrap value at the end of the fifth year of £1,000. Using the SYD method of depreciation show the charge each year.

5. P.G. buys a machine for £5,650. He estimates that the machine will last 5 years, after which time he will be able to sell it to G.B. for £150 cash.

Required:
Calculate the annual amount of depreciation chargeable to the profit and loss account using:
1) The straight line method
2) The reducing balance method
3) SYD
Show the balance sheet extract under each method for each of the five years.

DISPOSAL OF FIXED ASSETS
– selling business assets

WHAT IS MEANT BY DISPOSAL?

For one reason or another the business may decide to get rid of a particular machine or building prior to its reaching the end of its estimated useful life. For example, it may decide to replace an existing machine with a newer model or it may simply decide it no longer needs the particular machine. Thus, the machine's value in exchange (i.e. what it can realize immediately in cash) is greater than the machine's value in use (i.e. what it could expect to earn in revenue over its remaining useful productive life).

BOOKKEEPING ENTRIES ON ACQUISITION

When a fixed asset is purchased it is entered into the relevant fixed asset account at cost and cash is exchanged for the asset. That is, we

> **DEBIT   FIXED ASSET ACCOUNT AT COST**
>
> **CREDIT — CASH ACCOUNT WITH COST**

RECORDING DEPRECIATION

We then estimate how long the machine is likely to last and provide for the annual loss in value through charging depreciation.

> **DEBIT   — DEPRECIATION EXPENSE — PROFIT & LOSS ACCOUNT**
>
> **CREDIT — CUMULATIVE PROVISION FOR DEPRECIATION — BALANCE SHEET**

RECORDING DISPOSALS

If, however, we dispose of the asset we need to remove the asset from our books of account as follows:-

> **CREDIT — FIXED ASSET ACCOUNT AT COST B/S**
>
> **DEBIT   — DISPOSAL OF FIXED ASSET ACCOUNT AT COST P/L**

We also need to remove the cumulative provision for depreciation we have made over the period we held the asset, since we are no longer concerned with the fall in value of that particular asset. Therefore:-

---

DEBIT — **THE PROVISION FOR DEPRECIATION ACCOUNT — B/S** with the cumulative depreciation charged against that asset.

CREDIT — **THE DISPOSAL OF FIXED ASSET ACCOUNT — P/L** with the same amount.

Finally, we hopefully will have received some cash in exchange for the asset, therefore, we need to:-

---

DEBIT — **CASH ACCOUNT — B/S** with proceeds

CREDIT — **THE DISPOSAL OF FIXED ASSET ACCOUNT — P/L** with the cash proceeds

---

Having completed the above recording of the transactions we will be left with a difference in the Disposal Account, which if on the left hand side (DEBIT SIDE) will be a profit on disposal, and if on the right hand side (CREDIT SIDE) will be a loss on disposal.

EXAMPLE

X Ltd. bought a machine for £5,000 cash exactly 3 years ago. The Balance Sheet today shows the Net Book Value of the asset as £2,000. Thus the Balance Sheet Summary for that particular asset would be as follows:

	Cost £	Cumulative Provision for Depreciation	Net Book Value £
Machine	5,000	3,000	2,000

Y Ltd. paid £2,150 in cash for the machine. Show the Disposal Account.

Thus, following the steps described above:-

THE ACCOUNTS BEFORE DISPOSAL WOULD LOOK LIKE THIS:

FIXED ASSET — MACHINE A/C — B/S

		£ Dr			£ Cr
Year 1	Cash	5000	Year 1	Balance c/f	5000
Year 2	Balance b/f	5000	Year 2	Balance c/f	5000
Year 3	Balance b/f	5000			

PROVISION FOR DEPRECIATION A/C — B/S

Year 1	Balance c/f	1000	Year 1	Depreciation Exp.	1000
			Year 2	Balance b/f	1000
Year 2	Balance c/f	2000		Depreciation Exp.	1000
		2000			2000
			Year 3	Balance b/f	2000
				Depreciation Exp.	1000
					3000

DEPRECIATION EXPENSE A/C — P/L

		£ Dr			£ Cr
Year 1	Provision for Depreciation	1000	Year 1	Balance c/f to P/L A/C	1000
Year 2	Provision for Depreciation	1000	Year 2	Balance c/f to P/L A/C	1000
Year 3	Provision for Depreciation	1000	Year 3	Balance c/f to P/L A/C	1000

Notice, we have not yet closed off the Fixed Asset Account nor the Provision for Depreciation Account for Year 3. This is because we will now enter the Disposal Account as follows:-

THE ACCOUNTS AFTER DISPOSAL

FIXED ASSET — MACHINE A/C — B/S

Year 3 Balance b/f	5000		Year 3 Disposal A/C	5000

PROVISION FOR DEPRECIATION — MACHINE A/C — B/S

		Year 3 Balance b/f	2000
		Depreciation	
Year 3 Disposal A/C	3000	Exp.	1000
	3000		3000

DISPOSAL ACCOUNT

	£ Dr		£ Cr
Year 3 Fixed Asset – Machine a/c at cost	5000	Year 3 Provision for Deprec- iation.	3000
* Profit on Disposal transferred to P & L a/c	150	Year 3 Cash a/c — Proceeds	2150
	5150		5150

*Before this entry is made the excess of credit £5150 over debit £5000 indicates that a "profit" on disposal has appeared. This arises because earlier estimates of depreciation debited to the P & L A/c were overstated. The entry marked with the asterisk therefore effects a transfer to the P & L A/c as a corrective adjustment.

Thus, the profit on disposal is £150. Note the difference between the cash received and the Net Book Value of an asset will give you the profit or loss on disposal at a glance.

(i.e. CASH — NBV in this case 2150 – 2000 = £150)

SUMMARY

- This chapter explained the procedure for disposals of fixed assets.
- A profit on disposal is classed as Non-Trading Income and should be shown immediately below Gross Profit as an addition to profit.

e.g.	Gross Profit	X
	Add non-trading income	
	Profit on Disposal	X
		X
	Less Expenses	
	X	
	X	

- A loss would be treated as an expense. The loss could, however, be shown as extra depreciation. A profit could be treated as a credit to the expense of depreciation for management accounts.

SELF-CHECK QUESTIONS

1. Kirkpatrick Limited, sellers and repairers of motor vehicles, commenced business on 1 January 19–2. The company's balance sheet as at 31 December 19–3 included the following items in the fixed assets section:

	At cost	Aggregate depreciation	Net
	£	£	£
Motor vehicles	21,000	7,560	13,440

All the motor vehicles included above were acquired when the company commenced business, the vehicles were XYZ123 costing £10,000, ABC456 costing £7,000 and PQR789 costing £4,000. The company's policy up to 31 December 19–3 has been to provide depreciation at the rate of 20% per annum using the reducing balance method. However, it has now been decided to adopt the straight line method of providing for depreciation and to adjust the motor vehicles provision for depreciation at 1 January 19–4 in accordance with the new policy. In future, depreciation will be provided annually at the rate of 20% of the original cost of motor vehicles held at each accounting year end.

During 19–4, the following transactions took place involving motor vehicles (fixed assets):
31 March

Vehicle XYZ123 was badly damaged in a road accident. The insurance company decided that the vehicle was beyond repair and therefore paid Kirkpatrick Limited £7,100 in full settlement.
30 June
Vehicle RST765 bought for cash from Express Traders Limited. Kirkpatrick Limited paid a cheque for £8,300 in full settlement of the amount due which included the insurance of the vehicle for the year commencing 30 June 19-4 of £500.
30 September
Kirkpatrick Limited exchanged vehicle PQR789 for a new vehicle DEF432 and paid a cheque for £3,000 in full settlement. The list price of the new vehicle was £5,000.
10 October
Paid Quickspray Limited £200 for repainting DEF432 in the company's colours before it was used by Kirkpatrick Limited.

Required:
(a) Prepare the journal entries (or entry) required for the transaction of 30 September 19-4;
     Note: Narratives are required.   *(5 marks)*
(b) Prepare the following accounts in the books of the company for the year ended 31 December 19-4:
          Motor vehicles — at cost
          Motor vehicles — provision for depreciation
          Motor vehicles disposals
     Note: a separate account is opened for each vehicle disposal.
                                                          (15 marks)
                                                    (Total 20 marks)
                                                             [AAT]

2X. ADF Ltd. dispose of motor vehicles shown at cost in the balance sheet at 30.6. at £7,000. The cumulative depreciation provided against those vehicles to 30.6. was £4,000. The proceeds of the disposal was received by cheque £5,100 on that day.

You are required to:
(a) Show the Journal Entries required to record the above events.
(b) Show the Profit or Loss on Disposal in a Disposal Account.
                                                          (16 marks)

3. Since he commenced business on 1st January 19-9, Mr. I. Makeit has purchased three machines for his various manufacturing activities, viz.

Machine	Date of purchase	Cost £
A	20th January 19-9	3,200
B	18th April 19-0	6,000
C	11th June 19-1	4,200

Each machine was bought for cash.

Mr. Makeit's policy is to charge a full year's depreciation in the year of purchase irrespective of the date of purchase. He uses the diminishing balance method for calculating depreciation and the rates applicable to the three machines are as follows:

Machine	% rate
A	25
B	30
C	40

Required:
(a) A schedule showing the cost, each year's depreciation and the written down value of each machine at the end of each of the three years 19–9, 19–0 and 19–1.
(b) The Machinery Account and its related Depreciation Provision Account for the said three years.   [AAT]

4X. Brown is in business as a building contractor. At 1st May 19–2 he had three lorries, details of which are as follows:

Lorry Registration Number	Date Purchased	Cost	Accumulated Depreciation to Date
		£	£
BAB 1	1 July 19–9	16,000	9,000
CAB 2	1 January 19–1	21,000	8,000
DAB 3	1 April 19–2	31,000	6,000

During the year to 30th April 19–3, the following lorry transactions took place:
(a) BAB 1 was sold on 31st July 19–2 for £3,000 on cash terms. On 1st August 19–2 Brown replaced it with a new lorry, registration number FAB 4 for which he paid £35,000 in cash.
(b) On 15th December 19–2, the new lorry (FAB 4) was involved in a major accident, and as a result was completely written off. Brown was able to agree a claim with his insurance company, and on 31st December 19–2 he received £30,000 from the company. On 1st January 19–3 he bought another new lorry (registration number HAB 6) for £41,000.
(c) During March 19–3, Brown decided to replace the lorry bought on 1st April 19–2 (registration number DAB 3) with a new lorry. It was delivered on 1st April 19–3 (registration number JAB 6). He agreed a purchase price of £26,000 for the new lorry, the terms of which were £20,000 in part exchange for the old lorry and the balance to be paid immediately in cash.

Notes:
(i) Brown uses the straight line method of depreciation based on year end figures.

(ii) *The lorries are depreciated over a five-year period by which time they are assumed to have an exchange value of £1,000 each.*

(iii) *A full year's depreciation is charged in the year of acquisition, but no depreciation is charged if a lorry is bought and sold or otherwise disposed of within the same financial year.*

(iv) *No depreciation is charged in the year of disposal.*

(v) *Brown does not keep separate accounts for each lorry.*

Required:
(a) Write up the following accounts for the year to 30th April 19–3:
    (i) Lorries Account.
    (ii) Lorries Disposal Account.
    (iii) Provision for Depreciation on Lorries Account.
(b) Show how the Lorries Account and the Provision for Depreciation Account would be presented in Brown's Balance Sheet as at 30th April 19–3.   [AAT].

5. The vehicles and plant register of Hexagon Transport Ltd. shows the following vehicles in service at 30 September 19–3:

Registration No.	HT 1	HT 2	HT 3	HT 4	HT 5
Purchased during the year ended 30 September	19–9	19–0	19–1	19–2	19–3
Original cost	£800	£860	£840	£950	£980

Up to 30 September 19–3, the company had depreciated its motor vehicles by 20 per cent per annum on the diminishing balance system, but as from 1 October 19–3, it is decided to adopt the straight line method of depreciation, and to write all the vehicles down to an estimated residual value of £20 each over an estimated life of five years. The company wishes to adjust the accrued depreciation provisions on the existing vehicles in line with this policy.

During the year ended 30 September 19–4, the company has purchased vehicle HT 6 for £960 and sold HT 2 for £60.

A whole year's depreciation is provided for every vehicle on hand at the end of any accounting period.

You are required to:
(a) Reconstruct the entries for each vehicle in the register, as it appeared on 30 September 19–3.
(b) Calculate the necessary adjustments to be made in respect of the depreciation provisions on 1 October 19–3.
(c) Complete the entries in the register for the year to 30 September 19–4, showing clearly how you calculate any adjustment necessary in respect of the sale of HT 2. Calculations should be made to the nearest £1.   *(CIMA)*

6X. On 1 January, 19–5 John Smith purchased 6 machines for £1,500 each. His accounting year ends on 31 December. Depreciation at the rate of 10 per cent per annum on cost has been charged against income each year and credited to a provision for depreciation account.

On 1 January, 19–6 one machine was sold for £1,250 and on 1 January 19–7 a second machine was sold for £1,150. An improved model which cost £2,800 was purchased on 1 July, 19–6. Depreciation was charged on this new machine at the same rate as that on earlier purchases.

Required:
(a) The machinery account and the provision for depreciation account for 19–5, 19–6 and 19–7; and
(b) The entry for machines in the balance sheet at 31 December 19–7.   *[IOB]*

REDUCTION IN THE VALUE OF ASSETS
– the use of provision accounts

INTRODUCTION

We have already looked at depreciation. Depreciation is a charge for the use of a fixed asset. We charge an amount of depreciation each year to the profit and loss statement equivalent to our estimate of the asset value lost through consumption (use).

Other assets can also lose value. For example, let us turn to debtors. If the business makes credit sales to customers then that means that those customers owe the business the amount of the sale. Until they pay for the goods in cash they are called debtors. Debtors are an asset to the business, (strange as this may seem to someone coming new to accounting, but a business has a legal right to recover the amount. It is therefore an asset and will eventually turn into another asset BANK OR CASH). We discussed debtors briefly in the section on the balance sheet equation. It is necessary in many types of business to allow credit to customers so that sales can in fact grow which in turn leads to further investment in the business, so an expansion of sales may be a pre-requisite for the expansion of the business in total.

There are a number of important aspects with regard to debtors which will interest both the management of the organisation and the investor. There is the problem of working capital management which we will discuss later in the section on working capital. There is also the problem of the level of debtors in relation to other assets. The firm obviously does not want to over indulge one particular classification of asset because this has implications for the capacity of the business to actually produce and earn further amounts. For example, if we have four or five months' debtors on hand then this has cost implications for investment. It means in fact that the business will have to borrow from the bank at the going rate of interest for normal production funds which it would have obtained in the normal course of trade from its debtors (because the debtor would eventually turn into cash). The longer it takes the debtor to turn into cash the more it will cost the firm in terms of a bank loan, and its production and possibly its future expansion will suffer; it will limit its future expansion.

Finally, the longer a particular debtor remains on the balance sheet the less likely it is that the debtor will actually pay for the goods, so there is a problem of credit control.

BAD DEBTS

Any business that trades on credit terms will inevitably suffer what are called bad debts. These are simply debtors who fail to pay the amount that they owe to the business. As a result, these bad debts become an expense to the business rather than an asset. Obviously, if somebody owes you money and he never pays then you suffer a loss. This loss (expense) must be written off immediately the fact becomes known that the debtor is not going to pay, hence the prudence concept. There may be, in addition to what we call bad debts, what we consider doubtful debts. These are debtors about which we have some question mark — their ability to pay. It may be for example that we have heard on the grapevine that a particular customer is having cash flow problems or industrial relations problems, either of which is causing delayed payments. The longer the trouble occurs the less likely the debtor will pay. Therefore it is important to make a provision for the doubtful debt. We have already discussed the idea of what a provision is, in the section on depreciation.

Let me now summarise the bookkeeping entries for bad debts and doubtful debts. First of all, bad debts. A bad debt can be written off immediately it is known the debtor is not going to pay. The entry for this is as follows:-

---

DEBIT — BAD DEBT EXPENSE ACCOUNT (Profit & Loss)

CREDIT — DEBTORS (Balance Sheet)

The effect of this entry is to reduce debtors shown on the Balance Sheet by the amount which we consider to be irrecoverable and in turn by putting the loss in the Profit & Loss Statement as an expense we have reduced income by the amount not recoverable.

DOUBTFUL DEBTS

We have already discussed what a doubtful debt is. It is an amount owed by a debtor which we consider may be irrecoverable. It may be that we consider only part of the debt irrecoverable, in which case it is still prudent to make a provision for that part we consider irrecoverable. The entry for a doubtful debt is as follows:-

---

DEBIT — BAD DEBT EXPENSE ACCOUNT (Profit & Loss)

**CREDIT — PROVISION FOR DOUBTFUL DEBTS
(Balance Sheet)**

Once again this has the effect of reducing income in the Profit & Loss Statement by the amount of the doubtful debt and in the Balance Sheet the provision for doubtful debts is shown as a deduction from debtors, in other words we show debtors less the provision for doubtful debts and we show only the net debtor figure in the Balance Sheet.

Other assets apart from debtors can also lose value. It may be for instance that stock will lose value.

STOCK

Stock will be treated as a separate item later on in this book. Nevertheless it is appropriate to mention at this point the idea that stock does not always maintain its value. For example, certain stock items may become redundant, that is, no longer useful to the business. They may become obsolete, in which case they may no longer be of use to any business. A full discussion of how stock can lose value will take place later. It is sufficient to say here that the SSAP 9 which covers stock and work in progress states that stock should be placed in the Balance Sheet at the lower of cost or market value. In other words, if we realise that stock is obsolete or redundant, we ought to write the stock down from its cost figure which it would be shown at in the Balance Sheet, to its now new market value, if it has any. We will do this by

---

DEBIT   — COST OF SALES ACCOUNT — TRADING ACCOUNT

CREDIT — STOCK ACCOUNT — BALANCE SHEET

Alternatively, if you were uncertain about the value of stock, it may be prudent again to use the device of a provision in which case immediately we thought that stock may not realise its balance sheet value we would provide against such loss by debiting the income statement and crediting a provision account. We will see this later on.

SUMMARY — Reductions in the Value of Assets

— PROVISIONS are a means of taking account of a fall in value of an asset. They are a charge against income.

---

thus — DR —EXPENSE A/c — P/L

CR —PROVISION A/c — B/S

— Provisions are normally made for:-
        Depreciation
        Doubtful Debts
        Stock

SELF-CHECK QUESTIONS

1. A business commences on 1.1.19–6. The following debts are bad and written off on the dates shown. The year end is 31.12.19–6.

	£
31 May T. Bell	220
30 September R. Cook	128
30 November D B Ltd.	24

   On 31st December 19–6 the total debtors extracted from the ledger amount to £5,950. It is decided to make a provision for doubtful debts of £250.

   You are required to show:-
   1. The bad debts account.
   2. The provision for bad debts account.
   3. The charge to the profit and loss account.
   4. The relevant balance sheet figures for 31st December 19–6.

2. The closing debtors total at 31st December 19–6 for Ray is £3,500. Ray decides to make a provision for bad debts equivalent to 2% of the closing debtors. In addition he writes off £100 as a bad debt.

   You are required to show:
   1. The bad debts account.
   2. The provision for bad debts account.
   3. The charge to the profit and loss account.
   4. The relevant balance sheet figures for 31st December 19–6.

3X. Certain balances in a company's ledger at 30th June, 19–0 were:

	£
Debtors	20,000
Provision for bad debts	1,000
Stock of coke	630
Electricity accrued	920

During the year to 30th June, 19–1 the following transactions occurred:

	£
Sales on credit	200,000
Cash received from debtors	193,000
Certain debtors became bankrupt, and their debts were written off against the provision	3,000
Certain debts which had been written off as bad in previous years were recovered in cash and transferred to the provision	1,000
Purchases of coke	8,000
Payments for electricity for the year ended 30th April, 19–1	6,000

At 30th June, 19–1 the stock of coke was valued at £750, and the provision for bad debts was adjusted to be equal to 5% of the debtors. On 6th August, 19–1 the company paid its electricity account of £1,010 for the quarter ended 31st July, 19–1.

Required:
You are required to show the debtors, provision for bad debts and lighting and heating accounts in the company's ledger for the year ended 30th June, 19–1.   *(15 marks)*
                                                                                    (CIMA)

BANK RECONCILIATION
STATEMENTS – agreeing the bank
statement with the cash book

All businesses make payments in cash or by cheque and they will receive payments in cash or by cheque. In order to record these transactions the business will keep a Cash Book (ledger) as we have seen, with a separate column for cash, bank and discount transactions. Cash transactions are instant and therefore when cash is received or paid, the actual cash balance held by the firm will increase or reduce immediately. On the other hand when transactions pass through the bank account, timing differences may occur, or indeed there may be transactions passing through the bank account on a particular date about which we have no knowledge.

WHAT IS A BANK RECONCILIATION?

A bank reconciliation is a statement which results from comparing the entries in the business cash book with entries shown on the bank statement. The statement should clearly show why the balance shown in the cash book differs from that of the bank statement at a point in time.

— The reconciliation acts as an independent check on the accuracy of entries made in the cash book.

— Differences may occur for other reasons apart from errors. For example, differences occur because items:
a) shown in the cash book have not yet appeared on the bank statement owing to timing differences.
and
b) shown on the bank statement but not yet entered into the cash book. (e.g. direct debits, standing orders, credit transfers etc.)

— Where there is a difference between a particular item in the cash book and the bank statement then greater reliance should be placed on the bank statement.

TIMING DIFFERENCES

There are two major reasons why timing differences occur, which are:

1) Unpresented cheques: are payments recorded in the cash book which are not yet shown on the bank statement.

2) Uncredited lodgements: are receipts shown in the cash book of a business but not yet credited in the business bank account.

WHY DIFFERENCES CAN OCCUR BETWEEN CASH BOOK AND THE BANK STATEMENT IN DETAIL

1. Cheques received by the business will be entered in the Cash Book upon receipt and passed to the bank for payment. It will take the bank a few days to clear this cheque and place it upon your statement. These are referred to as **bank lodgements** not yet credited.

2. A business may write a cheque in settlement of a particular debt and this cheque payment will be recorded in the firm's Cash Book the same day it is issued. However it will take a couple of days in the post to reach the Creditor and he may take a day or two before he actually banks it, and the bank will take three days before they clear the cheque and enter it on the bank statement. These are called **unpresented cheques.**

3. **Standing Orders.** A standing order is an instruction to the bank to pay regularly a specific amount to a particular person, or business on specified dates. When writing up the Cash Book standing orders could be easily overlooked and may only be re-discovered when a bank statement is received.

    The amount on the standing order cannot be varied by the bank. Any change in the amount of the standing order has to be instructed from the customer.

4. **Direct Debits.** A direct debit results from a document giving authority to the recipient to claim any amount due from your bank. Unlike a standing order the amount is variable and the creditor has direct access to the funds in a customer's bank account, subject to an obligation to restore amounts wrongly claimed.

5. **Dishonoured Cheques.** A cheque may be received by a customer and entered into the firm's Cash Book and passed to the bank for payment. The bank may well enter the cheque on the firm's bank statement and pass the cheque to the drawer's bank for payment. The drawer's bank may return the cheque as unpaid. The following list gives an indication of some of the reasons why this may happen:

    a) The customer has insufficient funds in his bank account to cover the cheque.
    b) The customer forgets to sign the cheque.
    c) The cheque is undated.
    d) An alteration to a cheque which is unauthorised, i.e. the customer has forgotten to initial the alteration.
    e) If the cheque is more than 6 months old then the bank will not honour it. The drawer would have to issue a fresh cheque.
    f) The customer draws a cheque on a bank account which he has since closed between drawing the cheque and the business receiving the cheque.

g) Cheques written where the words and the numbers do not agree, i.e. the amount written in words on the cheque may differ from the numbers in the payment box.

6. **Stopped Cheques.** After obtaining the goods and making the cheque payment a customer may decide to stop payment on a cheque, without notifying the vendor. This situation may only come to light when the bank statement is received.

7. **Bank Charges.** These have a nasty habit of appearing on the business bank statement without prior knowledge being given to the business about the amount. They cannot, therefore, be written into the Cash Book until the Bank Statement is received.

8. **Credit Transfers.** Payments can be made directly from one bank account to another, if the payer has details such as the account number and the bank sorting code of the supplier, by filling in a Credit Transfer document. In such instances the business being paid may not actually know that they have been paid until they see the bank statement and the firm's Cash Book may only be written up by the receiver on receipt of the Bank Statement.

9. **Traders Credit.** Traders Credit is similar to a Credit Transfer.

10. **Cash Point.** Cash withdrawn using a card at a cash point.

PROCEDURE FOR RECONCILING

The procedure is a systematic check of the bank statement to the cash book and may be carried out as follows:

1) Check all the bank statements are present for the period you are reconciling. (Bank Statements are consecutively numbered, so check you have the sequence required; check balances carried forward and brought forward are correct).

2) Rule a line across the statement after the last entry within the accounting period you are reconciling.

3) Check the opening reconciliation to ensure that the opening balances you begin from in the period are the same and that all outstanding items shown on the last reconciliation statement have now been cleared.

4) Tick the receipt side of the cash book to the bank statement.

5) Tick the payment side of the cash book to the bank statement.

6) Adjust the cash book for errors and omissions found (unticked items on the bank statement will identify omissions and errors would also be discovered if incorrectly recorded items had been entered in either the cash book or on the bank statement in the ticking procedure).

REMEMBER THE CASH BOOK SHOULD BE A MIRROR IMAGE OF THE BANK STATEMENT, EVERY DEBIT IN THE CASH BOOK SHOULD HAVE A CORRESPONDING CREDIT ON THE BANK STATEMENT.

7) Balance off the cash book.

8) Write out the reconciliation statement by starting with the balance per the statement and ending with the balance per the cash book. (Note: you could do this by starting with the cash book balance and ending with the bank statement balance, it does not really matter).

9) Make adjustments for uncredited lodgements and unpresented cheques.

PRO-FORMA BANK RECONCILIATION

	£
Balance per bank statement as at - - / - - / - -	
Add: Bank Lodgements	
Deposits not credited	
Less: Unpresented Cheques	
Balance per Cash Book as at - - / - - / - -	

or alternatively:

	£
Balance per cash book as at / /	
Add back unpresented cheques	
Credit transfers (not yet on	
Bank Statement) — payments	_____
Less Bank lodgements /	_____
Balance per Bank Statement as at / /	======

EXAMPLE 1

Cash Book	£Dr			£Cr
May 27 Balance b/f	650	May 28 T. McDermott		70
		May 29 D. Johnson		120
		May 31 Balance c/f		460
	650			650
Jun 1 Balance b/f	460			

Bank Statement at 31.5

	Dr	Cr	Balance
May 27 Balance b/f			650 CR
May 31 T. McDermott	70		580 CR

ANSWER

Bank Reconciliation Statement at 31.5

	£
Balance per Bank Statement	580
Less unpresented cheque —	
D. Johnson	120
Balance per Cash Book	460

-556.45
-154.99

OR

Bank Reconciliation Statement at 31.5

	£
Balance per Cash Book	460
Add unpresented cheque —	
D. Johnson	120
Balance per Bank Statement	580

Remember the Bank Statement should be a mirror image of the Cash Book and vice versa.

EXAMPLE 2

Cash Book		£ Dr				£ Cr
June 27 Balance b/f		1,200	—	June 28 G. Souness		570
June 28 H. Jones		150		June 29 I. Rush		480
June 30 M. Hughes		400		June 30 Balance c/f		700
		1,750				1,750
July 1 Balance b/f		700				

440.96

Bank Statement at 30.6

	Dr	Cr	Balance
June 27 Balance b/f			1200 CR
June 28 Cheque		150	1350 CR
June 30 G. Souness	570		780 CR
June 30 Traders Credits		120	900 CR
June 30 Bank Charges	50		850 CR

436.85

ANSWER

Bank Reconciliation Statement at 30.6

		£
Balance per Bank Statement		850
Add: Bank Charges not in C.B.	50	
Bank Lodgements	400	
		450
		1400
Less: Unpresented Cheque — I. Rush	480	
Traders Credit	120	
		600
Balance per the Cash Book		700

OR

Bank Reconciliation Statement at 30.6

		£
Balance per Cash Book		700
Add unpresented cheque — I. Rush	480	
Add Traders Credit	120	
		1300
Less Bank Charges	50	
Less Bank Lodgement	400	
		450
Balance per Bank Statement		850

OR enter cash book to bring it up to date before the Reconciliation Statement is prepared. Agree to £770. First identify items on the Bank Statement not yet in the Cash Book and enter them in the Cash Book to obtain a new balance to agree to. Then simply remove those items from the Cash Book not on the Bank Statement in the Reconciliation Statement.

New Cash Book Balance

		£Dr			£Cr
30.6	Balance b/f	700	30.6	Bank Charges	50
	Traders Credit				
	bank	120		Balance c/f	770
		820			820

Bank Reconciliation Statement at 30.6

-556.45

	£	
Balance per Cash Book	770	
Add unpresented cheque	480	
	1250	
Less Bank Lodgement	400	
Balance per Bank Statement	850	CR

615.77
+ 81.18
696.95

SUMMARY — BANK RECONCILIATION STATEMENTS

Purpose To agree the balance in the Cash Book with the balance shown on the Bank Statement.

Two Basic Reasons Why Differences Occur

1. Timing differences, i.e. cheques received from Debtors entered in the Cash Book, but not yet deposited or entered on the Bank Statement (BANK LODGEMENTS) **OR** cheques sent to creditors entered in the cash book have not yet been presented to their bank for payment (UNPRESENTED CHEQUES).

2. Certain items may appear on the Bank Statement about which the firm/company have not been notified (i.e. no documentary initial record from which to write up the cash book) e.g.

   a) Bank Charges
   b) Standing Orders
   c) Direct Debits
   d) Credit Transfer — Traders Credit
   e) Dishonoured Cheques

QUESTIONS

1. CASH BOOK

		£Dr			£Cr
Dec 1	Balance b/f	1740	Dec 8	Brown	349
Dec 7	Clapton	88	Dec 15	Astbury	33
Dec 22	Robinson	73	Dec 28	Fuller	115
Dec 31	Johnston	249	Dec 31	Balance c/f	1831
Dec 31	Davis	178			
		2328			2328

-556. 45

BANK STATEMENT

		DR	CR	BALANCE
Dec 1	Balance b/f			1740
Dec 7	Cheque		88	1828
Dec 11	Brown	349		1479
Dec 20	Astbury	33		1446
Dec 22	Cheque		73	1519
Dec 31	Credit Transfer — CS		54	1573
Dec 31	Bank Charges	22		1551

2X. The cash book, bank columns, for January 19–4, of S. Simpson, sole trader is as follows:-

1984		£	1984		£
1 January	Balance	1,507.71	2 January	Electricity Board	43.10
9 January	Sales	1,370.00	2 January	John Jones Ltd.	149.10
17 January	Sales	168.54	4 January	Printers' Supplies Ltd	29.30
23 January	T. White Ltd.	310.00	5 January	Kingsway Products	37.08
24 January	Sales	150.00	12 January	Harold Smith Ltd.	138.32
30 January	Sales	44.70	17 January	Gray's Machines Ltd	645.10
31 January	Sales	210.00	24 January	Giant Displays	70.56
			26 January	P. Swann	124.64
			30 January	Deposit account	2,000.00
			30 January	Wages	320.40
			31 January	Balance	203.35
		3,760.95			3,760.95

On 6 February 19–4, S. Simpson received his bank statement for the previous month; the bank statement was as follows:
Mr. S. Simpson — Statement of Account with North Bank PLC., Main Street Branch, Westford.

Date 1984	Particulars	Payments £	Receipts £	Balance £
1 January	Balance			1,468.21
3 January	Bank Giro Credit		100.00	1,568.21
4 January	145688	149.10		1,419.11
5 January	145686	60.50		1,358.61
6 January	Charges	15.40		1,343.21
9 January	Standing order	12.00		1,331.21
10 January	Bank Giro Credit		1,370.00	2,701.21
11 January	145687	43.10		2,658.11
13 January	145690	37.08		2,621.03
17 January	Sundry Credit		168.54	2,789.57
18 January	145691	138.32		2,651.25
20 January	145689	29.30		2,651.95
23 January	Sundry Credit		310.00	2,931.95
26 January	Standing Order	44.00		2,887.95
27 January	Bank Giro Credit		150.00	3,037.95
30 January	Deposit account	2,000.00		1,037.95
30 January	Sundry Credit		44.70	1,082.65
31 January	145693	70.56		1,012.09

On 8 February 19–4, S. Simpson discovers that the sales debited in the cash book on 31 January 19–4 should read "£230.00" not "£210.00" and is advised by the bank that the standing order charge of £44.00 on 26 January was made in error and that the bank account has now been credited with £44.00.

Required:
Prepare a bank reconciliation statement as at 31 January 19–4.

(20 marks) [AAT]

3X. You are presented with the Bank Statement of McCartney, a sole trader, and a summary of his Bank Receipts and Payments for the month of January.

McCARTNEY — Summarized Bank Transactions for January
BANK ACCOUNT — Nominal Ledger

Date	Account Name	£Dr	Date	Account Name	£Cr
1.1	Balance b/f	2,500	1.1	A Ltd. — Creditor	500
	A. Jones — Debtor	1,000		Cheque No. (001)	
	S. Murphy — Debtor	1,250		Wages — Cheque (002)	600
	P. Parfitt — Debtor	750		Advertising — Cheque (003)	300
				JKS Ltd. — Creditor	
				Cheque (004)	500
			31.1	Balance c/f	3,600
		5,500			5,500

McCARTNEY — Bank Statement

Date	Detail	£Dr	£Cr	£Balance
1.1	Balance b/f		2,500	2,500 Cr
	Sundry Credit — A. Jones		1,000	3,500 Cr
	Cheque 001	500		3,000 Cr
	Cheque 003	300		2,700 Cr
	Cheque 004	500		2,200 Cr
	Sundry Credit — S. Murphy		1,250	3,450 Cr
	Bank Charges	25		3,425 Cr
	Standing Order — Rent	25		3,400 Cr
	Direct Debits	50		3,350 Cr
	Bank Giro Credit — Smith		100	3,450 Cr

Required:
You are required to:-
1. Draw up a Bank Reconciliation Statement for the month of January. *(14 marks)*
2. Give six reasons why differences may occur between the business organization records (i.e. Bank Account — Cash Book) and the Bank's Statement. *(6 marks)*

(Total 20 marks)

4. Hay has received his bank pass sheets for the year to 31st October
    19–3. At that date, his balance at the bank amounted to £14,130
    whereas his own cash book showed a balance of £47,330. His
    accountant investigated the matter, and discovered the following
    discrepancies:

    (a) Bank charges of £60 had not been entered in the cash book.
    (b) Cheques drawn by Hay and totalling £450 had not yet been
         presented to the bank.
    (c) Hay had not entered receipts of £530 in his cash book.
    (d) The bank had not credited Hay with receipts of £1,970 paid into
         the bank on 31st October 19–3.
    (e) Standing order payments amounting to £1,240 had not been
         entered in the cash book.
    (f) Hay had entered a payment of £560 in his cash book as £650.
    (g) A cheque received for £300 from a debtor had been returned by
         the bank marked "refer to drawer", but this had not been written
         back in the cash book.
    (h) Hay had brought down his opening cash book balance of £6,585
         as a debit balance instead of as a credit balance.
    (i) An old cheque payment amounting to £880 had been written
         back in the cash book, but the bank had already honoured it.
    (j) Some of Hay's customers had agreed to settle their debts by direct
         debit. Unfortunately, the bank had credited some direct debits
         amounting to £16,650 to another customer's account.

Required:
    (i)   Prepare a statement showing Hay's adjusted cash book balance
           as at 31st October 19–3.
    (ii)   Prepare a bank reconciliation statement as at 31st October
           19–3.
    (iii) State briefly the main reasons for preparing a bank reconciliation
           statement.   [AAT]

5X. The bank account for the month of September 19–3 for the firm of
    Rivers and Co. was as follows:

Bank Account

Sept.	Receipts	£	Sept.	Payments	Cheque no.	£
1	Balance b/d	271.94	3	Derwent Ltd.	052316	25.08
1	T. Hames	53.40	4	Severn Bros.	052317	31.72
1	Dove Enterprises	62.85	8	Clyde and Co.	052318	121.86
13	Isis PLC	1,793.48	9	Ribble Merchants	052319	1,374.29
20	Colne Electronics	2,404.37	13	Swale Associates	052320	10.35
			20	Don Engineering	052321	642.13
			24	Humber Water Authority	Direct Debit	32.00
			26	Arun Decorators	052322	90.44
			26	Tyne Borough Council	Standing Order	123.57
			27	Salaries transfers	—	940.60
			28	Wye and Sons Ltd	052323	4.30
			30	Balance c/d		1,189.70
		£4,586.04				£4,586.04
Oct.						
1	Balance b/d	1,189.70				

In early October the firm's bank sent a statement for the month of September 19–3, as shown below.

Statement of account with Mersey Bank Plc

Name: Rivers and Co. Current Account. *Date Issued:* 1st October 1983

Sept.	Description	Debit £	Credit £	Balance £
1	BCE			592.45
2	052315	85.16		507.29
5	052314	100.34		406.95
8	052316	25.08		381.87
12	DD (Medway Insurance)	26.26		355.61
13	CR		1,793.48	2,149.09
13	052318	121.86		2,027.23
15	052319	1,374.29		652.94
16	052317	31.72		621.22
20	CR		2,404.37	3,025.59
22	DD (Humber Water Authority)	32.00		2,993.59
23	052320	10.35		2,983.24
26	SO	123.57		2,859.67
28	TRFR	940.60		1,919.07
20	INT (Loan Account)	11.19		1,907.88
30	Bank charges	7.37		1,900.51
30	052321	642.13		1,258.38
30	BCE			1,258.38

Abbreviations: BCE = Balance. SO = Standing Order. CR = Credit.
TRFR = Transfer. INT = Interest.
DD = Direct debit (to Current Account).

Required:
Prepare the firm's Bank Reconciliation Statement as at 30th
September 19–3.   [ACCA]

6. **CASH BOOK**

		£Dr			£Cr
Dec 7	G. Souness	256	Dec 1	Balance b/f	870
Dec 14	M. Robinson	140	Dec 12	A. Hansen	80
Dec 29	D. Hodgson	370	Dec 28	P. Neal	450
Dec 31	S. Lee	418	Dec 29	Mercantile	95
Dec 31	Balance c/f	381	Dec 31	Bank Charges	70
		1565			1565

Bank Statement

		DR	CR	BALANCE
Dec 1	Balance b/f			870 OD
Dec 7	Cheque		256	614 OD
Dec 14	Cheque		140	474 OD
Dec 15	A. Hansen	80		554 OD
Dec 19	D. Hodgson — Traders			
	Credit		370	184 OD
Dec 19	Mercantile S. Order	95		279 OD
Dec 31	Bank Charges	70		349 OD

Required:
From the information given above you are required to draw up a bank
reconciliation statement.

CONTROL ACCOUNTS
– or totals accounts

PURPOSE OF CONTROL ACCOUNTS

Control accounts are a useful check to **detect fraud and error** in the system of accounting. This is because control accounts are usually the responsibility of an officer whose duties are segregated from the person who makes the entries in the day books or the ledgers. For example, the Invoice Clerk may enter an Invoice into the Sales Day Book. The Sales Day Book may then be totalled for a particular day and the Sales Ledger Clerk will enter the amounts into the Sales Account in the General Ledger and to the Debtors Personal Account in the Debtors Ledger. The person operating the Control Accounts will check the total in the Day Book and post the total to the Sales Ledger Control Account. Thus there is a check which prevents fraud or error. Computerised systems may update all accounts from one entry. Computerised systems therefore need program controls.

WHAT EXACTLY ARE CONTROL ACCOUNTS?

Control Accounts are totals accounts, this gives them a further major advantage which is that they **can be used to extract a Trial Balance quickly.** The Total Account (Control Account) may be used to extract, say, a Debtors figure for the Balance Sheet. This removes the need to total all the individual debtor accounts since the Control Account Balance should equal that total. It is important to ensure that this is the case by regularly reconciling the individual accounts with the Totals Account.

EXAMPLE: A firm makes the following sales on one day, 1.5.–5:

SALES DAY BOOK EXTRACT   SDB 5

Date	Invoice No.	Name of Customer	Amount £
1.5.–5	100	Abrahams	100.00
	101	Braun	50.00
	102	Charlton	75.00
	103	Davis	25.00
	104	Evans	50.00
		Sales Day Book Total	300.00

The Sales Day Book is alternatively referred to as a Sales Book or Sales Journal.

DEBTORS LEDGER ACCOUNTS

Abrahams

		£Dr	£Cr
1.5.–5	Inv. 100	100	
	SDB 5		

Brown

		£Dr	£Cr
1.5.–5	Inv. 101	50	
	SDB 5		

Charlton

		£Dr	£Cr
1.5.–5	Inv. 102	75	

Davis

		£Dr	£Cr
1.5.–5	Inv. 103	25	
	SDB 5		

Evans

		£Dr	£Cr
1.5.–5	Inv. 104	50	
	SDB 5		

DEBTORS CONTROL ACCOUNT

Date	Account Name	£Dr	Date	Account Name	£Cr
1.5.–5	Sales ·SDB 5	300			

Thus, it would be possible to refer to the control account to obtain a total for debtors and therefore, it would not be necessary to consult the individual debtor accounts. (sometimes called *'Personal Accounts'* because they refer to individuals).

It is possible to have Control Accounts for any accounts where there are a large number of transactions which make it useful. For example, Debtors, Creditors, Bank and Stock.

MISSING INFORMATION

Control Accounts are useful in deducing missing information. Supposing we knew the opening balance for Debtors £5,000 and the closing balance for Debtors, £3,500, and we also knew that cash received through the bank for all debtors was £20,000, we could work out the missing sales figure as follows.

DEBTORS CONTROL ACCOUNT

	£Dr		£Cr
Opening Balance b/f	5,000	Bank	20,000
Sales	?	Closing Balance c/f	3,500
	23,500		23,500

This could be a useful method of ascertaining the sales figure for a business organization which does not maintain full records. *(The sales figure missing is £18,500).*

THE CONTROL ACCOUNT

The Control Account is a total account. Therefore, the entry you make in the personal account of the debtor would be the same entry in the Control Account. However, the transaction affects the individual debtor, that is how it will affect the Control Account. Some people regard the Control Account as part of the double entry system and the personal account of the debtor as a memorandum account, i.e. just a note of detail as to who owes what.

DEBTORS CONTROL ACCOUNT EXAMPLE

From the following information prepare a Sales Ledger Control Account (note Sales Ledger and Debtors Ledger are synonymous)

		£
May 1	Sales Ledger Balances	5,000

Transactions in the month to May 31st

		£
May 31	Sales Day Book	47,620
	Bad Debts Written Off	320
	Cheques received from debtors	45,230
	Discount allowed	2,100
	Dishonoured cheques	100
	Goods returned by customers	500
	Balances in Sales Ledger set off against credit balances in the Purchase Ledger	250
	Sales Ledger Balances	?

The first step is to identify the effect of each transaction upon the Debtors Ledger Total.

1.   Sales Day Book £47,620, will this increase or reduce debtors owing? It will increase debtors which are an asset, therefore the opening balance will be brought forward on the debit side of the account, and an addition to this balance will also be a debit. Therefore, debit the Sales Day Book Total £47,620 to the Control Account.

> **DR — Debtors Control Account — £47,620**
>
> **CR — Sales Account General Ledger —   £47,620**

2.   Bad Debts Written Off £320. If a bad debt is written off it means you no longer have those debtors as an asset. Therefore, it is a reduction of debtors.

The accounting entry is:-

> **DR — Bad Debts Written Off — £320**
>
> **CR — Debtors Control Account —   £320**

3.   Cheques received from debtors will of course reduce the debtor total because they have now paid their debt.

The accounting entry is:-

> **DR — Bank Account — £45,230**
>
> **CR — Debtors Control Account —   £45,230**

4.   Discount Allowed £2,100. If you allow discount to a customer, this is an expense to the business and reduces the amount owed by the debtor. A reduction of a debtor.

The accounting entry is:-

> **DR — Discount Allowed Expense A/c — £2,100**
>
> **CR — Debtors Control Account   £2,100**

5.   Dishonoured Cheques £100. If a cheque is dishonoured by the bank it means that the debtor owing this amount needs to be placed back on the list of total debtors owing. It is therefore an increase in the debtor balance.

The accounting entry is:-

DR — Debtors Control Account — £100

CR — Bank Account —   £100

Note: Originally we would have assumed that the debtor paid and would have credited the debtor account with the amount paid and debited the bank account with the receipt. However, once we are informed that the bank has not honoured payment we must reverse those entries as above.

6.   Goods Returned by Customers £500. If a customer returns the goods it means that he no longer owes you money in exchange for those goods. Therefore, it reduces the total amount owed by debtors by the amount £500, i.e. the value of goods returned.

The accounting entry is:-

DR — Returns Inwards Account — £500

CR — Debtors Control Account —   £500

---

7.   Set Off Balances £250. Sometimes a business will buy goods from a supplier who may also be a customer for goods you sell. In these instances the supplier will have an entry in the Creditors (Purchase) Ledger and an entry as a customer in the Debtors (Sales) Ledger. It makes sense to offset the smaller amount in one of the ledgers to the other ledger so as to obtain a net amount either owing to the supplier or owed by the supplier as customer. Only the net difference need then be settled in cash/cheque and it removes the need to write a number of cheques. This entry is referred to as a contra entry, symbolised by ¢ alongside each ledger entry.

In this question we are told to set off the balances in the Sales Ledger against the credit balance in the Purchase Ledger. Thus, what this business is owed must be less than what it owes to the creditor. The effect is to reduce debtors by £250 and to reduce what is owed to the creditor by £250.

The accounting entry is:-

DR — Creditors Ledger —   £250

CR — Debtors Control Account —   £250

We are now in a position to complete the Control Account thus:-

		£Dr			£Cr
May 1	Balances b/f	5,000	May 31	Bad Debts	320
				Bank A/c	45,230
May 31	Sales A/c	47,620		Discount	
	Bank A/c	100		Allowed	2,100
				Returns	
				Inward	500
				Creditors	
				Ledger	250 ¢
				set off	
				balance	
				Balance	4,320
		52,720			52,720
June 1	Balance b/f	4,320			

If a list of all the personal accounts in the Debtors Ledger was extracted on 1st June it should agree in total with the balance of £4,320 obtained from the above Control Account. If it does not, investigation into each of the entries above will be required. Furthermore, a check on the balances obtained from each individual debtor may also be required until the error is discovered and rectified.

CREDITORS OR PURCHASE LEDGER CONTROL ACCOUNTS EXAMPLE:

From the following information prepare a Purchase Ledger Control Account.

		£
May 1	Purchase Ledger Balances	7,534
	Transactions during the month of May.	
May 31	Purchase Day Book	45,250
	Returns Outward	2,312
	Cheque paid to Suppliers	38,750
	Cash paid to Suppliers	200
	Discount received	350
	Balances in Purchase Ledger set off against Sales Ledger	
	Purchase Ledger Balances	?

The first step is to work out the effect upon the Purchase Ledger Balance at the start of each of the transactions detailed. That is, will it increase or reduce what is owed?

Note: The opening balance in the Purchase Ledger (Creditors) will of course be a credit balance b/f. It is a liability account. If you have difficulty understanding why it is an opening credit, refer back to the basic balance sheet equation.

1. Purchase Day Book £45,250. This is the total purchases made during the month and it will of course increase what is owed to creditors. It does, therefore, need to be added to the opening balance.

The accounting entry is:-

```
DR — Purchase Account General Ledger — £45,250

CR — Creditors Control Account —                    £45,250
```

2. Returns Outward £2,312. If you send goods back to a supplier then you no longer owe money for those goods. Therefore, the effect is to reduce what is owed to creditors.

The accounting entry is:-

```
DR — Creditors Control Account — £2,312

CR — Returns Outward —                    £2,312
```

3. Cheques paid to Suppliers obviously reduce the amount owed to creditors and will reduce the total balance owed.

The accounting entry is:-

```
DR — Creditors Control Account — £38,750

CR — Bank Account —                    £38,750
```

4. Cash paid to Suppliers has the effect of reducing the total creditors just as cheques do.

The accounting entry is:-

```
DR — Creditors Control Account — £200

CR — Cash Account —                    £200
```

5. Discount Received £350. If a supplier allows a discount it will reduce what the business must pay in cash/cheque to that supplier. The effect is therefore to reduce the liability of total creditors.

The accounting entry is:-

DR — Creditors Control Account — £350

CR — Discount Received Account —   £350
---

6. Set Off Balances. The concept of set off balances has already been explained in the Debtors Control example. In this instance the firm is owed more than it owes to its creditors and has decided to offset its liability to its supplier against what it is owed by that supplier as a customer. The effect is to reduce the liability of total creditors.

The accounting entry is:-

DR — Creditors Control Account — £500

CR — Debtors Ledger —   £500

We are now in a position to complete the Creditors Ledger Control Account and obtain the closing balance.

CREDITORS PURCHASE LEDGER CONTROL ACCOUNT

		£Dr			£Cr
May 31	Returns Out a/c	2,312	May 1	Balance b/f	7,534
	Bank A/c	38,750	May 31	Purchase a/c	45,250
	Cash A/c	200			
	Discount rec'd	350			
	Debtors Ledger set off balances	500 ¢			
	Balance c/f	10,672			
		52,784			52,784
			June 1	Balance b/f	10,672

Thus, the amount owed to Creditors has increased to £10,672. If the personal accounts for each creditor balance were totalled on an add list it should agree with the closing total balance. If it does not then investigation will ensue.

COMMON ERROR

A common error which occurs between the personal account and a control account is that of a TRANSPOSITION ERROR, i.e. £74 in one account and £47 in another. If a difference does occur it might be worthwhile checking for a transposition error. This is easily done since transposition errors are always divisible by 9 and the digits of the difference will add up to 9 also. For example £74 – £47 = £27.

$\frac{27}{9}$ = 3 and 2 + 7 = 9.

SUMMARY

— Control accounts are total accounts normally in the charge of a responsible officer.
— Control accounts help prevent fraud or error.
— A Trial Balance may quickly be extracted using control accounts.
— They are useful to find missing information.
— Control Accounts are normally prepared for Debtors, Creditors, Bank and Cash, Stock etc., where there are a large number of transactions.

SELF-CHECK QUESTIONS

1. Briefly explain what a control account is.
2. Why are control accounts useful?
3. Which side of the debtors control account are the following transactions recorded:-
   (a) Sales on credit
   (b) Bad Debts written off
   (c) Discount Allowed
   (d) Cash received
4. Which side of the creditor control account would:-
   (a) Discount received
   and
   (b) Returns outwards be shown?

QUESTIONS

1. Briefly explain the purpose of control accounts.

2. From the following information prepare a Sales Ledger Control Account:-

		£
January 1st	Sales Ledger Balances	6,500

Transactions in the month of January

		£
January 31st	Sales Journal	52,150
	Bad Debts written off	50
	Cash received from Debtors	2,100
	Cheques received from Debtors	49,100
	Discount Allowed	1,400
	Cheques dishonoured	150
	Returns Inwards Journal	150
	Balances in Sales Ledger set off against credit balances in the Purchase Ledger	350

The list of balances from the personal accounts of debtors shows a balance of £5,650 on 31st January.

3. (a) From the following information prepare a Creditors Ledger Control Account:-

		£
January 1st	Purchase Ledger Balances	5,250

Journals for the month

		£
January 31st	Purchase Day Book	42,150
	Returns Outward	1,400
	Cheques paid to Suppliers	41,500
	Cash paid to Suppliers	650
	Discount Received	250

The List of Balances extracted from the personal accounts of creditors showed a balance on the credit side at 1st February of £3,690.

(b) Can you suggest a reason why the balance you have obtained in the Control Account is different from the total on the add list of balances at 1st February?

4. From the following information prepare Control Accounts for Debtors and Creditors:-

		£
January 1st	Purchase Ledger Balances	9,240
	Sales Ledger Balances	8,250

The following transactions took place in the month to January 31st.

January 31st	Purchase Journals	44,250
	Sales Journals	52,560
	Cheques received from Debtors	49,350
	Cash paid to Suppliers	1,000
	Cash received from Debtors	500
	Cheques paid to Suppliers	45,100
	Bad Debts written off	150
	Discount Allowed	450
	Discount Received	600
	Returns Inward	500
	Returns Outward	275
	Balances in the Sales Ledger set off against Purchase Ledger Balances	220

5X. (a) From the following information you are required to prepare a Sales Ledger Control Account for the month of May 19–4 for T. Ltd.

May 1	Sales Ledger — debit balances	7,632
May 1	Sales Ledger — credit balances	44
May 31	Transactions for the month	
	Cash received	208
	Cheques received	12,478
	Sales	14,180
	Bad debts written off	612
	Discounts allowed	596
	Returns inwards	328
	Cash refunded to a customer who has overpaid his account	74
	Dishonoured cheques	58

The list of balances at the month end were:-

Sales Ledger — debit balances	7,758
Sales Ledger — credit balances	80

(c) Briefly explain the purpose of control accounts. *(16 marks)*

6X. From the following information supplied by Zee Ltd. you are required to prepare a Creditors Control Account showing the balance to carry forward at 31.1.19–6.

		£
January 1st	Purchase Ledger Balance b/f	105,650
During January	Purchase Journals	115,675
	Returns Outward	7,860
	Discount Received	10,850
	Payments by Cheque to Creditors	104,650
	Payments to Creditors by Cash	1,000

(10 marks)

WORKING CAPITAL
– managing cash flow

THE CONTROL OF WORKING CAPITAL

Ratios can be used to calculate the number of days it takes for stock to turnover; for debtors to turnover (become cash) and for creditors to turnover (be paid). There is a cost implication associated with the time it takes for working capital to turnover (i.e. stock; debtors and creditors).

Supposing it takes 4 months to turnover stocks and work-in-progress; 3 months for debtors to pay up and creditors are paid in a month. Let us also assume that the business has a bank overdraft facility paying interest at 15% per annum. Consider the true cost of funding the working capital to the business:-

	DAYS	INTEREST %
Stock turnover	120 × 15/365	= 4.93
Debtor turnover	90 × 15/365	= 3.70
Creditor turnover	(30) × 15/365	=(1.23)
WORKING CAPITAL NET	180	= 7.40

The net cost of using equal amounts of each component of working capital given the number of days it would take for each to turnover would be 7.40% in our example.

By using creditors to fund stocks and debtors we are in fact saving on the cost of incurring overdraft. If we now put some values into the balance sheet amounts for working capital we will be able to see the amounts saved in terms of pound notes. Assuming that the time taken remains the same we have:

					£ COST
Stock per balance sheet	£ 500,000	×	4.93	=	24,650
Debtors	300,000	×	3.70	=	11,100
Creditors	(200,000)	×	1.23	=	(2,460)
WORKING CAPITAL NET	600,000				33,290

Note: Our original calculations showed cost to the business of 7.40% but this figure took no account of the values for each element being financed. It assumed equal weightings but our example has used 5:3:2 respectively for stock debtors and creditors.

The cost of funding this level of working capital £600,000 for the cycle would amount to £33,290 equivalent to 5.55% of the net working capital.

ACTION TO REDUCE COSTS

It would pay the business to employ a Financial Controller a salary to reduce the cost of financing working capital. For example, if stock holding could be reduced to 60 days; debtors pursued such that they paid up in 60 days and payments to creditors delayed to 60 days then costs could be reduced as follows:

	ORIGINAL	REVISED
Stock	£500,000	£250,000 × 15% (60/365) = 2.47%
Debtors	300,000	£200,000 × 15% (60/365) = 2.47%
Creditors	200,000	£400,000 × 15% (60/365) = 2.47%
Net Working Capital	600,000	50,000

The cost of holding stock is	£6,164
debtors	4,932
creditors	(9,863)
Net Cost of Working Capital	1,233

The revised net cost of financing the working capital is now £1,233 resulting in a saving to the business of £32,057. A Financial Controller's salary could be paid from the savings made by the controller's actions.

SELF-CHECK QUESTIONS

1. What are the elements of working capital?
2. How can management of working capital improve cash flow?
3. Briefly explain how working capital can reduce bank overdraft charges?

ERRORS AND SUSPENSE ACCOUNTS
– checking the accuracy of a trial balance

There are various errors which can occur when recording accounting entries or upon transfer between accounts. It is important to distinguish between those entries which will affect the balance of the trial balance and those entries which still need rectification but do not prevent the debit and credit sides of the trial balance from agreeing.

When a trial balance will not balance we make it balance by opening a SUSPENSE ACCOUNT for the difference.

ERRORS AND OMISSIONS

Errors which do not affect the Trial Balance	Errors which do affect the Trial Balance
Original Entry	Undercast
Commission	Overcast
Principle	These effectively cause one sided entries.
Compensating error	
Omission	
Reversal	

ERRORS WHICH DO NOT AFFECT THE TRIAL BALANCE

1.   Original Entry An error of original entry is where a mistake is made as to the amount entered in the accounts both for debits and credits, e.g. a cash sale for £74.00 is entered in the books of account as follows:-

CR — Sales A/c	£47.00	
DR — Cash A/c		£47.00

In order to correct this you would need a journal entry as follows:-

JOURNAL				
Date	Description / A/c Name	Ref.	£Dr	£Cr
28.9	Sales A/c		47	
	Cash A/c			47
	Cash A/c		74	
	Sales A/c			74
	Correction to original entry			
	27.9 which was transposed.			
	Sales Invoice X134			
			121	121
OR				
	Cash A/c		27	
	Sales A/c			27
			27	27
Narrative:	Information as above plus: Originally entered as a sale of £47. It should have been £74.			

2. Commission An error of commission is where the person entering the details is careless, e.g. a sale of £50 to a debtor A. Kennedy is entered in R. Kennedy's account by mistake. To correct this a journal entry would be required as follows:-

CR — R. Kennedy	**£50**	
DR — A. Kennedy		**£50**

3. Principle This is where the person making the entries makes an error due to lack of knowledge or understanding, e.g. a disposal of fixed assets is wrongly entered as a sale, the amount being £500. To correct this the journal entry would be necessary as follows:-

DR — Sales A/c	**£500**	
CR — Motor Vehicles Disposal A/c		**£500**

4. Compensating Compensating error is where a one sided entry is made for the same sum of money for different items on both sides, debit and credit. For example, a sale for £500 cash is simply entered only in the sales account and a wage expense also for £500 is entered only in the wage account. The journal entry necessary to correct this would be as follows:-

DR — Cash	£500	
CR — Cash		£500

5.   Omission An omission will not affect the trial balance since both the entry for Dr. and Cr. are missed out.

6.   Reversal This is simply where the two entries are the wrong way round, e.g. a sale to a debtor for £500 should be made as follows: Cr. Sales £500, Dr. Debtor £500, and in fact the entries are made the wrong way round as follows: Dr. Sales £500, Cr. Debtor £500. The journal entry necessary to correct this error would be as follows:

DR — Debtor	£1,000	
CR — Sales		£1,000

ERRORS WHICH DO AFFECT THE TRIAL BALANCE

Undercasting and Overcasting. The Sales Day Book below has been overcast by £200.

SALES DAY BOOK			
Date	**Description**	**£Dr**	**£Cr**
28.9	Jones		500
	Smith		300
	Astbury		250
	Davis		170
	Balance c/f to Sales A/c	1420	
		1420	1420
	Overcast by £200.		

The Trial Balance extracted would look like this. A Suspense Account has been opened for the difference.

EXTRACT TRIAL BALANCE AT 28.9.–4

	£Dr	£Cr
Cash	1220	
Sales		1420
Suspense A/c	200	
	1420	1420

Once the over addition (overcast) has been discovered, the following Journal entry would correct the situation:

Journal to Correct		
DR — Sales A/c	£200	
CR — Suspense A/c		£200

Errors affecting the trial balance affect the Suspense Account.

SALES ACCOUNT

	£Dr				£Cr
Suspense A/c	200		28.9	S.D.B.	1420

CASH ACCOUNT

	£Dr	£Cr
Sales	1220	

SUSPENSE ACCOUNT

	£Dr		£Cr
Balance per T/B	200	Sales A/c	200

Note the Suspense Account has now been cleared.

SUMMARY

There are two types of error which are:-
1. Those that will make the debit and credit columns of the trial balance disagree

and 2. Those which although still errors will not affect the total debits from agreeing with the total credits.

TYPE 1 Undercasts and Overcasts
TYPE 2 Original Entry, Commission, Principle, Compensating errors, Omission, Reversal.

SUSPENSE ACCOUNTS are used as a 'dumping ground' account to make the trial balance agree until errors are discovered and rectified using journals.

Type 2 errors also need journals to correct them but they **do not** affect the suspense account.

EXAMPLE QUESTION

Your bookkeeper extracted a trial balance on 31.12.-3 which failed to agree by £660.00, the shortage being on the credit side of the trial balance. The suspense account was opened for the difference. In January 19–4 the following errors made in 19–3 were discovered.

1. The Sales Day Book had been undercast by £200.00.
2. Sales of £500.00 to S. Lee had been debited in error to J. Lees.
3. The Rent Account had been undercast by £140.00.
4. Discount received account had been undercast by £600.00.
5. The sale of a motor vehicle at book value had been credited in error to the Sales Account £720.00.

You are required to:-
1. Identify the type of error.
2. Show the journal entries necessary to correct the errors.
3. Draw up the Suspense Account after the journal entries have been made and the errors described have been corrected.
4. If the Net Profit for 19–3 was previously calculated at £15,800, show the calculation for the corrected Net Profit after the correction of errors.

ANSWER

1. Undercasting would affect the Trial Balance. T.B. Suspense Account.
2. Error of commission, would not affect the Trial Balance.
3. Undercasting would affect the Trial Balance.
4. Undercasting would affect the Trial Balance.
5. Error of Princple, would not affect the Trial Balance.
   Journals to Correct *(ignoring narratives)*

		£Dr	£Cr
1.	Dr. Suspense A/c	£200	
	Cr. Sales A/c		£200
2.	Dr. S. Lee	£500	
	Cr. J. Lees		£500
3.	Dr. Rent A/c	£140	
	Cr. Suspense A/c		£140
4.	Dr. Suspense A/c	£600	
	Cr. Discount Received		£600
5.	Dr. Sales A/c	£720	
	Cr. Sale of Asset A/c		£720

SUSPENSE ACCOUNT

£Dr			£Cr
Sales	200	Balance b/f	660
Discount received	600	Rent A/c	140
	800		800

STATEMENT OF CORRECTED NET PROFIT FOR THE
YEAR ENDED 31.12.–3

	£	£
Net Profit per the accounts		15,800
Add Sales Understated (1)	200	
Discount received undercast (4)	600	800
		16,600
Less		
Rent Undercast (3)	600	600
Corrected Net Profit for the year		16,000

QUESTIONS

1.   **JOHN WALK — TRIAL BALANCE AT 31.12.-4**

	£Dr	£Cr
Land and Buildings	10,500	
Motor Vehicles	5,500	
Stock 1.1.-4	3,150	
Debtors	4,100	
Cash	500	
Purchases	10,250	
Administration Expenses	500	
Light & Heat Expenses	200	
Rent & Rates Expenses	150	
Sales & Marketing Expenses	350	
Sales		12,750
Creditors		3,600
Loan		2,000
Capital		17,650
Suspense A/c	800	
	£36,000	£36,000

Notes:
1.   Stock at 31.12.-4 £2,750.
2.   Loan A/c overcast by £750.
3.   Administration A/c undercast by £50.

You are required to:
1.   Clear the suspense account, and produce:-
2.   A revised Trial Balance after the adjustments, and;
3.   A Trading and Profit and Loss Account and a Balance Sheet at 31.12.-4.

2.   To enable work to proceed on a firm's draft year end accounts a difference found in the trial balance was entered into a suspense account opened for the purpose. The draft Profit and Loss Account subsequently showed a profit for the year of £102,108 and the Suspense Account was shown in the draft balance sheet.

During audit the following errors were found which when corrected eliminated the Suspense Account entry:
(a)   One of the pages of the Sales Day Book totalling £5,138 had not been posted to Sales Account.
(b)   The year end stock sheets had been overcast by £1,100.
(c)   The last page of the Purchases Day Book totalling £7,179 had been posted to Purchases Account as £1,779.
(d)   No account had been taken of electricity consumed since the last meter reading, the estimated amount being £246.

(e) An invoice for £64 entered correctly in the Sales Day Book had been posted to the customer's account as £164.

(f) An entry in the Purchases Day Book of £82 had not been posted to the supplier's account.

(g) An error had been made in balancing the Petty Cash Book, the correct amount being £250, not £25.

(h) Loan Interest paid amounting to £500 had been posted to the Loan Account.

Required:

(i) Frame the necessary journal entries to clear the Suspense Account (narratives not required).

(ii) Prepare the Suspense Account showing the amount of the original difference.

(iii) Prepare a statement showing the corrected profit/loss for the year.

3X. Whilst you are preparing the annual accounts of Bramwell Factors for the year 19–2, the following matters have to be taken into account at 31st December:

(a) The provision for discounts allowed to debtors, which at present has a balance of £229.53, needs to be reduced to £157.40.

(b) Debts totalling £64.80 are now known to be bad and must be written off. However, an amount of £21.44 written off as a bad debt in the previous year has now been recovered in full, but the cheque has not yet been paid into the bank or posted to the accounts.

(c) Due to an oversight, discount has been allowed to a credit customer on the gross invoiced amount of £80.00 at the rate of 10%. A rate of 6% should have been used.

(d) Electricity accrued amounts to £36.71 whilst insurance premiums of £22.45 have been prepaid.

(e) In October 19–2 the business' employees received a general wages increase, backdated to July 19–2. There are now amounts of wages arrears, totalling £126.55, payable to former employees who left shortly before the wages award was announced and who have not yet been traced. It has been decided that the wage packets will be opened and the cash paid back into the bank until those ex-employees can be found.

(f) Amounts earned by employees in the last week of December 19–2 but not due to be paid until January 19–3, comprise wages £464.12 and salaries £301.70.

(g) During 19–2 the exterior of the warehouse was repainted at a cost of £5,000. The whole of this amount was wrongly debited to Premises account. It is the policy of Bramwell Factors to provide depreciation on the closing balances of fixed assets and this has already been done. The annual rate of depreciation on premises is

2%, calculated on the straight line basis and assuming no residual value.

(h) In December 19–2, Bramwell Factors had bought goods on credit from Conbrec Ltd. for £452.10 and had sold goods on credit to that same company for £163.04. These sums have been correctly posted to their respective accounts. These accounts are to be settled in contra at 31st December 19–2 and the remaining balance by cheque in January 19–3.

Required:
Prepare suitable entries in the Journal of Bramwell Factors to record each of the above matters at 31st December 19–2. (Your entries should also include items affecting the cash and bank accounts).

[ACCA]

4X. Edgeworth's profit is £7,600 on the Income Statement on the 30.6.–4. The following information has since come to light.

1) Purchase of a motor van for £3,500 has been entered as Motor Vehicle expenses.
2) Motor vehicle repairs amounting to £750 have been entered in the fixed asset account.
3) Cost of a factory extension £5,000 has been entered in the fixed asset account for land and buildings.
4) Legal costs incurred on a factory extension amounting to £500 have been entered as a legal expense.
5) Depreciation is to be provided as follows:-
Land & buildings   50 years Straight Line Basis
Motor vehicles   20% p.a. Straight Line Basis

Required:
1) Journal entries to make any corrections you think are necessary.
2) A revised income statement to 30.6.–4.   *(20 marks)*

5X. The first draft of the final accounts of Torkard Traders disclosed a net profit of £41,004 and a capital employed of £352,600, before providing for the manager's efficiency bonus, but including £8,928 (credit balance) for errors held in suspense.

H. Huthwaithe, the manager, receives a basic salary plus an annual bonus of £300 for every complete percentage point by which the net profit to capital employed percentage exceeds 10%. In this context, net profit is before charging the manager's bonus, and capital employed is defined as fixed assets plus working capital. The bonus calculation is not carried out until the figures have been audited.

During the course of the audit, it was discovered that:
(i) discounts allowed, £536, had been credited to discounts received;

(ii) the sale for cash, of some disused fixtures and fittings which had been completely written off in a previous year, had been credited to Fixtures and Fittings, £470;

(iii) an amount of £380 owed by M & Co. for goods supplied had been settled in contra against an amount of £850 owing to M & Co., but the ledger entries had not yet been made;

(iv) a glass carboy containing chemicals, which was kept in the warehouse, had sprung a leak. The resultant seepage had caused irreparable damage to stock valued at £800 but no account has yet been taken of this fact;

(v) due to an oversight, credit sales for the last three days of the accounting year, amounting to £1,575, have been completely omitted from the Sales Day Book;

(vi) in the Purchase Day Book, a sub-total of £27,183.54 had been carried forward as £37,183.54. Creditors, however, have been correctly posted;

(vii) a credit sale invoice of £978 had been entered in the Sales Day Book as £789;

(viii)a credit note from a supplier for £21 in respect of faulty goods, had not been posted;

(ix) the proprietor of Torkard Traders sometimes, for his convenience, abstracts cash from the till for personal purposes. During the year, this has amounted to £86. The bookkeeper states that he has 'reduced cash sales so that the cash book balances'.

Required:
(a) Recalculate the net profit and capital employed figures after the above errors have been corrected.   *(16 marks)*
(b) Calculate the manager's bonus.   *(4 marks)*
(c) Open the Suspense Account and post the eliminating entries.
                                                                 (3 marks)
                                                       (Total 23 marks)
                                                              [ACCA]

 **INCOMPLETE RECORDS**
– or single entry

PROCEDURE

Any analysis of incomplete records requires firstly the identification of what is missing. Problems of this nature usually require the following procedure:-

1. Preparing an opening balance sheet (possibly).
2. Writing up a cashbook from data supplied.
3. Use of control accounts to find missing figures (e.g. for sales or purchases).
4. Use of simple ratios (e.g. mark up or margin) to deduce figures which are not known.
5. Constructing a Trading and Profit and Loss Account and Balance Sheet to make the incomplete record, complete.

Incomplete records are sometimes referred to as single-entry accounts. This is because an entry for one account is often known. In such a case the other entry can always be deduced. For example, if you know that a business made a sale of goods for £10; then the dual aspect is the £10 received in cash as a result of the £10 goods sold. Thus:–

> **DR — CASH   £10**
>
> **CR — SALES   £10**

It is essential that you understand which two accounts are affected by the transaction. You may then make the necessary adjustments.

The following steps are necessary in dealing with questions on incomplete records:-

1.   Prepare an opening statement of affairs (Balance Sheet at the start). This is necessary when the opening capital of a business is not known or it may be that another balance sheet total is not known but could be deduced by preparing a balance sheet.

Remember the balance sheet equation
ASSETS = CAPITAL + LIABILITIES

[*Note: Revenue and Expenses are included as an addition to capital in the balance sheet. There is no need to include Expenses with Assets or Revenue with Liabilities since Revenue – Expenses = Profit which is an addition to capital.*]

So, if we want to find the capital at the start and we know the values of assets and liabilities, we can deduce the missing capital figure, thus:-

ASSETS £10,000 = CAPITAL? + LIABILITIES £7,000

Capital must of course be £3,000.

> **Remember Fixed Assets + Current Assets – Current Liabilities must equal Capital including reserves plus any Long Term loans.**

2.   Control Accounts may be required in order to obtain a missing figure.

For example, supposing we know that cheques received from debtors in a period amount to £20,000 and that the opening balance on the debtors control account was £100,000 and the closing balance is £130,000, we can deduce the missing figure for sales as follows:-

SALES OR DEBTORS LEDGER CONTROL ACCOUNT

	£Dr		£Cr
Balance b/f	100,000	Bank	20,000
SALES	?	Balance c/f	130,000
	150,000		150,000

Sales would of course be £50,000.

You could do the same kind of deduction for purchases, bank, cash, stock etc.

3.   It may also be necessary to calculate closing balances for bank and cash, to place on the closing balance sheet and you would, therefore, have to write up the cash book from information provided to obtain the necessary figures.

4.   Adjustments for accruals and prepayments will need to be dealt with in the normal way from the information supplied when constructing a Trading and Profit and Loss Account.

5.   Information with regard to simple ratios may be provided and you are expected to use these to deduce further information.

For example: if you are given a sales figure £10,000 and told that the margin is 25%, that is

$$\frac{Gross\ Profit}{Sales} \times \frac{100}{1} = 25\%$$

You can deduce the figure for gross profit as follows:-

$$\frac{Gross\ Profit}{£10,000} = 25\%$$

$$Gross\ Profit = 25\% \times £10,000$$
$$= \underline{\underline{£2,500}}$$

On the other hand you may be given the mark up which is

$$\frac{Gross\ Profit}{Cost\ of\ Sales} \times \frac{100}{1}$$

and you may know the cost of sales to be £7,500 but you are not given a sales figure or a profit figure.

Once again both can be deduced as follows:-

EXAMPLE:

$$\frac{Gross\ Profit\ as\ a\ \%}{Cost\ of\ Sales} = 33\frac{1}{3}\%$$

that is the mark up

$$\frac{Gross\ Profit}{£7,500} = 33\frac{1}{3}\%$$

$$Gross\ Profit = 33\frac{1}{3}\% \times £7,500$$
$$= \underline{\underline{£2,500}}$$

But since gross profit (GP) + cost of sales (COS) must equal the sales value, we can deduce the sales figure also
$$\underline{\underline{£2,500\ (GP) + £7,500\ (COS) = £10,000\ SALES}}$$

THE RELATIONSHIP BETWEEN MARK UP AND MARGIN

If we know the mark up but it is the margin we need to apply in the question, then we can find the margin by the following conversion:-

---

Mark up to Margin

$\dfrac{Gross\ Profit}{Cost\ of\ Sales}$ % given (mark up) but we want (margin) $\dfrac{Gross\ Profit}{Sales}$ %

thus $\dfrac{Gross\ Profit}{Cost\ of\ Sales + Gross\ Profit}$ % $\dfrac{Gross\ Profit}{Sales}$ %

therefore, if we know the mark up to be $33\frac{1}{3}\%$ we can convert thus

mark up $\dfrac{33\frac{1}{3}}{100}$ $\longrightarrow$ margin therefore $\dfrac{33\frac{1}{3}}{100 + 33\frac{1}{3}} = 25\%$

On the other hand we may wish to convert the margin to mark up and apply the result to the data to obtain a missing figure.

Margin to Mark Up

$$\text{margin} = \frac{\text{Gross Profit}}{\text{Sales}} \text{ \% given but we want mark up} = \frac{\text{Gross Profit}}{\text{Cost of Sales}} \text{\%}$$

$$\text{thus} \quad \frac{\text{Gross Profit}}{\text{Sales} - \text{Gross Profit}}\text{\%} \qquad \frac{\text{Gross Profit}}{\text{Cost of Sales}}\text{\%}$$

Using our example 25% margin converting to

$$\text{mark up} = \frac{25}{100 - 25} = \frac{25}{75} = 33\tfrac{1}{3}\%$$

Other simple ratios may also be used to deduce missing information, for example $\dfrac{\text{EXPENSES}}{\text{SALES}}\%$

EXAMPLE

Ricky is in business on his own account. On December 31st he invites good customers and friends to his premises to celebrate his first year in business. The party finished at 8.00 p.m. Ricky and some of the guests went on to a club. On arriving home at 3.00 a.m., he noticed a police car outside his house. The policeman greeted him with the news that his premises had been burnt to the ground. The suspected cause being a lighted cigarette left in some accounting ledgers. He was most distressed and immediately rang his accountant to tell him of the problem. The accountant, being a sympathetic chap, told him not to worry since he felt sure he would be able to reconstruct some financial statements from the business bank account and information that Ricky himself would be able to supply. At the meeting on the next day, the following information came to light:-

1.		£ 31.12.19–4	£ 31.12.19–5
	Stock	5,250	4,375
	Debtors	4,950	5,260
	Bank	3,200	?
	Cash	500	?
	Fixed Assets		
	Premises Net Book Value (NBV)	15,000	?
	Motor Van Net Book Value (NBV)	5,000	?
	Creditors	4,850	5,315

2. All business transactions apart from one or two specific items which Ricky had a note of, passed through the business bank account. Together the accountant and Ricky quickly obtained totals for the following:-

    a) Payments to creditors during the year amounted to £37,550.
    b) Payments received from debtors £72,340.
    c) Weekly wages paid £60 per week for 52 weeks.
    d) Rates £1,200.
    e) Electricity for light and heat in the respect of the period 30 September 19-5 — £900. The bill for the final quarter had not yet been received.
    f) Advertising expenditure — £2,250 for the year.
    g) Postage and stationery totalled £750 for the year, however, on investigating the premises during the morning after the fire, the franking machine was found intact and the meter showed that £49 of postage stamps was still unused.
    h) Ricky subscribed to a trade association. The fee is £20 each year. He has not paid his subscription for the year to December 19-5 as yet but he intends to. Furthermore, he did not pay his 19-4 subscription until February 19-5.
    i) Ricky received cash from sales £150 on 31.12.19-5 which he took home with him.
    j) Payments made by cheque to the local garage for petrol totalled £720 for the year. The last payment on this petrol account was made during October in respect of the quarter to the 30 September 19-5. The final quarter's bill has not yet been received.
    k) Road Tax for the year, paid by cheque in January, was £85 and Insurance £120.
    l) Drawings totalled to £4,600 by cheque.

    * No depreciation has been charged for the year in respect of premises or the motor van. The premises are to be depreciated by 2% on the net book value for the previous year. The motor van is to be depreciated by 20% per annum on the previous year's NBV.

    The Insurance company is expected to settle the claim on the basis of the accounts submitted by Ricky.

You are required to:
1. Prepare a Bank and Cash Control Account for the year 19-5.
2. Construct a Balance Sheet as at that date.
Note, however, before you can do so you will need to take the following appropriate steps:-
    1. Prepare a Bank and Cash Control Account for the year 19-5.
    2. Prepare an Opening Statement of Affairs (Capital).
    3. Prepare Debtors and Creditors Control Account (Sales & Purchases figures).
    4. Make appropriate adjustments.

ANSWER

1.   **RICKY — Opening Statement of Affairs**
                     i.e. Balance Sheet at 1.1.19–5.

Fixed Assets	£ Cost	£ Provision for Depreciation	£ NBV
Premises			15,000
Motor Vehicle			5,000
			20,000
Current Assets			
Stock	5,250		
Debtors	4,950		
Bank	3,200		
Cash	500		
		13,900	
Less Current Liabilities			
Creditors	4,850		
Accruals (Subs)	20		
		(4,870)	
Net Current Assets			9,030
Total Net Assets			29,030
Financed By			
Capital			29,030
Capital Employed			29,030

The following workings would have been necessary to obtain:-
*   a   The Closing Cash and Bank balances*
*   b   Sales*
*   c   Purchases*

a
Bank and Cash Control Accounts

| | **£Dr** | | | | **£Cr** | |
	Bank	Cash			Bank	Cash
Receipts	**Bank**	**Cash**	**Payments**		**Bank**	**Cash**
1.1 Balance b/f	3,200	500	Creditors		37,550	
Debtors	72,340		Wages (52 × 60)		3,120	
Cash Sales ¢		150	Rates		1,200	
			Light & Heat		900	
			Advertising		2,250	
			Postage & Stationery		750	
			Subscription 19–4		20	
			Road Tax		85	
			Insurance		120	
			Drawings		4,600	
			Petrol		720	
			Drawings	¢		150
			31.12 Balance c/f		24,225	500
	75,540	650			75,540	650

b
Control Account for Debtors and Creditors
Debtors Control A/c

	£Dr			**£Cr**
Balance b/f	4,950	Bank		72,340
Sales	72,650	31.12.19–5 Balance c/f		5,260
	77,600			77,600

c
Creditors Control A/c

	£Dr			**£Cr**
Bank	37,550	1.1 Balance b/f		4,850
		Purchases		38,015
31.12.19–5 Balance c/f	5,315			
	42,865			42,865

2.   **RICKY — Trading, Profit and Loss A/c**
                           year ending 31.12.19–5

		£	£
	Sales (b)		72,650
	+ Cash Sales		150
	Less Cost of Sales		72,800
	Opening Stock	5,250	
	Add Purchases (c)	38,015	
		43,265	
	Less Closing Stock	(4,375)	
	Cost of Goods Sold		(38,890)
	Gross Profit		33,910
	Less Expenses		
	Wages	3,120	
	Rates	1,200	
A	Light & Heat (900 + 300)	1,200	
	Advertising	2,250	
P	Postage & Stationery		
	(750 – 49)	701	
	Subscription	20	
	Road Tax	85	
	Insurance	120	
A	Petrol (M.V. running)		
	(720 + 240A)	960	
	Depreciation		
	Premises	300	
	Motor Vehicle	1,000	
		1,300	
	Total Expenses		(10,956)
	Net Profit		22,954

3.   **RICKY — Balance Sheet at 31.12.19-5**

	£ Cost	£ Provision for Depreciation	£ NBV
Fixed Assets			
Premises	15,000	300	14,700
Motor Vehicle	5,000	1,000	4,000
	20,000	1,300	18,700

Current Assets			
Stock	4,375		
Debtors	5,260		
Prepayments	49		
Bank (2)	24,225		
Cash (2)	500		
		34,409	
Less Current Liabilities			
Creditors	5,315		
Accruals	560		
		(5,875)	
		Net Current Assets	28,574
		Total Net Assets	47,234
Financed By			
Capital at 1.1.		29,030	
Add Profit		22,954	
		51,984	
Less Drawings		(4,750)	
		Capital Employed	47,234

QUESTIONS

1. You are required to deduce the missing figures in the table below from information supplied.

	Assets	Expenses	Capital	Liabilities	Revenue
i.	5,000	2,000	3,000	2,000	?
ii.	10,000	?	3,000	3,000	5,000
iii.	?	3,000	8,000	2,000	4,000
iv.	12,000	2,000	?	4,000	7,000
v.	20,000	5,000	15,000	?	5,000

2. State the margin from the following mark up's.

    i.   20%   ii.   30%   iii.   40%   iv.   50%   v. $33\frac{1}{3}$%
    vi. $\frac{1}{4}$ vii. $\frac{1}{8}$ viii. $\frac{1}{5}$ ix. $\frac{3}{5}$

3. State the mark up given the following margins.

    i.   25%   ii.   50%   iii.   30%   iv.   60%   v.   10%
    vi. $\frac{2}{5}$ vii. $\frac{3}{8}$ viii. $\frac{1}{3}$ ix. $\frac{1}{5}$

4. You are given the following trading account and asked to deduce the missing figures if the margin is 10%

	£
Sales	100,000
Less Cost of Sales	?
Gross Profit	?

5. Using the trading account supplied in question 4 and given a mark up of 50% deduce the missing figures for cost of sales and gross profit.

6. From the following three consecutive incomplete trading and profit and loss account summaries you are required to make them complete, using the information given below:-

	Year 1		Year 2		Year 3	
	£	£	£	£	£	£
SALES		100,000		?		?
LESS COST OF SALES						
Opening Stock	15,000					
Add Purchases	90,000		80,000		?	
	105,000		?		?	
Less Closing Stock	(?)		(?)		(?)	
Cost of Goods Sold		(?)		(70,000)		?
GROSS PROFIT		20,000		?		?
LESS EXPENSES		?		(5,000)	?	
NET PROFIT		?		?		6,000

Year 1 Expenses are 10% of Sales Value.

Year 2 The mark up on cost of sales is 25%.

Year 3 Purchases have increased 10% in volume terms over year 2 when each unit bought cost £1. Stock prices have also increased on average by 5% over the second year prices and purchases are deemed to have occurred evenly throughout year 3.

The mark up has increased to 33⅓% for year 3 and Net Profit is 5% of Sales.

7X. Gillespie was a sole trader in a retail business, all sales being made for cash. His draft balance sheet on Friday, 30 June 19-4 was as follows:

	£		£	£
Fixtures and fittings	2,800	Capital account		9,000
		Current account		1,000
Stock, at cost	7,200	Creditors:		
Balance at bank	1,960	Trade	1,360	
		Expenses	680	
Cash in hand	80			2,040
	12,040			12,040

Exactly eight weeks later, on the night of Friday 25 August 19-4, a fire occurred which destroyed all his stock, fixtures and fittings, financial books, records and papers, with the exception of the file of unpaid invoices and the cash box containing the unbanked cash that he had taken home with him.

His fire insurance policy included cover of his stock, at cost, not exceeding £10,000 and fixtures and fittings at an agreed value £2,700. He had not insured against loss of profit.

The cash in hand on 30 June 19-4 and all takings up to the close of business on 25 August 19-4 had been banked with the exception of:
(a)   £24 per week paid as wages;
(b)   £30 per week that he had withdrawn for personal expenses; and
(c)   £120 in the cash box taken home with him.

All payments for goods and business expenses, other than wages, were made by cheque.

The selling price of his goods was obtained by adding 30% to the cost price.

An analysis of his bank statement for the eight weeks ended 25 August 19-4 showed the following receipts and payments:

	£
Receipts:	
Cash banked	5,768
Payments:	
Creditors for goods supplied	2,800
Expenses	920

The total of unpaid invoices on 25 August 19-4 amounted to:

Goods	1,120
Expenses	280

You are required to prepare:
(a)   A statement, setting out his claim for loss of stock; and   *(15 marks)*
(b)   A profit and loss account for the eight weeks ended 25 August 19-4, and a balance sheet on that date assuming the claims for loss of stock and fixtures and fittings are admitted.   *(15 marks)*

8X. Victor Bingham commenced business as a retail grocer on 1st November 19-0 but has not kept a proper set of books of account. Most of his sales are for cash and a record of credit sales has been maintained.

A summary of the bank transactions for the year to 31st October 19-1 is as follows:-

Lodgements	£Dr	Payments	£Cr
Introduction of Capital	18,600	Fixtures & Fittings	8,005
Receipts from Credit Sales	18,178	Vehicles	4,000
Net Cash Sales (i.e. after		Stationery & Advertising	1,488
payments)	86,800	Personal Expenses	930
		Electricity	521
		Purchases for Resale	92,008
		Staff Wages	8,184
		Rent & Rates	2,108
		Insurance	620
		Legal Costs	645

In addition to making the following cash payments before banking the takings, Bingham also withdrew £110 each for living expenses.

Cash Payments	£
Sundry Expenses	496
Purchases for Resale	248
Staff Wages & Insurance	2,654

The following additional information is also available:-

(a)

	31.10.–1
	£
Stock on hand	9,920
Debtors	2,554
Creditors	5,456
Heating & Lighting Accrued (Electricity)	136
Rates Paid in Advance	164
Insurance Paid in Advance	10

(b)   Goods costing £960 had been taken by Bingham from stock for his own use, and depreciation is to be provided for at the rate of 20% on cost price per annum on fixtures and fittings, and on motor vehicles.

(c)   Assume a 52-week year.

You are required to:

1.   Prepare cash and bank accounts covering the year ended 31st October 19–1.   *(10 marks)*

2.   Prepare a Trading and Profit and Loss Account for the year ended 31st October 19–1, together with a Balance Sheet as at that date.   *(20 marks)*

(Total 30 marks)

[AAT]

9X. David Denton set up in business as a plumber a year ago, and he has asked you to act as his accountant. His instructions to you are in the form of the following letter:-

Dear Henry,

I was pleased when you agreed to act as my accountant and look forward to your first visit to check my records. The proposed fee of £250 p.a. is acceptable. I regret that the paperwork for the work done during the year is incomplete. I started my business on 1 January last, and put £6,500 into a business bank account on that date. I brought my van into the firm at that time, and reckon that it was worth £3,600 then. I think it will last another three years after the end of the first year of business use.

I have drawn £90 per week from the business bank account during the year. In my trade it is difficult to take a holiday, but my wife managed to get away for a while. The travel agent's bill for £280 was paid out of the business account. I bought the lease of the yard and office for £6,500. The lease has ten years to run, and the rent is only £300 a year payable in advance on the anniversary of the date of purchase, which was 1 April. I borrowed £4,000 on that day from Aunt Jane to help pay for the lease. I have agreed to pay her 10% interest per annum, but have been too busy to do anything about this yet.

I was lucky enough to meet Miss Prism shortly before I set up on my own, and she has worked for me as an office organiser right from the start. She is paid a salary of £3,000 p.a. All the bills for the year have been carefully preserved in a tool box, and we analysed them last week. The materials I have bought cost me £9,600, but I reckon there was £580 worth left in the yard on 31 December. I have not paid for them all yet, I think we owed £714 to the suppliers on 31 December. I was surprised to see that I had spent £4,800 on plumbing equipment, but it should last me five years or so. Electricity bills received up to 30 September came to £1,122; but motor expenses were £912, and general expenses £1,349 for the year. The insurance premium for the year to 31 March next was £800. All these have been paid by cheque but Miss Prism has lost the rate demand. I expect the Local Authority will send a reminder soon since I have not yet paid. I seem to remember that rates came to £180 for the year to 31 March next. Miss Prism sent out bills to my customers for work done, but some of them are very slow to pay. Altogether the charges made were £29,863, but only £25,613 had been received by 31 December. Miss Prism thinks that 10% of the remaining bills are not likely to be paid. Other customers for jobs too small to bill have paid £3,418 in cash for work done, but I only managed to bank £2,600 of this money. I used £400 of the difference to pay the family's grocery bills, and Miss Prism used the rest for general expenses, except for £123 which was left over in a drawer in the office on 31 December.

Kind regards,
Yours sincerely,
David.

Required:
You are required to draw up a Profit and Loss Account for the year
ended 31 December, and a Balance Sheet as at that date.

(22 marks)
[ACCA]

NON-PROFIT MAKING ORGANIZATIONS
– associations, clubs, charities, societies

ACCOUNTS FOR NON-PROFIT MAKING ORGANIZATIONS

So far, we have been concerned with preparing financial statements for sole traders, partnerships and limited companies, all of which are profit-making organizations. We now turn our attention to non-profit making organizations such as clubs, societies, associations and charities.

RECEIPTS AND PAYMENTS ACCOUNTS

Most non-profit making organizations will keep a record of cash receipts and payments. This equates to the cash book of profit-making organizations. It may not always take the form of a formalized cash book but that is nevertheless what the record of receipts and payments is. Receipts should be shown on the left hand side of the account (Dr.), and payments should be shown on the right hand side of the account (Cr.).

If the cash book is the only record that the organization holds, and members receive a copy of a receipts and payments account, this would be inadequate to present a true and fair view of the state of affairs for the organization in a specific year. This is so because receipts and payments accounts are simply a cash record and make no attempt to match the expenditure of a period with the income. One of the four fundamental accounting concepts, that is, the accruals concept or matching principle is ignored (SSAP 2). The following items are therefore not taken into account in a record of receipts and payments:-
1. Accounts receivable (debtors — members' subscriptions)
2. Accounts payable (creditors)
3. Accruals (members who have paid in advance)
4. Pre-payments
5. Provisions, e.g. depreciation
6. Stock balances not consumed, if any.

INCOME AND EXPENDITURE ACCOUNTS

This type of account overcomes the problems stated above and takes account of the matching principle. Thus the expenditure of a period is matched with the income of a period. At the end of this financial statement, there would not be a profit or loss but either:-
1. A surplus of income over expenditure; or
2. A surplus of expenditure over income.

Just as net profit or loss is transferred to the capital account in the balance sheet of a profit-making organization, so too is the surplus transferred to the capital account of the non-profit making organization. However, it is not called the capital account, it is called the **Accumulated Fund.**

TERMINOLOGY

PROFIT ORGANIZATION ◄────────►	NON-PROFIT ORGANIZATION
PROFIT	≡	SURPLUS OF INCOME OVER EXPENDITURE
LOSS	≡	SURPLUS OF EXPENDITURE OVER INCOME
CAPITAL	≡	ACCUMULATED FUND
BALANCE SHEET	≡	STATEMENT OF AFFAIRS

Sometimes, non-profit organizations will undertake trading activities from which it will earn a profit on the activity, e.g. a bar, café, dance, etc. Examination questions in this area will often ask you to complete a bar-trading account or some other kind of trading account for an activity undertaken by the organization. You will need to complete this before you can complete the income and expenditure account. All costs and clearly identifiable expenses for the trading activity should be placed in this account, as should the revenue from the activity. The profit made on trading should then be transferred as income to the income and expenditure account for the organization as a whole.

Sometimes you may be presented with an opening statement of affairs for the organization and details of transactions which have taken place throughout a period. You will then be asked to complete an income and expenditure account to begin with, together with an opening statement of affairs. Sometimes you may be expected to draw up an opening statement of affairs to obtain the figure for the accumulated fund at the start of the period. This is similar to questions on incomplete records. You need to list the assets and liabilities of the organization, at the start of the period. If you subtract the liabilities from the assets, this will give the opening accumulated fund. You may also have to write up a cash book so as to obtain a closing figure for bank and cash to place on the closing statement of affairs.

EXAMPLE

CHRIZELTON SPORTS CLUB

(1) **List of Balances**	31.12.-4 £	31.12-5 £
DEBTORS — members' subs	200	300
CREDITORS — bar stocks		500
ACCRUALS — members paid in advance		200
STOCK (BAR)	1,100	900

(2)
SUMMARY OF RECEIPTS & PAYMENTS

	Receipts	£Dr	Payments	£Cr
1.1.-5	Balance b/f	2,200	Cr. for Bar stock	2,750
	Subs from		Barman's wages	500
	members total	5,400	Honorarium to	
	Bar takings	4,200	Secretary	100
	Dance tickets	400	Printing &	
	Donations	10	Stationery	150
			Entertainers — dance	100
			Sundry items	5
			Glass washer machine for bar (bought in June)	150
			Balance c/f	8,455
		12,210		12,210

(3) The club owns a pavilion which was valued at £10,000 at 31.12.-4. It has been decided to depreciate this asset equally over its estimated useful life of 10 years.

(4) Any other equipment that the club buys is to be written off equally over a 3 year period.

(5) It is policy to charge a full year's depreciation on items bought during the year.

You are required to:-
1. Draw up a Statement of Affairs at 1.1.-5, showing the accumulated fund at that date.

2. Prepare a Bar-Trading Account for year ended 31.12.-5.

3. Prepare an Income and Expenditure Account for the year ended 31.12.–5.

4. Draw up a Statement of Affairs for the club as at 31.12.–5.

EXAMPLE ANSWER

The first step is to produce an opening statement of affairs (a balance sheet at the start – assets less liabilities = The Accumulated Fund) to find out the accumulated fund.

1.
CHRIZELTON SPORTS CLUB
Statement of Affairs at 1.1.–5

	£	£	£
		Provision for	
FIXED ASSETS	Cost	Depreciation	Net Book Value
Pavilion	—	—	10,000
CURRENT ASSETS			
Stock	1,100		
Debtors	200		
Prepayments	—		
Bank	2,200		
		3,500	
LESS CURRENT LIABILITIES			
Creditors	—		
Accruals	—	—	
Net Current Assets			3,500
Total Net Assets			13,500
FINANCED BY			
Accumulated Fund at 1.1.–5 [2]			

NOTES:
1. *We only have a value for the pavilion at 31.12.–4 and need only place the value in the N.B.V. column.*
2. *The Accumulated Fund must have funded the Total Net Asset position. The figure is obtained by adding the book values of fixed assets to current assets and taking away any liabilities the organization has.*

The second step is to write up the receipts and payments account (the cash book); to obtain a closing cash balance for the closing balance sheet. In this case we are already given this information so it is not necessary.

The third step is to prepare a bar trading account as follows:-

CHRIZELTON CRICKET CLUB — Bar Trading Account
for the year ended 31.12.19–5

	£	£
Sales		4,200
Less Cost of Sales		
Opening stock	1,100	
Add Purchases*	3,250	
	4,350	
Less Closing Stock	(900)	
Cost of Goods Sold		(3,450)
Gross Profit		750
Less Expenses		
Barman's wages	500	
Depreciation — glasswasher	50	
		550
Net Profit c/f to I & E A/c		200

Note: to obtain the purchases figure you needed to prepare a control account as below:-

PURCHASE CONTROL ACCOUNT

	£Dr		£Cr
Cash	2,750	Balance b/f	NIL
Balance c/f	500	PURCHASE A/c	3,250
	3,250		3,250

Also note that only those expenses relevant to bar trading are entered in the bar trading account.

The fourth step is to prepare the Income and Expenditure Account.

3.   **CHRIZELTON CRICKET CLUB**
Income & Expenditure Account for the year ended 31.12.19-5

	£	£
Income		
Subscriptions from members*		5,300
Profit from the bar		200
Dance tickets		400
Donations		10
		5,910
Less Expenditure		
Honorarium to secretary	100	
Printing and stationery	150	
Entertainers — Dance	100	
Sundries	5	
Depreciation:		
Pavilion	1,000	
		(1,355)
Surplus of Income over Expenditure		4,555

The subscriptions for the year are obtained as follows:-

DEBTORS CONTROL A/c — Subscriptions

	£Dr		£Cr
Balance b/f	200	Cash	5,400
Subscriptions in advance	200		
Subscriptions for year to		Balance c/f	300
I & E A/c	5,300		
	5,700		5,700

To summarise (subscriptions owed from the previous year) balance b/f + subscriptions paid by members in advance less subscriptions received in cash less balance c/f (subscriptions outstanding).

The final step is to prepare a closing balance sheet.

4.   **CHRIZELTON SPORTS CLUB**
                      Statement of Affairs at 31.12.19–5

	£	£	£
		Provision for	
Fixed Assets	**Cost**	**Depreciation**	**NBV**
Pavilion	10,000	1,000	9,000
Glass Washer	150	50	100
	10,150	1,050	9,100
Current Assets			
Stock (Bar)	900		
Debtors	300		
Prepayments	—		
Cash	8,455		
		9,655	
Less Current Liabilities			
Creditors	500		
Accruals	200		
		(700)	
Net Current Assets			8,955
Total Net Assets			18,055
Financed by:			
Accumulated fund at 1.1.–5		13,500	
Add Surplus of Income over expenditure		4,555	
Accumulated Fund at 31.12.–5			18,055

SUMMARY

1. Most non-profit making organizations will keep at least a Receipts and Payments Account (Cash Book).

2. An Income and Expenditure Account is more useful since it follows the concept of matching income and costs of a period. It takes account of:-
   1. Accounts Receivable and Payable, i.e. Debtors and Creditors.
   2. Accruals and Prepayments.
   3. Provisions.
   4. Changes in stock levels.

3. Important points to note:-
   — There is no profit but a surplus of income over expenditure or vice versa — expenditure over income.
   — Capital is called the Accumulated Fund.
   — The Balance Sheet is referred to as a Statement of Affairs.

QUESTIONS

1X. The following was a receipts and payments account prepared by the treasurer of the Mid-Cheshire Cricket Club for the year ended 31 December 19-4.

19-4	RECEIPTS	£Dr	19-4	PAYMENTS	£Cr
1.1	Cash in hand	20	31.12	Groundsman's fees	150
	Balances at bank as per bank statements:			Purchase of mowing machine	300
	Deposit a/c	446		Rent of ground	50
	Current a/c	120		Cost of teas	50
31.12	Bank interest on deposit account	6		Fares	80
	Donations and subscriptions	520		Printing and secretarial exp.	56
	Receipts from teas	60		Repairs to equipment and machinery	100
	Contributions to fares			Honoraria to secretary and treasurer for 19-3	40
	Sale of equipment	16		Balances at bank as per bank statements:	
	Net proceeds of dance	156		Deposit a/c	418
				Current a/c	30
				Cash in hand	50
		1,364			1,364

You are given the following additional information:

		On 1 Jan. 19–4 £	On 31 Dec. 19–4 £
(1)	Subscriptions due	30	20
(2)	Sums due for printing and secretarial expenses	20	16
(3)	Unpresented cheques, being payments for repairs	60	50
(4)	Interest on deposit accounts not yet credited on bank statements	—	4
(5)	Estimated value of machinery and equipment	160	350
(6)	For the year ended 31 December 19–4 the honoraria to the secretary and treasurer are to be increased by a total of £20 and the groundsman is to receive a bonus of £20.		

You are required to prepare:
(a) A computation showing the capital of the club on 1 January 19–4;   *(5 marks)*
(b) An income and expenditure account for the year ended 31 December 19–4; and   *(10 marks)*
(c) A balance sheet on that date.   *(5 marks)*

2X. The treasurer of the Wirral Cricket Club has prepared the receipts and payments account shown below. He would like to prepare a more appropriate financial statement and asks you as a friend if you could assist him.

Required:
1. Advise the treasurer what type of account you consider more appropriate and why.
2. Prepare the financial statement to illustrate your answer to 1 above. Show all workings.   *(20 marks)*

WCC Receipts and Payments Account for the
year ended 31.12.-3

	RECEIPTS	£Dr		PAYMENTS	£Cr
1.1.-3	Bank balance b/f	1,048		Bar supplies	7,924
				Wages:	
	Subscriptions	2,662		Groundsman	1,878
	Bar Sales	11,256		Barman	1,248
	Donations	240		Bar Expenses	468
				Repairs to	
				Clubhouse	238
				Ground upkeep	276
				Secretary Exp.	458
				Coach Hire	610
			31.12.-3	Bank balance c/f	2,106
		15,206			15,206

The treasurer also provides the following information:

		31.12.-2 £	31.12.-3 £
1.	Bar stock at cost	992	1,116
	Owing for bar supplies	588	680
	Bar Expenses owing	50	70
	Coach hire owing	—	65
	Subscriptions due	110	132

2. £80 subscriptions have been received in advance during 19-3.
3. The land was valued at 31.12.-2 at £8,000 and the Clubhouse at £4,000. The latter is to be depreciated at 10% p.a.
4. Equipment was valued at 31.12.-2 at £1,100 and is to be depreciated at 20% p.a.

3. As treasurer of your local tennis club you have just prepared a draft Receipts and Payments account, which is reproduced below.

The club committee decides, however, that it wishes its financial statements for 19-3 and subsequent years to be in the form of an Income and Expenditure account accompanied by a balance sheet and requests you to amend the 19-3 account accordingly.

Receipts and Payments Account
for the year ended 31.12-3

	£
Receipts:	
Cash in hand at 1st January, 19–3	100
Cash at bank at 1st January, 19–3: Current account	1,160
Deposit account	2,000
Members' subscriptions: 19–2	620
19–3	8,220
19–4	125
Interest on deposit account	85
Entry fees for club championship	210
Tickets sold for annual dinner/dance	420
Bank overdraft at 31st December, 19–3	4,000
	16,940
Payments:	
Groundsman's wages	4,000
Purchase of equipment (on 30th June, 19–3)	8,000
Rent for year to 30th September, 19–3	2,000
Rates for year to 31st March, 19–4	1,800
Cost of annual dinner/dance	500
Secretarial expenses	400
Prizes for club championship	90
Miscellaneous expenses	100
Cash in hand at 31st December, 19–3	50
	16,940

Additional information:
1. At 31st December 19–3, £700 was outstanding for members'
    subscriptions for 19–3.
2. During 19–2, £230 was received in respect of members'
    subscriptions for 19–3.
3. The cost of equipment purchased in previous years was:

	£
30th June, 19–2	5,000
1st January, 19–7	1,000
30th September, 19–1	1,000

4. The committee decides that equipment should be depreciated at
    the rate of 10% per annum on cost.
5. Rent has been at the rate of £2,000 per annum for the last two
    years and is not expected to change in the immediate future.
6. Rates of £750 for the six months to 31st March, 19–3 were paid
    on 2nd November, 19–2.

7. Interest of £250 on the bank overdraft had accrued at 31st December, 19–3.
8. Taxation is to be ignored.

You are required to prepare:
(a) The club's Income and Expenditure account for the year ended 31st December, 19–3; and
(b) The club's Balance Sheets as at 31st December, 19–2, and as at 31st December, 19–3.   *(35 marks)*
(CIMA)

4X. As the accountant of the Swallow Bowling Club, you have been presented with the following information for the year to 30th September 19–3:

Receipts	£	Payments	£
Cash in hand at 1.10-2	20	Club running expenses	770
Cash at bank at 1.10.-2	1,200	Cost of refreshments	180
Subscriptions	2,050	Christmas dance expenses	500
Bar receipts	3,600	Bar purchases	1,750
Christmas dance ticket sales	650	Lawn mower	600
Refreshment sales	320	Cash in hand at 30.9.-3	30
		Cash at bank at 30.9.-3	4,010
	7,840		7,840

Notes:

(a) Subscriptions

	In arrears £	In advance £
At 1.10.-2	100	50
At 30.9.-3	200	75

(b) Fixed Assets

	At 1.10.-2 £	At 30.9.-3 £
Club premises, at cost	50,000	50,000
Less Depreciation	35,000	37,500
	15,000	12,500

Depreciation is to be charged on the lawn mower at a rate of 15% per annum on cost.

(c) Bar stock at 30th September 19–2 was valued at £150 and £200 at 30th September, 19–3.

(d) Outstanding Expenses

	At 1.10.-2 £	At 30.9.-3 £
Bar purchases	300	400
Club expenses	250	200

(e) Rates paid in advance at 30th September 19–2 and at 30th September 19–3 amounted to £200 and £300 respectively.

Required:
Prepare the Club's Income and Expenditure Account for the year to 30th September 19–3, and a balance sheet as at that date.   *[AAT]*

5. The following is a summary of the receipts and payments for the year to 31st March 19–3 of the Scott Social Club:

	£
Receipts	
Club subscriptions	17,000
Donations	1,500
Christmas dance	850
Bar takings	27,000
Payments	
Rates	900
General expenses	26,200
Bar purchases	18,500
Christmas dance expenses	150

Other relevant information at the beginning and end of the year is as follows:

	1st April 19–2 £	31st March 19–3 £
Subscriptions due	900	600
Subscriptions paid in advance	50	100
Rates owing	450	500
Bar stock	2,000	2,500
Club premises (cost £50,000)	20,000	18,000
Furniture (cost £10,000)	3,000	2,000
Bank and cash in hand	1,600	2,200

Required:

(a) Prepare the Club's Bar Trading Account for the year to 31st March 19–3.

(b) Prepare the Club's Income and Expenditure Account for the year to 31st March 19–3, and a Balance Sheet as at that date. [AAT]

PARTNERSHIPS — AN INTRODUCTION
– the basic concepts

A partnership may consist of at least two people and up to a maximum of twenty people. There are exceptions to this maximum for professional partnerships such as accountants and solicitors where the rules of the profession forbid them from adopting other forms of organisation. Normally, there is a 'Partnership Deed' which specifies the rights, obligations and rewards for each of the partners. The deed is not a legal requirement and in the absence of such a deed, the rights, obligations and rewards are specified in the **Partnership Act 1890.**

THE LIMITED PARTNERSHIP

Be careful not to confuse limited partnerships with limited companies — they are not the same. A limited partnership is a special type of partnership whereby at least one of the partners must have unlimited liability and will therefore be responsible for the debts of the partnership. Partners having limited liability are often referred to as 'sleeping partners'. Sleeping partners do not, however, necessarily have to be limited partners. In the absence of a Deed of Partnership the rights, obligations and rewards are specified in the Limited Partnership Act 1907. Limited partners must not take part in the management of the firm. They merely invest capital in return for which they expect a share of the profits in accordance with the terms agreed in the deed.

THE DEED OF PARTNERSHIP

This will normally contain the following details:-
1. The Capital to be contributed by each partner.
2. The ratios in which profits or losses are to be shared (which need not necessarily be in the same proportions as the capital contribution.)
3. The rate of interest, if any, to be paid to the partners on their capital contribution prior to sharing out the profit or loss.
4. The rate of interest to be charged on drawings, if any.
5. Salaries to be paid to partners, if any.

SPECIAL POINTS TO NOTE WITH REGARD TO PARTNERSHIP ACCOUNTS

INTEREST ON CAPITAL

This is an incentive to a partner who may contribute more in the way of capital, assuming that the partners contribute equally towards the work of the business. It rewards a partner for his extra contribution of capital. The capital contributed by each partner will not necessarily be in their profit or loss sharing ratios. The rate of interest is a matter of agreement between the partners. The bookkeeping entry is:-

```
DEBIT   — PARTNERSHIP PROFIT AND LOSS
          APPROPRIATION ACCOUNT

CREDIT — THE RESPECTIVE PARTNER'S CURRENT
          ACCOUNT
```

Thus, it is income of the individual concerned and a charge to the Partnership.

INTEREST ON DRAWINGS

This is a charge against the individual and becomes income of the partnership. It may be looked at as an incentive for partners to leave money in the business or alternatively, as a disincentive for withdrawing capital.

```
DEBIT   — THE RESPECTIVE PARTNER'S CURRENT
          ACCOUNT

CREDIT — THE PROFIT AND LOSS APPROPRIATION
          ACCOUNT
```

SALARIES

In addition to a share of the profits some partners may receive a salary. For example, junior partners in firms of accountants or solicitors often receive a salary where their share of the profit may be insufficient to live on. Furthermore, some partners may take on additional duties for which it is only fair that they are rewarded and therefore a salary is paid. The entries are:-

```
DEBIT   — THE PROFIT AND LOSS APPROPRIATION
          ACCOUNT

CREDIT — THE RESPECTIVE PARTNER'S CURRENT
          ACCOUNT
```

CAPITAL AND CURRENT ACCOUNTS

Up to now dealing with sole trader accounts the net profit earned by the business has been added to the Capital Account. In the case of partnerships it is easier to deal with profit appropriation through means of a Current Account. The Capital Account remains fixed, that is to say that the balance brought down at the start of the year will be the balance carried forward at the end of the year. The Current Account, however, may be thought of as a floating Capital Account. The Balance Sheet Extract for a two person partnership consisting of Partners A and B would be as follows:-

Financed By	£	£	£
Capital Accounts –A	x		
–B	x	x	
Current Accounts –A	x		
–B	x	x	
			x

Note: It is not necessary to show any addition of profit to capital nor any drawings, since the balance on the Current Account will have already dealt with these.

THE APPROPRIATION ACCOUNT

This is simply the place where the net profit of the business is apportioned to those people entitled to a share of that profit. In this case the net profit is allocated to each of the partners after crediting any interest on drawings and after debiting any interest on capital or payment of a salary. The Appropriation Account containing these adjustments is shown immediately below the Trading and Profit and Loss Account. See the example below.

DISSOLUTION OF PARTNERSHIP

If one of the partners should decide to leave either voluntarily or involuntarily (e.g. death), then the partnership is automatically dissolved. If a new partner is introduced, the old partnership must be dissolved and a new one set up. This involves closing down the books of the business by paying all outstanding creditors, collecting all outstanding debtors and computing a final profit or loss for the firm. The steps involved in dissolution will be dealt with later.

EXAMPLE — PARTNERSHIP ACCOUNTS

Smith and Jones are in partnership sharing profits and losses equally.

TRIAL BALANCE AT 30.6.–6

	£Dr	£Cr
Buildings at Cost	50,000	
Fixtures at Cost	11,000	
Debtors	16,243	
Cash at Bank	677	
Stock 30.6.–5	41,979	
Purchases	85,416	
Carriage Out	1,288	
Discounts Allowed	115	
Loan Interest Cassidy	4,000	
Office Expenses	2,416	
Salaries & Wages	18,917	
Bad Debts	503	
Drawings Smith	6,400	
Jones	5,650	
Provision for Depreciation Fixtures		3,300
Creditors		11,150
Sales		123,650
Provision for Bad Debts		400
Loan from Cassidy (Long Term)		40,000
Capitals Smith		35,000
Jones		29,500
Current a/c Smith		1,306
Jones		298
	244,604	244,604

Notes and Instructions:
1. Stock at 30.6.–6 £56,340.
2. Expenses accrued office £96, wages £200.
3. Depreciate fixtures 10% on a reducing balance basis.
4. Reduce the provision for bad debts to £320.
5. Partnership salary £80 to Smith not yet paid.
6. Interest on Drawings Smith £180 and Jones £120.
7. Interest is to be paid on Capital account balances at 10% p.a.

Required:
A Trading & Profit & Loss Appropriation Account for the year ending
30.6.–6 and a Balance Sheet as at that date.

SMITH & JONES TRADING & PROFIT & LOSS
APPROPRIATION ACCOUNT FOR YEAR ENDED 30.6.–6

	£	£	£
Sales			123,650
Less Cost of Goods Sold			
Opening Stock		85,416	
Add Purchases		41,979	
		127,395	
Less Closing Stock		56,340	
			71,055
Gross Profit			52,595
Less Expenses			
Carriage Out		1,288	
Discount Allowed		115	
Loan Interest		4,000	
Office Expenses (2416 + 96)		2,512	
Salaries & Wages (18,917 + 200)		19,117	
Bad Debts	503		
Reduction in Provision	(80)	423	
Depreciation		770	
			28,225
Net Profit			24,370
ADD Interest on Drawings			
Smith			180
Jones			120
			24,670
LESS Salary			
Smith		80	
Interest on Capital			
Smith		3,500	
Jones		2,950	6,530
			18,140
Balance of Profits to be shared as follows:			
Smith		9,070	
Jones		9,070	
			18,140

CAPITAL ACCOUNT — SMITH

£Dr		**£Cr**
	Cash	35,000

CURRENT ACCOUNT — JONES

	£Dr		£Cr
Interest on Drawings	120	Balance b/f	298
Drawings	5,650	Interest on Capital	2,950
Balance c/f	6,548	Share of Profit	9,070
	12,318		12,318
		Balance b/f	6,548

CAPITAL ACCOUNT — JONES

£Dr		£Cr
	Cash	29,500

CURRENT ACCOUNT — SMITH

	£Dr		£Cr
Interest on Drawings	180	Balance b/f	1,306
Drawings	6,400	Salary	80
Balance c/f	7,376	Interest on Capital	3,500
		Profit Share	9,070
	13,956		13,956
		Balance b/f	7,376

SMITH & JONES BALANCE SHEET AS AT 30.6.–6

	£Cost	£Depn	£NBV
Fixed Assets			
Building	50,000		50,000
Fixtures	11,000	4,070	6,930
	61,000	4,070	56,930
Current Assets			
Stock	56,340		
Debtors 16,243			
Less Provision			
for Bad Debts 320	15,923		
Bank	677		
		72,940	
Current Liabilities			
Creditors	11,150		
Accruals (200 + 96)	296		
		11,446	
Net Current Assets or Working Capital			61,494
Total Net Assets			118,424
Financed By			
Capital Account Smith	35,000		
Jones	29,500		
		64,500	
Current Account Smith	7,376		
Jones	6,548		
		13,924	
			78,424
Loan (Cassidy)			40,000
Capital Employed			118,424

SUMMARY

1.   A partnership needs at least 2 people and no more than 20 except in the case of professional partnerships.

2.   Partnership Act 1890 relevant law.

3.   There are LIMITED PARTNERSHIPS
     — rare nowadays — where one or more partners' liability is limited, Limited Partnership Act 1907.

4.   Partners normally draw up a deed specifying rights, rewards and duties.

5. Important Accounting considerations
    – Interest on Capital
    – Interest on Drawings
    – Salaries for partners
    – Capital and Current Accounts
    – The Appropriation Account

QUESTIONS

1X. Dalglish and Rush were in partnership sharing profits in the ratio of 3:2, i.e. 3/5 to Dalglish and 2/5 to Rush. The following is a list of balances extracted from their books at 31.12.–3.

	£Dr	£Cr
Capital at 1.1.–3		
Dalglish		10,000
Rush		6,000
Current A/c at 1.1.–3		
Dalglish		2,000
Rush		1,000
Drawings:		
Dalglish	3,000	
Rush	2,500	
Premises	4,000	
Fixtures	2,000	
Stock at 1.1.–3	2,500	
Bad debts	200	
Purchases	16,000	
Sales		24,000
Debtors	6,000	
Creditors		3,000
Cash	800	
Wages	4,000	
Advertising	3,000	
Insurance	1,000	
Sundry Expenses	500	
Returns In	200	
Discount Allowed	300	
	46,000	46,000

Notes:
1. Stock on 31.12.19–3 — £2,800.
2. Depreciation is charged as follows:-
    Premises 10% per annum straight line basis.
    Fixtures 20% per annum straight line basis.

3. Interest is to be paid at 5% per annum on the partners' Capital accounts.
4. Wages accrued £500.
5. Provision for bad debts is to be made 2.5% on sales shown in the Trading and Profit and Loss Account.

Required:
1. Prepare a trading, profit and loss, appropriation account and partners' current accounts for the year ended 31.12.–3.
2. A Balance Sheet at 31.12.–3.
3. Briefly explain the accounting steps to be followed in dissolving the partnership should it become necessary.   *(30 marks)*

2X. **PARTNERSHIP**

DUM & DEE — Trial Balance at 31.12.–5

	£Dr	£Cr
Fixed Assets:		
Land and Buildings at cost	100,000	
Motor Vehicle at cost	20,000	
Current Assets:		
Stock at 1.1.–5	5,550	
Debtors	7,250	
Bank	3,200	
Cash	510	
Purchases	29,525	
Carriage inwards	100	
		300
Expenses:		
Administration:		
Wages & Salaries	7,500	
Office Repairs	500	
Telephones	350	
Rent & Rates of Office	1,800	
Sales & Marketing:		
Advertising	2,750	
Salesman's Salary	8,000	
Vehicle Running	2,150	
Discount Allowed	1,000	
Distribution:		
Vehicle Running	4,250	
Vehicle Repairs	1,100	
Carriage Outwards	1,000	
Finance: Bank Charges	550	
Sales		51,550
Creditors		7,650
Provision for Depreciation:		
Land & Buildings		30,000
Motor Vehicle		5,000
Partners Capital Accounts:		
Dum		50,000
Dee		40,000
Partners Current Accounts:		
Dum		8,185
Dee		4,400
	197,085	197,085

Notes:
1. Stock valued at cost 31.12.–5 was £5,385.
2. It is policy to charge depreciation as follows:-
    (a) Land & Buildings are to be written off in equal instalments over the estimated useful life which the partners deem to be 50 years.
    (b) Motor Vehicles are written off at 20% p.a. at cost. (75% of the vehicles are used for distribution purposes, the remainder are used as sales vehicles).
3. The partners have agreed to pay interest on fixed capitals at 5% p.a. They have also agreed to charge interest on drawings at 10% p.a.
4. Dee receives a salary of £5,000 p.a. in respect of extra duties he undertakes.
5. The partners have agreed to share Profits & Losses equally.
6. Drawings paid by cheque during the year, not included in the Trial Balance were as follows:-

	£
Dum	1,200
Dee	500

The money having been withdrawn from the bank, no entries have been made into the accounts as yet.
7. The Rent & Rates charge of £1,800 is in respect of the period from 1 January 19–5 to 30 June 19–6.
8. Further advertising expenses amounting to £750 were incurred. No invoice having yet been received and no cash having been paid.

Required:
1. Prepare a partnership Trading, Profit & Loss and Appropriation A/c for the year ended 31.12.–5.
2. Show the partners' Capital & Current Account at 31.12.–5.
3. Draw up a Balance Sheet for the partnership as at 31.12.–5.

(25 marks)

3. Dawn, Edith and Mandy are in partnership as Recreational Suppliers, sharing residual profits and losses in the ratio of 5:2:3 respectively. At 1st November 19–2 their capital and current account balances were:

	Capital Account £	Current Account £
Dawn	8,000	580 (credit)
Edith	10,000	350 (debit)
Mandy	12,000	210 (credit)

By agreement, partners are entitled to interest on capital at the rate of 5% per annum.

On 1st May 19–3, by mutual agreement, Dawn increased her capital by paying a further £2,000 into the partnership bank account, whilst Edith reduced her capital to £6,000, but left her withdrawn capital in the partnership as a loan bearing interest at 5% per annum.

Partners are allowed to withdraw from current accounts at any time during the financial year but are charged interest on the amounts involved. Details of drawings made and interest chargeable in respect of each partner for the financial year ended 31st October 19–3 are:

	Drawings £	Interest on Drawings £
Dawn	2,400	90
Edith	1,800	30
Mandy	3,000	25

Edith is remunerated for her participation in the running of the partnership by an annual salary of £2,500.

The trading profit (before interest) of Recreational Suppliers for the year ended 31st October 19–3 was £19,905.

Required:
(a) Prepare the profit and loss appropriation account for the partnership.
(b) Post to and balance the capital and current accounts of the individual partners.   [ACCA]

4. Ben, Ken and Len are in partnership sharing profits and losses in the ratio 3:2:1. The following is the trial balance of the partnership as at 30th September 19–3:

	£Dr	£Cr
Bad Debts Provision (at 1st October 19–2)		1,000
Bank and cash in hand	2,500	
Capital Accounts:		
Ben		18,000
Ken		12,000
Len		6,000
Current Accounts:		
Ben		700
Ken	500	
Len		300
Debtors and Creditors	23,000	35,000
Depreciation (at 1st October 19–2):		
Land and buildings		12,000
Motor vehicles		8,000
Drawings:		
Ben	4,000	
Ken	3,000	
Len	3,000	
Land and buildings, at cost	60,000	
Motor vehicles, at cost	20,000	
Office expenses	4,000	
Purchases	85,000	
Rates	4,000	
Sales		150,000
Selling expenses	14,000	
Stock (at 1st October 19–2)	20,000	
	243,000	243,000

You are provided with the following additional information:
1. Stock at 30th September 19–3 was valued at £30,000.
2. Fixed assets are written off at the following rates:
    Land and buildings 5% per annum on cost
    Motor vehicles 20% per annum on cost
3. At 30th September 19–3 an amount of £1,775 was owing for selling expenses.
4. Rates were prepaid by £2,000 as at 30th September 19–3.
5. A certain bad debt of £500 is to be written off.
6. The bad debts provision is to be made equal to 5% of outstanding debtors as at 30th September 19–3.

7. The partnership agreement covers the following appropriations:
    (a) Len is to be allowed a salary of £6,000 per annum.
    (b) Interest of 10% per annum is allowed on the partners' capital account balances.
    (c) No interest is allowed on the partners' current accounts.
    (d) No interest is charged on the partners' drawings.

Required:
(i)   Prepare the partners' trading, profit and loss and profit and loss appropriation accounts for the year to 30th September 19–3.
(ii) Write up the partners' current accounts for the year to 30th September 19–3, and bring down the balances as at 1st October 19–3.
(iii) Prepare the partnership balance sheet at 30th September 19–3.

[AAT]

 **ADMISSION OF NEW PARTNERS**
– spreading the risk and the rewards

THE NEED FOR NEW PARTNERS

As a business grows it may be necessary for it to take in a new partner either for his technical or entrepreneurial skills or simply to introduce extra capital. Whether the existing business is a sole trader or partnership, the admission of a partner brings a new firm into existence. It is essential to agree upon the terms of admission and the conditions of the new partnership.

TERMS OF ADMISSION

It may be agreed between two existing partners to admit a third party for a payment of £5,000 as his capital contribution and that the new partner would receive 25% of the profits of the new firm.

The accounting entries would be simple:-

DR — New Partnership Cash Book — £5000	
CR — New Partner's Capital Account —	**£5000**

It is, however, seldom so simple because the partner is being admitted to an already established business. The new partner would benefit from this. The old partners would forego the advantages by admitting a new partner in the way described above.

GOODWILL

This concept is that of goodwill. Goodwill will have been established by the partners in the old firm, from which the newly admitted partner will benefit. Not only would a new partner derive benefit from profit sharing but should the new partnership be sold, goodwill would be realized by the sale and he has the right to a share in its value. Owing to this it is usual for a new partner to pay for the privilege of admission to an existing business. The payment (premium) is made to the old members and may be regarded as compensation to them for the share of goodwill that will pass to the new partner at their expense. This premium is in addition to the capital the new partner will introduce to the new firm. The premium must not be confused with capital introduced. The cash or assets the new partner introduces will be credited to his Capital Account and debited to the relevant asset accounts.

VALUING GOODWILL

Goodwill like any asset value is only worth what a buyer is willing to pay. In practice a value is normally agreed upon by negotiation. Sometimes it will be 'a number of times the gross annual income of the business' say 1 to 1½. Alternatively, 'a number of times the average net profit' of the business.

EXAMPLE: A business has net profits for the last 5 years of £10,000, £11,000, £12,000, £13,000 and £14,000. It has been agreed by the parties that goodwill will be paid equivalent to 2 times the average net profit.

$$\text{in £000's}$$

$$\text{Therefore:-} \quad \frac{(10+11+12+13+14)}{5 \text{ years}} \quad = \quad £12,000 \times 2$$

= £24,000 is the premium agreed for goodwill.

ACCOUNTING TREATMENT OF GOODWILL

The premium is normally treated in one of three ways which are:-

1. No entries are made in the books of account of the new business and the premium is paid directly to the old partners who share the sum in their agreed profit sharing ratios.

2. The agreed payment for goodwill is paid into the new firm, but is paid out immediately to the old partners in accordance with their old profit sharing ratios. The only difference between methods 1 and 2 is that the second method records the transaction, the first does not. It may be the wish of the partners to record it.

3. The premium paid by a new partner into the firm remains in the business. The premium is the property of the old partners in their old profit sharing ratios.

The accounting entries would be as follows:-

DR — New Firm's Bank Account with receipt

CR — Each partners CAPITAL A/c with his proportion of the premium

---

The effect is to increase the Capital contribution of the old partners in the new firm.

USING A GOODWILL ACCOUNT

STEPS 1   Agree on the value of Goodwill.
        2   Open a Goodwill Account by debiting it with the agreed figure.
        3   Credit the old partners Capital a/c in their 'old' profit sharing ratios.
        4   Write down the Goodwill Account to 'zero' by crediting the account — debiting the new partners in their new profit sharing ratios.

MAINTAINING GOODWILL IN THE BOOKS OF ACCOUNT

Sometimes a new partner may be unable or find it inconvenient to pay the premium in cash and some other method of compensation must be devised to give the old partners a benefit for what they forego. Since no cash changes hands, the method of compensation becomes a series of bookkeeping entries to increase the old partners' claims on the new business. The resulting increase in the total asset value is represented by GOODWILL (This would be shown as an Asset in the Balance Sheet of the new firm.

IT IS NOT COMMON NOWADAYS TO RECORD GOODWILL IN THIS WAY. The valuation placed upon goodwill may be dubious and prudence would dictate that it is better to eliminate goodwill.

EXAMPLE QUESTION

John Brown was admitted to Smith and Jones Partnership. The agreed sum was to be paid £24,000 in cash. The agreed value of goodwill was £12,000. A goodwill account was not to be maintained in the books of account. Smith and Jones shared profits equally. The new partners would do the same.

You are required to:
Show the Goodwill Account clearing and the Partners Capital Accounts in the new firm.

ANSWER

STEP 1   GOODWILL ACCOUNT (ASSET A/c)

	£Dr	£Cr
Smith — ½	6,000	
Jones — ½	6,000	

Extract of CAPITAL ACCOUNT — OLD PARTNERSHIP (LIABILITY A/c)

£Dr		£Cr
	Smith — ½	6,000
	Jones — ½	6,000

These accounts would later be debited and the cash or bank accounts credited when the partners were paid in cash or by cheque.

STEP 2   GOODWILL ACCOUNT (ASSET A/c)

	£Dr		£Cr
Smith — ½	6,000	Smith — ⅓	4,000
Jones — ½	6,000	Jones — ⅓	4,000
		Brown — ⅓	4,000
	12,000		12,000

Extract of CAPITAL ACCOUNT — NEW PARTNERSHIP (LIABILITY A/c)

	£Dr				£Cr		
	S⅓	J⅓	B⅓		S	J	B
Goodwill	4,000	4,000	4,000	Cash			24,000
c/f			12,000				
	4,000	4,000	16,000		—	—	24,000

SUMMARY

1. New partners may introduce capital, knowledge, skill or a combination of these items.

2. The introduction of a new partner involves closing the books of the old partnership and opening the new.

3. Goodwill may exist from which a new partner would benefit and part of the total admission price is a payment for goodwill.

4. Valuing goodwill may be done in a number of ways. For example, a number of times turnover or averaged net profits over a number of years. The value is subject to agreement between partners.

5. The transaction involving goodwill will normally be a 'transient' one and it is not normal nowadays for partnerships to keep a goodwill account indefinitely.

QUESTION

1. Alan, Bob and Charles are in partnership, sharing profits and losses in the ratio 3:2:1 respectively.

   The balance sheet for the partnership as at 30th June 19–2 is as follows:

	£	£		£	£
Capital			**Fixed assets**		
Alan		85,000	Premises		90,000
Bob		65,000	Plant		37,000
Charles		35,000	Vehicles		15,000
			Fixtures		2,000
		185,000			144,000
Current account			**Current assets**		
Alan	3,714		Stock	62,379	
Bob	(2,509)		Debtors	34,980	
Charles	2,678	5,883	Cash	760	98,119
Loan — Charles		28,000			
Current liabilities					
Creditors		19,036			
Bank overdraft		4,200			
		242,119			242,119

Charles decides to retire from the business on 30th June 19–2, and Don is admitted as a partner on that date. The following matters are agreed:

(a) Certain assets were revalued — Premises £120,000
                                    — Plant   £35,000
                                    — Stock   £54,179

(b) Provision is to be made for doubtful debts in the sum of £3,000.

(c) Goodwill is to be recorded in the books on the day Charles retires in the sum of £42,000. The partners in the new firm do not wish to maintain a goodwill account so that amount is to be written back against the new partners' capital accounts.

(d) Alan and Bob are to share profits in the same ratio as before, and Don is to have the same share of profits as Bob.

(e) Charles is to take his car at its book value of £3,900 in part payment, and the balance of all he is owed by the firm in cash except £20,000 which he is willing to leave as a loan account.

(f) The partners in the new firm are to start on an equal fotting so far as capital and current accounts are concerned. Don is to contribute cash to bring his capital and current accounts to the same amount as the original partner from the old firm who has the lower investment in the business. The original partner in the old firm who has the higher investment will draw out cash so that his capital and current account balances equal those of his new partners.

Required:
(i)   Account for the above transactions, including goodwill and retiring partners' accounts.
(ii) Draft a balance sheet for the partnership of Alan, Bob and Don as at 30th June 19–2.   *[AAT]*

DISSOLUTION OF PARTNERSHIP
– breaking-up

STEPS INVOLVED IN DISSOLUTION OF PARTNERSHIPS

When a partnership is dissolved there are a number of steps which have to be followed, which are:

1. Pay off the creditors before any settlement is made between the partners.
2. Recover any monies owed to the business where possible.
3. Open a realization account. Transfer all the assets to the realization account, credit proceeds of each asset sold or realized and calculate a profit or loss on realization.
4. Transfer the profit/loss to the partners' capital and current account and repay the remaining capital to each of the partners.

N.B. Technically a partnership must be dissolved if one partner leaves or if a new partner enters. Therefore any changes made to the partners constitute dissolution of the partnership.

THE RULE IN GARNER v. MURRAY (not applicable in Scotland)

Sometimes, however, a partner's capital account ends up with a debit balance. Normally that partner will pay in sufficient cash to clear his indebtedness to the firm. Sometimes however, he may be insolvent and therefore unable to clear the balance. In the case of Garner v. Murray 1904 the court ruled that subject to any agreement to the contrary, the shortfall is to be shared by the other partners in the ratio of their last agreed capitals, that is, the credit balances on their capital accounts at the end of the last accounting period. Note the deficiency is not shared in the profit/loss sharing ratios.

Where a deed of partnership is drawn up it is common to find a clause rendering the rule in Garner v. Murray inoperative. It may well say that any deficiency is to be made up by the solvent partners in the profit/loss sharing ratios.

REALIZATION ACCOUNTS

The following steps normally take place using the realization account when the partnership is dissolved:-

1. The provision accounts, e.g. Depreciation, are transferred to the relevant asset account so that the net balance may be transferred to the realization account.

> **DR — PROVISION ACCOUNT**
>
> **CR — ASSET ACCOUNT**

2. The NBV's of the assets are transferred to the realization account.

> **DR — REALIZATION ACCOUNT**
>
> **CR — ASSET ACCOUNT**

3. Any assets which are sold:-

> **DR — BANK ACCOUNT with receipt**
>
> **CR — REALIZATION ACCOUNT with proceeds
> of disposal**

4. Other assets may be taken over by the partners. In those cases:-

> **DR — PARTNER'S CAPITAL ACCOUNT
> (with agreed value)**
>
> **CR — REALIZATION ACCOUNT**

5. Liabilities which are discharged

> **DR — LIABILITY ACCOUNT**
>
> **CR — BANK ACCOUNT**

6. Discounts on creditors.

> **DR — CREDITORS ACCOUNT**
>
> **CR — REALIZATION ACCOUNT**

7.   Dissolution costs.

DR — REALIZATION ACCOUNT

CR — BANK ACCOUNT

---

8.   There will now be a profit or loss on dissolution to balance the realization account. Providing there is no prior agreement this profit or loss will be shared according to the profit and loss sharing ratios of the partners. If it is profit the entries are:-

---

DR — REALIZATION ACCOUNT

CR — PARTNERS CAPITAL ACCOUNT

If it is a loss the reverse applies.

9.   The balances on the partners' current accounts need to be transferred to their capital accounts, normally by debiting the current account and crediting the capital account.

10.   At this stage any partner with a capital account in deficit, i.e. Debits exceeding Credits, must now pay in the cash amount necessary to cancel his indebtedness to the partnership.

DR — BANK ACCOUNT

CR — CAPITAL ACCOUNT

---

11.   The closing credit balances on the partners' capital accounts can now be paid to them:-

---

DR — CAPITAL ACCOUNT

CR — BANK ACCOUNT

The books of the partnership are now closed down.

EXAMPLE: Simple Dissolution of Partnership

A grocery business was doing particularly well and a competitor was keen to buy it. The firm was a partnership where the partners shared profits equally. The balance sheet at 31.12.-5, the date at which the partners decided to sell, was as follows:

THE BIG APPLE PARTNERSHIP BALANCE SHEET
AS AT 31.12.–5

	£Cost	£Depn.	£NBV
Fixed Assets			
Premises	10,000	3,000	7,000
Fixtures & Fittings	1,500	900	600
Motor Van	800	250	550
	12,300	4,150	8,150
Current Assets			
Stock	8,500		
Debtors	7,600		
Bank	3,200		
		19,300	
Current Liabilities			
Creditors	3,900		
		(3,900)	
Net Current Assets			15,400
Total Net Assets			23,550
Financed by			
Capital Accounts:			
Ted		6,000	
Tony		4,000	
Jim		3,000	
Willie		2,000	
			15,000
Current Accounts:			
Ted		2,080	
Tony		2,460	
Jim		2,120	
Willie		1,890	
			8,550
Capital Employed			23,550

The following assets were sold for cash:-

Premises	£9,000
Fixtures and Fittings	400
Stock	8,200
Debtors	7,500
Goodwill	12,000
TOTAL PROCEEDS	£37,100

Goodwill is the amount paid for a business over and above the book value. It will accrue as profit to the dissolved partnership and it will be treated in the books of the new business as an intangible asset in accordance with the Statement of Accounting Practice and the Companies Act 1985.

The intangible asset is shown on the balance sheet immediately before fixed assets as a separate category — goodwill. The new business should attempt to write off as an expense, the asset of goodwill as quickly as possible, since goodwill is a subjective and not an objective value and may therefore be difficult to realise.

The Motor Van was taken over by Jim at a valuation of £630. Creditors were paid in full and the bank account was closed.

Required:
1. The realization account.
2. The cash book.
3. The partners' current accounts.
4. The partners' capital accounts.

ANSWER

REALIZATION ACCOUNT

	£		£
Premises	7,000	Cash	37,100
Fixtures & Fittings	600	Jim Current a/c	630
Motor van	550		
Stock	8,500		
Debtors	7,600		
Profit on			
realization	13,480		
Ted 3,370			
Tony 3,370			
Jim 3,370			
Willie 3,370			
	37,730		37,730

CASH BOOK

	£		£
Balance b/f	3,200	Creditors	3,900
Realization	37,100	Partners Capital a/c	
		Ted	11,450
		Tony	9,830
		Jim	7,860
		Willie	7,260
	40,300		40,300

PARTNERS' CURRENT ACCOUNT

	Ted	Tony	Jim	Willie		Ted	Tony	Jim	Willie
Real-ization a/c			630		B/bf	2,080	2,460	2,120	1,890
Bal. c/f Capital Account	5,450	5,830	4,860	5,260	Real-ization	3,370	3,370	3,370	3,370
	5,400	5,830	5,490	5,260		5,450	5,830	5,490	5,260

PARTNERS' CAPITAL ACCOUNT

	Ted	Tony	Jim	Willie	B/bf	Ted	Tony	Jim	Willie
Bal. to Cash a/c	11,450	9,830	7,860	7,260	Bal.b/f	6,000	4,000	3,000	2,000
					Current a/c	5,450	5,830	4,860	5,260
	11,450	9,830	7,860	7,260		11,450	9,830	7,860	7,260

SUMMARY

1. A partnership must be dissolved if there is a change in membership of the partnership.

2. Creditors are paid, monies receivable are collected, assets may be sold or taken over by a partner at an agreed value and a profit or loss on dissolution will result.

3. The Rule in Garner and Murray (1904). Any shortfall after dissolution (subject to any agreement to the contrary) will be shared by solvent partners in the ratio of their last agreed capitals.

4. Realization Accounts are used to learn the steps.

QUESTIONS

1. John Graham, Bill Murphy and Bob Wilkins are trading in partnership together, sharing profits and losses equally. The balance sheet of the business as at 31st December 19-3 is as shown below:

Capital	£	£
Graham		70,000
Murphy		35,000
Wilkins		21,000
		126,000
Current accounts		
Graham	5,000	
Murphy	8,000	
Wilkins	(3,000)	
		10,000
Loan account		
Mrs. Wilkins		100,000
Net capital employed		£236,000

Represented by:	£	£
Fixed assets, at book value		
Land and buildings		450,820
Plant		77,115
Vehicles		18,065
		546,000
Current assets		
Stock	37,000	
Debtors	51,000	
	88,000	
Less Current liabilities		
Trade creditors	(91,400)	
Hire purchase on car	(3,000)	
Overdraft	(303,600)	
Working capital		(310,000)
Net assets		£236,000

The partnership business has made losses in recent years, and the bank and trade creditors are pressing for repayment of funds advanced to the business. Graham and Murphy consider the suggestion that they should inject more capital into the business, but decide against this plan. Wilkins is now bankrupt so cannot advance more funds. The partners decide to sell the business as at 31st December 19-3 to Exodus Plc., a company in the same trade.

The terms of the sale are as follows:
(a) Exodus Plc. agree to purchase the land and buildings, plant, two of the vehicles, and the stock, all for £501,000.
(b) The third vehicle, a car, which has a book value of £6,000, is to be taken by Murphy as part of his capital repayment. The price agreed for the car is £4,000, but Murphy also agrees to settle personally the hire purchase debt owing on the car.
(c) The partners collect the debts of their business, but because of their haste, £4,000 of bad debts are incurred, and £2,000 of cash discounts are allowed.
(d) The consideration is to be partly settled by Exodus Plc. by the payment of £368,600 in cash, and the assumption of the trade creditors (all except a personal contact of Graham who is owed £10,000 and is paid separately by the partnership). The balance of the consideration is to be settled by the issue of £1 ordinary shares in Exodus Plc at par to the partners.

Required:
Draft ledger accounts to close the books of the partnership.   [*AAT*]

2X. A record business, Hot Rod Records, had grown from strength to strength and in early 19–4 the partners decided to sell the business to one of their competitors. The balance sheet showed the following position, the partners sharing profits equally:

Hot Rod Records Balance Sheet at 30.6.19–4

Fixed assets	£Cost	£Depn.	£NBV
Lease	20,000	6,000	14,000
Fixtures and fittings	3,000	1,800	1,200
Motor van	1,600	500	1,100
	24,600	8,300	16,300
Current assets			
Stock		17,000	
Debtors		15,200	
Bank		6,400	
		38,600	
Current liabilities			
Creditors		7,800	
Net Current Assets (Working Capital)			30,800
Total Net Assets			47,100

Capital Accounts	£	£
Keith		12,000
Tony		8,000
Neil		6,000
Geoff		4,000
		30,000
Current Accounts		
Keith	4,160	
Tony	4,920	
Neil	4,240	
Geoff	3,780	
		17,100
		47,100

The following assets were sold for cash:

	£
Lease	18,000
Fixtures and fittings	800
Stock	16,400
Debtors	15,000
Goodwill	24,000
TOTAL PROCEEDS	74,200

The motor van was taken over by Neil at a valuation of £1,260. The creditors were paid in full and the bank account was closed.

Required:
1. The realization account. *(8 marks)*
2. The closing Cash Book. *(4 marks)*
3. Partners' Current Accounts after realization. *(4 marks)*

PARTNERSHIP AMALGAMATIONS
– merging the firms

AMALGAMATIONS

From a legal point of view the amalgamation involves the dissolution of the old firm and the creation of a new one. From a practical point of view the amalgamation can be effected by a revaluation of the individual assets of each firm and the incorporation of the revalued assets and the adjusted capital accounts in the books of the new firm.

EXAMPLE

Two partnerships have the following summarized balance sheets at 31.12 and they plan to merge.

Partnership		A		B
	£	£	£	£
Fixed Assets at NBV		10,000		15,000
Current Assets				
Stock	5,000		6,000	
Debtors	3,000		4,000	
Bank	2,000		2,000	
	10,000		12,000	
Less Current Liabilities	(2,000)		(3,000)	
Net Current Assets		8,000		9,000
		18,000		24,000
Financed by:				
Capitals —Fred		9,000	Sid	12,000
—Jim		9,000	Dick	12,000
Capital Employed		18,000		24,000

The terms of amalgamation were:-
1. The new Firm Z was to take over all the assets and discharge liabilities of the old firms.

2. Assets to be revalued as follows:-

	A	B
Fixed Assets	12,000	20,000
Stock	6,000	—
Debtors	2,500	—

3. Profits are to be shared in the new firm equally between partners, i.e. 25% each.

4. The capital of the new firm was to be contributed by the partners in their new profit sharing ratios.

5. Goodwill values were agreed £4,000 for A and £6,000 B.

6. Any deficiency of capital being made good in cash by the partners concerned. Any surplus would be paid in cash.

7. No account for goodwill is to be opened in the books, adjusting entries between the partners being made in the partners' Capital Accounts.

A. — REVALUATION ACCOUNT

	£ Dr reduction in value		£ Cr increase in value
Debtors		500	Goodwill 4,000
Profits shared			Fixed Assets 2,000
Fred — ½	3250		Stock 1,000
Jim — ½	3250	6,500	
		7,000	7,000

B. — REVALUATION ACCOUNT

	£ Dr		£ Cr
Profits shared			Goodwill 6,000
Sid — ½	5500		Fixed Assets 5,000
Dick — ½	5500	11,000	
		11,000	11,000

CAPITAL ACCOUNTS — A. — OLD FIRM

	£ Dr			£ Cr	
	Fred	Jim		Fred	Jim
			Balance b/f	9,000	9,000
Transfer to			Profit on		
new firm	12,250	12,250	Revaluation	3,250	3,250
	12,250	12,250		12,250	12,250

CAPITAL ACCOUNTS — B. — OLD FIRM

	£ Dr			£ Cr	
	Fred	Jim		Sid	Dick
			Balance b/f	12,000	12,000
Transfer to			Profit on		
new firm	17,500	17,500	Revaluation	5,500	5,500
	17,500	17,500		17,500	17,500

	F	J	S	D		F	J	S	D
					Transfer				
Goodwill	2,500	2,500	2,500	2,500	from old	12,250	12,250	17,500	17,500
Cash[3]			125	125					
Balance c/f[1]	14,875	14,875	14,875	14,875	Cash[2]	5,125	5,125	—	—
	17,375	17,375	17,500	17,500		17,375	17,375	17,500	17,500

Notes:
1. The capital of the new firm is to be 12,250 + 12,250 + 17,500 + 17,500 but contributed in the new ratios 25% each therefore:-

$$\frac{£59,500}{4}$$

$$= \underline{£14,875 \text{ each}}$$

2. Both Fred and Jim would have to contribute an extra £5,125 each to the new firm.

3. Sid and Dick would be entitled to withdraw £125 each in cash.

THE BALANCE SHEET OF Z. — NEW FIRM
AFTER AMALGAMATION WOULD BE:-

		£
Fixed Assets at NBV		32,000
Current Assets		
Stock	12,000	
Debtors	6,500	
Bank (4000 + 10250 – 250)	14,000	
	32,500	
Less Current Liabilities	(5,000)	
Net Current Assets		27,500
Total Net Assets		59,500
Financed by:		
Capitals —Fred	14,875	
Jim	14,875	
Sid	14,875	
Dick	14,875	
Capital Employed		59,500

QUESTION

1. John, Keith and Len are in partnership sharing profits in the ratio of 3:2:1 respectively.

A balance sheet for the partnership as at 31st March 19-3 is shown below:

	£	£		£
Capital accounts			Fixed assets	
John		100,000	Premises	100,000
Keith		80,000	Plant	52,000
Len		40,000	Office furniture	27,000
		220,000		179,000
Current accounts			**Current assets**	
John	6,450		Stock	29,500
Keith	14,978		Debtors	51,500
Len	(2,636)		Cash	10,412
		18,792		
Trade creditors		31,620		
		270,412		270,412

Len retired on 31st March 19-3, and John and Keith formed a company, Jake Ltd., to take over the business on that date.

Details of the changes agreed were as follows:

(a) The assets of the business, other than cash, were to be taken over by the company at a valuation of £284,000, but were to be recorded in the books of Jake Ltd. at the same book value as in the partnership books. Trade creditors were to be paid by the partnership.

(b) The authorized capital of Jake Ltd. was:
135,000 ordinary shares of £1 each.
65,000 12% preference shares of £1 each.

(c) The company raised a 16% debenture loan of £70,000 from a merchant bank.

(d) Jake Ltd. paid for its acquisition as follows:
(i) 135,000 ordinary shares issued to John and Keith to satisfy their capital accounts.
(ii) 16% debentures issued to John, Keith and Len to repay their current accounts.
(iii) The balance in cash.

Required:
(a) Calculate the current account balances of the partners to be satisfied by the issue of debentures.
(b) Draft journal entries to record these transactions in the books of Jake Ltd.
(c) Prepare a balance sheet for Jake Ltd. as at 1st April 19-3.

[AAT]

FINAL ACCOUNTS OF A LIMITED COMPANY
– an introduction

The two major disadvantages of partnerships are firstly that the number of members cannot exceed twenty and therefore finance may be difficult to raise, and secondly the liability of the partners is unlimited. To overcome these difficulties the alternative is to form a limited company. There needs to be at least two members, i.e. shareholders, but there is no maximum number. Limited companies are governed by the Companies Act 1985.

The major advantage of the limited company is that the member's liability is limited to the initial amount of share capital subscribed. For example, if as a member you subscribe £1,000 to a total share capital which was issued of £100,000, in the event of the company going into liquidation your only liability is the loss of the £1,000 initially subscribed. The equity stake that you would have in the business is 1/100 or 1%.

There are two types of limited company:-

1.   **Private limited company (LTD)**
2.   **Public limited company (PLC)**

There are more private companies than public companies. Many private companies are owned by family businesses which means that the directors of the company are usually the same people as the shareholders. In a public company, the shareholders will consist of members of the general public, institutions (pension funds, banks, trade unions etc.) or other companies. The directors of public companies tend to be professional managers, not shareholders.

There is a minimum share capital required for a PLC which currently stands at £50,000. There is no restriction in the case of a private limited company. A public company may trade its shares on the stock exchange, a private company does not invite the general public to subscribe to its shares. It may, however, be allowed to offer a small percentage of shares through the unlisted securities market (USM).

SPECIAL POINTS FROM THE ACCOUNTING POINT OF VIEW
Dividends
Shareholders receive their reward in the form of a dividend which is a proportion of the profits available for distribution after the payment of taxation and any retentions for future investment. The dividend is paid in proportion to the number of shares held by the member. Just like the partners received their rewards in the appropriation account so too do shareholders. For example, if the directors declared a 5% proposed dividend, this figure would be 5% of the issued share capital. The accounting entry in the case of a **proposed** dividend is:-

---

DR — P/L Appropriation Account

CR — Creditor (description — proposed dividend)

When the dividend was actually paid the entry would be:-

DR — Creditor

CR — Bank account

Transfers to Reserves

Any transfer to a reserve means that the directors do not wish to distribute that particular proportion of profit. This is because they may wish to retain sufficient income either for i) general purposes, in which case it would say to general reserve, or (ii) a specific reserve, e.g. fixed asset replacement reserve. In either case the accounting entry is:-

---

DR — P/L Appropriation Account
      (description — name of reserve)

CR — Appropriate named reserve
      (description — P/L appropriation)

APPROPRIATION OR CHARGE?

A reserve is an appropriation of profit and **not** a charge to it as is a provision. The retained profit in a limited company is referred to as the **profit and loss reserve** (undistributed profit)..

Directors' remuneration

This is the payment made to directors, i.e. their salary. Since directors are employees of the business, the charge for remuneration is simply an expense and is shown in the profit and loss account as such.

Debenture interest

Limited companies will borrow as well as have shareholders to finance the business. One such form of borrowing is for the company to issue debentures. They will be shown as loan capital in the finance part of the balance sheet, i.e. total amount of debentures issued and the interest paid on the debentures will be shown as an expense in the profit and loss account.

EXAMPLE

TVPM LTD. — TRIAL BALANCE AT 31.12-3

	£Dr	£Cr
Debtors	28,560	
Stock 31.12.-2	41,415	
Cash	16,255	
Machinery at cost	45,000	
Motor vehicles at cost	28,000	
Purchases	51,380	
Motor expenses	8,144	
Repairs to machinery	2,308	
Sundry expenses	1,076	
Wages and salaries	11,372	
Directors remuneration	6,200	
Issued share capital (£ ord. shares)		75,000
Creditors		22,472
Provision for depreciation 31.12.-2		
Machinery		18,000
Motor vehicles		12,600
Sales		92,500
Profit and Loss reserve 31.12.-2		6,138
General reserve		8,000
5% debentures		5,000
	239,710	239,710

NOTES:
1. The authorised share capital is £100,000.
2. Stock at 31.12.-3 £54,300.
3. Motor expenses owing £445.
4. Proposed ordinary dividend 20%.
5. Transfer £2,000 to general reserve.
6. Make a provision for the debenture interest payable.
7. Provide for depreciation of all fixed assets at 20% using the reducing balance basis.

You are required to prepare a trading and profit and loss and appropriation account for the year ended 31st December 19–3 and a balance sheet as at that date.

Appropriation Account. *This account follows on from the Trading and Profit and Loss Account. The heading should now be Trading and Profit and Loss and Appropriation Account for the period ending .... (note period could be substituted for month, year or whatever the period is).*

The appropriation account for a limited company shows how the net profit is shared between those entitled to it. Corporation Tax, Dividends and Transfers to Reserves are appropriations of profit. Appropriations are shares of not charges to profit.

TVPM LTD. — TRADING & PROFIT & LOSS & APPROPRIATION ACCOUNT FOR THE YEAR ENDED 31.12.-3

	£	£
Sales		92,500
Less cost of sales		
Opening stock	41,415	
Add purchases	51,380	
	92,795	
Less closing stock	(54,300)	
		(38,495)
GROSS PROFIT		54,005
Less Expenses		
Motor expenses (8144 + 445)	8,589	
Repairs to machinery	2,308	
Wages & salaries	11,372	
Directors' remuneration	6,200	
Sundry	1,076	
Debentures interest	250	
Depreciation — machinery	5,400	
— motor vehicles	3,080	
		38,275
NET PROFIT (before tax & transfers to reserves & dividends)		
Provision for tax		— *
NET PROFIT AFTER TAX (before dividends etc.)		15,730
Add /Profit & Loss reserve (from opening Balance Sheet)		6,138
		21,868
Transfer to general reserve	2,000	
Proposed ordinary dividend (20% × 75000) = 15,000		17,000
NET PROFIT RETAINED		4,868

The appropriation account begins here.

TVPM LTD. — BALANCE SHEET
FOR THE YEAR ENDED 31.12.-3

	£ Cost	£ Depn.	£ NBV
Fixed Assets			
Machinery	45,000	23,400	21,600
Motor vehicle	28,000	15,680	12,320
	73,000	39,080	33,920
Current Assets			
Stock	54,300		
Debtors	28,560		
Bank	16,255		
		99,115	

Less Current Liabilities			
Creditors		22,472	
Accruals			
Motor vehicle expenses	445		
Debentures	250	695	
Proposed dividend		15,000	
			(38,167)

NET CURRENT ASSETS	60,948
TOTAL NET ASSETS	94,868

Financed by

Shareholders funds	Authorised	Issued
£1 ordinary shares	100,000	75,000

Reserves

P&L reserve	4,868
General reserve	10,000
	89,868

Loan Capital

Debentures (5%)	5,000
	94,868

QUESTIONS

1X. The following trial balance at 31st December 19–6 is extracted from the books of Clay Ltd.

	£Dr	£Cr
Land and Buildings at cost	100,000	
Plant and Machinery at cost ?	40,000	
Motor Vehicles at cost ?	15,000	
Trade debtors	30,000	
Purchases	202,000 ✓	
Stock at 1.1.19–6	20,000 ✓	
Bad Debts written off	740	
Wages and Salaries 2	46,910	
Carriage Inwards	3,900	
General Expenses 2	22,900	
Cash in hand	1,160	
Bank balance		670
Authorized, issued and fully paid share 6		
capital; £1 ordinary shares		100,000
Provisions for depreciation (at 1.1.19–6)		
Plant and Machinery		8,000
Motor vehicles		6,000
Trade Creditors		25,840
Discounts — net		2,600
Sales		302,000 ✓
Provision for doubtful debts 3		1,100
5% Debentures 4		21,000
Profit and Loss Reserve at 1.1.19–6		5,900
General Reserve 5		9,500
	482,610	482,610

The following information is also provided:-
1. Stock at 31.12.19–6 was valued at £22,000.   c/s
2. At 31st December 19–6 wages owing amount to £490 and general expenses prepaid were £40.
3. The provision for doubtful debts is to be increased to £1,200.
4. Provision is to be made for debenture interest.
5. A further £6,000 is to be transferred to the general reserve.
6. The directors have proposed a dividend of 15% on the ordinary shares. (Note: dividends are paid on issued shares only).
7. Depreciation is provided as follows:-
    10% per annum on cost for plant and machinery.
    20% per annum on cost for motor vehicles.

Required:
1. Prepare a trading and profit and loss and appropriation account for Clay Ltd. for the year ended 31st December 19–6.
2. Construct a balance sheet for Clay Ltd. as at 31st December 19–6.

2. The following list of balances was extracted from the books of the
    Howton Company Ltd. at 31 December, 19–4.

	£	£
£1 ordinary shares		150,000
8% £1 preference shares		50,000
7% debentures		100,000
General reserve		65,000
Land and buildings at cost	111,000	
Plant and machinery at cost	382,000	
Undistributed profit at 1 January, 19–4		35,000
Share premium account		20,000
Stock at 1 January, 19–4	35,000	
Sales		290,000
Discounts allowed and received	3,200	4,600
Debtors and creditors	48,000	27,000
Provision for depreciation — plant and machinery		85,500
Bank	7,500	
Carriage inwards	1,100	
Purchases	165,000	
Suspense account		400
Wages	23,500	
Lighting and heating	2,900	
Office salaries	8,600	
Debenture interest	7,000	
Directors' fees	12,800	
Interim dividends		
ordinary (5%)	7,500	
preference (4%)	2,000	
Provision for doubtful debts		1,500
General expenses	11,900	
	829,000	829,000

Inspection of the books and records of the company yields the
following additional information.

(viii) On 31 December, 19–4, the company issued bonus shares to the
ordinary shareholders on a 1 for 10 basis. No entry relating to
this has yet been made in the books.

(ii) The authorised share capital of the company is 200,000 £1
ordinary shares and 50,000 8% £1 preference shares.

(iii) Stock at 31 December, 19–4 was valued at £41,000.

(iv) The suspense account (£400) relates to cash received for the sale
of some machinery on 1 January, 19–4. This machinery cost
£2,000 and the depreciation accumulated thereon amounted to
£1,500.

(v)   The directors, on the advice of an independent valuer, wish to revalue the land and buildings at £180,000, thus bringing the value into line with current prices.

(vi) Wages owing at 31 December, 19–4 amount to £150.

(vii) Depreciation is to be provided on plant and machinery at 10% on cost.

(viii) General expenses (£11,900) includes an insurance premium (£200) which relates to the period 1 April, 19–4 to 31 March, 19–5.

(ix) The provision for doubtful debts is to be reduced to 2½% of debtors.

(x)   The directors wish to provide for:
  (1) A final ordinary dividend of 5%
  (2) A final preference dividend
  (3) A transfer to general reserve of £15,000.

Required:
Prepare, *in vertical form,* the trading and profit and loss accounts of the Howton Company Ltd for the period ended 31 December, 19–4 and a balance sheet as at that date. Ignore taxation.   *(20 marks)*
                                                                           [ACCA]

3. The following trial balance as at 31 December 19–3 has been extracted from the books of XYZ Limited:

	£	£
Ordinary shares — 20,000 of £1 each		20,000
Profit and loss account		3,800
Sales		210,000
Purchases	160,000	
Rent and rates	9,000	
Light and heat	7,600	
Administrative expenses	11,300	
Motor vehicles: at cost	16,000	
provision for depreciation		3,000
Stock at 1 January 19–3	15,500	
Debtors	24,400	
Creditors		10,000
Balance at bank	3,000	
	246,800	246,800

Additional information relating to the year ended 31 December 19–3:

1. Since preparing the above trial balance, a bill has been received for rates of £2,000 for the half year ending 31 March 19–4.

2. The company has decided that a provision for doubtful debts be created of 2% of debtors as at 31 December 19–3.

3. Stock as at 31 December 19–3 has been valued at £13,500.

√4. Depreciation is provided annually on motor vehicles at the rate of 25% of the cost of vehicles held at each accounting year end.

√5. No entries have been made in the company's books for the sale on credit to Barry Dale of goods for £7,800 on 1 December 19–3; payment for the goods was received on 20 January 19–4.

6. It has been decided to transfer £5,000 to general reserve and to recommend that there be no dividends paid on the ordinary share capital for the year under review.

Required:
Prepare a trading and profit and loss account for the year ended 31 December 19–3 and a balance sheet as at that date.   *(20 marks)*
[AAT]

4X. Using the information given below you are required to prepare:

(a) Trading, profit and loss and appropriation accounts of ZDV Limited for the year ended 31st March 19–2.

(b) A balance sheet for the company at that date.

The trial balance of ZDV Limited at 31st March 19–2 was:

	Dr £'000	Cr £'000
Ordinary shares of f1, fully paid		1,000
Profit and loss account balance at 31st March 19–1		450
15% debentures		500
Freehold property (cost £400,000)	140	
Plant and equipment (cost £1,000,000)	860	
Stock of materials, at 31st March 19–2	500	
Work-in-progress, at 31st March 19–2	25	
Stock of finished goods, at 31st March 19–1	800	
Debtors	500	
Bad debts provision		20
Prepaid and accrued manufacturing expenses at 31st March 19–2	3	6
Cash at bank	90	
Creditors		700
Cost of finished goods manufactured during year	3,000	
Sales		4,000
Purchases of finished goods	100	
Administration expenses	248	
Marketing expenses	315	
Depreciation for year — unallocated	20	
Debenture interest	75	
	6,676	6,676

You are given the following information:
(a) Depreciation for the year, £100,000, has already been entered in the books. The basis of allocation among manufacturing, administration and marketing is in the proportions of 8:1:1.
(b) The stock of finished goods at the year-end was £900,000.
(c) Prepaid and accrued administration expenses were £7,000 and £19,000 respectively at 31st March 19-2.
(d) The bad debts provision is to be made equal to 5% of the debtors, and the adjustment is to be regarded as a marketing expense.
(e) Provision is to be made for:
    (i)   Corporation tax of £125,000 on the year's profit.
    (ii) A proposed dividend on the ordinary shares of £150,000; ignore advance corporation tax.   *(CIMA)*

 **STOCK VALUATION**
– and profit measurement

The valuation of stock may be undertaken either periodically or perpetually.

PERIODIC INVENTORY

If stock is valued periodically this means that at the end of an accounting period stock is valued at that point in time (see example below).

PERPETUAL INVENTORY

If stock is valued perpetually this means every time there is an addition to stock or an issue from stock that the stock is revalued (see example below).

STOCK VALUATION RULE

Stock is valued at the lower of cost or net realisable value (market value). This is stated in the Statement of Standard Accounting Practice No.9 (SSAP9). The statement follows the prudence concept of accounting, sometimes referred to as the principle of conservatism, for example, it would not show a true and fair view of the state of affairs if a business was to value stock in its balance sheet at cost £5000 if it could only obtain (realise) £4000 for that stock when sold. You can see that there would be a loss on sale of £1000. The prudence concept states that if you are aware or can foresee this kind of loss that you should act immediately. In the case of uncertainty as to the effect of the loss because of uncertainty in value, it may be sufficient to create a provision account. However, in the case of certainty in our example above, we should write down the value to a realisable amount.

The accounting entries are:-

```
DEBIT    — COST OF SALES A/C — £1000
CREDIT  — STOCK A/C —                £1000
```

DEFINITION OF COST

We have stated that stock is normally valued at cost or the net realisable value. We now need to clarify what we mean by cost.

SSAP9 — defines cost as "that **expenditure** which has been **incurred** in the **normal** course of business in bringing the product or service to its **present location and condition"**.

WHAT COSTS SHOULD BE INCLUDED?

1. The cost of purchase including import duties, carriage inwards, handling costs and any other directly related costs less any trade discounts, rebates or subsidies.
2. Costs of conversion (e.g. manufacture).

CONVERSION COSTS

These may include (1) direct costs other than raw materials, e.g. direct labour, direct expenses (e.g. royalties, commissions, patents); (2) production overheads; (3) other overheads for administration, sales and marketing, distribution or finance. **Only if** those particular overheads are directly attributable to the product or service in order to bring it to its present location and condition taking into account the particular circumstances of the business. The relevant portion only should be included in valuation. In reality few if any of these costs are ever included in valuation as they are difficult to identify and apportion satisfactorily; prudence would therefore dictate that we left them out.

PRODUCTION OVERHEADS

These are based on the 'normal level' of activity. Production overheads include such things as the rent of the factory for the production unit only, the rent for any production equipment which is not regarded as a direct expense, depreciation of machinery used in production, a works manager's salary, production foreman's salary, the wages of the indirect factory labour, light and heat for the factory, rates for the factory and other factory costs, not direct costs to a particular product.

THE MATCHING PRINCIPLE AND STOCK VALUATION

The principle states that the costs for a product in a particular period should be matched against the sales revenue obtained for that product in a particular period. It is sometimes called the accruals concept.

The cost of unsold or unconsumed stocks have been incurred in the expectation of obtaining future revenues (the going concern concept). Closing stocks are thus removed from the cost of sales in a period and are carried forward on the opening stocks of a future period for this very reason, i.e. to match cost and revenue. This is a reasonably straightforward process in the case of retailers but can be more complicated in the case of manufacturing. In a manufacturing company where a proportion of indirect production costs is included in stock valuation, then a proportion of those costs is also carried forward to a future period by means of the closing stock values. **It is most important to grasp this concept.**

THE MATCHING PRINCIPLE IN ACTION

	Opening stock	+ Purchases	− Closing stock	= Cost of sales
(1)	0	£500 −	£100 =	£400

If we did not follow matching principle

	Opening stock	+ Purchases	− Closing stock	= Cost of sales
(2)	0	£500	ignore closing stock =	£500 Costs i.e. cash accounting

This illustrates a difference between cash and profit. Supposing sales revenue in the period was £600 (actually received in cash also so as not to adjust for debtor)

	(1)		(2)
Sales	600		600
Less cost of sales	(400)		(500)
Gross Profit	200	Cash	100

Accruals Concept   **Cash or Non Accrual Concept**

METHODS OF STOCK VALUATION

1. First in first out — FIFO
2. Last in first out — LIFO
3. Average cost — AVCO
4. Highest in first out — HIFO
5. Next in first out — NIFO
6. Standard cost — SC
7. Unit cost — UC
8. Base stock
9. Adjusted selling price
10. Replacement price (current cost)

The most commonly used methods of valuation are FIFO, AVCO, SC and LIFO (this is more common in the USA).

FIRST IN FIRST OUT

Advantages
a) The values follow the physical movement of stocks, i.e. the idea of rotation.
b) The value is an actual price and may be readily linked with invoices.

c) It is relatively easy to calculate.
d) It is a recommended method of valuation per SSAP9.
e) Stock is valued in the balance sheet using more realistic prices.

Disadvantages
a) In times of rapidly rising prices, profits may be overstated in terms of current costs owing to historic costs of sales being matched with current sales revenue (this follows the historic cost convention). However, matching £'s with $'s from 1983 with £'s or $'s in 1988 is not to match like with like. For us to do so would involve some kind of current cost adjustment.
b) The comparison of costs between jobs is difficult since issues will be valued at different prices. Issue prices may not reflect current market values.
c) A large number of calculations may be necessary.

LAST IN FIRST OUT

Advantages of LIFO
1. Up to date prices are used when issues are made reflecting current values.
2. It's easy to calculate.
3. Actual prices stated on invoice are used.

Disadvantages
Comparisons of one job to another are difficult. A large number of calculations may be needed.
1. The advantage stated in 1 above does not apply when stocks are being run down. In this case older, out of date prices would be used.
2. The value of stocks stated on the balance sheet could be understated since it would be the older stock values.
3. In the UK LIFO is not an acceptable method of valuation for tax purposes (in the USA it is).
4. It is not a recommended method of valuation in the UK (SSAP9).
5. It does not follow normal distribution of physical stock items.

AVERAGE COST (AVCO)

Advantages of AVCO
1. It smoothes profits since an average of opening and closing stock values are taken.
2. It is relatively easy to calculate.
3. It is a recommended method in the UK (SSAP9).
4. Comparison of different jobs is made easier, relative to other valuation methods.

Disadvantages of AVCO
1. Because it is an average which is weighted, stock valuations may be distorted by the weights.

EXAMPLE:	**Qty.**	**Price**	**Total Value**
1.1.–6	100	5	500
30.6.–6	9	10	90
31.12.–6	1	50	50
	110		640

$$\text{Average} = \frac{640}{110} = \begin{array}{l} £5.82 \\ \text{each} \\ \text{unit value} \end{array}$$

This would affect profitability and balance sheet values.

2. The stock valuation unit prices would not be the same as any individual invoice price except by coincidence.

3. Although calculations may be relatively easy they may be time consuming as each time there is an addition to or an issue from stock, a new valuation is calculated.

4. Calculations need to be made to approximately four decimal places in order to achieve a fair degree of accuracy. The issue price may not reflect current economic values for reasons shown in Disadvantage 1.

STANDARD COSTING

Advantages of Standard Costing
1. Where a company operates a standard cost system, only additions to or issues from stock can be quickly taken account of by using a standard price.
2. Standard prices means that variances for control and action may be quickly identified, e.g. material price variances.
3. The system is easy to operate and avoids the problem of many different prices for the same stock item. This makes stock control easier and makes the costing system easier. (See Budgeting and Standard Costing).

Disadvantages of Standard Costing
1. If standards are not revised appropriately then calculations and variances will not be meaningful. It is however important not to revalue too frequently otherwise **standards** will become meaningless.
2. Issues may not be at current market values.
3. The lower of cost or net realisable value still applies.
4. The setting of standards takes time.
5. The price will not be an actual price and a variance will arise on issue.

EXAMPLE: STORES ISSUES AND GROSS PROFIT

The following is a record of receipts and issues of materials for XL Sports Co. during the six months to 30th June. All issues were sold at £20 per unit.

You are required to:
1. Record the receipts and issues in the stores ledger using
   (a) Perpetual Inventory — i.   FIFO
                             — ii. LIFO
                             — iii. AVCO
   (b) Periodic Inventory — iv. FIFO
                            — v.   LIFO
                            — vi. AVCO

2. Show the trading account for each method i. to vi., indicating the highest and lowest gross profits.

DETAILS	RECEIPTS	ISSUES
JAN 1st	10 units @ £10	
MAR 1st	20 units @ £10	
15th		15 units
MAY 5th	20 units @ £12	
25th		10 units
JUNE 1st	10 units @ £14	
30th		20 units

PERPETUAL INVENTORY

a(i) FIFO

Date	Receipts	Issues	Balance
1.1	10 units @ £10	—	10 units @ £10 = £100
1.3	20 units @ £10	—	30 units @ £10 = £300
15.3	—	15 units @ £10 = £150	Less 15 units @ £10 = £150
5.5	20 units @ £12	—	b/f 15 units @ £10 = £150 Add 20 units @ £12 = £240 c/f 35 units = £390
25.5	—	10 units @ £10 = £100	b/f 35 units = £390 Less 10 units = £100 c/f 25 units = £290
1.6	10 units @ £14	—	b/f 25 units = £290 Add 10 units = £140 c/f 35 units £430
30.6	—	20 units 5 @ £10 = 50 15 @ £12 = 180 20 230	b/f 35 units = £430 Less 20 units = £230 c/f 15 units = £200

(ii) **LIFO**

Date	Receipts	Issues	Balance
1.1	10 units @ £10	—	10 units @ £10 = £100
1.3	20 units @ £10	—	b/f 10 units @ £10 = £100 Add 20 units @ £10 = £200 c/f 30 units = £300
15.3	—	15 units @ £10 = £150	b/f 30 units = £300 Less 15 units = £150 c/f 15 units = £150
5.5	20 units @ £12	—	b/f 15 units £150 Add 20 units @ £12 = £240 c/f 35 units = £390
25.5	—	10 units @ £12 = £120	b/f 35 units £390 Less 10 units @ £12 = £120 c/f 25 units = £270
1.6	10 units @ £14	—	b/f 25 units = £270 Add 10 units @ £14 = £140 c/f 35 units = £410
30.6	—	20 units 10 units @ £14 = £140 10 units @ £12 = £120 20 units = £260	b/f 35 units = £410 Less 20 units = £260 c/f 15 units = £150

Note the difference between the FIFO and LIFO closing stock balances, both still have 15 units remaining but at different values.

Using the First In First Out system the closing balance comprises

1.6	10 units	£14 = £140
5.5	5 units	£12 = 60
	15 units	= £200

Using the Last In First Out system the closing balance comprises

1.3	5 units	£10 = £50
1.1	10 units	£10 = £100
	15 units	= £150

(iii) **AVCO**

Date	Receipts	Issues	Balance
1.1	10 units @ £10	—	10 units @ £10 = £100
1.3	20 units @ £10	—	b/f 10 units @ £10 = £100 Add 20 units @ £10 = £200 c/f 30 units £10 = £300
15.3	—	15 units @ £10	b/f 30 units @ £10 = £300 Less 15 units @ £10 = £150 c/f 15 units £10 = £150
5.5	20 units @ £12	—	b/f 15 units @ £10 = £150 Add 20 units @ £12 = £240 c/f 35 units ? = £390

Until 5.5 all receipts and issues were at £10 per unit and there was no need to calculate an average. At 5.5 however, we now have 35 units in stock valued at £390.

The average value = $\dfrac{£390}{35 \text{ units}}$ = £11.14 per unit

Date	Receipts	Issues	Balance
25.5	—	10 units @ £11.14 *Note the issue is at the calculated average value*	b/f 35 units £390 Less 10 units @ £11.14 = 111.40 c/f 25 units @ £11.14 = £278.60
1.6	10 units @ £14	—	b/f 25 units £278.60 Add 10 units @ £14 = 140.00 c/f 35 units £418.60

At 1.6 a new average price needs to be calculated thus:
$\dfrac{£418.60}{35 \text{ units}}$ = £11.96 per unit

Each stores item is now valued at this average price £11.96 per unit.

Date	Receipts	Issues	Balance
30.6	—	20 units @ £11.96	b/f 35 units = £418.60 Less 20 units @ £11.96 = 239.20 c/f 15 units £11.96 = 179.40

The closing stock of 15 units using Average Costing gives a unit value of £11.96 and a total £179.40.

The trading account for XL would look as follows:-

	FIFO	LIFO	AVCO
	£	£	£
SALES (45 units @ £20)	900	900	900.00
LESS COST OF SALES			
45 units @ cost	480	530	500.60
GROSS PROFIT	420	370	399.40

Note: 45 issues were sold at £20 per unit but the Cost of Sales differed for each method.

FIFO		LIFO		AVCO	
15 @ £10=	150	15 @ £10=	150	15 @ £10=	150.00
10 @ £10=	100	10 @ £12=	120	10 @ £11.14=	111.40
5 @ £10=	50	10 @ £14=	140	20 @ £11.96=	239.20
15 @ £12=	180	10 @ £12=	120		
COSTS					
45 units	480		530		500.60

PERIODIC INVENTORY

b   Using the periodic inventory method we simply need to choose a period end, which in this case is 30.6 and proceed thus:-

	RECEIPTS	ISSUES
1.1	10 @ £10	
1.3	20 @ £10	
15.3		15 units
5.5	20 @ £12	
25.5		10 units
1.6	10 @ £14	
30.6		20 units

The total receipts to the period end are:-

```
10×£10=  100
20×£10=  200
20×£12=  240
10×£14=  140
60 units  £680
```

During the period there were 45 issues. Ignore dates and proceed as follows:-

(iv) On a FIFO basis 10 @ £10 =   100
                             20 @ £10 =   200
                             15 @ £12 =   180

                             45 units   £480

(v)   On a LIFO basis 10 @ £14 =   140
                             20 @ ·£12 =   240
                             15 @ £10 =   150

                             45 units   £530

(vi) The average cost will be significantly different since the average is calculated only once over the whole period.

$$\frac{£680}{60 \text{ units}} = £11.33 \text{ per unit}$$

thus 45 issues at £11.33 = £509.85.

The trading accounts for (iv) and (v) are the same as for (i) and

                                           £

(vi) would be   Sales   900.00
                  Less Cost of Sales
                  (45   £11.33)   509.85

                  Gross Profit   390.15

2. For the purpose of demonstration it was easier to show the trading accounts earlier.

The highest gross profit was given by the FIFO method of inventory control. This is because older stock items at older stock prices were issued first.

The lowest gross profit was given by the LIFO method of inventory control. This is because newer stock item prices were issued to cost of sales first.

QUESTIONS

1. On 1 January a manufacturing business had 400 units of Material X in stores (cost £800). The following movements of Material X were recorded during the next three months:

		Receipts into Store		Issues to Workshops
		Units	Price per Unit £	Units
January	2	500	2.2	
	8			600
February	1	250	2.4	
	14	400	2.5	
	16			600
March	4	400	2.6	
	25			600

A physical count of Material X on 31 March showed only 50 units.

Required:

(a) Prepare a perpetual inventory account for Material X for the three months January to March, using FIFO method of valuation.

(10 marks)

(b) Explain what you understand by the term "cost accounting" and describe the benefits which a cost accounting system produces for an organisation. (You may refer to your own experience relating to costing systems in your answer.) *(15 marks)*

(Total 25 marks) [AAT]

2. The following information relates to the acquisition and issue of Material 2XA by Roe Limited, a small manufacturing company, for the three months to 31st March 19–4:

MATERIAL 2XA

Date	Acquisitions Quantity Kg	Price per Kg £	Issues Quantity Kg
1.1.-3	100	3.00	
15.1-3	200	4.00	
29.1-3			150
17.2.-3	400	4.50	
5.3.-3			450
16.3.-3	100	5.00	
31.3.-3			50

Note:
There was no material stock at 1st January 19-3.

Required:

(a) Calculate the closing stock value of MATERIAL 2XA using each of the following methods of pricing the issue of stock to production:
  (i)   First-in, first-out (FIFO).
  (ii) Last-in, first-out (LIFO).
  (iii) Periodic Simple Average.
  (iv) Periodic Weighted Average.
  (v)   Weighted Average.

(b) Examine the effect on gross profit of using the first-in, first-out (FIFO) and last-in, first-out (LIFO) methods of pricing the issue of stock to production assuming that price levels are rising. [AAT]

3. An evaluation of a physical stock count on 30th April, 19–2 in respect of the financial year ending on that date at Cranfleet Commodities has produced a figure of £187,033.

  The firm's bookkeeper has approached you, as the accountant, for assistance in dealing with the following matters to enable him to arrive at a final figure of closing stock for inclusion in the annual accounts:

(a) 320 components included at their original cost of £11 each can now be brought in for only £6 each due to over production by the manufacturer. This drop in price is expected to be only temporary and the purchase price is expected to exceed its original figure within 12 months. Cranfleet Commodities intends to continue selling the existing stock at the present price of £15 each.

(b) It has been discovered that certain items which had cost £5,657 have been damaged. It will cost £804 to repair them after which they can be sold for £6,321.

(c) On one stock sheet a sub-total of £9,105 has been carried forward as £1,095.

(d) 480 units which cost £1.50 each have been extended at £15.00 each.

(e) The firm has sent goods with a selling price of £1,500 (being cost plus 25%) to a customer on a sale or return basis. At 30th April 19–2, the customer had not signified acceptance, but the goods have not been returned, and consequently had not been included in the physical stock count.

(f) Included in stock were goods bought on credit for £4,679 from Byfleet Enterprises. At 30th April 19–2, Cranfleet Commodities had not paid this account.

(g) Byfleet Commodities had also sent some free samples (for advertising purposes only). These have been included in stock at their catalogue price of £152.

Required:
Taking account of such of the above facts as are relevant, calculate a closing stock figure for inclusion in the 19-2 annual accounts of Cranfleet Commodities, giving reasons for the action you have taken in each individual case.   [ACCA]

4X.a An importer deals only in one commodity and has recorded the following transactions for the first six months of the year.

Purchases

Date	Quantity Purchased Units	Gross Invoice Value £	Quantity Discount
February 1st	100	30,000	NIL
March 1st	200	60,000	2.5%
May 1st	300	90,000	5%

Sales

Date	Quantity Sold Units	Total Sales Value £
February	75	30,000
May	350	175,000

There was an opening balance at January 1st of 50 units, valued at £12,500.

Required:
(i)   Prepare the stores ledger account for the six months using the perpetual inventory system and the FIFO method of pricing issues.
(10 marks)
(ii) Prepare a trading account to show the gross profit for the period, using the FIFO method of valuation. *(2 marks)*
(iii) Prepare a trading account to show the gross profit for the period, using the LIFO method of valuation. *(4 marks)*

b. Production labour has traditionally been regarded as a directly variable cost.

Required:
Discuss the factors or circumstances which would make this treatment inappropriate. You may draw on your own experience in answering.
(9 marks)
(Total 25 marks)
[AAT]

5X. JERRY MANDA — Stock Valuation
Jerry Manda trades in paint as a retailer. You may assume that all his issues are sold. The following transactions take place during 19-5:

1st Jan.   20 units @ £20 each   ⎫   (STOCK AT START)
1st Jun.   15 units @ £25 each   ⎪
30th Sept.   10 units @ £30 each   ⎬   PURCHASES
31st Dec.   20 units @ £32 each   ⎭

1st Jun.   16 units   ⎫
30th Sept.   12 units   ⎬   ISSUES
31st Dec.   22 units   ⎭

The selling price per unit is £32.

Required:
1) Using the perpetual inventory method, calculate the Gross Profit using LIFO, FIFO and AVCO.
2) Briefly explain your findings.   *(16 marks)*
                                                          [Q&A]

6X. Jock had 100 litres of foam liquid in stock as at 1st October 19–2, purchased at £2 per litre. During the month to 31st October 19–2, the following changes occurred in the stock position:

PURCHASES

Date	Quantity litres	Cost per litre £
7.10.–2	200	2.50
14.10.–2	300	3.00
21.10.–2	50	4.00
28.10.–2	100	3.50

ISSUES

Date	Quantity litres
4.10.–2	80
11.10.–2	70
18.10.–2	250
25.10.–2	200

Required:
Calculate the value of the closing stock of foam liquid as at 31st October 19–2 using each of the following three methods of pricing the issue of materials to production:
(i)   First-in, first-out (FIFO).
(ii) Last-in, first-out (LIFO).
(iii) Weighted average.

Note:
The periodic weighted method is not required.   [AAT]

7X.a During the night of 30th April a fire at the premises of P Limited destroyed all the work-in-progress stock but not the raw materials nor the finished goods stocks.

A physical stocktaking on 1st May valued the stocks on hand as follows:

	£000
Raw materials	60
Finished goods	80

At 31st March the stocks on hand were:

	£000
Raw materials	30
Work-in-progress	20
Finished goods	50

During April, sales were £60,000 raw materials purchases £50,000, carriage on purchases of raw materials £8,000, and direct labour costs incurred £40,000. Production overhead absorption rate is 50% of the direct labour cost.

The sales and gross profits for the four months of December to March are shown below and it has been agreed with the insurers that the average gross profit over this period be used for the basis of a claim.

	Sales	Gross Profit
	£	£
December	53,000	12,340
January	42,000	11,920
February	47,000	10,860
March	54,000	13,880

Required:
You are required to determine the value of work-in-progress stock lost in the fire which will be the basis of a claim on P Limited's insurers. Present your answer in the form of a statement, showing your supporting calculations.   *(14 marks)*

b. A basic rule in stock valuation is that stock should be valued at the lower of cost and net realisable value, taking each item or group of similar items separately.

Required:
You are required, in the context of stock valuation for a manufacturer, to explain the terms 'cost' and 'net realisable value' as used in the above statement.   *(6 marks)*

(Total 20 marks)

(CIMA)

8. A shop stocks winter coats which sell at £55 each. To avoid over-stocking and because of limited space, the deliveries from four manufacturers, at differing prices, are made to the shop on a weekly basis at opening time on Monday mornings. During October the deliveries and sales of the coats were as shown below and there was an opening stock of 10 coats which had been purchased in September at £29 each.

Week No.	Coats bought		Number of coats sold Cost each
	Number		
		£	
1	20	30	15
2	30	33	33
3	40	29	35
4	30	35	39

Trading accounts are prepared monthly and from the information given above you are required to:
(a) Prepare stock records for the transactions based on the three methods of pricing issues listed below:
    (i)   FIFO;
    (ii) LIFO;
    (iii) Weighted average calculated at the end of the month (work to two decimal places of £1).
(b) Recommend which method you would advise the shop management to use and why.
(c) Show the gross margins to the nearest £1 and as a percentage of the sales turnover for each of the three methods of pricing issues.
(d) Comment on the type of information you would require to determine whether the gross margin figures are good, poor or indifferent.   **(25 marks)**
(CIMA)

9a. Three students, K, L and M, are equal partners in a joint venture which involves them, on a part-time basis, in buying and selling sacks of product F. The transactions for the six months ended 30th September were as stated below. You are to assume that purchases at the unit costs given were made at the beginning of each month and that the sales were made at the end of each month at the fixed price of £1.50 per sack.

Month	Purchases		Sales
	Sacks	Unit cost £	Sacks
April	1,000	1.00	500
May	500	1.20	750
June	1,000	1.00	Nil
July	Nil	—	600
August	500	1.20	650
September	500	1.30	600

In October the student partners held a meeting to review their financial position and to share out the profits but there was disagreement because each partner had priced the issues on a different basis. K had used FIFO, L had used LIFO and M had used a weighted average, basing his weighted average on the whole of the six months' purchases. It was, however, agreed that the stock remaining at the end of September should be stored until next April.

You are required to:
(i)   Show the records which each student kept of the transactions;
(ii) Show the amount each student ought to receive if the whole of the profit arising from each method of pricing the issues were distributed;
(iii) Comment briefly on the acceptability of the three different results arising from the transactions.

b. In the context of a manufacturing business, explain briefly what is meant **by the last sentence** of the following statement.

The Statement of Standard Accounting Practice No.9 on Stocks and Work-in-Progress (SSAP9) states in an explanatory note, paragraph 3 that 'In order to match costs and revenue, "costs" of stocks and work-in-progress should comprise that expenditure which has been incurred in the normal course of business in bringing the product or service to its present location and condition. Such costs will include all related production overheads, even though these may accrue on a time basis.'   *(25 marks)*
(CIMA)

MANUFACTURING ACCOUNTS
– building a product, building up cost

DEFINITION

Manufacturing is defined as the transformation of raw materials into a finished saleable product. The transformation process will have inputs of labour and overhead as well as materials. The owner of a manufacturing business could be a sole trader, a partnership or a Limited Company, or another form of ownership such as a Co-operative. Up to now we have been concerned only with retail businesses where a product for resale has been bought in from a wholesaler or a manufacturer. Our business organisations could have also been wholesale. Now we turn our attention to those businesses which make and sell their own products.

PURPOSE OF THE MANUFACTURING ACCOUNT

Before we can sell a product it has to be made. It is logical, therefore, that the Manufacturing Account is placed before the Trading and Profit and Loss Account.

The Manufacturing Account attempts to build up the product cost in a logical way. Raw materials are entered first, direct labour second, followed by any other direct costs (the costs which vary directly as a result of a change in output). These three component parts together are referred to as the **PRIME COST.** To the prime cost are added other overheads which can be traced directly to the factory or works unit (e.g. factory rent and rates, factory insurance, indirect labour — (foreman's salary etc.), indirect materials — (heat, light and power; factory repairs, factory depreciation and other factory costs).

WORK IN PROGRESS

If we were to stop production at any point in time we would find that we had some part finished units or incomplete units known as work in progress. Since these units will be sold in a future time period we need to remove them from the factory cost of production for the present period and hold them in the balance sheet under stock as an asset. Before we can do so we need to assess a value for the work in progress. In examination questions this is normally given. Nevertheless, it is important to understand that work in progress will contain within its value some material costs, some labour costs and some overhead costs. The exact amount of which will depend on the degree of completion.

MANUFACTURING ACCOUNT (BUILD UP OF COST)

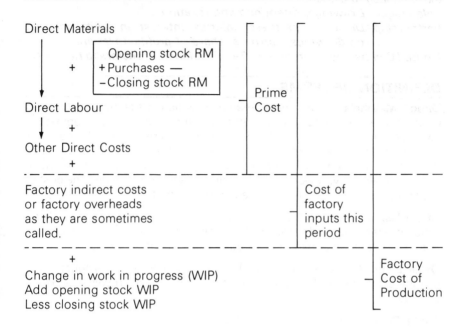

Direct Materials

+ | Opening stock RM
+ Purchases —
− Closing stock RM

Prime Cost

Direct Labour

+

Other Direct Costs

+

Factory indirect costs
or factory overheads
as they are sometimes
called.

Cost of factory inputs this period

+

Change in work in progress (WIP)
Add opening stock WIP
Less closing stock WIP

Factory Cost of Production

TRADING ACCOUNT

Sales
Less Cost of Sales
Opening stock
+ Add factory costs of production
− Less closing stock of finished goods
= Gross Profit

GROSS PROFIT

PROFIT AND LOSS ACCOUNT

Less expenses (non factory overheads)
Administration
Sales marketing and distribution
Finance

Net Profit

NET PROFIT

Appropriation Account if any:- This shows how net profit is shared between those entitled to a share.
Sole Trader = Drawings, retentions and taxation.
Partnership= Drawings, partners' salaries, interest on capital interest on drawings, partners' share of profits, taxation.
Limited Companies = Corporation Tax, Dividends, Transfers to Reserves.

DEFINITION OF TERMS

Direct Materials — are those materials which make up the finished product. They vary directly with output, for example, in making a cabinet the raw materials required might be wood, hinges, screws, varnish and other bought in components (maybe for decoration). If you produced one of these cabinets you would only need enough materials to produce one, if you produced 10 you would need 10 times as many materials. The cost of materials would therefore vary directly with output.

Direct Labour — This is the cost for labour (wages of production workers) which is directly related to the product. The cost of which will vary in output. It does not include supervisory or administrative labour costs.

Other Direct Costs — which may be traced directly to the product could include plant hire, tool hire, the hire of other machinery, royalty payments, patents, etc.

Prime Cost — this is the total of all direct costs.

Factory or Works Overheads — these are sometimes called the **factory indirect cost.** They are all those costs which are incurred in running the production unit but cannot be identified directly with a particular product, e.g. supervisory wages, cost of running a fork lift truck (wages, batteries — electricity, light, heat etc.).

Indirect Labour — supervisory wages, storekeeper's wages, maintenance wages and other factory clerical support staff (when referring to wages we mean wages or salaries in this case).

Indirect Materials — cleaning materials, maintenance materials including spare parts, lubricating oils, belt drives, consumable tools (screwdrivers, hammers and so on).

Differences in the Trading Account and Balance Sheet presentation
The Trading Account of a manufacturing business will contain a cost of sales as usual but the opening and closing stocks are finished goods stocks which have been manufactured. Purchases are replaced by the factory cost of production.

It is usual to classify the expenses in the Profit and Loss Account under major headings for Administration, Sales, Marketing, Distribution and Finance — interest on bank overdrafts, charges etc. This is because some costs may need apportioning between cost centres and the headings would represent cost centres. For example, rent and rates for the business in total may amount to £12,000 p.a., the factory portion may be 50% and the remaining 50% might be divided equally between administration offices and sales, marketing and distribution offices. This information would normally be extracted from the question for the purpose of examinations. Other expenses may also need apportioning as may accruals and prepayments which are relevant.

TRADING ACCOUNT OF A MANUFACTURING COMPANY

	£	£
Sales		X
Less Cost of Sales		
Opening Stock of Finished Goods	X	
Add Factory Cost of Production		
transferred in from Manufacturing A/c	X	
	X	
Less Closing Stock of Finished Goods	(X)	
Cost of Goods Sold		(X)
GROSS PROFIT		X

Balance Sheet — The Balance Sheet will contain three categories of stocks in a manufacturing company which are:-

     1. Raw Material Stocks
     2. Work in Progress Stocks
and
     3. Finished Goods Stock

BALANCE SHEET EXTRACT OF A MANUFACTURING COMPANY

	£	£	£
CURRENT ASSETS			
STOCKS — Raw Materials	X		
W.I.P.	X		
Finished Goods	X		
The total for all categories would be placed here		X	
Debtors		X	
Bank		X	
Cash		X	
			X

EXAMPLE

F. Ltd., a manufacturer, provides the following information for the year
ending 31.12.-3.

	£	
Sales	45,000	
WIP (1.1.-3)	2,000	
WIP (31.12.-3)	1,500	
Raw Materials (1.1.-3)	5,000	
Raw Materials (31.12.-3)	7,000	
Finished Good Stock (1.1.-3)	3,000	
Finished Good Stock (31.12.-3)	4,000	
Manufacturing Wages	5,000	
Licence fee on production	1,000	
Raw Material purchases	25,000	
Rent & Rates	3,000	(factory 5/6 office 1/6)
Insurance	2,100	(factory 2/3, office 1/3)
Depreciation		
Factory machinery	2,000	
Sales vehicle	500	
Office machinery	100	
Bank charges	100	
Salesman's salary	1,000	
Bad debts written off	100	
Discount allowed	100	
Profit on disposal of fixed asset	2,000	
Office salaries	1,000	
Administration Postage & Stationery	100	
Carriage Out	100	

F. LTD. — MANUFACTURING AND TRADING AND PROFIT AND LOSS ACCOUNT FOR THE YEAR ENDED 31.12.–3

	£	£
Factory Cost of Production*		35,400
Direct Materials		
Opening Stock Raw Materials	5,000	
Purchases	25,000	
	30,000	
Less Closing Stock Raw Materials	7,000	
Raw Materials consumed		23,000
Direct Labour		
Manufacturing wages		5,000
Direct Expenses		
Licensing Fee		1,000
PRIME COST		29,000
Factory Overheads (Indirect)		
Rent & Rates (5/6 3000)	2,500	
Insurance (2/3 2100)	1,400	
Depreciation on machinery	2,000	
		5,900
Change in WIP Stock		
Add Opening Stock	2,000	
Less Closing Stock	1,500	
		500
		35,400	35,400

Note: This figure is derived after having built up the totals for PRIME COST, FACTORY OVERHEAD and CHANGE IN WORK IN PROGRESS STOCK. The total is then transferred into the Trading Account.

	£	£
Sales		45,000
Less Cost of Sales		
Opening Stock of Finished Goods	3,000	
Add factory cost of production (transferred in from Manufacturing A/c)	35,400	
	38,400	
Less Closing Stock of Finished Goods	4,000	34,400
Gross Profit		10,600
Less Expenses (Overheads)		
Administrative		
Postage & stationery	100	
Office Salaries	1,000	
Rent & Rates 1/6	500	
Insurance 1/3	700	
Depreciation office equipment	100	
	2,400	
Sales, marketing, distribution		
Bad debts	100	
Salesman's salary	1,000	
Carriage out	100	
Depreciation sales vehicle	500	
Discount allowed	100	
	1,800	
Finance overheads		
Bank charges	100	
Total Overheads		4,300
Net Operating Profit		6,300
Add Non-Operating Income		
Profit on disposal of Fixed Assets		2,000
Net Profit Retained		8,300

EXAMPLE 2

Y Ltd. a manufacturer provides you with the following information in order to prepare a Manufacturing and Profit and Loss Account.

1.1.–3	Raw Material stocks	4,500
	WIP	1,200
	Finished Goods stock	7,500
	Purchase of raw materials in the year	30,000
	Manufacturing wages	5,200
	Factory Supervisor's salary	5,000
	Factory maintenance engineer	3,000
	Depreciation Plant & Machinery	5,000
	Delivery van	1,200
	Salesman's car	1,000
	Office Manager's car	800
	Accounting machinery	1,000
	Bank charges	200
	Loan Interest	500
	Bad debts	500
	Rent & rates	6,000
	Insurance	1,200
	Telephone	1,600
	Post & stationery	300
	Office salaries & wages	7,000
	Salesman's salary	5,000
	Carriage out	600
	Discount allowed	1,000
	Discount received	200
	Loss on disposal of fixed assets	300
	Carriage in on raw materials	200
	Stock at 31.12.–3	
	Raw materials	4,000
	WIP	1,500
	Finished goods	7,000
	Sales	90,000

Note:
1. Rent & Rates and Insurance is to be apportioned 1/4 administration, 1/4 sales office and 1/2 to factory.
2. Telephones are to be apportioned 10% to factory, 20% administration and 70% to the sales office.

Y LTD. — MANUFACTURING AND TRADING AND PROFIT AND LOSS ACCOUNT FOR THE YEAR ENDED 31.12.-3

	£	£
Factory Cost of Production		52,360
Direct Materials		
Opening Stock Raw Materials	4,500	
Purchases	30,000	
Carriage Inwards	200	
	34,700	
Less Closing Stock Raw Materials	4,000	
	30,700	
Raw Materials consumed		30,700
Direct Labour		
Manufacturing wages	5,200	5,200
PRIME COST		35,900
Factory Overheads (Indirect)		
Factory Supervisor's Salary	5,000	
Factory Maintenance Engineer	3,000	
Depreciation on P & M	5,000	
Rent & Rates	3,000	
Insurance	600	
Telephone	160	
		16,760
Change in WIP Stock		
Add Opening Stock	1,200	
Less Closing Stock	1,500	
		(300)	
		52,360	52,360
Sales		90,000
Less Cost of Sales		
Opening Stock Finished Goods	7,500	
Add Factory Cost of Production	52,360	
(transferred in from		
Manufacturing A/c)		
	59,860	
Less Closing Stock		
Finished Goods	7,000	
		52,860
Gross Profit		37,140

Add non trading income — Discount received		200
		37,340

Less Expenses (Overheads)

Administrative

Depreciation		
Office Manager's car	800	
Accounting machinery	1,000	
Rent & Rates	1,500	
Insurance	300	
Telephone	320	
Post & Stationery	300	
Office Salaries & Wages	7,000	
		11,220

Sales, Marketing, Distribution

Depreciation		
Delivery van	1,200	
Salesman's car	1,000	
Bad debts	500	
Rent & Rates	1,500	
Insurance	300	
Telephone	1,120	
Salesman's Salary	5,000	
Carriage Out	600	
Discount allowed	1,000	
		12,220

Finance Overheads

Bank charges	200	
Loan interest	500	
	700	
Total Overheads		24,140
Net Operating Profit		13,200
Less Non-Operating Income.		
Loss on disposal of fixed assets		300
Net Profit Retained		12,900

SUMMARY — MANUFACTURING ACCOUNTS

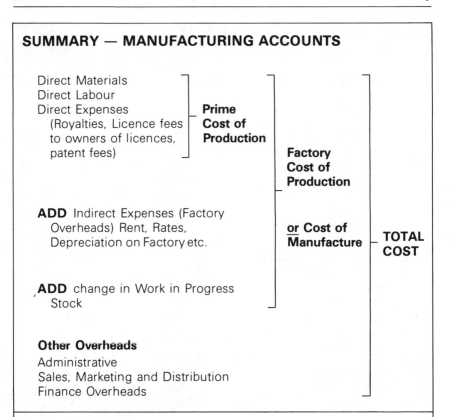

Direct Materials
Direct Labour
Direct Expenses
   (Royalties, Licence fees
   to owners of licences,
   patent fees)
   Prime Cost of Production

Factory Cost of Production

ADD Indirect Expenses (Factory
   Overheads) Rent, Rates,
   Depreciation on Factory etc.

or Cost of Manufacture

TOTAL COST

ADD change in Work in Progress
   Stock

Other Overheads
Administrative
Sales, Marketing and Distribution
Finance Overheads

Balance Sheet is also different from a retail business since it has three categories rather than one category of stock.

Stock— Raw Materials
      Work in Progress (WIP)
      Finished Goods

PRODUCTION FLOW

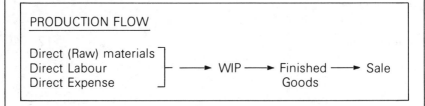

Direct (Raw) materials
Direct Labour
Direct Expense
   ⟶ WIP ⟶ Finished Goods ⟶ Sale

QUESTIONS

1X. Using the information given below, which relates to a manufacturing company Jones Limited, you are required to prepare a statement to show clearly:—   *(20 marks)*
  (a)   Cost of raw materials consumed.
  (b)   Prime cost.
  (c)   Cost of finished goods produced.
  (d)   Cost of finished goods sold.
  (e)   Gross Profit.
  (f)   Net Profit.
for the year ended 30 April 19–2.

		£
Raw Materials:	Stock at 1 May 19–1	45,000
	Purchases	154,000
	Stock at 30 April 19–2	49,000
Finished Goods:	Stock at 1 May 19–1	60,000
	Purchases	11,000
	Stock at 30 April 19–2	68,000
Work-in-progress:	at 1 May 19–1	21,000
	at 30 April 19–2	23,200
Sales		500,000
Manufacturing Wages		80,000
Manufacturing Expenses		30,300
Repairs & Maintenance of Plant & Machinery		18,500
Depreciation:	Factory	40,000
	General Office	8,000
	Sales Warehouse	9,000
Carriage outwards		6,600
Power		15,000
Light and Heat:	Factory	5,400
	General Office	800
	Sales Warehouse	3,300
Administration expenses		22,200
Selling and distribution expenses		31,100

2X. Summers Ltd. carries on a business as a manufacturer, the trial balance extracted from the books at 31st March 19–4 is as follows:-

	DR	CR
Drawings	1,600	
Light & heat Office	138	
Factory	1,445	
Manufacturing wages	9,918	
Office Salaries	2,116	
Advertising	856	
Stock Finished Goods (at 1.4.–3)	7,102	
WIP (at 1.4.–3)	3,500	
Finished Goods (at 1.4.–3)	7,278	
Sundry Expenses Office	399	
Factory	530	
Purchase of Raw Materials	49,944	
Salesman's Commission	880	
Premises at cost	4,050	
Plant (Cost 10,000)	7,500	
Trade Debtors	7,575	
Cash & Bank	2,013	
Office Machinery (Cost 1,000)	500	
Rent & Rates Office	69	
Factory	150	
Capital A/C		22,650
Bank Loan		5,600
Trade Creditors		7,733
Sales		71,580
	107,563	107,563

Notes:

1. A provision for bad debts is to be made equal to 4% of trade debtors.
2. Stocks at 31.3.–4 Raw Material   7,064
   WIP   2,500
   Finished goods 7,448
3. Depreciation is to be provided on plant 5% per annum on cost.
4. Office machinery valued at £400 on 31.3.–4.
5. Wages unpaid at 31.3.–4 £136. Advertising prepaid £48.

You are required to:

(a) Prepare a Manufacturing and Trading and Profit and Loss Account for the year ended 31st March 19–4.
(b) Prepare a Balance Sheet for Summers Ltd. as at 31st March 19–4.   *(20 marks)*
                                                                    [Q&A]

3X. The trial balance of YMB plc. at 30th June, 19–5 was as follows:

	Dr. £000	Cr. £000
Ordinary shares of £0.25 each, fully paid		50,000
6% preference shares of £1.00 each, fully paid		2,000
Share premium		8,000
Retained profit at 30th June, 19–4		36,120
Freehold land and buildings at cost	15,000	
Plant and equipment at cost	80,000	
Motor vehicles at cost	10,000	
Depreciation provisions at 30th June, 1984:		
— freehold land and buildings		7,200
— plant and equipment		12,500
— motor vehicles		2,000
Stocks at 30th June, 19–4:		
— materials	13,000	
— work-in-progress	84	
— finished products	9,376	
— packaging materials	18	
Trade debtors	23,000	
Provision for bad debts		1,000
Cash at bank	2,000	
Trade creditors		6,000
Sales		200,000
Purchases of materials	62,000	
Manufacturing wages	29,500	
Variable manufacturing overhead expenses	20,000	
Fixed manufacturing overhead expenses	34,895	
Variable distribution costs	2,702	
Fixed distribution costs	2,970	
Variable administration expenses	4,000	
Fixed administration expenses	14,155	
Preference dividend	120	
Interim ordinary dividend	2,000	
	324,820	324,820

You are given the following information:
1. There were no additions to fixed assets during the year.
2. Freehold land and buildings are to be depreciated at the rate of 2% per annum by the straight line method, assuming no residual value.
3. Plant and equipment are to be depreciated at the rate of 10% per annum on cost.
4. Motor vehicles are to be depreciated at the rate of 25% per annum by the diminishing (reducing) balance method.

5. The annual depreciation charges are to be allocated as follows:

	Land and buildings	Plant and equipment	Motor vehicles
Fixed manufacturing overhead expenses	75%	80%	—
Fixed distribution costs	10%	5%	80%
Fixed administration expenses	15%	15%	20%

6. The bad debts provision is to be increased by an amount equal to one per cent of sales. This item is to be regarded as a variable distribution cost.

7. Stocks at 30th June, 19–5, valued at full manufacturing cost where appropriate, were:

	£000
Materials	15,000
Work-in-progress	80
Finished products	10,900
Packaging materials (variable distribution costs)	20

8. Prepayments and accruals at 30th June, 19–5 were:

	Prepayments £000	Accruals £000
Manufacturing wages	—	500
Fixed administration expenses	900	1,100
Variable distribution costs	100	400

9. Provision is to be made for corporation tax at the rate of 50% of the net profit (advance corporation tax is to be ignored) and a final ordinary dividend of £0.02 per share.

Required:
You are required to prepare, for YMB plc's internal purposes, the following historic cost financial statements:
(a) A manufacturing, trading and profit and loss account, in vertical and columnar form, for the year ended 30th June, 19–5.   *(22 marks)*
(b) A balance sheet, in vertical and columnar form, as at that date.
(18 marks)
(Total 40 marks)
(CIMA)

4. From the information given below relating to the transactions of CQ Limited you are required to prepare:

(a) Manufacturing, trading and profit and loss accounts in vertical and columnar form for the year ended 30th September, 19–1.

(b) An appropriation account for the year ended 30th September, 19–1.

(c) A balance sheet as at 30th September, 19–1.

TRIAL BALANCE OF CQ LIMITED
AT 30th SEPTEMBER, 19–1

	Dr £000	Cr £000
Ordinary share capital		600
Share premium		100
Retained profit		270
Fixed assets, at cost	1,200	
Depreciation provision at 1st October, 19–0		380
Stocks at 1st October, 19–0:		
Materials	28	
Work-in-progress: department C	19	
department D	65	
Finished goods: product A (30,000 units)	125	
product B (10,000 units)	38	
Debtors	220	
Bad debts provision		8
Cash at bank	11	
Creditors		150
Sales product A (100,000 units)		600
product B (200,000 units)		1,400
Purchases of materials	380	
Purchases of product A (10,000 units)	72	
Wages: department C	99	
department D	297	
Royalties paid	197	
Manufacturing expenses	356	
Administration expenses	287	
Marketing expenses	84	
Interim dividend	30	
	3,508	3,508

You are given the following information:
1. The company manufactures and sells two products, A and B. During the year it has also purchased a quantity of product A from an external supplier.

2. The company has two manufacturing departments, C and D. Department C is concerned entirely with the manufacture of product A, but department D's costs should be apportioned between products A and B in the ratio of 1:29.

3. Royalties of £0.90 per unit of product A and of £0.60 per unit of product B are payable on the quantities sold.

4. During the year, materials costing £88,000 were issued to department C and £290,000 to department D. There was no discrepancy at stocktaking between the book and physical material stock.

5. Work-in-progress at 30th September 19–1 was valued at £20,000 for department C and £63,000 for department D.

6. Stocks of finished goods at 30th September 19–1 were valued at £84,000 for product A (20,000 units) and £188,000 for product B (50,000 units).

7. Depreciation is at the rate of 10% per annum on cost, and is to be apportioned among manufacturing, administration and market-ing in the proportions of 8:1:1. No fixed assets were purchased during the year.

8. The bad debts provision is to be made equal to 5% of the debtors. Any increase or decrease in the provision is to be treated as a marketing expense.

9. Prepaid expenses at 30th September 19–1 amounted to £2,000 for administration expenses and £3,000 for marketing expenses.

10. Accrued expenses at 30th September 19–1 amounted to £13,000 for royalties, £4,000 for manufacturing expenses and £3,000 for administration expenses.

11. Manufacturing expenses, including the share of depreciation, are to be apportioned between departments in proportion to the wages incurred in each department.

12. Administration expenses, including the share of depreciation, are to be apportioned between products in proportion to the number of products manufactured internally.

13. Marketing expenses, including the share of depreciation and the increase or decrease in the bad debts provision, but excluding royalties, are to be apportioned between products in proportion to the number of products (manufactured and purchased) sold.

14. Provision is to be made for corporation tax at the rate of 40% of the net profit, and for a proposed final dividend on the ordinary shares of £60,000.

Calculations should be made to the nearest £1,000.   *(50 marks)*
                                                            (CIMA)

5. You are required to correct where necessary the manufacturing, trading, profit and loss, and appropriation accounts of PGW Limited for the year ended 31st December, 19–0, and the balance sheet as at that date.

Manufacturing, Trading, Profit and Loss, and Appropriation Accounts of PGW Limited for the year ended 31st December, 19–0

	£000	£000	£000
Sales			10,100
Less: Returns outwards			60
			10,040
Stock of materials, at 31st December, 19–0			700
Purchase of materials		3,210	
Less: Returns inwards		100	
			3,110
			3,810
Less: Stock of materials, at 31st December, 19–9			650
Materials consumed			3,160
Carriage outwards			22
Manufacturing wages			850
Manufacturing expenses			1,275
Depreciation			380
Increase in work-in-progress			20
Cost of goods manufactured			5,707
Decrease in stock of finished goods			900
Cost of goods sold			6,607
Gross profit			3,433
Add: Income from investments			80
Carriage inwards			15
Discount allowed			240
			3,768
Less: Administration expenses			
Office salaries and expenses		860	
Rent received		20	
Depreciation		50	
			930
			2,838

Less: Marketing expenses:			
Advertising		1,010	
Salaries and commission		360	
Discount received		70	
Bad debt recovered	10		
Less: Bad debts written off	13		
		(3)	
Decrease in bad debt provisions		5	
Depreciation		50	
			1,492
Less: Debenture interest payable			80
Net profit before tax			1,266
Taxation			500
Net profit after tax			766
Less: Dividends paid		100	
Dividends proposed		200	
			300
Added to Reserves			466

Balance Sheet as at 31st December, 19–0

	£000	£000	£000
Fixed assets, at cost		4,800	
Less: Depreciation provision		1,800	
			3,000
Current assets:			
Stock of materials		650	
Work-in-progress		50	
Stock of finished goods		680	
Creditors	400		
Less: Bad debts provision	40		
		360	
Accrued expenses		20	
Bank overdraft		80	
		1,840	
Less: Current liabilities:			
Debtors	900		
Prepaid expenses	10		
Taxation	500		
Dividend paid	100		
		1,510	
			330
			3,330

	£000	£000
Ordinary share capital		2,000
Reserves:		
Balance, at 31st December, 19–9	1,800	
Add: Balance of unappropriated profit for year	466	
		2,266
Debentures		1,000
Investments		900
		6,166

In correcting these accounts you are to assume that:

1. the descriptions of all items are correct;
2. all values are correct except for profits before and after tax, profit added to reserves, and certain totals and differences;
3. the dates of items quoted in the profit and loss account are correct. *(20 marks)*
(CIMA)

THE PURCHASE OF A BUSINESS
– Takeovers an introduction

It is a frequent occurrence. It may be attractive to a buyer because it is an existing business which has an established track record and will have established 'goodwill'. The pattern of future trade may, therefore, be estimated with less uncertainty than that of a new business starting from scratch.

WHAT TYPE OF ORGANIZATIONS ARE TAKEN OVER?

The business taking over or being taken over may be owned by sole traders, partnerships or registered companies.

RECORDING THE PURCHASE

The purchase will be recorded in the books of the buyer whether the purchaser is a sole trader, partnership or company. The only difference will occur in the capital accounts and probably in the case of a company buying, it may wish to make payment in part or wholly through shares. Thus, purchase consideration is wholly or partly in shares.

AGREEING A PRICE

The purchase price will usually be based on particulars disclosed in a final 'agreed' balance sheet of the vendor. The buyer may request an independent valuation of the business assets. The agreement would also contain a reference to the limitation of liabilities, if they are to be taken over by the new business.

The seller may be asked to give a guarantee that liabilities will not exceed the figures on the agreed balance sheet or another agreed figure. The exact terms of the contract will vary depending on the nature, size and type of business and also on the desires and objectives of the two parties concerned.

ACCOUNTING PROCEDURE

Temporary accounts called:- THE BUSINESS PURCHASE ACCOUNT and THE VENDOR'S REALIZATION ACCOUNT are opened.

Let us look at an example where a sole trader takes over another sole trader.

EXAMPLE

Peter and Fred are both in business on their own account. Peter has agreed to buy Fred's business for £50,000 acquiring all assets except the cash at bank and assuming all the liabilities. Peter paid cash, borrowing £25,000 from the bank to supplement his own £25,000 cash.

The summarized balance sheets for the two businesses are given below:-

BALANCE SHEET AT 31.12.–6

	Peter £		Fred £
Fixed Assets			
Premises	50,000		30,000
Fixtures & Fittings	6,000		5,000
	56,000		35,000
Current Assets			
Stock		12,000	
Debtors 5,000		4,000	
Cash at Bank 6,000		1,000	
		17,000	
31,000			
Less Current Liabilities			
Creditors (12,000)		(8,000)	
Net Current Assets	19,000		9,000
Capital	75,000		44,000

Required:
1. The entries in the vendor's books (Fred) to record the sale.
2. The entries in the purchaser's books (Peter) to record the purchase.
3. The Goodwill on acquisition.
4. The Balance Sheet of Fred after the acquisition.

STEPS IN THE SELLER'S BOOKS
1. Close the asset accounts by crediting them and debit the Realization Account.

> **DEBIT** — **The Realization Account**
>
> **CREDIT** — **Relevant Asset Accounts**

2.
> **DEBIT** — **The Liability Account**
>
> **CREDIT** — **Realization Account**

3.
> **DEBIT** — **CASH ACCOUNT**
>
> **CREDIT** — **REALIZATION ACCOUNT**

with purchase consideration.

4. The consideration exceeds the assets given in exchange. There is a profit on realization which is treated as follows:-

> **DEBIT** — **REALIZATION ACCOUNT**
>
> **CREDIT** — **CAPITAL ACCOUNT**

5. The business is now closed down and the takeover complete as far as the seller is concerned.

STEPS IN THE BUYER'S BOOKS

1.
> **DEBIT** — **The relevant ASSET ACCOUNTS**
>
> **CREDIT** — **THE PURCHASE OF BUSINESS ACCOUNT**

with the value of acquired assets.

2.
> **DEBIT** — **The Purchase of Business Account**
>
> **CREDIT** — **The relevant liability accounts**

with the liabilities taken over.

3.
> **DEBIT** — **The Purchase of Business Account**
>
> **CREDIT** — **CASH ACCOUNT**

with the purchase consideration.

4. A credit balance on the Purchase of Business Account indicates GOODWILL, thus:

> **DEBIT** — **GOODWILL** — **Intangible Asset Account**
>
> **CREDIT** — **Purchase of Business Account**

A debit balance at this stage would be treated thus:-

DEBIT — **The Purchase of Business Account**

CREDIT — **A CAPITAL RESERVE ACCOUNT**

---

5. Extra funding for takeover

DEBIT — **CASH/BANK ACCOUNT with receipt**

CREDIT — **Source of Funding, e.g. CAPITAL A/c or LOAN A/c**

ANSWER

THE VENDOR — FRED
REALIZATION ACCOUNT

Items to be sold	£Dr	Receipts & liabilities	£Cr
Premises	30,000	Creditors	8,000
Fixtures & fittings	5,000	Purchase Consideration	
Stock	12,000	in Cash	50,000
Debtors	4,000		
Profit on realization to Capital A/c	7,000		
	58,000		58,000

FRED'S CAPITAL ACCOUNT

Cash (Purchase Consideration and Cash at Bank from Capital A/c)	51,000	Balance b/f	44,000
		Profit on Realization	7,000
	51,000		51,000

CASH AT BANK

Balance b/f	1,000	Balance c/f to Capital A/c	51,000
Purchase Consideration	50,000		
	51,000		51,000

PETER — PURCHASE OF BUSINESS ACCOUNT

	£Dr	Assets taken over	£Cr
Creditors	8,000	Premises	30,000
Purchase Consideration		Fixtures & fittings	5,000
— Cash	50,000	Stock	12,000
		Debtors	4,000
		Goodwill	7,000
	58,000		58,000

GOODWILL ACCOUNT (ASSET)

	£Dr		£Cr
Purchase of Business A/c from Fred at cost	7,000	Balance c/f	7,000

NOTE: GOODWILL IS SHOWN AS AN ASSET TO THE BUYER
and it is a profit to the seller.

CASH AT BANK

Balance b/f	6,000	To Fred for Purchase	50,000
Loan from Bank	25,000		
Capital	25,000	Balance c/f	
	56,000		56,000

CAPITAL ACCOUNT

		Balance b/f	75,000
Balance c/f	100,000	Cash	25,000
	100,000		100,000

BANK LOAN ACCOUNT

Balance c/f	25,000	Cash	25,000

PETERS — BALANCE SHEET AFTER TAKEOVER OF FRED

	£	£
FIXED ASSETS		
Intangibles — Goodwill		7,000
Tangible — Premises	80,000	
—Fixtures & fittings	11,000	
		91,000
		98,000
Current Assets		
Stock	32,000	
Debtors	9,000	
Cash at Bank	6,000	
	47,000	
Less Current Liabilities		
Creditors	(20,000)	
Net Current Assets		27,000
Total Net Assets		125,000
Financed by		
Capital	100,000	
Bank Loan	25,000	
Capital Employed		125,000

NOTES
- The Assets apart from goodwill and cash are the combined assets of the two businesses.
- The liabilities are the combined liabilities of Peter and Fred.
- Peter has had to borrow £25,000 from the bank and this is shown as a long term liability of the new business.
- Peter also had to put an extra £25,000 of his own cash into the business as capital.

The Business Purchase Account is a means of transferring assets and liabilities to the new business.

The balance of the Business Purchase Account after entering the purchase price and assets and liabilities taken over, is the value of the Goodwill acquired. If the price paid is less than the agreed values of assets less liabilities, then the credit balance should be treated as a CAPITAL RESERVE against which the value of assets might be written down, should the need arise.

THE PURCHASE OF A BUSINESS BY A COMPANY

An existing company may wish to buy another company (takeover) or a company may be formed specifically to take over another 'Going concern'.

METHODS OF PAYMENT

The purchase price may be paid in cash or partly in cash and partly in exchange for shares in the new company or wholly for shares.

The method of payment is agreed between the parties to the agreement prior to the takeover. The company may make a public share issue to raise the necessary capital to make the purchase. A statement in the prospectus (issued for the purpose of raising the capital) that the vendor (seller) is to be paid wholly **or** partly in shares may serve to encourage investors. This is because it may be taken by the investors as a sign of confidence by the vendor in the new ownership of the business.

Shares allotted as consideration for the purchase become part of the issued capital of the company.

TERMS OF CONTRACT

The terms of the agreement between the buyer and seller will determine the way in which the accounting entries are to be made. Remember the financial recording of economic events will reflect the agreement. The purchase price may well include a sum for goodwill. The total payment will be for Assets including goodwill less liabilities. The amount of goodwill will be agreed before the 'deal is struck'. The assets taken over may or may not include the cash and bank balance. Sometimes, it may be agreed that liabilities will be discharged by the old company before takeover. If liabilities are taken over it is usual for the seller to give a guarantee that they shall not exceed the figures in the agreed Balance Sheet. There may also be a clause restraining the vendor from starting a similar business within a certain agreed radius (location) of the present business.

However, the clause must not be held to be an unreasonable 'restraint of trade' — This is a very tricky area in practice.

QUESTION

1. A small company LB Ltd. is formed to take over DC's manufacturing business. LB Ltd. has an authorized share capital of £200,000 divided into 50 pence shares all of which are issued and fully paid. There is a premium of 20p per share. Fees and expenses paid in forming the company amounted to £500.

    The company took over all assets and liabilities with effect from 1st April 19-6 paying immediately a purchase price of £180,000.

Tangible assets taken over were valued as follows:-

	£	
Premises	60,000	
Machinery & Plant	30,000	
Vehicles	26,000	
Stocks	6,340	
Debtors	4,800	(book value £6,000)

Liabilities taken over amounted to £8,000. The company immediately bought new machinery at a cost of £40,000. One half of this price was paid immediately, the remainder will be paid in July 19-6.

Additional stocks were bought on credit for £10,800.

Required:
You are required to prepare the opening balance sheet for LB Ltd. as at 1st April 19-6.

FUNDS FLOW STATEMENTS — SSAP10
– sources and applications of funds

Statements of Sources and Application of Funds are now required in published financial statements for all companies with a turnover exceeding £25,000 per annum. This is a historic cash flow statement. By comparing the Balance Sheet at the start of a financial period with the Balance Sheet at the end of a financial period it is possible to deduce the movement of funds which have taken place during the period.

SOURCES OF FUNDS

These detail where cash has come into the business from, e.g.:-
> Trading
> Proceeds of a disposal of fixed assets
> Loans — long term (debenture issue, bank loan)
> Proceeds from the issue of shares (share capital plus any share premium)

APPLICATION OF FUNDS

This shows the way in which the cash has been spent, e.g.:-
> Acquisition of fixed assets
> Payment of taxation
> Payment of a dividend
> Repayment of a loan
> Repayment of share capital
> Other cash payments

THE WORKING CAPITAL POSITION

The Working Capital Position or rather the change in working capital over the two balance sheet dates should equal the difference between Sources of Funds less the Application of Funds.

Working capital is defined as current assets less current liabilities but excluding tax and dividends which are regarded as applications.

EXAMPLE

Z LTD. — BALANCE SHEET AT 31.12.19-4

	19-3 £		19-4 £
Fixed Assets			
Land and Buildings		40,000	64,000
Plant & Machinery at Cost	70,000		131,000
Less Depreciation Provision	(30,000)		(45,000)
		40,000	86,000
Current Assets			
Stock	100,000		122,000
Debtors	63,000		72,000
Cash	27,000		24,000
Less Current Liabilities			
Creditors	47,000		53,000
Current Taxation	17,000		27,000
Proposed Dividend	14,000		20,000
Net Current Assets		112,000	118,000
Total Net Assets		192,000	268,000
Financed By			
Ordinary Share Capital Issued	170,000		220,000
Reserves Profit & Loss	22,000		48,000
		192,000	268,000

Z LTD. — PROFIT AND LOSS EXTRACT FOR THE YEAR ENDED 31.12.19-4

	£
Net Profit before tax after charging depreciation	73,000
Less Corporation Tax	27,000
	46,000
Less Proposed Ordinary Dividend	20,000
Transferred to Profit and Loss Reserve	26,000

Z LTD. — STATEMENT OF SOURCES AND APPLICATION OF FUNDS FOR THE YEAR ENDED 31.12.19–4

Sources of Funds £

Profit before Tax	73,000	**A**
Add back non-cash items (Adjustments not involving the movement of funds)		
DEPRECIATION (for the year)	15,000	**B**
TOTAL GENERATED FROM OPERATIONS	88,000	**C**
FUNDS FROM OTHER SOURCES		**D**
Proceeds from Ordinary Share Issue	50,000	
	138,000	

Application of Funds

Purchase of Land and Buildings	24,000		**E**
Purchase of Plant and Machinery	61,000		**F**
Dividend Paid	14,000		**G**
Taxation Paid	17,000		**H**
		116,000	
INCREASE/(DECREASE) IN WORKING CAPITAL		22,000	**I**
Increase/(Decrease) in Stock	22,000		**J**
Increase/(Decrease) in Debtors	9,000		**K**
(Increase)/Decrease in Creditors	(6,000)		**L**
	25,000		
Movement in Liquid Funds (i.e. Change in Cash + Bank)	(3,000)		**M**
		22,000	

A Profit before tax is given in the profit and loss extract. It is the profit before tax but after charging depreciation.

B Non-cash items need to be added back to the profit since we are interested in deducting cash movements only. Non-cash items are such things as:-
Depreciation
Profit or Loss on the disposal of fixed assets
(Effectively a profit on disposal reduces the Net Profit before tax and a loss increases it.)

C Total Generated from Operations shows the funds obtained through the normal business activity (i.e. trading).

D Funds may also come in from non-trading activities such as the issue of shares or loans.
Share Capital (220 – 170) = £50,000 increase in funds.

E Purchase of Land and Buildings is obtained from the different cost figures given, i.e. (64,000 – 40,000) = £24,000.

F Purchase of Plant and Machinery (£131,000 – 70,000) = £61,000.

G Dividend Paid is obtained as follows:- On the closing balance sheet only the proposed dividend shown in the 19–4 Profit Statement is shown as a liability, therefore the liability shown on the 19–3 balance sheet must have been paid during the year.

H Taxation Paid is obtained in the same way as the dividend. The tax shown on the 19–4 balance sheet is the amount provided for 19–4 in the Profit and Loss Statement. Therefore, the liability shown on the 19–3 Balance Sheet must have been paid in cash during the year.

I Sources less Applications must give the total change in the working capital of the business.
An increase in an asset is a positive change in working capital, i.e. a debit, a reduction of an asset would be negative, i.e. a credit. Therefore, any increase in stock, debtors or cash is positive, and any reduction is negative and shown in brackets. An increase in a liability is negative and is therefore shown in brackets. A reduction of a liability is a positive change in working capital.

J Stock increased from £100,000 in 19–3 to £122,000 in 19–4, i.e. a change of £22,000 positive.

K Debtors increased from £63,000 to £72,000 over the year, i.e. a change of £9,000.

L Creditors increased from £47,000 to £53,000, i.e. a negative change of (£6,000).

M The change in the cash balance from £27,000 to £24,000 a reduction of £3,000, thus a negative change in working capital.

QUESTIONS

1. The following summarized information relates to Candle plc for the year to 30 September 19–4.

Profit and Loss Account for the year 30 September 19–4

	£'000	£'000
Net profit		312
Taxation		(104)
Net profit after taxation		208
Dividends:		
interim (paid on 1 April 19–4)	(14)	
final (proposed)	(35)	
		(49)
Retained profit for the year		£159

Balance Sheet at 30 September 19–4

	19–4		19–3	
	£'000	£'000	£'000	£'000
Fixed assets:				
Land and Buildings at cost	380		380	
less: Accumulated Depreciation	120		100	
		260		280
Machinery and Fittings at cost	500		225	
less: Accumulated Depreciation	156		85	
		344		140
		604		420
Current assets:				
Stocks	190		185	
Debtors	170		100	
Cash at bank	30		15	
		390		300
		£994		£720
Financed by:				
Capital and reserves:				
Called up share capital		300		250
Revenue reserves		10		10
Profit and loss account		274		115
		584		375
Debenture stock:				
10% debenture stock		60		50
Deferred taxation		85		70
Current liabilities:				
Creditors	147		25	
Taxation	68		100	
Proposed dividend	35		70	
ACT on proposed dividend	15		30	
		265		225
		£994		£720

Additional information:
1. During the year some machinery was sold for £6,000. Its original cost was £25,000 and its net book value at 30 September 19-3 was £10,000.
2. The standard rate of income tax is 30%.

Required:
(a) Prepare a statement of source and application of funds for the year to 30 September 19-4 in a format that accords with best practice.   *(20 marks)*
(b) Summarize briefly the use of such a statement by financial analysts.   *(5 marks)*
                                                          (Total 25 marks)
                                                                  [AAT]

2. A friend of yours who owns a newsagent's and confectionery business has asked for your help. He is very worried because he suspects that a shop assistant is stealing money from his till. He comments as follows:

"For the year to 31st March 19-2 my shop made a profit of £8,600 and yet I have had to ask the bank for an overdraft", then adds "Will you check the figures for me please?" You agree to help and he supplies the following information.

Nick's Newsmart — Balance sheets as at 31st March

19–1		Fixed assets	19–2	
£	£		£	£
16,000		Premises, at cost	16,000	
3,600		**Less** Depreciation	3,900	
	12,400			12,100
3,000		Fixtures and fittings, at cost	8,200	
1,000		**Less** Depreciation	1,300	
	2,000			6,900
	14,400			19,000
		Current assets		
5,400		Stocks – magazines, periodicals etc.	8,060	
1,480		– sweets, tobacco etc.	3,240	
2,200		Debtors – trade	4,900	
140		– other	420	
6,400		Bank	–	
280		Cash	500	
15,900			17,120	
		Less **Current liabilities**		
4,200		Creditors – trade	3,600	
100		– other	120	
–		Bank overdraft	4,000	
4,300			7,720	
	11,600	**Working capital**		9,400
	£26,000	**Net assets employed**		£28,400
24,600		Opening capital	26,000	
6,800		**Add** Net profit	8,600	
31,400			34,600	
5,400		**Less** Drawings	6,200	
	£26,000	Closing capital		£28,400

You confirm that he has not disposed of any fixed assets during the year.

Required:
Prepare a Statement of Source and Application of Funds (Funds Flow Statement) to show Nick where his profit has gone.   [ACCA]

3X. From the information given below relating to GLS Limited you are required to list all the sources from which the company obtained finance during the year ended 31st August 19–8, and show the amount raised from each source.

Balance sheets of GLS Limited at 31st August

	19-7		19-8	
	£'000	£'000	£'000	£'000
Fixed assets				
Freehold land and buildings, at cost	100		–	
Less Depreciation	20		–	
		80		
Leasehold land and buildings, at cost	–		50	
Less Depreciation	–		1	
				49
Plant and equipment, at cost	300		1,200	
Less Depreciation	250		320	
		50		880
		130		929
Investments, at cost		60		
Current assets				
Stocks and work-in-progress	300		200	
Debtors	100		100	
Cash at bank	10		–	
	410		300	
Less Current liabilities				
Creditors	40		70	
Bank overdraft	–		94	
Taxation	60		60	
Acceptance credits	–		5	
	100		229	
Net Current assets		310		71
		500		1,000
Share capital				
Preference shares of £1 each, fully paid	–		50	
Ordinary shares of £1 each, fully paid	200		320	
		200		370
Reserves				
Capital redemption reserve fund	40		–	
Share premium	20		40	
Surplus on sale:				
Freehold land and buildings	–		120	
Investments	–		20	
Government grants	30		50	
Retained profits	210		250	
		300		480
Debentures		–		100
Loan: ICFC		–		50
		500		1,000

You are given the following information:

(a) No plant and equipment was sold or scrapped during the year.
(b) On 1st September 19–7, the freehold land and buildings were sold and leased back from the purchaser.
(c) A bonus issue of ordinary shares on the basis of one new share for every five held has been made. The capital redemption reserve

fund was used for this purpose.
(d) The preference shares were issued for cash at par.
(e) An issue of £1 ordinary shares was made at a price of £1.25 per
     share.
(f) The debentures were issued at par.   *(CIMA)*

4X. The draft accounts of the Flaker Airfreight Company for the year to 30
     June 19–4 are as follows:

	19–4		19–3	
	£	£	£	£
Balance sheet				
Freehold premises at cost		250,000		150,000
Plant, at cost	420,000		250,000	
Less Depreciation	160,000		110,000	
		260,000		140,000
Debtors		160,000		120,000
Stock		240,000		200,000
		910,000		610,000
Capital		690,000		440,000
Long-term loans		100,000		100,000
Trade creditors		90,000		60,000
Bank overdraft		30,000		10,000
		910,000		610,000
Profit and loss account				
Sales revenue		1,050,000		850,000
Trading profit		157,000		122,000
Less Depreciation	50,000		40,000	
Loan interest	7,000		7,000	
		57,000		47,000
Net profit for the year		100,000		75,000

Required:
(a) Rearrange the above Balance Sheets of Flaker Airfreight into a
     presentable format.   *(4 marks)*
(b) Draw up a Statement of Sources and Application of Funds for
     the year ended 30 June 19–4.   *(16 marks)*
(c) Show your workings clearly where appropriate on a separate
     working paper.   *(4 marks)*
(d) Briefly comment upon the change in working capital over the
     year. You may use working capital ratios to support your
     analysis.   *(6 marks)*
                                              (Total 30 marks) [Q&A]

INTERPRETATIONS OF FINANCIAL STATEMENTS
– using accounting ratios

PURPOSE

Accounting ratios are used so that comparisons can be made quickly between different time periods for the same business or between different businesses in the same time periods. We need to be careful when making comparisons to ensure that they are meaningful by comparing like with like. For example, it would not be useful to make a direct comparison between pounds and dollars from 1968 with pounds or dollars in 1988 since they are not the same thing (the purchasing power is totally different). Although we refer to accounting ratios they may be expressed as fractions or percentages as well as ratios in order to achieve a specific purpose.

PROBLEMS WITH MAKING COMPARISONS

1. When we compare the closing financial statements of a current period with a previous period, even if only twelve months earlier, we need to remember and be aware of the fact that what we are measuring cannot possibly be exactly the same thing. For example, distortion may have taken place owing to rising price levels (inflation).

2. Sometimes the accounting policies applied by the organization will have changed, thereby making comparison between periods difficult. For example, a change in depreciation policy. If we are making comparisons between companies for the same periods of time, we would need to take account of the different accounting policies in order to make the comparisons meaningful. This is not always possible as we are limited by the amount of disclosure in the published financial statements. Therefore accuracy may be sacrificed and meaningful comparison limited.

3. When comparing different businesses the financial periods do not always coincide so direct comparison cannot be made. Nevertheless, intelligent estimates can often prove useful.

4. The nature and type of business may vary between accounting periods. Therefore, when making comparisons, we need to understand and take account of such changes in order to obtain meaningful results.

5. It should be remembered that ratios are records of past events. They are historical measures. Therefore, if we use ratios to obtain a trend we should remember their limitations in predicting future events. They will only be useful indicators of future events if there are no changes in the business structure, products sold, markets engaged in and the economic environment. Remember, it cannot be stressed enough that

they are measuring historic events, their predictive powers are limited and they should not be taken in isolation. They may, of course, be used as part of a financial forecast providing factors which affect their accuracy as predictors are also considered.

TYPES OF ACCOUNTING RATIO

We may classify the main accounting ratios as follows:-
1.   Profitability ratios.
2.   Liquidity ratios.
3.   Capital structure.
4.   Asset turnover.
5.   Investment ratios.

PROFIT MARGIN RATIOS

$$\frac{\text{Gross Profit}}{\text{Sales}} \qquad \frac{\text{Net Profit}}{\text{Sales}}$$

$$\frac{\text{Operating Profit}}{\text{Sales}} \qquad \frac{\text{General Overheads}}{\text{Sales}}$$

$$\frac{\text{Factory Cost}}{\text{Sales}} \qquad \frac{\text{Marketing Overheads}}{\text{Sales}}$$

$$\frac{\text{Material Cost}}{\text{Sales}} \qquad \frac{\text{Administration Overheads}}{\text{Sales}}$$

$$\frac{\text{Labour Cost}}{\text{Sales}} \qquad \frac{\text{Production Overheads}}{\text{Sales}}$$

i.e. $$\frac{\text{Operating Profit 31.12.–4 + Operating Profit 31.12.–5}}{2}$$

= Average Operating Profit

$$\frac{\text{Operating Assets 31.12.–4 + Operating Assets 31.12.–5}}{2}$$

= Average Operating Assets

LIQUIDITY/SOLVENCY RATIOS

Current Ratio $= \dfrac{\text{Current Assets}}{\text{Current Liabilities}}$ $\dfrac{\text{C.A.}}{\text{C.L.}}$

Acid Test $= \dfrac{\text{CA – Stock}}{\text{CL}}$

Average Stock turnover $= \dfrac{\text{Cost of Goods Sold}}{\text{Average Stock held}}$ (COGS)

Average Collection Period $= \dfrac{\text{Debtors}}{\text{Sales}} \times$ no. days

Average Payment Period $= \dfrac{\text{Creditors}}{\text{Purchases}} \times$ no. days

CAPITAL STRUCTURE

LONGER TERM – Various measures for gearing

Gearing Ratio $= \dfrac{\text{Fixed Interest Capital}}{\text{Fixed Interest Capital + Equity}}$

Gearing Ratio $= \dfrac{\text{Shareholders equity}}{\text{Total Assets}}$

Gearing Ratio $= \dfrac{\text{Long term debt + current liabilities}}{\text{Total Assets}}$

Capital Gearing at Market Values $= \dfrac{\text{Total Market Value of Preference Shares + Market Value of Debentures}}{\text{Total Equity Market Value}}$

Interest coverage Ratio $= \dfrac{\text{Profit before tax + interest}}{\text{Interest charges for period}}$

Other Supporting Ratios

ASSET TURNOVER RATIOS

$\dfrac{\text{Sales}}{\text{Operating Assets}}$ $\dfrac{\text{Sales}}{\text{Current Assets}}$

$\dfrac{\text{Sales}}{\text{Fixed Assets}}$ $\dfrac{\text{Sales}}{\text{Stocks}}$

$\dfrac{\text{Sales}}{\text{Liquid Assets}}$ $\dfrac{\text{Sales}}{\text{Debtors – Creditors}}$

INVESTMENT RATIOS

$$\text{Earnings Per Share (EPS)} = \frac{\text{Profit after tax less preference dividend (gross)}}{\text{No. of Ordinary Shares}}$$

SSAP 3 recommends that all listed Companies show EPS in their financial statements.

$$\text{Dividend Yield} = \frac{\text{Nominal Share Value} \times \text{Dividend \%}}{\text{Market price per share}}$$

$$\text{Dividend Cover or Payout Ratio} = \frac{\text{Profit after tax} - \text{Preference dividend gross}}{\text{Gross Equity Dividend}}$$

$$\text{Price earnings (PE)} = \frac{\text{Market price per share}}{\text{EPS}}$$

$$\text{Earnings Yield} = \frac{\text{EPS}}{\text{Market price per share}} \times 100\%$$

EXAMPLE using ratios for interpretation

X LTD. BALANCE SHEET AS AT 31st DECEMBER

	19–4		19–5	
		£		£
FIXED ASSETS				
Land and Buildings	100,000		120,000	
less Depreciation	50,000	50,000	51,200	68,800
Plant and Machinery	30,000		25,000	
less Depreciation	9,000	21,000	10,000	15,000
Motor Vehicles	20,000		20,000	
less Depreciation	4,000	16,000	6,000	14,000
		87,000		97,800
CURRENT ASSETS				
Stock	7,500		5,000	
Debtors	5,500		6,000	
Bank and Cash	1,500		2,000	
	14,500		13,000	
CURRENT LIABILITIES				
Trade Creditors	6,000		5,000	
Other Creditors	1,000		1,000	
Net Current Assets		7,500		7,000
Total Net Assets		94,500		104,800
FINANCED BY				
EQUITY CAPITAL				
Ordinary Share Capital	60,000		60,000	
Reserves	14,500		23,800	
	74,500		83,800	
LOAN CAPITAL				
5% Debentures	20,000		21,000	
CAPITAL EMPLOYED		94,500		104,800

X LTD. PROFIT AND LOSS SUMMARY
FOR THE YEAR ENDED 31.12

	19–4		19–5	
		£		£
Sales		90,000		100,000
Less Cost of Sales		50,000		52,000
Gross Profit		40,000		48,000
Less Expenses				
Administration Overheads	9,000		15,000	
Sales and Marketing Overheads	10,000		11,000	
Distribution Overheads	7,000		9,000	
Finance Overheads	3,000	29,000	1,700	36,700
Net Profit from operation		11,000		11,300
Add Profit/(Loss) on Disposal		NIL		(2,000)
of fixed assets				
Retained Profits		11,000		9,300
transferred to Reserves				

COMPARING THE TWO BALANCE SHEETS OF X LTD.

Just by looking at the two years' balance sheets for X Ltd. we are able to deduce the following:-

1) There has been an addition to the fixed asset category for land and buildings in the sum of £20,000.

2) There has been a reduction in the fixed asset category for plant and machinery in the sum of £5,000.

3) The only change detectable in the fixed asset category for motor vehicles is the increase in depreciation, hence the charge for using the asset for one extra year. It could be that there has been an increase to the fixed asset which is equally cancelled out by a disposal. At this stage, however, we are not in a position to confirm or refute this.

4) Stock holding has been reduced at the balance sheet date in 19-5 by £2,500 over the previous year total.

5) Debtors have increased by £500 in 19-5.

6) Bank and Cash balances have increased by £500.

7) Trade Creditors (i.e. those creditors for stock items (Purchaser) have been reduced by £1,000.

8) Other creditors (which could include tax and various expense creditors, e.g. utilities) have remained unchanged in total.

9) Reserves have increased by £9,300. This is probably due to X Ltd. retaining the same sum in profit from its profit and loss statement.

10) Finally, there has been an injection of loan capital from a further issue of 5% Debentures £1,000 which has also helped to finance the expansion of the business by increasing its fixed assets in Land and Buildings.

11) If we look at the total change in the balance sheet value it has increased from £94,500 to £104,800, a change of £10,300. This is represented by a net increase in the business's fixed assets of £10,800 and a reduction in working capital of £500. Looking at this from the other side of the coin; reserves have increased by £9,300 making a total change in equity of £9,300 and then added to that the increase in loan capital due to the issue of a further £1,000 worth of 5% Debentures results in the overall increase of £10,300.

COMPARING THE PROFIT AND LOSS SUMMARIES OF X LTD.

1) Sales turnover has increased by approximately 11% in the year to 31.12.19–5 (i.e. $1 - \frac{100}{90}$ 11% or $\frac{10}{90} \times \frac{100}{1} = 11.11\%$) an increase of £10,000.

2) Cost of making those sales has increased by £2,000, i.e. $\frac{2,000}{50,000} \times \frac{100}{1} = 4\%$.

3) Gross Profit has increased by £8,000, i.e. $\frac{8,000}{40,000} \times \frac{100}{1} = 20\%$.

There are two ways to compare expenses, firstly against the previous year totals:-

4) Administration expenses have increased by £6,000, i.e. $\frac{6,000}{9,000} \times \frac{100}{1} = 66.67\%$.

5) Sales and Marketing expenses have increased by £1,000, i.e. $\frac{1,000}{10,000} \times \frac{100}{1} = 10\%$.

6) Distribution expenses have increased by £2,000, i.e. $\frac{2,000}{7,000} \times \frac{100}{1} = 28.57\%$.

7) Finance overheads have decreased by £1,300, i.e. a reduction in percentage terms of $\frac{1,300}{3,000} \times \frac{100}{1} = -43.33\%$.

8) In 19–5 total expenses have increased by £7,700 over the 19–4 total, an overall increase in percentage terms of $\frac{7,700}{29,000} \times \frac{100}{1} = 26.55\%$.

The second way to compare expenses is to take account of the change that may have occurred in sales volume – turnover; and to measure each expense category as a percentage of turnover as follows. This is probably a more meaningful measure, since it takes account of the fact that it may cost more in terms of expenditure in absolute terms to make more sales and therefore, in order to compare 'like with like' we ought to measure expenditures in relative terms and hence as a percentage of sales value.

PROFITABILITY RATIOS

		19–4	19–5
		%	%
1 $\dfrac{\text{Cost of Sales}}{\text{Sales}} \times \dfrac{100}{}$		55.55	52.00

There has been a 3.55% reduction in the cost of making sales in 19–5. This could be due to a reduction in the cost of materials owing to larger discounts or falling prices or it could be that material usage in the product is more efficient or a less expensive grade of materials has been used. It could also be due to lower labour costs; maybe the plant is able to produce more output in the same number of given hours thus not incurring extra labour costs (i.e. better plant utilization causing a fall in unit cost). Alternatively, a fall in wage rates could have caused the reduced costs. There may be other reasons too, in addition to those stated above.

				19–4	19–5
				%	%
2	$\dfrac{\text{Gross Profit}}{\text{Sales}}$	×	$\dfrac{100}{1}$	44.45	48.00

This is the corollary of the Cost of Sales/sales ratio. Profitability at the Gross Margin stage has increased in 19–5 over 19–4 by 3.55%. This will be for the same reasons mentioned in 1 above.

3   $\dfrac{\text{Expense Classification}}{\text{Sales Turnover}}$ as a %

	19–4	19–5
	%	%
Administration	10.00	15.00
Sales and Marketing	11.11	11.00
Distribution	7.78	9.00
Finance	3.33	1.70

It can be seen that even when we have taken account of changing sales (prices and volume – we do not know the detail as to whether the change in total sales were due to price increases or quantities sold), that administration costs have increased to 15% a 50% increase over the previous year. The reasons for such a change would be the subject of investigation by management if they calculated the ratio. They would require a breakdown of the costs making up administration to see if anything could be done to control them. Similarly distribution costs have risen by 15.68% on the previous year ($\frac{9.00}{7.78}$ –1 × 100) as a percentage of turnover. Sales and Marketing costs have remained static and Finance costs have fallen by about 50%.

4   $\dfrac{\text{Net Operating Profit}}{\text{Sales}}$ × $\dfrac{100}{1}$ =   %

19–4

$\dfrac{11,000}{90,000}$ × $\dfrac{100}{1}$ = 12.22%

19–5

$\dfrac{11,300}{100,000}$ × $\dfrac{100}{1}$ = 11.30%

The operating profit has fallen by 7.52% despite an improvement at the gross margin of 3.55%; operating expenses have increased overall; resulting in a net profit reduction.

It might be useful to look at the two years in percentages at this stage to see the changes more clearly.

	19–4	19–5	Change on
	%	%	previous year
Sales	100.00	100.00	—
Cost of Sales	55.55	52.00	–3.55
Gross Profit	44.45	48.00	+3.55

Expenses:

Administration	10.00	15.00	+5.00
Sales & Marketing	11.11	11.00	−0.11
Distribution	7.78	9.00	+1.22
Finance	3.33	1.70	−1.63
Net Profit	12.23*	11.30	−0.93

*This difference of 0.01% is due to rounding.

Comparing the two profit statements in this way we can observe the major differences and areas for further investigation and control.

RETURN ON CAPITAL EMPLOYED

There are a number of ways to measure a rate of return on capital employed. For comparability it is essential that the measure used is consistent between different periods and different business organizations.

One way is to measure $\dfrac{\text{Net Profit (after tax)}}{\text{Total Assets}}$

Total Assets are all fixed assets plus working capital (i.e. current assets less current liabilities). If working capital is negative it should be ignored. There are two problems with using this measure:-

1) The net profit after tax is after charging loan interest (debentures, mortgages, loans, overdrafts.). The return on capital employed will be distorted by the interest charges if they are material. That is, the return is understated.

2) Total Assets will include intangibles such as goodwill. Such assets are liable to fluctuations in value and subjective.

To overcome these problems a better measure is:–

$$\dfrac{\text{Net Operating Profit}}{\text{Operating Assets}}$$

Operating profit ignores such things as interest charges and non-trading income (profits on disposal, investment income etc.).

USE OF ASSETS — RATIOS

		19–4			19–5		
Land and Buildings : Sales	50,000 : 90,000	1 :	1.8	68,800 : 100,000	1 :	1.5
Plant and Machinery : Sales	21,000 : 90,000	1 :	4.3	15,000 : 100,000	1 :	6.7
Motor Vehicles : Sales	16,000 : 90,000	1 :	5.6	14,000 : 100,000	1 :	7.1
Fixed Assets : Sales	87,000 : 90,000	1 :	1.0	97,800 : 100,000	1 :	1.0
Stock in Trade : Sales	7,500 : 90,000	1 :	12.0	5,000 : 100,000	1 :	20.0
Debtors : Sales	5,500 : 90,000	1 :	16.4	6,000 : 100,000	1 :	16.7
Cash at Bank : Sales	1,500 : 90,000	1 :	60.0	2,000 : 100,000	1 :	50.0
Current Assets : Sales	14,500 : 90,000	1 :	60.0	2,000 : 100,000	1 :	50.0
Current Assets : Sales	14,500 : 90,000	1 :	6.2	13,000 : 100,000	1 :	7.7

These ratios assess asset utilization. They show how effective management have been in using the assets at their disposal; they are in effect efficiency ratios. An external analyst could use a simple ratio of asset to sales.

In our example total fixed assets to sales value is low at 1:1. We are measuring the utilization a business is obtaining from its investment in fixed assets. It may be the case that better management of the business could improve this ratio – hence more efficient use of assets. Nevertheless, one needs to be extremely careful in making glib statements since the value of assets shown in the balance sheet are dependent upon historic cost value and depreciation policy. Thus, the value of sales in 19–4 pounds is being measured against pounds from previous periods. We are not therefore, measuring like with like. It may be that efficiency ratios would be better measures if they were at current cost values.

Furthermore, in making comparisons between different businesses or different time periods, we need to ensure that depreciation policies are consistent. This is difficult if not impossible for an external analyst.

LIQUIDITY

CURRENT ASSETS : CURRENT LIABILITIES

This is a simple liquidity measure. It measures whether or not a business has enough current assets to meet its current liabilities.

		19–4		19–5
$\dfrac{\text{CURRENT ASSETS}}{\text{CURRENT LIABILITIES}}$	$= \dfrac{14,500}{7,000} =$	2.07:1	$\dfrac{13,000}{6,000} =$	2.17:1

Current assets are those which are or will become liquid within twelve months with liabilities due for payment in that time. A creditor will want to make sure that the business has sufficient current assets to meet its obligations. It is often said that as a rule of thumb a ratio of 2:1 is appropriate. However, this can be misleading since it depends on the nature of the business and type of industry. In our example, it would appear that X Ltd. had sufficient current assets to meet current liabilities in both periods. For every £1 liability it had £2.17 in current assets in 19–5.

THE ACID TEST OR QUICK RATIO

$$\frac{\text{Current Assets less Stock in Trade}}{\text{Current Liabilities}}$$

This is a better measure of liquidity since it may take time for stock to become a sale, thus a debtor and eventually be turned into cash. It is essential for a business to ensure it can meet its obligations in cash at the due dates. A ratio which showed current assets less stock to be lower than the current liabilities may signify that the business is over-trading.

X LTD.

		19–4		19–5
$\dfrac{\text{Current Assets} - \text{Stock}}{\text{Current Liabilities}}$	$= \dfrac{14,500 - 7,500}{7,000} =$	1:1	$\dfrac{13,000 - 5,000}{6,000} =$	1.33:1

In 19–4 liquid assets were 1:1, that is for every £1 in liquid assets the business had a current liability of £1. In 19–5 this position improved to £1.33 in current assets (less stock) for every £1 in current liabilities.

These ratios are likely to prove more useful to external analysts since management would be inclined to plan and control their liquidity by preparing cash flow forecasts (cash budgets).

STOCK TURNOVER

We could measure this by dividing sales by stock in trade but there is a problem in so far as stock is at cost and sales includes profit. To overcome this we measure sales at cost which is, of course, the cost of goods sold which is then divided by stock. The stock figure used should be an average for the period. A true averaged stock holding figure which is representative is usually known to management but for external analysts the next best approximation is obtained by averaging opening and closing stocks. Using X Ltd. an external analyst would obtain an average thus:–

$$\frac{7,500 + 5,000}{2} = 6,250$$

and measuring stock turnover for 19–5 would get:–

$$\frac{\text{Cost of Goods Sold}}{\text{Stock in Trade}} = \frac{52,000}{6,250} = 8.32 \text{ times}$$

This can also be measured in terms of the number of days stock on average which is held at the balance sheet date, assuming that production remains at a similar level and other things being equal:–

$$\frac{365 \text{ days}}{8.32 \text{ times}} = 43.87 = 44 \text{ days}$$

We could have obtained this figure first by using:–

$$\frac{\text{Stock}}{\text{Cost of Goods Sold}} \times \frac{\text{Number of days}}{\text{in the period}}$$

Supposing as management we thought that closing balance sheet figures for stock were representative of average stockholding during those years we could compare the two years thus:–

STOCK TURNOVER	19–4		19–5	
No. of Times =	$\frac{50,000}{7,500}$ =	6.67	$\frac{52,000}{5,000}$ =	10.40
Days =	$\frac{7,500}{50,000} \times 365$ =	54.75	$\frac{5,000}{52,000} \times 365$ =	35.10

Comparing the two years it can be seen that stock turnover has increased from 6.67 to 10.40 and that the number of days now being held in stock has fallen to 35.10. This is good on the face of it since the business is now tying up less money in stocks.

DEBTOR TURNOVER

It is important to know the collection period for debtors, that is, how long it takes on average for a sale to be turned into cash. We calculated that in 19–4 for every £16.40 sold £1 was owed by debtors and in 19–5 it was £16.70 to £1, a marginal improvement.

In terms of the number of days it takes for an average debtor to pay, we can obtain this for each year as follows:–

$$
\begin{array}{ll}
\text{Number of days for} & \dfrac{365}{16.4} = \\[2mm]
\text{a debtor to pay in cash} &
\end{array}
\left.\phantom{\dfrac{365}{16.4}}\right\} 22.3
\qquad
\dfrac{365}{16.7} =
\left.\phantom{\dfrac{365}{16.7}}\right\} 21.9
$$

$$
\underline{\textbf{OR}} \quad \dfrac{\text{Debtors}}{\text{Sales}} \times 365 \quad \dfrac{5{,}500}{90{,}000} \times 365 =
\left.\phantom{\dfrac{5500}{90000}}\right\}
\qquad
\dfrac{6{,}000}{100{,}000} \times 365 =
\left.\phantom{\dfrac{6000}{100000}}\right\}
$$

The collection period has been reduced in 19–5 to 21.9 days.

It is the average debtor balance during the period over which sales are made which the analyst should use to obtain a measure. I have assumed the closing balance sheet figures to be a proxy for that average.

An external analyst might obtain an average for 19–5 by adding the opening and closing debtor balances from the balance sheet and divide by two. Thus for 19–5 the figures used would be:–

$$
\frac{5{,}500 + 6{,}000}{2} \quad = \quad 5{,}750
$$

$$
\frac{5{,}750}{100{,}000} \times 365 \quad = \quad 20.99 \text{ days}
$$

It does not materially alter the analysis in this case. However, in a company where debtor balances change significantly throughout a period and between two balance sheet dates it would alter the analysis.

CREDITOR TURNOVER

It is important for management and creditors to assess how quickly on average a business pays its suppliers for goods and services.

For trade creditors; those supplying stock in trade this can be measured as follows:-

$$
\frac{\text{Trade Creditors}}{\text{Purchases}} \quad \times \quad \text{No. of days}
$$

$$
\text{or} \quad \frac{\text{Purchases}}{\text{Trade Creditors}} \quad = \quad \text{No. of times in a period}
$$

For X Ltd.   19–5

    Number of days $\dfrac{5,000}{49,500}$ × 365   =   36.9 days

    Number of times $\dfrac{49,500}{5,000}$ =   9.9 times

Purchases for 19–5 can be obtained by taking the cost of goods sold and opening and closing stocks for the period thus:–

Opening Stock + Purchases – Closing Stock = Cost of Goods Sold
7,500 + ? – 5,000 = 52,000

therefore:–

PURCHASES = Closing Stock + Cost of Goods Sold – Opening Stock
49,500 = 5,000 + 52,000 – 7,500

On average, trade creditors are being paid in 37 days. An external analyst may average creditors as we did for stock and debtors to obtain $\frac{5,500}{49,500}$ × 365 = 40.55 days.

Note: we can only calculate this ratio for 19–5 since we do not have the purchase figures or sufficient detail from which to deduce the figure for 19–4.

The same analysis could be done for other creditors. For example, for service creditors the calculation would be:–

$$\frac{\text{Creditors}}{\text{Expenses bought in, in the period}} \times \frac{\text{No. of days}}{\text{in the period}}$$

We do not have sufficient detail of the expenses bought in, in either year.

THE WORKING CAPITAL RATIO

We can obtain a rough measure regarding the number of days it takes for working capital to turnover.

X LTD.	19–4 days	19–5 days
STOCK	55	42
DEBTORS	22	22
LESS TRADE CREDITORS	?	(37)
		27

Again, we are only able to analyze 19–5.

CAPITAL STRUCTURE

The analysis of the capital structure of a business is of particular interest to creditors, shareholders and competitors.

NET WORTH/TOTAL ASSETS

Net Worth is Ordinary Shares and Preference Shares plus reserves OR
Total Assets less Current and Long Term Liabilities.
Total Assets are Fixed plus Current Assets.

X LTD.   19–4   19–5

$$\frac{74,500}{101,500} \ = \ 1:1.36 \qquad\qquad \frac{83,800}{110,800} \ = \ 1:1.32$$

This means that the shareholders' stake in the business is approximately
75% in each year. It has actually strengthened from 73.5% in 19–4 to
75.8% in 19–5. This is known as a measure of gearing.

FIXED ASSETS/NET WORTH

This shows the proportion of fixed assets funded by shareholders.

	19–4	19–5
X LTD.	87,000:74,500 = 1.17 : 1	97,800:83,800 = 1.17 : 1
	or 85.6%	or 85.6%

The position has not changed significantly over the two years analyzed.

LONG AND SHORT TERM DEBT/TOTAL ASSETS

This is also a measure of gearing. The ratio measures the proportion of
debts to total assets; it is the 'other side of the coin' to the previous
measurement of Net Worth/Total Assets. If that ratio for 19–5 showed the
shareholders' interest to be 75% then this ratio should be 25% since the
sum of the parts must equal 100% (i.e. NET WORTH + DEBT = TOTAL
ASSETS).

X LTD.   19–4   19–5

$$\frac{27,500}{101,500} = 1:3.7 \qquad\qquad \frac{28,000}{110,800} = 1:4$$
                          OR 27%   OR 25%

A company which has a large proportion of debt funding total assets is said
to be highly geared. X LTD. is low geared. As a 'rule of thumb':–

zero geared	=	no borrowed funds
low geared	=	0 – 30%
medium geared	=	31 – 49%
high geared	=	50% +

INTEREST COVERAGE RATIO

This measures the extent to which profit may decline before a company is
unable to meet its interest repayments on loans etc. Since interest charges
are an allowable tax expense, it is profit before tax which is used in the
calculation.

$$\frac{\text{Profit before tax} + \text{Fixed Interest Charges}}{\text{Interest charges for the period}}$$

Looking at X Ltd. the only fixed interest charges the company appears to have is the 5% debenture interest. This charge, we assume, must be included in Finance Overheads.

Debenture Interest   19-4 = 5% × 20,000 = 1,000
                      19-5 = 5% × 21,000 = 1,050

There is no tax shown in the statements and the net profits before tax are £11,000 and £11,300 respectively.

		19-4		19-5
Interest Cover	= $\dfrac{12,000}{1,000}$	12 : 1	$\dfrac{12,350}{1,050}$	11.8 : 1

On average, profits could fall 12 times or to $\frac{1}{12}$th of the current level and the business would still be able to pay its interest charges.

INVESTMENT RATIOS

These are of interest to investors, analysts and the financial managers interested in the market price of shares quoted on the stock exchange. In the case of X Ltd., let us assume that:–

1) There is no liability to income tax for the year.
2) The number of ordinary shares issued are 120,000 at a nominal value of 50 pence per share = £60,000. They must have been issued at par since there is no share premium account on the balance sheet.
3) The current market prices at 31.12.-4 = £1.00 and at 31.12.-5 = £1.20.

Note: it is only PLC's which are quoted on the Stock Exchange.

EARNINGS PER SHARE = $\dfrac{\text{PROFIT after tax} - \text{Preference Dividend (gross)}}{\text{Number of Ordinary Shares Issued}}$

X LTD. 19-4   = $\dfrac{11,000 - 0}{120,000}$ = 9.16 pence
                                                    or £0.09 per share

        19-5   = $\dfrac{11,300 - 0}{120,000}$ = 9.42 pence
                                                    or £0.09 per share

This ratio has remained fairly stable over the two years in question. It shows that each ordinary share has earned 9 pence in profit. This is not necessarily the amount that the shareholder will receive as a dividend, since dividend policy is decided by the directors. (See SSAP3, Chapter 59).

DIVIDEND YIELD measures the real rate of return on the investment in shares since it is based on market prices and not nominal share values.

In the case of X Ltd., let us assume that a dividend is declared at 5% of the nominal value of the shares issued for both 19-4 and 19-5.

$$\text{DIVIDEND YIELD} = \frac{\text{Nominal Share Value} \times \text{Dividend \%}}{\text{Market Price per Share}}$$

X LTD.
19-4 $\qquad = \dfrac{£0.50 \times 5\%}{£1.00} = 2.5\%$

19-5 $\qquad = \dfrac{£0.50 \times 5\%}{£1.20} = 2.08\%$

It can be seen that the real rate of return on the investment in X Ltd. declined in 19-5 as a result of the change in market value of the shares.

DIVIDEND COVER OR PAYOUT RATIO

This indicates the proportion of profits retained and paid out as dividend by the business in a period.

$$\text{DIVIDEND COVER} = \frac{\text{Profit after Tax} - \text{Preference dividend gross}}{\text{Gross Equity Dividend}}$$

For X Ltd., using our previous assumptions, the gross equity dividend or the dividend on ordinary shares was:- £0.50 × 5% per share, that is, 2½ pence per share gross (before tax). There are 120,000 (£0.50) shares; the total dividend paid would be:-

$$120,000 \times £0.025 = £3,000$$

The ratio for 19-4 is $\qquad = \dfrac{11,000 - 0}{3,000} = \quad 3.7 \text{ times}$

Alternatively, as a payout measure, 27.27% of net profit is paid out as dividend, or put another way, 72.73% was retained in the business.

for 19-5 $\qquad = \dfrac{11,300}{3,000} = \quad 3.8 \text{ times}$

That is to say that the dividend paid out was covered by 3.8 times the amount paid in net profit. Alternatively, 26.55% of net profit paid as a dividend which means that 73.45% must have been retained within the business.

PRICE EARNINGS RATIO

This ratio is an indicator to an investor of the value placed upon a share by the market. It is very important if a company is about to make a new share issue, since an investor may decide to invest or not to invest on the basis of what amount is normally earned by each share in relation to its market price. Remember, investors will be comparing this ratio with other possible investments.

$$\text{PRICE EARNINGS} = \frac{\text{Market Price per Share}}{\text{Earnings per Share}}$$

$$\text{X LTD.} \quad 19\text{-}4 \quad = \quad \frac{£1.00}{£0.0916} \quad = \quad 10.9$$

$$19\text{-}5 \quad = \quad \frac{£1.20}{£0.0942} \quad = \quad 12.7$$

The lower the price earnings ratio, the more attractive the investment might be not taking into account other things.

This ratio would not be considered in isolation and the potential or existing shareholder would be interested in the payout ratio also to see what proportion of the earnings he could expect to receive. A business with a higher PE ratio may be more attractive because its dividend policy is more attractive.

Return on Capital Employed (ROCE)

$$= \frac{\text{PROFIT}}{\text{INVESTMENT}} \quad \times \quad 100\%$$

$$\frac{\text{SALES}}{\text{Investment}} \quad \times \quad \frac{\text{Profit}}{\text{Sales}} \quad \times \quad 100\%$$

$$\frac{\text{OPERATING PROFIT}}{\text{OPERATING ASSETS}} = \frac{\text{Operating Profit}}{\text{Sales}} \quad \times \quad \frac{\text{Sales}}{\text{Operating Assets}}$$

Various definitions of Capital Employed
1) Total Capital
2) Long Term Capital (i.e. Total Capital — Current Liabilities)
3) Shareholders' Total Capital (i.e. Share Capital + Reserves)
4) Shareholders' Equity (i.e. Ordinary Shares + Reserves)

Note: you may use $\dfrac{\text{average operating profit}}{\text{average operating assets}}$

This is done by using opening and closing balance sheet figures.

SUMMARY — RATIO ANALYSIS

Ratios are useful in both internal and external financial statements to summarise key relationships.

They need to be:
1) Prepared regularly and in a consistent manner.
2) Consistent with other firms in the same industry if inter-firm comparisons are to be made.
3) Interpreted accurately. For this reason if they are considered in isolation they will be much less use. Remember they are historic measures, they may therefore lead to fallacious future predictions if used in isolation.

WHAT RATIOS? Prepare those ratios most useful to the situation you are trying to analyse.

QUESTIONS

1. Stephen House, the principal shareholder of Hilltown Traders Limited, is very concerned that although the company's net profit has increased in the past year the bank is reluctant to continue the company's overdraft facility.

    The summarized results of Hilltown Traders Limited for the last three financial years are as follows:

Trading and profit and loss accounts — years ended 31 December

	19–2 £'000	19–3 £'000	19–4 £'000
Turnover	100	130	150
less: Cost of sales	80	110	125
Gross profit	20	20	25
less: Administrative expenditure	4	6	7
Distribution expenditure	6	5	5
	10	11	12
Net Profit	10	9	13

Balance sheets as at 31 December

	19–2 £'000	£'000	19–3 £'000	£'000	19–4 £'000	£'000
Fixed assets		60		60		60
Current assets:						
Stock	10		24		40	
Debtors	6		7		9	
Balance at bank	2		—		—	
	18		31		49	
Current liabilities:						
Creditors	8		9		13	
Bank overdraft	—		3		4	
	8		12		17	
Net current assets		10		19		32
Net capital employed		70		79		92
Capital:						
Ordinary share capital		50		50		50
Reserves		20		29		42
		70		79		92

Required:

(a) Calculate five financial ratios of Hilltown Traders Limited which will indicate to the company those aspects which have improved and those which have weakened in the past three years.

(14 marks)

(b) Outline three significant and distinct limitations of financial ratios. *(6 marks)*

(Total 20 marks) [AAT]

2. White and Black are sole traders. Both are wholesalers dealing in a similar range of goods. Summaries of the profit calculations and balance sheets for the same year have been made available to you, as follows:

Profit and loss accounts for the year

	White		Black	
	£'000	£'000	£'000	£'000
Sales		600		800
Cost of goods sold		450		624
		150		176
Administration expenses	64		63	
Selling and distribution expenses	28		40	
Depreciation – equipment and vehicles	10		20	
– buildings		102	5	128
Net profit		48		48

Balance sheets as at end of the year

	White		Black	
	£'000	£'000	£'000	£'000
Buildings		29		47
Equipment and vehicles		62		76
Stock		56		52
Debtors		75		67
Bank balance		8		
		230		242
Creditors	38		78	
Bank balance		38	4	82
		192		160

Required:

Compare the performance and position of the two businesses on the basis of the above figures, supporting your comments where appropriate with ratios and noting what further information you would need before reaching firmer conclusions. [ACCA]

3. Carlton Construction Plc have tendered for the contract to build an
    office block for Amalgamated Air Traffic Plc. Their price of
    £1,245,000 is the lowest among the rival alternatives, and their
    completion time of 10 months is acceptable.

    As an Accounting Technician employed by Amalgamated Air Traffic
    Plc you have been asked in December 19–3 to review the most recent
    published accounting statements of Carlton Construction Plc in order
    to discover any information concerning the financial situation of the
    building company which will have a bearing on the award of the
    contract, which is scheduled to be decided at a board meeting in
    January 19–4.

Carlton Construction Plc
Balance Sheet as at 31st March 19–3

	Cost £	Depreciation £	Net £
Fixed assets			
Land and buildings	230,000	40,000	190,000
Plant	520,000	100,000	420,000
Vehicles	50,000	30,000	20,000
	£800,000	£170,000	630,000
Current assets			
Stock		41,850	
Work-in-progress		258,490	
Debtors		57,600	
Cash		14,821	
			372,761
			£1,002,761
Represented by:			
Capital			
£1 ordinary shares, fully paid			200,000
Reserves			183,422
			383,422
Long term loan 15% debentures			
(repayable June 19–4)			250,000
Current liabilities			
Trade creditors		153,473	
Overdraft		184,647	
Taxation		31,219	
			369,339
			£1,002,761

Required:
(a) Explain the constituent parts of the current asset "work-in-
    progress" in the balance sheet.
(b) Use SIX suitable ratios to analyse the financial position of
    Carlton Construction Plc, note significant points which should
    be drawn to the attention of your board.   [AAT]

4X.   **ZERO LTD. — Summarised Trading & P/L Account**

	31.5.-3 £		31.5.-4 £
Sales	30,000		34,000
Cost of Sales			
Opening Stock	8,000	10,000	
Purchases	22,000	30,000	
Closing Stock	10,000	15,000	
	20,000		25,000
Gross Profit	10,000		9,000
Less Expenses	8,000		9,100
Net Profit	2,000		(100)

ZERO LTD. — Balance Sheet Summaries

	31.5.-3 £		31.5.-4 £
FIXED ASSETS			
Cost	100,000	100,000	
Depreciation	40,000	62,000	
NBV	60,000		48,000
CURRENT ASSETS			
Stock	10,000	15,000	
Debtors	5,000	9,000	
Cash	500	400	
	15,500	24,400	
CURRENT LIABILITIES			
Trade Creditors	6,000	4,000	
Other Creditors	1,000	—	
Net Current Assets	8,500		20,400
	68,500		68,400
FINANCED BY			
£1 Ordinary Shares	50,000		50,000
PROFIT and LOSS RESERVE	18,500		18,400
	68,500		68,400

You are required to:—
1. From the above summarised Balance Sheets and Trading and Profit & Loss Accounts for two years of Zero Ltd., you are required to advise the management about their performance. Use and explain the purpose of any accounting ratios you consider useful in your analysis.
2. The management of working capital is often said by businessmen to be the most important factor to control in order to control the business. Explain what working capital is and say what you understand by this statement.
3. Explain the term RESERVE as used in accounting.

(30 marks) [Q&A]

5X. The net assets of three unconnected companies are financed as follows, as at 31 December 19-4:

	X PLC		Company Y PLC		Z PLC	
	£'000	£'000	£'000	£'000	£'000	£'000
Share capital						
Authorised						
Ordinary shares of £1.00 per share		12,000		—		—
Ordinary shares of £0.25 per share		—		6,000		6,000
8% preference shares of £1.00 per share		—		4,000		4,000
		12,000		10,000		10,000
Called up and issued						
Ordinary shares of £1.00 per share £0.75 paid		6,000		—		—
Ordinary shares of £0.25 per share fully paid		—	4,000		1,000	
8% preference shares of £1.00 per share, fully paid		—	4,000		2,000	
		6,000		8,000		3,000
Reserves						
Share premium account (raised on issue of ordinary shares)			500		200	
General reserve	1,000		—		1,300	
Fixed asset revaluation reserve	2,000		—		—	
Fixed asset replacement reserve	—		1,000		—	
Profit and loss account	1,000		500		1,500	
		4,000		2,000		3,000
Shareholders' funds		10,000		10,000		6,000
10% Debenture stock		—		—		4,000
		10,000		10,000		10,000

For all three companies, the profit before interest and tax is estimated at £5,000,000 for the next 12 months ended 31 December 19-5. The capital structure of each company will remain unaltered.

Taxation on profits after interest is an effective rate of 40%. Assume that an ordinary dividend of 12% of the paid up share capital will be paid.

Required:
For each of the three companies,
(a) Prepare the estimated profit and loss accounts for the year ended 31 December 19-5. *(4 marks)*
(b) Calculate
  (i) basic earnings per share for the year ended 31 December 19-5,
  (ii) gearing ratio as at 31 December 19-4. *(8 marks)*
(c) Briefly explain, in relation to gearing, the effects on earnings of substantial changes in profit after tax. *(4 marks)*

Marks will be awarded for workings which must be shown.

(Total 16 marks)
[ACCA] [Q&A]

VALUE ADDED TAX
– a simple indirect tax

Taxation is a major worry for most small businessmen and an inconvenience to many large organizations. Nevertheless, taxation is necessary to finance Government Expenditure and is the major way in which income is redistributed from those with ability to earn income for themselves to those unable to derive their own income.

VALUE ADDED TAX

This is an indirect tax. It is a tax placed on the supply of goods and services. It was introduced in 1973 to replace Purchase Tax and as part of a 'harmonisation' programme to bring the U.K. in line with the E.E.C.

There are a number of free booklets issued by H.M. Customs and Excise, who are the authority responsible for administering V.A.T. The most important of these guides is:-

No. 700   General Guide

Currently, there are two rates of tax in operation. Zero and 15%. In addition, certain goods and services are exempted from V.A.T.

It is important to distinguish between those goods which are exempt from the tax and those which are zero rated. Zero rated goods are subject to V.A.T. but at 0%. The Government may decide to implement a lower rate than 15% at some stage, which might bring 0% items in the taxable band, that is, above 0% but below 15%. Or it may decide to make all items chargeable at the standard rate. Items which are exempt are simply not subject to V.A.T.

From a trading point of view this has important implications. Let us, for example, take the case of publishing books. Books are currently zero rated and therefore purchases of goods used in production may be claimed as an **INPUT** if the publisher is registered for V.A.T. The **OUTPUTS** (i.e. Sales) are subject to V.A.T. at 0%. The trader is, therefore, able to claim the INPUT taxes he has paid, back from H.M. Customs. If publishing was exempt from the scope of the tax, the trader would not be able to register for V.A.T. and would therefore be unable to claim back any V.A.T. suffered on his purchases.

VALUE ADDED AT STAGES

V.A.T. is a staged tax and V.A.T. is paid at every stage. However, it is the ultimate consumer of the goods or services who suffers the tax. For example, supposing a manufacturer who is V.A.T. registered and falls within the scope of the tax buys in Raw Materials for £10 plus V.A.T. at 15%, he then "adds value" by manufacture (i.e. converting the materials into a saleable form). Thus he incurs labour and overheads in manufacture amounting to £10 and then adds 25% for his profit before selling to a wholesaler. The wholesaler then adds his profit margin of 50% and passes the goods to the retailer who adds 20% to the goods and sells to the customer.

STAGE 1	Manufacturer	£	£
	Goods (Raw Materials)	10	
	Input Tax V.A.T.		1.50

The cheque he pays to the supplier will be £11.50 (i.e. £10 for goods, £1.50 V.A.T.), the supplier will pay over to H.M. Customs £1.50.

STAGE 2	Manufacturing Costs	£
	Raw Materials	10.00
	Labour & Overheads	10.00
	Profit Mark-up 25%	5.00
		25.00
	V.A.T. at 15%	3.75
	TOTAL INVOICE	28.75

Thus, the wholesaler will pay the manufacturer £25 for goods and £3.75 V.A.T. which the manufacturer will pay over to H.M. Customs & Excise.

However, the manufacturer has already suffered tax of £1.50 on the inputs and has now charged £3.75 on his outputs. Since the manufacturer is not the final point of consumption, he need only pay over the net difference between tax suffered on his input costs and the tax charged on outputs.

	£
INPUTS	1.50
OUTPUTS	3.75
Paid to H.M. Customs by Manufacturer	2.25

STAGE 3	£	£ VAT	
Wholesaler buys goods	25.00	3.75	paid to Manufacturer
Profit Mark-up 50%	12.50		(INPUTS)
Price of Goods	37.50		
Plus VAT at 15%	5.62	5.62	(OUTPUTS) charge
TOTAL INVOICE	43.12	1.87	to Retailer

Thus the wholesaler needs only pay over the net difference which is £1.87 V.A.T.

STAGE 4	£	£ VAT
Retailer buys goods	37.50	5.62 INPUTS
Profit Mark-up 20%	7.50	
Price of Goods	45.00	
Plus VAT at 15%	6.75	6.75 OUTPUTS
TOTAL INVOICE	51.75	1.13

Thus the retailer needs to pay over £1.13 in V.A.T.

The ultimate consumer has paid £6.75 in V.A.T. and he is unable to get any of that back.

SUMMARY — V.A.T. at each stage

	£
Raw Materials Supplier	1.50
Manufacturer	2.25
Wholesaler	1.87
Retailer	1.13
PAID IN TOTAL TO H.M. CUSTOMS by the above	6.75

VOLUNTARY REGISTRATION

Traders may register voluntarily for VAT if it is to their advantage, even though their turnover is less than the requirement for registration. This is normally advantageous if the goods sold (outputs) by the trader are zero rated but the purchases (inputs) are subject to Value Added Tax.

COMPULSORY REGISTRATION

It is compulsory to register where the turnover of the business is in excess of the figure currently stated by HM Customs and Excise in their literature. In 1990 the annual turnover requirement is £25,400 for registration and less than £24,400 for deregistration.

VAT TERMINOLOGY

Inputs	are purchases and expenses incurred by the business.
VAT on Inputs	is the tax paid or payable on any purchase or expense incurred by the business.
Outputs	are the sales made by the business.
VAT on Outputs	is the tax paid or payable on sales.

Tax Point = The transaction date for tax purposes.

If the output VAT is greater than the input VAT the difference is payable to HM Customs and Excise. Until it is paid the amount payable should be shown as a CREDITOR on the business balance sheet.

If the input VAT is greater than the output VAT the difference is receivable from HM Customs and Excise in the form of a repayment. Until payment is received the amount receivable should be shown as a DEBTOR on the balance sheet of the business.

HOW WILL I KNOW WHAT TO PAY OR IF A REPAYMENT IS DUE?

If you look back at the example of S. Lee (Chapter 13) you will see that all entries made regarding every transaction had a dual aspect, i.e. DOUBLE ENTRY. VAT requires an account in the Nominal Ledger and any entries regarding VAT will be made therein as follows:

> **DR — VAT Inputs (Purchases/Expenses) to VAT A/c**
>
> **CR — VAT Outputs (Sales) to VAT A/c**

At the end of an accounting period the balance extracted from this account if on the DEBIT side (i.e. left hand side) of the account will be the amount payable to HM Customs and Excise. If the balance on the VAT account is on the CREDIT side (i.e. right hand side) of the account, then this amount will be repayable to the business from HM Customs and Excise.

SUMMARY OF VAT

It can be seen that VAT is as we said, a tax at every stage, and that the ultimate consumer suffers the full impact of the tax. Currently, you need to register for VAT if your turnover is above £25,400 per annum.

QUESTIONS

1. A company buys and sells goods, some of which are:
   (a) subject to VAT at the standard rate of 15%;
   (b) zero rated (those where no VAT is chargeable on sales but any VAT charged on purchases is recoverable);
   (c) exempt (those where no VAT is chargeable on sales and where any VAT charged is not recoverable).

   You are given the following information:
   1. The balance on the VAT account at the end of July was £4,700. This amount was paid on 30th August.
   2. Purchases, including VAT at 15%, during the quarter were:
      £69,000 for standard rated goods;
      £ 6,900 for zero rated goods;
      £ 2,300 for exempt goods.

3. Sales, not including VAT, during the quarter were:
£100,000 for standard rated goods;
£ 10,000 for zero rated goods;
£ 5,000 for exempt goods.
4. All items purchased are for resale.

Required:
You are required to write up a company's Value Added Tax account, sales account and purchases account in its ledger for the months of August, September and October, and to show the balance out-standing on the VAT account at the end of the quarter.

(10 marks) *(CIMA)*

2X. Mudgee Ltd issued the following invoices to customers in respect of credit sales made during the last week of May 19–7. The amounts stated are all net of Value Added Tax. All sales made by Mudgee Ltd are subject to VAT at 15%.

Invoice No	Date	Customer	Amount £
3045	25 May	Laira Brand	1,060.00
3046	27 May	Brown Bros	2,200.00
3047	28 May	Penfold's	170.00
3048	29 May	T Tyrrell	460.00
3049	30 May	Laira Brand	1,450.00
			£5,340.00

On 29 May Laira Brand returned half the goods (in value) purchased on 25 May. An allowance was made the same day to this customer for the appropriate amount.

On 1 May 19–7 Laira Brand owed Mudgee Ltd £2,100.47. Other than the purchases detailed above Laira Brand made credit purchases of £680.23 from Mudgee Ltd on 15 May. On 21 May Mudgee Ltd received a cheque for £2,500 from Laira Brand.

Required:
(a) Show how the above transactions would be recorded in Mudgee Ltd's Sales Book for the week ended 30 May 19–7.
(b) Describe how the information in the Sales Book would be incorporated into Mudgee Ltd's double-entry system.
(c) Reconstruct the personal account of Laira Brand as it would appear in Mudgee Ltd's ledger for May 19–7.

[AAT]

ACCOUNTING FOR SERVICES
– and segment reports

SERVICES

The tertiary sector of the economy does not supply goods but provide services. Examples are:-

professional services	— accountants, lawyers, insurance, banks etc.
personal services	— hairdressing, beauticians, dentists, transport, travel, entertainment, restaurants and hotels.

Over a twenty year period from 1964 to 1984 this sector of the economy increased output by about 54%. Manufacturing industrial output increased by about 15% over the same period. It is the second largest growth area in the U.K. after agriculture, forestry and fishing.

DIFFERENCES BETWEEN SERVICE ACCOUNTS AND OTHERS

1) Service industries may not have a trading account which separates the cost of goods sold from expenses so as to report a gross profit, since a pure service does not sell goods. Pure services would have a profit and loss account which shows income from the sale of services less all costs and expenses to arrive at a net profit. The concept of gross profit may not apply. Some services may supply goods in addition to a service and therefore, the concept of gross profit does apply. The choice of accounting report will depend on what is considered to be most appropriate given the circumstances.

2) In a business which supplies a number of different services it may be appropriate to segment the services into particular categories and report a profit for each separable part of the business. For example, an Interior Decorating and Design business may be split into the two areas:- (i) decorating and (ii) design services. Let us look at a brief example:-

EXAMPLE

— Supposing Arthur completed and invoiced decorating work amounting to £5,000 in a year to 31.12 and design services £3,000.
— The cost of materials supplied in decorating (paint, paper etc.) amounted to £2,000.
— Expenses incurred are:-

— Wages — decorating	£1,000
— Rent and Rates	£1,500
— Insurance	£ 60
— Printing & Stationery	£ 100
— Motor Vehicles	£1,000
— Sundries	£ 40
— Telephone	£ 150
— Office Wages	£1,000

— It is policy to charge general expenses for the business as a whole — 50% to decorating and 50% design since they use the services provided equally.

ARTHUR'S PROFIT AND LOSS ACCOUNT
for the year ended 31.12 — (may look like this)

	DECORATING		DESIGN		TOTAL	
Income from sale of services		5,000		3,000		8,000
Less Cost of Materials consumed		2,000		—		2,000
Gross Profit		3,000		3,000		6,000
Less Costs and Expenses						
Wages — decorating	1,000		—		1,000	
— office	500		500		1,000	
Rent and Rates	750		750		1,500	
Insurance	30		30		60	
Printing and Stationery	50		50		100	
Motor Vehicle Running	500		500		1,000	
Telephone	75		75		150	
Sundries	20		20		40	
		2,925		1,925		4,850
Net profit		75		1,075		1,150

Note: In reporting the two segments (similar to departmental accounts), the design part of the business does not really have a gross profit and if it was reported separately; that is if it was only a design business it would be reported thus:-

	£	£
Income from the sale of design services		3,000
Less **Costs and Expenses**		
Wages	500	
Rent and Rates	750	
Insurance	30	
Printing and Stationery	50	
Motor Vehicle Running	500	
Telephone	75	
Sundries	20	
		1,925
Net Profit		1,075

WORK IN PROGRESS

Some service businesses such as accounting, lawyers, architects and design may incur costs and expenses in a period for which revenue will be recognized in a following period. The matching principle (accruals concept) says that those costs and expenses should be matched with the revenue and thus not recognized also until the following period. The purpose of including work-in-progress is to eliminate those costs from the present period and transfer them to the period in which they should be recognized.

EXAMPLE

Supposing an accounting practice had fee income of £20,000; Wages and Salaries £10,000; Rent and Rates £2,000; Indemnity Insurance £200; Motor Vehicle running £1,000; Telephone £500; Stationery and Postage £800; the work-in-progress brought forward from the previous period is £1,500 (the income of which is now recognized in the £20,000 total income); work-in-progress to carry forward to the next period is £2,000.

The income statement of the practice for the present period may look like this:-

	£	£
Fees Invoiced (or Total Billings)		20,000
Less **Costs and Expenses:**		
Wages and Salaries	10,000	
Rent and Rates	2,000	
Indemnity Insurance	200	
Motor Expenses	1,000	
Telephone	500	
Stationery and Postage	800	
	14,500	
Add: Work in Progress b/f	1,500	
	16,000	
Less: Work in Progress c/f	2,000	
		14,000
NET PROFIT		6,000

Note the Income is called by different names in different types of service industry.

Examples are:— Advertising = Total Billings
Lawyers = Costs (paradoxically solicitors call their income costs).
Accountants = Fees

Furthermore, it is often difficult to obtain an accurate figure for work-in-progress.

QUESTIONS

1. The XL Company Limited sells its own trading stamps to shops, garages and other establishments, and operates a number of shops at which members of the public can purchase goods with their books of stamps. In its accounts the company does not recognize that a profit has been made until this exchange of goods for stamps has been made in its shops.

Required:
(a) The trading and profit and loss accounts of the XL Company Limited for the year ended 31st December, 19–0.
(b) The closing trial balance of the XL Company Limited as at 31st December, 19–0 after the preparation of the trading and profit and loss accounts.
(c) The trading account of the PQ Garage Limited for the year ended 31st December, 19–0.

The trial balance of the XL Company Limited at 1st January 19–0 was as follows:

	£'000	£'000
Ordinary share capital		1,600
Retained profit		500
Fixed assets, at cost	1,300	
Aggregate depreciation		520
Stock in trade	900	
Sundry creditors		400
Cash at bank	420	
Trading stamps issued but not exchanged for goods		1,600
Investments	2,000	
	4,620	4,620

During the year to 31st December, 19–0 the following summarized transactions took place.

	£'000
Purchase of investments for cash	1,500
Purchases on credit	3,550
Payments to creditors	3,500
Sales of trading stamps for cash	5,900
Trading stamps exchanged for goods	5,000
Cost of goods exchanged for trading stamps	3,500
Business expenses paid in cash	1,170
Depreciation of fixed assets for the year	130
Investment income received in cash	200

The PQ Garage Limited buys trading stamps from the XL Company Limited which it issues to customers on purchases at the garage. On 1st January, 19–0 it held a stock of stamps valued at £200. During the year to 31st December, 19–0 the following summarized transactions took place:

	£'000
Purchase of trading stamps for cash	2.1
Sales	100.0
Cost of petrol and other merchandise sold	75.0

The stock of trading stamps held at 31st December, 19–0 was valued at £300.   *(CIMA)*

2. The profit and loss account for the year ended 31st December, 19–8 of DQ Holidays Limited, a company which provides holidays at several resorts in Spain, is as follows:

	£		£
Agents commission	90,600	Sales of holidays	906,000
Hire of aeroplanes	105,000	Net loss for the year	10,000
Coaches from airport to resorts	7,000		
Hotel accommodation	581,400		
Salary and expenses of resort representatives	32,000		
Brochures, advertising head office and other common costs	100,000		
	916,000		916,000

The managing director has complained to you, as chief accountant, that the form of presentation of this profit and loss account does not tell him where or why the net loss has been incurred and is of little use for management purposes.

Required:
You are required to re-design the profit and loss account, using also the information given below, so that it will overcome the complaints of the managing director.

You are given the following information:
(a) The public book their holidays with the company through local travel agents who were paid a commission of 10% of the gross price of the holiday.
(b) Holidays were offered at six resorts in Spain, namely P, Q, R, S, T and U.
(c) Only one hotel was used in each resort.
(d) Flights were from Luton Airport to three airports in Spain, as follows:

Airport	For resorts	Annual cost
X	P and Q	30,000
Y	R and S	40,000
Z	T and U	35,000

(e) Separate coaches were used for the journey from the Spanish airport to each resort hotel. The annual costs of these were:

To resort	£
P	1,100
Q	900
R	1,400
S	1,100
T	1,700
U	800

(f) The annual costs of hotel accommodation at each resort were:

Resort	£
P	305,900
Q	153,200
R	22,600
S	45,500
T	10,200
U	44,100

(g) A separate representative was employed at each resort, and the annual costs were:

Resort	£
P	5,000
Q	4,500
R	6,000
S	5,500
T	5,700
U	5,300

(h) Sales of holidays at the various resorts were:

Resort	£	
P	480,000	
Q	244,000	
R	30,000	
S	60,000	
T	24,000	
U	68,000	*(CIMA)*

**HIRE PURCHASE
TRANSACTIONS**
– an introduction

INTRODUCTION

The purpose of this section is to explain clearly the accounting treatment of
hire purchase transactions. Technically and legally when a hire purchase
contract is made the purchaser does not become the owner of the asset
which is the subject of the agreement until the final payment is made. Thus,
he is hiring the asset until the final payment which secures purchase. The
seller under such agreements does, however, make a sale as soon as there
is a contract which legally obligates a buyer to pay certain amounts. The
other legal aspects of hire purchase contracts are beyond the scope of this
book and not necessary for our purpose.

THE SELLER UNDER THE AGREEMENT

When a 'deal is struck' the seller has sold goods which have a sale value for
the goods element and over and above this a finance charge for the credit
which is extended. During the term of the agreement the buyer will repay
both the goods value and the interest charged on the credit. The amount of
interest payable each period will be the subject of the original agreement.
There may also be a clause regarding early settlement by the buyer which is
in effect allowing a reduction of interest for prompt payment (a discount).

In the books of the seller the following entries will be necessary:-

1) In the period the sale is made the full sale price will be entered as a sale
    and shown in the Trading Account for the period. This price does not
    include any interest element.

2) The agreed interest charged to the buyer for each period is credited to
    an income account for HP interest receivable in the relevant period.
    The HP interest income recognized in each period is shown in the
    trading account since it is received as a result of trading.

3) The cost of goods sold will be transferred to the trading account in the
    normal manner, and the stock account reduced by the amount of cost
    of sale.

4) In the balance sheet there will be a debtor at the end of each financial
    period until settlement is made in full. The debtor consists of two
    elements:-
    (a) The sale value of goods still to be paid by the buyer at the
         balance sheet date; and
    (b) The interest receivable in respect of the finance charge under the
         HP agreement.

THE BUYER UNDER THE AGREEMENT

Although according to legal 'form' the buyer does not own the asset under the HP agreement, according to commercial reality ('substance') the buyer may use the asset as he sees fit and is to all intents and purposes able to exercise the same control through use that an owner would be able to. In accounting for such assets it has long been the custom for substance to rule over form and treat the asset as if it is owned by the buyer. The way in which this is achieved is as follows:-

1) The asset acquired under a hire purchase agreement is placed in the balance sheet at cost excluding interest charges and is depreciated in line with company policy in the normal way.

2) The outstanding balance owed to creditors for the asset at the balance sheet date consists of two elements:-
   (a) The sale price outstanding on the goods bought; and
   (b) The interest payable under the terms of the HP agreement at the balance sheet date.

   These two amounts taken together represent the liability outstanding against the particular asset and it is normal to show them as a deduction against the book value of the asset to show a 'true and fair' view of the ownership interest in that asset at the balance sheet date.

3) The hire purchase interest charged and capital sum repaid each accounting period effectively reduces the liability by that amount paid in cash.

4) Hire Purchase Interest is a charge to the Profit and Loss Account for the period in which the interest falls due. It is an expense just like bank interest or loan interest. It is therefore, a charge against revenue.

THE PROVISION FOR UNREALIZED PROFIT

A seller may decide that it is prudent for some reason not to recognize all the profit on the HP Cash Price during the period in which the sale is made. The seller would need to deduct from the sale the amount of profit thought to be uncertain and credit a provision for unrealized profit which effectively is offset in the balance sheet against those debtors. It is similar to a bad debt provision.

DR — TRADING ACCOUNT

CR — PROVISION FOR UNREALIZED PROFIT ACCOUNT — B/S

Such a provision may be calculated thus:-

$$\frac{\text{Cash to be collected}}{\text{Total Sale Price including HP interest}} \times \text{GROSS PROFIT}$$
Inclusive of interest
before provision

EXAMPLE

G. Ltd. sells a car to M. Ltd. on 1.1.–6 under a hire purchase agreement. The cash price for the car is £10,000 and finance charges are £2,200 in total for the period of 2 years. Repayments are to be made in 24 equal instalments after taking account of the deposit paid in cash of £2,000 at the outset. The cost of goods sold is £7,000.

Show how this transaction is recorded:-
1) In the books of the seller; and
2) In the books of the buyer.

1. SELLER — G. LTD.

YEAR 1 — TRADING ACCOUNT

	£	£
SALES at cash price		10,000
Add HP Interest for the year		1,100
		11,100
Less Cost of Sales		7,000
GROSS PROFIT		4,100

M. LTD. — HP DEBTOR ACCOUNT

1.1.–6	Sale at cash price	10,000	1.1.–6	Cash — deposit	2,000
	HP interest receivable	2,200	31.12.–6	Cash — capital	4,000
				Cash — interest	1,100
			31.12.–6	Balance c/f — capital	4,000
				— interest	1,100
		12,200			12,200

However, the interest element of the transaction needs further consideration. The sale at cash price has been contracted but the interest is a reward to the seller for allowing credit. At the end of the first year the interest earned is £1,100. The total interest charged over the two year period is £2,200 but the second year's interest has not yet been earned and the debtor shown in the balance sheet needs to be reduced by this amount of interest as yet unearned.

The best way to deal with this is as follows:-

G. LTD. — HP SALES ACCOUNT

	£Dr		£Cr
Trading A/c — Cash Price	10,000	Debtors	12,200
Interest Suspense A/c	2,200		
	12,200		12,200

The first step is to clear all the interest to a suspense account. This enables it to be sorted out into income recognized and income not yet earned, without cluttering other accounts, thus:-

G. LTD. — HP INTEREST SUSPENSE A/c

	£Dr		£Cr
Trading A/c (1st Yr. Interest)	1,100	HP Sales A/c	2,200
Interest not earned	1,100	(interest element)	
	2,200		2,200

THE BALANCE SHEET EXTRACT FOR G. LTD. would now show:-

CURRENT ASSETS	£	£
Debtors — HP instalments not yet due	5,100	
Less Provision for Interest not yet earned	(1,100)	4,000

Supposing G. Ltd. decided to create a provision for unrealized profit thus:-

$$\frac{\text{Cash to be collected}}{\text{Total Cash Collectable}} \quad \times \quad \text{Total Gross Profit}$$

$$= \quad \frac{5,100}{12,200} \quad \times \quad 4,100 \quad = \quad £1,714$$

DR — TRADING ACCOUNT

CR — PROVISION FOR UNREALIZED PROFIT

The Trading Account would now look like this:-

	£	£
Sales at Cash Prices		10,000
HP interest		1,100
		11,100
LESS COST OF SALES	7,000	
Provision for unrealized profit	1,714	
GROSS PROFIT (taken this period)		2,386

THE BALANCE SHEET EXTRACT AT 31.12.–6
FOR G. LTD.

CURRENT ASSETS	£	£
Debtors — HP instalments not yet due	5,100	
Less Provision for unrealized profit	(1,714)	
		3,386

2. BUYER'S BOOKS — M. LTD.

FIXED ASSET — VEHICLES at Cost

		£Dr			£Cr
1.1.–6	G. Ltd.	10,000			

G. LTD. — CREDITOR

		£Dr			£Cr
1.1.–6	Cash — deposit	2,000	1.1.–6	Fixed Asset — Vehicles	10,000
31.12.–6	Cash Instalments	5,100	31.12.–6	HP Interest	1,100
	Balance c/f	4,000			
		11,100			11,100
31.12.–7	Cash	5,100	1.1.–7	Balance b/f	4,000
			31.12.–6	HP Interest	1,100
		5,100			5,100

HP INTEREST — EXPENSE A/c

		£Dr			£Cr
31.12.–6	G. Ltd.	1,100	31.12.–6	Profit and Loss A/c	1,100
31.12.–7	G. Ltd.	1,100	31.12.–7	Profit and Loss A/c	1,100

Suppose the policy of G. Ltd. was to depreciate motor vehicles at 20% p.a. on cost; the provision for depreciation for the two years would look like this:-

PROVISION FOR DEPRECIATION — VEHICLE A/c

		£Dr			£Cr
31.12.–6	Balance c/f	2,000	31.12.–6	Profit and Loss A/c Depreciation Expense	2,000
31.12.–7	Balance c/f	4,000	1.1.–7	Balance b/f	2,000
			31.12.–7	Profit and Loss A/c Depreciation Expense	2,000
		4,000			4,000

M. LTD. — BALANCE SHEET EXTRACTS

31.12.-6
FIXED ASSET

Motor Vehicles at Cost	10,000
Less Provision for Depreciation	2,000
Net Book Value	8,000
Less owing on HP*	4,000
	4,000

*The amount shown as outstanding at the balance sheet date does not include any interest since it has been paid for the year to 31–12–6 and the interest for the next year is not yet a liability.

FIXED ASSET

Motor Vehicles at Cost	10,000
Less Provision for Depreciation	4,000
Net Book Value	6,000

The asset is fully owned at 31.12.–7. There is no HP liability outstanding.

QUESTIONS

1. Bulwell Aggregates Ltd. wish to expand their transport fleet and have purchased three heavy lorries with a list price of £18,000 each. Robert Bulwell has negotiated hire purchase finance to fund this expansion, and the company has entered into a hire purchase agreement with Granby Garages Plc on the 1st January 19–1. The agreement states that Bulwell Aggregates will pay a deposit of £9,000 on 1st January 19–1, and two annual instalments of £24,000 on 31st December 19–1, 19–2, and a final instalment of £20,391 on 31st December 19–3.

   Interest is to be calculated at 25% on the balance outstanding on 1st January each year and paid on 31st December each year.

   The depreciation policy of Bulwell Aggregates Ltd. is to write off the vehicles over a four-year period using the straight line method and assuming a scrap value of £1,333 for each vehicle at the end of its useful life.

   The cost of the vehicles to Granby Garages is £14,400 each.

   Required:
   (a) Account for the above transactions in the books of Bulwell Aggregates Ltd., showing the entries in the Profit and Loss Account and Balance Sheet for the years 19–1, 19–2, 19–3 and 19–4.

(b) Account for the above transactions in the books of Granby Garages Plc, showing the entries in the Hire Purchase Trading Account for the years 19–1, 19–2, 19–3. This is the only hire purchase transaction undertaken by this company.

Calculations to the nearest £.   [AAT]

2X. Rock commenced business on 1 September 19–3 selling televisions and videos on cash and hire purchase terms. The following summarized trial balance was extracted from his books of account as at 31 August 19–4:

	£ Dr	£ Cr
Bank overdraft		8,475
Capital (cash introduced on 1 September 19–3)		50,000
Cash sales: televisions (600 at £300 each)		180,000
Creditors		121,000
Debtors	1,000	
Drawings	16,000	
Fixed assets at cost	45,000	
Hire purchase debtors: televisions	105,000	
videos	342,000	
Hire purchase sales: televisions (350 at £400 each)		140,000
Hire purchase sales: video (380 at £1,260 each)		478,800
Purchases:		
televisions (1,000 at £150 each)	150,000	
videos (400 at £350 each)	140,000	
Retailing expenses	179,275	
	£978,275	£978,275

Additional information
1. During the year, Rock purchased 1,000 televisions at a cost of £150 each. He sold them either on cash terms for £300 each or on hire purchase. The hire purchase terms were an initial deposit of £100, followed by two annual instalments of £150 each, payable by the customer on the first and second anniversary respectively of the date of purchase of the television.
2. Rock had also purchased 400 videos for £350 each. Although he was prepared to sell them on cash terms (for £1,000 each), all the video sales had been on hire purchase. An initial deposit of £360 was required, followed by two annual instalments of £450 each, payable by the customer on the first and second anniversary respectively of the date of purchase of the video.
3. In the annual accounts, Rock decided to take credit for gross profit on hire purchase sales in accordance with the following policy:
     a)   televisions: to allow for both the ordinary gross profit and hire purchase interest in proportion to the total cash collected from customers sold televisions on hire purchase terms; and

b) videos: to take the ordinary gross profit on videos sold on hire purchase in the year of sale, and to apportion the interest on hire purchase equally over the two years of the agreement.

4. Depreciation is to be provided on fixed assets at 20% per annum on cost.

Required:

(a) Prepare columnar trading, profit and loss accounts for the year to 31 August 19–4, and a balance sheet as at that date, for
   i)   televisions,
   ii) videos, and
   iii) the business as a whole, and a combined profit and loss account for the year to 31 August 19–4.   *(17 marks)*

(b) Prepare a balance sheet as at 31 August 19–4.   *(8 marks)*
          (Total 25 marks)
          [AAT]

3X. RJ commenced business on 1 January 19–8. He sells refrigerators, all of one standard type, on hire purchase terms. The total amount, including interest, payable for each refrigerator, is £300. Customers are required to pay an initial deposit of £60, followed by eight quarterly instalments of £30 each. The cost of each refrigerator to RJ is £200.

The following trial balance was extracted from RJ's books as on 31 December 19–8.

Trial Balance

	£	£
Capital		100,000
Fixed Assets	10,000	
Drawings	4,000	
Bank overdraft		19,600
Creditors		16,600
Purchases	180,000	
Cash collected from customers		76,500
Bank interest	400	
Wages and salaries	12,800	
General expenses	5,500	
	£212,700	£212,700

850 machines were sold on hire-purchase terms during 19–8.

The annual accounts are prepared on the basis of taking credit for profit (including interest) in proportion to the cash collected from customers.

Required:

Prepare the hire purchase trading account, and the profit and loss account for the year 19–8 and balance sheet as on 31 December 19–8. Ignore depreciation of fixed assets. Show your calculations.
          [ICSA]

 **BILLS OF EXCHANGE**
– paper for goods

DEFINITION OF BILLS OF EXCHANGE

The Bills of Exchange Act 1882 defines a bill of exchange as:- "An unconditional order in writing, addressed by one person to another, signed by the person giving it, requiring the person to whom it is addressed to pay on demand, or at a fixed or determinable future time, a sum certain in money to or to the order of, a specified person or to bearer".

EXAMPLE   **SAN FRANCISCO 25/5/1988**

90 days after the above date please pay to my order the sum of One Thousand Pounds sterling for value received.

To: Arnold Limited, London   **Signed: Tony**

The circumstances of the bill may be as follows:-

1) Arnold Limited owe Tony £1,000.

2) Tony is the drawer since he made out the bill and sent it to Arnold Limited.

3) Arnold Limited would write "accepted" on the bill and return it to Tony. Arnold the drawee now becomes the acceptor.

4) Tony no longer has a debt owing by Arnold but a bill of exchange which is negotiable, that is, it may be sold to a third party either at face value or at a discount.

5) Supposing Tony sold it to his bank for £900 the difference £100 would be the discount charge.

6) On August 24th the bank present the bill to Arnold Limited who would pay £1,000; the face value of the bill to the bank.

7) If Arnold did not pay, the bill is said to be dishonoured and the bank would have recourse to Tony who sold it to them. Tony would have to pay the bill.

RETIRED BILLS

Sometimes a bill may be paid before maturity and a rebate is given for early settlement. Alternatively, the bill may be retired and replaced by a new bill taking its place.

Let us now consider the recording of the above transactions, firstly if the bill ran to maturity without negotiation.

DRAWER'S BOOK

ARNOLD LTD. — DEBTOR A/c

		£Dr			£Cr
25 May	Sales	1,000	25 May	Bill Receivable	1,000

BILLS RECEIVABLE A/c — DEBTOR

		£Dr			£Cr
25 May	Arnold Ltd.	1,000	24 August	Bank	1,000

BANK

		£Dr		£Cr
24 August	Bill Receivable	1,000		

ACCEPTOR'S BOOKS

So far as the acceptor is concerned, regardless of whether or not the bill is negotiated, only two things happen:-
1) The debt is acknowledged by acceptance; and
2) It is discharged by payment.

In Arnold Ltd.'s books:-

TONY — CREDITOR

		£Dr			£Cr
25 May	Bills Payable	1,000	25 May	Purchases	1,000

BILLS PAYABLE — CREDITOR

24 August	Bank	1,000	25 May	Tony	1,000

BANK — (ASSET) A/c

		24 August	Bills Payable	1,000

NEGOTIATED BILLS

Now let us consider the drawer's books if the bill is negotiated to a third party. In this case B. Ltd.

ARNOLD LTD.

		£Dr			£Cr
25 May	Sales	1,000	25 May	Bills Receivable	1,000

BILLS RECEIVABLE — DEBTOR

		£Dr			£Cr
25 May	Arnold Ltd.	1,000	27 May	B. Ltd.	1,000

BANK

		£Dr			£Cr
27 May	B. Ltd.	1,000			

DISCOUNTED BILLS

Supposing the bill was discounted, then the entries would be as follows in the books of the drawer – (note: the acceptor's books do not change).

ARNOLD LTD.

		£Dr			£Cr
25 May	Sales	1,000	25 May	Bills Receivable	1,000

BILLS RECEIVABLE

		£Dr			£Cr
25 May	Arnold Ltd.	1,000	26 May	Bank	1,000

BANK

		£Dr			£Cr
26 May	Bills Receivable	1,000	26 May	Discounting Charge	100

DISCOUNTING CHARGES — EXPENSE A/c

		£Dr
26 May	Bank	100

The discounting charges account is a finance expense just like overdraft interest or it may be regarded as similar to a settlement discount.

 **JOINT VENTURE ACCOUNTS**
– a marriage of convenience

DEFINITION

A joint venture is a partnership which may be between two or more sole traders, two or more partnerships, two or more limited companies or between any combination. For example, between a partnership and a limited company. It is formed to undertake a particular trading operation or speculation and its scope is restricted to that particular purpose.

The rights, rewards, duties and obligations of each adventurer (this is what each party to the venture is called) are normally specified in a written agreement between the parties.

LARGE SCALE VENTURES

If the business is on a large scale to warrant the opening of a separate set of books for the venture, then they will be in accordance with normal partnership accounts.

SMALLER VENTURES

Each adventurer will record in his own books the transactions he undertakes on behalf of the joint enterprise.

WHAT ACCOUNTS WOULD EACH ADVENTURER NEED TO MAINTAIN?

Each adventurer would open a Joint Venture Account in his own books. This is a personal account with a co-adventurer(s).

DR — Joint Venture A/c — with payments and charges

CR — Joint Venture A/c — with receipts and other credit items

---

When the venture is completed each adventurer would send a copy of his own account to his co-adventurer.

The separate accounts of each adventurer are then combined into a single Joint Venture Account, which is in effect a Profit and Loss Account for the venture. It will show each adventurer's profit share. Each adventurer would debit his own venture account with his share of the profit, or credit a Loss. The contra entry being in the Joint Venture — Profit and Loss Account.

EXAMPLE

Brown and Dalglish enter into a joint venture to purchase and sell books. They agree that all expenses and profits will be shared equally. Brown buys the books paying £10,000 by cheque. Dalglish gives Brown a cheque for £5,000; his proportion of the cost. Dalglish pays £500 for advertising. Brown pays warehousing charges £200; carriage inwards on books £50; and sundry expenses £5. Brown is allowed £50 to pay office expenses. Dalglish sells 75% of the goods for £10,400 in cash. Brown sells the remainder for £3,200 cash.

You are required to:
Prepare the Joint Venture Account and the appropriate ledger accounts for Brown and Dalglish.

ANSWER TO EXAMPLE QUESTION

Joint Venture A/c in Books — DALGLISH and BROWN

	£	£
Proceeds of Sale		**13,600**
Less Cost of Sales		
Opening Stock	—	
Add Purchases	10,000	
Carriage Inwards	50	
	10,050	
Less Closing Stock	—	
Cost of Goods Sold		(10,050)
GROSS PROFIT		**3,550**
Less Expenses		
Warehousing	200	
Sundry Expenses	5	
Office Expenses	50	
Advertising	500	
		(755)
Net Profit for Venture		2,795
Adventurers' profit share:-		
Brown — ½	1397⁵⁰	
Dalglish — ½	1397⁵⁰	
		2,795

IN BROWN'S BOOKS

Joint Venture with Dalglish

	£Dr		£Cr
Cash — purchase of goods	10,000	Cash received from Dalglish	5,000
Cash — warehouse charge	200	for purchases — ½ share	
Cash — sundry expenses	5	Cash proceeds from Sales	3,200
Cash — carriage expenses	50	**Cash received from Dalglish**	**3,502⁵⁰**
Office allowance	50		
Profit share — ½	1,397⁵⁰		
	11,702⁵⁰		11,702⁵⁰

IN DALGLISH'S BOOKS

Joint Venture with Brown

	£Dr		£Cr
Cash to Brown for	5,000	Cash Proceeds from Sales	10,400
purchases — ½ share			
Cash — Advertising	500		
Profit share — ½	1,397⁵⁰		
Cash paid to Brown	**3,502⁵⁰**		
	10,400		10,400

1. The profit share and the cash transfer between the adventurers are known only after the preparation of the Joint Venture Account.
2. The cash transfer is a balancing figure to clear the account.

SUMMARY

– A joint venture is a partnership between two or more organizations who combine for the purpose of undertaking a particular project. – The scope of the venture is clearly defined normally in a written agreement between the parties.

– Each adventurer would keep a record of payments, charges and receipts within his own book of account.

– Profit shares can only be identified after a single Joint Venture Account has been prepared.

– Having prepared a single Joint Venture Account and ascertained the profit share, this may be included in each adventurer's personal account with his co-adventurer and the balance left on the account can be cleared by means of a cash payment or cash receipt, to or from a co-adventurer.

A SIMPLE SHARE ISSUE
– paper for money?

People may subscribe for shares in a company in return for a 'share of profit'. For example, if the total number of ordinary shares issued by a company is 1,000 and a person subscribes (buys) 100 shares, then that person is entitled to $\frac{100}{1000} \times$ Profit distributed. It should be noted that the profit available for distribution may not be the same amount as that actually distributed. This is because directors may decide to retain a proportion of profit for expansion, to take account of inflation or for some other reason.

IMPORTANT POINTS

1. The company may issue shares to a subscriber in exchange for cash or other assets (e.g. a business — takeovers are sometimes achieved in this way).
2. The payment for shares may be in instalments or in a single payment.
3. The value of shares issued may be at
   a) par (e.g. £1 ordinary shares issued at £1).
   b) a premium (e.g. £1 ordinary shares issued at £1.50).
   Note: Shares are not normally issued at a discount.

ISSUE AT PAR EXAMPLE

1,000 ordinary shares at £1 each issued in exchange for cash or cheque.

The accounting entries are:-

DR — CASH OR BANK A/C	£1,000	
CR — SHARE CAPITAL A/C		£1,000

ISSUE AT A PREMIUM

1,000 ordinary shares at a nominal value of £1 issued in exchange for cash or cheque at £1.50 each share.

The accounting entries are:-

DR — CASH OR BANK A/C	£1,500	
CR — SHARE CAPITAL A/C with value at par		£1,000
— SHARE PREMIUM A/C with the premium		500

Note: a share premium account is a reserve.

AN ISSUE IN EXCHANGE FOR A BUSINESS

1,000 ordinary shares issued at a premium £1 ordinary shares at £2 in exchange for freehold property of another business.

The accounting entries are:-

DR — FIXED ASSET Freehold Property A/c £2,000	
CR — SHARE CAPITAL A/C at par	£1,000
— SHARE PREMIUM A/C reserve	£1,000

AN ISSUE BY INSTALMENTS — EXAMPLE

50,000 ordinary shares having a nominal value of £1 per share, issued at an issue price of £1.50 per share, payable as follows:-

On application	1st May 30p per share
On allotment	1st June 60p per share
On first and final call	1st September 60p per share

Note: payments on 1st June will include the premium.

Supposing there are 76,000 shares applied for and the following scenario took place:-

1. 25,000 shares allotted in full.
2. 50,000 share applications are granted half.
3. 1,000 share applications are refused.
4. 500 applicants did not pay the call and their shares were forfeited on 1st November and resold on 1st December for £2 per share.

STEP 1

An Application Account (Debtor) is opened in respect of potential shareholders, therefore:-

DR — Application A/c £15,000	
(50,000 × £0.30)	
CR — Share Capital	£15,000

STEP 2

More applications than shares available, therefore 76,000 applicants at £0.30 = £22,800 received in cash.

DR — CASH A/C	£22,800	
CR — Application A/c		£22,800

STEP 3

Unsuccessful applicants have their cash returned. 1,000 applicants at £0.30.

DR — Application A/c	£300	
CR — CASH A/C		£300

STEP 4

(a) Applicants for 50,000 shares receive only 50% = 25,000. Therefore, 25,000 × £0.30 must be returned to the applicants in respect of cash paid for the shares they did not get.

DR — Application A/c	£7,500	
CR — CASH A/C		£7,500

(b) Alternatively, the cash could be used to cover part of the sums due on allotment and offset. For example, each successful subscriber has paid £0.30 per share and still owes £1.20 per share. Thus, the 30 pence on the shares not allotted to these applicants could be used to reduce what they owe £1.20 – £0.30 leaving £0.90 to pay. In this case the entries would be:-

DR — Application A/c	£7,500	
CR — Allotment A/c		£7,500

Note: an Allotment A/c is also a Debtor A/c.

STEP 5

Once applications have been granted it is essential to set up another debtors account for monies still receivable. Such an account is called an Allotment Account.

(a) Sums due are 50,000 × £0.60 = £30,000.
(b) Or in the event of 4b above — 25,000 × £0.60 = £15,000
                                                   — 25,000 × £0.30 =   £7,500
                                                                                   £22,500

```
DR  —  Allotment A/c          £30,000
CR  —  Share Capital A/c                    £5,000
    —  Share Premium A/c                   £25,000
```

In case (a) The full amounts would be due

```
Cash A/c              £30,000
Allotment A/c                        £30,000
```

In case (b) Only £22,500 is now due since £7,500 was received earlier.

```
Cash A/c              £22,500
Allotment A/c                        £22,500
```

EITHER WAY AT THIS STAGE THE BALANCE SHEET EXTRACT IS:—

	£
Current Assets	
Cash	45,000
Financed by:	
Share Capital	20,000
(50,000 Ordinary shares of £1)	
40 pence paid	
Share Premium	25,000
	45,000

STEP 6
Set up a CALL A/c which is a debtor a/c. The amounts due on first and final call are 50,000 × £0.60 = £30,000.

```
DR  —  CALL A/c              £30,000
CR  —  Share Capital A/c                   £30,000
```

500 applicants failed to pay the call and forfeited their shares. (500 × £0.60) = £300. Since £30,000 is due, this must mean only £29,700 is received in cash.)

STEP 7
Therefore, the cash received on call would be £29,700 recorded as follows:-

DR — CASH A/C	£29,700	
CR — CALL A/C		£29,700

STEP 8
The forfeited shares can no longer form part of the issued share capital and must be temporarily withdrawn (awaiting re-issue), and taken to a forfeited share account (set up for this purpose) which is a capital reserve.

DR — Share Capital A/c	£500	
CR — Forfeited Shares A/c		£500

STEP 9
The call account may now be cleared by transferring the remaining £300 to the forfeited shares account. This represents the 500 shares at £0.60 which failed to answer the call.

DR — Forfeited Shares A/c	£300	
CR — Call A/c		£300

STEP 10
The forfeited shares are now to be re-issued for £2 each; that is 500 × £2 = £1,000 to be paid in cash on 1st December. To set up the re-issue, 500 £1 nominal value shares must be transferred out of the forfeited share account back to the share capital account.

DR — Forfeited Shares A/c	£500	
CR — Share Capital A/c		£500

STEP 11
The actual cash received for the shares is £1,000. It should, therefore, be noted that the company have now received £2 per share from the new shareholders in addition to £0.90 from the original applicant who failed to pay the final call and forfeited.

The bookkeeping entry dealing with the receipt is:-

DR — CASH A/C	£1,000	
CR — Forfeited Shares A/c		£1,000

STEP 12
The forfeited shares account will now have a debit balance of £700. This balance represents the amount received in excess of the nominal value of the 500 £1 shares. That is:-

$$
\begin{array}{llll}
& & £ & \\
500 \times £0.90 & = & 450 & \text{original applicant} \\
500 \times £0.50 & = & 250* & \text{new shareholder.}
\end{array}
$$

***Note:** in the case of the new applicant it is not 500 × £1 = £500 (i.e. offer price £2 less nominal £1) which is the premium since the first applicant had paid the original premium (£0.50 × 500 = £250) in the £0.90 paid. Therefore, the new applicant is only responsible for the new premium (£2 − £1.50) = £0.50 × 500.

As such, the excess is the same as a share premium and once the shares are sold this balance on the forfeited share account should be transferred to the share premium account, thus:-

DR — Forfeited Shares A/c	£700	
CR — Share Premium A/c		£700

Thus the T Accounts would look like this:-
references in brackets refer to Journal steps.

SHARE CAPITAL ACCOUNT

		£Dr			**£Cr**
Forfeited Shares A/c	(8)	500	Application A/c	(1)	15,000
			Allotment A/c	(5)	5,000
			Call A/c	(6)	30,000
Balance c/f		50,000	Cash A/c	(10)	500
		50,500			50,500

SHARE PREMIUM ACCOUNT (RESERVE)

	£Dr			**£Cr**
		Allotment A/c	(5)	25,000
Balance c/f	25,700	Forfeited Shares A/c	(12)	700
	25,700			25,700

APPLICATION ACCOUNT (DEBTOR)

		£Dr			£Cr
Share Capital A/c	(1)	15,000	Cash A/c	(2)	22,800
Cash A/c	(3)	300			
Cash A/c	(4a)	7,500			
		22,800			22,800

ALLOTMENT ACCOUNT (DEBTOR)

		£Dr		£Cr
Share Premium A/c	(5)	25,000	Cash A/c	30,000
Share Capital A/c	(5)	5,000		
		30,000		30,000

CALL ACCOUNT (DEBTOR)

	£Dr			£Cr
Share Capital A/c	30,000	Cash A/c	(7)	29,700
		Forfeited Share A/c	(9)	300
	30,000			30,000

FORFEITED SHARES ACCOUNT

		£Dr			£Cr
Call A/c	(9)	300	Share Capital A/c	(8)	500
Share Capital A/c	(10)	500	Cash A/c	(11)	1,000
Share Premium A/c	(12)	700			
		1,500			1,500

CASH ACCOUNT

		£Dr			£Cr
Application A/c	(2)	22,800	Application A/c	(3)	300
Allotment A/c	(6)	30,000	Application A/c	(4a)	7,500
Call A/c	(7)	29,700			
Forfeited Shares A/c	(11)	1,000	Balance c/f		75,700
		83,500			83,500

THE FINAL BALANCE SHEET EXTRACT

	£
CURRENT ASSETS	
Cash	75,700
FINANCED BY:	
Share Capital	50,000
(£1 ordinary shares issued) and fully paid	
Share Premium	25,700
	75,700

CONCLUSION

In practice, the application and allotment accounts may be combined as one account. The forfeiture of shares does not often arise nowadays.

QUESTIONS

1. JHP Limited is a company with an authorized share capital of £10,000,000 in ordinary shares of £1 each, of which 6,000,000 shares had been issued and fully paid on 30th June, 19–1.

    The company proposed to make a further issue of 1,000,000 of these £1 shares at a price of £1.40 each, the arrangements for payment being:
    (a) 20p per share payable on application, to be received by 1st July 19–1.
    (b) Allotment to be made on 10th July 19–1, and a further 50p per share (including the premium) to be payable.
    (c) The final call for the balance to be made, and the money received, by 30th April 19–2.

    Applications were received for 3,550,000 shares and were dealt with as follows:
    (i)   Applicants for 50,000 shares received an allotment in full.
    (ii) Applicants for 300,000 shares received an allotment of one share for every two applied for; no money was returned to these applicants, the surplus on application being used to reduce the amount due on allotments.
    (iii) Applicants for 3,200,000 shares received an allotment of one share for every four applied for; the money due on allotment was retained by the company, the excess being returned to the applicants.
    (iv) The money due on final call was received on the due date.

    Required:
    You are required to record these transactions (including cash items) in the journal of JHP Limited.   *(CIMA)*

INTERNAL ACCOUNTS

The trading and profit and loss account produced for internal purposes may be very detailed, showing expenses analysed under various headings. For example, Production, Administration, Selling, Marketing and Distribution and Financial Overheads, and others as appropriate. A company's published report which is presented to the members (shareholders) at a General Meeting and filed with the registrar of companies is a somewhat abbreviated statement prepared in accordance with one of the formats specified in the Companies Act 1985. The formats are given at the end of this chapter.

Let us now look at an example showing firstly how information might be presented for internal distribution and secondly, how the presentation would be modified for publication.

The Trial Balance of A Company Plc
at 31.12.19–6

	£000s Dr	£000s Cr
Purchases	1,000	
Carriage Inwards	56	
Wages and Salaries	94	
Settlement Discounts Allowed	20	
Advertising	30	
Insurance	20	
Carriage Out	72	
Commissions on Sales	35	
Debenture Interest	8	
Rent and Rates	60	
Light and Heat	40	
Repairs and Maintenance	12	
Directors' Salaries	120	
Interim Dividend (2.0p per share paid 30.9.–6)	6	
Fixtures and fittings at Cost	150	
Motor Vehicles at Cost	80	
Trade Debtors	450	
Stock at 1.1.–6	250	
Goodwill at Cost	350	

		1,950
Discount Received		72
Provisions for Depreciation:		
Fixtures and Fittings		85
Motor Vehicles		50
Trade Creditors		190
Share Capital Issued (50p shares)		150
Profit and Loss Reserve		66
Share Premium Reserve		150
Bank overdraft		40
8% Debentures 19–4 to 19–9		100
	2,853	2,853

Notes:
(i) The insurance shown in the trial balance is for the period 1st January 19–6 to 30th April 19–7.
(ii) Accruals are required for wages £6,000; salesman's commissions £5,000 and auditor's remuneration £15,000.
(iii) It is policy to charge depreciation as follows:-
    Fixtures and fittings 10% per annum on cost
    Motor vehicles 20% per annum on the reducing balance basis.
(iv) Stock at 31.12.19–6 is valued at £350,000.
(v) A final dividend was proposed at 5.00p per share.
(vi) Corporation tax on profit for the year is expected to be £70,000.

Let us present the trading and profit and loss account for the year ended 31.12.19–6 for internal use.

A Company Plc Trading and Profit and Loss Account
for the year ended 31.12.19–6

	£000's	£000's	£000's
Sales			1,950
Less Cost of Sales			
Opening Stock (1.1.–6)	250		
Add Purchases	1,000		
Carriage Inwards	56		
		1,306	
Less Closing Stock		(350)	
			956
Gross Profit			994
Less Expenses			
OCCUPANCY COSTS			
Rent and Rates	60		
Insurance (prepaid ¼ × 20 = 5)	15		
Repairs and Maintenance	12		
Light and Heat	40		
Depreciation fixtures and fittings	15		
		142	

ADMINISTRATION COSTS			
Wages and Salaries (94 + 6A)	100		
Directors' remuneration	120		
Auditors' remuneration A	15		
		235	
SELLING AND DISTRIBUTION			
Advertising	30		
Salesmen's Commission (35 + 5A)	40		
Carriage Outwards	72		
Depreciation Motor Vehicles	6		
		148	
FINANCE COSTS			
Discount allowed	20		
Discount received	(72)		
Debenture interest	8		
		(44)	
TOTAL EXPENSES			481
NET PROFIT FROM OPERATIONS			513
Corporation tax (provided)			(70)
NET PROFIT AFTER TAX available to			
ordinary shareholders			443
DIVIDENDS			
— paid (2.00p × 2 × 150,000) =	6		
— proposed (5.00p × 2 × 150,000) =	15		
			(21)
RETAINED PROFIT			422
ADD PROFIT AND LOSS RESERVE			66
TRANSFERRED to			
Profit and Loss Reserve at 31.12.–6			488

Note: A = Accrual

Some points to note with regard to company accounts:

(i)   Directors' remuneration — directors are employees of the company, as such remuneration is an expense to the company in exactly the same way that wages and salaries are an expense for other employees.

(ii) Debenture interest — this is interest payable on a loan and is therefore charged to the company as an expense.

(iii) Corporation tax — all companies are required to pay tax on their profits. Since companies are bodies corporate, the tax is called corporation tax. Tax is not an expense, it is an appropriation of profit. In questions of this nature the tax will normally be given and complex calculations are therefore not normally required.

(iv) Dividends — the owners of a company are its shareholders. They do not have drawings, they receive dividends. It is the directors who decide dividend policy. For example, whether or not a dividend should be declared, if so, how much and when it is to be paid. There might be an interim dividend payment as well as a final payment. The directors recommend what is to be paid and the members of the company (the shareholders) need to approve this recommendation at the AGM.

Dividends are always paid at xp per share.

Dividends are not expenses, they are appropriations of profit.

(v) The discount received although a settlement or cash discount as it is sometimes called was treated as offsetting other finance costs in this case rather than shown as non-trading income and added immediately below gross profit. This is because it was felt to be more appropriate for internal management accounts. The discount allowed was treated as a finance expense rather than a discount for selling — see discounts for further explanations.

PUBLISHED FINANCIAL STATEMENTS

We have now prepared accounts suitable for internal distribution, however, we have not fulfilled the statutory obligation placed upon the company by the Companies Act 1985, which is to produce a profit and loss account and balance sheet in accordance with one of the prescribed formats. To satisfy this requirement, we now need to aggregate certain figures so that we can present a published statement in accordance with format 1. Note: there are actually 4 formats laid down in the Companies Act, all of which are equally acceptable.

Format 1 — Profit and Loss Statement is:
1. Turnover
2. Cost of Sales
3. Gross Profit or Loss
4. Distribution Costs
5. Administrative Expenses
6. Other Operating Income
7. Income from Shares in Group Companies
8. Income from Shares in Related Companies
9. Income from Other Fixed Asset Investments
10. Other interest receivable and similar income
11. Amounts written off investments
12. Interest payable and similar charges
13. Tax on profit or loss of ordinary activities
14. Profit or loss on ordinary activities after taxation
15. Extraordinary income
16. Extraordinary charges
17. Extraordinary profit or loss
18. Tax on extraordinary profit or loss
19. Other taxes not shown under the above items
20. Profit or loss for the financial year.

Using the information we already have, we do not need figures for 6 to 11 inclusive nor for items 15 to 19 inclusive, since this company does not have any of those items to account for. We do need to aggregate in order to obtain items 2, 4 and 5.

The Act gives no guidance as to what should be included under each heading, some accountants would include selling costs within distribution costs, others may not. For the purposes of this exercise we will assume the following:-

(i)   Insurance in respect of the Administration Offices amounts to 30% of the total charge; the shop areas 20% and motor vehicles 50%.

(ii) The book value of motor vehicles used by the salesforce is £10,000, the other vehicles are used for distribution.

(iii) Of the total repairs and maintenance expenditure £7,000 is in respect of shop premises and the remainder, offices.

(iv) Light and heat is ¾ shops; ¼ offices.

(v)   Depreciation of fixtures and fittings is all in respect of shop premises. Details necessary for motor vehicle allocation are given in Note (ii) above.

(vi) Rent and rates for administrative offices amounted to £10,000 and £50,000 for shops.

Analysis of Costs for Publication

	£000's Cost of Sales	£000's Distribution Costs	£000's Administration Costs
Purchases	1,000		
Stock Adjustment	(100)		
Carriage Inwards	56		
Discounts net	(52)		
Wages and Salaries	100		
Advertising	30		
Insurance	5.5	5	4.5
Carriage Outwards		72	
Sales Commission	40		
Rent and Rates	50		10
Light and Heat	30		10
Directors' Remuneration			120
Repairs and Maintenance	7		5
Auditors' Remuneration			15
Depreciation			
— Fixtures and fittings	15		
— Motor Vehicles	2	4	
	1,183.5	81	164.5

**A Company Plc — Trading and Profit and Loss Account
for the year end 31.12.19-6** (in accordance with
format 1 C.A.1985 — suitable for publication)

		£000's
1	TURNOVER	1,950.0
2	COST OF SALES	(1,183.5)
3	GROSS PROFIT	766.5
4	DISTRIBUTION COSTS	(81.0)
5	ADMINISTRATIVE EXPENSES	(164.5)
12	DEBENTURE INTEREST PAYABLE	(8.0)
13	TAX ON PROFIT OF ORDINARY ACTIVITIES	(70.0)
14	PROFIT ON ORDINARY ACTIVITIES AFTER TAX	443.0
20	PROFIT FOR THE FINANCIAL YEAR	443.0
	UNDISTRIBUTED PROFIT FROM PREVIOUS YEAR	66.0
	DIVIDENDS PAID AND PROPOSED	(21.0)
	UNDISTRIBUTED PROFITS CARRIED FORWARD	488.0

THE FINAL ACCOUNTS OF LIMITED COMPANIES: BALANCE SHEETS

The Companies Act 1985 sets out two formats for the balance sheet, one vertical and one horizontal. In this text we have chosen to show the vertical style format since this is the most widely used in the U.K. For examination purposes the vertical format is the most appropriate.

Balance Sheet – Format 1

		£000's		
		£	£	£
A	CALLED UP SHARE CAPITAL NOT PAID*			X
B	FIXED ASSETS			
I	Intangible assets			
	1 Development costs	X		
	2 Concessions, patents, licences, trade marks and similar rights and assets	X		
	3 Goodwill	X		
	4 Payments on account	X	X	
II	Tangible assets			
	1 Land and buildings	X		
	2 Plant and machinery	X		
	3 Fixtures, fittings, tools and equipment	X		
	4 Payments on account and assets in course of construction	X	X	
III	Investments			
	1 Shares in group companies	X		
	2 Loans to group companies	X		
	3 Shares in related companies	X		
	4 Loans to related companies	X		
	5 Other investments other than loans	X		
	6 Other loans	X		
	7 Own shares	X	X	X
C	CURRENT ASSETS			
I	Stock			
	1 Raw materials and consumables	X		
	2 Work in progress	X		
	3 Finished goods and goods for resale	X		
	4 Payments on account	X	X	
II	Debtors			
	1 Trade debtors	X		
	2 Amounts owed by group companies	X		
	3 Amounts owed by related companies	X		
	4 Other debtors	X		
	5 Called up share capital not paid*	–		
	6 Prepayments and accrued income**	–	X	
III	Investments			
	1 Shares in group companies	X		
	2 Own shares	X		
	3 Other investments	X		

			X	
IV	Cash at Bank and in Hand		X	
			X	
D	PREPAYMENTS AND ACCRUED INCOME**		X	
			X	
E	CREDITORS AMOUNTS FALLING DUE WITHIN ONE YEAR			
	1 Debenture loans	X		
	2 Bank loans and overdrafts	X		
	3 Payments received on account	X		
	4 Trade creditors	X		
	5 Bills of exchange payable	X		
	6 Amounts owed to group companies	X		
	7 Amounts owed to related companies	X		
	8 Other creditors including taxation and social security	X		
	9 Accruals and deferred income***	–	X	
F	NET CURRENT ASSETS (LIABILITIES)			X
G	TOTAL ASSETS LESS CURRENT LIABILITIES			X
H	CREDITORS AMOUNTS FALLING DUE AFTER MORE THAN ONE YEAR			
	1 Debenture loans	X		
	2 Bank loans and overdrafts	X		
	3 Payments received on account	X		
	4 Trade creditors	X		
	5 Bills of exchange payable	X		
	6 Amounts owed to group companies	X		
	7 Amounts owed to related companies	X		
	8 Other creditors including taxation and social security	X		
	9 Accruals and deferred income***	–	X	
I	PROVISIONS FOR LIABILITIES AND CHARGES			
	1 Pensions and similar obligations	X		
	2 Taxation, including deferred taxation	X		
	3 Other provisions	X	X	
J	ACCRUALS AND DEFERRED INCOME***		X	X
				X
K	CAPITAL AND RESERVES			
I	Called up share capital			X
II	Share premium account			X
III	Revaluation reserve			X
	1 Capital redemption reserve	X		
	2 Reserve for own shares	X		
	3 Reserves provided for by the articles of association	X		
	4 Other reserves	X		X
V	PROFIT AND LOSS ACCOUNT			X
				X

(*); (**); (***) These items may be shown in either of the two positions indicated.

Format 2 — Type of Expenditure Format

		£	£	£
1.	Turnover			X
2.	Change in stocks of finished goods and in work in progress			(X)
3.	Own work capitalised*			X
4.	Other operating income			X
				X
5.	(a) Raw materials and consumables	X		
	(b) Other external charges and overheads	X		
			X	
6.	Staff costs:			
	(a) Wages and salaries	X		
	(b) Social security costs	X		
	(c) Other pension costs	X		
			X	
7.	(a) Depreciation and other amounts written off tangible and intangible fixed assets	X		
	(b) Exceptional amounts written off current assets	X		
			X	
8.	Other operating charges		X	
				(X)
				X
9.	Income from shares in group companies		X	
10.	Income from shares in related companies		X	
11.	Income from other fixed asset investments		X	
12.	Other interest receivable and similar income		X	
				X
				X
13.	Amounts written off investments		X	
14.	Interest payable and similar charges		X	
				(X)
	Profit or loss on ordinary activities before taxation			X
15.	Tax on profit (or loss) on ordinary activities			(X)
16.	Profit (or loss) on ordinary activities after taxation			X
17.	Extraordinary income		X	
18.	Extraordinary charges		(X)	
19.	Extraordinary profit (or loss)		X	
20.	Tax on extraordinary profit (or loss)		(X)	
				X
				X
21.	Other taxes not shown under the above items			(X)
22.	Profit (or loss) for the financial year			X
	Dividends paid and proposed			(X)
	Transfers to (from) reserves			(X)
	Retained profit (or loss) for the financial year			£X

*Own work capitalised represents the amount of work or costs which are incurred in producing a product which is to be treated as a fixed asset.

BUDGETING — AN INTRODUCTION
– Forecasting, Planning and Control

DEFINITION

A budget is a plan or a forecast expressed in financial terms. It is normally for a definite period of time, e.g. most organizations will prepare an annual budget which will normally be split down into smaller control periods – say one month. To prepare a budget for a longer period than one year is probably unrealistic since so many variables will change. For example, the range of products sold, distribution areas covered, price, output and cost. Planning for a period longer than 12 months is more the province of the corporate plan, which is designed to give management an indication of the longer term direction of the business.

FIXED OR FLEXED BUDGETS

Budgets may be either fixed or flexed. A fixed budget is set at the start of the budget period and is unable to be adapted to changes in volume or price. A flexed budget on the other hand is adjusted for volume and price as or when necessary.

ZERO BASED BUDGETING

Another technique of budgeting developed by the Canadians during the 1960s and used extensively throughout the U.S.A. is zero based budgeting. The organization will begin its estimations for each category of expense from a zero base, unlike ordinary budgets which usually start their estimate from a previous year's actual expenditure and increase it by a set percentage.

THE BUDGETING PROCESS

An organization will normally have a member of the accounting department acting as budget officer. His job is to make the individual managers, who are responsible for particular budget areas, aware of these responsibilities, for example, if variances between actual and budgeted figures do exist then they will be expected to take responsibility by giving explanations and, more importantly, by taking action to ensure budgetary control is maintained for future periods. An organization will normally have a number of sub budgets. It will begin by the Sales Director compiling forecast sales figures in value and volume terms, and possibly by geographical area, demographical area and by product. Having compiled the sales budget and returned it to the budget officer, the rest of the budgeting process may begin. Production budget will be the next area of responsibility; this will encompass the stores. The major objective of the production budget is to ensure that the sales output targets can be realistically achieved given product capacity. Scheduling of production is important, for example it may be that to hit peak demand during the summer months the factory will need to produce goods regularly during winter and spring and store them. Furthermore, co-operation is essential in setting a budget since what the production department can purchase will be dependent on the available resources, therefore having stated what they need to maintain sales targets, this information will be used by the budget officer for the cash flow budget he will construct. He will then need to co-ordinate the other sub budgets, i.e. administration department expenses, sales, marketing and distribution expenses and so on, in order to compile the finance costs, for example if the cash flow forecast produced negative figures for any month it means that some kind of finance needs to be obtained. It might simply mean a bank overdraft, it might mean a loan, an issue of debentures or a further subscription of capital – whatever the alternative chosen, the cost implication must be built into the overall budget.

THE MASTER BUDGET

When all the budgets are co-ordinated by the budget officer, the outcome is normally called a master budget. A master budget will have a budgeted profit statement, a budgeted balance sheet, a budgeted cash flow statement and possibly a forecast statement of source and application of funds statement prepared for the period in question.

THE CAPITAL EXPENDITURE BUDGET

The one thing not mentioned so far is the capital expenditure budget. As well as expenditure on revenue items during the budget period the business may decide to buy new plant and machinery, premises etc. The requirements for new plant and machinery will be obtained from the production manager, who may also decide to prepare an efficiency usage budget.

MOTIVATION

A good budget, i.e. a realistic budget, will act as a motivator to the managers responsible to achieve the targets. A badly constructed budget that no-one believes in will simply act as a de-motivator. There must be co-operation between the different areas of responsibility, for example, it might help the production department if the sales and marketing department could give an estimate of expected demand prior to the commencement of the production budget. Co-ordination is therefore essential.

Targets must be realistically set, that is they must be achievable, otherwise as previously suggested, budgets may become a demotivator rather than an incentive for management and the advantages which budgetary control might yield will be eroded.

THE BUDGET PERIOD

In most businesses the budget period is for one year and it normally coincides with the financial year of the business. There is no reason, however, why the budget period could not be shorter, for example, cash budgets may often be preferred for three month or six month periods. A crucial factor is that a specific period of time is chosen, which is most suitable to the business in question. Budgets which are drawn up for a period longer than one year may tend to lose impact and deviate from their original objective, because the time period is too long to estimate activities with accuracy. For example, variances may be due to:-

Internal Factors
1. The organization may change.
2. Productive capacity may change owing to the purchase of new plant etc.
3. Sales and Marketing policy may become more effective thus penetrating new markets or by increasing market share.
4. Other personnel may become more or less effective.
5. Constraints originally imposed when the budget was set, may have been removed, e.g. shortage of capital for expansion.

External Factors
1. Market conditions may change.
2. Government policy with regard to the industry or the particular type of business may also change, e.g. increased or reduced taxation, legislation and general attitude.
3. Inflation.

These lists are not exhaustive but rather they give an indication of the considerations to be made when budgets are formulated, and furthermore show why longer periods than one year are difficult to plan for. Nevertheless most businesses of medium or large size will tend to plan for a period of 5 years. This is often referred to as the corporate plan. The annual budget will be only one component in that plan.

The corporate plan is designed to focus attention on the longer term direction. It may therefore be regarded as a policy document or as an executive plan, rather than an operational plan which is what the budget is.

THE BUDGET MANUAL

Many firms will lay down their budget procedures which may include:-

1. Allocating areas of responsibility to job holders.
2. Specifying procedures to be followed.
3. Defining the authority and responsibility of particular personnel with regard to the target set in process.

This manual formalizes the budgeting process and makes it clear what is expected of various staff in the budget setting process.

LIMITING FACTORS

There may be a principal budgeting factor which will determine the overall levels of activity shown in the plan, e.g. if a firm makes several products, it may only be possible to make more of one product at the expense of foregoing production of another product. That is to say, there is an opportunity cost. This may be due to a shortage of capital, or of a particular type of labour, or of a particular type of machine availability, or a scarcity of materials. Providing you can identify the limiting factors you can take account of them in the plan. Linear programming is a mathematical technique which is able to assist management in this area.

It is important for management to know what effect the limiting factor will have upon other areas of the business and hence on the overall plan.

The limiting factor may also be external, such as limited demand for the product or a limited supply of essential material.

TYPES OF BUDGET

The master budget, which is the overall plan for the business, will be made up from a number of subsidiary budgets which may include the following:-
1. The Sales Budget.
2. The Production Budget.
3. Various Departmental Budgets or Functional Budgets, e.g. administration, personnel and management services, research and development etc.
4. Capital Expenditure, i.e. proposed new investment which will take place over the next new budget period.
5. Cash budget.
6. Plant utilisation budget.

Having defined the budget areas which yield sources of revenue and incur expenditure, business needs to combine them to formulate the overall plan, i.e. the Master Budget.

SALES BUDGET

It will be the responsibility of the Sales and Marketing director to provide a forecast of sales by product and perhaps by area in conjunction with a responsible officer from the accounting department who has overall responsibility for co-ordinating the budget. Some businesses will have a Budget Committee responsible for preparation and co-ordination of budgets. The committee should comprise the Chief Executive and functional heads or delegated officers and have a Budget Officer nominated to administer the budget programme.

At the outset it is important to establish with each target setter that he is responsible for achiving the target set. This will have the effect of dampening any over-enthusiastic, over-optimistic target setter. In formulating the sales and marketing plan, the following factors may be taken into account:–

1. Past trends – by product, by area.
2. Any changes on the horizon, e.g. extra demand due to increased marketing.
3. Any changes in preference or taste by consumers which may result from
   a) General public attitude.
   b) Government action.
   c) Advertising etc.
   d) Changes in H.P. regulations.
4. Competition – substitutes – complementary goods.
5. Changes in population, e.g. age structure or pattern of distribution.
6. Import or export restrictions.
7. Redistribution of income or wealth which gives different sectors of the community more or less spending power.
8. Discount policies and differential pricing, i.e. different customers might buy the same product at different prices.

After thorough analysis of the expected total sales for the budget period in terms of value and volume, most businesses will subdivide the plan further into smaller control periods, e.g. months. Having exploded the aggregate figures to obtain this microanalysis, factors such as seasonal fluctuations, marketing campaigns and so on must be taken into account. These shorter control periods allow for prompt action when variances to the plan occur.

There might be a similar budget summary showing sales by area or sales by salesman if areas differ in size. This would be to analyse the effectiveness of the product by area and the sales and marketing of the product by area. Unacceptable variances could trigger action on the part of management, e.g. if sales dramatically fell below budgetary targets for one particular product in one particular area, management may decide to invoke a substantial marketing campaign for that product in that area. A sales budget is no different than any other budget insofar as it is a useful tool to management to plan and control the business. To be effective the information base on which the plan is set must be good, i.e. relevant, realistic and timely.

A budget summary may also be done by product or area in volume terms as opposed to value. It is also useful to have an analysis of sales by customer and product.

THE PRODUCTION BUDGET

The production manager will be expected to provide this budget. It is based on the details provided by the sales budget and on the expected movement in finished goods stocks. It will detail the quantity of each product to be produced. The inputs such as Direct Materials, Direct Labour, other

Variable Overheads and any allocated fixed overheads (via absorption rate) will be costed to obtain the cost of production. The production manager will have to liaise with the Sales Department, Stores Management and the officer responsible for the budget from the accounts department in order to achieve his objective, budgets cannot be prepared in isolation.

The objective of the Production Manager is to satisfy demand estimated by the Sales Department. This may mean designing a budget that gives a steady throughput of goods. On the other hand, if the business is seasonal it may mean estimating for production periods when output is very low and other periods when the factory is producing a very high quantity.

Once the production budget is completed, stock levels can be estimated for each section of the budget period. Remember, it is the objective of Stores Management to ensure supply and avoid stockouts whilst keeping costs to a minimum. There are a number of techniques available to assist them in these conflicting objectives.

One of the latest techniques is **Material Resource Planning (MRP)** which is now a practical as well as a theoretical proposition, which the advent of microcomputers has made possible. Previously the calculations would have taken too long. There is also the traditional economic order quantity and ABC analysis. The management must co-ordinate all of these techniques which are most appropriate to their needs, within their operational plans. (See Inventory Control).

CAPITAL EXPENDITURE BUDGET

It may be decided at Board level to build a new plant, to buy a new fleet of lorries, to buy new ships, to buy aeroplanes, to buy new machinery, buildings etc. It is necessary to plan the financing of this capital expenditure over a period of years and also take account of the cost in the present budget period, e.g. if loans are to be taken on, what will the cost of the loan be each month, that is, how much cash will be consumed by the new equipment and how will it affect profitability?

PLANT UTILIZATION BUDGET

Once the production budget has been drawn up it will give an indication as to how the plant and machinery within the factory will be utilized, e.g. it may be as a small factory which consists of twelve production lines will not use a particular production line during the budget period whilst another production line will be greatly overloaded, a decision might be made by management to remove the under-utilized line and replace it with a line capable of producing the goods currently manufactured on the over-utilized line. This information therefore could be used as an input to the Capital Expenditure Budget.

OTHER BUDGETS

Similarly, other department heads will need to estimate the cost of providing the services which they provide during the budget period. For example, administration, distribution, research and development etc.

CASH BUDGETS

In the next chapter we look at cash budgets in some detail. Suffice here to summarise the position. Having formulated the budget plans we are in a position to forecast receipts and payments for the budget period and the times at which maximum and minimum cash usages will occur. It is important to prepare a cash budget in order to arrange temporary finance to cover periods when funds flow is below normal so as to ensure that liquidity is maintained. Cash is the life blood of the business and therefore management of this resource is essential to its survival.

THE MASTER BUDGET

After all the sectional budgets have been completed, the overall budget may be co-ordinated by the budgeting officer to give a master budget in the form of a forecast profit statement and a forecast balance sheet at the end of the period. This master budget will be presented to the Board of Directors and senior management for their approval.

BUDGETARY CONTROL

At the start of a budget period each manager with budget responsibility will be given a copy of his budget which is divided into control periods, i.e. weeks and months. This clearly indicates the targets the manager must achieve. At the end of each control period the management accountant will prepare a statement of actual results by categories shown on the budget. As a result variances will be indicated and special attention needs to be paid to those which are unfavourable. This information needs to be timely in order to be effective, significant variance may demand further explanation and it is the role of the management accountant to illicit the appropriate information and explain the results both to the manager concerned and to senior management. Corrective action may then be taken.

MANAGEMENT BY EXCEPTION

In order to avoid too much detail which may be costly in terms of management time given the benefits achieved, it might be more appropriate to report only those matters which deviate significantly from the budget and by implication assume that the other matters not reported are satisfactory. Therefore only the exceptions to the normal rule will be reported.

FIXED BUDGETS

A fixed budget is designed to remain unchanged regardless of the volume of output or turnover attained. Once the budget is approved by the Board targets set will form the basis of comparison with actual results. A fixed budget may be considered unrealistic and therefore unachievable because of this inflexibility. For example, the following matters may significantly alter throughout the budget period and therefore make the set target inappropriate:

1. If the volume of output changes so too will variable costs.
2. If the volume of output changes so too will turnover.

Thus these matters will affect the sales, production, plant utilisation, cash and may also affect capital expenditure and other functional budgets.

FLEXIBLE BUDGETS

A flexible budget is designed to recognise the difference in behaviour between fixed and variable costs in relation to changes of output or turnover. The budget will therefore be amended each control period in line with the level of current activity.

SELF-CHECK QUESTION

(a)   Explain what is meant by the terms 'fixed budget' and 'flexible budget' and state the main objective of preparing flexible budgets.

(5 marks)

(b)   (i)   Prepare a flexible budget for 19–6 for the overhead expenses of a production department at the activity levels of 80%, 90% and 100%, using the information listed below.

(12 marks)

1. The direct labour hourly rate is expected to be £3.75.
2. 100% activity represents 60,000 direct labour hours.
3. Variable costs:

Indirect labour	£0.75 per direct labour hour
Consumable supplies	£0.375 per direct labour hour
Canteen and other welfare services	6% of direct **and** indirect labour costs

4. Semi-variable costs are expected to correlate with the direct labour hours in the same manner as for the last five years which was:

Year	Direct labour hours		Semi-variable costs £	
19–1	64,000		20,800	
19–2	59,000		19,800	
19–3	53,000		18,600	
19–4	49,000		17,800	
19–5	40,000	(estimate)	16,000	(estimate)

5. Fixed costs:

	£
Depreciation	18,000
Maintenance	10,000
Insurance	4,000
Rates	15,000
Management salaries	25,000

6. Inflation is to be ignored.

(ii) Calculate the budget cost allowance for 19–6 assuming that 57,000 direct labour hours are worked.   *(3 marks)*
(Total 20 marks)
(CIMA)

QUESTIONS

1X. R. Limited manufactures three products: A, B and C.
You are required:
(a) using the information given below, to prepare budgets for the month of January for:
(i)   sales in quantity and value, including total value;
(ii) production quantities;
(iii) material usage in quantities;
(iv) material purchases in quantity and value, including total value;
(N.B. Particular attention should be paid to your layout of the budgets.)

(b) to explain the term principal budget factor and state what it was assumed to be in (a) of this question.

Data for preparation of January budgets
Sales:

Product	Quantity	Price each £
A	1,000	100
B	2,000	120
C	1,500	140

Materials used in the company's products are:

Material	M1	M2	M3
Unit cost	£4	£6	£9
Quantities used in:	units	units	units
Product: A	4	2	–
B	3	3	2
C	2	1	1

Finished stocks:

Product	A	B	C
Quantities			
1st January	1,000	1,500	500
31st January	1,100	1,650	550
Material stocks:	M1	M2	M3
	units	units	units
1st January	26,000	20,000	12,000
31st January	31,200	24,000	14,400

(20 marks)
(CIMA)

2. Outline
    (a) the objectives of budgetary planning and control systems.
        (7 marks)
    (b) the organisation required for the preparation of a master budget.
        (10 marks)
        (Total 17 marks)
        (ACCA)

3. In the preparation of budgets it is important to separate controllable costs from non-controllable costs.
    (a) Distinguish between
        (i) controllable costs, and
        (ii) non-controllable costs.   *(6 marks)*
    (b) Sketch a Budget Statement, which is to be presented on a monthly basis, for a small workshop, showing four controllable costs and four non-controllable costs.   *(8 marks)*
    (c) Outline the duties of a Budget Committee.   *(8 marks)*
        (Total 22 marks)
        (AAT)

COST CONTROL
– the essentials for managing the business

WHY RECORD COSTS?

A primary function of cost data is to enable control of the costing units of an enterprise. To analyse a costing unit's performance effectively, it is necessary to know the costs which the unit is responsible for. Accountants need to develop reporting systems which reflect cost behaviour according to responsibility so as to Plan, Control and Direct the business.

COST CENTRES

Costing units are often referred to as COST CENTRES. Often the variable costs of the cost centre are considered to be the major controllable costs. Nevertheless, several fixed and semi-fixed costs may be controllable, especially if the levels of these costs can be influenced by decisions made in the current time period (examples are some selling and marketing overheads, some administration costs, some factory overheads such as indirect labour and some finance overheads such as interest on an overdraft).

CONTROLLABLE AND NON-CONTROLLABLE COSTS

Some costs are within the control of managers having responsibility for a function, product or process usually called a 'Cost Centre'. Some costs in the managers area of responsibility may be outside of his control but may be influenced by a manger in another area. For example, a Production Manager may have responsibility for production and output of the unit but his output may be influenced by the quality of materials supplied as input to the unit for which the Purchasing Manager has responsibility. Controllable costs are usually seen to be variable costs since they are direct costs changing with output. This is because this type of cost has immediate results for cost savings if we reduce a direct cost of production whereas fixed costs by their nature remain fixed for specific time periods and are not affected by changes in output. Ultimately all costs within an enterprise fall within someone's control even if only to a limited extent. For example, somebody has to take decisions on what to spend money and when to spend it. Take the case of fixed overheads in relation to rental of premises; it was someone's decision in the organization to commit the business to the spend for a fixed time period. If we extend time horizons all costs are controllable even long-term investment plans. However, when we think in terms of controllable and non-controllable costs we are normally referring to operational cost control and the time period is shorter, usually one year (the current financial period), or for savings to be effected over two to three years.

Below I have listed some examples of costs which I consider could fall within the heading of controllable cost:

CONTROLLABLE COSTS: Ineffective time down to managers having cost implications could include the following items:

- Excessive Product Variety in final product or components used.
- Lack of standardisation
- Design changes
- Bad Planning
- Lack of co-ordination and control
- Shortage of materials
- Plant breakdown
- Shortage of tooling
- Incorrect tooling / bastardised equipment
- Tools, plant, machinery in bad condition
- Bad working conditions
- Accidents (Excessive number)
- Scrap (Excessive)
- Waste (Excessive)
- Absenteeism
- Lateness
- Idleness
- Careless work
- Accidents

COST REDUCTION

In order to reduce costs and know the effect of cost reduction on the bottom line (Profit position) you need to know how costs behave in the organization.

COST ELEMENTS: There are certain elements of costs which are common to all organizations which can be classified as follows:

Direct Costs = Variable Costs = Marginal Costs = Product Costs

MATERIALS + LABOUR + ANY DIRECT EXPENSES

Direct Costs are those costs which change directly as a result of changes in output.

Indirect Costs = Fixed Costs = Overhead Costs = Period Costs

Indirect Costs are those costs which do not change owing to changes in output.

Thus Materials, Labour and Overheads are the elements of cost.

PRODUCT COSTS: These are the direct costs which change as the units of output increase or reduce. Direct Materials to make each unit + Direct Labour Costs incurred as a result of making each extra unit together with any expenses which can be directly traced to the product form the total direct costs of production which are often referred to as PRIME COSTS OF PRODUCTION.

PERIOD COSTS: Are the costs incurred by the organization which are not directly related or traceable to the product. They are time based costs incurred for particular time periods. For example: Rent and Rates for premises are time based and not dependent on units of product produced. Other time based costs would include such things as: Salaries; Depreciation; Bank Charges; Loan Interest; Non-Product Labour Costs etc.

PRODUCT OR PERIOD COST?

In differentiating between period and product costs it is important to recognize the nature of the business. For example, a leasing cost could ordinarily be classified as a period cost. If, however, the lease cost was incurred for a specific job or contract undertaken it would then be treated as a direct cost for that particular job or contract (i.e. unit of output).

ABSORPTION COSTING

Period costs need to be recovered in the products that have been produced in the period and this is achieved by absorbing overheads into a product based upon some reasonable estimate of time and usage of the particular overhead to be attributed to the product cost. This is known as "Absorption Costing".

There are many ways to apportion overheads. For example, overheads incurred in respect of premises for say light and heat may be apportioned according to the floor area. If one production unit took up 60% of the floor space and the remainder was taken up by another unit then it would seem reasonable to apportion the overheads for light and heat in the ratio 60 : 40. The cost of overheads incurred by plant & machinery could be apportioned according to the Net Book Values of the machinery. A service such as a canteen could apportion its overheads to user departments based upon the number of people in each user department using the facility.

ABSORPTION RATES:

There are a number of common ways to recover overheads for a particular job, contract or process which include:

   % Direct Labour or £ per direct labour hour
   % Direct Materials or £ per unit of direct material consumed
      The cost unit bases (overhead cost / number of units)
   % Prime Cost of Production

SEMI-VARIABLE OR SEMI-FIXED COSTS:

Some costs do not fit easily into either category of fixed or variable cost but rather are a mixture having part fixed and part variable. For example, an expense having a standing charge (fixed by period) for rental of equipment and a usage charge for the number of units of service consumed (variable cost) such as: Gas; Electricity; Water; Telephone etc.

STEP-VARIABLE COSTS:

Some costs remain fixed for given time periods or up to a certain level of output but then as the scale changes further fixed costs need to be incurred to produce more. For example, one machine might cost $100,000 and be capable of producing 100,000 units in a year. To produce 100,001 units might require an additional fixed cost of $100,000 to acquire a new machine.

COST EFFECTIVE:

Being cost effective is not purely about cost reduction but it is about reducing costs by obtaining better value for money. If you can reduce the cost of a component in manufacture without reducing quality then this is being cost effective. If at the micro-level in production everyone in the organization thinks in terms of obtaining the same quality product from a reduced spend then the cost savings made at the macro-level that is the finished product in total cost could be substantial and increase profitability. For example, if in building an aeroplane savings in costs accrue from materials bought in; from materials being used in the manufacture more effectively; from bought in components; from manufactured components. If more components and more aircraft can be produced in a given time this will reduce the Labour cost element in each unit produced (i.e. increased productivity) then this means that the total cost of producing the aircraft is reduced. If the selling price remains the same it means higher profitability.

Being cost effective can give room for manoeuvre in business. For example, if cost savings are effected it gives opportunities not only to increase profits on each unit but also to negotiate more easily on price if need be. If the business is exposed to external risk, for example by trading in dollar currencies, a U.K. business is subject to risks beyond its direct control and changes in the exchange rate can adversely affect profitability and saleability of a product. By being cost effective, exposure to external risks can to some extent be minimized owing to the flexibility the cost savings allow. It is not suggested that all risk is removed by being cost effective.

A man who knows the cost of everything but the value of nothing is not much use. Remember, it is about maintaining value and reducing cost to increase margins. Increased margins secure the long term future of the business. It therefore makes sense as a shareholder; a manager; a supervisor; a worker; to be cost effective.

ACTION POINTS

What can Management do?

1)   Consider those areas within which costs are incurred which fall directly within your sphere of responsibility and briefly classify the costs into a) Direct Costs; and b) Indirect Costs.

2)   Consider costs which you are able to exercise some control over and list them.

3)   Consider other costs which are not directly controllable by you and try to identify a person who is able to exercise control.

4)   Consider what steps you can take to influence the person identified in 3) above to be more cost effective.

5)   Classify cost savings you have identified as being directly within your control under the following headings:

MATERIALS; MEN; TIME

These are basically the same as the cost elements identified earlier only then we referred to them as: materials; labour and overheads.

COST SAVING AND MANAGERS

CONTROLLABLE COSTS: Ineffective time down to managers could include the following items:

MATERIAL COSTS:
- Use of poor or inferior quality materials
- Unsuitable materials acquired and used in a product or process
- Excessive product variety either in final product or in components
- Failure to standardize product range and components used in the "Bill of Materials"
- Holding excessive quantities of varieties of stocks and work-in-progress
- Lack of standardization in procedures, practice or working methods which gives rise to large variances in the quantities of material used in a product or process
- Design changes not introduced quickly enough or too many changes introduced causing increased costs
- Failure to plan or bad planning in material resourcing: stores, production and procurement
- Failure to co-ordinate and control planned activities in any area of material resourcing
- Material shortages and stock-outs
- Use of incorrect tooling causing material scrap, spoilage and waste
- Excessive scrap
- Excessive waste
- Excessive spoilt work

- Failure to source suitable suppliers to procure the right materials in the right place at the right time and to ensure supplies are not threatened by having alternative suppliers
- Failure to keep abreast of changes in material structures and development of substitute materials which have similar properties to existing materials used but may be available at lower cost
- deterioration / obsolescence / theft of materials

LABOUR COSTS:

- Incorrect grades of labour used on a product or process causing material waste or increased cost through extra time taken or through increased cost of the grade used
- Lateness causing losses in output
- Absenteeism excessive
- Idleness
- Idle time
- Careless work
- Excessive labour turnover
- Excessive spoilt work or low output owing to a failure by managers to identify training needs
- Inadequate or non-existent Manpower Planning and a failure to recruit and retain people with relevant skills and knowledge
- Lost time through accidents which could have been prevented through training or supervision
- Communication failure

TIME LOST:

- Lack of planning and co-ordination
- Material and component shortages
- Poorly organized work areas
- Poor and inadequate storage
- A failure to safeguard assets giving rise to deterioration or theft
- Poor or inadequate training
- Poor or inadequate communication
- Breakdown of plant and machinery
- Lateness, Absenteeism, Accidents and poor supervision etc.
- Bad working: conditions / practices / procedures
- Shortage of suitable tooling
- Incorrect or inadequate tooling
- Tooling / plant / equipment in poor condition
- Failure to invest in new technology, plant and equipment
- Failure to recognize market opportunities giving rise to lost income (Opportunity Cost, as Economists say)

COST OR INVESTMENT?

A strive to reduce costs must not cause a failure to invest in the future of the business. Areas at particular risk in cost cutting exercises are: Training &

Development, Research & Development, Investment in new plant, equipment and technology, Market Research and Product Development. These are the very items which can secure the long term future but which can be cut in the short term with little immediate impact.

An investment is an outlay of money which will yield benefits in the form of a future income stream to the business over a number of years. If an initial cash outlay does not produce an income stream over future time periods as well as the current financial period it is a cost or expense to the business in the current financial period. Note there can be no guarantee that any outlay will produce a future income since the future is uncertain.

COSTS AND THEIR EFFECT UPON PROFITABILITY

Supposing direct costs can be reduced by 5%, the effect upon Gross Profit would be as follows:

	%	% (1)
SALES REVENUE	100	100
COST OF SALES	50	45
GROSS PROFIT	50	55

Direct costs are included in the cost of sales figure and you can see that a 5% reduction in cost of sales has had the effect of increasing the gross profit by 5%. The cost saving will immediately result in increased profits.

Let us look at a further example and assess how we are able to improve the bottom line by increasing selling prices and hence revenue by 5%; reducing direct costs for materials and labour each by 5% and reducing overhead costs by 5% say by reducing discounts allowed on sales:

	% (0)	% (1)
SALES REVENUE	100	105
LESS COST OF SALES		
Direct Materials	25	20
Direct Labour	25	20
GROSS PROFIT	50	65
LESS OVERHEAD EXPENSES	25	20
NET PROFIT	25	45

You can see the dramatic effect of the cost savings and the changed selling price taken together has been to increase profitability by 20% from position (0) to position (1). This represents an increase in profitability of 80% at the "bottom line" 45/25 × 100/1 – 100%. Even if we are unable to change the selling price but could reduce costs by the above percentages it would improve the net profit in position (1) to 40% and as a percentage change on position (0) represents improved profitability of 60%.

CASH BUDGETS
– essential forecasts to keep the business alive

Cash flow is the life blood of the business — without cash, no matter how profitable a business may be, it cannot continue.

Cash is needed to pay suppliers (Trade Creditors) and expenses. It is important therefore to ensure liquidity, that is that the business will have enough cash to meet its liabilities when payments are due. This demands cash planning (or cash budgeting). Cash planning and control will also involve managing the working capital of the business.

WORKING CAPITAL CYCLE

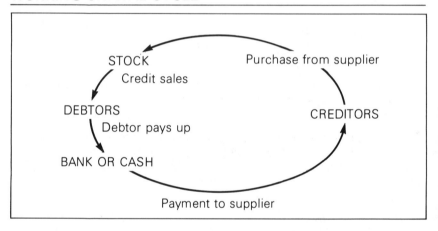

EXAMPLE OF A CASH FLOW FORECAST

Kennedy commences in business with £5,000 of his own money on 1st January 19–6.
He buys a machine for cash £2,000 paid 1st January.
He rents a shop for £4,000 p.a. The rent is payable quarterly in advance commencing 1st January.
He buys stock for resale on credit terms, £3,000 in January, £3,000 in March and £3,000 in May. Payment is made in cash to suppliers one month after purchase, e.g. January paid February. This is called one month in arrears.

The following expenses are incurred and paid in the same month:

Wages   £250 p.m.
Advertising   £300 p.m.

Other expenses: Rates (est.) £80 p.m. Settlement for the whole year is expected by 30th June.

The machinery is to be depreciated on a straight line basis over its estimated useful life of 5 years.

Sales for each of the 6 months:-

January	£3,000
February	£2,000
March	£4,000
April	£3,500
May	£5,000
June	£4,000

Payment is expected from debtors one month after sale.

Gross Margin is 60%, i.e. Gross Profit as a % of sales value is 60%.

KENNEDY — CASH FLOW FORECAST FOR 6 MONTHS TO 30.6.–6

	J	F	M	A	M	J	J
Cash balance b/f	5000	1450^A	900^B	2350^C	1800^D	4750^E	5240^F
Receipts							
Debtors	—	3000	2000	4000	3500	5000	
Others							
— investments							
— capital							
	£5000	£4450	£2900	£6350	£5300	£9750	
	(1)	(3)	(5)	(7)	(9)	(11)	
Payments							
Creditors (stock)	—	3000	—	3000	—	3000	
Rent	1000	—	—	1000	—	—	
Rates	—	—	—	—	—	960	
Advertising	300	300	300	300	300	300	
Wages	250	250	250	250	250	250	
Capital expenditure							
Machinery	2000						
	£3550	£3550	£550	£4550	£550	£4510	
	(2)	(4)	(6)	(8)	(10)	(12)	

The balances to carry forward in cash to the start of the next period are obtained by deducting cash payments from cash receipts.

A	(1) —(2)	=	balance c/f £1450
B	(3) —(4)	=	balance c/f £900
C	(5) —(6)	=	balance c/f £2350
D	(7) —(8)	=	balance c/f £1800
E	(9) —(10)	=	balance c/f £4750
F	(11) —(12)	=	balance c/f £5240

$$\text{MARGIN} = \frac{\text{Gross Profit}}{\text{Sales}} \times \frac{100}{1}$$

Therefore, the Gross Profit is:-

$$= \quad 60\% \text{ (margin)} \times £21500 \text{ (sales)}$$
$$= \quad £12900$$

Cost of Sales = Sales 21500 – Gross Profit 12900
Cost of Sales = 8600

FORECAST
TRADING AND PROFIT AND LOSS ACCOUNT
FOR PERIOD ENDED 6 MONTHS TO 30.6.-6

	£Dr	£Cr
Sales		21,500
Less Cost of sales		8,600
Gross Profit (i.e. Margin 60% of sales)		12,900
Less Expenses		
Rent	2,000	
Rates	480	
Advertising	1,800	
Depreciation	200	
Wages	1,500	
		5,980
Net Profit		£6,920

FORECAST
BALANCE SHEET AS AT 6 MONTHS TO 30.6.-6

	£Cost	£Depn.	£NBV
Fixed Assets			
Machinery	2,000	200	1,800
Current Assets			
Stock	400		
Debtors	4,000		
Prepayments	480		
Cash	5,240		
		10,120	
Less Current Liabilities			
Net Current Assets			10,120
Total Net Assets			11,920
Financed By			
Capital		5,000	
Add Retained Profit		6,920	
Capital Employed			11,920

QUESTIONS

1. **BUDGETS**

During the year to 31.12.–6 the following budgeted information is available.

1. Land and buildings are expected to depreciate £5000, motor vehicles 20% per annum on cost.
2. The following information is available with regard to each of the four quarters.

Sales	Purchases
Quarter 1 = £10,000	Quarter 1 = £8,000
2 = £12,000	2 = £8,000
3 = £12,000	3 = £8,000
4 = £16,000	4 = £8,000

3. Total expenses are expected to be £12,000 paid at £1,000 per month in the month they are incurred.
4. Debtors are expected to pay two months after the date of sale. Sales are to be made evenly throughout the quarter.
5. Creditors are paid two months after the date of purchase. These are also to be made evenly throughout the quarter.

Required:
1. A cash budget for each quarter.
2. Forecast profit statement for the year.
3. Forecast balance sheet as at 31.12.–6.
4. Ratios showing profitability/liquidity.
   Note: the last two years Profit and Loss and Balance Sheet summaries are given below.

BALANCE SHEET SUMMARIES

	19–4 £	19–5 £
Fixed assets		
Land and building	30,000	25,000
Motor vehicles	15,000	12,000
Current assets		
Stock	10,000	7,000
Debtors	9,000	5,000
Cash	1,000	500
Current liabilities		
Creditors	(8,000)	(3,000)
	57,000	46,500

Financed by

Capital	40,000	40,000
Profit	7,000	(2,500)
	47,000	37,500
Loan	10,000	9,000
	57,000	46,500

PROFIT AND LOSS SUMMARISED INFORMATION

	19-4 £	19-5 £
Sales	50,000	50,000
Cost of Sales	35,000	35,000
Gross Profit	15,000	15,000
Net Profit	5,000	(9,500)

2X. The following information relates to XY Limited:

Month	Wages incurred £000	Materials purchases £000	Overhead £000	Sales £000
February	6	20	10	30
March	8	30	12	40
April	10	25	16	60
May	9	35	14	50
June	12	30	18	70
July	10	25	16	60
August	9	25	14	50
September	9	30	14	50

(i) It is expected that the cash balance on 31st May will be £22,000.
(ii) The wages may be assumed to be paid within the month they are incurred.
(iii) It is company policy to pay creditors for materials three months after receipt.
(iv) Debtors are expected to pay two months after delivery.
(v) Included in the overhead figures is £2,000 per month which represents depreciation on two cars and one delivery van.
(vi) There is a one-month delay in paying the overhead expenses.
(vii) 10% of the monthly sales are for cash and 90% are sold on credit.
(viii) A commission of 5% is paid to agents on all the sales on credit but this is not paid until the month following the sales to which it relates; this expense is **not** included in the overhead figures shown.
(ix) It is intended to repay a loan of £25,000 on 30th June.

(x) Delivery is expected in July of a new machine costing £45,000 of which £15,000 will be paid on delivery and £15,000 in each of the following two months.

(xi) Assume that overdraft facilities are available if required.

Required:
You are required to prepare a cash budget for each of the three months of June, July and August.   *(14 marks)*

(b) 'Experts stress that one of the most vital uses of management accounts is regularly to monitor cash flow — moneys coming into the company each month minus moneys going out.'
(Financial Times – 8th March, 1983)

You are required to comment on the above statement and include in your answer the chief benefits obtained from the preparation of cash budgets.   *(6 marks)*
(Total 20 marks) *(CIMA)*

3X. The following information is available:

At 31.12.19–5	£	
Debtors	100,000	(2 months' sales)
Stocks	40,000	(1 month's cost of sales)
Creditors for Material purchases	40,000	(1 month's purchases)

	19–6	
	Period 1	Period 2
Budgeted Sales	£50,000	£50,000

N.B. (i) Purchases for the final period 19–5 amounted to £40,000.
(ii) Cost of sales are entirely materials, and amount to 80% of sales value.

It has been suggested that efficient working capital can improve an organisation's cash flow position, and management reviewing the position at the beginning of January 19–6 propose that the level of debtors, stock and creditors should be changed as follows to take effect immediately, i.e. to be operational for the end of Period 1.

Debtors	—	1 month's sales
Stocks	—	½ month's cost of sales
Creditors	—	2 months' purchases

All sales and purchases are on credit terms.

Required:
(i) Show the cash flows for each of the periods in 19–6 assuming that the proposed levels for debtors, stock and creditors are introduced to be operational for the end of Period 1. *(6 marks)*

(ii) Explain how a reduction in the level of debtors and stocks might be achieved by a business.   *(6 marks)*
(Total 12 marks) [AAT]

COST, VOLUME & PROFIT
– the unknown elements of business

The cost of the product or service you sell will depend on how much of the product or service you sell. For example, intuitively, the less of a product or service you sell then the higher the price you would like to charge in order to achieve a certain level of profitability.

ELASTICITY

However, the higher the price you charge, the less of the product or service you might be able to sell. This idea is what Business Economists refer to as Elasticity of Demand. If the product is highly elastic because it has a large number of substitutes, i.e. products which could satisfy the customer equally well, then a price increase in this type of product would cause a fall in the quantity demanded by the consumer. Products which are highly elastic are those which are sold in very competitive market places (e.g. computer industry). Economists refer to such markets as being perfectly competitive or almost perfectly competitive, since no market is perfectly competitive. If, on the other hand, the product or service is highly inelastic, i.e. does not have many substitutes, then an increase in price will have little effect on the quantity demanded, e.g. monopoly or near monopolies are able to increase price in this way (e.g. electricity).

ECONOMIES OF SCALE

Why is it necessary to charge higher prices for a low volume of output? Well, this is because you are unable to spread your costs especially your FIXED COSTS over a large number of units, thus the cost of each individual unit is increased. Furthermore, because you are only able to buy in small quantities you may not be eligible for discounts which bulk buyers are able to achieve. For example, if you own one High Street clothes shop and you approach a manufacturer to buy 50 or 100 of a particular type of shirt you are unlikely to be able to reduce the price to what Marks & Spencer Plc would be able to achieve buying quantities of, say, 50,000. Thus, because of their scale of operations, Marks & Spencer are able to achieve purchasing economies. Economists refer to this phenomenon as 'Economies of Scale', i.e. economies obtained purely because of the size of the operation. Nevertheless, do not be misled into thinking that the bigger the better, because size has its problems too. The larger an organization becomes might mean it is more difficult to manage and co-ordinate activities and thus 'Diseconomies of Scale' arise. It may be for example because the production operation is too big for one site, you spread production over several sites, some of which are not as efficient as others, thus increasing production costs and distribution costs may also be increased because the production units are spread over a larger area.

SELLING

How will I know what price to charge in order to achieve a satisfactory level of profit and make sure that sales do not slump? It is the market place that determines the price at which goods and services exchange. Nevertheless, you may be able to influence the market by advertising your product and service to the appropriate people in order to inform them of your product or service and also in an attempt to influence them to buy. Therefore, it is not price alone which influences potential customers but other factors such as the preferences and taste of buyers (e.g. quality), the availability of the goods compared with competitors (i.e. delivery dates), and the after-sales service offered, if appropriate. British industry has often been criticised for being too concerned with price competitiveness, and although this is important it may not always be the most important factor.

You should research your market and see what your competitors offer in the way of non-price incentives to buy, such as after-sales service and look at the prices they charge. This will give you some guideline as to the reasonableness of the prices you hope to charge. Also take into account how well established the competitors are in the market place, since it may be more difficult than you think to enter the market. Customers are very conservative creatures, especially in some industries, and as such may be reluctant to change their suppliers even though you offer a better product at a lower price. This is where your advertising campaign is crucial in persuading people that you too are a respectable firm offering a good product at a reasonable price.

FIXED AND VARIABLE COSTS

What about price? Well, before you can say whether or not you are able to sell the product or service at a certain price, you need to know with a high degree of accuracy what your costs are. There are basically two types of cost you need to identify:

1. **Fixed costs** — those which do not vary with output, and
2. **Variable costs** — those which do vary with output.

Fixed Costs are such things as rent, rates, machinery depreciation, (not the running costs), that is costs which do not vary with output over a given period. Of course in the longer term, as John Maynard Keynes (the famous economist) said, all costs are variable. What he meant by this statement was simply that fixed costs themselves may change over a longer time period, e.g. you may increase the size of premises or add to machinery which means that your fixed costs vary with the scale of operation. Nevertheless, it is important to distinguish between costs which vary with output and those which do not. This is because we are then able to identify profitability at different levels of output.

EXAMPLE

Supposing we estimate sales this year to be 100,000 units at 50 pence each selling price. The Fixed Costs we identify as rent, rates and depreciation on machinery, and these total £15,000. In addition, we estimate that in order to achieve our sales target we will incur variable costs (labour, material and other variable costs, e.g. electricity, maintenance on machinery, distribution, sales and marketing etc.) of £35,000. In order to achieve this sales level the plant and machinery in the factory is only working at 50% of its full capacity. What is our expected profit or loss?

INCOME STATEMENT AT 50% CAPACITY

	£
Sales: (100,000 units at 50p)	50,000
Less Variable Costs	35,000
Contribution to fixed overheads	15,000
Less Fixed Costs	15,000
Profit or (Loss)	Nil

Therefore, at 50% capacity given a sales level of £50,000 (100,000 units) and the cost structure indicated we would break even, i.e. no profit, no loss.

How does the cost structure break down?

Selling Price per unit	=	50p
Variable Cost per unit	=	35p
Contribution per unit	=	15p

Fixed costs cannot be allocated in this way since they do not vary with output and if we make one unit we incur £15,000 and if we make 200,000 units we incur £15,000.

Suppose we did try to allocate fixed costs, then the cost breakdown would be:—

Selling Price per unit	=	50p
Variable Cost per unit	=	35p
Contribution	=	15p
Less Fixed Cost per unit	=	15p
Profit per unit	=	Nil

However, supposing we only achieved 40% capacity, i.e. 40% × 200,000 = 80,000 units (this is because 50% = 100,000, therefore 100% = (100,000 × 2) = 200,000 units).

	£
Sales (80,000 × 50p)	40,000
Less variable costs (80,000 × 35p)	28,000
Contribution	12,000
(1) Fixed Overheads (80,000 × 15)	12,000
Profit per unit	Nil

(1) This calculation is, however, fallacious since we have attempted to make fixed costs variable and by so doing we have undercharged the fixed costs by (15,000 — 12,000) = £3,000.

PRICES

If we set our prices on the basis of allocating fixed costs in this way, we might say that 50p was enough to charge because even if we fall 10% below the estimated production level of 50% capacity we would break even. Of course, we know we would not because we have separated fixed and variable costs. In fact at 40% capacity we would make a £3,000 loss.

(100,000 – 80,000) × contribution per unit
i.e. 20,000 units of lost contribution at
15p per unit   =   £3,000

This is because we have failed to cover £3,000 of fixed costs.

If we know for certain that our level of sales was going to be 80,000 units, then if we wanted to break even we would have to either cut costs or increase the selling price. Let us suppose that we could not cut costs, then by how much must the selling price increase?

$$\frac{£3,000}{80,000 \text{ units}}$$ =   3.75p per unit

thus increased contribution   =   3.75p
+ original contribution   =   15.00p
                                                   18.75p

Selling price   =   Variable cost +
                                                   Contribution
thus 53.75p   =   35p + 18.75p

PROFIT

Suppose we wanted to achieve a certain level of profit, say £5,000, then we would need to estimate the selling price as follows:-

$$\frac{\textbf{FIXED COST + VARIABLE COSTS + PROFIT}}{\textbf{VOLUME OF OUTPUT}} = \begin{array}{c}\textbf{Selling}\\\textbf{Price}\end{array}$$

Thus at 40% capacity

$$\text{Variable Cost} = \frac{£15,000 + 28,000 + £5,000}{80,000}$$

$$= \frac{£48,000}{80,000 \text{ units}}$$

$$= 60 \text{ pence per unit}$$

This is because the Selling Price   **(SP)**
is equal to the   Fixed Costs   (FC)
plus the   Variable Costs   (VC)
plus the   Profit   (P)

Therefore   TOTAL SALES   =   FC + VC + P

Therefore   SP   = $\left(\dfrac{FC + VC + P}{No. \, of \, Units}\right)$

(CONTRIBUTION = SP — VC)

Alternatively, supposing we estimated output to be at the 50% level then sales in total would be 100,000 units.

VARIABLE COSTS 100,000 × 35p   =   £35,000
FIXED COSTS UNCHARGED AT   =   £15,000

Therefore: Total Costs   =   FC + VC
                           =   £15,000 + £35,000
                           =   £50,000

Suppose we require a profit of 20% on Total Cost, then profit is 20% × £50,000 = £10,000.

What does the selling price have to be?

$$SP = \frac{FC + VC + P}{UNITS}$$

$$= \frac{35,000 + 15,000 + 10,000}{100,000}$$

$$= \underline{\underline{60p \text{ per unit}}}$$

Thus, the selling price you charge will depend on:—
1. **The level of output achieved.**
2. **Your cost structure.**
3. **The profit you require, and**
4. **What the market will bear.**

NOTE:
(a) If you cannot cover your costs or make a required profitability level because the price you need to charge is too high for the market to bear, then you will have to drop out of the market or if you are not already in, then do not enter.

(b) Other firms may still be able to achieve their objectives in terms of profitability in the same market that you have to withdraw from because they achieve economies of scale which effectively change their cost structure in a favourable way. That is, lower unit costs.

If we know the contribution each unit makes towards our fixed overhead costs then we are able to determine at what point in terms of sales quantity (volume) we will break even.

$$\text{Thus Break Even point} = \frac{\text{FIXED OVERHEAD COSTS}}{\text{CONTRIBUTION PER UNIT}}$$

$$\text{Quantity} = \frac{£15,000}{15p \text{ per unit}}$$

$$\text{Quantity} = \underline{\underline{100,000 \text{ units}}}$$

It should be noted that the underlying assumption in our calculations is that variable costs vary proportionately with output which is fair enough because they will do within limits. Nevertheless, the variable cost per unit may fall beyond a certain output owing to economies of scale being achieved or they may increase beyond a certain point owing to diseconomies of scale.

GRAPHICAL REPRESENTATION

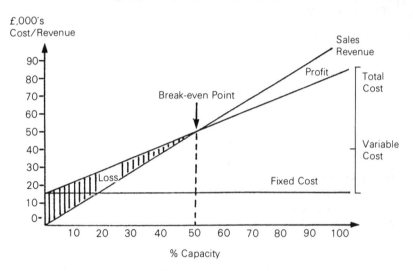

£,000's
Cost/Revenue

% Capacity

Having estimated the level of sales (given cost and selling prices) necessary to break even or give a sufficient return (profit), you need to make decisions with consideration to the available alternatives.

1. Is the Sales Target achievable (given other competitors)?
2. Could I sell more through effective marketing?
3. Is the price right or would I sell more at a lower price, and if so would it increase my total profitability?
4. Is all the effort worth my while or would I be better doing something else?

OPPORTUNITY COST OF THE BUSINESS

This is the alternative you have to forego in order to undertake the business venture in question. For example, if you have been made redundant and decide to open a wine war with your £20,000 in redundancy pay, you are giving up the other things you could invest in or buy with that £20,000. You do, therefore, need to consider very carefully the range of opportunities open to you and this can only be done by collecting as much information as possible about those alternatives. Supposing you went into business with the £20,000 and earned only £2,000 profit in your first year. If you could have invested that money in Local Authority Bonds, a Bank or a Building Society where interest rates were above 10% per annum, you would have been better off. Nevertheless, you may be taking a longer term view, and looking at your investment over a longer 'time frame' in which case you expect your business to grow and become more profitable than the short term opportunities you have foregone. Therefore, the longer term 'opportunity gains' outweigh the short term 'opportunity loss'.

QUESTIONS

1X. The following data relate to a company:

Sales	Delivery costs
£000	£000
80	16
85	11
115	21
160	16
205	23
280	18
290	27
330	32
390	30
450	37
470	25
550	35

You are required to:
(a) (i)   plot these costs on a graph;
    (ii) draw on the graph the 'line of best fit';
    (iii) state the approximate level of fixed costs.   *(15 marks)*
(b) State and explain a formula which may be used for predicting future delivery costs for any level of sales. (**Note:** figures are not required.)   *(5 marks)*
(Total 20 marks)   *(CIMA)*

2X. Explain what you understand is meant by the term 'capacity' in the context of volume and profit relationship.

MARGINAL OR DIRECT COSTING
– planning for profit

DEFINITION

The term 'marginal costing' is borrowed from Economics. The marginal cost is the cost of producing 1 extra unit of output. Owing to this, it is concerned only with variable costs or direct costs, that is, the direct cost for materials, labour and any other direct costs consumed in making the product. Marginal costing is, therefore, a powerful tool for decision making with regard to pricing and output. Regardless of whether you are an advocate of the marginal cost approach or the absorption cost approach, both have their part to play in the costing system.

Marginal costing is extremely useful for short term decisions affecting price and output. It must be remembered, however, that in the longer term, for an organization to remain in business, it must recover its overhead costs.

EXAMPLE

X Limited makes one product. Each unit of product consumes the following direct costs:–

$$\text{Direct Labour } – £2$$
$$\text{Direct Material } – £3$$

The product sells for £15 per unit. The total estimated fixed overheads for the year amount to £100,000. You are required to:–

1. Calculate the contribution for each unit produced.
2. Calculate the break even point for X Ltd.
3. Graph the information on a break-even chart.
4. Show the margin of safety on the chart if 12,000 units are produced.
5. Draw a profit/volume chart.
6. Calculate the profit/volume ratio.

1.

		£
SELLING PRICE PER UNIT		15
LESS DIRECT COSTS		
LABOUR	2	
MATERIAL	3	
		(5)
CONTRIBUTION PER UNIT		10

2. $\dfrac{\text{Fixed Costs}}{\text{Contribution}} = \dfrac{100,000}{10} = 10,000$ units for Break Even

3.

Qty.	Sales Rev	VC	Cont.	FC	Profit
0	0	0	0	100,000	(100,000)
2,000	30,000	10,000	20,000	100,000	(80,000)
4,000	60,000	20,000	40,000	100,000	(60,000)
6,000	90,000	30,000	60,000	100,000	(40,000)
8,000	120,000	90,000	80,000	100,000	(20,000)
10,000	150,000	50,000	100,000	100,000	B/E
12,000	160,000	60,000	120,000	100,000	20,000
14,000	210,000	70,000	140,000	100,000	40,000

4.

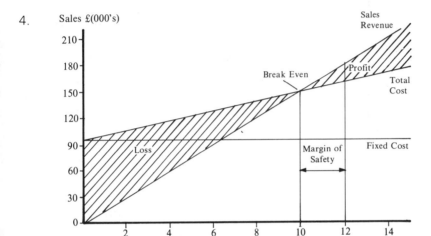

CONTRIBUTION – This is the difference between the selling price and the variable costs. Thus, it is the contribution each unit sold makes towards fixed overheads until break-even point is reached, it then becomes a profit.

5. **PROFIT/VOLUME CHART**

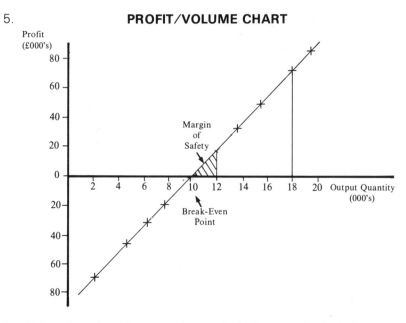

6. Although referred to as the profit/volume ratio it is in fact the contribution/sales ratio.

$$£10 \;:\; £15$$
$$\therefore \text{P/V Ratio} = 2 \;:\; 3 \qquad (\text{P/V \% = } 66\tfrac{2}{3}\%)$$

Every £3 in sales will earn a contribution of £2.

Margins of Safety *may be defined as the difference between budgeted or actual output and the break-even point.*

EXAMPLE QUESTION

A.B.C. Ltd. make one major product which sells for £14 per unit. The fixed costs of A.B.C. Ltd. are £400,000, the direct costs are materials £6 per unit and labour £4 per unit. In the coming year it is estimated that 105,000 units of the product will be sold. The sales director further estimates that sales of the product could be increased by 20% in overseas markets if the selling price was dropped by 40%. Currently 35% of the product is accounted for by overseas trade.

Required:
1. Calculate the contribution per unit.
2. Calculate the break-even point.
3. Graph the information in the form of a break-even chart.

A.B.C. Ltd.

1.

	£
Sales per Unit	14
Less	
Labour 4	
Materials 6	
	(10)
Contribution per Unit	£4

2.

$$\text{Break even} = \frac{\text{Fixed Costs}}{\text{Contribution}} = \frac{400,000}{4} = \underline{100,000}$$

3.

Quantity	Sales Rev.	VC	Contribution	FC	Profit
0	0	0	0	400,000	(400,000)
10,000	140,000	100,000	40,000	400,000	(360,000)
20,000	280,000	200,000	80,000	400,000	(320,000)
30,000	420,000	300,000	120,000	400,000	(280,000)
40,000	560,000	400,000	160,000	400,000	(240,000)
50,000	700,000	500,000	200,000	400,000	(200,000)
60,000	840,000	600,000	240,000	400,000	(160,000)
70,000	980,000	700,000	280,000	400,000	(120,000)
80,000	1,120,000	800,000	320,000	400,000	(80,000)
90,000	1,260,000	900,000	360,000	400,000	(40,000)
100,000	1,400,000	100,000	400,000	400,000	0
110,000	1,540,000	110,000	440,000	400,000	40,000

A.B.C. BREAK EVEN CHART

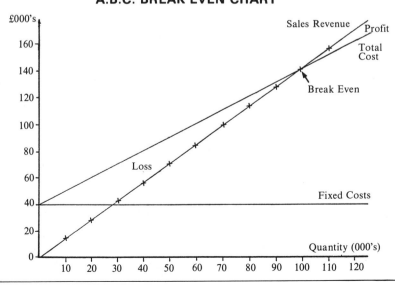

LIMITATIONS OF BREAK EVEN CHARTS

1. Variable costs may not vary in direct proportion to the volume of production or sales. Reasons for this could be:-
   1. Purchasing discounts for greater quantities of direct materials.
   2. Extra direct labour costs may require overtime work.
   3. Short notice material requirements may cost more per unit.

Note: It may still, however, be the case that over time such variations still conform to the 'norm'. That is, that gains and losses in unit costs cancel each other out. Therefore, a straight line relationship still exists. It may, however, be the case that the straight line relationship only holds true within bands.

Scattergraphs could be used to achieve approximations.

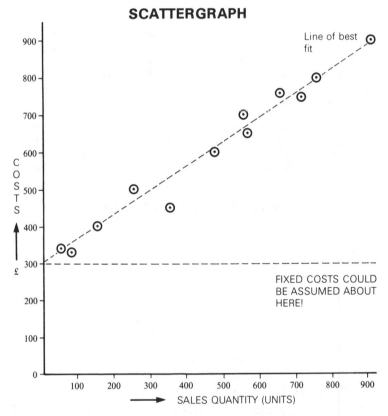

SCATTERGRAPH

Note: A straight line approximation is obtained by plotting points ⊙

2. Sales Revenue would not necessarily increase uniformly with output. To gain additional sales a business might need to give discounts. The Sales Revenue for each unit of output would differ.

3. Multi-product organizations are problematic, since the contribution per unit achieved by each product is likely to be different. A change in the product mix/sales mix by month would invalidate the previous break even chart. Also problems described in 1 and 2 would further complicate matters.

Note: One way round this problem would be to draw a break even chart for each product. The problem then is how to apportion fixed costs by product.

4. Fixed Costs are only fixed within certain limits of output. For example, there may be no need to increase fixed costs in the range from 0 to 100,000 units of output. This range is known as the **RELEVANT RANGE.** If, however, the business needs to produce somewhere between 100,001 units to 200,000 it may require additional machinery, additional storage and warehousing, additional factory space etc. Thus increase in output beyond certain limits could cause an increase in fixed costs.

5. Inflation defined as the changing price level of fixed and variable costs would invalidate the chart, if such changes were frequent.

Break-even charts can still be useful providing that managers are aware of the limitations and take account of them.

CONTRIBUTION AND THE LIMITING FACTOR

It may be that a business is not able to increase its contribution indefinitely owing to a constraint (limiting factor). Limiting factors could be:-
  1. Limited production capacity.
  2. Limited demand for the product.
  3. Limited available labour hours.
  4. Limited available materials.

QUESTIONS

1X. Cagney Ltd make one product which sells currently at £12 per unit. Direct Labour costs £5 per unit and Direct Materials cost £4 per unit. The Fixed Overheads for the year are estimated to be £1,500.

From the above information you are required to:
  1. Calculate the contribution to fixed overheads.   *(2½ marks)*
  2. Calculate the required output to break-even.   *(2½ marks)*
  3. Prepare a budgeted profit statement for the year at an output level of 550 units.   *(5 marks)*
  4. Give the 'margin of safety' at 550 units of output. *(2½ marks)*
  5. Draw a Break-Even Chart which clearly shows:-
     (a) The Break-Even Point.
     (b) The Margin of Safety at 550 units of output.   *(10 marks)*

6. Draw a Profit/Volume Graph which clearly shows:–
    (a) The Break-Even Point.
    (b) The Margin of Safety at 550 units of output.   *(10 marks)*
7. Calculate the Profit/Volume Ratio.   *(2½ marks)*
                                                         (Total 35 marks)
                                                              (Q&A)

2.

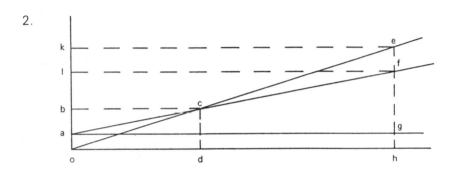

UNITS OF PRODUCT Z

o to h represents budgeted sales units for the period

By the use of the letters in the graph above, identify the point, line or area on the graph which represents each of the following items or quantities.
(i)   sales revenue at any volume.
(ii)   fixed costs at any volume.
(iii) break-even point in £ sales.
(iv)   margin of safety in units.
(v)   budgeted sales revenue.
(vi)   budgeted variable cost, and
(vii) budgeted profit.   *(10 marks)*
                                                              (AAT)

3. A manufacturing company with a single product has the following sales and production results over three financial periods:–

	Period 1 000 units	Period 2 000 units	Period 3 000 units
Sales	50	60	40
Production	70	40	60

The selling price per unit has remained at £10, and direct material and direct labour costs per unit at £5. All manufacturing overheads are absorbed into product cost at predetermined rates per unit of output. Any under/over absorbed balances are transferred to profit and loss in the period in which they arise. Variable manufacturing overhead absorption was predetermined at a rate of £1 per unit in each period.

Fixed manufacturing overheads were expected to be £180,000 per period. Normal capacity is 60,000 units of output per period.

Manufacturing overheads actually incurred were as follows:–

	Period 1 £000's	Period 2 £000's	Period 3 £000's
Variable	68	45	60
Fixed	180	180	180

Assume that no further overheads are incurred (i.e. other than manufacturing overheads).

Required:
(a) Calculate the expected break-even point per period.   *(3 marks)*
(b) Calculate the profit/loss that arose in each of the three periods.
(8 marks)
(c) Reconcile your answers to (a) and (b) above, clearly demonstrating, explaining fully the reasons for, and commenting briefly upon, any differences encountered.   *(11 marks)*
(Total 22 marks)
(ACCA)

4. (a) A company located in the Far East manufactures a digital watch which has a variable cost of $6. It sells to distributors in world markets, and budgets to sell the following quantities at the quoted selling prices in the coming trade period.

	Quantities (thousands)	Selling Price (dollars) $
Asia	500	10
North America	600	12
Western Europe	1,000	13
Africa	400	8

The capacity of the factory is 3 million watches.

The fixed costs for the trading period are $11,400,000.

A marketing exercise has been conducted in South America and it is forecast that a low selling price would enable that market to absorb the surplus production.

Management requires a profit of $1 for each watch sold.

Required:
What is the lowest price at which the surplus production could be sold in South America?   *(18 marks)*

(b) Marginal costing techniques require that all costs be classified as either variable or fixed.

Required:
What problems would arise in making this classification?
What particular constraints would you apply when considering the use
of Marginal costing?   *(10 marks)*
                                                    (Total 28 marks)
                                                          (AAT)

5X. (a) From the following information you are required to construct
         (i)   a break-even chart, showing the break-even point and the
               margin of safety;
         (ii) a chart displaying the contribution level and the profit level;
         (iii) a profit-volume chart.

Sales	6,000 units at £12 unit	=	£72,000
Variable costs	6,000 units at £7 unit	=	£42,000
Fixed costs		=	£20,000

                                                        (9 marks)

    (b) State the purposes of each of the three charts in (a) above.
                                                        (6 marks)

    (c) Outline the limitations of break-even analysis.   *(5 marks)*
    (d) What are the advantages of graphical presentation of financial
         data to executives?   *(2 marks)*
                                                    (Total 22 marks)

MARGINAL AND ABSORPTION COSTING
– A question of overheads and stock values

DIFFERENCE BETWEEN MARGINAL AND ABSORPTION COSTING

In a manufacturing business, we have already seen that costs are built up in the manufacturing account and factory overheads are charged to that account (i.e. Factory Indirect Expenses). This is a full cost system, since all factory overheads are absorbed in the cost of the product. This full (absorption) cost system may be alright for determining profitability in a past period but might lead to a misleading decision about a future project. Let us see why:–

EXAMPLE

Excess Ltd. produce 5,000 units of oil per annum. The costs are made up as follows:

	£
Direct Labour	10,000
Direct Material	5,000
Direct Expenses	1,000
Factory Overheads	10,000
PRODUCTION COST	26,000
Administration Overheads	2,500
Sales & marketing Overheads	2,500
Finance Overheads	1,000
TOTAL COST	32,000

All the units are sold for £10 each   =   £50,000

$$\text{PRODUCTION COSTS per unit} = \frac{£26,000}{5,000 \text{ units}} = £5.20$$

The factory is currently only working at 40% capacity and the Sales Director has been on a trade delegation in Europe to try and increase sales. When he came back he said that a German company were interested in buying 5,000 units if they were offered a discount of 50%, and they would pay carriage to Germany, in view of the large quantity ordered. "This would mean selling each unit at £5," says the Managing Director. "Impossible. If only we could cut our costs to become more competitive, we'd be able to take the order, but as we know, it costs us £5.20 per unit to produce, which means we would lose 20 pence on each unit sold." The accountant tells the two directors that he would like to analyse the costs before making a decision. The other directors agree. Below is an outline of the results he came up with.

	Order Rejected £		Order Accepted £
Sales (5,000 × £10)	50,000	5,000×£10 5,000×£5	75,000
LESS VARIABLE COSTS			
Direct Labour 10,000			
Direct Material 5,000			
Direct Expense 1,000			
	(16,000)		(32,000)
CONTRIBUTION	34,000		43,000
LESS FIXED OVERHEADS	16,000		16,000
NET PROFIT	18,000		27,000

When the figures are presented to the Managing Director, he says, "This is marvellous, it means we can accept the order and we increase our profit by £9,000. How can this be?" At this point the accountant offers a thorough explanation as follows:–

1. We have increased our production to 80% capacity which still allows 20% downtime for maintenance and allows for breakdown. We do not have to incur any further fixed costs. For example, no extra machines need to be bought.

2. Sales would increase by 5,000 units at £5 = £25,000.

3. Some of our costs are variable and will therefore change in line with the number of units produced.

        DIRECT LABOUR   5,000 units × £2 p.u.   =   £10,000
        DIRECT MATERIAL 5,000 units × £1 p.u.   =   £ 5,000
        DIRECT EXPENSES 5,000 units × 20p p.u.   =   £ 1,000

        TOTAL VARIABLE COSTS   £16,000

        Thus INCREASE IN SALES REVENUE   £25,000
        LESS INCREASE IN COSTS   16,000

        INCREASE IN PROFIT   £ 9,000

"Wait a minute," says the Managing Director. "You have not included any costs for Administration, Sales and Marketing, Finance costs or Factory Overheads."

"Well, that is because those costs do not vary with output," says the accountant. "Since most of our overheads consist of people's salaries and wages, it costs us no more, whether we process one order or one thousand.

The same may be said of invoices and finance costs. Furthermore, we don't need extra staff to accept this order, therefore all those costs are fixed."

"Well, that's it then – we accept," says the Managing Director.

TYPES OF COST (FIXED, VARIABLE and SEMI-VARIABLE)

Of course in real life it may be the case that we have fixed costs and variable costs like those described above. We may, however, have other costs which we call semi-variable costs. Semi-variable costs may remain fixed but only within limits.

In our example Excess Ltd. we assumed that variable costs were 100 per cent variable. It may, however, be the case that if production output rose by 100 per cent as in our example, some costs may increase by 100 per cent, e.g. raw material costs, but direct labour incurred on running the machines may not increase at all, especially if the factory is staffed for 100% capacity and is currently only running at 40%. If it doubled to 80% Direct Labour costs may not increase at all, or only increase at a lower rate than 100% variability. That is to say, if it costs £10,000 to produce 5,000 units it may not necessarily cost £20,000 to produce 10,000 units (which 100% variability assumes). It may only cost £12,000, i.e. 20% variability.

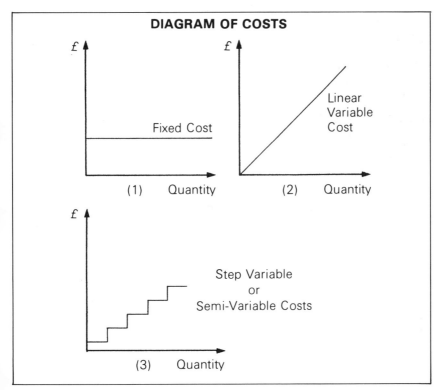

Some costs, like those shown in the diagram, increase in steps and are known as step variable costs. Machine costs may remain fixed up to a certain output but once we exceed that output we may have to use another machine to produce the extra output, thus increasing costs. Labour costs may also be step variable costs.

SUNK COSTS

These are past costs which do not affect a future decision. For example, once a business has bought a machine to produce certain goods the cost is a past cost and should not affect a decision in costing future output.

THE EFFECT ON PROFIT OF MARGINAL AND ABSORPTION VALUATIONS OF INVENTORY

EXAMPLE
1. A firm sells 1,000 units @ £10 per unit each year.
2. Direct Labour costs £3 per unit throughout.
3. Direct Material costs £3 per unit throughout.
4. Fixed Factory Overhead amounts to £4,000 per annum.
5. In year 1 Production is 1200 units.
   In year 2 Production is 1500 units.
   In year 3 Production is 500 units.

REQUIRED:
The Gross Profit for each of the three years on
1. A Marginal Cost basis.
2. An Absorption Cost basis.
3. A brief explanation as to why the two methods give different profit.

EXAMPLE ANSWER

YEAR 1	Marginal Cost		Absorption Cost	
	£		£	
Sales (1000 @ £10)		10,000		10,000
LESS VARIABLE COST				
Direct Labour (1200 @ £3)	3,600		3,600	
Direct Material (1200 @ £3)	3,600		3,600	
Total Variable Cost	7,200		7,200	
LESS CLOSING STOCK (MC)				
$\frac{200}{1200} \times 7200$	1,200			
	6,000			
FACTORY OVERHEAD	4,000	10,000	4,000	
PRODUCTION COST (AC)			11,200	

LESS CLOSING STOCK (AC)

$\dfrac{200}{1200}$ x 11,200   1,867

                                                                             9,333

GROSS PROFIT   NIL   667

YEAR 2	Marginal Cost		Absorption Cost	
	£		£	
Sales (1000@£10)		10,000		10,000
LESS VARIABLE COST				
Direct Labour (1500@£3)	4,500		4,500	
Direct Material (1500@£3)	4,500		4,500	
Total Variable Cost	9,000		9,000	
Add Opening Stock b/f	1,200			
	10,200			
LESS CLOSING STOCK (MC)				
$\dfrac{700}{1500}$ x 9,000	4,200			
	6,000			
Factory Overhead	4,000	10,000	4,000	
Production Cost (AC)			13,000	
Add Opening Stock b/f (AC)			1,867	
			14,867	
LESS CLOSING STOCK (AC)				
$\dfrac{700}{1500}$ x 13,000			6,067	
				8,800
GROSS PROFIT		NIL		1,200

YEAR 3	Marginal Cost		Absorption Cost	
	£		£	
Sales (1000@£10)		10,000		10,000
LESS VARIABLE COST				
Direct Labour (500@£3)	1,500		1,500	
Direct Material (500@£3)	1,500		1,500	
TOTAL VARIABLE COST	3,000		3,000	
ADD OPENING STOCK b/f	4,200			
	7,200			

LESS CLOSING STOCK (MC)		
$\frac{200}{500}$ x 3,000	1,200	
	6,000	
Factory Overhead	4,000 10,000	4,000
Production Cost (AC)		7,000
Add Opening Stock b/f		6,067
		13,067
LESS CLOSING STOCK (AC)		
$\frac{200}{500}$ x 7,000		2,800
		10,267
GROSS PROFIT	NIL	(267)

Thus, the only year in which a loss appeared to occur under absorption costing during the three year period was in the final year, when production fell and destocking took place. This is because the absorbed overheads from previous years have now hit the income statement.

3. On the marginal cost basis there is no profit and no loss shown. Thus we have a break even position. We can prove this as follows:

Selling Price per unit		£10
Less Variable Cost per unit		
Direct Labour	£3	
Direct Material	£3	6
CONTRIBUTION TO FIXED OVERHEADS		4

Therefore $\dfrac{\text{Fixed Overhead}}{\text{Contribution per Unit}} = \dfrac{£4,000}{£4} = 1000 \text{ units}$

The absorption cost profit statement differs from the marginal cost statement, insofar as the value of stock includes the factory overhead. In the marginal cost statement factory overhead is not included in the stock valuation and is treated as a time expense rather than a production expense.

You will see that the Gross Profit of £667 in year 1 using Absorption Costing is achieved because the factory overhead of £4,000 has not all been included as an expense of this period. 200/1200 × 4000 = 667 has been carried forward in the valuation of closing stock to the next trading period and will only be charged as an expense to Cost of Sale when those 200 units are sold.

QUESTIONS

1. Tom Foolery Limited have been trading for three years. The Management Accountant is interested in comparing the profits using (1) Absorption Costing and (2) Marginal Costing. He supplies you with the following summarised information and asks you to draw up clear financial statements showing the difference for each year.

    1. Sales were: 8,000 units at £20 each in Year 1
                          9,000 units at £20 each in Year 2
                          14,000 units at £20 each in Year 3

    2. Production was: 9,000 units in Year 1
                          11,000 units in Year 2
                          15,000 units in Year 3.

    3. Fixed Factory Overhead is £15,000 per annum.
    4. Direct Labour costs per unit were £5 throughout.
    5. Direct Material costs per unit were £3 throughout.
    6. Variable Overheads were £4 per unit throughout.
    7. Administration, Sales & Marketing, Distribution and Finance expenses totalled:

Year 1	Year 2	Year 3
£15,000	£18,000	£21,000

These are time expenses which are not to be absorbed into stock values.

2. (a) Comment briefly on the two most important features which you consider distinguish marginal costing from absorption costing.

   (b) For decision making purposes, a company uses the following figures relating to product B for a one-year period.

Activity:	50%	100%
Sales and production, in thousands of units	200	400
	£000	£000
Sales	1,000	2,000
Production costs:		
Variable	400	800
Fixed	200	200
Selling, distribution and administration expenses:		
Variable	200	400
Fixed	300	300

The normal level of activity for the current year is 400,000 units. The fixed costs are incurred evenly throughout the year and actual fixed costs are the same as budgeted.

There were no stocks of product B at the start of the quarter in which 110,000 units were produced and 80,000 units were sold.

From each of the questions (i) to (iv) below, you are required to select the appropriate answer. You must support each answer with an explanatory calculation.

(i)   The amount of fixed production costs absorbed by product B in the first quarter, using absorption costing, is:

£
1   80,000
2   40,000
3   110,000
4   55,000
5   None of these.

(ii) The over/(under) absorption of fixed production costs in the first quarter is:

£
1   (5,000)
2   5,000
3   10,000
4   15,000
5   None of these.

(iii) The net profit (or loss) for the first quarter using absorption costing, is:

£
1   (115,000)
2   50,000
3   (175,000)
4   125,000
5   None of these.

(iv) The net profit (or loss) for the first quarter, using marginal costing, is:

£
1   35,000
2   (340,000)
3   65,000
4   (115,000)
5   None of these.

(20 marks)
(CIMA)

3. Two decision making problems are faced by a company which produces a range of products and absorbs production overhead using a rate of 200% on direct wages. This rate was calculated from the following budgeted figures:

		£
Variable production costs	. . . . . .	64,000
Fixed production costs	. . . .	96,000
Direct labour costs	. . . .	80,000

Problem 1

The normal selling price of product X is £22 and production cost for one unit is:

		£
Raw materials	. . . .	8
Direct labour	. . . .	4
Production overhead	. . . .	8
		£20

There is a possibility of supplying a special order for 2,000 units of product X at £16 each. If the order were accepted the normal budgeted sales would not be affected and the company has the necessary capacity to produce the additional units.

Problem 2

The cost of making component Q, which forms part of product Y, is stated below:

		£
Raw material	. . . .	4
Direct labour	. . . .	8
Production overhead	. . . .	16
		£28

Component Q could be brought from an outside supplier for £20.

Required:

You are required, assuming that fixed production costs will not change, to:
(a) state whether the company should:
    (i) accept the special order in Problem 1;
    (ii) continue making component Q or buy it from outside in Problem 2;
    both your statements must be supported by details of costs;
(b) comment on the principle you have followed in your cost analysis to arrive at your answers to the two problems.

(15 marks)
(CIMA)

LABOUR COSTING
– Direct or Indirect Costs?

DEFINITION OF LABOUR COSTING

Labour costing is not just the cost of wages, but includes all associated costs of employing people –

    The employer's NIC

    Any employment insurance paid by employer.

    Holiday or sickness cover.

    Sick pay.

    Pension contributions made by employer on behalf of employee.

    Other benefits provided by employer –

    private health insurance, bonus or commission payments.

    staff canteen, day release, other training, recruitment costs, protective clothing.

    Idle time (time paid for by the business not spent on jobs owing to such things as no work available, machine breakdown, stock-out of materials etc.)

CLASSIFICATION OF LABOUR COSTS

Costs may be classified as direct or indirect.

DIRECT COSTS

These are labour costs which vary as a result of a change in output, such labour costs are product costs and not period costs. In practice, it can be difficult to distinguish between direct and indirect labour costs. It must be practicable and cost efficient to set up a system of data collection to identify and classify direct costs.

In a manufacturing business, direct wage costs would consist of those wages paid to factory operatives. In a service industry, it would be the cost of wages paid to those people who directly perform the service, e.g. Train Drivers, Aeroplane Pilots, Truck Drivers, Postal Operatives etc.

INDIRECT COSTS

These are period costs and would not change as a result of increased or reduced output. For example, salaried administrators, marketing personnel, factory supervision, and others not involved directly in producing the product or service.

It is usual to also classify the following as indirect labour costs:–

    Employer's National Insurance Costs

    Holiday pay

    Sick pay

    Overtime payments

    Idle time

However, the treatment of such costs is dependent on the recording systems employed, the accuracy of recording and the policy of the management.

BOOKING TIME

The need to record attendance is somewhat obvious but there is also the need to identify and record time spent by employees on work of a direct nature and work of an indirect nature. Cost code numbers would usually be used for this purpose. It is an essential part of the management process that all time is recorded and analysed so that management are kept informed of the reasons for any idle time.

At the end of each week activity time could be reconciled with attendance time thus:–

Attendance for Factory Employees

		Total Hrs.
	50 Production Workers at 40 hours	2000
	Add Overtime Hours	
	10 Production Workers at 10 hours	100
*	Total Hours Worked	2100

Activity Record

Code No.		
011	Direct Hours (booked to jobs/products etc.)	1500
022	Indirect Hours (repairing and cleaning machines)	200
021	– (Supervision)	100
030	Idle Time – (due to breakdowns of machines)	300
*	Total Hours Worked	2100

*If these totals fail to agree, management should investigate the reasons. It may be, for example, that all activity time has not been recorded properly.

Activity time may be recorded using:–
- Daily Time Sheets – Mechanical Methods (e.g. Clock Cards)
- Weekly Time Sheets – Electronic Methods
- Job Cards (or Job Tickets)
- Idle Time Cards

METHODS OF REMUNERATION

There are two basic types of remuneration system, which are:
(1) Time Rates; and
(2) Piece Rates.

TIME RATES

In this type of system an employee is paid an hourly/weekly/monthly or annual rate, regardless of the amount of work performed. The advantages of such a method are:

(1) It is easy to operate and simple to understand for both employer and employee.
(2) It may have the advantage that better quality work is done by an employee since there is not pressure of time for task completion.

There are also disadvantages:

(1) An employee still has to be paid if his output is nil or low in comparison to others whose output may be higher. There is no incentive for an employee to do work quickly.

There may in fact be incentive for an employee to delay jobs either to avoid unpleasant work or to stretch it out into an overtime period. The only time that these disadvantages are possibly overcome is when an employee sees his long term future bound up with that of the employer.

(2) The employer might have to incur high supervision costs to overcome the problem stated in (1) above.

(3) Time-rate system may demotivate efficient staff who see their colleagues idling their time away. Hence there is no reward for efficiency.

(4) A high level of dissatisfaction owing to (3) above could cause high labour turnover with high recruitment costs and the cost of training, which could be high in the case of skilled employees. There could also be a cost in terms of cost output.

THE APPROPRIATENESS OF TIME RATES

(1) Where skill and accuracy are essential factors then time rates may be appropriate, since quality is more important than speed.

(2) It is often difficult to measure, with accuracy, the output of certain groups of workers, e.g. office staff.

(3) For people undergoing training or apprenticeships, the output could be erratic and the purpose is for those employees to obtain a skill, therefore whilst in training, speed may not be an essential quality.

(4) Where the costs of other wage payment systems would be higher than time rates, time rates would be appropriate.

(5) Where an employee is unable to produce more output owing to a constraint such as, the speed of a machine, then it would be more equitable to use a time rate system. Other constraints could be such things as: the interdependence of productive units, for example, unit B is unable to produce until it receives a transfer of output from unit A

PIECE RATES

Employees are paid according to the number of units of output they produce. The simple piece rate is simply the number of units produced × rate per unit. There may be differential piece rates, the first so many units being paid at one rate per unit and once certain quantities are exceeded, different rates per unit apply. A progressive piece rate system might be structured as follows – Higher rates being paid for higher outputs.

0 – 100	@	£1.00	p.u.
101 – 200	@	£1.20	p.u.
201 – 300	@	£1.50	p.u.

There could be a mixture of piece rates with a guaranteed time rate, as a compromise between the two systems.

Advantages of the Piece Rate System:
(1) Effort and efficiency are rewarded. The employee has an incentive to produce more.
(2) Less supervision should be required.
(3) Owing to increased productivity the overhead cost absorbed into each unit of output should fall, therefore cutting the cost per unit and giving the employer an edge in keen pricing.

There are also disadvantages:
(1) Because speed is rewarded and less supervision assumed, quality control becomes a higher cost.
(2) Piece workers may adopt a satisficing approach, thus when a required wage is reached, they become satisfied and are not therefore keen to produce any more. As a result, plant and machinery may be left idle.
(3) A proper piece rate system will demand careful planning in setting standard times and measuring work done by O & M or work study (organization and methods). This may involve lots of management time and hence cost rates may have to be agreed with an appropriate Trade Union. If for any reason standard times are found to be too high and standard rates of pay too high, then it is extremely difficult or impossible to re-negotiate.
(4) Piece rates could cause over-production.

BONUS SCHEMES (PREMIUM BONUS SCHEMES)

Often employers will pay bonuses for time saved on particular jobs. Hence there is an incentive to the worker to complete the job more quickly. Such a bonus system demands that a time allowance for the performance of a job is accurately measured, since the bonus will be based on that allowance. A bonus is a payment over and above the payment made for the normal time allowance. Hence, if bonus targets are not achieved, the employee still receives his normal pay. The two major bonus schemes to be aware of are:–

THE HALSEY BONUS SCHEME

$\frac{1}{2}$ Time Saved   ×   Day Rate Per Hour

ROWAN BONUS SCHEME

$\frac{\text{Time Taken}}{\text{Time Allowed}}$ ×   Time Saved   ×   Day Rate Per Hour

EXAMPLE

X Limited have decided that the time allowance for producing 80 units is 8 hours. The normal daily rate paid to Jones, an employee, is £20. – He manages to produce 100 units in one 8 hour day. Calculate the total wages that would be paid to Jones under
(1)   The Halsey Bonus Scheme; and
(2)   The Rowan Bonus Scheme.

(1) $\frac{1}{2}$ × 2 hours × £2.50 = £2.50

(2) $\frac{8}{10}$ × 2 × £2.50 = £4.00

Under the Halsey method his wages are: £22.50
Under the Rowan method his wages are: £24.00

Bonus schemes such as the Halsey & Rowan Schemes are called Premium Bonus Systems. They are a combination of piece rate and time rate. The piece rate element enters into the equation through "time saved". A major disadvantage with such schemes is the complexity of calculations and scepticism on the part of employees that the management has 'done them'! Often an organization will simply have a bonus pay rate which is easily understood by employees and employer and related to time spent or units produced.

EXAMPLE 2

B Limited pay an hourly rate of £3. Standard number of hours in the week is 40. The normal output for each worker is expected to be 400 units. During a particular week Brown, an employee, turned out 420 units, and Smith 450 units. Calculate the total wages due to both Brown and Smith under the following bonus schemes:–
(1)   The Halsey method; and
(2)   The Rowan Method.

BROWN
(1)   Halsey
$\frac{1}{2}$ time saved × Day rate per hour.

units produced per hour = $\frac{400}{40}$ = 10; Time Saved = 20 units = 2 hours

$\frac{1}{2}$ × 2 hrs × £3 = £3   total wages = (40 × 3) + 3
                                                    = £123

(2) Rowan method

Time Taken × Time Saved × Daily Rate Per Hour.
Time Allowed

$\dfrac{40 \text{ hrs}}{42 \text{ hrs}}$ × 2 hrs × £3 = £5.71

∴ total wages = (40 × 3) + 5 = <u>£125.71</u>

SMITH

(1) Halsey method

$\dfrac{1}{2}$ × 5 hrs × £3 = £7.50; ∴ <u>total wages (40 × £3 + £7.50) = £127.50</u>

(2) Rowan method

$\dfrac{40 \text{ hrs} \times 5 \text{ hrs} \times £3 = £13.33}{45 \text{ hrs}}$; ∴ <u>total wages 40×£3+£13.33=£133.33.</u>

NOTE: There are other bonus schemes, e.g. Halsey Weir is simply a variation on Halsey using ⅓ time saved rather than ½.

PROFIT SHARING SCHEMES

There are many such schemes, but the basic principle is that employees receive a bonus based on the profit of the organization. Sometimes profitability may be further broken down, into profit centres. That is to say easily identifiable contributing units and the bonus is paid to employees within each profit centre by apportioning the profit of that centre to them. Often this is done based on grading and length of service of the employee. It is possible to link profit sharing to the budgeting process, for example, if a sales department manages to exceed sales targeted in the sales budget, then as part of the profit sharing scheme, it may be possible to acknowledge this by giving an appropriate reward.

There are alternative forms of profit sharing to a straight cash payment, such as an opportunity for employees to be given or buy shares in the company. The major argument in support of this method is that it gives employees a stake in the company. How watertight the logic of this argument is depends on the attitudes of employees towards holding shares for supposed future benefit as against selling the shares for immediate gain.

From an employee point of view, the profit sharing scheme, where an employee is given shares, could be more attractive since any gain made on the sale of such shares would be subject to Capital Gains Tax and not Income Tax. The employee is exempt from CGT up to a limit of £5,000 in 1990. Once the exemption limit is passed it is still taxed at a lower rate. From the employer's point of view a share scheme may have lower costs since national insurance contributions may be avoided. The major disadvantage is the market fluctuation of a share.

Cash Profit Sharing Schemes may cause the employer a problem in terms of meeting the cash payment, since profit is not cash and the cash may well be required for investment in fixed assets or working capital.

Advantages of Such Schemes:
(1) To motivate employees to work harder?
(2) Employees feel part of the organization?

Disadvantages of Such Schemes:
(1) Aspirations of employees are raised to the point of expectation.
(2) It places pressure on employers to meet obligations in terms of payments.

Such schemes can be divisive, leading to antagonism and de-motivation. A scheme not only needs to be fair, it needs to be seen to be so. Both objectives in practice are difficult to achieve.

INCENTIVE SCHEMES

The basis of such schemes is that a financial incentive is given to employees according to results achieved, the objective being to raise output. The ingredients for a good scheme are as follows:–
(1) Co-operation of the work force is necessary.
(2) Employees need to be educated in order to allay fears and suspicions, for example, the introduction of the scheme equating with redundancies.
(3) It must be fully understood and relatively easy for employees to check their payment.
(4) Targets set should be realistic. An average employee should be able to reach the normal standard of output.
(5) The amount of bonus paid should be sufficient to stimulate greater output.
(6) Quality control is an essential part of the scheme. Output must not increase at the expense of quality.
(7) Employees should not be penalized when situations outside of their control cause a reduction in their output. It will therefore be necessary to measure such occasions and make a payment in lieu of bonus.
(8) The payment of such bonuses must be made promptly in order to act as an incentive.
(9) The labour cost per unit produced should fall even though total labour costs will rise.

There are alternatives to paid incentives such as free holidays, gifts, etc.

INDIVIDUAL OR GROUP INCENTIVE SCHEMES

Incentive schemes may be measured for individuals or groups of employees.

INDIVIDUAL INCENTIVE SCHEMES

Individual incentive schemes may be the best, since they can act as a time motivator to the individual concerned. The individual would not be penalized by poor group performance. The problems with an individual scheme are:–

(1)   Individual measures may be difficult to achieve.
(2)   Corporate goals become secondary to individual goals.
(3)   Individuals may find it difficult to co-operate with colleagues especially if team work is necessary.

GROUP INCENTIVE SCHEMES

Group schemes are easier to measure and can weld a feeling of team spirit. There are still problems:

(1)   Individuals may feel that they have little influence over group activities and hence incentive is removed.
(2)   Some groups will feel special, while some may feel alienated. The jealousy between groups could reduce overall output.

The most important factors with regard to incentive schemes are:
(1)   How well they are designed; and
(2)   How well they are managed – it is management's role to ensure incentive schemes do exactly what they set out to do. If there is management failure, then incentive schemes are worse than useless, they are in fact costly and harmful.

WORK STUDY

This is a technique designed to study the most economical way to perform tasks. Work study engineers will record the systems and methods currently employed. They will measure the work done, evaluate performance and suggest improved methods.

WORK MEASUREMENT

Work study engineers will record the time it takes to perform a particular task, given normal conditions. These normal times will be supplemented by allowances for rest periods, and an overall standard would be set for a particular task or set of tasks. Once a standard is established it can be used as a measure of productivity and also to implement any bonus or incentive schemes that the firm may wish to operate.

JOB EVALUATION

There are various methods of job evaluation, but they are all designed to achieve one objective which is to estimate the value of each particular job in an organization, in comparison with other jobs in the organization. The evaluation would normally involve the ranking of jobs in order of importance. The types of thing usually considered in an evaluation are:

(1) Skill required to perform the job.
(2) Level of training and education required.
(3) Experience necessary.
(4) Intelligence.
(5) The physical and mental effort.
(6) The responsibility of the job holder.

Each of these items is normally given an allocation of points. The individual jobs then looked at are rewarded a proportion of the maximum points allowable, in accordance with the evaluation. The points will then be totalled for each job and the total number of points will determine the salary paid.

EXAMPLE 3

JOB EVALUATION OF COST ACCOUNTS CLERK

	Maximum Score Possible	Actual Score
Skill	5	2
Training	8	4
Education	8	4
Experience	5	2
Intelligence	5	2
Responsibility	7	2
Physical Effort	6	1
Mental Effort	6	4
TOTAL SCORE	50	21

GRADES, POINTS PAY SCHEME

Grade	Point Score for Job	Salary Scale
1.	0 – 10	£5,000 – £7,999
2.	11 – 20	£8,000 – £9,999
3.	21 – 30	£10,000 – £11,999
4.	31 – 40	£12,000 – £14,999
5.	41 – 50	£15,000 – £20,000

The criteria for the allocation of points for specific knowledge, skills and experience required would be clearly defined in the scheme. In our example, there is no reason for the figures chosen. They are there simply to illustrate how the points are used in evaluation.

It should be pointed out however that such schemes have their critics, and problems they highlight with regard to job evaluation are:–

(1)   They take no account of the market place. Jobs are a function of the demand for goods and services supplied by the organization. In order to place a value on a job, which will determine pay structures, one must not lose sight of the added value which is produced by that job.
(2)   Job evaluation schemes tend to be highly subjective. It becomes a matter of opinion rather than fact, as to the points which are allocated for the various knowledge, skills and experience requirements.
(3)   Job evaluation schemes have no influence over external factors such as collective bargaining or the demand for labour in the job market. Another external influence could be government guidelines on pay policy.

It should be noted that job evaluation schemes evaluate jobs not people.

MERIT RATING

A merit rating system places value on the person and not the job. It is similar in so far as points are allocated for particular qualities, which are said to be desirable in an employee, for example, punctuality, reliability, initiative. Again, such schemes are purely subjective and they involve judgements being made by managers in the organization.

WAGE PAYMENTS

The total wage payment made by the business would consist of the gross pay, plus overtime payments, plus any bonuses paid. This gross pay would be calculated from clock cards, time sheets or other records of hours worked or pieces completed. The number of hours or the number of pieces completed would then be multiplied by the rate per hour or the rate per piece.

EXAMPLE

In a standard week of 40 hours, the hourly rate of pay for an employee is £4. Overtime is paid at time and a half and this employee worked 10 hours extra. The gross pay would be made up as follows:–

$$
\begin{array}{lll}
\text{40 hrs at standard rate} & = £4 \times 40 = & £160 \\
\text{10 hrs at overtime rate} & = £6 \times 10 = & \underline{£\ 60} \\
\\
\text{Gross Pay} & & \underline{\underline{£220}}
\end{array}
$$

In addition to the gross pay to the employee, the employer may also have to pay employer's national insurance contributions (NIC) and any benefits in kind, that the business is obliged to pay according to the contract of employment, e.g. Pension schemes, Health insurance, BUPA, etc.

The net pay of the employee will be arrived at after certain authorized deductions from gross pay are made. They are:-
(1)   Income tax under PAYE.

(2) NIC of the employee.
(3) Contributions to any superannuation schemes.
(4) Voluntary deductions such as payments to charities, private health
     insurance, trade unions, sports and social clubs, additional voluntary
     contributions (AVC's) on a pension scheme.

Using the previous example:

		£
Gross Pay		220

Less: Deductions

Income Tax	60	
NIC	19	
Pension Fund	20	
Trade Union	1	
		100
NET PAY		120

In addition to this the employer pays £20 towards the pension fund on
employee's behalf and NIC £23.

ENTRIES IN THE LEDGER

The entry in the books of the account, if only this one person was employed,
would be as follows:-

	£Dr	£Cr
GROSS WAGES (including employer's contributions)	263	
Inland Revenue PAYE		60
NIC Employee		19
Employer		23
Pension Fund Employer		20
Employee		20
Trade Union		1
Bank		120
	263	263

**NOTE: The other accounts for Inland Revenue, NIC, Pension and
Trade Union would be debited and the bank account credited when
payments are made.**

INTERNAL CONTROL IN A WAGE SYSTEM

In order to prevent any fraud the risks can be minimized by a system of internal controls, which do the following:–

(1) Segregation of duties where possible, e.g. the person calculating the wages should not be the person handling the cash or filling the wage packets. In a small organization, there may be no alternative.

(2) By installing a proper system for authorising wage payments and deductions thereon, e.g. clock cards should be initialled or signed by the employee's immediate supervisor to confirm that the work has been done. All deductions from pay packets, apart from statutory deductions for tax and NIC, should be authorized by the employee, signing a document which is held in his personnel records.

(3) Checks should be made when wage packets are handed out, e.g. employees should sign for their wage packet and the person handing out the packet should check the signature against a specimen signature held on file. It is also useful in a large organization if staff present identity cards or have their managers in attendance at a pay out.

(4) Unclaimed wages should be held in safe custody for employees who are unable to claim on that day. The period they are held on site should only be short. If they remain unclaimed for more than a reasonable length of time, the money should be re-banked. There will be procedures specifying reasonable time periods etc.

(5) It is also advisable that from time to time managers of the business or designated personnel, e.g. the internal auditor, should carry out spot checks at a wage payout to ensure that all personnel being paid, actually exist.

LABOUR TURNOVER

This is expressed as the number of employees leaving in a period divided by the average number of people employed times 100 to give a percentage, for example, the workforce on 1st January 19–6 was 500. At 31st December 19–6 it was 480. New starters during the year were 10 and people who left during the year were 30. Calculate the labour turnover.

$$\text{LABOUR TURNOVER \%} = \frac{\text{Number of Employees leaving in a period}}{\text{Average Number of Employees}} \times \frac{100}{1}$$

$$\text{Labour turnover} = \frac{30}{\left(\frac{500+480}{2}\right)} \times 100 = 6.122\%$$

REASONS FOR LABOUR TURNOVER

(1) Dissatisfaction with the job, the pay or the conditions of employment.

(2) Friction between colleagues or management.

(3)   Lack of promotion opportunities.
(4)   Early retirement schemes.
(5)   Ill health or personal problems, e.g. marriage failure.
(6)   Redundancy.
(7)   To take advantage of a better opportunity.

COSTS OF LABOUR TURNOVER

Apart from lost production and low morale, other costs will result such as:–
(1)   Advertising and interviewing costs for personnel.
(2)   Training costs.
(3)   Any removal expenses or subsistence allowances involved in obtaining new personnel.
(4)   The organization may have to pay higher wages to attract personnel.
(5)   Administration costs, e.g. maintaining staff records, wage payments and bank details, pension administration, changing names on stationery, and so on.
(6)   There may be an increase cost due to scrap and defective work produced by new labour.
(7)   Low morale could cause increased sick leave or industrial action or deliberate machine breakdowns.
(8)   Machine breakdowns could also occur through misuse and lack of training in the case of new employees.

If labour turnover is high then the disruption to normal products or services offered by the business, could be so great as to lose custom.

HOW TO REDUCE LABOUR TURNOVER

It is management's responsibility to find ways in which the effects of labour turnover can be minimized.
(1)   The collection and analysis of regular statistics is essential in larger organizations. They may give insight to the reasons why people left, e.g. was labour turnover avoidable, was it voluntary or involuntary? The answers to such quetions may help. In the case of people who left voluntarily, they may not always give the real reasons as to why they left.
(2)   Plan the increase or reduction in a firm's labour requirement.
(3)   Improve recruitment and selection to avoid discontent or unsuitability.
(4)   Give due consideration to incentive schemes.
(5)   Ensure that the working environment is appropriate.
(6)   Consider the transfer of discontented or disruptive staff to another department where both parties (the management and the employee) may gain.
(7)   Consider fringe benefits (pension schemes, subsidized meals, health care, sports & social facilities).
(8)   Improve human relations between management and the workforce.

LABOUR COSTING

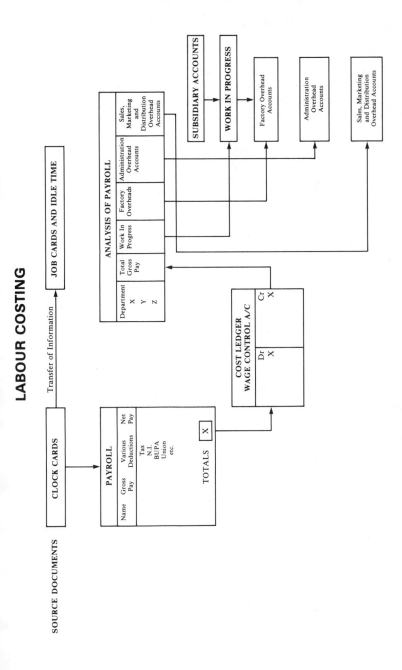

OVERHEADS
– The burden of fixed costs in relation to output

Overheads are costs which are not directly attributable to production, therefore overheads may be regarded as fixed costs. They are also referred to as indirect costs. Overheads are usually time based expenses; they are usually a common cost, in so far as the cost may be shared by a number of departments (e.g. light and heat).

MANUFACTURING OVERHEADS = indirect factory costs. Examples of such costs are: indirect materials, indirect labour, employment costs (sick pay, holiday pay, idle time, bonuses, National Insurance Contributions), rent, rates, insurance, light, heat and power, depreciation, repairs and maintenance.

THE NATURE OF THE PROBLEM

All businesses incur overheads, that is those costs which cannot be traced directly to a unit of output. If we were to cost on a marginal or direct basis only, the selling price less direct costs would yield a contribution to overheads. The rule in marginal costing states "that if the contribution is positive then it's worth doing". This approach is fine for short term decision making or where a product is itself a marginal product (i.e. not the mainstream of the business). The problem facing any business is to ensure that the contributions obtained from mainstream products will be sufficient, not only to cover overhead costs but also to make a contribution to profit. In order to achieve this objective it is essential that overheads are recovered in the selling price. How do we do this?

ABSORPTION

The method of recovering overheads to ensure that they are included in costing and pricing decisions is known as absorption costing. Overheads are traced to the product by the use of an overhead absorption rate, which is designed to recover a fair share of overhead from each unit of output.

$$\text{OVERHEAD ABSORPTION RATE} = \frac{\text{TOTAL OVERHEAD COST}}{\text{LEVEL OF ACTIVITY (i.e. output)}}$$

DEFINITION OF ABSORPTION COSTING

The CIMA define it as 'a principle whereby fixed as well as variable costs are allotted to unit costs and total overheads are absorbed according to activity level. The term may be applied where:

    (a)   production costs only, or

(b)   costs of all functions are so allotted.'

A share of fixed overhead costs are added to the marginal cost of the product (i.e. Direct Costs).

USEFULNESS OF ABSORPTION COSTING (or FULL COSTING as it is sometimes called).

(1)   STOCK VALUATION – SSAP 9 states that costs of stock and Work in Progress should comprise those costs which have been incurred in the normal course of business in bringing the product (or service) to its present location and condition. Such costs will include all related production overheads. Stocks are therefore valued at full factory cost, providing of course this is lower than net realizable value (selling prices).

(2)   PRICING – Although price setting is ultimately a marketing decision, it is essential for a business to ensure it does at least cover the full cost of production. Full cost is only known if a proportion of overheads are included as well as direct costs of production.

(3)   PROFITABILITY can be measured by product.

CHOICE OF ABSORPTION METHOD

Overheads may be recovered by using different methods of absorption. The method chosen should take account of:–
(1)   The accuracy in applying overhead rates to units of output, so as to recover the overhead equitably.
(2)   It should be simple to understand and easy to calculate.
(3)   If the business is organized departmentally, then it is better to apply departmental rates of recovery rather than factory-wide rates.
(4)   Since many indirect costs are period costs, account needs to be taken of time as well as the level of activity.

Basis of recovery could be:–
(1)   **UNITS OF PRODUCT** = Overhead rate per unit.
(2)   **DIRECT LABOUR HOURS** = Overhead rate per direct labour hour.
(3)   **DIRECT MACHINE HOURS** = Overhead rate per machine hour.
(4)   **DIRECT MATERIAL COST OF PRODUCTION** = Overhead rate % of direct material.
(5)   **DIRECT LABOUR COST OF PRODUCTION** = Overhead rate % of direct labour cost.
(6)   **PRIME COST OF PRODUCTION** = Overhead rate % of prime cost.
(7)   **STANDARD HOURS** = Overhead rate per standard hour.

NOTE: Items 1 to 6 would apply to a product costing system which is historical or normal. Item 7 would only be used if a standard costing system was in operation.

EXAMPLE

X Ltd manufactures two products, A and B. Details are as follows:–

	Product A (£)	Product B (£)
Direct Material Cost	20	40
Direct Labour Cost – Machining	£2 per hour	£2 per hour
Hours Required	12 hours	24 hours
Assembly Costs	£1.50 per hour	£1.50 per hour
Hours Required	6 hours	6 hours
Budgeted Output	250,000	150,000

Total Budgeted Overheads for year   500,000

REQUIRED

Calculate overhead absorption rates on the following basis:–
1. Rate per unit
2. Rate per direct labour hour
3. Rate per machine hour
4. Percentage of direct material
5. Percentage of direct wages
6. Percentage of prime cost.

N.B. based on budgeted figures.

1 Rate per unit $= \dfrac{\text{Total Budgeted Overhead}}{\text{Total Units Budgeted}} = \dfrac{£500,000}{400,000 \text{ units}} = £1.25$

2 Rate per direct labour hour $= \dfrac{\text{Total Budgeted Overhead}}{\text{Total Direct Labour Hours}} = \dfrac{£500,000}{9,000,000 \text{ DLH}} = £0.055$

$$\begin{array}{ll} \text{For A} = 18 \times 250,000 & \text{For B} = 30 \times 150000 \\ \qquad = 4,500,000 & \qquad = 4,500,000 \end{array}$$

3 Rate per machine hour $= \dfrac{\text{Total Budgeted Overhead}}{\text{Total Machine Hours}} = \dfrac{£500,000}{6,600,000 \text{ M/hrs}} = £0.076$

4 % of direct material $= \dfrac{\text{Total Budgeted Overhead}}{\text{Total direct material cost}} = \dfrac{£500,000}{£11,000,000} = 4.545\%$

5 % of direct wages $= \dfrac{\text{Total Budgeted Overhead}}{\text{Total direct wage cost}} = \dfrac{£500,000}{£16,800,000} = 2.976\%$

6 % of prime cost $= \dfrac{\text{Total Budgeted Overhead}}{\text{Total Prime Cost}} = \dfrac{£500,000}{£27,800,000} = 1.798\%$

COMPARISON OF THE DIFFERENT METHODS

1. PER UNIT OF OUTPUT

This is easy to calculate and easy to understand, but is only suitable for a single product firm. In a multi-product firm it would cause an inequitable allocation of overheads. It ignores cost weightings of products.

2. PER DIRECT LABOUR HOUR

This is suitable where labour is the major resource input. It is simple to calculate and easy to understand. It does take account of time (hence period costs). It is, however, dependent upon accurate labour records being maintained, which may be expensive. The benefits must outweigh the costs. Since work is measured in units of time, it is suitable in businesses where production is not uniform.

3. MACHINE HOURS
This is a suitable method when machine hours are the major resource input. It has the advantage of being related to time. There could be a problem in cases where production does not utilize any machine hours, since they would not be charged any overhead. Hence machine production would unfairly absorb all overheads.

4. PERCENTAGE OF DIRECT WAGES
Easy to understand and simple to calculate. Most suitable for large companies employing the same or similar grades of labour where pay is fairly standard. The method would cause an inequitable distribution of overheads if the business had many different grades of labour on different pay structures, e.g. if low paid grades of labour were used on a particular job, overhead absorptions would be unfairly charged at the same rate, as if higher paid grades of labour were used. Useful when labour costs represent a high proportion of total product cost.

5. PERCENTAGE OF DIRECT MATERIALS
Easy to calculate and simple to understand. It is only suitable where the cost of materials input into each unit of output is the same. Otherwise it suffers from the same problems as percentage of direct wages (i.e. in this case, different grades of materials). It ignores time which is probably the most important factor in choosing an overhead absorption rate.

6. PERCENTAGE OF PRIME COST
Simple to understand and easy to calculate. The problem is that it ignores time. It does however take account of weights in the cost of materials and labour.

HISTORICAL, NORMAL AND STANDARD ABSORPTION RATES

HISTORICAL
These are based on past events, hence past costs. The overhead rate is calculated at the end of a cost period.

EXAMPLE

The costing records for a period reveal that total overheads during that period amounted to £36,000. The total number of direct labour hours in the period was 9,000. Four jobs were completed during the period and consumed the following direct labour hours:–

Job A	1,000 hours
Job B	3,000 hours

| | Job C | 2,000 hours |
| | Job D | 3,000 hours |

The Historical Overhead Rate would be calculated thus:–

$$\frac{£36,000}{9,000 \text{ hours}} = £4.00 \text{ per direct labour hour.}$$

		Total Overhead Charge Per Job
Job A 1,000 hrs × 4	=	£4,000
Job B 3,000 hrs × 4	=	£12,000
Job C 2,000 hrs × 4	=	£8,000
Job D 3,000 hrs × 4	=	£12,000
Total Overheads	=	£36,000

DISADVANTAGES OF HISTORICAL RATES

1. They delay production cost evaluations, since overheads cannot be charged to Work in Progress until the end of an accounting period.
2. The overhead rate might vary from period to period. Some overheads are fixed and do not vary with activity. Recovery rates would change from period to period and hence product costs would change from period to period.

EXAMPLE: Products Costs

	Period 1	Period 2
	£	£
Direct Labour	36,000	24,000
Overheads		
Fixed	72,000	72,000
Variable	36,000	24,000
	108,000	96,000

Factory overheads recovery rate: per hour direct labour.

	£	£
Fixed	2.00	3.00
Variable	1.00	1.00
	3.00	4.00

This could lead to inconsistent product costing and inconsistent product pricing. Exactly the same job in January could cost twice as much in February, owing to changing levels of activity (volume).

NORMAL RATES

In order to overcome the disadvantage of historical rates, often a pre-determined factory overhead rate is used. An overhead rate can be predetermined using budgeted figures as a basis, as shown below:–

$$\text{Predetermined Overhead Rate} = \frac{\text{Budgeted Overhead}}{\text{Budgeted Activity Level}}$$

ADVANTAGES
1. The rate need be calculated only once in an accounting period, that is, the budget period.
2. Product costs can be calculated more promptly, thus overhead costs can be charged at the same time that direct costs can be charged to the product, hence Work in Progress can be calculated quickly and overheads can be included in Work in Progress.

DISADVANTAGE
The major problem with predetermined rates is that actual overheads will hardly ever be the same as budgeted overheads. Hence, an under or over absorption would occur.

(UNDER)/OVER ABSORPTION
EXAMPLE:

	Period 1 £	Period 2 £
Budgeted overheads	100,000	90,000
Actual overheads	90,000	100,000
(UNDER)/OVER ABSORPTION	10,000	(10,000)

Overheads which are absorbed are charged to Work in Progress. Any over absorption would effectively be profit. Any under absorption would result in a loss.

VOLUME VARIANCE

One reason why budgeted and actual figures might not agree would be due to a difference in the level of activity between budget and actual.

1. **A FAVOURABLE VARIANCE** = This when the actual level is greater than the budgeted level.

2. **AN UNFAVOURABLE VARIANCE** = This is when the actual level is less than the budgeted level.

SPENDING OR EXPENDITURE VARIANCE

Such a variance occurs due to price changes.

1. **FAVOURABLE VARIANCE** = This occurs when actual costs or expenses are less than budget.

2. **UNFAVOURABLE VARIANCE** = This occurs when actual costs or expenses are greater than budget.

EXAMPLE OF VOLUME/PRICE VARIANCE ANALYSIS

	Year 1 £	Year 2 £
Sales (10,000 × £10)	100,000	

Supposing we are told that sales are expected to rise by 20% in volume terms for Year 2 and prices are expected to rise on average by 10%.

Determine the sales value for Year 2 showing the effect of the volume and price changes.

Volume increase (10,000 × 1.2) = 12,000 units × Price increase (£10 × 1.1) = £11
Year 2 Sales = 12,000×£11
= £132,000

Volume gives the measure of efficiency.

STANDARD

A standard is a predetermined cost for a particular unit which is scientifically derived.

DEPARTMENTAL OVERHEADS

Most organizations will have two types of department:–
1. **PRODUCTION DEPARTMENT.** Those currently engaged in the conversion of raw materials into finished products or manufactured goods.

2. **SERVICE DEPARTMENT.** Those not directly engaged in the production process but nevertheless provide necessary support services, e.g. centralized computing, personnel and management services.

The purpose of allocating overheads via departmental rates are to obtain:–
1. Responsibility accounting and cost control.
2. Accuracy in the costing of products.

USING DEPARTMENTAL RATES

The budgeted overheads is selected at the selected output level. This total overhead then needs to be split into various departments. At this initial stage service departments will have to be apportioned with overheads. It is necessary to recharge service department overheads to production departments which use those services. The basis of charge is discussed below. The final step is to work out departmental rates based on the level of activity and the overheads each department needs to recover. At the end of an accounting period it will be necessary to analyse and deal with under or over absorption.

TERMINOLOGY

1. **ALLOCATION:** a charge to a cost centre with overheads that are the direct result of that cost centre. For example, a factory foreman's wage would be entirely chargeable to the factory concerned.

2. **APPORTIONMENT:** most overheads will require apportionment in accordance with the use made by recognized user departments. They are jointly shared facilities. For example, centralized computer services. It can be seen that apportionment is the most difficult to deal with, whereas an allocation is self-explanatory. The basis of apportionment should be equitable, practicable and yield more benefits than its costs.

BASIS OF APPORTIONMENT — examples

1. Floor area – rent, rates, heat, light, repairs & maintenance, depreciation on buildings.
2. Number of employees – personnel department, accounts department etc; canteen.
3. Volume, weight or quantity of materials – stores personnel, warehousing costs.
4. Book values or cost of equipment – depreciation, insurance of equipment, etc.
5. Technical estimates (or export estimates) – occupancy costs, service centres.
6. Number of machines – depreciation, insurance of equipment, maintenance costs, supervision.
7. Number of radiators – heat.
8. Number of lights etc. – light.
9. Value of materials – carriage inwards.
10. Any other reasonable basis.

SOURCES OF INFORMATION

1. Statistics relating to the factory – e.g. occupancy details, who occupies where, and floor area or volume.
2. Personnel statistics, number of employees, total departmental breakdown, personnel establishment versus in post.
3. Statistics regarding production, plant, machinery and equipment. This may be available from work study engineers, e.g. capacity, average

output, output over a period from machinery or by department or cost centre.

4.   Accounting records. The plant register, the property register, the patent register. And from original documents, purchase invoice, stores requisitions, payroll analysis etc.

BASIS OF APPORTIONING OVERHEADS — EXAMPLE

Suggest a reasonable basis of apportioning costs for the following service departments:-

Suggested Possible Basis

1 Stores	– Number of requisitions, number of units handled, by value of materials handled.
2 Canteens	– Number of employees, labour hours, labour costs.
3 Machine repairs & maintenance	– Book value of machinery, number of machines, machine hours.
4 Estate management services	– Floor area.

QUESTION

1.   Compare and contrast the following business costs and basis of absorption.

Business A produces a single product.

Direct Material Costs	£20 per unit
Direct Labour Costs	
– Machining	£2 per hour 3 hours used to produce each unit
– Assembly & Finishing	£1.75 per hour 2 hours used to produce each unit
Budgeted Output for Year	100000 units
Total Budgeted Overheads	£400000

Business B produces 2 products Y and Z

Direct Material Costs	£10 for Y and £30 for Z
Direct Labour Costs	
– Machining	£2 per hour Y 0 hours Z 5 hours
– Assembly & Finishing	£1.80 per hour Y 4 hours Z 1 hour
Budgeted Output for Year	100000 units Y 200000 units Z
Total Budgeted Overheads	£750000.

REQUIRED

1.   Calculate overhead absorption rates for A and B (as before 1 to 6).
2.   State which method you would advise for business A and why?
     State which method you would advise for business B and why?

JOB COSTING
– for products and services

Job Costing is a method of specific order costing similar to batch and contract costing. Up to now we have been concerned with marginal and absorption costing which is to do with the way in which the business values its stock in total. We have followed the stock from its raw material state to its manufactured state. For simplicity in most of the examples it has been assumed that we have only produced one product; in reality there may be more than one product. Depending on the type of product, the business will either use job costing or process costing as a system. Within either system the firm could use either marginal or absorption costing, and they may value stocks on a FIFO, LIFO, AVCO or standard cost basis (see Stock Valuation) when pricing issues. Note: Marginal costing is not a costing system, neither is absorption costing. It is merely the approach we use. Job costing can also be used for costing a service and where the word product is used in this chapter one could equally substitute service.

JOB COSTING OR PROCESS COSTING?

Job costing systems exist in business where products are made singly or in batches. Each job is clearly and easily distinguishable from other jobs, and goods are usually made or services provided to particular customer specifications. A classic example of where a job costing system may be employed is printing, e.g. personalised stationery for customers, company reports, books etc. The materials used and the labour consumed are easily traceable to a particular job. The documentation in such a system must be designed to facilitate the recording of materials, labour and any overhead. Normally job tickets or job cards (see example later) are used.

Process costing is relevant in the manufacture of petrochemicals, whereby the flow of production undergoes different processes which may yield different outputs at different stages in the production process. Once again suitable documentation needs to be designed to record the processes.

JOB COSTING EXAMPLE

Inky Ltd. is involved in a printing business producing a number of small pamphlets for various customers. He recently estimated that he is likely to incur £15,000 of fixed overhead (i.e. rates, rent, indirect staffing and other indirect costs) during his current financial year. Clutterbug, one of his principal customers, requests a quote on a new pamphlet to advertise the small business advisory service. He estimates that he will need 2,000 of these pamphlets. Following the discussion with Inky it is estimated that the following materials will be required:

1. 6,000 sheets of paper costing £2 per ream (500 sheets per ream).
2. Ink – 4 units @ £5 per unit.
3. Typesetting & Design – 6 pages @ £8 per page.
4. 4,000 staples @ £5.

Inky further estimates it will take half an hour to set up the machine and two and a half hours to run and complete the job. The labour therefore will be as follows:

> 1 hour skilled labour at £5 per hour
> 3 hours semi-skilled labour at £2 per hour

Inky further estimates that owing to current temperamental machinery and in view of his previous knowledge, he should allow 10% flexibility in material costs for wastage.

REQUIRED
The estimated cost of the job for Clutterbug.

Inky has decided to recover overheads on the basis of direct labour hours. He has further estimated that budgeted direct labour hours will be 6,000 for the year.

$$\text{Direct Labour hour basis for Overhead Absorption Rate (OAR)} \begin{cases} = \dfrac{£15,000 \quad \text{Total Estimated Annual Cost}}{6,000 \quad \text{hours of direct labour}} \\[2em] = £2.50 \text{ overheads per labour hour} \end{cases}$$

The following job sheet can be used for a quote and can then be used when the job is carried out to give details of the actual costs which might differ from the quote. Variances could be identified and acted upon.

INKY LTD.	JOB SHEET			Job No.				
				Date				
	BUDGET			ACTUAL			Total	
	Qty.	Price	Total	Qty.	Price	Total	Price Variance	
DIRECT MATERIAL								
Paper	12 units	2.00	24.00					
Ink	4 units	5.00	20.00					
Staples	4 units	5.00	5.00					
Typesetting & Design (brought in)	6 units	8.00	48.00					
TOTAL DIRECT MATERIAL			97.00					
Add Allowance Wastage 10%			9.70					
DIRECT LABOUR								
Skilled	1 unit	5.00	5.00					
Unskilled	3 units	2.00	6.00					
DIRECT OVERHEADS	—	—	—					
PRIME COST			117.70					
Overheads Recovered	4 units	2.50	10.00					
Total Estimated Cost			127.70					
Add Required Profit Mark-up 50%			63.85					
ESTIMATED SELLING PRICE			191.55					

Alternative Design of Job Sheet

INKY LTD.	JOB SHEET					No.	
						Date Commenced	
Code No.	Description	Unit	Qty	Price £	Value £	Date Completed	
						NOTES	
P001	Paper	1 rm.	12	2.00	24.00		
I001	Ink	1 unit	4	5.00	20.00		
TD001	Typesetting & Design	1 page	6	8.00	48.00		
S001	Staples	—			5.00		
LS001	LABOUR Skilled	1 hour	1	5.00	5.00		
L001	Semi-skilled	1 hour	3	2.00	6.00		
O001	OVERHEADS	1 hour	4	2.50	10.00		
W001	Wastage Allowance	Material	10%	9.70	9.70		
	FULL COST				£127.70	Completed by	
	Add Profit Mark Up 50% on cost				63.85		
	Estimated Selling Price				191.55		

SELF-CHECK QUESTION

1X.   In order to identify the costs incurred in carrying out a range of work to customer specification in its factory, a company has a job costing system. This system identifies costs directly with a job where this is possible and reasonable. In addition, production overhead costs are absorbed into the cost of jobs at the end of each month, at an actual rate per direct labour hour for each of the two production departments.

One of the jobs carried out in the factory during the month just ended was Job No. 123. The following information has been collected relating specifically to this job:–

400 kilos of Material Y were issued from stores to Department A. 76 direct labour hours were worked in Department A at a basic wage of £4.50 per hour. 6 of these hours were classified as overtime at a premium of 50%.

300 kilos of Material Z were issued from stores to Department B. Department B returned 30 kilos of Material Z to the storeroom being excess to requirements for the job.

110 direct labour hours were worked in Department B at a basic wage of £4.00 per hour. 30 of these hours were classified as overtime at a premium of 50%. All overtime worked in Department B in the month is a result of the request of a customer for early completion of another job which had been originally scheduled for completion in the month following.

Department B discovered defects in some of the work, which was returned to Department A for rectification. 3 labour hours were worked in Department A on rectification (these are additional to the 76 direct labour hours in Department A noted above). Such rectification is regarded as a normal part of the work carried out generally in the department.

Department B damaged 5 kilos of Material Z which then had to be disposed of. Such losses of material are not expected to occur.

Total costs incurred during the month on all jobs in the two production departments were as follows:–

	Department A	Department B
	£	£
Direct materials issued from stores*	6,500	13,730
Direct materials returned to stores	135	275
Direct labour, at basic wage rate†	9,090	11,200
Indirect labour, at basic wage rate	2,420	2,960
Overtime premium	450	120
Lubricants and cleaning compounds	520	680
Maintenance	720	510
Other	1,200	2,150

Materials are priced at the end of each month on a weighted average basis. Relevant information of material stock movements during the month, for materials Y and Z, is as follows:–

	Material Y	Material Z
Opening Stock	1,050 kilos (value £529.75)	6,970 kilos (value £9,946.50)
Purchases	600 kilos at £0.50 per kilo 500 kilos at £0.50 per kilo 400 kilos at £0.52 per kilo	16,000 kilos at £1.46 per kilo
Issues from stores	1,430 kilos	8,100 kilos
Returns to stores	–	30 kilos

*This includes, in Department B, the scrapped Material Z. This was the only material scrapped in the month.
†All direct labour in Department A is paid at a basic wage of £4.50 per hour, and in Department B £4.00 per hour. Department A direct labour includes a total of 20 hours spent on rectification work.

Required:
(a) Prepare a list of the costs that should be assigned to Job No.123. Provide an explanation of your treatment of each item.   *(17 marks)*
(b) Discuss briefly how information concerning the cost of individual jobs can be used.   *(5 marks)*
   (Total 22 marks)
   (ACCA)

QUESTION

2(a) A printing firm is proposing offering a leaflet advertising service to local traders.
The following costs have been estimated for a batch of 10,000 leaflets:
   Setting-up machine: 6 hours at £10 per hour.
   Artwork: £20 per batch.
   Paper: £1.80 per 100 sheets.
   Other printing materials: £15.
   Direct labour cost: 4 hours at £6 per hour.
Fixed Overheads allocated to this side of the business are £1,000 per annum and recovered on the basis of orders received, which are expected to be 2 per week for 50 weeks in the year.
The Management requires 25% profit on selling price.

Required:
(i) A price to be quoted per 1,000 leaflets for batches of 2,000; 5,000; 10,000; and 20,000 leaflets.
(ii) The individual cost per leaflet at the various batch quantities.
   (12 marks)

(b) Draft a memorandum addressed to the printing-room manager
     informing him of the kind of costing information you will be providing
     him with as from 1 January 19–4. Your memorandum should explain
     the purpose of this information and the nature of any subsequent
     action he should be able to take.   *(10 marks)*
                                                          (Total 22 marks)
                                                                   (AAT)

CONTRACT COSTING
– Costing major projects or long term contracts

The CIMA define contract costing as follows: "That form of specific order costing which applies where work is undertaken to customers' special requirements and each order is of long duration compared with those to which job costing applies. The work is usually of a constructional nature. In general the method is similar to job costing, although it has certain distinctive features."

DISTINCTIVE FEATURES

Each contract is given a separate number and because the cost units are likely to be large, in order to maintain adequate control the work needs to be broken down and a number of sub-orders will be allocated to each contract. Costs will be recorded against each sub-order and the postings to the various sub-orders will be summarised on the main order. The total will represent the cost of the contract to date.

A greater proportion of costs can be allocated to the cost units, as a result the overhead to be absorbed is relatively small. In addition many costs which we have considered indirect will be treated as direct for the purpose of contracting costing. We can consider these further under the following headings:

a) **Direct Material** These are normally ordered for specific contracts and delivered to the site where the work is done. As a result the cost of materials will be charged directly to the contract. Smaller items may be requisitioned from a central store owned by the contractor and charged out in the normal manner.

b) **Direct Labour** The wages of those workers whose efforts and skills are applied directly to the contract will be treated as direct, e.g. labourers, engineers, carpenters etc. (craftsmen). Time and attendance will be recorded in the normal way and some kind of time sheet will be prepared.
   Other remuneration paid to site clerks, foreman and site administrative staff will NOT be regarded as overheads but they will be charged directly to the cost of the contract.

c) **Direct Expenses** It is often necessary to sub contract work to outside specialists. The invoice amounts will be charged directly to the contract.

Plant and Machinery Normally this will be an item of capital expenditure but they may be charged to the contract, e.g. bulldozers, cranes, cement mixers etc. may have been bought specifically for that contract. If the item will be used for other contracts then following the matching principle we should charge only that proportion consumed on that contract. This may be done through depreciation. Similarly if plant is sold at the end of the contract then the contract needs to be credited with the proceeds.

There is another method which is used to deal with plant and machinery where the contracts are for shorter periods, that is to hire out plant and machinery at an hourly or daily rate to the contract from a central pool.

Other Services Plant hire and stores may not be the only central service provided, e.g. window frames and doors may be made at a central workshop and transferred to site as and when required. If the workshop is unique to that contract it will need to be treated as a cost centre, and material, labour and overhead costs will be recorded and charged to the contract via that cost centre. If it is a central unit providing the service to a number of contracts then it will be more usual to invoice costs to the particular contract.

Overheads These will be relatively small in the case of contracts, since many of the costs will be treated direct to the contract. Where they do occur, e.g. central stores, central administration etc., they can be charged either using an overhead absorption rate or simply written off to the costing profit and loss account, by some agreed allocation.

Progress Payments Where contracts are of long duration, financing becomes a major problem, therefore the contractor will demand progress payments at regular intervals or when the work reaches particular stages. The contractor will issue an invoice on the basis of work completed to date. The customer will require the valuation to be supported by an architect's or quantity surveyor's certificate. Even so a percentage of the invoice will be retained by the customer in case damage occurs from faulty workmanship not evident at the time of invoice. This is known as **retention money** and gives the customer some protection.

Profit on Uncompleted Contracts Because contracts are of long duration and may cover a number of financial periods it is necessary to calculate profit on the contract to date. However, we need to take account of the prudence concept and therefore not anticipate profits which have not yet been earned, and to be aware that major defects could severely alter the profit situation. An arbitrary proportion is used, for example:-

$$\text{Estimated Profit} = \frac{2}{3} \text{ Notional Profit} \times \frac{\text{Cash received}}{\text{Value of work certified}}$$

EXAMPLE

Prepare a contract cost account from the following data.

	£
Materials purchased specifically for the contract	121,000
Stores issued	9,500
Materials returned to the stores	440
Materials transferred to other contracts	360
Book value of plant sent to site	24,000
Sub contract work	8,000
Direct wages	37,000
Direct expenses	4,600
Architect fees	2,500
Overhead absorbed	6,200
Valuation of work certified by architect	200,000

At the year end the following valuations were made:–

Materials on site	9,700
Cost of work done not yet certified	7,000
Plant on site	18,000
Accrued charges	640
Prepayments	200

The amount invoiced to the customer is based on the valuation of the work certified to the architect less a retention of 10%.

ANSWER TO EXAMPLE

CONTRACT COST ACCOUNT

	£Dr		£Cr
Purchases	121,000	Material returns	440
Stores issued	9,500	Material transfers to	
Plant	24,000	other contracts	360
Sub Contract work	8,000	Value of work	
Direct Wages	37,000	certified	200,000
Direct Expenses	4,600	Stock c/f	9,700
Architect Fees	2,500	Work in progress	
Overhead absorbed	6,200	c/f	7,000
Accrued charges		Plant c/f	18,000
c/f	640	Prepayment c/f	200
Costing Profit &			
Loss	13,356		
Profit Suspense c/f	8,904		
	235,700		235,700
Stock c/f	9,700	Accrued charges c/f	640
WIP c/f	7,000	Profit suspense c/f	8,904
Plant c/f	18,000		
Prepayment c/f	200		

WORKINGS:

$$\text{Estimate Profit} = \frac{2}{3} \text{ Notional Profit} \times \frac{\text{Cash Received}}{\text{Value of work certified}}$$

$$= \frac{2}{3} \times 22,260 \times \frac{180,000}{200,000}$$

$$= 13,356 \text{ — to Costing P \& L}$$

Profit to Suspense Account $= 22,260 - 13,356$

$$= £8,904$$

QUESTIONS

1. (a) Outline the special problems which are experienced when accounting for long term contracts, and explain the rules adopted by best accounting practice to overcome these problems.

(12 marks)

(b)   Bradmore Builders Ltd are a firm of building contractors. In the
      present conditions of slack trade they have only one current
      contract. Operating data for the contract for the year ended 30
      June 19–4 is as follows:

Contract	A
	£
Contract Price	620,000
Value of work certified	570,000
Cash received from Contractee	480,000
Work in Progress at 1 July 19–3	447,850
Costs incurred during the year:	
Materials	46,412
Labour	31,283
Overhead excluding depreciation	12,513
Plant – Valuation at 1 July 19–3	83,465
Plant – Valuation at 30 June 19–4	87,220
Plant – Purchased during year 19–3/4	21,478
Cost of work not yet certified	3,458

The contract is nearing completion and the quantity surveyors
estimate that a further £25,000 will be incurred to complete the
job, and that any plant remaining on the site will be sold for
£70,000 at completion. No further plant purchases are planned
for this contract.
The Work in Progress figure for the contract as at 1 July 19–3
included an estimated profit of £26,480.

Required:
Draft the appropriate ledger accounts to record the transactions
disclosed above in the books of Bradmore Builders Ltd; and
show how they would appear in the Balance Sheet as at 30 June
19–4.   *(11 marks)*
                                                        (Total 23 marks)
                                                                   (AAT)

2.   (a)   XY Construction Limited is building an extension to a college
          operated by the Education Authority. Work on the college
          extension commenced on 1st April, 19–1 and after one year, on
          31st March, 19–2, the data shown below were available.

Required:
(i)   Prepare the account for the contract for the year ended 31st
      March, 19–2;
(ii) Show in relation to the contract an extract from the balance
      sheet as at 31st March, 19–2.

During the year:

	£000
Plant sent to site	100
Direct materials received at site	460
Direct wages incurred	350
Direct expenses incurred	45
Hire of tower crane	40
Indirect labour costs	70
Supervision salaries	42
Surveyors fees	8
Service costs	18
Hire of scaffolding	20
Overhead incurred on site	60
Head office expenses apportioned to contract	70
Cash received from the Education Authority	1,000

	£000
At 31st March, 19–2	
Value of plant on site	75
Work certified, valued at	1,250
Cost of work not certified	250
Wages accrued	30
Service costs accrued	2
Materials unused on site	40

(b) Discuss the valuation of work-in-progress, with particular
reference to contract building work.   *(CIMA)*

PROCESS COSTING
– Chemicals and Beer?

DEFINITION

This is defined by the CIMA as:
"That form of operation costing which applies where standardised goods are produced.

> The cost per unit is ascertained as follows:–
>
> $$\frac{\text{costs incurred during the period}}{\text{no. of units produced during the period}}$$

WORK IN PROGRESS

There is usually going to be some work which is not completed at the end of a costing period. Therefore, following the matching principle of accounts, not all the costs from a period can be transferred to the next process since some of those costs relate to partially completed work which we therefore have to calculate.

EQUIVALENT UNITS

(the CIMA define equivalent unit as follows — "A notional quantity of completed unit substituted for an actual quantity of incomplete physical units in progress when the aggregate work content of the incomplete units is deemed to be equivalent to that of the substituted quantity. For example, 200 units 50% complete = 100 equivalent units, the principle applies when operation costs are being incurred and apportioned between WIP and completed output")

EXAMPLE

A manufacturing process consists of process A, B and C during a 4-week period 1000 units of product are completed.

The following information is available:

	Process £A	£B	£C
Direct Materials	4,000	2,000	1,000
Direct Wages	3,000	1,400	1,000
Direct Expenses	500	200	–

Indirect production costs were £5,000 and are to be apportioned on the basis of direct wage costs.

Note:
The output from process A is the input to process B, and the output from process B is the input to process C.

Prepare the process accounts, ignoring any WIP.

The inputs to each process (direct labour, material, expenses and overheads) are placed as debits in the account. The output is shown on the right hand side as a credit being transferred to the next process.

PROCESS A — ACCOUNT

	£Dr				£Cr	
	C.P.U.	Amount			C.P.U.	Amount
Direct Materials	4.00	4,000				
Direct Wages	3.00	3,000				
Direct Expenses	0.50	500				
Production Overhead	2.77	2,778	Output transferred to B	10.27	10,278
	10.27	10,278			10.27	10,278

PROCESS B

	C.P.U.	Amount			C.P.U.	Amount
Input from A	10.27	10,278				
Direct Materials	2.00	2,000				
Direct Wages	1.40	1,400				
Direct Expenses	0.20	200				
Production Overhead	1.30	1,296	Output transferred to C	15.17	15,174
	15.17	15,174			15.17	15,174

PROCESS C

	C.P.U.	Amount			C.P.U.	Amount
Input from B	15.17	15,174				
Direct Materials	1.00	1,000				
Direct Wages	1.00	1,000	Process			
Production Overhead	0.92	926	Total Cost	18.09	18,100
	18.09	18,100			18.09	18,100

BASIC FEATURES OF PROCESS COSTING

1. The total output for a period is accumulated.
2. The output is measured (quantity and value).

3. The average unit cost of output is measured.
   Two normal ways to deal with Work in Progress:
   a) The Average Cost Method (AVCO)
   b) First in First Out (FIFO)

EXAMPLE

A firm makes a product which undergoes 3 processes X, Y and Z. The input to Y is the output from X, the input to Z is the output from Y. Direct materials cost £10 per unit for process X, £5 for process Y, £3 for process Z. X used 1000 units, Y. 500 and Z. 100.

Direct wage costs for all 3 processes are £2 per hour. X used 500 hours, Y 300 and Z 200.

Direct expenses cost £1 per unit for X, £0.50 for Y and Zero for Z.

Indirect production costs were £10,000 and are to be apportioned on the basis of direct wage costs.

Prepare the process accounts, ignoring WIP.

PROCESS X

	£Dr C.P.U.	£Dr Amount		£Cr C.P.U.	£Cr Amount
Direct Materials	10.00	10,000			
Direct Wages	1.00	1,000			
Indirect Costs	5.00	5,000			
Direct Expenses	1.00	1,000	Output Transferred to Y	17.00	17,000
	17.00	17,000		17.00	17,000

PROCESS Y

	£Dr C.P.U.	£Dr Amount		£Cr C.P.U.	£Cr Amount
Input from X	17.00	17,000			
Direct Materials	5.00	2,500			
Direct Wages	1.20	600			
Direct Expenses	0.50	250			
Indirect Costs	6.00	3,000	Output Transferred to Z	29.70	23,350
	29.70	23,350		29.70	23,350

PROCESS Z

	£Dr				£Cr	
	C.P.U.	Amount			C.P.U.	Amount
Input from Y	29.70	23,350				
Direct Materials	3.00	300				
Direct Wages	4.00	400				
Indirect Costs	20.00	2,000	Process Cost		56.70	26,050
	56.70	26,050			56.70	26,050

EXAMPLE

Average Cost Per Unit with Work in Progress at the End

Process A – Opening WIP – UNITS = 0
Units Introduced this period   =   50,000
Units Finished   =   40,000
Units Uncompleted   =   10,000

COSTS INCURRED: £
Materials   100,000
Labour   67,500
Overhead   67,500

A technical estimate of WIP is given at the end of the period
           where Materials are 100% complete
           Labour and Overheads are 50% complete

PROCESS OF CALCULATION

1. Prepare the process account and reconcile the unit columns.
2. Convert the production into equivalent units, at this stage ignore any costs.
3. Costs charged to the process.
4. Costs per equivalent unit.
5. Evaluation:
   a) The work introduced and completed.
   b) The WIP uncompleted at the end of the period.
6. The final process account.

PROCESS A

1.

	£Dr				£Cr	
	C.P.U.	**Value**			**C.P.U.**	**Value**
Raw Materials			Completed (40,000)			
(50,000 units)	2.00	100,000	Work in Progress c/f			
Labour		67,500	(10,000 units)			
Overheads		67,500				
		235,000				235,000

2. Equivalent Units

In	Out		Material	Labour	Overhead
50,000		Work in Progress b/f	—	—	—
	40,000	Completed	40,000	40,000	40,000
	10,000	Work in Progress c/f			
		100% Materials	10,000		
		50% Labour & Overheads		5,000	5,000
50,000	50,000		50,000	45,000	45,000

3.

WIP b/f	NIL	NIL	NIL
COSTS	£100,000	£67,500	£67,500
TOTALS	100,000	67,500	67,500

4.

Cost per equivalent unit	$\dfrac{100,000}{50,000 \text{ (units)}}$	$\dfrac{67,500}{45,000}$	$\dfrac{67,500}{45,000}$
	= £2	£1.50	£1.50

VALUE OF INPUTS	Material = £100,000	Labour = £67,500	Overhead = £67,500
LESS VALUE OF COMPLETED UNITS	Material = £80,000	Labour = £60,000	Overhead = £60,000
VALUES OF WORK IN PROGRESS	20,000	7,500	7,500

Therefore: Total Value of WIP = £35,000.

ACCOUNTING FOR LOSSES

Sometimes the inputs may be greater than the outputs in a process, the loss must be analysed to determine the cause. Possible causes are:-
1. Theft;
2. Wastage (for example, evaporation, shrinkage);
3. Scrap (usually insignificant (in sales) – note scrap does have a recovery value).
4. Spoiled work which fails to meet quality control.
5. Defective units.

LOSS
There are 2 types:-
1. Normal; and
2. Abnormal.

1. A **normal loss** is an uncontrollable loss and is accepted as being a part of production. It should therefore be expected and allowed for in planning. The cost of such loss should be borne by the expected output, and the sales value of the expected loss is either treated as other income or credited direct to the process account. For example: evaporation, ullage.

> The average cost per unit without WIP would be:-
>
> $$\frac{\text{Cost Incurred} - \text{Sales Value of Normal Loss}}{\text{Units Introduced} - \text{Expected or Normal Loss}}$$

DISTINGUISHING BETWEEN WASTE and SCRAP

Waste is defined as a substance of no value.

"Scrap is a disregarded material having some recovery value which is normally disposed of without further treatment (other than reclamation handling) or reintroduced into the production process as raw materials." (ICMA).

All units lost are credited in the process account but in the case of scrap the saleable value is also credited after deducting handling costs.

EXAMPLE

Assume that 5000 litres of a material is introduced in the first process at 10p per litre.
Direct Wages £200
Production Overheads £100
Normal Loss = 5% of input and has no saleable value and is in wastage.

PROCESS ACCOUNT

	Litres	C.P.U.	Amount		Litres	C.P.U.	Amount
Direct Materials	5,000	0.10	500	Normal Loss (Waste)	250	—	—
Direct Wages			200				
Production Overheads			100	Output transferred to			
				process Z	4,750	0.168	800
	5,000	—	800		5,000	—	800

Using the same information in the above example, let us now assume that there is a recovery value of 2p per unit for the normal loss, i.e. scrap.

	Litres	C.P.U.	Amount		Litres	C.P.U.	Amount
Direct Materials	5,000	0.10	500	Normal Loss (Scrap)	250	0.02	5
Direct Wages			200	Output transferred to			
Production Overheads			100	process Z	4,750	0.167	795
	5,000	—	800		5,000	—	800

DR — Normal Loss A/c with quantity for wastage or recovery for scrap (Quantity and Value)

CR — Process A/c

ABNORMAL LOSSES

A loss exceeding a normal loss must by definition be an abnormal loss, thus by separating abnormal losses from the expected or normal loss it focuses management attention in order to control the business by taking action to avoid abnormal losses in future. If however, abnormal losses are a frequent occurrence it may be time for management to reconsider the allowance for normal loss, since maybe their original estimates were too optimistic. A credit entry has to be made for an abnormal loss in the process account. To do so, the cost of the loss needs to be apportioned between good production and abnormal loss. As a result, the cost per unit of abnormal loss must be identical to the unit cost of good production.

EXAMPLE

Using the information in the previous example and assuming a normal loss of 5% which has a recovery value of 2p per unit (i.e. scrap), let us assume that actual good production amounted to 4,600 units. Draw up the process account.

We do not yet know the values for normal loss (scrap) nor abnormal loss. We may calculate these thus:–

$$\begin{array}{lrl}
\text{Input} & 5,000 & \text{units} \\
\text{Output} & (4,600) & \text{units} \\
\hline
 & 400 & \\
\text{Normal (5\%)} & (250) & \\
\hline
\text{Abnormal Loss} & 150 & \text{units} \\
\hline
\end{array}$$

Abnormal Loss $= \dfrac{150}{4750} \times 795 = 25.11$ $\left(\begin{array}{c} \therefore 769.89 \text{ is used to} \\ \text{balance} \end{array} \right)$

Good production $= \dfrac{4600}{4750} \times 795 = 769.89$ rounded to 770 for simplicity of illustration.

DR — Abnormal Loss A/c

CR — Process A/c

	Litres	C.P.U.	Amount		Litres	C.P.U.	Amount
Direct Materials	5,000	0.10	500	Normal Loss (Scrap)	250	0.02	5
Direct Wages			200	Output transferred to			
Production Overheads			100	Process Z	4,600		770
				Abnormal Loss	150		25
	5,000		800		5,000		800

ABNORMAL GAIN

Where the quantity lost in the process is less than expected by the management, that is, it is less than the normal loss, it should be treated as an abnormal gain. Thus the difference between the normal loss and any abnormal gain would be the actual loss.

DR — Process A/c

CR — Abnormal Gain A/c

EXAMPLE

Using the information from our previous examples, assuming a 5% normal loss with a recovery value of 2p per unit that this time actual output is 4,800 units, prepare the process account.

	Litres	C.P.U.	Amount		Litres	C.P.U.	Amount
Direct Materials	5,000	0.1	500	Normal Loss (Scrap)	250	0.02	5
Direct Wages			200				
				Output transferred			
Production Overheads			100	to Process Z	4,800	0.167	803.37
Abnormal Gain	50	0.167	8.37				
	5,050	—	808.37		5,050	—	808.37

NOTE

We would take the following steps in order to calculate the abnormal gain:–
1. Calculate the normal loss.
2. Obtain a unit cost for expected good production.
3. Multiply the unit cost for expected good production by the actual output quantity.
4. The value of the abnormal gain may then be obtained in one of two ways:
    a) by deducting the value of inputs from the value of outputs – you can obtain the total value of the abnormal gain; or alternatively
    b) by multiplying the unit quantity for the abnormal gain by normal good production unit price.

THE EFFECT ON THE NORMAL LOSS ACCOUNT OF AN ABNORMAL GAIN

NORMAL LOSS A/c

	£Dr		£Cr
Process A/c	5	Scrap sales (200 × 0.02)	4
		Abnormal Gain	1
	5		5

ABNORMAL GAINS A/c

	£Dr		£Cr
Normal Loss A/c	1.00	Process 1	8.37
Costing P/L A/c c/f	7.37		
	8.37		8.37

This has taken account of the fact that we now only have 200 units of normal loss to sell as scrap at a recovery of 2p each, i.e. actual inputs 5,000 units less actual outputs 4,800 units which leaves scrap sales of 200 units. Normal loss however was estimated to be 250 units – with a loss of only 200, an abnormal gain of 50 units was thereby made. The scrap sales account would be debited with the amount sold and credited with cash received and any profit made transferred to the costing Profit and Loss Account.

JOINT PRODUCTS

Some processes might produce two or more products each having sufficiently high saleable value to merit recognition as a product in its own right. They are only separately identifiable from a point which is called the **split off point** or point of separation. Up to that point all costs are JOINT COSTS and need apportioning on a suitable basis.

The most common methods of apportioning joint costs are:–
1. By sales value – where costs are apportioned relative to their selling price;
2. By market value or notional market value at the split off point; and
3. By physical measurement, e.g. weight or volume.

Where physical measurement is not used then market value is preferred to sales value since the sales value may be distorted owing to different weights of further processing costs.

EXAMPLE
(a) Explain briefly the distinction between joint products and by-products.

(b) Discuss briefly the problems involved in calculating the cost of manufacture of joint products with particular reference to the apportionment of pre-separation point costs.

A common method of apportioning these pre-separation point costs is by physical measurement: outline two other methods.

(c) In a process line of the JP Manufacturing Company Limited, three joint products are produced. For the month of October the following data were available:

Product	X	Y	Z
Sales price per kilogram	£5	£10	£20
Post-separation point costs	£10,000	£5,000	£15,000
Output in kilograms	2,500	1,000	1,500

Pre-separation point costs amounted to £20,000.

The joint products are manufactured in one common process, after which they are separated and may undergo further individual processing. The pre-separation point costs are apportioned to joint products, according to weight.

You are required:
(i) to prepare a statement showing the estimated profit or loss for each product and in total;
(ii) as an alternative to the costing system used in (i) above, to present a statement which will determine the maximum profit from the production of these joint products.

The sales value of each product at separation point is as follows:

$$X = £3 \qquad Y = £4 \qquad Z = £6$$

(CIMA)

EXAMPLE ANSWER

1. Pre-separation costs are apportioned by weight of output in kilos:

$$X = \frac{2,500 \text{ kilos}}{5,000 \text{ kilos}} \times £20,000 \text{ pre-separation costs} = \textbf{£10,000}$$

$$Y = \frac{1,000}{5,000} \times £20,000 = \textbf{£4,000}$$

$$Z = \frac{1,500}{5,000} \times £20,000 = \textbf{£6,000}$$

2.
JP Manufacturing Company Ltd.

Statement of Estimated Profit & Loss for Joint-Products X, Y and Z for the month of October

	X		Y		Z		Total
Output in kilograms	2,500		1,000		1,500		5,000
	£		£		£		£
Selling price per kilo	5		10		20		
Sales	12,500		10,000		30,000		52,500
Apportioned costs[1]	10,000		4,000		6,000		20,000
Subsequent costs	10,000		5,000		15,000		30,000
Total costs	20,000		9,000		21,000		50,000
Profit/(Loss)	(£7,500)		£1,000		£9,000		£2,500

3. "Marginal costing" is applied to determine which products to sell at the split-off point and which it would be more profitable to process further.

Calculation of Profit/(Loss) on Sale at Split-off Point

PRODUCT	X	Y	Z
Final selling price	£5	£10	£20
Less Additional processing costs	4	5	10
"Market" value at split-off or point of separation	£1	£5	£10
But Selling price at split-off point	3	4	6
Profit/(Loss)	£2	(£1)	(£4)

Workings:

Post-Separation/Subsequent Processing costs
Kilograms of weight

$$X = \frac{£10,000}{2,500 \text{ kilos}} = \textbf{£4 per kilo}$$

$$Y = \frac{£5,000}{1,000 \text{ kilos}} = \textbf{£5 per kilo}$$

$$Z = \frac{£15,000}{1,500 \text{ kilos}} = \textbf{£10 per kilo}$$

Product X should be sold at the separation point since it makes a "profit" of £2 per kilogram over "market value". Products Y and Z should be processed further, as follows:–

4. **Statement of Estimated Profit for Product X sold at separation point and Products Y and Z sold after further processing**

	X	Y	Z	Total
Output in kilos	2,500	1,000	1,500	5,000
	£	£	£	£
Selling price per kilo	3	10	20	
Less Additional processing costs per kilo	–	5	10	
Contribution per unit	3	5	10	
Total contribution*	7,500	5,000	15,000	27,500
Less Pre-separation costs				20,000
Maximum Profit from Production of Joint Products				£7,500

WORKINGS – Contribution per unit × output
e.g. £3 × 2,500 = 7,500 for X.

BY-PRODUCTS

The CIMA define a by-product as follows:- "A product which is recovered incidentally from the material used in the manufacture of recognized main products, such a by-product having either a net realizable value or useable value which is relatively low in comparison with the saleable value of the main products. The preferred costing treatment is to deduct net realizable value from cost of production".

SELF-CHECK QUESTIONS

1X AB Chemicals Limited produces a compound by mixing certain ingredients within two separate processes. For a particular week the recorded costs were:

      Process 1   – Material: 2,000 kilogrammes at £2 per kilogramme
                             Labour: £360
                             Process plant time: 24 hours at £200 per hour
      Process 2   – Material: 3,100 kilogrammes at £6 per kilogramme
                             Labour: £240
                             Process plant time: 40 hours at £76.30 per hour.

Indirect production overhead for the week amounted to £2,400 and is absorbed on the basis of labour cost.

   Normal outputs are: Process 1   80% of input
                         Process 2   90% of input

Discarded materials have scrap values of £0.30 per kilogramme from Process 1 and £1.50 per kilogramme from Process 2. Assume that sales of scrap are made for cash during the week.

There was no work-in-progress at either the beginning or end of the week.

Output during the week was 1,400 kilogrammes from Process 1 and 4,200 kilogrammes from Process 2.

Required:
You are required to:
(a) Show the accounts for:
     (i) Process 1;
     (ii) Process 2;
     (iii) abnormal gain/loss;
     (iv) profit and loss – relating to transactions in any of the above accounts;
     (v) finished goods.   *(16 marks)*

(b) Explain, in relation to process costing, the concept of 'equivalent units' and give a simple example using your own figures.
                                        (4 marks)
                                (Total 20 marks)
                                          (CIMA)

2X A manufacturing company makes a product by two processes and the data below relates to the second process for the month of April.

A work-in-progress balance of 1,200 units brought forward from March was valued, at cost, as follows:

	£
Direct materials, complete	10,800
Direct wages, 60% complete	6,840
Production overhead, 60% complete	7,200

During April, 4,000 units were transferred from the first process to the second process at a cost of £7.50 each, this input being treated as direct material within the second process.

Other costs incurred by the second process were:

	£
Additional direct materials	4,830
Direct wages	32,965
Production overhead	35,538

3,200 completed units were transferred to finished goods store. A loss of 520 units, being normal, occurred during the process. The average method of pricing is used.

Work-in-progress at the end of April consisted of 500 completed units awaiting transfer to the finished goods store and a balance of unfinished units which were complete as regards direct material and 50% complete as regards direct wages and production overhead.

You are required to:
(a) Prepare for the month of April the account for the second process;   *(14 marks)*

(b) Present a statement for management setting out the:
(i) cost per unit of the finished product, by element of cost and total;
(ii) cost of production transferred to finished goods;
(iii) cost of production of completed units awaiting transfer to finished goods;
(iv) cost of uncompleted units in closing work-in-progress, by element of cost and in total.   *(6 marks)*
(Total 20 marks)
(CIMA)

QUESTIONS

---

3. A process costing £200,000 produces 3 products – A, B & C. Output details are as follows:

Product A	6,000 litres
Product B	10,000 litres
Product C	20,000 tonnes

Each product may be sold at the completion of the process as follows:

	Sales value at the end of the first process
Product A	£10 per litre
Product B	£4 per litre
Product C	£10 per tonne

Alternatively, further processing of each individual product can be undertaken to produce an enhanced product thus:

	Subsequent Processing Costs	**Sales Value After Final Process**
Enhanced Product A	£14 per litre	£20 per litre
Enhanced Product B	£2 per litre	£8 per litre
Enhanced Product C	£6 per tonne	£16 per tonne

Required:
(a) Explain the following terms:
 (i)   normal process loss,
 (ii) joint Product,
 (iii) by Product, and
  state the appropriate costing treatments for normal process
  loss and for by products.   *(10 marks)*

(b) Calculate the apportionment of joint process costs to products
  A, B and C above.   *(8 marks)*

(c) Explain whether the initial process should be undertaken and
  which, if any, of the enhanced products should be produced.
                                                            (7 marks)
                                                     (Total 25 marks)
                                                                (AAT)

4. (a) In a process costing system state what is meant by:
  (i)   normal loss, and
  (ii) abnormal loss, and indicate how you would treat these items
    in the cost accounts.

(b) A company makes one product which passes through two
  processes. From the data given below which relates to period 4,
  you are required to show the transactions which would appear in
  the two process accounts, finished goods account, abnormal loss
  account and the abnormal gain account.

  Process No. 1
  Material: 5,000 kilogrammes at £0.5 per kilogramme
  Labour: £800
  Production overhead 200% on labour

  Process No. 2
  Materials: 4,000 kilogrammes at £0.8 per kilogramme
  Labour: £1,753
  Production overhead 100% on labour

Normal losses are 20% of input in process 1 and 10% of input in process 2 but without further processing any losses are able to be sold as scrap for £0.3 per kilogramme from process 1 and £0.7 per kilogramme from process 2.

The outputs for period 4 were:
3,800 kilogrammes from process 1
7,270 kilogrammes from process 2

There was no work in process at the beginning or end of period 4 and no finished goods stock at the beginning of the period.

(20 marks)

(CIMA)

5. A company assembles and finishes a product using two bought-in components. Details of the make-up of the standard variable production cost of one unit of finished product are as follows:–

Component	Number of units of component per unit of finished product	Cost per unit of component (£)
A	4	1.00
B	1	3.50

There is no allowance for wastage of components.
Direct labour for assembling and finishing: 1.5 hours at £3.00 per hour.
Variable production overhead: absorbed on a direct labour hour basis at a rate of £2.00 per hour.

Production information for the month just ended is as follows:–

Units of product: completed, 10,250
closing work-in-process, 400 (these incorporate all components, but only 50% of direct labour and variable overhead costs)
opening work-in-process, 250 (these incorporate all components, but only 60% of direct labour and variable overhead costs)

Number of components used: component A, 42,000
component B, 10,460
(Components are charged to work-in-process at standard price, material price variances having been identified on purchase).

Hours worked: 15,070.

Required:
(a) Prepare the process account for the month just ended (variances should be identified in as much detail as possible from the information provided). *(15 marks)*

(b) Contrast the process account prepared in (a) above with that which would be prepared in a non-standard process costing system.
(7 marks)
(Total 22 marks)
(ACCA)

STANDARD COSTING & VARIANCE ANALYSIS
– a means of planning and control

Many organisations operate a standard costing system. Standard cost is a predetermined estimate which is compared with actual costs as they are incurred. The difference between the two is described as a variance. A favourable variance occurs when the actual cost is lower than the standard cost, an unfavourable variance (also referred to as an adverse variance) is when the actual cost exceeds the standard. Standard costs may be calculated on several different assumptions as indicated below.

STANDARDS

A Basic standard is used over long periods of time and trends can be determined. It is an underlying standard from which a *current standard* can be developed.

Ideal standards These are used taking no account of breakdowns, wastage, stoppages, idle time, strikes etc. They would be the standard if everything ran smoothly. They are very seldom used in practice because they are unrealistic. An ideal standard assumes the most favourable conditions possible.

Attainable standards These do take account of breakdowns, wastage, stoppages, idle time etc., and are designed to give a realistic picture. These are the most widely used type of standard in practice. This is a *'Normal Standard'* or an *Expected Standard.*

Current standards Sometimes a current standard may be introduced in order to take account of short term price fluctuations or use fluctuations. You may therefore suspend the attainable standard for a short time and use the current standard because you think the current standard more realistically reflects the position. It is a standard established for use over a short period of time, related to current conditions.

Material Standard – Paper
This takes into account the mix of the types of paper, the estimated price change for the next period and the time of the price change.
        Original Price £2.00   Future Price £2.40
The paper may be purchased in equal quantities thus a standard price would fall between the £1.80 and £2.40 at £2.20.

INVOICE RECEIVED	£
20 units material a actual cost of 2.30 p.u.	46.00
+ VAT a 15%	6.90
Payable	52.90

THE WAY IT WOULD BE CODED MIGHT BE:-

Codes

8200	20 units a 2.20	44.00
1000	Price variance of Raw Material	2.00
9000	VAT	6.90
		52.90

Where the following codes for processing the invoice in the computer system are as follows:-

1000   Price variance of raw material
8200   Standard purchase cost of raw material
9000   VAT

an attainable standard for raw materials may be set as follows:

1. Calculate the current weighted average price for purchases, i.e. in proportion to usage.

2. Take account of any known forthcoming price increases or reductions, e.g. supposing you currently buy paper for between £1.80 and £2.40 per unit and it is consumed in equal amounts at the various prices then the weighted average price would be £2.10. Supposing you also expect prices in the budgeted period to increase on average by 10% with effect from halfway through the year then you might decide to add a further 10½p for this. Rounded in above example to 10p. (See above example.)

MATERIAL PRICE VARIANCE

Price Variance = **Actual Quantity × Actual Price
– Actual Quantity × STD Price**

OR = **(Standard Price – Actual Price)
× Actual Quantity
(SP – AP) × AQ**

MATERIAL USAGE VARIANCE

= **Actual Quantity × STD Price**
− STD Quantity × STD Price

OR = **(Standard Quantity − Actual Quantity)**
× Standard Price
(SQ − AQ) × SP

DIRECT WAGE RATE VARIANCE

= **(Standard Rate per hour − Actual Rate)**
× No. of hours worked
(SR − AR) × AH

DIRECT WAGE EFFICIENCY VARIANCE

= **(Standard no. of hours − Actual**
no. of hours) × Standard rate per hour
(SH − AH) × SR

EXAMPLE

The standard cost information for the production of one unit of product X
is as follows:

Direct Materials   5 kilograms of Material Y @ 60p per
kilogram.

During a certain cost period 4,000 units of X were manufactured and the
material used in production was 20,200 kilograms of Y at a total cost of
£11,716. Calculate the material cost variance and separate the results into
a price and usage variance.

	£
STD Direct Materials	12,000
(4,000 × £3)	
Actual Cost	11,716
	284 F

(Favourable Variance)

The question now arises − was it a price or material usage variance?

Price Variance
= (SP − AP) × AQ
= (£0.60 − £0.58) × 20,000
= £404 (Favourable Price Variance)

Price Variance   £404 (F)

Material Usage Variance
$$(SQ - AQ) \times SP$$
$$(20,000 - 20,200) \times £0.60 = £120 \text{ (Adverse Material Variance)}$$

Taking the two constituent variances together we have a Net Favourable Material Cost Volume of £284 (F).

REASONS FOR MATERIAL PRICE VARIANCE

1. Efficient or inefficient buying.
2. A reduction in production may mean smaller amounts purchased, therefore a loss of quantity discounts. The reverse may also be true.
3. The need to acquire emergency supplies may lead to higher prices.
4. Changing quality of the material purchased.
5. The loss of a source of supply which was inexpensive.
6. External factors, e.g. if you buy from abroad, exchange rates. Other factors – inflation.

REASONS FOR USAGE VARIANCE

1. Inefficiency by an operator using the material (if not watching a machine and a fault occurs, e.g. in printing – operative may fail to turn off machine in time to minimise quantity of paper spoilt).
2. Spoilages – due to insufficient maintenance of machinery.
3. Substitution of poor quality material resulting in lost production.
4. Change in the methods of production which makes the standard being used obsolete.
5. Inadequate storage, causing damage.
6. If the actual mix of materials in the product change then the usage variance would change also.

DIRECT WAGE COST VARIANCES

Using the same example direct wage costs at standard for product X 3 hours at £2 per hour.

4,000 units were produced in 11,750 hours, at a labour cost of £24,675. Thus the actual hourly rate paid was £2.10.

	£
STD Direct Wages	24,000
(4,000 units @ £6 p.u.)	
Actual Cost	24,675
	(675) A

(Adverse Variance)

Direct Wage Rate Variance   £
   (SR – AR) × AH
   = (2 – 2.10) × 11750   =   1,175   A

Direct Wage Efficiency Variance
   (SH – AH) × SR
   = (12,000 – 11,750) × 2   =   500   F
                                             _____
                                              (675) A

                                       (Adverse Variance)

REASONS FOR WAGE RATE VARIANCES

1. Pay rises which have not been budgeted for.
2. Using different grades of labour whose rates differ from those specified in the standard cost of the product.

REASONS FOR LABOUR EFFICIENCY VARIANCES

1. The efficiency or inefficiency of the labour employed on production. This may arise from using different grades of labour from those who normally do the job, for example, trainees.
2. A change in production methods.
3. Machine breakdowns.
4. Correction of spoiled work.
5. Bad production planning, e.g. machines not available when required or material stockouts.
6. The purchase of new or more efficient machinery leading to better labour utilisation.

VARIABLE PRODUCTION OVERHEAD VARIANCE

This is the difference between the standard variable production overhead absorbed in the actual production and the actual variable production overhead. There can be no quantity variance, this is because the standard and the actual are measured using the same level of output, e.g. the budgeted variable production overhead for the month of June is £15,000 for a budgeted production of 12,000 units. The actual figures were £14,600 variable overhead expenditure for an actual production of 12,500 units.

VARIABLE OVERHEAD PRODUCTION VARIANCE

	£
Standard Cost of Actual Production	
$£15,000 \times \dfrac{12500}{12000}$	15,625
Actual Cost	14,600
Variable Production Overhead Variance	1,025 F

FIXED PRODUCTION OVERHEAD VARIANCE

This is defined in the CIMA terminology as "The difference between the standard cost of fixed overheads absorbed in the production achieved whether completed or not and the fixed overhead attributed and charged to that period." It consists of two elements; a volume variance and an expenditure variance.

VOLUME VARIANCE

= (Actual Hours – Budgeted Hours) × Budgeted Absorption Rate

EXPENDITURE VARIANCE

= (Budgeted Fixed Overhead – Actual Fixed Overhead)

EXAMPLE

The budgeted fixed overhead for May was £12,000.
The budget output in terms of standard hours was 5,000 hours. The actual fixed overhead was £12,300 and the actual production expressed in standard hours 5,500.

Fixed Budgeted Overhead absorbed

$$\frac{5,500 \times £12,000}{5,000 \text{ hrs}} \quad \text{i.e. } £2.40 \qquad = \qquad 13,200$$

Actual Fixed Overhead   12,300
                                                            ―――――
                                                             900 F

Volume Variance
= (Actual Hours – Budgeted Hours) × Budgeted Absorption Rate
                                                              £
= (5,500 – 5,000) × 2.40
= 500 × 2.40   1,200 F

Expenditure Variance
= 12,000 – 12,300   300 A
                                                            ―――――
                                                             900 F

SALES VARIANCES

Operating Profit Variance due to Sales	
Sales Price Variance (ACT SP – STD SP) × ACT Q	Sales Volume Variance (ACT Q – Budgeted Q) × STD Unit Operating Profit

EXAMPLE

A business manufactures a single product. The budget for May gives the following information relating to sales:

Quantity   10,000 units
Selling Price   £20 p.u.
Standard Cost   £14 p.u.

During the month 9,600 units were sold and the invoiced value of sales £196,800 = £2.05 per unit.

Calculate

1. The operating profit variance due to sales.
2. The sales price variance.
3. The sales volume variance.

Reasons for a Sales Price Variance

1. Offering a discount.
2. Changing selling price.

OPERATING PROFIT VARIANCE

	£
a) Budgeted Operating Profit	
10,000 units × £20 p.u. – £14 p.u.)	60,000
b) Actual Sales	196,800
c) Standard Cost of Actual Sales	
9,600 (actual sales) × £14 (standard cost)	134,400
d) Margin between Actual Sales and Standard	
Cost of Sales (b) – (c)	62,400
Operating Profit Variance due	
to Sales (60,000 – 62,400)	2,400 F

	£
Sales Price Variance	
(ACT SP – STD SP) × ACT Q	
(20.5 – 20) × 9,600	
0.50 × 9,600 = 4,800 F	4,800 F
Sales Volume Variance	
(ACT Q – Budgeted Q) × STD Unit Operating Profit	
(9,600 – 10,000) × £6	
–400 × 6 = 2400 A	2,400 A
	2,400 F

REASONS FOR VOLUME VARIANCE

The budget sales figure is not achieved for various reasons. For example:
- More fierce competition in the market place hence a loss of markets to competitors.
- New products introduced causing a change in buying preferences, hence lost sales (makes the product obsolete).
- Production hold ups which prevent the achievement of target delivery dates.

This list is not exhaustive and you might like to consider other reasons, drawing on your own experiences.

QUESTIONS

1. (a) Explain the difference between:
        (i) sales variances; and
        (ii) sales margin variances.
        Which do you consider to be more useful to management and why?

   (b) Some cost accounting textbooks refer to 'idle time variance' within the context of direct wages while others refer to idle time as an overhead cost item. Which view do you support and why?
                                                               (20 marks)
                                                                  (CIMA)

2. The following details of Product B are provided:

Standard Cost	£
Direct material – 2 lb. at £2 per lb.	4.0
Direct wages – 1 hour of work	1.0
	5.0
Standard Selling Price	10.0

   The budgeted product and sales are 1,000 units for each of the 13 reporting periods in the year.
   In the 7th reporting period the actual results were as follows:

		£
Sales	980 units sold for	10,200
Material purchases (all used)	2,000 lb. costing	5,000
Labour	800 hours paid and worked	1,000

   Required:
   (a) Prepare a report of performance for the period in a form suitable for presentation to management. Your report should briefly provide possible explanations for the results.   *(17 marks)*

(b) Explain what you understand by the terms "forecast" and "budget", distinguishing carefully between them.   *(8 marks)*
(Total 25 marks)
(AAT)

3. A company manufactures two products called 'Kob' and 'Kleg'. Each uses two kinds of materials, 'Alloy' and 'Composite', and two grades of labour, grade I and grade II.

At the beginning of a 4 week period the following stocks were recorded:

Kob	**Kleg**	**Alloy**	**Composite**
16 units	9 units	187 kilos, value £935	60 kilos, value £480

Planned specifications for each product are:

	Kob	**Kleg**
Alloy (£5 kilo)	3 kilos	1 kilo
Composite (£8 kilo)	1 kilo	4 kilos
Grade I Labour (£4 hour)	30 minutes	15 minutes
Grade II Labour (£5 hour)	24 minutes	48 minutes

Overheads are recovered at 100% of labour cost.
Actual transactions for the 4-week period were:

Material purchases	Alloy	900 kilos costing £5,400
	Composite	870 kilos costing £6,003

Materials issued to production:	Alloy	890 kilos
	Composite	810 kilos
Grade I Labour:	142 hours costing £568	
Grade II Labour:	200 hours costing £960	
Overheads, total:	£1,596	

	Kob	**Kleg**
Transfer to Finished Stock	208 units	152 units
Sales	210 units	135 units

There was no work in progress at beginning or end of the period and no losses in production.

You are required to calculate:
(i)   the standard cost of one unit of each product.   *(5 marks)*
(ii)   a) material usage variances for each material.
       b) material price variances for each material.
       c) labour efficiency variance for each grade of labour.
       d) wages rate variance for each grade of labour.
       e) overhead variance in total.   *(10 marks)*
       Note: assume materials are issued on the FIFO basis.
(iii) the Finished Goods Stock valuation at standard cost at the end of the period.   *(6 marks)*

(iv) the Material Stock Valuation at standard cost at the end of the period. *(7 marks)*
(Total 28 marks)
(AAT)

4. This diagram reflects material costs within a standard costing system. Assume that all the variances are unfavourable.

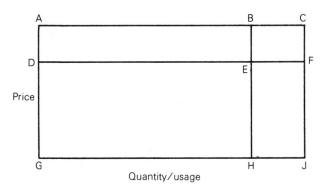

(a) state which rectangle(s) represent the:
   (i) standard cost;
   (ii) actual cost;
   (iii) material price variance;
   (iv) material usage variance;
   (v) material cost variance. *(9 marks)*
Note: Your answer should be stated in the form of the letters representing each corner of each rectangle; it is not necessary to draw the diagram.

(b) give a short explanation of:
   (i) principal budget factor;
   (ii) the membership and functions of a budget committee.
(6 marks)
(Total 15 marks)
(CIMA)

CAPITAL INVESTMENT — APPRAISAL
– buying fixed assets

DEFINITIONS OF CAPITAL INVESTMENT

It has been defined by many business economists in the following terms:
1. A creative search for investment opportunities.
2. A means of strategic planning, that is, long term planning.
3. As part of a budgeting process in short to medium term planning.
4. A realistic estimation of the economic value of individual projects.

In this section we are mainly concerned with the last of these definitions. Project evaluation has to be undertaken by all business whether formally or informally.

INVESTMENTS AND OPPORTUNITY COST

The cost of following one course of action may well be the lost value of the opportunity foregone. Economists refer to this as opportunity cost. For example, given that an organisation has limited resources and competing projects such as: (a) to build a new factory, or (b) to undertake further research; if it chooses project (a) the opportunity cost (i.e. the alternative foregone) would be project (b). This is an example of projects which accountants refer to as 'mutually exclusive'. On the other hand there may be projects which because of the method of funding or because of the nature of the project are independent of one another, but this is unusual, if resources are scarce. Again in this section we are concerned with projects which are 'mutually exclusive'.

PURPOSE

The main objective of any investment decision is to obtain a return on the investment greater than the outlay at the start. Of course it may take some time to obtain the return, and therefore account must be taken of the changing value of money. Pound notes in 1985 will not have the same value in terms of purchasing power as, say, pound notes in 1990. Discounted Cash Flow (DCF) techniques of investment appraisal may take account of this.

Methods:
1. The Payback Method
2. Discounted Cash Flow —Net Present Value
                          —Internal Rate of Return
3. The Accounting Rate of Return (Book Rate)

THE PAYBACK METHOD

The criterion for investment using this method is how quickly the investment cost will be returned. For example, if we have two investment alternatives both costing £10,000 initially and returns as follows, which alternative should we choose?

Time	A £	B £
Year Initial Outlay	– 10,000	– 10,000
Year 1 Cash Receipts	+ 3,000	+ 1,000
Year 2	+ 2,000	+ 3,000
Year 3	+ 5,000	+ 3,000
Year 4	+ 2,000	+ 3,000

Investment opportunity A repays the initial outflow of cash by the end of the third year, whereas B is not repaid until the end of the fourth year. Using our criterion for the Payback Method we would choose A.

Supposing the two investment opportunities had cash flow streams as follows:

	A £	B £
Year 0 Initial Outlay	– 10,000	– 10,000
Year 1 Cash Receipts	5,000	1,000
Year 2	4,000	3,000
Year 3	1,000	6,000

Now which alternative investment opportunity should we choose? Using our Payback Method criterion, i.e. how quickly the initial outlay is repaid, we cannot differentiate between A and B. Both investments look equally attractive. This is because the Payback Method takes no account of the time value of money. As we stated earlier, pound notes in year one may not be worth the same as pound notes at the end of year three owing to rising price levels (inflation).

DEFINITION OF TERMS

Discounted Cash Flow (DCF)

The value of future expected cash receipts and expenditures at a common date which is calculated using NET PRESENT VALUE (NPV) OR INTERNAL RATE OF RETURN (IRR).
Application: CAPITAL INVESTMENT APPRAISAL — SECURITIES INVESTMENT.

1. **Payback.** Finds the period of time projects have to run before their original investment (Cash Outlay) is returned.

2. **Internal Rate of Return (Discounted Cash Flow).** Finds the average return on investment earned through the life of the investment. It

determines the discount rate that equates the present value of future cash flows to the cost of the investment.

3. **Net Present Value (Discounted Cash Flow).** Applies a rate of discount (interest rate) based on the marginal cost of capital to future cash flows to bring them back to the present.

4. **Accounting Rate of Return (or Book Rate of Return).** Measures profit on the project each year by the projects total investment cost to give a rate of return. This is not a discounted cash flow method of appraisal.

NET PRESENT VALUE (NPV)

The formula for **compound interest** is:-

$$A = P(1+r)^n$$

where A is the Amount
P is the Principal (or Present Value)
r is the rate of interest
n is the time period

EXAMPLE

If we invest £100 at 10% per annum what will the compound accumulated interest be in 5 years?

For the present value, we need to transpose the formula as follows:-

$$P = \frac{A}{(1+r)^n}$$

Using the above example, what would £161.05 at the end of year 5 be worth in present value terms today (i.e. time 0), given an annual rate of interest of 10%?

Working back we can prove this:-

$$A = P(1+r)^n$$
$$= 100(1+.10)^5 \quad \text{therefore} \quad P = \frac{£161.05}{(1.10)^5}$$
$$= £161.05 \qquad\qquad\qquad\qquad = £100$$

Supposing a firm could invest its funds at 10% per annum for the next 5 years in a bank, or it could adopt a new project to produce goods for sale. The estimated cash flow for the 5 year period being as follows:-

Year End	1	2	3	4	5
Amount £	−10,000	+2,000	+2,500	+3,000	+4,000

Would the investment in the project be worthwhile?

To find out if the project is worthwhile we will discount the returns at 10% per annum (i.e. the alternative rate at which we could invest capital to see if it is a better investment).

Thus, we need to know the discount rate for each year:-

Year	1	2	3	4	5

$$\frac{1}{(1.10)^1} + \frac{1}{(1.10)^2} + \frac{1}{(1.10)^3} + \frac{1}{(1.10)^4} + \frac{1}{(1.10)^5}$$

The Discount Factor is:

	.909	.826	.751	.683	.621

We then need to multiply the outflows and inflows by the Discount Rate

Thus:	Year 1	$-10,000 \times .909$	$=$	-9090
	2	$+2000 \times .826$	$=$	$+1652$
	3	$+2500 \times .751$	$=$	$+1878$
	4	$+3000 \times .683$	$=$	$+2049$
	5	$+4000 \times .621$	$=$	$+2484$
		NET PRESENT VALUE		-1027

The project is not worth investing in since it yields a negative NPV. If, however, the NPV was positive, we would accept it.

Let us suppose that the cost of the funds, that is, the **Cost of Capital** was only 5%, given the same cash flows, would the project be worthwhile?

Let us make a similar appraisal on this basis.

	Cash Flow		**Discount Rate**		**NPV £**
Year 1	$-10,000$	$\times$	.952	$=$	-9520
2	$+ 2,000$	$\times$	.907	$=$	$+1814$
3	$+ 2,500$	$\times$	.864	$=$	$+2160$
4	$+ 3,000$	$\times$	.823	$=$	$+2469$
5	$+ 4,000$	$\times$	.784	$=$	$+3136$
Net Present Value					$+ \quad 59$

Yes, the project is worth accepting since it yields a positive Net Present Value.

Problems in Practice
1. Cash flows are subject to uncertainty.
2. Interest rates are also uncertain, and therefore the cost of capital.

Advantages of the NPV Rule
1. The method does take account of the 'time value' of money.
2. Relatively easy to calculate.

THE INTERNAL RATE OF RETURN

DEFINITION

Internal Rate of Return (Discounted Cash Flow). Finds the average return on investment earned through the life of the investment. It determines the discount rate that equates the present value of future cash flows to the cost of the investment.

Taking the following example:

Year	Project A £	Project B £
0	- 10,000	- 10,000
1	+ 5,000	+ 1,000
2	+ 4,000	+ 3,000
3	+ 1,000	+ 6,000
4	+ 2,000	+ 3,000

Formula for Net Present Value:

$$NPV = \sum_{0}^{\infty} \frac{A}{(1 + r)^n}$$

where A = Cash Flows
       n = the number of periods over which the project will run
       r = The Discount Rate

$\sum_{0}^{\infty}$ = Sum of these cash flows from time zero (0) to infinity (whenever you place the time limit).

We need to choose a discount rate that equates the inflows in each of the years one to four with the cash outflow at the start.

Let us try 10%.
$-10,000 + 5,000 (.909) + 4,000 (.826) + 1,000 (.751) + 2,000 (.683)$
$-10,000 + 9966$
$= -34$

10% p.a. is just a little too high, we need therefore to try a lower rate. Let us try 8%.
$= -10,000 + 5,000 (.926) + 4,000 (.857) + 1,000 (.794) + 2,000 (.735)$
$= -10,000 + 10,322$
$= +322$

We know that the IRR lies somewhere between 8 and 10% p.a. If we take the lower rate (8) and add the difference between the highest rate we chose (10) and the lower rate (8) which is 2 and multiply this by the difference we obtained at the lower rate, +322, divided by the total difference between the two rates, we will obtain the IRR. That is:- **[(–34 + 322) = 356]**

$$8 + (2 \times \frac{322}{356}) \quad = \quad \underline{\underline{9.81}}$$

CHECK THAT THIS IS CORRECT:-

$$
\begin{aligned}
9.81\% &= -10{,}000 + 5{,}000 \,(.911) + 4{,}000 \,(.829) \\
&\qquad + 1{,}000 \,(.755) + 2{,}000 \,(.687) \\
&= -10{,}000 + 10{,}000 \\
&= \underline{\underline{0}}
\end{aligned}
$$

The Internal Rate of Return on this project is therefore $\underline{\underline{9.81\%}}$.

You can now attempt to evaluate project B in exactly the same way.

What is the significance of the IRR? Well, if the firm can borrow capital at a lower rate than 9.81% p.a. it will find the project worthwhile.

A cash stream equivalent to that in project A could be obtained if the firm could invest £10,000 today at a return of 9.81% p.a. for 4 years.

The IRR differs from other discounting methods for the following reasons:-

1. It does not obtain a cash figure to determine whether or not an investment should be undertaken, but rather seeks to find a discount rate at which the NPV is zero.

2. It takes no account of the absolute size of a project investment cost, nor its total cash returns. It is a measure expressing the net returns as a percentage of investment cost.

3. The criterion for acceptance or rejection of a project is that the IRR must be greater than some other rate. For example, if we had two projects, A and B, and A had an Internal Rate of Return of 9.81% and B had an Internal Rate of Return of 8.00%, Project A would be preferred but neither would be acceptable if a higher rate of return than 9.81% was required as a cut-off when retaining available capital finance.

THE ACCOUNTING RATE OF RETURN or BOOK RATE OF RETURN

This is:-

$$\frac{\text{Average Annual Net Profit after Tax}}{\text{Average Investment}}$$

Thus, if we know that the average net profits after tax for each of three years were as follows, and that also the Book Value of the investment, i.e. Capital

Employed is also as follows, we can calculate the Accounting Rate of Return.

Year	Average Net Profit	Capital Employed
1	£1,000	£12,500
2	£1,000	£11,000
3	£1,000	£10,000

Year	1	2	3

$$\frac{1000}{12500} = 8\% \qquad \frac{1000}{11000} = 9\% \qquad \frac{1000}{10000} = 10\%$$

Over a three year period the Accounting Rate of Return would be:-

$$\frac{\left(\dfrac{1000 + 1000 + 1000}{3}\right)}{\left(\dfrac{12,500 + 11,000 + 10,000}{3}\right)}$$

$$= \frac{1000}{11183}$$

$$\simeq 9\%$$

PROBLEMS

The measure deals with book values for capital employed. Therefore, rate of return on investment may be inaccurate and is subject to variations because:

a) Net Book values are based on historic cost and take no account of changing price levels.

b) Profits include allocations such as depreciation and other provisions which may distort the decision.

c) From the point of view of an investment decision it is better to consider cash flows which do not suffer from the drawbacks mentioned in (a) and (b) above.

QUESTIONS

1. The following data is supplied relating to two investment projects, only one of which may be selected:

	Project A £	Project B £
Initial Capital Expenditure	50,000	50,000
Profit (loss) year 1	25,000	10,000
2	20,000	10,000
3	15,000	14,000
4	(10,000)	26,000
Estimated resale value end of year 4	10,000	10,000

Notes:
1) Profit is calculated after reducting straight line depreciation.
2) The cost of capital is 10%.
3) Present value £1 received at the end of Year 1   0.909
         2   0.826
         3   0.751
         4   0.683
         5   0.620

Required:
(a) Calculate for each project
   (i) average annual rate of return on average capital invested;
   (ii) payback period;
   (iii) net present value.   *(12 marks)*
(b) Briefly discuss the relative merits of the three months of evaluation mentioned in (a) above.   *(10 marks)*
(c) Explain which project you would recommend for acceptance.
                                              (3 marks)
                     (Total 25 marks) [AAT]

2. (a) With reference to capital investment decisions by businesses explain:
   (i) Net Present Value.   *(3 marks)*
   (ii) The Cost of Capital.   *(3 marks)*

(b) An electronics company is contemplating launching a home security system. The following information is available:

Market Research and Development Costs are £250,000 and are to be considered as 'sunk' costs.

New Plant and Machinery will cost £1.4 millions and will have no resale value at the end of its life of five years.

Sales are forecast as follows:

During year	Quantities Sold	Selling Price (each) £
1	5,000	200
2	8,000	205
3	25,000	205
4	16,000	210
5	5,000	210

Costs are forecast as follows:
Labour £20 a unit in Year 1, rising by £1 per unit each succeeding year.
Materials £120 a unit which will remain for 3 years rising by 10% in Year 4 and by a further £18 in Year 5.
Other costs will be £25 a unit and are expected to remain at this level throughout the life of the project.

The cost of capital to the company is 12%.

Evaluate whether it is worthwhile undertaking this proposal.
(22 marks)
[AAT]

(All calculations to nearest £1,000)
Note: PV OF 1 AT 12%.

Year 1:	0.893
Year 2:	0.797
Year 3:	0.712
Year 4:	0.635
Year 5:	0.567

(Total 28 Marks)
[AAT]

3X. The management of a hotel group is deciding whether to scrap an old but still serviceable machine bought five years ago to produce fruit pies, and replace it with a newer type of machine.

It is expected that the demand for the fruit pies will last for a further five years only and will be as follows:

	Produced and Sold number of pies
Year 1	40,000
Year 2	40,000
Year 3	30,000
Year 4	20,000
Year 5	20,000

The fruit pies are currently sold for £3 per pie. Each machine is capable of meeting these requirements.

Data for the two machines are as follows:

	Existing Machine £	New Machine £
Capital Cost	320,000	150,000
	Per Unit	Per Unit
Operating Costs:		
Direct Labour	£0.6	£0.40
Materials	£0.6	£0.60
Variable Overheads	£0.3	£0.25
Fixed Overheads:		
Depreciation	£0.8	£1.00
Allocated costs (100% direct		
labour costs)	£0.6	£0.40
	£2.9	£2.65

Unit operating costs, fixed overhead costs and selling price are expected to remain constant throughout the five year period.

Required:
(a) Using data relating ONLY to the new machine
   (i) Calculate the payback period of the new machine.
   (ii) Calculate the net present value of the new machine.
   N.B. The hotel group expects that its cost of capital will be 20% p.a. throughout the period. *(10 marks)*
(b) Assume that the existing machinery could be sold for £130,000 immediately, if it was replaced. Show, using present value calculations, whether the existing machine should be replaced by the new machine.

Note	PV	20%
	Year 1	0.833
	2	0.694
	3	0.579
	4	0.482
	5	0.402

(8 marks)

(c) Assume that no new machinery can be purchased, but that an outside caterer has offered to supply all of the hotel group's requirements for fruit pies at a price which compares favourably with the group's own cost of producing the pies. What factors other than price would need to be considered before making a decision whether to accept the offer. *(7 marks)*

(Total 25 marks)
[AAT]

VALUE ADDED STATEMENTS
– input-output analysis

The production of a value added statement was recommended by the Accounting Standard Committee (ASC) 'Corporate Report' (1975). Some companies include one in their Annual Published Report.

DEFINITION

It is a statement which shows the difference between input values and output values, whereby the net difference is shown as value added, that is, value contributed by different groups in the enterprise **and** the way in which rewards are shared to providers of capital, management and employees etc. It is a way of reporting income for all the groups contributing to the performance of the enterprise.

EXAMPLE

TOTO LTD. —
Profit and Loss and Appropriation Account for the year ended 31.12.

	£	£
Turnover		100,000
Cost of Sales[1]		40,000
Gross Profit		60,000
Less Expenses:		
Selling + Distribution Costs[1]	12,000	
Administrative Expenses[1]	24,000	
		36,000
		24,000
Interest Payable		(1,000)
Profit on Ordinary Activities before tax		23,000
Tax on profit from ordinary activities		(7,000)
Profit after tax		16,000
Add Profit and Loss Reserve b/f		50,000
		66,000
Transfer to General Reserve	5,000	
Proposed Ordinary Dividend	6,000	
		(11,000)
Profits transferred to P/L reserve		55,000

Note:		£
1. The costs for Cost of Sales		40,000
Selling + Distribution		12,000
Administration		24,000
Total		76,000
They comprise:		
Factory wages, pension and employee benefits	26,000	
Management salaries, pension and employee benefits	16,000	
Depreciation	8,000	
Other costs bought in from outside the organization	26,000	
		76,000

We now have all the information we need to prepare a Value Added Statement as follows:-

TOTO LTD. —
Statement of Value Added for the year ended 31.12

	£	£
Turnover		100,000
Less: Bought in materials and services		26,000
VALUE ADDED		74,000
APPLIED THE FOLLOWING WAY		
To Employees —		
— Factory Wages, Pensions and Employee benefits	26,000	
— Management Salaries, Pensions and benefits	16,000	
		42,000
To Providers of Capital —		
— Interest on Loans	1,000	
— Dividends to Shareholders	6,000	
		7,000
To Government —		
— Corporation Tax Payable		7,000
To Provide for maintenance and expansion of assets		
— Depreciation	8,000	
— Retained Profits (including general reserve)	10,000	
		18,000
		74,000

QUESTIONS

1X. A company has presented profit and loss information to its employees as follows:

	£000	£000	£000
Sales of a company's products during the year amounted to			1,000
The value of the externally purchased materials and services used in earning these sales was:			
Direct material content of products sold		300	
Indirect materials and services concerned with:			
manufacturing	70		
administration	16		
selling and distribution	50		
		136	
			436
The value added by the company during the year was:			564
This value added was applied in the following way:			
To pay employees their wages, pensions and fringe benefits:			
Directly concerned with manufacturing the product		150	
Indirectly concerned with:			
manufacturing	100		
administration	124		
selling and distribution	40		
		264	
			414
To pay providers of capital:			
Interest on: debentures		20	
bank overdraft		4	
Dividends to Shareholders on:			
preference shares		4	
ordinary shares		10	
			38
To pay corporation tax due			10

To provide for maintenance and expansion
  of assets:
    Depreciation of fixed assets concerned
      with:

manufacturing	80		
administration	10		
selling and distribution	10		
		100	
Retained profits		2	
			102
Value added			564

Required:
You are required, using information from the above extract, to prepare
the company's profit and loss and appropriation accounts for the year
in question in as much detail as possible. *(10 marks)*
(CIMA)

ROYALTY ACCOUNTS
– payments for rights

DEFINITION

A royalty is a payment received in respect of a right being given by the owner to someone else wishing to exploit that right for profit. Remuneration is normally agreed on the basis of use, for example, percentage of sales value, cost value, weight or quantity.

ACCOUNTING TREATMENT

In such cases where a fixed amount per unit is paid, the accounting treatment is straightforward. The payer of the royalty treats it as a trading expense in a royalty account and the recipient as income.

Royalties are paid for such things as:-
1) A publisher remunerating an author.
2) Rights to minerals and the extraction thereof.
3) Using a patent.
4) Licensed production (e.g. Coca Cola; Pilkington's Glass).

COMPLICATIONS

It is really only complications which give rise to difficulties. Such complications arise when there is a minimum amount agreed as payable per period regardless of usage. Such agreements are common in mining and the oil industry and guarantee a minimum income to the owner of the rights regardless of production. When payments are made which are not represented by use of the right, they are known as **"SHORT WORKINGS"**.

SHORT WORKINGS

In cases where 'short workings' are agreed it is often stated in the agreement that short workings from one period may be carried forward to a future period to be offset against the royalty charges of that future period. There is normally a limit to the number of years that such short workings may be carried forward. After such time they are irrecoverable and must be written off as an expense.

EXAMPLE

The lessee of a quarry has agreed to pay £1 per ton for extracted ore. The minimum rent has been agreed at £500 per annum. Any short workings are recoupable only, within one year following the year in which they occur. The following table gives details of tonnage extracted, royalty payments and short workings. Note: the amount payable must not be less than £500 in any year.

YEAR	TONS EXTRACTED	PAYABLE	SHORT WORKINGS c/f	recouped	irrecoupable
1	540	540	—	—	—
2	460	500	40		
3	560	520		40	
4	480	500	20		
5	500	500			20

Translating the table into accounts we get:-

ROYALTIES EXPENSE ACCOUNT

		£Dr			£Cr
YEAR 1	LESSOR	540	YEAR 1	OPERATING ACCOUNT	540
YEAR 2	LESSOR	460	YEAR 2	OPERATING ACCOUNT	460
YEAR 3	LESSOR	560	YEAR 3	OPERATING ACCOUNT	560
YEAR 4	LESSOR	480	YEAR 4	OPERATING ACCOUNT	480
YEAR 5	LESSOR	500	YEAR 5	OPERATING ACCOUNT	500

SHORT WORKINGS ACCOUNT

YEAR 2	LESSOR	40	YEAR 3	LESSOR - (recouped amount)	40
YEAR 4	LESSOR	20	YEAR 5	Profit and Loss A/c (now irrecoverable)	20

LESSOR ACCOUNT

		£Dr			£Cr
YEAR 1	Cash	540	YEAR 1	ROYALTIES	540
YEAR 2	Cash	500	YEAR 2	ROYALTIES	460
				Short Workings c/f	40
		500			500
YEAR 3	Short Workings recouped	40	YEAR 3	ROYALTIES	560
	Cash	520			
		560			560
YEAR 4	Cash	500	YEAR 4	ROYALTIES	480
				Short Workings c/f	20
		500			500
YEAR 5	Cash	500	YEAR 5	ROYALTIES	500

The operating account for each of the 5 years would have the following royalty expenses:-

YEAR 1 £540; YEAR 2 £460; YEAR 3 £560; YEAR 4 £480; YEAR 5 £500.

The profit and loss account for year 5 would show the irrecoverable amount for short workings which must now be written off as an expense £20.

The Balance Sheet for years 2 and 4 would have current assets for short workings recoupable shown:- Year 2 £40 and Year 4 £20. Note: the treatment of short workings is similar to that of prepayments.

OPERATING ACCOUNTS

This could be termed a production account or manufacturing account. All costs relating to a particular operation are collected together in an operating account. Royalties in our example are a cost of operating the quarry; they are a direct expense in producing output. The irrecoverable short workings are not an operating expense but are in fact a cost for not operating. In such cases the expense is not direct but indirect and is a 'time based' expense which should be charged to the profit and loss account for the period.

ROYALTY INCOME

A royalty is paid for the use of a right that another party has agreed to license for a fee. The income in such cases is usually classified as non-trading income. This is because the royalty paid is received as a result of someone else trading in the product or service which is the subject of those rights. It is non-trading income and shown as such immediately below gross profit of the receiving business.

QUESTIONS

1. BDL p.l.c. manufactures and sells a product which incorporates a feature which has been patented by MFJ p.l.c. The agreement between the two parties allowing BDL p.l.c. to use the patent, contains the following conditions:

    1. The agreement came into force on 1st January, 19–0.
    2. For every calendar year ending 31st December, BDL p.l.c. should pay to MFJ p.l.c. a royalty of £2 for every product manufactured during the year.
    3. A minimum payment of £15,000 should be made by BDL p.l.c. to MFJ p.l.c. for each calendar year.
    4. If, for a calendar year, the minimum payment exceeds the royalties due as calculated under condition 2, then the difference shall be carried forward and recouped from royalties in excess of

the minimum payment during the following calendar year, but not thereafter.

On 1st January, 19–1, BDL p.l.c. entered into an agreement with CHA p.l.c. containing the following conditions:

A. CHA p.l.c. had the right to manufacture and sell the product, which incorporated the patented feature, under its own brand name.
B. For this right CHA p.l.c. agreed to pay a royalty of £5 for every product sold during the calendar year ending 31st December.
C. A minimum payment of £6,000 should be made by CHA p.l.c. to BDL p.l.c. for each calendar year.
D. If, for a calendar year, the minimum payment exceeds the royalties due as calculated under condition B, then the difference shall be carried forward and recouped from royalties in excess of the minimum payment during the following calendar year, but not thereafter.

Details of the quantities of product sold during each year and in stock at each 31st December, are as follows:

	BDL p.l.c.		CHA p.l.c.	
	Sales	Stock	Sales	Stock
19–9	—	—	—	—
19–0	3,000	2,000		
19–1	3,500	4,500	800	200
19–2	8,000	3,500	900	150
19–3	8,020	3,000	1,380	250

Ignore VAT.

Required:
You are required to journalise the above transactions in the books of BDL p.l.c., showing each year separately.   *(20 marks)*
(CIMA)

BRANCH ACCOUNTS
– including Foreign Branches

As an organization grows or diversifies its activities it may become necessary or advantageous to control operations by using a system of departmental or branch accounting. Each department or branch can be treated as a separate cost centre and profitability can be measured by branch as well as a whole. Banks, Estate Agents, Building Societies and retail shops usually operate systems of branch accounting.

DEPARTMENTAL ACCOUNTS (see Accounting for Services)

Trading and Profit and Loss Accounts can be prepared for each separate department within an organization (e.g. a department store). One problem from an accounting point of view is how to allocate shared common costs (the overheads). Facilities such as a staff canteen, personnel and administration, lighting and heating need to be apportioned between the departments. Overheads can be apportioned in some equitable way usually based on time or use.

Examples could be:-
(a)   canteen – number of employees per department
(b)   personnel & administration – number of employees
(c)   light and heat – metred by department or square footage (floor area)
(d)   insurance – value of items insured in each department as a percentage
           of total cost
(e)   rent and rates – floor area
(f)   store advertising – charged as percentage of sales value.

COMMISSION PAYMENTS

Often such payments are made to department branch managers based on a percentage of net profit either before or after charging the commission. If commission is payable after charging commission it can be calculated thus:

$$\frac{\% \text{ commission}}{100\% + \text{commission} \%} \times \begin{array}{l} \text{NET PROFIT} \\ \text{before commission} \end{array}$$

For example, commission of 10% is to be paid on the net profit before charging commission which is £5,000. The calculation would be:-

$$\frac{10}{110} \times £5000 = £454.55$$

This makes the net profit after charging commission £4545.45 and you can see that 10% commission is indeed £454.55.

BRANCH ACCOUNTS (maintained at Head Office)

The Head Office (H.O.) keeps all accounting records and control branch stocks and operations precisely. Goods may be sent to the branch recorded at:-
- selling price at the branch
- cost price plus a percentage mark-up
- cost price to the H.O.

The first of these methods is most common.

RECORDS NEEDED

The Head Office will need the following accounts:-
- Branch Stock Control Account
- Branch Mark-up or Adjustment Account
- Goods sent to Branch Account

and possibly:-
- Branch Bank and Cash Control Accounts
- Branch Debtors Accounts (if credit allowed to customers)
- Branch Expense Accounts

In our example, the branch stock account is maintained at selling price as follows:-

Dr –	Goods sent to branch
Cr –	Sales
–	Returns to Head Office
–	Shortages or mark-downs

The balance on the branch stock account should always be equivalent to the stock of unsold goods at selling prices.

The branch mark-up account is effectively the branch trading account and entries would be made as follows:-

Branch Mark-Up Account

DEBIT	CREDIT
Goods returned to H.O.	MARK-UP = POTENTIAL GROSS PROFIT
Goods lost in transit	
Goods destroyed	
Goods marked down	
Mark-up on unsold goods at the end of a period c/d	
Profit and Loss Account	

Sometimes a question on branch accounts will require the profit and loss account for the branch. The profit can be deduced from the Branch Mark-Up Account and any further expenses for the branch deducted to arrive at the net profit for the branch.

The Goods sent to Branch Account is maintained at Cost Price and would contain the following entries:-

Goods sent to Branch Account

DEBIT	CREDIT
Goods returned to H.O. at Cost	Goods sent to Branch at Cost

At the end of the period it is closed off to the Head Office Purchases Account (or Trading Account) to reduce H.O. Cost of Sales.

EXAMPLE QUESTION

Thatcher has been trading with main premises in London and a branch at Grantham. All purchases are made by the Head Office and goods are invoiced to the branch at the expected selling price (cost plus 25%). The following details for the period are available:-

	£
Opening stock at branch (selling prices)	10,000
During the period:	
Goods sent to branch (at cost)	60,000
Cash Sales (includes goods marked down)	55,000
Credit Sales	10,000
Returns to H.O. (at cost)	2,000

Required:
(a)   The Branch Stock Control Account
(b)   Branch Mark-Up Account
(c)   Goods Sent to Branch Account
(d)   Debtors Account in the H.O. books.

SOLUTION TO THATCHER

The first step is to establish the price (cost) relationship before launching into the answer.

		%
H.O. Cost	=	100
Mark-up	=	25
Selling Price	=	125

Opening stock (balance b/f on the Branch Stock Control Account) is at selling price and the balance b/f on the Mark-Up Account must be calculated (i.e. anticipated gross profit in respect of the opening stock).

$$\frac{25}{125} \times 10,000 = 2,000 \quad [A]$$

Branch Stock Control Account (at selling prices)

	£Dr			£Cr	
Balance b/f	10,000		Goods returned to H.O.		
Goods sent to branch:			– at cost	2,000	[D]
– at cost	60,000	[E]	– add mark-up 25%	500	[B]
– add mark-up 25%	15,000	[C]	Cash Sales	55,000	
			Branch Debtors	10,000	[F]

Branch Mark-Up Account

	£Dr			£Cr	
Branch stock control a/c mark-up on returned goods	500	[B]	Balance b/f	2,000	[A]
			Branch Stock Control a/c mark-up on goods sent to branch	15,000	[C]

Goods Sent to Branch Account

	£Dr			£Cr	
Branch Stock Control a/c Goods returned to H.O.	2,000	[D]	Branch Stock Control a/c Goods sent to Branch	60,000	[E]

Branch Debtors Account

	£Dr		£Cr
Branch Stock Control Branch Debtors	10,000	[F]	

ACCOUNTS MAINTAINED BY THE BRANCH AS A SEPARATE ENTITY

Where branches are treated as separate entities the branch will keep independent records and produce its own trading and profit and loss accounts and balance sheets. The business as a whole will need to combine all branch accounts to produce the company trading and profit and loss account and balance sheet.

Usually, the Head Office will establish the branch by transferring necessary assets for the branch to operate as a semi-independent entity. The H.O. will record this transfer in a H.O. Branch Current Account. The Branch will open up a H.O. Current Account. The branch current account balance in the H.O. balance sheet is an asset which represents the H.O. investment in the branch (the net worth). The credit balance in the branch H.O. Current Account shows the ownership or capital of the branch.

EXAMPLE SEPARATE HEAD OFFICE AND BRANCH BOOKS

JH Ltd. opened a new branch on January 1st and the following assets were transferred from the Head Office to the branch:-

	£	
Freehold Premises	20,000	
Fixtures (Cost £5,000)	3,000	Net Book Value
Motor Vehicles (Cost £10,000)	7,000	Net Book Value
Cash at Bank	5,000	

The branch which will keep independent records installed additional Fixtures and Fittings at a cost of £1,000.

Show these transactions recorded in:-
(a) the Branch Current Account in the H.O. Ledger
(b) the Branch Ledger Accounts.

SOLUTION TO JH LTD.

(a) HEAD OFFICE BOOKS

Branch Current Account

	£Dr		£Cr
Freehold Premises	20,000	Provisions for depreciation:-	
Fixtures	5,000	– Fixtures	2,000
Motor Vehicles	10,000	– Motor Vehicles	3,000
Bank	5,000	Balance c/d	35,000
	40,000		40,000

(b) BRANCH BOOKS

H.O. Current Account

	£Dr		£Cr
Provisions for depreciation:-		Freehold Premises	20,000
– Fixtures	2,000	Fixtures	5,000
– Motor Vehicles	3,000	Motor Vehicles	10,000
Balance c/d	35,000	Bank	5,000
	40,000		40,000

Note: the H.O. Current Account in the Branch records is a mirror image of the H.O. Branch Current Account.

Freehold Premises at Cost

	£Dr	£Cr
H.O. Current A/c	20,000	

Fixtures and Fittings at Cost

	£Dr	£Cr
H.O. Current A/c	5,000	
Bank	1,000	

Motor Vehicles A/c at Cost

	£Dr		£Cr
H.O. Current A/c	10,000		

Provision for Depreciation – Fixtures and Fittings A/c

	£Dr		£Cr
		H.O. Current A/c	2,000

Provision for Depreciation – Motor Vehicles A/c

	£Dr		£Cr
		H.O. Current A/c	3,000

Bank Account

	£Dr		£Cr
H.O. Current A/c	5,000	Fixtures and Fittings	1,000

CENTRAL PURCHASING

Often organizations, if they are very large, may decide to purchase goods centrally through a Head Office function to achieve buying economies of scale. In such cases the Head Office will transfer goods to branches at cost or at a marked-up price which enables the H.O. to make a profit by supplying branches. The branch will make a profit when it marks-up the H.O. Price to the final customer.

AGREEMENT OF H.O. AND BRANCH RECORDS

The balance in the H.O. books (usually a debit) should agree with the balance in the branch books (usually a credit). However, agreement may not be achieved owing to errors which need correction or goods in transit which have not been recorded in both sets of records.

EXAMPLE GOODS IN TRANSIT

During January the following transactions were recorded in JH Ltd at Head Office:-

	£
Goods sent to branch – at cost	20,000
Goods returned to H.O. – at cost	1,000
Remittances from branch	42,000
H.O. Expenses charged to the branch	4,000

Transactions recorded by the branch were as follows:-

	£
Goods received from H.O. at cost	18,500
Goods returned to H.O. at cost	1,000
Remittances to H.O.	44,000

SOLUTION TO JH LTD

Since both branch and H.O. maintain independent records you can see that (a) the branch has only recorded £18,500 of goods received from H.O. and (b) H.O. have only recorded £42,000 remittances. To reconcile the current accounts the chargeable expenses have to be entered by the branch and the items in transit are carried down as balances in the branch current account in the H.O. books.

(a) **HEAD OFFICE BOOKS**

Branch Current A/c

	£Dr		£Cr
Balance b/f	35,000	Goods returned from branch	1,000
Goods sent to branch	20,000	Bank remittances from branch	42,000
Expenses	4,000	Goods in transit c/d	1,500
		Cash in transit c/d	2,000
		Balance c/d	12,500
	59,000		59,000

(b) **BRANCH BOOKS**

H.O. Current Account

	£Dr		£Cr
Goods returned to H.O.	1,000	Balance b/f	35,000
Bank Remittances	44,000	Goods received from H.O.	18,500
Balance c/d	12,500	Expenses	4,000
	57,500		57,500

Note the items in transit have not affected the branch records.

PREPARING THE FINAL ACCOUNTS

A trial balance will be extracted from the Head Office and Branch Ledgers from which final accounts for the period can be prepared for the Head Office; the Branch and the combined business. It is usual, nowadays, for these final accounts to be prepared in columnar form.

EXAMPLE

Trial balances for H.O. and Branch were extracted from the relevant ledgers as at 31st December:-

	Head Office		Branch	
	£Dr	£Cr	£Dr	£Cr
Capital at 1st January		51,500		
Head Office Current Account				20,000
Branch Current Account	27,500			
Stock at 1st January	5,000			
Sales		79,000		40,500
Purchases	50,000			
Goods sent to branch at cost		20,000		
Goods from H.O. at cost			18,500	
Goods returned to H.O.	1,000			1,000
Freehold Premises – cost	25,000		20,000	
Fixtures and Fittings – cost	10,000		6,000	
– depreciation		5,000		2,000
Motor Vehicles – cost	12,000		10,000	
– depreciation		6,000		3,000
Expenses	20,000	4,000	8,000	
Short Term Investment Account	10,000			
Bank	5,000		4,000	
	165,500	165,500	66,500	66,500

Notes:
Information which has not been taken into account in the trial balances extracted above, is as follows:-
(a) Head Office expenses apportioned to the branch amounting to £4,000 has not been recorded in the Branch records.
(b) Goods in transit to the branch at the year end were £1,500.
(c) Cash in transit to H.O. at the year end was £2,000.
(d) Depreciation is to be provided at the rate of:-
   (i) 10% p.a. on the cost of Fixtures and Fittings
   (ii) 20% p.a. on the cost of Motor Vehicles.
(e) The closing stocks of goods were valued at cost:-
   (i) Head Office £4,000
   (ii) Branch   £1,000

Required:
(a) A draft trading and profit and loss account for the Head Office, the Branch and the Combined Business in columnar form for the year to 31st December.
(b) Draft Balance Sheets as at 31st December for the Head Office; the Branch and the Business Combined in columnar form.

SOLUTION TO FINAL ACCOUNTS

The following steps should be followed in solving branch accounting problems:
1 Establish the price structure between the H.O. and branches (Not required in this example).
2 Open working accounts for the H.O. and Branch Current Accounts.

3 Prepare in columnar form:
  (a) the Branch Trading Account not including transit items
  (b) the H.O. Trading Account not including transit items
  (c) the Combined Trading Account
  (d) the draft Profit and Loss Accounts for the Branch; the H.O. and the Business Combined
  (e) Finally reconcile the current accounts using them to transfer the branch profit/loss from the branch appropriation account to the H.O. appropriation account. The H.O. profit/loss carried down should now be the same as the combined profit/loss carried down.

4 Prepare the closing balance sheets in columnar form for the Branch; the Head Office and the business combined. Note: the current account balances will cancel each other out and do not appear in the combined balance sheet.

DRAFT TRADING ACCOUNTS IN COLUMNAR FORM

	H.O. £	Branch £	Combined £		H.O. £	Branch £	Combined £
Opening Stock	5,000	–	5,000	Sales	79,000	40,500	119,500
Add: Purchases	50,000	–	50,000	Goods to Branch	19,000[2]		
Goods from H.O.		17,500[1]					
	55,000	17,500	55,000				
Less: Closing Stocks	4,000	1,000	6,500[3]				
	51,000	16,500	48,500				
therefore,							
GROSS PROFITS c/d	47,000	24,000	71,000				
	98,000	40,500	119,500		98,000	40,500	119,500

1 Goods from H.O. (18,500 – 1,000 Returns)
2 Goods to Branch (20,000 – 1,000 Returns to H.O. from Branch)
3 £4,000 + £1,000 + £1,500 (Goods in transit) = £6,500
  Gross Profit is the balancing figure.

DRAFT PROFIT AND LOSS ACCOUNTS IN COLUMNAR FORM

	H.O. £	Branch £	Combined £		H.O. £	Branch £	Combined £
Expenses	16,000	12,000	28,000	Gross Profit b/d	48,000	23,000	71,000
Depreciation:							
– Fixtures & Fittings	1,000	600	1,600				
– Motor Vehicles	1,200	1,000	2,200				
therefore, NET PROFITS	28,800	10,400	39,200				
	47,000	24,000	71,000		48,000	23,000	71,000

Note expenses and depreciation are cross cast to obtain the combined figures.

Workings: 10% × £10,000 = £1,000   *Depn F+F H.O.*
Depreciation   10% × £6,000   = £600   *Depn F+F B.*
               20% × £12,000 = £1,200   *Depn MV. H.O.*
               20% × £10,000 = £1,000   *Depn MV. B.*

Expenses: H.O. from T/B = £20,000 – £4,000 = £16,000
           Branch from T/b plus adjustment = £8,000 + £4,000 = £12,000.

DRAFT P & L APPROPRIATION ACCOUNTS

	H.O. £	Branch £	Combined £		H.O. £	Branch £	Combined £
H.O. Current a/c		10,400		Net Profit b/d	28,800	10,400	39,200
Balance c/d	39,200		39,200	Br. Current a/c	10,400		
	39,200	10,400	39,200		39,200	10,400	39,200

HEAD OFFICE BOOKS

Branch Current Account

	£Dr		£Cr
Balance b/f	27,500	Goods in transit c/d	1,500
P & L Appropriation A/c		Cash in transit c/d	2,000
– Branch Profit	10,400	Balance c/d	34,400
	37,900		37,900

BRANCH BOOKS

H.O. Current Account

	£Dr		£Cr
		Balance b/f	20,000
		Expenses chargeable to Branch	4,000
Balance c/d	34,400	P&L Appropriation a/c – Branch Profit	10,400
	34,400		34,400

DRAFT BALANCE SHEETS IN COLUMNAR FORM

	H.O. £	Branch £	Combined £		H.O. £	Branch £	Combined £
Freehold Premises	25,000	20,000	45,000	Capital	51,500	–	51,500
Fixtures & Fittings NBV	4,000	3,400	7,400	Profit	39,200	–	39,200
Motor Vehicles NBV	4,800	6,000	10,800				
Branch Current A/c	34,400						
Stock	{ 4,000	1,000	6,500				
Goods in Transit	{ 1,500						
Short Term Investment A/c	10,000						
Bank	{ 5,000	4,000	11,000				
Cash in transit	{ 2,000						
	90,700	34,400	90,700		90,700	34,400	90,700

HEAD OFFICE MARK-UP

The above example transferred goods from the H.O. to the Branch at cost but many questions and real life situations require an understanding of goods transferred at some marked-up price. In such situations both the H.O. and the Branch will make a profit on the goods transferred. The price structure is the key to solving problems of this nature and it is essential to establish this at the start.

EXAMPLE OF PRICE STRUCTURE

	£	
Head Office Cost	100	
H.O. profit on transfer to branch	20	H.O. Mark Up $\frac{1}{5}$
Cost to Branch	120	
Branch Profit	10	Branch Mark Up $\frac{1}{12}$
Selling Price	130	

Once this price structure has been established you are able to calculate or deduce gross profits; closing stocks; and any stock shortages.

PROVISIONS FOR UNREALIZED PROFIT

This is made up of two elements in the H.O. Balance Sheet:-
and (1)   the provision in respect of branch closing stock deducted from the branch current account
and (2)   the provision in respect of goods in transit needs to be removed from the goods in transit.

This is to: (a) remove the profit on goods marked up by the H.O. which the branch has not yet sold (hence not realized) and (b) where goods are in transit between H.O. and the branch (hence the H.O. will have marked up the goods but the branch will not have sold them and therefore, profit is unrealized).

A provision for unrealized profit must be made by the Head Office as follows:-

	£Dr	£Cr	
H.O. Profit & Loss A/c	X		P+L
Provision for unrealized profit A/c		X	B/S
This creates the provision for unrealized profit for closing stocks held by the branch and for goods in transit.			

Once this adjustment has been made to the H.O. books it is not necessary to do anything with either the branch or the combined Trading and Profit and Loss. You should note that sometimes branches may purchase stocks from external sources as well as the H.O. In such cases it is essential to exclude any externally purchased stock from the adjustments for unrealized profit since externally purchased stocks will not contain any element of unrealized profit.

FOREIGN BRANCHES ACCOUNTS

The only difference in dealing with foreign branches is that when the trial balances for the H.O. and branches are drawn up that they will be stated in local currencies. In order to amalgamate the figures it will be necessary to translate foreign currencies to that of the Head Office currency.

SSAP20 FOREIGN CURRENCY TRANSLATION

Gives some general guidance on how this can be achieved.

A Fixed Assets converted at the exchange rate ruling when the assets were bought. This is known as the *TEMPORAL METHOD* (AT THE TIME THE TRANSACTION TAKES PLACE). Thus if fixed assets are acquired at different points in time the exchange rates ruling at the times of acquisition should be used.

B Depreciation should be dealt with on the same basis as for the fixed assets to which the fall in value is charged.

C Current Assets and Current Liabilities should be translated at the rate ruling at the date of the trial balance. This is known as the *CLOSING METHOD*.

D Opening stock in the Trading Account – should be translated at the rate ruling at the previous balance sheet date (i.e. the opening position for the period concerned).

E Goods transferred from H.O. to Branch or vice versa should use the actual figures shown in the Goods sent to Branches Account in the H.O. books.

F Any remaining trading and profit and loss account items (other than depreciation, opening and closing stocks or goods sent to or returned by the branch) should be translated at the average rate for the period covered by the accounts.

G H.O. Current Account – at the same figures shown in the Branch Current Account in the H.O. books.

When all transactions and events have been translated or converted into the desired currency the debit and credit columns of the trial balance will not normally be in agreement. This is because of the exchange rates applied. It will be necessary to include a balancing item known as 'Difference on Exchange Account'. The balance on this account will be shown in the Profit and Loss Account as a profit or loss on exchange.

EXAMPLE CONVERSION OF CURRENCIES IN A TRIAL BALANCE

You are required to convert the trial balance shown below into the currency of the UK (H.O.) in accordance with the guidance provided by SSAP 20.

Exchange Rates given are:
1st January 19–5

1st January 19–5	$2 = £1
1st January 19–7	$2^{50} = £1
1st January 19–9	$3 = £1
31st December 19–9	$2^{60} = £1

In the absence of any further information the average rate for the year 19–9 could be assumed as $3 + 2^{60} ÷ 2 = $2^{80}. In practice it would be better to take an average at weekly or monthly intervals to overcome any distortions (extremes) that two readings may give.

Trial Balance as at 31st December 19–9

	$Dr	$Cr	Exchange Rate	£Dr	£Cr
Fixed Assets at NBV					
Acquired 1st Jan. 19–5	20,000		$2 = £1	10,000	
Acquired 1st Jan. 19–7	10,000		$2^{50} = £1	4,000	
Stock at 1st Jan. 19–9	7,000		$3 = £1	2,333	
Administration Expenses	5,000		$2^{80} = £1	1,786	
Selling & Distribution Expenses	8,000		$2^{80} = £1	2,857	
Sales		50,000	$2^{80} = £1		17,857
Goods from H.O.	9,000		£ per account invoiced by H.O. books	5,000	
H.O. Current A/c		19,000	£ per account in H.O. books		10,000
Debtors	10,000		$2^{60} = £1	3,846	
Creditors		5,000	$2^{60} = £1		1,923
Bank	5,000		$2^{60} = £1	1,923	
	74,000	74,000			
Balancing Item Difference on Exchange A/c					1,965
				31,745	31,745

Note the closing stock will be converted at the closing rate when the Trading Account is drawn up.

In our example shown above the balancing item on conversion 'the Difference on Exchange Account' is shown as a gain or a profit on exchange.

QUESTION

1X.   RST Limited is a family-controlled company which operates a chain of retail outlets specialising in motor spares and accessories.

Branch stocks are purchased by a centralised purchasing function in order to obtain the best terms from suppliers.

A 10% handling charge is applied by head office to the cost of the purchases, and branches are expected to add 25% to the resulting figure to arrive at normal selling prices, although branch managers are authorised to reduce normal prices in special situations. The effect of such reductions must be notified to head office.

On 1 April 19–6, a new branch was established at Derham. The following details have been recorded for the year ended 31 March 19–7:

	£
Purchase cost to head office of stock transferred to Derham	82,400
Derham branch sales: cash	89,940
credit	1,870
Stocks transferred from Derham to other branches, at normal selling prices	3,300
Authorised reductions from normal selling prices during the year	2,250

All records in respect of branch activities are maintained at head office, and and branch profit margin is dealt with through a branch stock adjustment account.

Required:
(a)   Prepare
      ((i) the branch stock account (maintained at branch selling prices)
      (ii) the branch stock adjustment account
      The **book stock** should be taken for this part of the question.
(b)   List four of the possible reasons for the stock difference revealed when a physical stocktaking at the Derham branch on 31 March 19–7 showed stock valued at selling prices amounting to £14,850.
(c)   State which of the following is the figure to be included in RST Limited's balance sheet at 31 March 19–7, for Derham branch stock:
      (i)   £11,138
      (ii) £11,880
      (iii) £10,800
      (iv) None of these.
      Justify your choice with appropriate calculations.

(CIMA)

CONTAINERS AND PALLETS

INTRODUCTION – WHAT ARE CONTAINERS?

Crates, Cartons, Pallets, Boxes, Bottles, Cylinders, Barrels and Packets are
all containers for goods. Some containers are disposable in which case the
supplying firm incurs the cost as a cost of sales. Other containers are,
however, returnable by customers, for example, pallets, bottles, crates and
kegs or gas cylinders. In order to encourage customers to return such
re-usable containers, a firm will often charge a deposit which it will refund
as and when the containers are returned in a re-usable condition. If the
container is returned damaged the deposit is retained.

STOCK ACCOUNTS FOR CONTAINERS

Where a firm supplies goods in returnable containers it will need to
maintain a stock account.

EXAMPLE

	£
Stock of containers at 1st January	450
Containers bought in January	1,200
Containers sent to customers in January	1,500

Prepare the stock account for containers.

SOLUTION

The stock account would look like this:-

Containers Stock Account

1st JAN	Balance b/d	450	JAN	ISSUED TO CUSTOMERS COST OF SALES A/c	1,500
JAN	BANK (OR CREDITOR)	1,200	31st JAN	Balance c/d	150
		1,650			1,650

In our example we have charged the containers issued to customers to cost
of sales assuming that the containers would not be returned. The
containers may be charged to a manufacturing account if the containers
formed an integral part of the manufacture of goods and hence
inseparable from the products they contained.

RETURNABLE CONTAINERS

Where containers are returnable and deposits paid by customers are refundable the accounting records must show two things:- (a) the stock of containers at a point in time and (b) the amounts owing to customers for returnable deposits. The stock account is a current asset account and the returnable deposits are recorded in a containers suspense account which is a current liability.

Usually when containers are issued with a returnable deposit, time limits and other conditions such as the container returned must be in a re-usable condition are specified to encourage customers to look after the container and return it within a reasonable time.

EXAMPLE

1 During January 60 pallets were bought for cash at £2 each pallet.
2 50 pallets were issued to customers who were charged £3 per pallet as a returnable deposit.
3 40 pallets were returned from customers who had each paid £3 per pallet.
4 5 pallets were damaged and sold as scrap at £1 each.
5 10 pallets had been retained by customers who have decided not to claim the refundable deposit.
6 There are 30 returnable pallets still with customers.
7 There are 15 pallets at the warehouse at the end of January.

Container Stock A/c

	£rate	qty	£value		£rate	qty	£value
January				January			
Cash 1	2	60	120	Container Suspense a/c (retained by customers) (5)	3	10	30
				Cash: damaged pallets sold. (4)	1	5	5
P&L A/c: Profit on hire of pallets.			5	P & L A/c Cost of pallets used.	NOT APPLICABLE IN THIS EXAMPLE		
				Stock c/d in: Warehouse (7)	2	15	30
				With Customers (6)	2	30	60
		60	120			60	125

Note the profit on the hire of pallets is the balancing item.

Container Suspense A/c

	£rate	qty	£value		£rate	qty	£value
January							
Debtors – pallets credited to customers ②	3	50	150	Debtors: pallets charged to customers	3	90	270
Container Stock A/c – pallets held by customers ⑤	3	10	30				
Deposits on pallets refundable ⑥	3	30	90				
		90	270			90	270

Balance Sheet Summary at end of January

	£
Current Assets – Stock of Pallets	90
Current Liabilities – Refundable deposits	90

It is merely coincidence that these two values are the same in this example.

You should note that although a specific number of pallets may be bought these pallets are re-usable and, therefore, the same pallets can be hired out time and time again.

QUESTION

1X.   S Limited delivers its product to customers in returnable containers. These are invoiced to the customer at £20 each and, if returned in good condition within six months, are credited in full. The containers are purchased for £10 each.

At 30 June 19–6, there were 2,000 containers held in S Limited's warehouse and provision was made in the 19–6 accounts for an estimated liability in respect of 5,500 containers in customers' hands. During 19–7, 1,250 new containers were purchased and 120 were scrapped.

8,750 containers were charged to customers and 9,050 containers were returned within the six-month period.

At 30 June 19–7, the physical stocktaking showed 3,390 containers in the warehouse and information derived from customers indicated that there was a potential liability in respect of 4,950 containers. The stocks of containers are valued at cost price.

Required:
Prepare the containers stock account and the containers suspense account necessary to record these transactions in the books of S Limited.

(CIMA)

THE REGULATORY FRAMEWORK

INTRODUCTION

External users of accounting information published by companies want to be able to rely on those statements to be sure that reported profits and losses; and balance sheets presented by the company show a true and fair view of the state of affairs. The external auditors report appended to such statements is a statutory requirement (Companies Act 1985) and provides the users of those statements with an independent (outside of the company view) opinion as to whether or not the statements presented show a true and fair view.

External auditors are qualified accountants and members of the Institute of Chartered Accountants in England and Wales; Ireland or Scotland; The Chartered Association of Certified Accountants or some other overseas professional body recognised by the Department of Trade & Industry (DTI) for the purpose of allowing their members to practise as auditor in the U.K. An auditor must not be connected with the company he is auditor of, for obvious reasons, since the auditor could not be considered to hold an independent opinion if that person also held a position as a director or officer of the company.

COMPANIES ACT 1985

There is by law a requirement for all limited companies to have their financial statements subjected to an external audit. It is often said that this is the price the members of that company pay for having limited liability. Legislation which is passed through the European Parliament also finds its way into English Company Law and in recent years a number of EC Directives as they are called have meant considerable changes to the Companies Acts have had to be accommodated.

THE ACCOUNTING PROFESSION AND SELF REGULATION

Legislation is one way in which financial statements can be regulated. However, the accounting profession itself can regulate members' activities and provide rules which all members must obey or risk disciplinary action against them by their professional body. The professional bodies do not just provide rules for members to follow but will also assist by giving guidance to members on how to apply those rules and regulations sensibly. There is co-operation between the major professional accounting bodies in the U.K. through the Consultative Committee for Accountancy Bodies (CCAB). It should be noted, however, that there are some smaller professional accounting bodies which have been excluded from CCAB and some professional bodies although not accountants as such that should have been given an opportunity to take part and co-operate in forming a sensible debate on accounting issues.

STATEMENTS OF STANDARD ACCOUNTING PRACTICE

In 1970 the Accounting Standards Committee was formed to develop Statements of Standard Accounting Practice (SSAP's). These standards are intended to establish common guidelines and principles by which all financial statements should be drawn up. SSAP's are not a legal requirement and cannot therefore, be enforced through the law and it is the responsibility of the professional bodies that passed the SSAP to ensure that their members comply. Since auditors are members of professional bodies they will audit any financial statements in accordance with the Companies Acts and any relevant SSAP's.

The Dearing Committee has put forward recommendations for the future of how SSAP's should be formulated and applied. The main objectives being to share the cost burden of the standard making and enforcement process more fairly between those who benefit from it and less onerous to the professional bodies. Secondly, to give SSAP's more weight in the business world.

STATEMENTS OF RECOMMENDED PRACTICE

Statements of Recommended Practice (SORP's) are developed in the public interest and set out current best accounting practice. The primary aim of a SORP is to reduce differences and variety in the accounting treatment of matters with which they deal and thus help users of financial statements by improving the quality of information presented. SORP's are issued on subjects it is not considered appropriate to issue an accounting standard at the time.

SORP's may be developed and issued by the Accounting Standards Committee (ASC) or alternatively developed by an "industry" group representative of the industry concerned and offered to the ASC for approval. This approval process is known as franking. Unlike SSAP's, SORP's are not mandatory on members of the governing bodies of the ASC.

INTERNATIONAL ACCOUNTING STANDARDS

The International Accounting Standards Committee (IASC) came into existence on 29 June 1973 as a result of an agreement by accountancy bodies in Australia, Canada, France, Germany, Japan, Mexico, the Netherlands, the United Kingdom and Ireland and the United States of America. The business of the IASC is conducted through a Board comprising representatives of up to thirteen countries and up to four organizations having an interest in financial reporting.

The objectives of the IASC are to:-

(a) formulate and publish in the public interest accounting standards to be observed in the presentation of financial statements and to promote their worldwide acceptance and observance, and

(b) work generally for the improvement and harmonization of regulations, accounting standards and procedures relating to the presentation of financial statements.

The members of the IASC agree to support these objectives by using their best endeavours:-

(i)   to ensure that published financial statements comply with International Accounting Standards in all material respects and disclose the fact of such compliance

(ii)   to persuade governments and standard setting bodies that published financial statements should comply with International Accounting Standards in all material respects

(iii) to persuade authorities controlling securities markets and the industrial and business community that published financial statements should comply with International Accounting Standards in all material respects and disclose the fact of such compliance

(iv)   to ensure that the auditors satisfy themselves that the financial statements comply with International Accounting Standards in all material aspects

(v)   to foster acceptance and observance of International Accounting Standards internationally.

THE ACCOUNTING STANDARDS BOARD (ASB)
(established 1st August 1990)

In August 1990 David Tweedie will be the first Chairman of this new self-regulatory body which replaces the Accounting Standards Committee (ASC). The ASB is the outcome of the Dearing Committee recommendations reported in September 1988. The main recommendations were:-

- to replace the ASC with a smaller committee – the ASB
- to give more weight to ASB pronouncements (but there is still no statutory backing for SSAP's).

In the 21 year life of the ASC 25 SSAP's were issued and 52 Exposure Drafts (ED's). Nine of these ED's were issued in 1990. Also two SORP's and numerous franked SORP's were issued. The ASC lost face with industry over inflation accounting (SSAP's 7 and 16) and its fate was sealed after failing to find satisfactory solutions to such problems as goodwill (including brand values), merger accounting, deferred taxation and pension costs.

It remains to be seen if the ASB can succeed where the ASC failed without having statutory backing for enforcement.

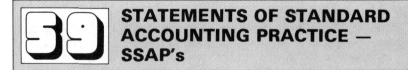

STATEMENTS OF STANDARD ACCOUNTING PRACTICE — SSAP's

BACKGROUND

During the late 1960s there were a number of cases which led to general unrest amongst financial writers, institutions, investors and other interested parties. The major case that comes to mind is the takeover of Associated Electrical Industries by the General Electric Company. AEI had resisted the takeover by GEC for most of the year and produced a forecast profit statement during the tenth month of their financial year which showed a profit of £10m. Nevertheless GEC did take over AEI and not long after the takeover within a matter of weeks GEC showed that AEI had made a loss of £4½m. The total difference therefore between the two statements is £14½m. £9½m of this difference was said to be due to adjustments which remain matters substantially of judgement arising from different accounting policies between the two firms. The other £5m difference was said simply to be matters of fact. There is not really a problem on the matters of fact, since you would expect a reported statement to be slightly different to a forecast statement. The important things to take account of in this case were:

1. That AEI were in the tenth month of the year, so they only had two months to run, and in that two months £5m difference was due to matters of fact.

2. The other £9½m difference which is the more important factor and the one that most people would have been upset about, is the different accounting policies operated by GEC to show a reduced profit of £9½m. There was much pressure at the time for consistency to be shown in financial statements and the profession were very worried that unless it did something to regulate itself it would in fact have regulation imposed upon it by the government through legislation.

So in 1970 the Institute of Chartered Accountants led the way by forming an Accounting Standard Steering Committee which in 1971 became the Accounting Standards Committee (ASC) and since that date they have been initiating Statements of Standard Accounting Practice (SSAP's). There are representatives on this committee from the Institute of Chartered Accountants of England and Wales, the Institute of Chartered Accountants of Scotland, the Institute of Chartered Accountants in Ireland, the Chartered Association of Certified Accountants, the Institute of Cost and Management Accountants and the Chartered Institute of Public Finance and Accounting. The members of these bodies are expected to comply and observe the SSAP's as far as possible in the financial statements that they prepare, which are intended to give a "true and fair" view of the financial position of an organization. If there are significant departures from accounting standards then these must be disclosed and an explanation must be given as to why there is a departure from the Standard. Normally the effect of departure should also be quantified, unless it would be misleading to do so. For audit purposes financial statements are expected to be in accordance with Statements of Standard Accounting Practice and organizations risk an audit qualification if they depart from Statements of Standard Accounting Practice.

Let us now turn our attention to a brief summary of the SSAP's in operation.

A full list of SSAP's is given at the end of this section. Before we move into the summary it is perhaps worthwhile just mentioning the way a standard is achieved. First of all the committee draft what is called an Exposure Draft (ED). The Exposure Draft is then sent to interested parties both inside and outside the profession for comment. As a result of the comments, amendments may be made where appropriate and the Statement of Standard Accounting Practice would then be the result.

SSAP1. Accounting for the results of associated companies. This was the first standard issued by the committee in January 1971. It has since been amended in August 1974 and completely revised in April 1982. This Standard specifies the way in which the results of associated companies must be reported in the financial statements of the other company.

SSAP2. Disclosure of accounting policies. This Standard came into force on the 1st January 1972. The aim of the Standard was to improve the quality of the information disclosed in financial statements. This was to be achieved by clear disclosure of accounting policies. The standard was not revolutionary – in fact, most good financial statements already complied with the requests of this standard. It specified a number of fundamental accounting concepts:

1. The going concern concept.
2. The accruals concept.
3. The consistency concept.
4. The concept of prudence.

For more information on these concepts see the section in this book on Accounting Concepts and Conventions, where the above four fundamental concepts are fully explained.

The standard also mentioned accounting bases. These are the particular methods developed for applying the fundamental accounting concepts to financial transactions. For example, for determining the accounting period in which revenue and costs should be recognised in the Profit and Loss Statement or for determining the amounts at which any material items should be disclosed in the Balance Sheet. An example of different accounting bases would be in the case of depreciation where perhaps we may choose the reducing balance method as a base, or we may choose the straight line method as a base.

SSAP3 Earnings Per Share (EPS). This standard applies to stock exchange listed companies. It seeks to ensure that when EPS figures are used that they are prepared on a consistent basis. (See chapter on ratios). The theory is straightforward. Earning Per Share is the Net Profit for the year divided by the number of ordinary shares entitled to that profit. The calculation of net profit excludes minority interests (in the case of groups) and any preference dividends. Extraordinary items should also be excluded (see SSAP6). The net profit is after taxation.

There are some practical difficulties with regard to associated companies, taxation and changes in share capital.

SSAP4 Accounting Treatment of Government Grants. This standard is designed to achieve consistency in the treatment of grants relating to capital expenditure. The purpose is to relate the grant to the asset and its estimated useful life.

There are two ways to achieve the aim of consistency and the matching of costs and revenues in this context.

1. **REDUCE THE COST OF THE ASSET** by the amount of the grant and depreciate the net cost

OR

2. **DEFERRED CREDIT** – The alternative is to treat the asset at cost and depreciate on the full cost and to treat the grant as deferred income which is credited to the profit and loss account over the life of the asset. The effect is the same either way, the net charge for depreciation will be reduced by the amount of the grant written back each period. It is the presentation which is different.

SUMMARY

METHOD 1 Reducing Asset Cost – The Balance Sheet would show:-

	£
FIXED ASSETS AT COST	x
LESS GOVERNMENT GRANT	(x)
Net Cost	x
Less Depreciation	(x)
Net Book Value	x

METHOD 2 DEFERRED CREDIT –
BALANCE SHEET SUMMARY

	£Cost	£Depn.	£NBV
FIXED ASSETS	Full x	x	x
CURRENT ASSETS	x		
LESS CURRENT			
LIABILITIES	(x)		
NET CURRENT ASSETS			x
Total Net Assets			x
FINANCED BY			
Share Capital	x		
Profit and Loss Reserve	x		
		x	
Government Grant			
Reserve	x		
Less write back to			
Profit and Loss	(x)	x	
Long Term Loans		x	
CAPITAL EMPLOYED			x

SSAP5 Accounting for Value Added Tax (VAT). VAT was introduced in the UK on 1st April 1973. This standard came out a year later. The current registration figure at the time of writing is £25,400 (August 1990). There are currently two rates of tax:-

1. **Zero Rate**
2. **Standard Rate 15%**

Some suppliers are zero rated and therefore, no tax is charged on supplies (outputs) which are zero rated, e.g. books. However, the inputs used to produce such goods and services may well be subject to the tax at standard rate (15%). In such cases a trader is able to reclaim the tax suffered on inputs in full.

Where supplies (outputs) are at standard rate and inputs are also at standard rate, the difference between tax on inputs and tax on outputs is payable to HM Customs and Excise or receivable from HM Customs and Excise. (See chapter on VAT).

Some items fall outside the scope of the tax and are exempt supplies. Any inputs taxed in creating the exempt outputs cannot be reclaimed since they do not come within the scope of the tax. Tax on these inputs is, therefore, a cost to the business.

The same is true for non-registered traders, they do not have to charge VAT on outputs but they cannot recover VAT on inputs from HM Customs and Excise.

The standard requires that any 'material' amount of VAT irrecoverable included in fixed assets or expenses should be disclosed by way of note in the financial statements.

SUMMARY OF VAT STANDARD RULES		
Treatment of	**Registered trade**	**Non-registered**
TURNOVER	Excluding VAT	No VAT charged
EXPENSES	Excluding VAT	Include VAT charged
SPECIAL CASES (expenses/assets)	Include VAT as non allowed items	–
FIXED ASSETS	Excluding VAT recoverable (include non-recoverable VAT)	Include VAT
DEBTOR OR CREDITOR for VAT	NOT NECESSARY TO SHOW SEPARATELY – MANY BUSINESSES, HOWEVER, CHOOSE TO DO SO.	–
CAPITAL Commitments Note	Include non-recoverable VAT	Include VAT

SSAP6 Extraordinary Items and Prior Year Adjustments.

Extraordinary items are those items which are outside the normal activity of the business, the amount of which is material, and which is not expected to recur frequently or regularly. If an item does not fulfil all three criteria it may be classed as an 'exceptional' item and not extraordinary.

Examples of Extraordinary Items would include:–

1.   Profit or Loss on the sale of long term investments.
2.   A loss caused through the expropriation of assets (a nationalization of part of the global business in a particular area).
3.   Discontinuance of a significant part of the business.

PRIOR YEAR ADJUSTMENTS are permitted in only two circumstances:–
1.   To show a 'truer and fairer' view of previous years' financial statements where a change of accounting policy would have made a material difference to the interpretation of those accounts.
OR
2.   Because you want to correct a fundamental error in a prior period. That is, where the error invalidates the previous set of financial statements.

SSAP8 The Treatment of Taxation under the Imputation System in the Accounts of Companies. This standard is designed to achieve uniformity in the published accounts of companies with regard to corporation tax. The following items should be included in the profit and loss account charge for tax. If the items are material, they should be shown separately.

1. The charge for Corporation Tax on profits for the year.
2. Tax attributable to Franked Investment Income (i.e. tax credits which are added to the cash dividends received on investments held by the company).
3. Irrecoverable Advance Corporation Tax.
4. Any overseas tax relief.
5. Total overseas tax relieved and unrelieved, identifying the tax due on the payment of dividends.

The standard also requires that Advance Corporation Tax on proposed dividends, whether it is recoverable or irrecoverable, should be shown as a current liability on the Balance Sheet.

SSAP9 Stocks and Work in Progress. Stocks and Work in Progress should be stated at cost or net realizable value, whichever is the lower. Cost is defined as "that expenditure which has been incurred in the normal course of business in bringing the product or service to its present location and condition. This expenditure should include, in addition to the cost of purchase, such costs of conversion as are appropriate to the location and condition."

Net Realizable Value is the actual or estimated selling price (net of trade but before settlement [cash] discounts) less all further costs to completion and all costs to be incurred in marketing, selling and distribution.

Cost means all expenditure, including production overheads, incurred in bringing the product to its present location and condition.

Cost of Purchase includes import costs, handling costs and other directly attributable costs less trade discounts, rebates and subsidies. Sometimes, there are hidden rebates, for example, a baker's dozen – 13 items delivered but only 12 invoiced. Thus, the cost should be shown as being for 13 items.

Costs of conversion includes all direct costs and production overheads. Overheads for selling, distribution and administration are not normally included, but exceptionally where a product is made to order, selling expenses may be included as a cost in calculating the value of a part made item. Fixed overheads, including depreciation, are charged in the cost of conversion.

Methods of allocating changing costs to stock issues include:–

1. First In First Out FIFO
2. Last In First Out LIFO — this is not recommended in the SSAP.
3. Average Cost

4.   Standard Cost
5.   Base Stock – not recommended in the SSAP.
6.   Replacement Cost

(See Stock Valuations – Chapter).

Long Term Contract Work in Progress
Valuation should be based on cost including production overhead and any attributable profit. Prudence dictates that, say, only two-thirds of the profit is taken in the current period. See Contract Costing. Any foreseeable losses should be provided in full. Full details of gross values and progress sums deducted should be given in the balance sheet or disclosed in a note thereto, to give an indication of the size of the contract. Architects' certificates or those of a quantity surveyor as to the value of completed work are useful but do not in themselves provide all the information unless they are on a 'cost plus basis'.

SSAP10 Statements of Source and Application of Funds. This is an historic funds (cash) flow statement which indicates sources of funds to the business over a past period and how those funds were applied. (See Sources and Application of Funds – Chapter 00).

The minimum disclosure the statement requires are:–
>   Net Profit or Loss
>   Adjustments for items not using funds (e.g. depreciation)
>   Dividends Paid
>   Acquisitions and Disposals of Fixed Assets
>   Amounts raised for long-term capital (e.g. share issue)
>   Redemptions of Long Term Capital
>   Change in Working Capital
>   Movement in Net Liquid Funds

SSAP12 Accounting for Depreciation
DEFINITION: 'Depreciation is the measure of wearing out, consumption or other loss of value of a fixed asset whether arising from use, effluxion of time or obsolescence through technology and market changes'.

The word 'cost' has been carefully avoided in the standard definition so that the standard may be equally applied to current cost accounting. It refers to a loss in value. All assets which have a finite life should be depreciated. This includes freehold buildings but not the land they stand on. Assets that waste away or wear out such as leases, mines, quarries, oil and gas fields, having a pre-determined life, should be amortized. The cost should be matched with the revenues obtained from the asset (SSAP2). The rate at which depreciation is charged will be dependent on cost/value of the asset; the type of asset; its estimated useful life and any residual value. (For methods of depreciation see the chapter on Depreciation).

The standard requires that the following be disclosed:–
1.   The method of depreciation chosen.

2. The estimated useful life of the asset or rate of depreciation.
3. The total depreciation charged for the period.
4. The gross amountof depreciable assets together with the accumulated charges for depreciation to date.

SSAP13 Accounting for Research and Development
DEFINITIONS:

Pure Research — This is original investigation undertaken to gain new technical knowledge. It may not have a practical application.

Applied Research — As above but it is intended to have a practical application.

Development — Using the technical knowledge to produce new products but prior to the commencement of commercial production. For example, building a prototype.

As a general rule, research and development costs should be written off immediately. One of the basic accounting concepts is objectivity (i.e. measurability); if we were to treat R & D as an asset the amount of write off each period would be a subjective measure, as would the amount of charge to carry forward to set off against future revenues. It is also prudent to do so but it does contravene the matching principle.

The only exception to this general rule is that development expenditure only which meets criteria carefully laid down may be treated as an intangible asset and the cost amortized over future periods against the revenue earned by the project. This does, therefore, take account of the matching principle.

The Criteria:–
1. There must be a clearly defined project.
2. The expenditure on the project must be separately identifiable.
3. The project must be certain to come on line as a product and must be commercially and environmentally viable (environmentally viable means it will not be thwarted owing to pollution of some kind, e.g. noise/lead).
4. The expected revenues must cover the costs.
5. The business must have the necessary resources to see the development through.
6. Once written off, it must not be written back.

SSAP14 GROUP ACCOUNTS
BASIS OF CONSOLIDATION
The standard requires consolidated accounts to be prepared covering the holding and all subsidiary companies unless there are exceptional circumstances (see below).

Standard accounting policies should be applied throughout the group or if this is not practicable, disclosure of the differences and the effects quantified where they are material.

The Companies Act requires that the group has a common accounting date but there is provision for the Department of Trade and Industry to give exemption from this. Where different dates are applied, the standard requires an adjustment be made for any abnormal transactions in the intervening period.

Exclusion from Consolidation
1. When activities are so dissimilar that consolidation would be misleading.
2. When the Holding Company, although owning half the shares (equity), either does not have half the votes or some other restriction on its ability to appoint the majority of shareholders.
3. When the subsidiary operates under severe restrictions which reduces effective control by the holding company.
4. When control is temporary.

Such exclusions must be disclosed with details of the circumstances.

SSAP15 Accounting for Deferred Taxation. Permanent differences and timing differences will affect the reported Net Profit figure before Tax compared with profits assessed to Corporation Tax for the same accounting period. The standard is designed to take account of these.

PERMANENT DIFFERENCES – Gains which are not chargeable to tax or expenses which are not tax deductible in computing assessable profits.

TIMING DIFFERENCES
1. Short term differences
2. Accelerated Capital Allowances*
3. Surpluses on revaluations of fixed assets
4. Gains on disposals of fixed assets which are 'rolled over'.

*These will eventually disappear as Government Budgetary Policies take effect.

SSAP16 Current Cost Accounting (CCA). Since July 1985 this is no longer a compulsory standard. (See the chapter on Alternative Asset Valuations). More than 50% of companies required to provide CCA were not doing so.

The standard required publication of a current cost balance sheet and profit and loss account by all companies listed on the Stock Exchange and other companies meeting the following three criteria:-
1. **Turnover exceeding £5 million.**
2. **A balance sheet total over £2.5 million.** (Fixed Assets at book value plus current assets but not deducting current liabilities).
3. **UK employees in excess of 250.**

It is now a voluntary standard. Those that wish to produce CC Accounts should do so in accordance with the standard.

Four adjustments to historic cost accounts are necessary:–
1. **Cost of Sales Adjustment**
2. **Depreciation Adjustment**
3. **Monetary Working Capital Adjustment**
4. **Gearing Adjustment.**

SSAP17 Accounting for Post-Balance Sheet Events. Events often occur after the balance sheet date which provide evidence of the amount of liabilities or the value of assets at the balance sheet date. Such events may often affect the way in which users of financial statements interpret them. This standard seeks to identify which post balance sheet events need disclosure.

The terms **Adjusting** and **Non-adjusting** events are used. One should ask the question: Are they relevant to the period and to the interpretations users may place upon the financial statements? If so, the differences are material and they require those accounts to be adjusted.

Examples of Adjusting Events:
1. Subsequent determination of a purchase price or proceeds from the sale of assets made before the year end.
2. The discovery of errors or frauds which show the financial statements to be incorrect.
3. Sale proceeds from stock which affect the balance sheet values for stock at the year end. Thus, Net Realizable Values materially lower than cost values in the balance sheet.

Non-adjusting events do not affect the year ended.

SSAP18 Accounting for Contingencies. 'A contingency is a condition which exists at a balance sheet date, where the outcome will be confirmed only on the occurrence or non-occurrence of one or more uncertain future events. A contingent gain or loss is a gain or loss dependent on a contingency.'

In accordance with the concept of prudence, contingent losses should be provided for and contingent gains should not be taken into account until they are realized.

SSAP19 Accounting for Investment Properties. Investment properties should be included in the balance sheet at their open market value. The standard does not require a revaluation every year, but where such properties are a substantial proportion of the total assets of a major enterprise the valuation would normally be:–

1. Annually by persons qualified who have recent and relevant local experience; and
2. At least every five years by an external valuer.

The standard requires disclosure of the names or qualifications of the valuers, together with their bases of valuation. If the valuer is an employee or officer of the company or group which owns the property, it should be disclosed.

The exceptions are:
1. Where an investment property is held on a lease of 20 years or less, it should be depreciated on the normal basis.
2. The standard does not apply to charities.

SSAP20 FOREIGN CURRENCY TRANSLATION
This standard deals with foreign currency translations, that is, the means by which financial information in one currency is expressed in another currency.

Translation should be distinguished from conversion which is the exchange of currency, whereas translation deals with simply measuring financial data in a different currency and does not involve actual conversion of currency.

There are two main methods of translation which are:–
1. The Temporal Method; and
2. The Closing Rate/Net Investment Method.

THE TEMPORAL METHOD
The rules for translation under this method are:–
1. Monetary Assets and Liabilities at the balance sheet date (The Closing Rate of Exchange is used).
2. Non-Monetary Assets at the exchange rate on the date of purchase (i.e. time of purchase thus temporal rate).
3. Profit and Loss Account items at the rate on the date the transaction takes place or alternatively at an average rate for the period if rates do not fluctuate significantly.

Exchange differences should be reported as part of the profit from ordinary operations (unless they are due to extraordinary items per SSAP6).

Note that under SSAP20 a difference on exchange could occur when stocks are translated, since stock for the Profit and Loss Account could be translated at an average rate whilst they will be translated at the purchase date for the balance sheet.

THE CLOSING RATE/NET INVESTMENT METHOD
The rules for translation are:–
1. Balance Sheet items translated at the closing rate of exchange (i.e. the exchange rate at the Balance Sheet date).
2. Profit and Loss Account items at the closing rate or an average rate.

All exchange differences should be treated as movements on reserves.

SSAP20 CRITERIA FOR WHICH METHOD TO USE
1. The extent to which the cash flows of the foreign enterprise have direct impact on those of the investing company.
2. The extent to which the functioning of the foreign enterprise is directly dependent on the investing company.
3. The currency in which most of the trading transactions are denominated.
4. The major currency to which the operation is exposed in its financial structure.

The temporal method is used where the foreign transactions are best regarded as extensions of home operations. Differences on exchange which are mainly due to profit and loss items, are rightly treated as part of the profit or loss for the year.

SSAP21 ACCOUNTING FOR LEASES AND HIRE PURCHASE
The growth of leasing in recent years has led to the need for a standard to establish uniform accounting treatment.

There are two types of lease which are:–
1. **Operating leases;** and
2. **Finance leases**

OPERATING LEASES
This is where there is an intention by the lessor to lease the asset to several lessees during the life of the asset.

FINANCE LEASES
These transfer substantial risks and rewards of ownership during the life of the asset although legally the asset remains the property of the leasing company.

The standard recommends that operating leases be dealt with in accordance with legal ownership. The rental is treated as an expense by the lessee, income by the lessor and the asset is recorded as such in the books of the lessor.

In the case of finance leases, it was decided that the treatment reflects "substance over form" and the same sort of treatment as for hire purchase agreements be given. The accounting treatment reflects what actually happens rather than the legal formality.

For both **finance leases** and **hire purchase** agreements the treatment is to:–
1. Record the asset in the balance sheet of the lessee or hirer (not including the interest element).
2. The interest element is charged to the profit and loss account over the period of the agreement and should not be shown as part of the value of the asset.
3. The asset should be valued as the lower of either:–
   (a) the present cash value of minimum future payments under the

agreement (using a commercial rate of interest for discounting purposes); or

(b) the 'true and fair' value of the asset if it was to be bought outright excluding H.P. or leasing.

This effectively removes the interest element from value. The difference between the asset value determined in (a) or (b) and the total future payments must be interest. Interest is then charged to the profit and loss account over the life of the agreement.

4. Depreciation charged against the asset will be based upon the lower of the lease life or the estimated life of the asset.

There is a problem with regard to apportioning the interest charges over the life of a lease or hire purchase agreement. The standard gives examples of three methods which could achieve this:–

1. **Actuarial Method**
2. **Sum of the digits**
3. **Straight Line Method**

The straight line method is not recommended if the amounts involved are large since it would be incorrect to charge interest equally in each year (contravenes the matching principle). However, where sums are not large it is acceptable.

More interest will be payable in early years when the sum outstanding is higher. As time goes by the total sum will be reduced by the annual sum paid (excluding interest) and thus interest paid should be less in future periods. This should be reflected by the accounting treatment. The actuarial method will be most accurate. Nevertheless, the sum of the digits method is simpler to operate and will yield acceptable results if the interest charges are small and the agreement is not for a long time period.

EXAMPLE

An agreement to lease a machine for its expected life of 5 years was made on 1st January 1986. The terms of the lease were as follows:–

1. Four years
2. Rental payment £25,000 per annum in arrears
3. A fair value for the machine was estimated to be £79.247.

The difference between total payments 4 × £25,000 = £100,000 and the value estimated at £79.247 is the interest implied, which is £20,753. This sum of £20,753 needs to be charged to the profit and loss account each year and the liability to the lessor is shown on the balance sheet at the end of each year. In the table below you can see the interest chargeable each year to the profit and loss account, for each of the methods specified in the standard.

The interest of £20,753 is equivalent to a charge of 10% per annum on the true cost of the asset.

METHOD 1 — ACTUARIAL METHOD

Year		£
	1st January 19-6 — Liability	79,247
	Add Interest for 19-6	7,925
		87,172
	Less Payment at 31.12.-6	25,000
1	Liability at 31.12.-6	62,172
	Add Interest for 19-7	6,217
		68,389
	Less Payment at 31.12.-7	25,000
2	Liability at 31.12.-7	43,389
	Add Interest for 19-8	4,339
		47,728
	Less Payment at 31.12.-8	25,000
3	Liability at 31.12.-8	22,728
	Add Interest for 19-9	2,272
		25,000
	Less Payment at 31.12.19-9	25,000
4	Liability at 31.12.19-9	NIL

METHOD 2 — SUM OF THE YEARS DIGITS

Year			Annual Interest Charge to P/L £	Liability at Year End £
19–6	1	$\frac{4}{10}$ × 20,753	8,301	62,548
19–7	2	$\frac{3}{10}$ × 20,753	6,226	43,774
19–8	3	$\frac{2}{10}$ × 20,753	4,151	22,925
19–9	4	$\frac{1}{10}$ × 20,753	2,075	NIL
	10	TOTAL CHARGE	20,753	

METHOD 3 — STRAIGHT LINE

$$\frac{£20,753}{4} = £5,188.25 \text{ p.a.}$$

Liability at Year End	1 £59,435	2 £39,623	3 £19,811	4 NIL

DISCLOSURE IN THE ACCOUNTS OF THE LESSEE

The asset should be shown gross for each major class of asset together with related depreciation for each finance lease. Alternatively, the items may be grouped with owned assets providing disclosure is given by way of a note to the accounts. The liability (net of future interest) should be disclosed separately either on the balance sheet or by way of note. The interest element must be disclosed separately in the profit and loss account or by way of note. The requirements of this standard only apply if the lessee or lessor engage in a significant amount of leasing.

DISCLOSURE IN THE ACCOUNTS OF THE LESSOR

1. The net investment in finance leases and hire purchase contracts must be shown.
2. The gross value of assets held under operating leases together with accumulated depreciation on those assets must be shown.
3. The accounting policies with regard to leases and hire purchase agreements need to be shown.
4. The cost of assets acquired for the purpose of finance leases must be disclosed.

Disclosure requirements became effective for periods commencing on or after 1st July 1984. The accounting treatments became effective from 1st July 1987.

SSAP22 ACCOUNTING FOR GOODWILL

The reasons for developing this standard were the many different treatments reflecting the differences of opinion in dealing with goodwill. Should goodwill appear as an asset on the balance sheet? Should it be written off? Over what period should the amortization (write off) take place? The standard addressed these problems.

Goodwill is defined as the difference between the value of a business in total as a going concern and the total book values of the separable assets less liabilities. The value of a business to prospective buyers is the price they are willing to pay to obtain the business which will be determined to a large extent by the profits they expect to make over a number of years. (See Income, Value and Capital). The value of the business could therefore be greater than the total net worth of tangible assets. The excess is goodwill. For goodwill to be present it is often said that there must be 'super profit'. This means that the profits are expected to be greater than the return expected from separable assets.

There are problems in valuing goodwill (some of which have been discussed elsewhere in the text) which are:-

1. It cannot be realized separately from the other assets of the business.
2. How can it be objectively valued? (Goodwill could disappear overnight if a particular 'company' or person took over the business – owing to all sorts of reasons – can it therefore, be passed on?)
3. Following on from 2 above; the value of goodwill may change dramatically in a very short period of time.

The standard distinguishes between purchased and non-purchased goodwill. Non-purchased goodwill should not be brought into the balance sheet as an asset. Therefore, only purchased goodwill may be treated as an asset or it may be written off to profit and loss or accumulated reserves. The standard recommends that purchased goodwill should not be recorded as an asset but written off immediately to accumulated reserves. It recommends the write off against reserves since a write off against profit would distort that year's trading position.

The standard does allow for goodwill to be capitalized but it does not allow this to be permanent. The goodwill should be amortized over its expected useful economic life. The guidelines in appendix 1 of the standard are vague with regard to what may reasonably be regarded as 'useful economic life'. It defines this as 'the period over which benefits may reasonably be expected to accrue from that goodwill in the acquired company, which existed and was identified at the time of acquisition'.

The guideline goes on to state:-
1. Purchased goodwill will be replaced by newly created (earned) goodwill post acquisition.
2. In estimating useful economic life no account should be taken of renewed goodwill since it is not purchased.

3. The life of goodwill is dependent upon the factors which created it and these should be taken into account when determining the write off period –
e.g. personality of previous owner
reputation of product or service and customer relations.

Thus, the treatment of purchased goodwill still involves many subjective judgements.

Other important points covered in the standard are:–
1. The value of separable assets used to determine goodwill is not necessarily the book values but rather a fair value. That is the cost if purchased separately elsewhere.
2. Goodwill should not include any value for intangible assets – patents, licences or franchise rights.
3. Once a decision has been reached with regard to the value of goodwill, it should not subsequently be increased in value.
4. A company may treat different acquisitions differently. For example, if a company adopts the immediate write off for one acquisition it may still capitalize goodwill on a different purchase.

DISCLOSURE
The standard requires the following to be disclosed:–
1. Accounting policy towards goodwill.
2. The amount of recognized goodwill on acquisition during a year should be stated separately if the amounts are material.
3. Where purchased goodwill is capitalized it should be shown as a separate intangible asset. Movements in the goodwill account should be shown by way of a note to the balance sheet.
4. The chosen period of amortization should also be disclosed. This is also required by the Companies Act 1985.

The standard became effective for all financial statements beginning on or after 1st January 1985.

SSAP23 ACCOUNTING FOR ACQUISITIONS AND MERGERS
This standard lays down rules designed to clarify when alternative methods to the normal method of acquisition may be used.

THE ACQUISITION METHOD
The parent company for a group must incorporate assets of the subsidiary at an up-to-date revaluation as at the date of purchase. The difference between the purchase consideration and the revalued separable assets less liabilities is goodwill (to be treated in accordance with SSAP22).

If the purchase is made by issuing shares either in part or whole, then a fair value must be placed upon them and are stated in the value of the investment shown in the parent company's books. The difference between fair and nominal value will of course be credited to a share premium in the normal way.

In the consolidated accounts of the group the investment in the subsidiaries is omitted as is the share capital of the subsidiaries. The share premium will appear in the consolidated balance sheet, but pre-acquisition reserves of the subsidiaries do not. This is because they have already been included in the net worth at the date of acquisition and are included in the goodwill at the date of acquisition. Only the group share of post acquisition retentions may be included in group reserves. The effect of this is that the reserves of the subsidiaries become non-distributable as a dividend and the share premium account of the parent company. These provisions protect the creditors of the parent company.

If an acquiring company pays in cash then it simply acquires assets for cash and reserve accounting may be limited to that of goodwill. There are no share premiums involved. As such if the acquiring company subsumed the pre-acquisition reserves into group accounts and attempted to pay dividends out of such reserves then creditors might suffer from this fund depletion.

If, however, a share exchange takes place for the acquisition then no funds change hands and it was felt that the acquisition treatment was inappropriate. Merger accounting is more appropriate and S56 of the Companies Act 1985 gives relief from the rules described above providing certain conditions are met.

THE MERGER METHOD
The main difference between acquisition and merger accounting is that in the latter reserves are distributable. The consolidated accounts are simply an amalgamation of the parent and subsidiaries accounts. It is not necessary to revalue assets. There is no need for a share premium account since shares exchanged are recorded at nominal values. If shares are not exchanged on an equal basis then any difference between nominal values is adjusted in group reserves. All reserves are shown in the group balance sheet. Under these circumstances nothing has taken place to reduce distributable profits as would happen under acquisition accounting. This is attractive to companies because reserves are not affected and lower charges to future group profits will result since assets did not require a revaluation nor was any goodwill account required.

SSAP23 requires the following conditions to be fulfilled before merger accounting is acceptable:-
1. An offer is made to all ordinary shareholders and holders of other voting shares of the company being acquired.
2. The offering company must not have held 20% or more of the equity or voting shares immediately before the offer is made.
3. The offer results in a holding of not less than 90% of the equity shares and that the holding constitutes 90% of the voting power.
4. Not less than 90% of the purchase consideration must be in the form of shares and not more than 10% cash.

NOTE: SSAP23 applies to group accounts only, and the system of merger accounting is merely allowed if conditions are met; it is not compulsory.

DISCLOSURE
1. Names of combining companies.
2. Details of shares exchanged and any other purchase consideration.
3. The method of accounting used – acquisition or merger.
4. Nature and amount of significant accounting adjustments made by the combining companies to achieve consistency in the group statements.

If merger accounting is used in addition the following must be stated in the year of the merger:–
1. The fair value of the consideration given.
2. The amounts of pre and post acquisition profits.
3. An analysis of any extraordinary items between pre and post acquisition profits, giving details as to which party in the merger it refers to.

The statement is effective for accounts beginning on or after 1st April 1985.

STATEMENTS OF STANDARD ACCOUNTING PRACTICE
 1   Accounting for associated companies
 2   Disclosure of accounting policies
 3   Earnings per share
 4   The accounting treatment of government grants
 5   Accounting for value added tax
 6   Extraordinary items and prior year adjustments
 7   Current Purchasing Power – now withdrawn
 8   The treatment of taxation under the imputation system in the accounts of companies
 9   Stocks and Work-in-Progress
10   Statements of source and application of funds
11   Deferred Tax – now withdrawn (see 15)
12   Accounting for depreciation
13   Accounting for research and development
14   Group accounts
15   Accounting for deferred taxation
16   Current Cost Accounting – the only non-compulsory standard
17   Accounting for post balance sheet events
18   Accounting for contingencies
19   Accounting for investment properties
20   Foreign currency translation
21   Accounting for leases and hire purchase contracts
22   Accounting for goodwill
23   Accounting for acquisitions and mergers
24   Accounting for charities
25   Segmental Reporting (the last to be issued by ASC)

 **INCOME, CAPITAL AND VALUE**

ACCOUNTING INCOME

Accounting income is sometimes equated with profit. The term income when used in this way is reflected in the increase in the Capital Account which has occurred between the beginning and the end of the trading period. A change in capital value therefore is measured by the capital value at the start of the trading period. The difference between the two is the income that the business entity has earned during the period. Therefore, if a company has capital at the start of the period of £100,000 and by the end of the period this capital has increased to £120,000, the income during the period, that is the profit earned during the period, must have been £20,000. This is subject to the proviso that such an increase has not been affected by the introduction of new capital or the withdrawal of funds.

ECONOMIC INCOME AND CAPITAL MAINTENANCE

Not a great deal has been written about accounting income apart from the fact that it is evidenced by an increase in the capital value from the start to the end of the period. On the other hand, very much has been written about economic income and two of the most important theories were discussed by Irving Fisher and Sir John Hicks. Let us look at Hicks' definition of income. Hicks said something to the effect that income was the amount of money that one could consume during the period and still be left with as much capital at the end of the period as one had at the start of the period. Therefore, the change in value of the individual's capital between the beginning and the end of the period could be stated as follows:

Income = Consumption + Capital at the End — Capital at the Beginning

Hicks talked about this concept being the idea of 'well-offness'; in other words capital an individual could consume during the period and still be as well off at the end of the period as he was at the start of the period. The economic definition of income does not suffer distortion from the change in price levels. Accounting income does however suffer such distortion since pounds at the beginning of a period may be rather different in value from pounds at the end of a period owing to inflation. If we consider what an individual can buy at the beginning of a period with his capital and say to ourselves, at the end of a period he is still able to buy equally as much but has also consumed £10,000 during the period, then his economic income during the period would have been £10,000. This idea of economic income as Hicks defined it can only be measured at the end of a period, since one can only then measure how much better off one is when one has decided that capital has been expanded.

If we were to estimate the income stream at the start of a particular period, this is known as ex-ante income. If on the other hand we measure income at the end of the period this is known as ex-post income. Ex-ante income would be the same as ex-post income if during our estimation the value of the future net receipts did not alter from the start of the period to the end of the period. The importance of this particular measurement of income to the decision maker, be it the management of the organization or the shareholder, can be quite dramatic. Where we have a condition of certainty economic income is an ideal concept for financial reporting. The present value of the organization's future net receipts may be capitalised and this will provide the investor with a basis for decision-making. Uncertainty, however, which tends to be the real world situation, prevents us using such measurements of economic income because of the assumptions which we have to make in order to achieve the measurement. In other words, economic income contravenes the convention of objectivity. It is for this reason that accountants do not attempt to value the firm. If accountants were to measure economic income then they would have to be valuers as well as accountants.

Although there are practical limitations to the economic concept of income, it does nevertheless stress an important point to the decision maker. First of all, under the historic cost convention accounting is simply measured in monetary terms, and therefore in times of inflation it may be that the organization decides to pay part of its money income to the shareholders as a dividend when it may in fact in real terms be eating into the capital of the business. For example, if an organization began with £100,000 of capital at the start of the year and during the year there was inflation at 10% per annum, at the end of the year the organization would have to maintain its capital position by showing £110,000 in its Capital Account. If during the year the organization earned £20,000 in accounting income, that is to say £20,000 profit, and it decided to pay out the £20,000 profit, one can easily see that the idea of capital maintenance has been contravened. In other words, the organization would be left with only £100,000 at the end of the period, whereas to maintain the original real wealth £110,000 would be required.

THE ENTITY CONCEPT OF CAPITAL

It is implicit in this concept that there are no persons with claims to ownership of the assets or with personal responsibility for the discharge of liabilities. The entity is an abstraction – usually a corporate body which has an artificial legal personality. It follows that the balance sheet equation is expressed as Assets = Liabilities. Liabilities are of course sub-divided according to priorities which would be observed in the event of liquidation, first preferential and secured creditors, later unsecured trade creditors and eventually – if there is a residue of assets – shareholders. Any profit which arises merely increases the amounts attributable to the shareholders. Under this concept profit is generated by the organization as its functions are performed by its employees in mobilising resources for satisfaction of customers' requirements under co-ordination and control of its officers. The sets of assets and liabilities, though at all times they are equal in value, are in a constant state of change as business activity proceeds.

THE PROPRIETARY CONCEPT

This focuses on the owners of the business, those people that own the equity. A business may be financed partly by debt capital and partly by equity capital, equity being the money that the owners put in. The difference between the entity concept, which concentrates on the business as an operating unit, and the proprietary concept, which concentrates on the purpose of the business being to make profits for its shareholders, is simply a matter of differing emphasis. Nevertheless when the assets are valued by a different convention the differing concepts of capital will have important implications for capital maintenance and profit. The distinction between the entity concept and the proprietary concept was taken account of in SSAP16 on current cost accounting. The distinction that was made in SSAP16 was between current cost operating profit which takes account of the entity concept of capital maintenance, and the current cost profit attributable to ordinary shareholders which applies to the proprietary concept of capital maintenance. (Note: SSAP16 has now been withdrawn. A further Exposure Draft ED35 was never approved and ED38 is still under discussion at the time of writing). The difference between these two measures of profit is that in the proprietary use, shareholders receive not only their proportionate share of the current cost profit but also any excess of current cost profit arising from the use of loan capital over and above the interest payable on loan capital.

WHY DO WE MEASURE INCOME AT ALL?

Profit is an important measure in financial statements for the following reasons:

1) It indicates to the shareholders of the business the nature of the company's dividend and retention policies.
2) It helps creditors and investors to decide whether they can safely lend money to the business, or in the case of investors whether in fact they should invest in the business, because
3) Income is a measure of the efficiency of the company's management – are they using the assets of the business in the most efficient way in order to maximise profit?
4) Past profits may act as a guide to the shareholder or prospective investor or management as to forecasts about future profits.
5) Profit is used by the government as a means of imposing corporation tax.
6) Measuring income helps management to decide their pricing policies, their investment policies (do they wish to expand or should they close particular plants, etc.), and their output policies. **However, the**

management of the organization will have other information which will assist in addition to the measurement of income in the making of these decisions; for example, they will have access to cost structures and other management accounts which the external user of the financial statements will not have.

Income does have a variety of uses and a variety of users, but the measurement of income depends on the methods used to value capital and on any method involving accounting for price level changes.

ASSET VALUATION ALTERNATIVES

The topic of valuation is both complex and controversial. Accountants have not traditionally been associated with the concept of value; this has been more the province of the economist. Traditionally accountants have concerned themselves with recording assets at historic cost and allocating such costs to particular 'income periods'. Nevertheless, financial measurements of assets and liabilities must by definition be concerned with value. Value itself is a complex concept, and whole books have been devoted to the topic. Value is essentially a subjective matter; for example, what represents value to one person may well be regarded as worthless by someone else. As accountants, however, we need to be scientific and hence objective about values. Therefore, how do we measure value objectively? It is important to emphasise that this chapter is no more than a brief introduction to some of the major concepts and complexities involved with determining value.

WHY DO WE NEED TO KNOW VALUE?

It is important to know the value of assets, in order to make decisions about those assets. For example, if we take a proprietorship view of the business, the shareholders will want to know whether they should be buying more shares in the business, holding on to the shares they have, or selling shares and making an investment in a more profitable alternative. If investors are able to establish a value for the business, then they are more easily able to make such a decision. Alternatively taking the entity viewpoint in order to establish the value of the business enterprise we must assess how effectively the business is using the assets at its disposal to produce an acceptable income stream.

HISTORIC COST

Most financial statements prepared by accountants are drawn up using the 'historic cost convention' except where expressly stated, for example, under SSAP16 where current costs are used instead. As such, assets are taken into the business at their entry cost to the business and so far as fixed assets are concerned they are then reduced in 'book value' terms each income period by charging depreciation (see Depreciation). Traditionally, therefore, the value shown in the reported Balance Sheet of a business is referred to as 'book value'. Practising accountants have always been aware of the fact that this 'book value' may differ significantly from either the actual value to the business through use (i.e. its economic value) or from the value in exchange for cash (i.e. net realizable value). Furthermore, if the business had to replace the asset at current costs, this would also differ from the book value.

It is argued that historic cost is an objective measure and that documentary evidence can always be seen to substantiate value, e.g. purchase invoice. It therefore has the advantage of auditability; it is easy to verify.

The major disadvantage of historic cost valuation is that in times of changing price levels, for example in times of inflation, the value of assets stated in historic monetary terms will be severely undervalued. It is further argued that because assets are valued in historical monetary terms and depreciation is charged on the same basis, profits may be overstated at the cost to the shareholders of not maintaining sufficient capital within the business.

This last point needs a little further explanation by means of a simple example.

Supposing a business sets up with £1,000 invested by shareholders. Assets of machinery are bought with this £1,000 which have an estimated useful life of 10 years and will have no scrap value at the end of the tenth year. It is further estimated that the machinery will wear out evenly over the period. It is also estimated that the business will earn £100 profit in each year in present value money terms. Currently the shareholders are representative of the typical consumer as portrayed by the Retail Price Index (i.e. they buy the same range of goods in the same proportions as the weightings in the index). Furthermore, the Retail Price Index has risen by 100% by the end of the fifth year. Let us now look at the Balance Sheet at the start under the historic cost convention and the Balance Sheet at the end of the fifth year.

Historic Cost Balance Sheet at Time 0

Assets	£	Financed by	£
Machinery	1000	Shareholders Funds	1000

Historic Cost Depreciation

$$\frac{\text{COST less SCRAP VALUE}}{\text{Estimated life of Asset}} = \frac{£1000 - NIL}{10}$$

Annual Charge = £100 per annum

Historic Cost Balance Sheet at the End of Year 5

Fixed Assets	£	Financed by	£
Machinery at Cost	1000	Original Share Capital	1000
Less Provision for		Add Retained Profits	500
Depreciation	500		
NET BOOK VALUE	500	Shareholders' Funds	1500
Current Assets less			
Current Liabilities			
Working Capital	1000		
	1500	**TOTAL EQUITY**	1500

In monetary terms the shareholders' funds which equal their total equity have been increased by £500 profit. In current value terms, however, taking the proprietorship point of view, the shareholders' capital has not been maintained and in fact no profit has been made in current cost terms. In order to maintain capital at the end of the fifth year given that the Retail Price Index had increased by 100% the shareholders would now need £2,000 as an equivalent investment to that made at the start, of £1,000.

The Current Cost Balance Sheet would be as follows:

Current Cost Balance Sheet at the End of Year 5

Fixed Assets	£	Financed by	£
Machinery Revalued		Shareholders' Funds	
at Current Cost	2000		
Less Provision for		Original money	
Depreciation	1000	put in	1000
NET BOOK VALUE	1000	Capital Maintenance	
WORKING CAPITAL	1000	Reserve	1000
			2000
	2000		2000

Thus capital has been maintained in current value terms using the capital maintenance reserve. In order to bring the assets to current value terms we need to revalue the machinery in some way. This has been done.

NET REALIZABLE VALUE

An alternative view of valuation is obtained if we focus attention on exit value rather than the entry value of assets. How much money would the asset realize, if sold? Realizable values have the following advantages:

1) They are easily understood, in so far as the value of the asset is the money which the asset can realize when sold.
2) Opportunity cost is easily measured since we are able to compare the value in exchange (realizable value) against the (going concern) value in use. Furthermore, we can estimate the alternative investments foregone as a result of holding on to a particular asset. For example, if we knew a particular asset would realize £1,000 in cash, then the opportunity cost of holding the asset (that is the alternative investments we forego) might be placing the £1,000 in a deposit account earning 10% interest per annum.
3) Realizable values do not conjure up future values to measure the present value.

Realizable value does, however, place emphasis upon the business selling its assts, and therefore stresses the concept of liquidation rather than that of the business enterprise as a going concern. It does, therefore, place undue stress upon the asset values in exchange rather than the asset value in use.

REPLACEMENT COST

Replacement cost value focuses attention once again upon the entry value of an asset to the business. It does, therefore, overcome the problem of over-emphasis on the realizable value of an asset in exchange (i.e. as might be adopted for the purpose of a statement of affairs in the event of bankruptcy or company liquidation) and emphasizes the value in use at current replacement cost to the business (as would be appropriate to a going concern).

CURRENT COST ACCOUNTING

The Statement of Standard Accounting Practice Number 16 (see SSAP's) requires that four adjustments be made to historic cost figures which are:–

1) Cost of Sales Adjustment (COSA)
2) Depreciation Adjustment (DA)
3) Monetary Working Capital Adjustment (MWCA)
4) Gearing Adjustment (GA)

COST OF SALES ADJUSTMENT

The purpose of this adjustment is to remove paper profit which is misleading during periods of rising prices. For example, stock items bought at the beginning of a period may have doubled in cost per unit by the end of a period. In comparing the opening and closing stock position to obtain a stock adjustment under the historic cost convention, no account would be taken of this. Like is not compared with like.

In order to overcome this problem SSAP16 uses a specific index applicable to stock values and attempts to restate Opening and Closing Stock figures at an average price for the period. It assumes that purchases and sales occur at an average price level throughout the year. Effectively this brings all items in the trading account to a common measure at a common date. It is argued that like is compared with like. During periods of rising price levels the effect of this adjustment is to reduce profit by taking account of rising prices for cost of sales (stocks).

THE DEPRECIATION ADJUSTMENT

Under the historic cost convention the fixed assets are stated at cost and this may not reflect the current cost of replacing that asset. Similarly depreciation is charged on the basis of historic cost. It is argued that historic cost is the only objective measure.

Under current cost accounting fixed assets are revalued (using a specific inflation rate – index for the particular asset – using either a mid year or end of year rate) and depreciation is charged (in accordance with policy) on the revised value.

The depreciation adjustment for the year is the difference between current cost depreciation and historic cost depreciation.

MONETARY WORKING CAPITAL ADJUSTMENT (MWCA)

In times of rising prices, debtors are likely to increase in total as a result. Stocks are excluded since they are dealt with by the Cost of Sales Adjustment. Similarly, creditors increase for the same reason as debtors. If debtors are higher than creditors then the company will require more cash to finance them. The MWCA takes account of this fact by restating opening and closing debtors and creditors to an average price level for the year. Average debtors less average creditors for the period, gives the monetary working capital. An index may be applied to restate the figures at an average price level for the period.

If there is an increase in monetary working capital, this is assumed to be due to volume once the changing price levels have been taken care of by restating MWCA at mid point prices. The volume increase is then deducted from the total increase so as to leave a remainder which is due to price changes only and this is the adjustment which is then deducted from historic cost profit to allow for inflation.

THE GEARING ADJUSTMENT

The Cost of Sales Adjustment, Depreciation Adjustment and Monetary Working Capital Adjustment aim to identify profits which may safely be distributed to shareholders. The adjustments take no account of holding gains. CCA is based on the concept of capital maintenance using specific indices for prices of specific assets. In times of rising prices, the company will gain in 'real' terms by having long term loans since it will repay those loans at a future date in pounds of lesser value. On the other hand, the lenders would lose because of inflation. Following this logic it makes sense to increase historic cost profit by reducing the three adjustments mentioned above, taking account of the benefits bestowed upon the company by borrowing in times of rapidly rising prices. This is done by applying the gearing ratio to the three adjustments.

The average gearing is calculated for the period by restating opening and closing long term capital employed by using the revaluation in the CCA balance sheet. The ratio is:-

$$\frac{\text{net borrowing}}{\text{shareholders' funds + long term capital employed}}$$

If the gearing ratio should turn out to be negative, it is not applied.

Once the adjustment is made by applying the ratio to the COSA, DA and MWCA, it is added to the historic cost profit and the COSA, DA and MWCA are deducted to give a current cost profit attributable to shareholders.

The CCA Balance Sheet will contain monetary assets and liabilities at their historic figure (since such commitments do not change as a result of rising price levels). Fixed assets and stock will be stated at their current cost. The surplus due to revaluation is a holding gain which is placed in a current cost reserve shown separately as the balance sheet.

EXAMPLE

IC Snoflake Ltd. was formed on 1 January 19–5 with issued ordinary share capital of £40,000 and 12% loan stock of £20,000. It acquired fixed assets for £30,000 and stock for £10,000 and began trading. Its "final accounts" produced at the end of the first year and prepared on the **historic cost** basis, appeared as follows:-

Profit and Loss Account for the year ended 31 December 19-5

	£	£
Sales		60,000
Less: Cost of Sales	36,000	
Depreciation	3,000	
Loan Stock interest	2,400	
Miscellaneous expenses	1,600	
		43,000
		17,000
Deduct Ordinary Dividend paid (15%)		6,000
Retained Profit		11,000

Balance Sheet as at 31 December 19-5

	£	£
Fixed Assets (net)		27,000
Current Assets		
Stock	14,000	
Debtors	15,000	
Bank	20,000	
Cash in hand	5,000	
	54,000	
Less: Current Liabilities		
Creditors	10,000	
		44,000
		71,000
FINANCED BY		
Issued Ordinary Share Capital		40,000
Reserves		
Retained Profit		11,000
		51,000
12% Loan Stock		20,000
		71,000

The following additional information is also available:–

1. Stock prices rose evenly by 30% during the year. The closing stock was purchased at the end of October 19-5.

2. Replacement fixed assets of the type purchased on 1 January would have cost £40,000 on 31 December.

3. Stock prices had risen by 7½% over the average credit period for debtors and creditors.

You are required to:
(a) Prepare accounts for IC Snoflake Ltd. on the basis prescribed in SSAP 16.

(b) Briefly state, in your own words, why you feel it is important to adjust accounts for inflation.

IC SNOFLAKE LTD. — WORKING PAPER

1 COST OF SALES ADJUSTMENT

Historic Cost of Sales	£36,000
Stock Prices rose by	30%
Stock turnover[1]	3 times per annum

$$^1 \text{ Stock Turnover} = \frac{\text{Average Stock}}{\text{Cost of Sales}} = \%$$

$$\text{or} \quad = \frac{\text{Cost of Sales for year}}{\text{Average Stock for year}} \quad \text{times per annum} \quad \text{i.e.} \left(\frac{\text{Opening Stock} + \text{Closing Stock}}{2}\right)$$

$$= \frac{£36,000}{\left(\dfrac{£10,000 + £14,000}{2}\right)}$$

$$= 3 \text{ times per annum}$$

$$\text{COSA} \quad = \quad \frac{30\%}{3} \quad \times \quad £36,000 \quad = \quad £3,600$$

JOURNAL:–	£Dr	£Cr
Cost of Sales	3,600	
Current Cost Reserve		3,600

2 REVALUATION OF STOCK

Closing Stock = £14,000
Revalued Stock = £14,000 × (30% × $^2/_{12}$*) = 700

*Average Prices rose by 30%; we are told that the stock at close was purchased at 31st October; thus, prices will have risen on average by $^2/_{12}$ × 30% that is through November and December as a proportion of the 12 months in the year. The average price rise over those two months is therefore 5%.

The total stock after revaluation is £14,700.

JOURNAL:–	£Dr	£Cr
Stock	700	
Current Cost Reserve		700

3 DEPRECIATION ADJUSTMENT

	£ Historic	£ Current	£ Current Cost Adjustment
Cost	30,000	40,000	10,000
Depreciation	3,000	4,000	1,000
Net Book Value	27,000	36,000	9,000

JOURNALS:–

	£Dr	£Cr
i. Depreciation Expense	1,000	
Current Cost Reserve		1,000
ii. Fixed Asset at Cost	10,000	
Current Cost Reserve		10,000

Note: the extra depreciation necessary using Current Cost Accounting is
£1,000 and that is the depreciation adjustment necessary.

It is also necessary to revalue the fixed assets on the current cost balance
sheet represented by journal ii.

4 THE MONETARY WORKING CAPITAL ADJUSTMENT

	£
Debtors	15,000
Creditors	10,000
	5,000

$$\text{MWCA} = 7\tfrac{1}{2}\% \times £5,000 = £375$$

JOURNAL:–	£Dr	£Cr
Current Cost P/L MWCA	375	
Current Cost Reserve		375

5 GEARING ADJUSTMENT

			£
	HISTORIC COST CAPITAL EMPLOYED	=	71,000
ADD ADJUSTMENTS	FIXED ASSETS REVALUED	=	9,000
	STOCK ADJUSTMENT – Revaluation	=	700
	CURRENT COST CAPITAL EMPLOYED	=	80,700

$$\text{Gearing Percentage Adjustment} = \frac{\text{Borrowed Funds – Cash}}{\text{Current Cost of Capital Employed}} \times \frac{100}{1}$$

$$= \frac{(£44,000 + £20,000) - (£5,000 + £25,000)}{£80,700} \times \frac{100}{1}$$

$$= 42.13\%$$

This is then applied to the total of the COSA + DA + MWCA which is
£3600 + £1000 + £375   =   £4975
                                      × ·4213

The Gearing Adjustment is therefore   =   £2096

This is added back to the other adjustments to take account of the gains
obtained in using borrowed funds during periods of rising prices.

6 TOTAL CURRENT COST RESERVE

	£
Cost of Sales Adjustment	3,600
Stock revaluation	700
Fixed Asset revaluation	9,000
Monetary Working Capital Adjustment	375
Depreciation Adjustment	1,000
Less the Gearing Adjustment	(2,096)
Current Cost Reserve	12,579

IC SNOFLAKE LTD. —
CURRENT COST OPERATING STATEMENT
for year ended 31.12.19-5

	£	£
Historic Cost Operating Profit (before interest and dividends)		19,400
Less Current Cost Adjustments:		
Cost of Sales	3,600	
Depreciation	1,000	
Monetary Working Capital	375	
Gearing	(2,096)	
		2,879
Current Cost Operating Profit (before interest and dividends)		16,521
Less Interest		2,400
Current Cost Operating Profit (attributable to shareholders)		14,121
Less Dividend		6,000
Current Cost Retained Profit		8,121

IC SNOFLAKE LTD. — CURRENT COST BALANCE SHEET
at 31.12.19–5

	£ Cost	£ Depreciation Provision	£ Net Book Value
FIXED ASSETS			
	40,000	4,000	36,000
CURRENT ASSETS			
Stock	14,700		
Debtors	15,000		
Bank	20,000		
Cash	5,000		
		54,700	
LESS CURRENT LIABILITIES			
Creditors		(10,000)	
NET CURRENT ASSETS			44,700
TOTAL NET ASSETS			80,700
FINANCED BY			
Ordinary Share Capital Issued		40,000	
Add Reserves:-			
Profit and Loss c.c.	8,121		
Current Cost Revaluation	12,579		
		20,700	
Shareholders' funds		60,700	
12% Loan Stock		20,000	
Capital Employed			80,700

You may now attempt part (b) of the example yourself.

SELF-CHECK QUESTIONS

1X 'One can imagine a science fiction society in which money's purchasing power and the relative worth of assets never vary. In such a sleepy setting, historical accounts would be admirable. In the world as we know it they invite criticism. When prices are rising briskly traditional accounts are beset by several ailments . . .'

You are required to:
Identify and discuss the weaknesses suffered by historical cost accounts during a period of rising prices. *(25 marks)*
(AAT)

2X Lennon Limited was set up on 1st January 19–5 with a share capital of £100,000 and loan capital £25,000. It purchased fixed assets, having an estimated useful life of eight years, for £80,000 and commenced trading. The financial statements prepared on an Historic Cost basis for the first year are given below:–

LENNON LIMITED

Historic Profit and Loss Account
for the year ended 31.12.-3

	£	£
Sales		180,000
Less cost of sales		80,000
Gross profit		100,000
Less Operating expense	40,000	
Depreciation	10,000	
		50,000
Net operating profit (before interest and dividends)		50,000
Less interest		2,500
Net profit attributable to shareholders		47,500
Dividend paid		12,500
Retained profit		£35,000

LENNON LIMITED

Historic Cost Balance Sheet
as at 31.12.-3

	£	£	£
Fixed Assets	Cost	Depreciation	N.B.V.
	80,000	10,000	70,000
Current Assets			
Stock	50,000		
Debtors	30,000		
Cash	30,000		
		110,000	
Less Current Liabilities			
Creditors		20,000	
			90,000
			£160,000
Financed by:			
Share Capital			100,000
Reserves (P/L)			35,000
Shareholders' Funds			135,000
Debentures			25,000
			£160,000

The following additional information is also available:-
1. Stock prices rose evenly by 15% during the year. Average Stock Turnover is three times per annum.
2. Replacement Fixed Assets of the type purchased on 1st January would have cost £96,000 on 31st December.

3. Stock prices had risen by 2% over the period represented by the average age of debtors and creditors.

Required:

You are required to prepare financial statements for Lennon Limited in accordance with the standard Statement of Accounting Practice on Current Cost Accounting (SSAP 16).   *(30 marks)*
                                                                          (Q&A)

APPENDIX I
ACCOUNTANCY EXAMINATIONS AND YOU

BEFORE THE EXAM

You will be studying the subject matter of the examination. It is therefore essential that you are familiar with the syllabus for your examination. You should obtain a copy well in advance from the examining body.

You may be studying alone at home with recommended texts, following a correspondence course or receiving formal instruction at a college. It is harder to study at home and you need to approach the subject in a methodical manner by devising a work programme to ensure you cover topics on the syllabus within set times. Whatever your route of study the key to success is your ATTITUDE to study. You need to be DETERMINED to succeed. Success inevitably costs; it costs your time and effort. There are no 'free rides'. Look at it this way, why waste any time, money or effort on taking a course of study or in suffering in an examination in which you stand no chance or little chance of success. Therefore, if you are going to spend time, effort and money, put yourself in with a good chance of success by attacking the problem in a systematic and determined way.

REGULAR study in a SYSTEMATIC way is essential to your success, more so, in accounting than other subjects which you may think you can 'CRAM' for, although I would not recommend that either.

During your course, you should:-

1   PLAN your study time each week.

2   SET the work you want to cover.

3   ALLOW extra time to revise topics previously studied, so as they 'stick'.

4   HAVE all the tools to hand — Notes, texts, calculators, pens, pencils, rulers etc.

5   ENVIRONMENT — a comfortable, quiet room with no distractions from the job at hand is essential, where you will not be interrupted.

6   DO NOT WASTE time. It is a valuable commodity and a finite one. Start work immediately — Do not decide to read a paper, doodle, watch T.V. or whatever, during your study time. You should be strict with yourself on this issue.

7   PRESENT any work you do in a neat manner, pay attention to detail. Students often present work to me which is untidy and

would be unacceptable in an examination. The reasons (excuses) I receive vary from — "I did it quickly" — "It's only rough" — "I wanted to see it was right before I wrote it in ink" etc. You should get into the habit of writing your answers neatly and in ink — not pencil. Your speed will improve and you will be in shape to take the exam. Pencils are not usually accepted in examination scripts therefore, **do not** get into the habit of using them. Just like joggers are attempting to fine tune their bodies for fitness, you are getting your examination technique into shape.

8   Where you are following a formal course of study, ensure that you take good notes that are good enough to jog your memory about important points. Rewrite them when you get home, if necessary. Always read them and practise any questions or techniques set.

9   Organize your file into topic areas in line with the syllabus you are studying. Any questions you do on each topic should be at the end of your notes on the topic, so as not to 'mess' up the text.

10 Take notice of the weightings given to each topic when allocating your study time. For example, if 5% of the syllabus is devoted to Depreciation, then it might be an idea to allocate 5% of your total study time to that topic. However, you should not be too rigid, since it takes different people different amounts of time to grasp a particular topic. The message is not to spend an inordinate amount of time on any single item.

11 FINAL EXAM — You should prepare for this by obtaining past questions and doing as many of those questions as possible without reference to notes. This book should have helped you in your approach to questions. I would recommend you to obtain at least 4 to 6 past papers. You should, however, ensure that the examination papers set in the past are going to be similar to the one you are taking. OR HAVE THERE BEEN SYLLABUS CHANGES?

11.1   Attempt at least one complete paper under examination conditions. Answer questions correctly, neatly and in the time.

11.2   Study your answers and see where and why you went wrong, noting improvements you could make.

DURING THE EXAM

1   Ensure you arrive in plenty of time.

2   Do not try reading notes immediately before the exam, they will only confuse you. If you don't know it now, it's too late for this one.

3   Ensure you have the necessary tools with you to do a good job (pen, pencil, rubber, ruler, calculator etc.)

4   Ensure you have your examination reference number and identification.

5   When you receive the paper, read the instructions carefully. Note how many questions you need to answer.

6   READ quickly through all the questions, marking those you think you can best answer. Ask yourself the following:- How many questions do I need to answer? Are any questions compulsory? How many marks are allocated to each question and each section of the question?

7   Allocate your time in proportion to the possible marks you can earn. Remember, in a three hour exam you could earn a possible 100%, therefore, each percentage point should be earned in no more than 1.8 minutes, i.e.   A question worth 20 marks should therefore have a time allowance of 36 minutes (20 × 1.8). This planning is essential to the most effective use of your time and should take no longer than 5 minutes.

8   Do not waste time. Remember if you score half marks on all the required questions, you will pass the examination. It is essential you do not spend time inefficiently trying to squeeze an extra 10% from a question by spending a further 20 minutes over and above the allowed time for that question.

9   Make sure you answer the question the examiner set and cover the relevant points.

10 Attempt all the questions you need to. If the paper asks you to complete five questions all worth 20 marks each — DO FIVE. If you only do four, you immediately write off 20 possible marks. Therefore, ensure you keep an eye on the time and answer all the questions you need to.

AFTER THE EXAM

Forget about it unless you're into unnecessary pain and self torture. Post mortems at this stage do not achieve anything.

Finally, GOOD LUCK!

APPENDIX II
MULTIPLE CHOICE QUESTIONS

1 A Balance Sheet is
   a A Ledger
   b A Trial Balance
   c A Statement of Assets and Liabilities at a point in time
   d A Statement of Profitability

2 Which of the following items could not be obtained from a balance sheet?
   a Value of assets
   b Outstanding Liabilities
   c Cumulative depreciation
   d Gross Profit

3 Which of the following is an asset?
   a Creditors
   b Capital
   c Machinery
   d Maintenance
   e None of these

4 Which of the following is a liability?
   a Debtors
   b Profit
   c Fixtures
   d A credit balance on the cash account
   e None of these

5 Capital is best described as:-
   a An asset account of the business
   b A loan account of the business
   c A liability account of the business
   d A current asset
   e None of these

6 After preparing a balance sheet a cheque was issued to a creditor for £100. The
   following alteration to the balance sheet would be required:-
   a Increase debtors by £100
   b Decrease bank account £100 and Increase Debtors by £100
   c Decrease bank account £100 and Decrease creditors by £100
   d Decrease Creditors by £100

7 The state of affairs of a business at a point in time is shown by:-
   a The Trading Account
   b The Profit and Loss Account
   c The Cash Book
   d The Balance Sheet
   e None of these

8 Premises £50,000 shown as part of the balance sheet totals means:-
   a The premises cost £50,000
   b The business owns an asset valued at £50,000 in the books of account
   c The business has spent £50,000 on premises
   d The business uses premises worth £50,000 but does not necessarily own them.

9 Fixed Assets are assets:-
   a which continually increase in value
   b which remain in a 'fixed' location

    c which were bought at a fixed price
    d which the business intends to keep and use in the business over a long period of time

10 Current Assets are assets:-
    a that are held in cash
    b which can be easily moved
    c excluding fixed assets which continually change form
    d which cannot easily be turned into cash

11 Current liabilities are:-
    a All liabilities of the business
    b Long term liabilities only
    c Liabilities falling due within one year
    d Mortgages

12 Working Capital is the difference between
    a Fixed and Current Assets
    b Equity Capital and Loan Capital
    c Cash in the bank and Cash held at the business
    d Current Assets and Current Liabilities
    e None of these

13 Another name for Net Current Assets is:-
    a Working Capital
    b Total Assets
    c Total Net Assets
    d Capital Employed

14 Stocks and WIP + Debtors + Bank and Cash Less Creditors and other short term liabilities would best be described as:-
    a Capital
    b Net tangible assets
    c Working Capital
    d Net Liabilities
    e None of these

15 Goods costing £300 sold for £500 on credit terms would:-
    a Increase creditors by £300 and reduce stock by £500
    b Increase debtors by £500
    c Increase creditors by £500
    d Increase debtors by £500, reduce stock by £300 and increase Capital by £200
    e Increase debtors by £500 and reduce stock by £500

16 Liquid Assets are:-
    a Cash Only
    b Cash and anything that can be turned into cash quickly
    c Net Current Assets
    d Fixed Assets plus Capital
    e None of these

17 Retained Profit is shown on the balance sheet as:-
    a An addition to capital
    b An increase in bank and cash
    c A Current Asset
    d Capital Employed

18 Drawings by a sole trader are:-
    a An expense
    b A reduction in capital
    c A liability
    d A reduction in profit
    e None of these

19 The depreciation shown on the balance sheet is:-
    a An expense for wear and tear of the asset
    b The Net Book Value or Written Down Value
    c The cumulative total for depreciation which has been written off the cost of the asset to date
    d None of these

20 Amortization is:-
    a Type of Fixed Asset
    b Similar to depreciation usually indicating a fall in the value of an asswet, which has a definite life such as a lease.
    c An increase in the value of an asset which has a definite life such as a lease.
    d A Reserve Account
    e None of these

21 A provision is:-
    a A reserve
    b An amount retained to provide for a liability or loss where there is uncertainty as to timing or amount.
    c An amount retained to provide for a loss which is certain in value but not in timing.
    d Purchase of stocks

22 A reserve is:-
    a An amount set aside out of profit for a specific purpose
    b Represented by asset values which exceed liabilities
    c Hidden Stocks
    d Money held in an undisclosed account of the business

23 A Day Book is:-
    a A Ledger Account
    b A book of prime entry where items are recorded prior to posting the relevant ledger accounts.
    c A daily listing of all moneys received and paid out
    d None of the above

24 Which of the following does not constitute a separate ledger:-
    a Sales
    b Purchases
    c Fixed Assets
    d Cash
    e Nominal or General

25 The total of the Sales Day Book is posted to:-
    a the debit of the creditors accounts
    b the credit of the sales account and the debit of the relevant customer accounts.
    c the debit of the sales account and the credit of the cash account.
    d it is not posted to the ledger.

26 In the trial balance Sales would be shown on the:-
    a debit side
    b both debit and credit sides
    c credit side
    d credit side only if they were credit sales

27 A debit balance of £500 on D. Campbell's account in the books of Thomas means that:-
    a Campbell owes Thomas £500
    b Thomas owes Campbell £500
    c That Campbell has paid Thomas
    d That Thomas has paid Campbell
    e None of these

28 A credit note received from a supplier would first be entered in:-
    a The Sales Ledger

b   The Sales Returns Day Book
c   The Purchase Day Book
d   The Purchase Returns Day Book

29   A credit note sent to a customer would first be entered in:-
a   The Sales Ledger
b   The Sales Returns Day Book
c   The Purchase Day Book
d   The Purchase Returns Day Book

30   A sales return £50 wrongly posted to the credit of the Purchase Returns Account, but posted correctly to the debtors account would make the following difference to a Trial Balance:-
a   No difference, both sides still agree
b   The credit side would be £50 more than the debit side
c   The debit side would be £100 less than the credit side
d   The debit side would be £100 more than the credit side

31   If a proprietor takes goods costing £500 for his own use, this would be recorded as:-
a   An expense to the business £500
b   Private drawings £500
c   A reduction in cash £500
d   A reduction in capital £500 and a reduction of stock £500
e   A reduction of stock £500

32   A reduction of capital by a sole trader is described as:-
a   An expense
b   An increase in liabilities
c   A reduction of cash
d   Drawings
e   None of these

33   A proprietor withdraws cash for his own use. The ledger accounts affected are:-
a   Debit Cash, Credit Bank
b   Debit Cash, Credit Expenses
c   Credit Bank, Debit Drawings
d   Credit Cash, Debit Drawings
e   Credit Capital, Debit Cash

34   A proprietor buys a motor vehicle on credit for use in his business. The transaction should first be recorded in:-
a   The Cash Book
b   The Nominal Ledger
c   The Purchase Day Book
d   The Journal
e   None of these

35   Invoices received for the purchase of goods would be entered first in:-
a   The Cash Book
b   The Sales Day Book
c   The Purchase Account
d   The Purchase Day Book
e   The Purchase Returns Day Book

36   When a debtor pays in cash the ledger entries would be:-
a   Dr Debtor, Cr Bank
b   Dr Debtor, Cr Cash
c   Dr Cash, Cr Debtor
d   Dr Cash, Cr Creditor

37   When a creditor is paid by cheque the ledger entries would be:-
a   Dr Creditor, Cr Bank
b   Dr Creditor, Cr Cash

c Dr Debtor, Cr Cash
d Dr Debtor, Cr Creditor

38 When a debtor returns goods the ledger entries would be:-
    a Dr Sales, Cr Creditor
    b Dr Sales Returns, Cr Cash
    c Dr Sales Returns, Cr Debtor
    d Dr Purchase Returns, Cr Debtor

39 Which of the following may be classified as capital expenditure:-
    a Purchase of Goods for Resale
    b Payments for Wages and Salaries
    c The purchase of Premises
    d Repairs to Premises

40 An owner of a business pays £2000 by cheque in wages for work carried out on an extension to his factory. The ledger entries should record this thus:-
    a Debit Wages, Credit Cash
    b Debit Wages, Credit Bank
    c Debit Factory Premises – Fixed Asset, Credit Bank
    d None of these

41 An owner of a business pays £2000 cash in wages to extend his house. The ledger entries needed are:-
    a Debit Wages, Credit Cash
    b Debit Wages, Credit Bank
    c Debit Premises, Credit Cash
    d Debit Repairs, Credit Cash
    e No need for any entries in the ledger

42 A cash discount received for prompt settlement would be shown in:-
    a Discount Received Account, The relevant Creditors Account and the Cash Book.
    b Discount Allowed Account, The Purchase Account and the Cash Book.
    c Discount Received Account and The Cash Book only.
    d None of these

43 Cash discount is given when:-
    a goods are bought for cash
    b goods are paid for by cash or cheque
    c accounts are settled promptly in accordance with the terms on the invoice.
    d dealing with other businesses in the same trade

44 Trade discount is given for:-
    a Cash
    b Prompt settlement
    c Businesses in the same or similar trade or industry
    d Bulk purchase

45 Trade discount is recorded in:-
    a The Sales or Purchase Day Book only
    b The Sales Day Book, Purchase Day Book and Ledger
    c It is not recorded
    d The Cash Book only

46 An invoice shows a total goods value before VAT of £600 less a trade discount of 30% and a cash discount of 5% for payment within 30 days. Assuming payment is made within the terms of settlement and VAT is applied at 15% to the invoice total, then the cheque paid is for:-
    a £600
    b £458.85
    c £448.50
    d £489

47   An invoice for goods purchased £100 allowed trade discount of 20%. The discount
     would be recorded as follows:-
     a   Dr Creditor, Cr Discount Received
     b   Dr Purchases, Cr Discount Received
     c   Dr Discount Allowed, Cr Creditor
     d   It is not necessary to record trade discount in the ledger

48   An invoice for goods bought £500 allowed a cash discount of £50 for prompt
     settlement. The discount would be recorded in the ledger as follows:-
     a   Dr Creditor, Cr Discount Received
     b   Dr Creditor, Cr Discount Allowed
     c   Dr Discount Received, Cr Creditor
     d   Dr Discount Allowed, Cr Creditor

49   A bank overdraft is shown as a:-
     a   Debit balance in the bank account
     b   Credit balance in the bank account
     c   Debit balance in the Capital Account
     d   None of these

50   A business receives a loan £10,000 by cheque. The ledger entries are:-
     a   Debit Loan Account, Credit Creditor
     b   Debit Cash, Credit Capital
     c   Debit Bank, Credit Loan Account
     d   Debit Bank only

51   An account being debited would be increased if it is:-
     a   An asset account
     b   A liability account
     c   A capital account
     d   A loan account

52   An account being debited would be reduced if it is:-
     a   An asset account
     b   A cash account
     c   An expense account
     d   A liability account

53   An account being credited is increased if it is:-
     a   A liability account
     b   An asset account
     c   An expense account
     d   None of these

54   An account being credited is reduced if it is:-
     a   A liability account
     b   An asset account
     c   A creditor
     d   A capital account

55   Which account is not of the same type as the others? – that is the odd one out.
     a   Wages and Salaries
     b   Carriage Out
     c   Discount Allowed
     d   Fixtures and Fittings

56   Which account is not of the same type? – that is the odd one out.
     a   Creditor
     b   Capital
     c   Loan
     d   Debtor

57 Which account is not of the same type? – that is the odd one out.
    a Land and Buildings
    b Fixtures and Fittings
    c Plant and Machinery
    d Stock

58 Which account is not of the same type? – that is the odd one out
    a Depreciation
    b Bad Debts
    c Wages and Salaries
    d Sales

59 Prepayments are shown as:-
    a A current liability
    b An expense
    c Revenue
    d A current asset

60 Accruals are shown as:-
    a A current liability
    b A current asset
    c Revenue
    d A provision

61 Rates paid in advance are shown as a:-
    a Debit balance on the rates account
    b Credit balance on the rates account
    c A current liability
    d They are not recorded in the rates account

62 Rates shown in the Profit and Loss Account should be:-
    a The total rates paid in the period
    b The total rates that have been paid and are payable for the period, i.e. what is due.
    c The actual rates that should have been paid in the period
    d The total rent due.

63 If a company has a financial year to 31st December and rates from 1st April in that year to 31st March following the year end amount to £2,400, the Profit and Loss Account would show rates as:-
    a £2,400
    b £1,800
    c £3,000
    d £1,600

64 Gross Profit is:-
    a Sales less Sales Returns
    b Net Profit less Expenses
    c Sales less Closing Stock
    d Sales less Cost of Goods Sold

65 Annual Turnover is usually regarded as:-
    a The number of times something occurs in a period
    b A technical term for turning a ledger page
    c The yearly sales total
    d A sale which occurs once every year

66 The Cost of Goods Sold is:-
    a Purchases
    b Sales
    c Opening Stock less Closing Stock
    d Stock at start, plus purchases less stock at the end

67 The Gross Profit to Sales ratio expressed as a percentage is 20% and sales for the
    period are £10,000. The Gross Profit is:-
    a   £20,000
    b   £50,000
    c   £2,000
    d   £200

68 Another name for the Gross Profit to Sales ratio is:-
    a   The mark-up
    b   The acid test
    c   The current ratio
    d   The margin

69 Net Profit is:-
    a   The increase in cash
    b   Sales less all expenses
    c   Sales less cost of goods sold
    d   Gross Profit less expenses

70 Which of the following items would not appear in the Profit and Loss Account:-
    a   Carriage Out
    b   Discount Allowed
    c   Purchase of Premises
    d   Interest received

71 Goodwill if shown in a balance sheet is shown as:-
    a   A Tangible Asset
    b   A Current Asset
    c   An Intangible Asset
    d   Capital

72 Purchased Goodwill may best be defined as:-
    a   That amount paid as purchase consideration in excess of the value of tangible
    assets
    b   A Current Asset
    c   A Liability
    d   None of these

73 If the closing stock in the trading account is understated, the gross profit will be:-
    a   Understated
    b   Overstated
    c   Not be affected
    d   Double the previous figure

74 If the stock at the end of a period shown in the trading account is overstated, then the
    gross profit will be:-
    a   Overstated
    b   Understated
    c   Not affected
    d   Half the original figure

75 Gross Profit is £7,500 and sales are £75,000. The gross profit to sales ratio expressed
    as a percentage is:-
    a   1%
    b   5%
    c   10%
    d   20%

76 If the Gross Profit to sales percentage is 60% then Gross Profit as a percentage of Cost
    of Sales is:-
    a   150%
    b   50%
    c   40%

d   37.5%

77 If Gross Profit to Sales is 25% and Sales are £78,000, the Gross Profit is:-
    a   £7,800
    b   £19,500
    c   £26,000
    d   £58,500

78 Gross Profit as a percentage of Cost of Sales is 25%. The Sales are £132,000. The Gross Profit is:-
    a   £33,000
    b   £44,000
    c   £13,200
    d   £26,400

79 During the past year a firm's average stock has been £12,000 at cost, the mark-up has been 50% and sales have been £54,000. The firm's rate of stock turnover during the past year has been:-
    a   4.5
    b   3.0
    c   2.25
    d   1.5
    e   None of the above

80 Which, if any, of the following items would be classified as capital expenditure:-
    a   Withdrawals of cash by the owner for his own use
    b   Redecoration of existing premises
    c   Lighting and heating costs for the factory during the year.
    d   Several cars for resale, purchased by a motor dealer
    e   None of the above

81 Net sales for a business were £97,000. Average debtors throughout the year were £8,000. Assuming all sales were on credit, the average collection period was:-
    a   12 days
    b   24 days
    c   30 days
    d   37 days
    e   None of the above

82 Using the reducing balance method, the depreciation for the year at 20% for a motor vehicle which cost £8,000 now valued at £4,800 would be:-
    a   £960
    b   £640
    c   £1,600
    d   £240
    e   None of the above

83 If a posting of the correct amount is made on the correct side, but in the wrong class of account, it is an error of:-
    a   Original entry
    b   Reversal of entries
    c   Commission
    d   Compensation
    e   None of the above

84 Which, if any, of the following would increase the working capital of a sports shop?
    a   The purchase on credit of rugby balls
    b   The receipt of cash from a debtor
    c   Payment by cheque to a creditor
    d   The sale for cash of a delivery van
    e   None of the above

85   Which, if any, of the items below appear in the sales ledger control account?
    a   Cash sales
    b   Returns outwards
    c   Provision for bad debts
    d   Customers' dishonoured cheques
    e   None of the above

86   In a limited company's balance sheet the equity shareholders interest includes:-
    a   Issued preference share capital
    b   Authorised ordinary share capital
    c   Dividends paid to shareholders
    d   Reserves
    e   None of the above

87   One of the purposes of the trial balance is to ascertain:-
    a   The accounting records are correct in every detail
    b   The owner has enough cash left in the business
    c   Certain types of mistakes have not occurred
    d   The profit made by the business
    e   None of the above

88   Which, if any, of the following items appearing in the final accounts of a manufacturer,
form part of the prime cost of manufacture?
    a   Royalties paid out on a production process
    b   Carriage on fnished goods
    c   Factory Overheads
    d   Work in progress (at factory cost)
    e   None of the above

89   Fixed Assets are best described as:-
    a   Land and Buildings
    b   Those assets which a business intends to keep and use to produce revenue over a
number of years.
    c   Assets which do not move
    d   Plant and Machinery
    e   Those assets which are regarded as capital investment.

90   Current Assets are best described as:-
    a   Assets currently in use
    b   Stock and Debtors
    c   Those assets which a business intends to use within a period of twelve months,
       e.g. Stock, Debtors, Bank and Cash.
    d   Working Capital
    e   Net Current Assets

91   Current Liabilities are best described as:-
    a   Those liabilities which are payable immediately.
    b   Those liabilities which will be paid within 5 years
    c   Those liabilities which will be paid within a period of twelve months.
    d   Creditors
    e   Long term Loans

92   The Margin is best described as:-
    a $\dfrac{\text{Gross Profit}}{\text{Sales}} \times \dfrac{100}{1}$

    b $\dfrac{\text{Cost of Sales}}{\text{Sales}} \times \dfrac{100}{1}$

    c $\dfrac{\text{Sales}}{\text{Gross Profit}} \times \dfrac{100}{1}$

d $\dfrac{\text{Net Profit}}{\text{Gross Profit}}$ × $\dfrac{100}{1}$

e $\dfrac{\text{Sales}}{\text{Cost of Sales}}$ × $\dfrac{100}{1}$

93 The Mark Up is best described as:-

a $\dfrac{\text{Profit}}{\text{Selling Price}}$ × $\dfrac{100}{1}$

b $\dfrac{\text{Gross Profit}}{\text{Cost of Sales}}$ × $\dfrac{100}{1}$

c $\dfrac{\text{Net Profit}}{\text{Gross Profit}}$ × $\dfrac{100}{1}$

d $\dfrac{\text{Gross Profit}}{\text{Sales}}$ × $\dfrac{100}{1}$

e $\dfrac{\text{Sales}}{\text{Cost of Sales}}$ × $\dfrac{100}{1}$

94 CAPITAL is best described as:-
   a The funds that the owners of a business have invested in it.
   b Fixed Assets
   c Cash
   d Stock and Cash
   e Profit

95 LONG TERM LIABILITIES are best described as:-
   a Those liabilities which are not current and which will be paid over periods longer
      than one year
   b Those liabilities which are not current
   c Debentures
   d Long Term Loans
   e Bank Overdrafts

96 CAPITAL EMPLOYED is best described as:-
   a Fixed Assets and Current Assets
   b All the money used in a business
   c Owners' funds plus profits retained plus any Loans the business has.
   d Everything the business has
   e Money invested in the bank

97 GROSS PROFIT is best described as:-
   a The Trading Profit or Loss
   b Sales Revenue less the Cost of Goods sold in a period
   c Sales Revenue less all costs
   d The profit after all expenses are paid
   e The Cost of Sales Account

98 The Balance to carry forward on a Sales Ledger Control Account is:-
   a The Total Purchases
   b The Total Sales
   c The Total for Debits and Credits
   d The Total Creditors
   e The Total Debtors outstanding

99 Given opening debtors b/f £8,500, sales £20,000 and the balance to c/f £5,000 the
   amounts received from debtors in the period must have been:-
   a £25,000
   b £20,000
   c £15,000
   d £28,500

    e £23,500

100 The Sales Day Book may also be called:-
    a The Purchase Day Book
    b The Sales Ledger
    c The Debtors Control Account
    d The Sales Journal
    e The Sales Invoice

101 Sales Invoices are first entered into:-
    a The Purchase Day Book
    b The Journal
    c The Cash Book
    d The Debtors Control Account
    e The Sales Day Book

102 A debit balance in the cash book of £500 brought forward at the start of a period shows that:-
    a Cash had been overspent by £500
    b The total cash spent was £500
    c The total cash received was £500
    d The business has £500 cash in hand
    e None of these

103 A credit balance in the cash book of £100 brought forward at the start of a period shows that:-
    a Cash had been overspent by £100
    b The total cash paid out was £100
    c The total cash received was £100
    d The business has £100 cash in hand
    e None of these

104 An invoiced amount owing at the end of an accounting period is described as:-
    a A Prepayment
    b An Asset
    c Debtors
    d An Accrual
    e None of these

105 An invoice paid in respect of a future accounting period may be described as:-
    a An Accrual
    b Creditors
    c A Liability
    d A Prepayment
    e None of these

APPENDIX III
ANSWERS TO MULTIPLE CHOICE QUESTIONS

1c	35d	69d	103a
2d	36c	70c	104d
3c	37a	71c	105d
4d	38c	72a	
5c	39c	73a	
6c	40c	74a	
7d	41e	75c	
8b	42a	76a	
9d	43c	77b	
10c	44c	78d	
11c	45a	79c	
12d	46b	80e	
13a	47d	81e	
14c	48a	82a	
15d	49b	83e	
16b	50c	84d	
17a	51a	85d	
18b	52d	86d	
19c	53a	87c	
20b	54b	88a	
21b	55d	89b	
22b	56d	90c	
23b	57d	91c	
24c	58d	92a	
25b	59d	93b	
26c	60a	94a	
27a	61b	95a	
28d	62c	96c	
29c	63b	97b	
30c	64d	98e	
31d	65c	99e	
32d	66d	100d	
33d	67c	101e	
34d	68d	102d	

APPENDIX IV

PRESENT VALUE AND ANNUITY TABLES

TABLE A Present Value of 1

Periods	1%	2%	3%	4%	5%	6%	7%	8%	9%	10%
1	0.990	0.980	0.971	0.962	0.952	0.943	0.935	0.926	0.917	0.909
2	0.980	0.961	0.943	0.925	0.907	0.890	0.873	0.857	0.842	0.826
3	0.971	0.942	0.915	0.889	0.864	0.840	0.816	0.794	0.772	0.751
4	0.961	0.924	0.888	0.855	0.823	0.792	0.763	0.735	0.708	0.683
5	0.951	0.906	0.863	0.822	0.784	0.747	0.713	0.681	0.650	0.621
6	0.942	0.888	0.837	0.790	0.746	0.705	0.666	0.630	0.596	0.564
7	0.933	0.871	0.813	0.760	0.711	0.665	0.623	0.583	0.547	0.513
8	0.923	0.853	0.789	0.731	0.677	0.627	0.582	0.540	0.502	0.467
9	0.914	0.837	0.766	0.703	0.645	0.592	0.544	0.500	0.460	0.424
10	0.905	0.820	0.744	0.676	0.614	0.558	0.508	0.463	0.422	0.386
11	0.896	0.804	0.722	0.650	0.585	0.527	0.475	0.429	0.388	0.350
12	0.887	0.788	0.701	0.625	0.557	0.497	0.444	0.397	0.356	0.319
13	0.879	0.773	0.681	0.601	0.530	0.469	0.415	0.368	0.326	0.290
14	0.870	0.758	0.661	0.577	0.505	0.442	0.388	0.340	0.299	0.263
15	0.861	0.743	0.642	0.555	0.481	0.417	0.362	0.315	0.275	0.239
16	0.853	0.728	0.623	0.534	0.458	0.394	0.339	0.292	0.252	0.218
17	0.844	0.714	0.605	0.513	0.436	0.371	0.317	0.270	0.231	0.198
18	0.836	0.700	0.587	0.494	0.416	0.350	0.296	0.250	0.212	0.180
19	0.828	0.686	0.570	0.475	0.396	0.331	0.277	0.232	0.194	0.164
20	0.820	0.673	0.554	0.456	0.377	0.312	0.258	0.215	0.178	0.149
21	0.811	0.660	0.538	0.439	0.359	0.294	0.242	0.199	0.164	0.135
22	0.803	0.647	0.522	0.422	0.342	0.278	0.226	0.184	0.150	0.123
23	0.795	0.634	0.507	0.406	0.326	0.262	0.211	0.170	0.138	0.112
24	0.788	0.622	0.492	0.390	0.310	0.247	0.197	0.158	0.126	0.102
25	0.780	0.610	0.478	0.375	0.295	0.233	0.184	0.146	0.116	0.092

TABLE A (contd.) — Present Value of 1

Periods	11%	12%	13%	14%	15%	16%	17%	18%	19%	20%
1	0.901	0.893	0.885	0.877	0.870	0.862	0.855	0.847	0.840	0.833
2	0.812	0.797	0.783	0.769	0.756	0.743	0.731	0.718	0.706	0.694
3	0.731	0.712	0.693	0.675	0.658	0.641	0.624	0.609	0.593	0.579
4	0.659	0.636	0.613	0.592	0.572	0.552	0.534	0.516	0.499	0.482
5	0.593	0.567	0.543	0.519	0.497	0.476	0.456	0.437	0.419	0.402
6	0.535	0.507	0.480	0.456	0.432	0.410	0.390	0.370	0.352	0.335
7	0.482	0.452	0.425	0.400	0.376	0.354	0.333	0.314	0.296	0.279
8	0.434	0.404	0.376	0.351	0.327	0.305	0.285	0.266	0.249	0.233
9	0.391	0.361	0.333	0.308	0.284	0.263	0.243	0.225	0.209	0.194
10	0.352	0.322	0.295	0.270	0.247	0.227	0.208	0.191	0.176	0.162
11	0.317	0.287	0.261	0.237	0.215	0.195	0.178	0.162	0.148	0.135
12	0.286	0.257	0.231	0.208	0.187	0.168	0.152	0.137	0.124	0.112
13	0.258	0.229	0.204	0.182	0.163	0.145	0.130	0.116	0.104	0.093
14	0.232	0.205	0.181	0.160	0.141	0.125	0.111	0.099	0.088	0.078
15	0.209	0.183	0.160	0.140	0.123	0.108	0.095	0.084	0.074	0.065
16	0.188	0.163	0.141	0.123	0.107	0.093	0.081	0.071	0.062	0.054
17	0.170	0.146	0.125	0.108	0.093	0.080	0.069	0.060	0.052	0.045
18	0.153	0.130	0.111	0.095	0.081	0.069	0.059	0.051	0.044	0.038
19	0.138	0.116	0.098	0.083	0.070	0.060	0.051	0.043	0.037	0.031
20	0.124	0.104	0.087	0.073	0.061	0.051	0.043	0.037	0.031	0.026
21	0.112	0.093	0.077	0.064	0.053	0.044	0.037	0.031	0.026	0.022
22	0.101	0.083	0.068	0.056	0.046	0.038	0.032	0.026	0.022	0.018
23	0.091	0.074	0.060	0.049	0.040	0.033	0.027	0.022	0.018	0.015
24	0.082	0.066	0.053	0.043	0.035	0.028	0.023	0.019	0.015	0.013
25	0.074	0.059	0.047	0.038	0.030	0.024	0.020	0.016	0.013	0.010

TABLE B Present Value of Annuity of 1

Periods	1%	2%	3%	4%	5%	6%	7%	8%	9%	10%
1	0.990	0.980	0.971	0.962	0.952	0.943	0.935	0.926	0.917	0.909
2	1.970	1.942	1.913	1.886	1.859	1.833	1.808	1.783	1.759	1.736
3	2.941	2.884	2.829	2.775	2.723	2.673	2.624	2.577	2.531	2.487
4	3.902	3.808	3.717	3.630	3.546	3.465	3.387	3.312	3.240	3.170
5	4.853	4.713	4.580	4.452	4.329	4.212	4.100	3.993	3.890	3.791
6	5.795	5.601	5.417	5.242	5.076	4.917	4.767	4.623	4.486	4.355
7	6.728	6.472	6.230	6.002	5.786	5.582	5.389	5.206	5.033	4.868
8	7.652	7.325	7.020	6.733	6.463	6.210	5.971	5.747	5.535	5.335
9	8.566	8.162	7.786	7.435	7.108	6.802	6.515	6.247	5.995	5.759
10	9.471	8.983	8.530	8.111	7.722	7.360	7.024	6.710	6.418	6.145
11	10.368	9.787	9.253	8.760	8.306	7.887	7.499	7.139	6.805	6.495
12	11.255	10.575	9.954	9.385	8.863	8.384	7.943	7.536	7.161	6.814
13	12.134	11.348	10.635	9.986	9.394	8.853	8.353	7.904	7.487	7.103
14	13.004	12.106	11.296	10.563	9.899	9.295	8.745	8.244	7.786	7.367
15	13.865	12.849	11.938	11.118	10.380	9.712	9.103	8.559	8.061	7.606
16	14.718	13.578	12.561	11.652	10.838	10.106	9.447	8.851	8.313	7.825
17	15.562	14.292	13.166	12.166	11.274	10.477	9.763	9.122	8.544	8.024
18	16.398	14.992	13.754	12.659	11.690	10.828	10.059	9.372	8.756	8.204
19	17.226	15.678	14.324	13.134	12.085	11.158	10.336	9.604	8.950	8.362
20	18.046	16.351	14.877	13.590	12.462	11.470	10.594	9.818	9.129	8.511
21	18.857	17.011	15.415	14.029	12.821	11.764	10.836	10.017	9.292	8.649
22	19.660	17.658	15.837	14.451	13.163	12.042	11.061	10.201	9.442	8.772
23	20.456	18.292	16.444	14.857	13.489	12.303	11.272	10.371	9.580	8.883
24	21.243	18.914	16.936	15.247	13.799	12.550	11.469	10.529	9.707	8.985
25	22.023	19.523	17.413	15.622	14.094	12.783	11.654	10.675	9.823	9.077

TABLE B (contd.) — Present Value of Annuity of 1

Periods	11%	12%	13%	14%	15%	16%	17%	18%	19%	20%
1	0.901	0.893	0.885	0.877	0.870	0.862	0.855	0.847	0.840	0.833
2	1.713	1.690	1.668	1.647	1.626	1.605	1.585	1.566	1.547	1.528
3	2.444	2.402	2.361	2.322	2.283	2.246	2.210	2.174	2.140	2.106
4	3.102	3.037	2.974	2.914	2.855	2.798	2.743	2.690	2.639	2.589
5	3.696	3.605	3.517	3.433	3.352	3.274	3.199	3.127	3.058	2.991
6	4.231	4.111	3.998	3.889	3.784	3.685	3.589	3.498	3.410	3.326
7	4.712	4.564	4.423	4.288	4.160	4.039	3.922	3.812	3.706	3.605
8	5.146	4.968	4.799	4.639	4.487	4.344	4.207	4.078	3.954	3.837
9	5.537	5.328	5.132	4.946	4.772	4.607	4.451	4.303	4.163	4.031
10	5.889	5.650	5.426	5.216	5.019	4.833	4.659	4.494	4.339	4.192
11	6.207	5.938	5.687	5.453	5.234	5.029	4.836	4.656	4.486	4.327
12	6.492	6.194	5.918	5.660	5.421	5.197	4.988	4.793	4.611	4.439
13	6.750	6.424	6.122	5.842	5.583	5.342	5.118	4.910	4.715	4.533
14	6.982	6.628	6.302	6.002	5.724	5.468	5.229	5.008	4.802	4.611
15	7.191	6.811	6.462	6.142	5.847	5.575	5.324	5.092	4.876	4.675
16	7.379	6.974	6.604	6.265	5.954	5.668	5.405	5.162	4.938	4.730
17	7.549	7.120	6.729	6.373	6.047	5.749	5.475	5.222	4.990	4.775
18	7.702	7.250	6.840	6.467	6.128	5.818	5.534	5.273	5.033	4.812
19	7.839	7.366	6.938	6.550	6.198	5.877	5.584	5.316	5.070	4.843
20	7.963	7.469	7.025	6.623	6.259	5.929	5.628	5.353	5.101	4.870
21	8.075	7.562	7.102	6.687	6.312	5.973	5.665	5.384	5.127	4.891
22	8.176	7.645	7.170	6.743	6.359	6.011	5.696	5.410	5.149	4.909
23	8.266	7.718	7.230	6.792	6.399	6.044	5.723	5.432	5.167	4.925
24	8.348	7.784	7.283	6.835	6.434	6.073	5.746	5.451	5.182	4.937
25	8.422	7.843	7.330	6.873	6.464	6.097	5.766	5.467	5.195	4.948

TABLE C Future Value of 1

Periods	1%	2%	3%	4%	5%	6%	7%	8%	9%	10%
1	1.010	1.020	1.030	1.040	1.050	1.060	1.070	1.080	1.090	1.100
2	1.020	1.040	1.061	1.082	1.102	1.124	1.145	1.166	1.188	1.200
3	1.030	1.061	1.093	1.125	1.158	1.191	1.225	1.260	1.295	1.331
4	1.041	1.082	1.126	1.170	1.216	1.262	1.311	1.360	1.412	1.464
5	1.051	1.104	1.159	1.217	1.276	1.338	1.403	1.469	1.539	1.611
6	1.062	1.126	1.194	1.265	1.340	1.419	1.501	1.587	1.677	1.772
7	1.072	1.149	1.230	1.316	1.407	1.504	1.606	1.714	1.828	1.949
8	1.083	1.172	1.267	1.369	1.477	1.594	1.718	1.851	1.993	2.144
9	1.094	1.195	1.305	1.423	1.551	1.689	1.838	1.999	2.172	2.358
10	1.105	1.219	1.344	1.480	1.629	1.791	1.967	2.159	2.367	2.594
11	1.116	1.243	1.384	1.539	1.710	1.898	2.105	2.332	2.580	2.853
12	1.127	1.268	1.426	1.601	1.796	2.012	2.252	2.518	2.813	3.138
13	1.138	1.294	1.469	1.665	1.886	2.133	2.410	2.720	3.066	3.452
14	1.149	1.319	1.513	1.732	1.980	2.261	2.579	2.937	3.342	3.797
15	1.161	1.346	1.558	1.801	2.079	2.397	2.759	3.172	3.642	4.177
16	1.173	1.373	1.605	1.873	2.183	2.540	2.952	3.426	3.970	4.595
17	1.184	1.400	1.653	1.948	2.292	2.693	3.159	3.700	4.328	5.054
18	1.196	1.428	1.702	2.026	2.407	2.854	3.380	3.996	4.717	5.560
19	1.208	1.457	1.754	2.107	2.527	3.026	3.617	4.316	5.142	6.116
20	1.220	1.486	1.806	2.191	2.653	3.207	3.870	4.661	5.604	6.727
21	1.232	1.516	1.860	2.279	2.786	3.400	4.141	5.034	6.109	7.400
22	1.245	1.546	1.916	2.370	2.925	3.604	4.430	5.437	6.659	8.140
23	1.257	1.577	1.974	2.465	3.072	3.820	4.741	5.871	7.258	8.954
24	1.270	1.608	2.033	2.563	3.225	4.049	5.072	6.341	7.911	9.850
25	1.282	1.641	2.094	2.666	3.386	4.292	5.427	6.848	8.623	10.835

TABLE C (contd.) — Future Value of 1

Periods	11%	12%	13%	14%	15%	16%	17%	18%	19%	20%
1	1.110	1.120	1.130	1.140	1.150	1.160	1.170	1.180	1.190	1.200
2	1.232	1.254	1.277	1.300	1.322	1.346	1.369	1.392	1.416	1.490
3	1.368	1.405	1.443	1.482	1.521	1.561	1.602	1.643	1.685	1.728
4	1.518	1.574	1.630	1.689	1.749	1.811	1.874	1.939	2.005	2.074
5	1.685	1.762	1.842	1.925	2.011	2.100	2.192	2.228	2.386	2.488
6	1.870	1.974	2.082	2.195	2.313	2.436	2.565	2.700	2.840	2.986
7	2.076	2.211	2.353	2.502	2.660	2.826	3.001	3.185	3.379	3.583
8	2.305	2.476	2.658	2.853	3.059	3.278	3.511	3.759	4.021	4.300
9	2.558	2.773	3.004	3.252	3.518	3.803	4.108	4.435	4.785	5.160
10	2.839	3.106	3.395	3.707	4.046	4.411	4.807	5.234	5.695	6.192
11	3.152	3.479	3.836	4.226	4.652	5.117	5.624	6.176	6.777	7.430
12	3.498	3.896	4.335	4.818	5.350	5.936	6.580	7.288	8.064	8.916
13	3.883	4.363	4.898	5.492	6.153	6.886	7.699	8.599	9.596	10.699
14	4.310	4.887	5.535	6.261	7.076	7.988	9.007	10.147	11.420	12.839
15	4.785	5.474	6.254	7.138	8.137	9.266	10.539	11.974	13.590	15.407
16	5.311	6.130	7.067	8.137	9.358	10.748	12.330	14.129	16.172	18.488
17	5.895	6.866	7.986	9.276	10.761	12.468	14.426	16.672	19.244	22.186
18	6.544	7.690	9.024	10.575	12.375	14.463	16.879	19.673	22.901	26.623
19	7.263	8.613	10.197	12.056	14.232	16.777	19.748	23.214	27.252	31.948
20	8.062	9.646	11.523	13.743	16.367	19.461	23.106	27.393	32.429	38.338
21	8.949	10.804	13.021	15.668	18.822	22.574	27.034	32.324	38.591	46.005
22	9.934	12.100	14.714	17.861	21.645	26.186	31.629	38.142	45.923	55.206
23	11.026	13.552	16.627	20.362	24.891	30.376	37.006	45.008	54.649	66.247
24	12.239	15.179	18.788	23.212	28.625	35.236	43.297	53.109	65.032	79.497
25	13.585	17.000	21.231	26.462	32.919	40.874	50.658	62.669	77.388	95.396

APPENDIX V
GLOSSARY OF ACCOUNTING TERMS

Absorption. This is a system of costing designed to attribute overhead costs (indirect costs) to a particular product, service or cost centre. There may be a number of different bases for apportioning overheads. For example: a business may decide to absorb a particular overhead on the basis of Labour Hours. To do so a rate of absorption would be applied (see rate).

For example: $\dfrac{\text{Total Overheads per cost centre}}{\text{Number of Labour Hours}}$

would give an hourly rate at which to absorb the overhead. The overhead rate × the number of labour hours per product/job would give the overhead charge in total.

Account. A chronological record by name or type of 'account' classification for assets, expenses, capital, liabilities and revenue. It is a record of monetary transactions relating to specific time periods or persons. Debits are posted to the left-hand-side of an account and credits are posted to the right-hand-side in accordance with the accounting equation.

Account Balance: The excess of debits over credits or vice-versa in any account.

Accountant. A person who practises accountancy.

Accounting. The objective of accounting is to identify, measure and communicate economic information to permit informed judgements and decisions by users of the information.

Financial Accounting is the process of recording and classifying assets, liabilities, capital, expenses and revenue. The Ledgers are the place where this is done.

Management Accounting is the process of using financial information in order to plan, control and make decisions to assist management in achieving their objectives. Accounting involves theories, concepts and methodology.

Accounting bases. The methods used to apply an accounting concept. For example: the accounting year; choice of depreciation method; choice of stock valuation method LIFO, FIFO, AVCO. The base chosen is a matter of Accounting Policy.

Accounting equation. Assets + expenses = capital + liabilities and revenue.

Accounting period. The time period, usually a month or one year, to which financial statements are related.

Accounting policies. The specific accounting bases (methods) selected and consistently followed by a business management as being, in their opinion, appropriate to its circumstances and best suited to present a true and fair view of the financial position.

Accounts payable. Amounts owed to suppliers for the purchase of goods and services: also called creditors.

Accounting principles. The rules and conventions which form the basis on which financial statements are prepared — historic cost, periodicity, the matching principle (accruals concept), prudence or conservatism, the going concern, consistency, objectivity, etc.

Accounting ratio. A relationship between two significant figures. For example, current assets to current liabilities. Some ratios are expressed as percentages since this is more meaningful. For example: gross profit to sales.

Accounting standards. A set of rules binding upon members of the accountancy profession. The aim is to achieve consistency and to reduce the variety of accounting practices so that comparability of financial statements is achieved. See Statements of Standard Accounting Practice SSAP.

Accounts receivable. Amounts customers owe to an organization for goods and services supplied: also called debtors.

Accruals. Expenses which have been consumed but which have not been paid for at the accounting date. An accrual will increase liabilities or reduce assets.

Accruals convention. The convention whereby revenue and costs are matched (that is, recognised as they are earned or incurred, not as money is paid or received).

Accumulated depreciation. The part of the original cost of a fixed asset which has been regarded as a depreciation expense in successive profit and loss accounts: cost less accumulated depreciation = net book value.

Accumulated fund. The capital of a non-profit making organization.

Acid Test. A ratio comparing liquid assets with current liabilities. It is measured thus: $\dfrac{\text{current assets less stock}}{\text{current liabilities}}$ sometimes called the quick ratio.

Activity ratios: Ratios used to analyze a firm's effectiveness in using specific resources: examples include stock or work in progress turnover ratios.

Added value = Sales less bought in materials.

Advance Corporation Tax (ACT). That part of corporation tax payable in advance of the mainstream payment calculated on dividend payments as follows = $\dfrac{\text{Tax Rate}}{1 - \text{Tax Rate}} \times \text{DIVIDEND GROSS}$

Amalgamation. Two or more companies joining together.

Amortization. Similar to depreciation: usually used for writing off, as an expense, to profit and loss account, the capital cost of acquiring leasehold property.

Annual General Meeting (AGM). A meeting of a company required by statute (CA1985) at which the audited financial statements are presented to the members of the company. There must not be more than 15 months between each AGM.

Annual return. A return required to be made each calendar year to the Registrar of Companies by all companies. The return contains sections on shareholdings, directors, indebtedness and other matters and must include the Annual Accounts.

Annuity. A fixed sum payable each year for a number of years.

Appropriation account. An account following the profit and loss account of partnerships and companies which shows the appropriation or division of the profit amongst the parties entitled.

Articles of association. The internal rules for the running of a company. All companies must have Articles. Many adopt table A (a model set in the Companies Act 1948) with modifications.

A.S.C. (the Accounting Standards Committee). A committee of the C.C.A.B. which produces SSAP's (statements of standard accounting practice). The procedure is for A.S.C. to produce an Exposure Draft for public comment, to amend the draft where required after public comment and to issue the SSAP. The several bodies of accountants then accept the SSAP and it becomes mandatory on the members of the accounting bodies.

Assets. The resources of business that are expected to give benefit in future time periods and that can usefully be expressed in money terms, e.g. land & buildings, plant & machinery, stock, debtors, bank & cash.

Asset turnover. $\text{ASSET TURNOVER} = \dfrac{\text{TURNOVER}}{\text{Average Net Assets}}$ to give an indication of capital usage.

Asset value. A term which expresses the value of assets less liabilities of a company attributable to one ordinary share.

Associated company. A company which is not a subsidiary of an investing company but one in which the investing company has a long term interest and has substantial influence over its affairs. Usually the investing company must have between 20% and 50% of the equity capital of a company for it to be an associated company.

Attributable profit. That part of the total expected profit on a contract which may be considered as a fair representation of profit earned on work completed to date. (See Percentage Complete).

Audit committee. A committee of top management or directors not related to any finance function whose objective is to independently review internal control procedures highlighted in the audit report or management letter.

Auditor. One who carries out an audit. In the UK statutory audits may only be undertaken by a member of one of the following bodies: Institute of Chartered Accountants in England and Wales (or Scotland or Ireland); The Chartered Association of Certified Accountants or one who is recognized by the Department of Trade and Industry as having equivalent overseas qualifications.

Auditing. An independent examination by an auditor, and expression of opinion as to the truth and fairness of the financial statements of a business taking into account any relevant statutory obligations.

Authorized capital. The amount of capital stated in the Memorandum of Association. The company cannot issue more than the authorized capital but the amount may be increased if certain procedures are followed. Authorized capital is usually divided into shares of a specific monetary value and into different classes such as preference and ordinary shares. It is issued share capital that forms part of the balance sheet.

Average cost (AVCO). A method of valuing fungible assets (notably stock) at average (simple or weighted) input prices.

Bad debts. Debts which are irrecoverable and therefore included in the profit and loss account as an expense.

Bad debt provision. A sum set aside out of profit (an expense) to allow for non-payment by a percentage or proportion of debtors usually based on previous experience.

Balance sheet. A financial statement showing the state of affairs of a business at a point in time in terms of assets, liabilities and owner's equity.

Bank Reconciliation statement. A statement which explains the difference in the balance shown by a cash book from that shown by a bank statement. The differences are caused by differences in timing.

Bankruptcy. A legal status imposed upon a person by a court, either on his own petition or on the petition of his creditors. Usually a trustee is appointed to receive and realize the assets of the bankrupt and to distribute the proceeds to his creditors in accordance with the law.

Base stock. A method of valuing individual stock items which assumes that there is always an irreducible minimum quantity in stock. That quantity is valued at the price which prevailed when the line was first stocked, possibly many years earlier. The balance is valued on Lifo or other method. SSAP9 disapproves of the base stock method.

Bill of Exchange. "An unconditional order in writing, addressed by one person to another, signed by the person giving it, requiring the person to whom it is addressed to pay on demand, or at a fixed determinable future time, a sum certain in money to or to the order of, a specified person or to bearer."

Bond. A formal written document that provides evidence of long term indebtedness, e.g. debentures.

Bonus Issue. An issue of new shares to existing shareholders made possible by the capitalization of reserves. No payment is made for the shares. Also referred to as a scrip issue, a capitalization issue or a stock dividend.

Bookkeeping. The process of recording transactions in the books of account, using the system known as double entry bookkeeping.

Book value. The value is the original cost less accumulated depreciation. It is also called net book value and written down value. Book values are rarely the same value as saleable value.

Bought ledger. BOUGHT LEDGER = PURCHASE LEDGER.

Budget. Examples are the sales budget, purchases budget, cash budget, expense budget and the master budget. A financial plan (forecast) for a particular part of the business or the whole business used to gain direction, control the business and make the decisions.

Called-up capital. When shares are issued the sums due may be payable by instalments either at fixed dates or at the directors' discretion. A request for repayment is known as a call. Share capital which has been paid or requested is known as the called-up capital.

Capital. Assets less liabilities owned by a person or business.

Capital allowances. A tax allowance for items of capital expenditure. The effect is to reduce taxable profits by the amount of allowance. In effect capital allowances are a formal recognition of depreciation to replace the accounting methods of depreciation in assessing taxable profit. The rates at which assets may be written down in value are the subject of the Chancellor of the Exchequer's budget. Over the years different rates have been applied to different classes of asset. Until recently it was possible for a business to write off 100% of the cost in the year of acquisition. The rate for most items is now 25% per annum on a reducing balance basis.

Capital Expenditure. Expenditure on assets which provide benefits over a number of financial years by earning revenues. Fixed Assets are items of capital expenditure. If the item bought will be used over longer than one accounting period (a year) then it should be regarded as capital expenditure and its use charged via a depreciation expense.

Cash budget. A calculation of expected future receipts and payments to determine the net inflows or outflows for each time period (monthly for example).

Capital Budget. A programme for financing long-term outlays such as an investment in plant and machinery (fixed assets).

Capital redemption reserve. A capital reserve created by a transfer from revenue reserves on the occasion of redemption of redeemable share capital.

Capital reserve. A liability to shareholders that cannot be paid either because the law prohibits it or because the directors or the Articles so determine. Capital reserves are represented by some of the assets on the other side of the balance sheet; they are not themselves assets! For example, goodwill would be an asset represented by such a reserve.

Cash. Coins and banknotes are strictly cash but often in everyday terminology people refer to money in a bank account as cash.

Cash Book. The double entry account used to record cash transactions and also transactions with the bank.

Cash discount. The granting of a reduction in the amount payable by a debtor to induce prompt payment. It is also called a settlement discount.

Cash flow accounting ignores accounting concepts and deals only in cash payments and receipts.

Cash flow. The difference between cash inflows and cash outflows. A cash flow statement is a statement that shows the receipts and payments of cash over a period.

C.C.A.B. The consultative committee of the accounting bodies — the means through which the accounting bodies co-operate.

Cheque. A bill of exchange drawn on a banker and payable on demend.

Clock card. Cards used in a factory to record the time worked by a worker.

Common stock. Ordinary shares.

Company. Legal personality whose affairs are regulated by the Companies Acts. Sometimes called a corporation (Ltd or Plc).

Compensating error. A bookkeeping term for two separate errors, the effects of which cancel each other out. Thus the errors do not give rise to a difference in the trial balance.

Conglomerate. A holding company which has diversified interests through its own or its subsidiary companies activities.

Conservatism. An accounting convention whereby revenue and profits are not anticipated, but provision is made for all known liabilities (expenses and losses). Sometimes called prudence.

Consideration in accounting usage, the amount to be paid for a business. The consideration may be in cash or other assets or securities. See takeovers.

Consignment. Usually the despatch of goods. In a restricted sense the sending of goods to an agent for him to sell; the ownership of the goods being retained by the consignor until the goods have been sold by the consignee.

Consistency. An accounting concept whereby there is consistency of accounting treatment of like items within each accounting period and from one period to the next.

Consolidated accounts. The combination of individual companies financial statements into one group statement. This is done in accordance with established rules and the relevant accounting standards.

Contingent liabilities. A potential obligation or liability that depends on some future event beyond the control of the firm.

Contra (against). A bookkeeping entry that offsets a corresponding entry. Thus a Dr. cancels a Cr, e.g. a transfer from bank (Cr) to cash (Dr) symbolised by c.

Control account. A memorandum (not part of the double entry system) account, the balance of which reflects the total balances of many related subsidiary accounts which are part of the double entry system, e.g. debtors control.

Convertible loan stocks. Loan stock with the right of the holder to convert the loan stock into equity shares under certain conditions in accordance with terms agreed.

Conversion cost. Part of the cost of stock comprising: costs which are specifically attributable to units of production, in bringing the product or service to its present location and condition, taking account of the circumstances (manufacturing costs). See SSAP9.

Copyright is an intangible asset which grants an exclusive right to the owner of intellectual property to produce and sell that property. The right usually applies to written material; artistic works, (including Film, TV, Video); music (including recordings) and computer programs.

Copyright can also be transferred to the heirs of the owner after death for a limited period of time, say 50 years. (See Royalty).

Corporation. A legal entity which is separate from the persons comprising its membership.

Corporation tax. A tax payable on the income and profits of companies and certain other entities including clubs and societies.

Corporate report. A company report. Also a document published by the accounting profession. (See the index).

Cost accounting. That area of accounting that deals with the collection, analysis, control and evaluation of costs.

Cost of capital. This may be calculated for a particular business by using a weighted average of its cost of debt and classes of equity (sometimes the equity cost may be calculated using a proxy such as the opportunity cost of the equity — i.e. what it could have earned in interest if invested elsewhere).

Cost of sales. The cost price of goods sold in a period. Also called Cost of Goods Sold (C.O.G.S.). The purchase price of goods sold or their cost of manufacture. The cost of sales will usually be obtained by the following calculation. Opening stock + purchases + carriage inwards – returns out – closing stock. In the case of manufacture it is the same calculation except that purchases would be replaced by direct labour + direct materials + direct overheads = prime cost + indirect factory (manufacturing) overheads + opening WIP – closing WIP = Production Cost of Finished Goods. **Note:** Cost of Sales in published accounts includes other costs for selling and distribution etc.

Cost plus. The cost of a product plus the profit required which is usually a fixed percentage on cost.

Credit. The right hand side of a double entry account.

Credit control. Measures and procedures instituted by a business that trades on credit to ensure that customers pay their accounts.

Credit note. A document issued by a supplier giving credit to his debtor for goods returned or overcharges.

Creditors. Those to whom a firm owes money, that is, accounts payable.

Creditors settlement period. A liquidity ratio which may indicate the ability of a business to pay its debts as they fall due. Calculated by (creditors/goods supplied on credit in the year) × 365 if expressed in days.

Cumulative preference shares. A share where dividend rights are carried forward if the business does not generate enough profit to pay a dividend during one or more years. These dividends must be paid before any subsequent dividends are distributed to ordinary shareholders.

Current accounts for partners record the movements in capital that take place from accounting period to period. The fixed capital account remains fixed having the starting capitals unchanged. The balance remaining on the current account represents the undrawn profit of the partner concerned and is effectively part of his capital contribution.

Current assets. Those assets which the management intend to convert into cash or consume in the normal course of business within one year.

Current cost accounting. A system of accounting which recognizes the changing value of money by measuring profits, assets and liabilities in current cost terms in accordance with SSAP16.

Current liabilities. Debts or obligations that will be paid within one year. The Companies Act 1985 prefers the expression Creditors — amounts falling due within one year.

Current ratio. An accounting ratio to measure liquidity, calculated as current assets total divided by current liabilities total.

Cut-off items of income and expense are correctly ascribed to the appropriate accounting periods by allocating a date at which transactions for one period are 'cut-off' from transactions of a future period.

Cycle. The time taken to complete a transaction or set of similar transactions from "birth to death". That is initial record to final record. For example, the working capital cycle is the time it takes a business to turn stock into cash. That is stock to sale to Debtor to Bank or Cash.

Data. Facts and figures (Latin = given).

Day book. A book of prime entry. From the daybooks postings are made to the double entry system, sometimes referred to as Journals, for example, the sales day book lists all sales invoices on a particular day.

Debenture. A document which creates or acknowledges a debt. Debenture deeds issued by companies usually contain details of the loan and have clauses concerning payment of interest, repayment of capital, security, if any. It is also called a bond.

Debit note. A document sent to a person, usually a supplier, whose account it is intended to be debited. Usually it reports a short delivery or overcharge and seeks a credit note as a response. Only the credit note is entered in the books.

Debt. A sum due by a debtor to a creditor, either for goods and services bought or a loan.

Debtors. Those who owe money to a business. Customers who buy on credit terms are debtors.

Debtors payment period. A calculation of the average time taken by credit customers to pay their debts. It is usually calculated by (debtors/credit sales for a year) × 365 to give a result in days.

Deferred liabilities. Liabilities that exist but where payment has been postponed to some unknown future date, e.g. deferred taxation.

Delivery note. A note sent by a supplier to accompany the goods. Often it is in duplicate and the carrier retains a copy signed by the recipient to act as evidence of good delivery. Sometimes called an advice note.

Depletion method. A method of depreciation applicable to wasting assets such as mines or quarries. The amount of depreciation in a period is a function of the quantity extracted in the period compared to the total resource available.

Deposit account. An account with a bank, building society or other financial institution which earns interest.

Depreciation is a measure of the wearing out, consumption or other loss of value of a fixed asset whether arising from use, effluxion of time or obsolescence through technology and market changes. Depreciation should be allocated to accounting periods so as to charge a fair proportion of cost to each accounting period during the expected useful life of the asset. Depreciation includes amortization of fixed assets whose useful life is pre-determined (e.g. leases) and depletion of wasting assets (e.g. mines).

Diminishing balance (also reducing balance). A method of depreciation whereby the cost of the asset is written off over its expected life by the application of a percentage to the written down value or net book value.

Direct costs. Those costs which vary directly with output and can be directly identified with specific jobs, products or services, e.g. direct labour.

Directors. These are the people who manage the company on behalf of the owners (the shareholders'). They are elected by the members of the company (shareholders). Together the directors form the Board of Directors.

Disclosure. The provision of information necessary to ascertain all the financial facts important enough to influence the judgement of an informed user of financial statements.

Discount. The amount of what the full price of an item is reduced by. Debentures can be issued or redeemed at a discount. Bills of Exchange may be discounted by a third party; that is sold at less than their face value.

Discount allowed is an expense to the business. It can be trade discount allowed to a customer by virtue of being in the same line of business. Alternatively, it can be a cash or settlement discount allowed for prompt settlement of a debt.

Discount received may either be classified as non-trading income in the case of a cash or settlement discount or simply treated as a reduction in the cost of a purchase if it is a trade discount.

Dissolution of partnerships. The break up of a partnership.

Dividend. This is a payment made to a shareholder out of the profits of a company. The total dividend is proportionate to the shares held. For example: 5.5 pence per share; if 100 shares were held the total dividend would be 100 × 5.5p = £5.50. It is the directors who determine dividend policy.

Dividend cover. A measure of the extent to which the dividend paid by a company is covered by its earnings (profits).

Dividend yield. A measure of the revenue earning capacity of an ordinary share to its holder. It is calculated by dividend per share as a percentage of the market or quoted price of the share.

Double entry bookkeeping. A method of record keeping whereby every transaction is recorded twice in the books of account (debit and credit); devised by an Italian monk Luca Paciola.

Doubtful debts. A charge to profit and loss account to recognize the probable loss to be suffered because a debt is likely to prove uncollectable. The debts remain in the books (unlike actual bad debts) but are contra'd by an account with a credit balance called a provision for doubtful debts.

Drawings. Cash or goods withdrawn from a business by a sole proprietor or partner for his own use.

Dual aspect. Every transaction has two aspects. Every debit has a credit. For example, paying a supplier for goods bought on credit involves reducing the supplier's liability by debiting his credit account and also reducing the asset of cash by crediting the cash account of the business paying.

Earnings. Another word for profit, used particularly for company profits.

Earnings per share. A performance measure used by investment analysts. The measure is calculated by total profits divided by total number of ordinary shares and is stated in the profit and loss accounts of quoted companies. Its calculation and presentation is the subject of SSAP3.

Earnings yield. An indicator of interest to investors. Calculated by earnings per share as a percentage of the quoted share price (market price).

Entity concept states that the business entity should be considered as separate from the owners of the business.

Equity. The ordinary shares or risk capital of a business.

Exceptional items. Items which are of abnormal size or incidence but are not extraordinary items because they derive from the ordinary activities of the company. They might include abnormal charges for bad debts, write offs of stocks and work in progress and abnormal provisions for losses on long term contracts. Exceptional items should be separately disclosed.

Extraordinary items. Those items which derive from events or transactions outside the ordinary activities of the business and which are both material and expected not to recur frequently or regularly. They may include profits or losses arising from discontinuance of a significant part of a business or the sale of an investment not held for sale. Extraordinary items are shown separately after the results derived from ordinary activities have been computed. See SSAP6.

Factoring. Debtors are sold to a factoring company who pay say 90% of the sum owed to the business immediately. The factoring company then become responsible for collecting the full debt on the due dates. The difference between what they pay for the debt and what they receive is their profit. Factoring improves cash flow. Such services are only available to businesses who can fulfil certain criteria with regard to turnover and size etc.

F.I.F.O. First in first out; a method for stock issues.

F.I.I. franked investment income; dividends from UK companies received by other UK companies. These dividends have been paid from profits which have already suffered corporation tax and do not have to suffer additional corporation tax.

Financial statements. Balance sheets, profit and loss accounts, income and expenditure accounts, funds flow statements and other statements which provide information of a financial nature to interested parties about business performance.

Fiscal year. The government's financial year from 6th April to the following 5th April (FISC = purse).

Fixed assets. Business assets which have a useful life extending over more than one accounting period. For example, land and buildings, plant and machinery, motor vehicles and fixtures and fittings.

Floating charge. A lender to a company has a right (lien) over the assets generally of the company which gives the lender priority of repayment from the proceeds of sale of the assets in the event of insolvency.

Franchise. A license to supply some good or service, rights to which are held by the originator of the good or service. Examples of franchises are McDonalds, Burger King, Kwik Fit exhaust systems.

Freehold. The best title to ownership of land.

Fundamental accounting concepts. The broad basic assumptions which underline periodic financial statements. SSAP2 names four: The going concern, prudence, accruals, and consistency.

Fungible assets. Assets which are indistinguishable one from another. In the case of a stock line which is fungible it is not possible to determine which consignment it came in and consequently what its input cost was. Therefore assumptions such as FIFO or LIFO have to be made.

Futures. Contracts for the sale and purchase of commodities at an agreed price and for delivery and settlement at an agreed future date.

Gearing (leverage in U.S.) A company which is heavily reliant on borrowing is said to be high geared and a company which is largely equity financed is said to be low geared.

General ledger. Also referred to as the NOMINAL ledger. This ledger holds those real (property) and nominal accounts not held in the Purchase Ledger, Sales Ledger or Cash Ledger. Personal accounts of suppliers are held in the Purchase Ledger and personal accounts for customers are held in the Sales Ledger.

Gilt-edged securities. Securities and investments with negligible risk of default in interest or capital. Principally government securities.

Going concern. An accounting convention which assumes that the enterprize will continue in operational existence for the foreseeable future. This means in particular that the profit and loss account and balance sheet assume no intention or necessity to liquidate in the foreseeable future.

Goodwill. An intangible asset representing the value of the whole business in excess of the tangible assets which comprise. Goodwill should appear in the balance sheet only if it had an input cost to the business.

Gross profit. The excess of sales price over the cost of the goods sold.

Ground rent. Rent paid for land as opposed to rent paid for buildings. Ground rents usually apply when land is let on long leases, e.g. 99 years.

Group. A set of interrelated companies usually consisting of a holding company and its subsidiary and maybe sub-subsidiary companies.

Group accounts. The financial statements of a group wherein the separate financial statements of the member companies are combined into consolidated financial statements.

Hire purchase. A method of financing the acquisition of assets whereby the purchaser pays by instalments, repaying the amount borrowed plus interest on the borrowing. In law the ownership (purchase) of the goods does not pass to the buyer until the last instalment has been paid. Until the last payment is made the goods are deemed to be hired.

Historical cost. The accounting convention whereby inputs to the business are recorded at cost.

Imprest. A fixed amount of money used to meet petty cash (or other) expenditures for a period. At the end of the period the imprest is made up again to its original figure.

Income and expenditure accounts. Financial statements which measure and report the income and expenditure of a period of a non trading body such as a club, society, charity or professional body, using the accruals concept.

Incomplete records. Accounting which deals with the production of financial statements which do not have full double entry bookkeeping. Sometimes called single entry.

Income statement. Any financial statement which measures and reports the revenues, expenses and net income of an enterprise. Examples are profit and loss accounts and income and expenditure accounts.

Income tax. A tax imposed on the income of individuals and partnerships. The tax is collected from employed persons by means of the P.A.Y.E. (pay as you earn) system.

Indirect cost. Labour, material and expense costs which cannot be identified with particular products. They are 'fixed costs'; also called overheads.

Information. Meaningful data used to report, plan, control and take decisions.

Insolvency. The state of being unable to pay debts as they fall due. Also used to describe the activities of practitioners in the fields of bankruptcy, receivership and liquidation.

Intangible assets. Assets which have long term value, but which have no physical existence. Examples are goodwill, copyright, patents and trademarks.

Interest. The price paid by a borrower to a lender for the use of borrowed money.

Interim dividend. Many companies pay a dividend in respect of a financial year in two instalments. The final dividend is paid after the year end when the results are known. The interim dividend is paid during the year usually after the results for the first half of the year are known.

Inventory. A detailed list of articles of any kind. It is often used as another word for stock.

Investments. A class of asset consisting of shares or loan stocks of companies, financial institutions or the government.

Invoice. A document issued or services bought, to a buyer giving details of the transaction of the goods.

Issued capital. That part of the authorized capital of a company which has actually been issued to shareholders.

Journal. A daily record from which transactions enter into a business's accounting system. From the data in a journal the entries in the double entry system are made. There may be a main journal and subsidiary journals such as a sales journal. Day books are sometimes referred to as journals.

Leasehold. Land rented from the owner of the freehold. Leases can be for any period. Leases with less than 50 years to run are called short leases and other leases are called long leases. It is possible to buy a leasehold interest in the property and when this has occurred the cost appears on the balance sheet. It is then amortized (depreciated) over the period of the lease.

Ledger. The place where double entry accounts are recorded. The Ledger is usually divided into sections dealing with Sales, Purchases, Cash and all other transactions in the General Ledger. Real and nominal accounts are contained in the General Ledger and personal accounts in the Debtors or Creditors, i.e. Sales or Purchases.

Leverage (Gearing UK). This measures the proportion of equity as opposed to debt in the financial structure of the business.

Liabilities. Amounts owed to entities external to the business which have been incurred as a result of past trading transactions or events. Liabilities need to be discharged at a future date by the business paying for past services or goods consumed. LONG TERM — greater than one accounting year. CURRENT — due in less than one accounting year.

L.I.F.O. That method of stock valuation based on Last In First Out.

Limited companies. Companies registered under the Companies Acts in which the liability of the members is limited to the amount unpaid on the share capital or to a specific amount in the case of companies limited by guarantee. Identified by the initials Ltd. and Plc.

Liquidation. The break-up of a company. The process of turning assets into cash to discharge liabilities. The break-up value is the net realizable value of assets less total debts. The proceeds are then distributed to those entitled to them in accordance with the rules of liquidation.

Liquidity. The ease of turning assets into cash.

Liquidity ratios. Measures which are supposed to determine the ability of a business to meet its liabilities in cash when they fall due. Examples are the Current Ratio, The Acid Test, Debtor and Creditor payment periods.

Listed companies. Companies whose shares are quoted on a recognised stock exchange or (paradoxically) on the unlisted securities market.

Long term contracts. Contracts entered into for manufacture or building of a single substantial entity or the provision of a service where the time taken to manufacture, build, or provide is such that a substantial proportion of all such contract work will extend for a period exceeding one year.

Long term liabilities. Obligations expected to be paid after one year. The Companies Act 1985 refers to creditors — amounts falling due after more than one year.

Management accounting. The provision and interpretation of information which assists management in planning, controlling, decision making and appraising performance.

Manufacturing accounts. Financial statements which detail the total costs of production in a period.

Market value. The amount an asset would realise if sold in the open market.

Mark up percentage. Gross profit as a percentage of cost of goods sold.

Matching convention. See Accruals Concept.

Materiality. A convention dictating that an accountant must judge the impact and importance of each transaction (or event) to determine its proper handling in the accounting records.

Memorandum of association. All companies have a document which outlines a company's constitution and defines the scope of a company's powers.

Minority interests. The interests in the assets of a group relating to shares in group companies not held by the holding company or other members of the group.

Modified accounts. Shortened versions of full financial statements which The Companies Act permits small and medium sized companies to file in preference to full accounts. Full accounts must however be produced for shareholders.

Money measurement. The accounting convention that requires all assets, liabilities, revenues and expenses to be stated in monetary amounts.

Mortgage. A transaction in which an asset (usually land) is given as security for a loan. The effect is that the mortgagor (borrower) cannot dispose of the asset without first repaying the loan and that the mortgagee has, in the case of default, priority of payment from the proceeds of sale of the asset.

Negotiable instruments. A document of title that can be freely negotiated (transferred) by delivery or delivery with endorsement. Examples are bills of exchange and promissory notes.

Net book value. The balance sheet value of an asset, that is, cost or valuation less accumulated depreciation.

Net realisable value. The actual or estimated selling price of an asset (net of trade but before cash discounts) less all further costs to completion and all costs to be incurred in marketing, selling and distribution.

Net worth. The difference between total assets and total external liabilities of a business equivalent to the capital of the owners of that business.

Nominal ledger. A division of the ledger which contains the nominal accounts and usually also real accounts and the capital account.

Nominal value. The face value of a share or debenture as stated in the memorandum. It may not always be the same as issue price which may be at a premium and par value will almost never be the market value which is quoted.

Objectivity. A principle requiring that accounting information be free from bias and verifiable by an independent party. Historic cost is said to be objective, whereas it is argued that CCA statements are not.

Obsolescence. The ending of an asset's useful life for reasons other than deterioration. Obsolescence is caused by new technology and market changes and is an increasing problem.

Operating cycle. The period of time it takes a firm to buy inputs, make or market a product and collect the cash from a customer.

Opportunity cost. The cost of the alternative foregone.

Ordinary shares. The equity capital of a company. The holders of these shares are entitled to the balance of the distributed profit and in a winding up to the balance of the assets after all other claims have been met.

Overdraft facility. An arrangement with a bank whereby the account holder can draw up to an agreed amount beyond the amount lodged with the bank. It is in effect a short term source of funding.

Overtrading. A business is said to be overtrading when its working capital is expanding causing liquidity problems. Success causes overtrading. Overtrading can be avoided by careful cash planning (budgeting).

Owners equity. The capital of a business attributable to the owners of the business.

Paid up capital. That part of a company's share capital which has been both called up and paid up.

Partnership. The relationship which subsists between persons carrying on a business in common with a view to profit.

Par value. An amount specified in the memorandum of association for each share and imprinted on the face of each share certificate. It is the figure which appears on the balance sheet for share capital. As a value it has no significance. Nominal value means the same.

Patent. An intangible asset permitting its owner to have exclusive rights to use, manufacture and sell a product or process.

Periodicity. An accounting convention that assumes that for reporting purposes the life of an enterprise can be divided into discrete time periods such as years.

Perpetual inventory. A method of maintaining records of stock held, on a continuous basis.

Petty cash. A fund used to make small cash payments, usually kept on the imprest system.

Post balance sheet events. Those events both favourable and unfavourable that occur between the balance sheet date and the date at which the financial statements are approved by the board of directors. They can be adjusting or non adjusting events.

Posting. The process of entering up double entry accounts from the data in books of prime entry (Day books).

Preference shares. A class of share capital in which shareholders are entitled to a fixed rate of dividend in priority to ordinary shareholders and to priority in a winding up over other classes of shareholders.

Premium. An amount paid in excess of par or nominal value. Premiums can arise on issues and redemptions of shares and debentures.

Prepayments. An amount paid in advance of the time for which the item is chargeable to the profit and loss account.

Price earnings ratio. A ratio of interest to investment analysts. The stock exchange quoted price of a share divided by the earnings per share.

Prime cost. The total of direct costs.

Prime entry. Books of are day books or journals. They are the first place a transaction is recorded before posting accounts.

Prior year adjustments. Material adjustments applicable to earlier years arising from changes in accounting policies or from the correction of fundamental errors.

Private company. Any company that is not a public company.

Private ledger. That part of the ledger which contains nominal and real accounts of a confidential nature.

Profitability ratios. Ratios designed to measure the success or otherwise of a business for particular accounting periods. Examples are the return on capital employed ratio; Gross Profit to Sales; Net Profit to Sales.

Pro forma. A preliminary invoice giving the usual details of the sale, requiring payment before the goods are despatched.

Promissory note. A negotiable instrument containing a promise to pay the holder a sum of money at a specified date, e.g. £1.

Pro rata. In proportion to.

Prospectus. A document offering shares or debentures to the public or a section of the public. Prospectuses must meet the requirements laid down by the Companies Acts and the Stock Exchange.

Provision. Provisions for liabilities or charges are defined in the Companies Act 1985 as any amount retained as reasonably necessary for the purpose of providing for any liability or loss which is either likely to be incurred, or certain to be incurred but uncertain as to amount or as to the date on which it will arise. Retained in this context means treated as an expense in the profit and loss account.

Public company. A public company is a company which states in its memorandum that it is a public company, ends its name with the designation 'public limited company' or plc. and has a minimum share capital of £50,000.

Quick ratio (= acid test ratio) current assets less stocks over current liabilities. An indication of liquidity.

Quoted company. A company whose shares are traded on the Stock Exchange or the unlisted securities market. The price of the company's shares is quoted in the Stock Exchange daily official list and in serious newspapers such as the Financial Times.

Ratio analysis. The use of mathematical relationships to study a firm's liquidity and profitability. Ratios can be compared with those of previous years or with budgeted figures or with other businesses.

Real accounts. Double entry accounts for assets with actual physical existence, e.g. stocks, fixed assets, tangible assets.

Realisable value. The amount that an asset can be sold for.

Realisation convention. An accounting convention which states that a profit should not be taken as accruing in connection with an asset until that asset has been sold and turned into cash or into a legally enforceable debt. Q. When is a sale a sale? A. When it is recognised in law.

Receivership. The appointment of receiver to take over an asset which is the subject of a charge given to a lender. A receiver can be appointed by a court or by the lender when the terms of the loan deed allow.

Redemption. The repayment of shares or debentures.

Reducing balance. A method of depreciation whereby the cost is charged to the profit and loss account over its useful life by the application of a percentage to the Net Book Value (reduced balance) or Written Down Value.

Registrar of Companies. A civil service department located in Cardiff which maintains a file for each registered company. Companies have a legal obligation to file numerous documents with the registrar. Company files are open to the inspection of members of the public.

Reserves. A company has reserves if its assets exceed its specific liabilities. Reserves are thus liabilities to shareholders, arising primarily from undistributed profits.

Residual value. See Salvage value below.

Replacement cost. The cost at which an identical asset could be purchased or manufactured. SSAP9 dictates that replacement cost should not be used for stock valuation.

Retentions. Undistributed profit : retained profit after distribution to shareholders or transfers to reserves.

Return on Capital Employed. A ratio measuring income as a percentage of the capital used to generate the income. It is a difficult concept to use and objectively measure because Income and Capital are themselves problematic to define.

Revenue. Sales income for goods or services.

Revenue expenditure. An expenditure that gives benefits only in the current accounting period.

Rights issue. An invitation to existing shareholders to subscribe for new shares in the company.

Sales journal (= sales day book). A book of prime entry in which the details of sales invoices are entered chronologically. From the sales journal, entries are posted to the customers' accounts and in total to the sales account.

Sales ledger. A division of the ledger in which an account is kept for each credit customer. Also called a Debtors ledger.

Sales mix. The relative proportions of products that sum to total sales.

Salvage value (= residual value). The amount that a business expects to receive upon disposal of an asset at the end of the asset's useful life.

Scrip issue (= bonus issue). An issue of shares to existing shareholders involving no payment of money. A book entry crediting share capital and debiting reserves is made.

Secret Reserves. A practice which is no longer acceptable in the UK whereby a business understated profit and overstated a liability in order to establish secret reserves. The same result could be achieved by understating asset values and profit.

Secured Loans. A loan which is granted by the lender in return for receiving security against the loan. This security usually takes the form of pledging a particular asset (fixed charge) or assets generally (floating charge). This means that one way or another the lender's position is protected if the business fails to repay the loan.

Securities. Financial assets such as shares, debentures and loan stocks.

Segment Reports. A line of activity or a particular section of the business for which separately identifiable costs and/or revenues can be reported. For example, by product, location, department, customer or geographical area.

Sensitivity analysis. Measuring how particular results would be affected by changes in input variables.

Settlement discount. A reduction in the amount payable offered to a debtor to induce rapid payment. A cash discount is the same thing.

Share capital. This is the amount of money initially subscribed to a limited company in suitable discrete divisions. For example, shares may be different classes, preference or ordinary, and in units 10p, 50p, £1 or some other appropriate split. Authorized share capital is stated in the company's Memorandum and Articles of Association, this is the number and classes of share that the company is able to issue. Issued share capital is the amount currently issued and forming the capital of the company.

Shareholders are individuals, institutions or other corporate bodies who collectively hold preference or ordinary shares in the company.

Shareholders Equity. Total Assets less Total Liabilities (= Net Worth).

Sinking Fund. Sums of money set aside on a regular basis in a separate custodial account used to redeem debt securities, meet specific obligations or to replace specific assets. It is no longer a common practice.

Source document. The original record of any transaction.

S.O.R.P. Statement of recommended practice, a statement of accounting practice produced by the A.S.C. and approved by the accounting bodies.

Spreadsheet. A ledger sheet on which a company's financial statements are shown in columns and rows (e.g. Income Statements, Balance Sheets, Sales Analysis, Cost Reports, Cash Flow Statements). Electronic spreadsheets are now a common feature of computerized financial systems. Any time a number is changed, all other numbers are automatically adjusted by the software (program). Useful in budgeting or for making "what if?" decisions.

S.S.A.P. Statement of standard accounting practice, statements of accounting practice are mandatory on members of the accounting bodies.

Standard cost. Periodically predetermined costs calculated from management's estimates of expected levels of costs and of operations and operational efficiency and the related expenditure. Standard costs can be compared with actual costs and the variances analysed.

Standing order. An instruction to a bank to make specific payments at specified intervals, e.g. subscriptions, rates, rent or mortgages.

Statement of affairs. A listing, with values, of assets and liabilities. A balance sheet is a formal statement of affairs.

Statutory books. The Companies Act requires that the following books be kept: Proper Books of Account, a register of directors and secretaries, a register of all charges (fixed or floating), minute books for general meetings, minute books for directors or managers, an indexed register of shareholders, an indexed register of directors' interests and those of spouses or infant children, a register of directors' service contracts, an indexed register of shareholders who hold an interest of 5% or more of the nominal value of voting share capital. They are collectively called the statutory books.

Step Variable Cost (= Semi-Variable Cost). A variable cost which changes sharply at specific levels of activity because their acquisition is in discrete quantities.

Stewardship. An arrangement where the property of one party (e.g. the shareholders of a company) is entrusted to and managed by another party (e.g. the directors). Stewardship reporting is the accounting by means of financial statements by the management to the owners.

Straight line. A method of depreciation that allocates the cost of a depreciable asset, less any residual value, over the estimated useful life in equal instalments.

Subsidiary company. A company of which more than half of the equity capital is owned by another company.

Substance over form. An accounting convention whereby a transaction is accounted for in accordance with its substance or commercial reality rather than its legal form.

Sum of the years digits. A depreciation method that allocates the cost less salvage value of a depreciable asset over its useful life in steadily diminishing instalments (SYD).

Sunk cost. A past cost which has no relevance to future decisions. A historic cost.

Surrogate (= a substitute).

Suspense account. An account used as a 'dumping ground' for a difference in total debits and credits in a trial balance as a result of bookkeeping errors.

T-account. A form of presentation of a double entry account named for its shape — debit on the left, credit on the right and title at the top.

Tax credit. The tax imputed to a dividend payment. No further tax is payable on the dividend unless the recipient is liable to higher rates. Shareholders receive a tax credit certificate.

Trade discount. Reductions in sales price given to favoured customers, special classes of customer or for bulk purchase. Accounting is always on the net amount of the invoice in such cases.

Trademarks. An intangible asset consisting of the right to exclusive use of a particular mark or motif.

Trading account. A financial statement which measures the gross profit of a period. Sales less Cost of Sales = Gross Profit.

Transaction. An event that affects the financial position of a business and needs recording in the double-entry system.
Transfer price. A price charged by one segment of a business for a product or service supplied to another segment of the same business.
Transposition errors. Posting errors in which digits are transposed, e.g. 16 entered as 61.
Trend. Financial analysts often try and identify a trend by comparing the same variables over different time periods.
Trial balance. A listing in two columns (debit balances and credit balances) of all the balances in all the accounts held by the business.
True and fair view. The Companies Act requires that the balance sheet and profit and loss account of a company must give a true and fair view. Truth and fairness are not defined in the act.
Turnover = total sales in a period.
Unquoted investments. Investments which are not quoted or traded on a stock exchange. They are usually shares or debentures in private limited companies.
Unsecured creditors. Creditors who do not have the security of a charge over assets of the business.
Variance. The difference between budgeted or standard costs and actual figures, for sales revenue, materials, labour and overheads.
Variable cost = A cost that changes directly as a result of a change in output. (also called direct or marginal cost).
Venture capital = risk capital. In return for taking a risk venture capitalists would receive one or a combination of profit, preferred stock, common stock and royalties on sales.
Voting stock = common stock or equity.
Voucher. A document which supports any journal or ledger entry, e.g. Petty Cash Vouchers.
Warranty. This is a promise made by a seller or manufacturer to remedy any deficits regarding product quality or performance. Warranties may give rise to contingent liabilities if a customer makes a claim under warranty.
Wasting assets = mines, quarries, oilwells or other mineral rights may be regarded as wasting assets. They are assets with finite lives which are exhausted as goods are produced and materials extracted.
Weighted average. An average which is calculated giving regard to the number of items (weightings) in each group or range.

	Weights	Value	W × V
For example:	2 units	£10	20
	4 units	£20	80
Total	6		100

The weighted average $\sum \dfrac{w \times v}{w} = \dfrac{£100}{6} = 16\frac{2}{3}$

Winding up. A term applied to the closure of a company. Assets are liquidated and cash proceeds distributed to those who have claims in order of priority. Also called liquidation.
Window dressing. A term which describes accounting trickery designed to present a more favourable view to users of financial statements than actually exists. For example, by concealing liabilities, removing revenue or expenses from one period to another to show the most favourable view or changes in accounting policy such as depreciation to delay write offs. Window dressing may or may not be fraudulent.
Working Capital = Current Assets minus Current Liabilities. It is also called Net Current Assets.
Work-in-progress. It is the goods started but not fully completed during an accounting period. Such inventory has to be valued. It is also called work-in-process.
Write off. To reduce the value of an asset by writing off the fall in value, as an expense.
Written down value = Net Book Value. Cost of an asset less cumulative depreciation.
Yield. Return on an investor's capital invested. It is usually expressed as a percentage.
Zero Based Budgeting. A method of setting budgets starting from a zero base and justifying all expenditures and revenues. Each budget category is looked at on its merits rather than simply looking back to a previous accounting period and adding say 10% or some other fixed increase.

APPENDIX VI
ANSWERS TO QUESTIONS

CHAPTER 15

1.

(a) **STRAIGHT LINE METHOD**

Annual Depreciation = $\dfrac{\textbf{Cost} - \textbf{Scrap Value}}{\textbf{Estimated useful life of the asset}}$

Annual Depreciation = $\dfrac{£5000 - £1000}{5 \text{ years}}$

= £800 p.a.

The rate at which depreciation has to be charged may be calculated thus:-

RATE = $\dfrac{100\%}{\text{Estimated Value Life of Asset}}$

= $\dfrac{100}{5}$

= 20% p.a. (on cost – scrap value)

OR   Cost Scrap

$\dfrac{100\% - 20\%}{5} = \dfrac{80}{5}$

= 16% on cost

(b) **REDUCING BALANCE METHOD**

To calculate a rate use the following formula:-

Rate = $1 - \sqrt[n]{\dfrac{S}{C}}$

where n = estimated life of asset
      S = scrap value
      C = cost of asset

Using previous example details:-

$$\text{Rate} \quad = \quad 1 - \sqrt[5]{\dfrac{1000}{5000}}$$

$$= \quad 1 - \sqrt[5]{0.20}$$

$$= \quad 1 - 0.7247$$

$$\underline{\text{Rate} \quad = \quad 0.275 \text{ or } 27.5\% \text{ p.a.}}$$

Calculation for Annual Depreciation Charge

	Cost/Reduced Balance	Annual Depn.	NBV at end of year
Yr. 1	5000 × 27.5%	1375	3625
Yr. 2	3625 × 27.5%	997	2628
Yr. 3	2628 × 27.5%	723	1905
Yr. 4	1905 × 27.5%	524	1381
Yr. 5	1381 × 27.5%	381	1000

(c) **GRAPH OF EXAMPLE — STRAIGHT LINE DEPRECIATION**

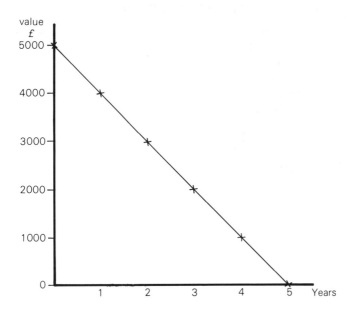

£NBV Y	TIME X
4200	1
3400	2
2600	2
1800	4
1000	5

2.

REDUCING BALANCE

$$\text{Rate} = 1 - \sqrt[n]{\frac{S}{C}}$$

$$= 1 - \sqrt[8]{\frac{650}{6250}} \quad = 1 - \sqrt[8]{0.104}$$

$$= 1 - 0.7536$$

Rate $= 0.2464$ or 24.6% p.a.

Calculation for Annual Depreciation Charge

	Cost/Reduced Balance	Annual Depn.	NBV at end of year
Yr. 1	6250 × 24.6%	1538	4712
Yr. 2	4712 × 24.6%	1159	3553
Yr. 3	3553 × 24.6%	874	2679
Yr. 4	2679 × 24.6%	659	2020
Yr. 5	2020 × 24.6%	497	1523
Yr. 6	1523 × 24.6%	375	1148
Yr. 7	1148 × 24.6%	282	866
Yr. 8	866 × 24.6%	213	653

STRAIGHT LINE METHOD

$$\text{Annual Depn.} = \frac{£6250 - 650}{8}$$

Annual Depn.   =   £700 p.a.

£NBV	TIME
6250	0
5550	1
4850	2
4150	3
3450	4
2750	5
2050	6
1350	7
650	8

The straight line method gives the best profit at the end of 5 years. This method is the most widely used and also is the simplest of the two.

3.

$$\text{Rate} = \frac{100\%}{8}$$

Rate   =   12.5%

$$\text{Annual Depreciation} = \frac{£4000 - \text{NIL}}{8 \text{ yrs.}}$$

Annual Depreciation   =   £500 p.a.

£NBV	TIME
3500	1
3000	2
2500	3
2000	4
1500	5
1000	6
500	7
—	8

BALANCE SHEET EXTRACT at the end of each year

Yr. 1	FIXED ASSETS	£ COST	£ DEPN.	£ NBV
	Machine	4000	500	3500

Yr. 2	FIXED ASSETS	£ COST	£ DEPN.	£ NBV
	Machine	4000	1000	3000

Yr. 3	FIXED ASSETS	£ COST	£ DEPN.	£ NBV
	Machine	4000	1500	2500

Yr. 4	FIXED ASSETS	£ COST	£ DEPN.	£ NBV
	Machine	4000	2000	2000

Yr. 5	FIXED ASSETS	£ COST	£ DEPN.	£ NBV
	Machine	4000	2500	1500

Yr. 6	FIXED ASSETS	£ COST	£ DEPN.	£ NBV
	Machine	4000	3000	1000

Yr. 7	FIXED ASSETS	£ COST	£ DEPN.	£ NBV
	Machine	4000	3500	500

Yr. 8	FIXED ASSETS	£ COST	£ DEPN.	£ NBV
	Machine	4000	4000	—

4.

	Depn. amount p.a.	Accum. Depn.			NBV
Yr. 1 $5/15 \times 4000$	1333	1333	(2667 + 1000)	=	3667
Yr. 2 $4/15 \times 4000$	1067	2400	(1600 + 1000)	=	2600
Yr. 3 $3/15 \times 4000$	800	3200	(800 + 1000)	=	1800
Yr. 4 $2/15 \times 4000$	533	3733	(267 + 1000)	=	1267
Yr. 5 $1/15 \times 4000$	267	4000	(NIL + 1000)	=	1000

$\underline{15}$

5.

1) **STRAIGHT LINE**

Annual Depreciation $= \dfrac{5650 - 150}{5}$

$= \dfrac{5500}{5}$

Annual Depreciation $= £1100$

TIME		NBV
Yr. 1	£4550	
Yr. 2		£3450
Yr. 3		£2350
Yr. 4		£1250
Yr. 5		£ 150

BALANCE SHEET EXTRACT

FIXED ASSET	COST £	DEPN. £	NBV £
Yr.1 Machine	£5650	£1100	4550
FIXED ASSET			
Yr.2 Machine	£5650	£2200	3450
FIXED ASSET			
Yr.3 Machine	£5650	£3300	2350
FIXED ASSET			
Yr.4 Machine	£5650	£4400	1250
FIXED ASSET			
Yr.5 Machine	£5650	£5500	150

2) **REDUCING BALANCE METHOD**

Rate $= 1 - \sqrt[n]{\dfrac{S}{C}}$

where n = no. of years useful life
S = scrap value
C = cost of the asset

$= 1 - \sqrt[5]{\dfrac{150}{56}}$

$= 51.6\%$ per annum

	Cost/reduced balance	Annual Depn.	NBV at end of year
Yr. 1	5650 × 51.6%	2915	2735
Yr. 2	2735 × 51.6%	1411	1324
Yr. 3	1324 × 51.6%	683	641
Yr. 4	641 × 51.6%	331	310
Yr. 5	310 × 51.6%	160	150

BALANCE SHEET EXTRACT

FIXED ASSET	COST £	DEPN. £	NBV £
Yr.1 Machine	£5650	£2915	2735

FIXED ASSET			
Yr.2 Machine	£2735	£1411	1324

FIXED ASSET			
Yr.3 Machine	£1324	£ 683	641

FIXED ASSET			
Yr.4 Machine	£ 641	£ 331	310

3) **SYD METHOD**

Cost £5650　　　　Scrap £150
Amount to depreciate　£5500

	Depn. amount p.a.	Accum. Depn.	NBV
Yr. 1 5/15×5500	£1833	£1833 (3667 + 150)	£3817
Yr. 2 4/15×5500	£1467	£3300 (2200 + 150)	£2350
Yr. 3 3/15×5500	£1100	£4400 (1100 + 150)	£1250
Yr. 4 2/15×5500	£ 733	£5133 (367 + 150)	£ 517
Yr. 5 1/15×5500	£ 367	£5500 0 + 150)	£ 150

The Net Book Values would be the balance sheet value at the end of each year.

CHAPTER 16

1.

(a) 19-4 — 30.9 Dr MV disposal PQR789 £2,400, MV provision for depreciation £1,600, Cr MV at Cost £4,000. Dr MV at cost £2,000, P and L account £400, Cr MV disposal PQR789 £2,400. It is not necessary to journalise cash transactions.

(b) MV at Cost Account Fixed Asset. Dr Balance b/f £21,000, Bank (7,800 + 3,000) = £10,800, Sundries £2,000, Bank — Q Ltd. £200. Cr

MV disposal XYZ123 £10,000, Sundries £4,000, Balance c/f £20,000. Totals £34,000.

MV Provision for Depreciation Dr MV Disposal XYZ123 £4,000, Sundries £1,600, Balance c/f £6,800, Cr Balance b/f £7,560, P and L depn. adj. £840, Profit and Loss £4,000, Totals £12,400. MV Disposal Account XYZ123 Dr MV Cost £10,000, P and L £1,100, Cr MV Provision for depreciation £4,000, Bank £7,100, Totals £11,100.

MV Disposal Account PQR789 Dr Sundries £2,400 from Journals above, Cr Sundries from Journals above £2,400.

3.

A

	Cost	Annual Depn.	Cumulative Depreciation	NBV
19–9	3,200	800	800	2,400
19–0	3,200	600	1,400	1,800
19–1	3,200	450	1,850	1,350

C

	Cost	Annual Depn.	Cumulative Depreciation	NBV
19–1	4,200	1,680	1,680	2,520

Provision for Depn. Machinery

12.–9	c/f	800	12.–9	P/L	800
			1.–0	b/f	800
12.–0	c/f	3,200	12.–0	P/L	2,400
		3,200			3,200
			1.–1	b/f	3,200
12.–1	c/f	6,590	12.–1	P/L	3,390
		6,590			6,590

B

Cost	Annual Depn.	Cumulative Depreciation	NBV
6,000	1,800	1,800	4,200
6,000	1,260	3,060	2,940

Machinery a/c at Cost

1.–9	Bank A	3,200	31.12.–9	c/f	3,200
1.–0	b/f	3,200			
4.–0	Bank B	6,000	12.–0	c/f	9,200
		9,200			9,200
1.–1	b/f	9,200			
6.–1	Bank C	4,200		c/f	13,400
		13,400			13,400

5.

(a) Reduced balance HT1 800 less 160, 128, 102, 82, 66 = 262, HT2 860 less 172, 138, 110, 88 = 352, HT3 840 less 168, 134, 108 = 430, HT4 950 less 190, 152 = 608, HT5 980 less 196 = 784. Straight line HT1 800 less 5 × 156 = 20, HT2 860 less 4 × 168 = 188, HT3 840 less 3 × 164 = 348, HT4 950 less 2 × 186 = 578, HT5 980 less 192 = 788.

(b) Necessary Adjustments Dr Provision for Depreciation HT5 = 4, Cr Provision for Depreciation HT1 = 242, HT2 = 164, HT3 = 82, HT4 = 30.

(c) Depreciation 19–4: HT1 NIL, HT3 164, HT4 186, HT5 192, HT6 188. Loss on disposal of HT2 is 128.

CHAPTER 17

1.

1. Bad Debts: Dr total 372, Cr Profit and Loss 372.
2. Provision for Bad Debts: Cr 250 Profit and Loss, Dr 250, Balance c/f.
3. Profit and Loss Account: Bad Debts Dr 372, Doubtful Debts Dr 250. Total charge 622.
4. Debtors £5,950 less provision for doubtful debts £250. Net Debtors £5,700.
   Note: The bad debts were written off prior to the ledger balance of £5,950 being extracted from the ledger.

2.

1. Bad Debts: Dr total 100, Cr Profit and Loss £100.
2. Provision for Bad Debts: Cr 70 Profit and Loss, Dr Balance c/f 70.
3. Profit and Loss Account: Bad Debts written off 100, Doubtful Debts 70, Total charge 170.
4. Debtors 3,500 less bad debts written off = 3,400 less provision for doubtful debts 70 = 3,330.

CHAPTER 18

1.

CASH BOOK

		£Dr			£Cr
Dec 31	Balance b/f	1831	Dec 31	Bank Charges	22
Dec 31	Credit Transfer – CS	54	Dec 31	Balance c/f	1863
		1885			1885
Jan 1	Balance b/f	1863			

BANK RECONCILIATION STATEMENT 31.12.

	£	£
Balance per Cash Book		1863
Add unpresented cheque – Fuller		115
		1978
Less Bank Lodgements Johnstone	249	
Davis	178	427
Balance per Bank Statement		1551

4.

(i) Cash Book adjustments Dr Balance b/f 47,330, (c) 530, (f) 90, Cr (a) 60, (e) 1,240, (g) 300, (h) 13,170 (l) 880, (j) Direct Debit adjustment 32,300. Totals 47,950.

(ii) Reconciliation Balance per C/B 32,300, less D.D. 16,650, Lodgements not yet credited 1,970, add unpresented cheques 450, Balance per Bank Statement 14,130.

6.

	£	
Balance per Cash Book	381	(OD)
Add unpresented Cheque — P. Neal	450	
	69	
Less Bank Lodgement	418	
Balance per Bank Statement	349	OD

CHAPTER 19

1.

The purpose of Control Accounts is to prevent error and fraud and thereby act as a control. Furthermore, it is a quick and easy way to extract totals for a trial balance, e.g. Debtors, Creditors.

2.

DEBTORS CONTROL ACCOUNT

1.1	Balance b/f	6,500	31.1	Bad Debts	50
31.1	Sales	52,150		Cash A/c	2,100
	Bank Account			Bank A/c	49,100
	(dishonoured			Discount	
	cheque)	150		Allowed	1,400
				Returns In	150
				Creditors	
				Ledger set	
				off balances	350
				Balance c/f	5,650
		58,800			58,800
1.2	Balances b/f	5,650			

3.

(a)   **CREDITORS CONTROL ACCOUNT**

31.1	Returns Out	1,400	1.1	Balance b/f	5,250
	Bank Account	41,500	31.1	Purchase	42,150
	Cash Account	650		A/c	
	Discount Rec'd	250			
	Balance c/f	3,600			
		47,400			47,400

(b)   It could be the result of a transposition error since the difference is £90. Further investigation would be required.

4.

DEBTORS CONTROL ACCOUNT

		£Dr			£Cr
1.1	Balance b/f	8,250	31.1	Bank Account	49,350
31.1	Sales Account	52,560		Cash Account	500
				Bad Debts	150
				Discount Allowed	450
				Returns Inward	500
				Purchase Ledger C	220
				Balance c/f	9,640
		60,810			60,810
1.2	Balance b/f	9,640			

CREDITORS CONTROL ACCOUNT

		£Dr			£Cr
31.1	Cash Account	1,000	1.1	Balance b/f	9,240
	Bank Account	45,100	31.1	Purchase A/c	44,250
	Discount Rec'd	600			
	Returns Outward	275			
	Debtors Ledger	220 C			
	Balance c/f	6,295			
		53,490			53,490

CHAPTER 21

1.

SUSPENSE ACCOUNT

	£Dr		£Cr
Balance c/f	800	Loan Account	750
		Administration	50
	800		800

LOAN ACCOUNT

Suspense	750	Balance c/f	2000
Balance c/f	1250		
	2000		2000
		Balance b/f	1250

ADMINISTRATION ACCOUNT

Balance c/f	500		
Suspense	50	Balance c/f	550
	550		550
Balance b/f	550		

JOHN WALK — REVISED TRIAL BALANCE AT 31.12.-4

	£Dr	£Cr
Land and Buildings	10,500	
Motor Vehicle	5,500	
Stock 1.1.–4	3,150	
Debtors	4,100	
Cash	500	
Purchases	10,250	
Administration Expenses	550	
Light and Heating Expenses	200	
Rent and Rates Expenses	150	
Sales and Marketing Expenses	350	
Sales		12,750
Creditors		3,600
Loan		1,250
Capital		17,650
	£35,250	£35,250

JOHN WALK — TRADING AND PROFIT & LOSS ACCOUNT
FOR THE PERIOD ENDED 31.12.-4

	£	£
Sales		12,750
Less Cost of Sales		
Add Opening Stock	3,150	
Purchases	10,250	
	13,400	
Less Closing Stock	2,750	
		10,650
Gross Profit		2,100
Less Expenses		
Administration	550	
Light & Heating	200	
Rent & Rates	150	
Sales & Marketing	350	
		1,250
Net Profit/(Loss)		£ 850

JOHN WALK — BALANCE SHEET AS AT 31.12.-4

Fixed Assets	**£ Cost**	**£ Depn.**	**£ NBV**	
Land and Buildings	10,500	—	10,500	
Motor Vehicle	5,500	—	5,500	
	16,000		16,000	
Current Assets				
Stock	2,750			
Debtors	4,100			
Cash	500			
		7,350		
Less Current Liabilities				
Creditors	3,600	(3,600)		
Net Current Assets on Working Capital			3,750	
			19,750	
FINANCED BY				
Capital	17,650			
Net Profit	850			
	18,500			
Loan	1,250			
Capital Employed			19,750	

2.

Journals Dr Suspense 5,138, Cr Sales 5,138, Dr Purchase 5,400, Cr Suspense 5,400, Dr Suspense 100, Cr Debtors 100, Dr Suspense 82, Cr Creditors 82, Dr Petty Cash 225, Cr Suspense 225, Input the journals to clear Suspense, Dr Balance b/f 305 (a) 5,138, (e) 100, (f) 82, Cr (c) 5,400, (g) 225. The account clears. Totals 5,625.

CHAPTER 22

1.

i. £2000   ii. £1000   iii. £11,000   iv. £3000   v. £5000.

2.

i. $\dfrac{20}{100+20} = 16.67\%$ ii. $\dfrac{30}{100+30} = 23.08\%$

iii. $\dfrac{40}{100+40} = 28.57\%$ iv. $\dfrac{50}{100+50} = 33\frac{1}{3}\%$

v. $\dfrac{33\frac{1}{3}}{100+33\frac{1}{3}} = 25\%$ vi. $\dfrac{1}{4+1} = \frac{1}{5}$

vii. $\dfrac{1}{8+1} = \frac{1}{9}$ viii. $\dfrac{1}{5+1} = \frac{1}{6}$

ix. $\dfrac{3}{5+3} = \frac{3}{8}$

3.

i. $\dfrac{25}{100-25} = 33\frac{1}{3}\%$ ii. $\dfrac{50}{100-50} = 100\%$

iii. $\dfrac{30}{100-30} = 42.86\%$ iv. $\dfrac{60}{100-60} = 150\%$

v. $\dfrac{10}{100-10} = 11\%$ vi. $\dfrac{2}{5-2} = \frac{2}{3}$

vii. $\dfrac{3}{8-3} = \frac{3}{5}$ viii. $\dfrac{1}{3-1} = \frac{1}{2}$

ix. $\dfrac{1}{5-1} = \frac{1}{4}$

4.

Cost of Sales £90,000   Gross Profit £10,000.

5.

Margin $= \dfrac{50}{100+50} = 33\frac{1}{3}\%$ ∴ Cost of Sales £66,667

Gross Profit £33,333

6

Year 1 Cost of Goods Sold 80,000; Closing Stock £25,000; Expenses £10,000; Net Profit £10,000.

Year 2 Opening Stock = Yr. 1 Closing Stock b/f £25,000. Gross Profit if £70,000 Cost of Sales given a margin of 20% (i.e. deduced from mark up) then £70,000 represents 80% (if GP + COS = 100%) $\therefore$ G.P. = £17,500. Working back closing stock must be £35,000, sales must be £87,500 and net profit £12,500.

Year 3 Opening Stock = £35,000 (b/f closing stock Yr. 2). Purchases 80,000 units £1 each in Yr. 2 if increased by 10% in volume (1.1 × 80,000) = 88,000 units bought in Year 3 at £1 × 1.05 (i.e. 5% price increase on Year 2 purchased averagely throughout the year $\therefore$ O.K. to use average price increase).

88,000 units £1.05 = £92,400.

If Net Profit is £6,000 and this represents 5% of Sales

$$\left(1\% = \frac{6,000}{5\%} = £1,200 \times 100 = £120,000 \text{ Sales} \right)$$

If mark up is 33⅓% then margin $= \frac{33\frac{1}{3}}{100+33\frac{1}{3}} = 25\%$

thus Gross Profit 25% × £120,000 = £30,000

Expenses £30,000 – £6,000 = £24,000
Cost of Goods Sold = £90,000
Closing Stock £37,400

CHAPTER 23

3.

(a) Income: Members' subs (230 + 8,220 + 700) = 9,150, Interest 85, Championship net receipt (210 – 90) = 120, total income 9,355. Expenditure: Rent 2,000, Rates (375 + 1,800 – 450) = 1,725, Depreciation 600, Groundsman's Wages 4,000, Secretary's Expenses 400, Miscellaneous 100, Interest on overdraft 250, Loss on dinner dance (420 – 500) = 80. Total expenditure 9,155, Surplus to accumulated fund 200.

(b) Opening Statement at 1.1.–3. Equipment at cost 7,000, less provision for depreciation 5,725, net book value 1,275. CA subs (debtors) 620, prepayments rates 375, Cash at bank — deposit 2,000, Current a/c 1,160, Cash in hand 100, CL subs in advance 230, Accrued rent 500. Accumulated Fund 4,800.
BALANCE SHEET at 31.12.–3. Equipment cost 15,000, less provision for depreciation 6,325, net book value 8,675, CA Subs 700, prepaid rates 450, Cash in hand 50, CL overdraft 4,000, Subs in advance 125, Accrued rent 500, Accrued bank interest 200. Total

Net Assets 5,000. Accumulated fund 4,800 + Surplus for year 200.
Total Accumulated Fund at 31.12.-3 = 5,000.

5.

Bar Trading Account: Sales 27,000, Less Cost of Sales: O/S 2,000, add
Purchases 18,500, less C/S 2,500 = 18,000. Gross Profit 9,000.
Income and Expenditure Account: Income: Bar Profit 9,000, Subscription
(17,000 + 50 – 900 + 600 – 100) = 16,650, Donations 1,500, Christmas
Dance Net (850 – 150) = 700. Total 27,850.
Expenditure: Rates (900 – 450 + 500) = 950, General Expenses 26,200,
Depreciation — premises 2,000, furniture 1,000. Deficit 2,300.
Balance Sheet (Statement of Affairs) at 31.3.-3. FA Premises Cost 50,000,
Depreciation 32,000, Net Book Value 18,000, Furniture cost 10,000,
Depreciation 8,000, Net Book Value 2,000. CA Bar Stock 2,500, Subs due
600, Bank and Cash 2,200, CL Cubs in advance 100, Accrued rates 500.
Total Net Assets 24,700. Accumulated Fund at 1.4.-2 27,000 less deficit
for year 2,300 = 24,700. Accumulated Fund at 1.4.-2 (900 – 50 – 450 +
2,000 + 20,000 + 3,000 + 1,600) = 27,000.

CHAPTER 24

3.

(a) P and L appropriation account Net Profit for year 19–5.

	D	E	M	Total
DR Salary		2,500		2,500
DR Interest on Capital	450	400	600	1,450
CR Interest on drawings	(90)	(30)	(25)	(145)
DR Balance of Profits 5 : 2 : 3	8,000	3,200	4,800	16,000
	8,360	6,070	5,375	19,805

(b) Capital Accounts DR (D) 10,000, (E) 4,000 loan, 6,000 c/f, (M)
12,000. CR b/f (D) 8,000, Cash 2,000, (E) b/f 10,000, (M) b/f
12,000.
Current Accounts DR (D) Drawings 2,400, c/f 6,540, (E) b/f 350,
Drawings 1,800, c/f 3,920, (M) Drawings 3,000, c/f 2,585, CR (D)
b/f 580, Profit Share (D) 8,360, (E) 6,070, (M) 5,375.

4.

(a) BKL Trading Account: Sales 150,000 Less Cost of Sales: O/S
20,000, add Purchases 85,000, less C/S 30,000 = Gross Profit
75,000. Office expenses 4,000, Rates 2,000, Selling expenses
15,775, Bad debts 500, Doubtful debts provided for 125,
Depreciation: L and B 3,000, Motor Vehicles 4,000. Total expenses
29,400, Net Profit 45,600. Appropriation Account: Dr Salaries
L6,000, Interest on Capitals B1,800, K1,200, L600. Balance of
profits shared 3:2:1 B18,000, K12,000, L6,000.

(b) Current Accounts: Dr Balance b/f K500, Drawings B4,000, K3,000, L3,000; Balance c/f B16,500, K9,700, L9,900, Cr Balance b/f B700, Salary L6,000, Interest on Capitals B1,800, K1,200, L600. Profit B18,000, K12,000, L6,000.

(c) BALANCE SHEET at 30.9. FA Land and Building Cost 60,000, Depreciation 15,000, Net Book Value 45,000; Motor Vehicles Cost 20,000, Depreciation 12,000, Net Book Value 8,000. CA Stock 30,000, Debtors 21,375, Prepayment 2,000, Bank and Cash 2,500. CL Creditors 35,000, Accruals 1,775, NCA 19,100. Total Net Assets 72,100, Capital Accounts B18,000, K12,000, L6,000. Current Accounts B16,500, K9,700, L9,900. Total Capital Employed 72,100.

CHAPTER 25

1.

(i) CAPITAL ACCOUNTS — Alan Dr's — Goodwill 18,000, Cash 30,023, balance c/f 66,377, Cr's — balance b/f 85,000, revaluation 29,400. Bob Dr's — Goodwill 12,000, balance c/f 72,600, Cr's — balance b/f 65,000, revaluation 19,600. Charles Dr's — Car 3,900, Loan 40,900. Cr's — balance b/f 35,000, revaluation 9,800. Don Dr's — Goodwill 12,000, balance c/f 70,091. Cr's cash 82,091.
CURRENT ACCOUNTS — Alan Dr's — balance c/f 3,714. Cr's — balance b/f 3,714. Bob Dr's — balance b/f 2,509, Cr balance c/f 2,509. Charles Dr's — Loan 4,678, Cr balance b/f 4,678.
REVALUATION ACCOUNT — Dr's — Plant 2,000, Stock 8,200, Debtors 3,000, Profit A 29,400, B 19,600, C 9,800. Total 72,000. Cr's — Premises 30,000, Goodwill 42,000. Total 72,000.
LOAN ACCOUNT — Charles — Dr balance c/f 20,000, cash 25,578. Cr Current Account 4,678, Capital Account 40,900.

(ii) BALANCE SHEET at 30.6 — F.A. Premises 120,000, Plant 35,000, Vehicles 11,100, Fixtures 2,000, CA Stock 54,179, Debtors 31,980, CL Creditors 19,036, Overdraft 4,950. Capital + Current Accounts total 210,273, Loan — Charles 20,000. Totals 230,273.

CHAPTER 26

1.

REALIZATION ACCOUNT Dr Land B 450,820, Plant 77,115, M.V. 18,065, Stock 37,000, Debtors 51,000, Cr Exodus 501,000, M Car 4,000, Debt Settlement 45,000, Loss G 28,000, M 28,000, W 28,000. Totals 634,000.
CAPITAL ACCOUNTS (combining current and capital (fixed) on dissolution). Dr Balance b/f Current W 3,000, Car M 4,000, Losses shared G 28,000, M 28,000, W 28,000, W balance: G 6,667, M 3,333. Following

the rule in Garner and Murray Exodus plc A/c. Dr Consideration 501,000, Cr Cash 368,600, Creditors 81,400, Ordinary Shares G 40,333, M 10,667, Totals 501,000. Shares taken in Exodus G 40,333, M 10,667, Cr Balances b/f Capital 70,000, M 35,000, W 21,000, b/f Current Balances G 5,000, M 8,000, HP Car M 3,000, W to G 6,667; W to M 3,333. CASH ACCOUNT Dr Debtors 45,000, Exodus 368,600, Cr Balance b/f 303,600, Creditors 10,000, Mrs W 100,000. Totals 413,600.

CHAPTER 27

1.

(a) Balances J 18,450, K 22,978, L 1,364. The overall gain was £24,000 shared 3:2:1 and added to balances b/f on current accounts.

(b) Journal entries Dr's — Premises 100,000, Plant 52,000, Furniture 27,000, Stock 29,500, Debtors 51,500, Goodwill 24,000. Cr — JKL Acquisition A/c 284,000. Dr — JKL Acquisition A/c 284,000. Cr — Ordinary Shares 135,000, Share premium 45,000, Debentures 42,792, Cash 61,208 — Loan from bank — Dr Cash, Cr Debentures.

(c) Balance Sheet at 1st April — FA Premises 100,000, Plant 52,000, Furniture 27,000, Goodwill 24,000, CA — Stock 29,500, Debtors 51,500, Cash at bank 8,792. Share capital — 135,000, Share Premium — 45,000, Debentures — 112,792.

CHAPTER 28

2.

Howton Ltd TP&L year ended 31.12.19–4. Sales 290,000. Cost of Sales:- Opening stock 35,000. Purchases 165,000. Carriage in 1,100 less Closing Stock 41,000. Gross Profit 129,900. Add back provision for doubtful debts no longer required as non-trading income 300 and Discount Received 4,600. Sub-total 134,800. Less Expenses: Wages 23,650 (23,500 + 150A). Office Salaries 8,600. Directors' fees 12,800. General expenses 11,850. Lighting & Heat 2,900. Depreciation machinery 38,000. Loss on disposal of machinery 100 (effectively extra depreciation). Discount Allowed 3,200. Debenture interest 7,000. Total 108,100. Net Profit available for appropriation 26,700. APPROPRIATION A/C Dividend paid interim 5% Ordinary 7,500 8% preference (for 6 months) 2,000 Dividends proposed 5% final ordinary (nominal value 165,000) = 8,250, 8% final preference (6 months) 2,000 transfer to general reserve 5,000 sub-total 24,750. Retained profit this year 1,950 add b/f undistributd P&L reserve at 1st Jan. 35,000. undistributed P&L reserve c/f at 31.12.19–4 (Balance Sheet) 36,950 BALANCE SHEET AT 31.12.19–4 F.A. Land (at valuation) 180,000. P&M at cost 380,000 less cumulative depreciation 122,000 NBV 258,000. Total F.A. 438,000, C.A. Stock 41,000, Debtors and prepayments less provision 46,850, Bank 7,500, Total 95,350. Less C.L. Creditors and accruals 27,150. Proposed Dividends 5% ordinary 8,250, *% preference 2,000. Total 37,400. N.C.A. 57,950. Total 495,950 Less Long term liability Loan Capital 7%. Debentures 100,000. Total 395,950. Called up and issued shared capital £1 ordinary shares 165,000. 8% preference shares 50,000, sub-total 215,000. Reserves: Share premium 5,000. Revaluation reserve 69,000. General reserve (65,000 + 5,000) 70,000. Undistributed profit 36,950, sub-total 180,950. Total 395,950.

3.

XYZ Ltd. Trading and Profit and Loss and Appropriation — Sales 217,800, Cost of Sales O/S 15,500, Purchases 160,000, C/S 13,500, Gross Profit 55,800, Rent and rates 10,000, Light and heat 7,600, Administration 11,300, MV depreciation 4,000, Provision for doubtful debts 644, Total 33,544, Net Profit 22,256, Appropriation — General Reserve 5,000, Retained profit 17,256, add profit and loss reserve 3,800 transferred to the profit and loss reserve at 31.12 £21,056.

BALANCE SHEET — FA M.V. net 9,000, CA Stock 13,500, Debtors net 31,556, Bank 3,000, CL — Creditors and accruals 11,000, Total 46,056, SC — 5,000, general reserve 5,000, P + L reserve 21,056, Total 46,056.

CHAPTER 29

1.

(a)   Total receipts 1,550 units, value 3,740, issues 1,900, value 4,410, closing balance 50 units, value 130.

(b)   CIMA definition – "That part of management accounting which establishes budgets and standard costs and actual costs of operations, processes, department or products and the analysis of variances, profitability or social use of funds. — Benefits — to plan, control and make decisions; to price products; determine optimum output levels; to know the cost of production or service units".

2.

(a)   (i)   FIFO Total receipts 800 units, value 3,400; Total issues 650 units, value 2,675, balance 150 units, value 725.
      (ii) LIFO Total receipts 800 units, value 3,400; Total issues 650 units, value 2,850; balance 150 units, value 550.
      (iii) Periodic simple average issue price £4,125; closing balance valued at £618.75.
      (iv) Periodic weighted average price £4.25; closing balance £637.50.
      (v)   Weighted average issues 150 units, value 550; 450 units, value 1,923; 50 units, value 232; closing balance 150 units at 4.63 = 695.

(b)   FIFO gives higher profits than LIFO since the older stock prices will be those issued on a FIFO basis, thus making cost of sales lower. In times of rising price levels FIFO will also give a more realistic valuation of the stock remaining since the most recent purchases will not yet be issued.

3.

Stock valuation at 30.4. Provisional figure 187,033. (a) No action; (b) 5,657 + 804 = 6,461 total cost value 6,321, write off — 140; (c) + 8,010; (d) – 6,480; (e) + 1,200; (f) No action; (g) – 152, amended stock value 189,471.

8.

Opening balance 10 at 29 = 290. Total receipts 120 units, 3,800 value; issues 122 units, 3,810 value; remaining balance 8 units at 35 = 280.

9.

(a) (i) FIFO — K — receipts 3,500 units, 3,850 value; issues 3,100, 3,330 value; balance at close 400 units at 1.30 = 520.
LIFO — L receipts 3,500 units, 3,850 value; issues 3,500 units, 3,450 value; balance at close 400 units at 1.00 = 400.
WEIGHTED AVERAGE – M $\frac{£3,850}{3,500 \text{ units}}$ = £1.10 per unit.

(ii) Closing stock values K 400 at £1.30 = 520; L 400 at £1.00 = 400; 400 at £1.10 = 440. Profit K — FIFO = 440; L — FIFO =400; M — AVCO = 413.33.

(iii) LIFO not acceptable for tax purposes in UK and not recommended per SSAP9. It does, however, give the most appropriate profit during times of rising prices since the costs and revenues which are matched in the income statement are closer to the same time period. FIFO although acceptable by the UK tax authorities and recommended per SSAP9 will overstate profit during periods of rising prices. Weighted average falls between FIFO and LIFO and is acceptable by I.R. and SSAP9.

(b) Costs accruing on a time basis are period costs, i.e. fixed costs. Stock valuation systems allow for such costs by absorption — See stock valuations and SSAP9 in this text.

CHAPTER 30

4.

(a)

Materials consumed (000's)	88 C,	290 D,	total	378
Wages (000's)	99 C,	297 D,		396
Manufacturing expenses	114 C,	342 D,		456
Add opening WIP	19 C,	65 D,		84
Less closing WIP	20 C,	63 D,		83
Transfer to product A	32 C,	(32) D,		—
Cost of finished goods	332	899,		1231
Trading Account — Sales	600 A,	1400 B,		2000
Cost of Sales — O/S	125 A,	38 B,		163
F.G. transferred in from Mfctg.	332 A,	899 B,		1231
Purchased F.G.	72 A,	—		72
Closing Stocks	84 A,	188 B,		272
Profit and Loss Account				
Gross Profit	155 A,	651 B,		806
Administration Expenses	75 A,	225 B,		300
Marketing Expenses	32 A,	64 B,		96
Royalties Expenses	90 A,	120 B,		210
Net Profit/(Loss) before tax	(42) A,	242 B,		200

(b) Appropriation Account
Profit this year before tax 200, Corporation Tax 80, Profit after tax 120,

Dividends paid and proposed 90, Retained profit this year 30, add retained profit b/f 270, retained profit c/f 300.

(c) BALANCE SHEET F.A. net 700, C.A. Stock RM 30, WIP 83, FG 272, Debtors net 209, Prepayments 5, Bank 11, CL — Creditors 150, Accruals 20, Taxation 80, Proposed Dividend 60, NCA 300, TOTAL 1,000, SC 600, S Premium 100, Reserve P + L 300, Total 1,000.

5.

Sales 10,100, less returns in 100, Cost of Sales O/S 650, Purchases 3,210, less returns out 60, Carriage in 15, less C/S 700, Materials consumed 3,115, Manufacturing Wages 850, Man. Expenses 1,275, Depreciation (Factory) 380, Increase in WIP (20). Cost of FG manufactured 5,600, decrease in FG stock 900, COGS 6,500, Gross Profit 3,500, Admin. Exp. — Office salaries 860, Depreciation 50, Marketing and distribution — Advertising 1,010, Salaries and Commission 360, Depn. 50, Bad Debts w/off 13, recovered (10), decrease in provision (5), Carriage out 22, Total 1,430; Finance Exp. — Discounts allowed 240 less received 70, net 170. Total Expenses 2,520; Operating profit 980, add non-trading income — rent received 20, investment income 80, less debenture interest payable 80, Profit before tax 1,000, Taxation 500, Profit after tax 500, less dividends paid and proposed 300, Transferred to P & L Reserve 200.

CHAPTER 31

1.

FA Goodwill 60,860, Premises 60,000, P & M 70,000, Vehicles 26,000, CA Stocks 17,140, Debtors 6,000 – 1,200, Bank 28,200 — CL Creditors 28,000 = Net Current Assets or Working Capital 22,140 = Total 239,000. Share capital 200,000, share premium 40,000, Profit and Loss Reserve (1,000) — this deficit is the preliminary expenses owing to company formation for LB Ltd.

CHAPTER 32

1.

(a) Sources of Funds (000's) — Profit before tax 312, Adjustments not involving the movement of funds — Depreciation 106, Loss on sale of machinery 4, Total generated from operations 422. Funds from other sources — Share issue 50, Debenture issue 10, Disposal of F.A. 6, Total sources 488, Application of those funds — Dividends paid 84, Tax paid 136, Purchase of F.A. 300; Total 520. Sources less application (32) represented by a decrease in Working Capital — Stocks + 5, Debtors + 70, Creditors — 122, Movement in net liquid funds — Increase in cash 15, Total (32).

(b) Useful since it summarises the cash position, it links profit to cash. It is, however, a historical cash flow statement and therefore not a present or future predictor. It shows where cash came into the business from and how it was applied — revenue and capital items are disclosed. See SSAP10.

2.

Sources of Funds — Net profit before tax 8,600, Adjustments not involving the movement of funds — Depreciation 600, Total from operations 9,200. Applications — F+F 5,200, Drawings 6,200, Net decrease in working capital (2,200), Increase in stock 4,420, Increase in debtors 2,980, Increase in creditors 260, Decrease in net liquid funds (220 – 10,400) 10,180 = (2,200).

CHAPTER 33

1.

(a)

	19-2	19-3	19-4
Gross Profit/Sales	20.00%	15.38%	16.67%
Net Profit/Sales	10.00%	6.92%	8.67%
Net Profit/Capital Employed	14.29%	11.39%	14.13%
CA/CL	2.25 . 1	2.58 : 1	2.88 : 1
Acid Test CA – S/CL	1 : 1	.78 : 1	.69 : 1
Debtor turnover	21.9 days	19.7 days	21.9 days
Stock turnover (using closing (point measure) balance as average)	8 times yr	4.6 times	3.1 times
or Average Stock/Cost of Sales	8 times	6.5 times	3.9 times
	45.6 days	56.4 days	93.6 days

(b) Limitations — the changing value of money is ignored, relative rather than absolute amounts are considered, they do not take account of different accounting policies — for a full discussion refer to the chapter.

2.

	W	B
1 Gross Profit/Sales	25%	22%
2 Net Profit/Sales	8%	6%
3 R.O.C.E.	25%	30%
4 Stock turnover	8 times yr.	12 times yr.
5 Debtor turnover	45.6 days	30.6 days

6 Creditor payment period — unable to calculate this since purchases figure not shown and not possible to deduce in this case.

B. earned same net profit as W but on a higher turnover, this is reflected in ratios 1 and 2 above. B has a 5% better returns on his investment; but B's average stockholding is higher than W's. B has better credit control than W, reflected by ratio 5. You may consider other points for discussion, both of a general and a specific nature. For further comparison/analysis — required — Accounting policies — depreciation; opening stocks to deduce purchases and calculate credit turnover. Cost and depreciation on Fixed

Assets. Aged Debtors and breakdown Trade and other — same for Creditors. Changes in market conditions or sources of supply which affected performance for the year. Cash Flows. Time and effort spent by each proprietor in earning profit.

3.

(a) Current Assets less Current Liabilities (stock, debtors, prepayments, bank and cash less Trade Creditors and other creditors less than one year, together with accrued expenses).

(b) (i) Current ratio CA:CL ≙ 1.
   (ii) Acid Test CA-S:CL = 1:5.
   (iii) Gearing ratio Longterm debt/Longterm capital = 39% $\left(\frac{250,000}{633,422} \times \frac{100}{1}\right)$. The more highly geared a business is the greater the pressure in difficult periods since debt commitments must be met (interest and repayments).
   (iv) Fixed Assets/Shareholders' Funds 1:64:1, most investment of SF is in FA.
   (v) S.C. to EQUITY = .52:1 — It would appear that the company is making large retentions, presumably to fund growth.
   (vi) Current Assets form a low proportion of total assets CA/TA = 37%. You would expect a construction company to have a larger proportion of CA to TA if it is active due to stockholding.

CHAPTER 34

1.

VAT a/c Dr's (³⁄₂₃ × 69,000) = 9,000, Bank VAT paid 4,700, balance c/f 6,000; Cr's balance b/f 4,700; 15,000 Sales (100,000 + 15%). Zero rated and exempt supplies do not affect what is owed or receivable. The balance outstanding at 30th August payable to HM Customs and Excise is £6,000.
SALES a/c Cr's 100,000; 10,000; 5,000.
PURCHASE a/c Dr's 60,000; 6,900; 2,300.

CHAPTER 35

1.

(a) Stamps for Goods — 5,000, less Cost of goods O/S 900, Purchases 3,550, C/S 950, Gross Profit 1,500, Expenses 1,170, Depreciation 130, Net Profit 200, add non-trading income from investments 200.

(b) Trial balance Dr's FA at cost 1,300, Stock 950, Cash at Bank 350, Investments (intangible assets) 3,500, Total 6,100, Cr's Ord. S.C. 1,600, retained profit 900, (Cumulative) Depreciation provision 650, Creditors 450, provision for unredeemed stamps 2,500, Total 6,100.

(c) Trading Account for the year ended 31.12. — Sales 100,000, Cost of petrol and other merchandise sold 75,000, Gross profit 25,000, less Cost of trading stamps, Opening stock 200, add Purchases 2,100, less Closing Stock 300, Net profit 23,000.

2.

Analysed Profit and Loss Account

	P	Q	R	S	T	U	Total
Sales by resort (000's)	480	244	30	60	24	68	906
Costs by resort							
Agents Commission (10%)	48	24.4	3	6	2.4	6.8	90.6
Hotel Accommodation	305.9	153.2	22.6	45.4	10.2	44.1	581.4
Coaches	1.1	0.9	1.4	1.1	1.7	0.8	7.0
Reps.	5	4.5	6	5.5	5.7	5.3	32
Total Costs	360	183	33	58	20	57	711
Gross Profit	120	61	(3)	2	4	11	
		120		(3)		4	
		181		(1)		15	195
Hire of planes		(30)		(40)		(35)	(105)
Contribution		151		(41)		(20)	90
Less Overheads (FC)*							(100)
Net loss for the year							(10)

*brochures, advertising, head office and common costs.

CHAPTER 36

1.

(a) Bullwell's Books
Lorry a/c Dr's Granby Garage 54,000 (3 lorries 18,000), Interest a/c Dr's Granby 81 – 11,250, 82 – 8,063, 83 – 4,078. Cr's P/L 11,250, 8,063, 4,078. Cash Book Cr's Granby 9,000; 24,000; 24,000; 20,391.
Granby Garages Yr.1: Dr — Cash 9,000, Cash 24,000, balance c/f 32,250, Cr — Lorries 54,000, Interest 11,250. Totals 65,250.
Yr.2: Dr's Cash 24,000; balance c/f 16,313, Cr's balance b/f 32,250; interest 8,063. Totals 40,313.
Yr.3: Dr's Cash 20,391, G balance b/f 16,313, Interest 4,078.

Provision Depreciation a/c, Dr Balance c/f 12,500, Cr P/L 12,500, Dr balance c/f 25,000, Cr balance b/f 12,500, P/L 12,500, total 25,000. Yr.3 balance c/f 37,500, Cr balance b/f 25,000, P/L 12,500, total 37,500. 4 Dr balance c/f 50,000, Cr balance b/f 37,500, P/L 12,500.

Balance Sheet Extract	81	82	83	84
Vehicles at cost	54,000	54,000	54,000	54,000
less Depn. to date	12,500	25,000	37,500	50,000
NBV				
HP Debt outstanding	32,250	16,313	—	—
Charge to profit				
Interest	11,250	8,063	4,078	—
Depn.	12,500	12,500	12,500	12,500
	27,750	20,563	16,578	12,500

MV Calc. Int. (25% — 45,000) (25% × 32,250) (25% × 16,313)

(b) Granby's Books

Bulwell a/c 19-1 — Dr HP Sales 54,000, HP Int. 11,250, Total 65,250. Cr Bank deposit 9,000; Bank instalment 24,000; Balance c/f 32,250. 19-2 — Dr Balance b/f 32,250, HP Int. 8,063, Total 40,313. Cr Bank instalment 24,000, Balance c/f 16,313. 19-3 — Dr Balance b/f 16,313, HP Int. 4,078. Totals 20,391. Cr Bank instalment 20,391.

Bank a/c Dr 9,000 Bulwell, 24,000 B. 19-2 — 24,000 B. 19-3 — 20,391 B.

HP interest a/c Dr 19-1 — HP Trading 11,250, Cr Bulwell 11,250. 19-2 — HP Trading 8,063. Cr Bulwell 8,063. 19-3 — D. HP Trading 4,078. Cr Bulwell 4,078.

HP Trading a/c. Dr. 19-1 — Gen. Trading a/c. 43,200, Provision for unrealised profit c/f 6,450, Gross Profit 15,600 to P/L. Total 65,250. Cr HP Sales 54,000, HP int. 11,250. 19-2 — Dr's Provision for unrealised profit c/f 3,263, GP to P/L 11,250. Total 14,513. Cr — Provision for unrealised profit b/f 6,450, HP int. 8,063. Total 14,513. 19-3 — Dr GP to P/L 7,341. Cr Provision for unrealized profit b/f 3,263, HP interest 4,078, Total 7,341.

Calculation of provision — unrealized profit

$$\text{Margin} \quad \frac{10,800}{54,000} \times \frac{100}{1} = 20\% \quad \left(\begin{array}{c} \text{i.e. } 54,000 - 43,200 \\ = 10,800 \end{array} \right)$$

20% × 32,250 = 6,450; 20% × 16,313 = 3,263

CHAPTER 41

2.

(a) (i)

		A	B	C	Total
	Sales budget – quantities	1,000	2,000	1,500	
	selling price	£100	£120	£140	
	sales value	£100,000	£240,000	£210,000	£550,000

(ii)

		A	B	C
	Production budget quantities			
	sales	1,000	2,000	1,500
	Add c/s	1,100	1,650	550
	Less o/s	(1,000)	(1,500)	(500)
	Production	1,100	2,150	1,550

(iii) Material Usage budget –

	M1 Units per Product	M2 Units per Product	M3 Units per Product
Production Quantity			
A 1,100 × 4 =	4,400	2 = 2,200	– = –
B 2,150 × 3 =	6,450	3 = 6,450	2 = 4,300
C 1,550 × 2 =	3,100	1 = 1,550	1 = 1,550
Usage	13,950	10,200	5,850

(iv) Materials purchase budget

	M1	M2	M3
Usages	13,950	10,200	5,850
Add c/s	31,200	24,000	14,400
Less o/s	(26,000)	(20,000)	(12,000)
Purchase Quantity	19,150	14,200	8,250
Price per Unit	× £4	× £6	× £9
Purchase Values	£76,000	£85,200	£74,250

Total Purchase Value £236,050.

(b) The term is also known as the key or limiting factor. It is a constraint. When there are no stated limiting factors it is assumed that sales is the principal budget factor. It could be stated as a shortage of man hours – labour constraint; machine hours – production constraint, material in short supply etc.

3.
These points are discussed in the text.

4.
(a) (i) Known as managed costs because they can be influenced by decisions of managers, e.g. Most variable costs are controllable since the decision on how many to produce will affect cost.
  (ii) Costs beyond the control of managers. Most fixed costs are non-controllable.

(b)   **Department A Budget**

	This Month			Year to Date		
	Budget	Actual	Variance	Budget	Actual	Variance

Controllable Costs
  Direct Labour
  Direct Materials
  Direct Expenses
  Total
Non-Controllable Costs
  Rent
  Rates
  Depreciation
  Total
Overall Costs						

(c)   The role of the committee is fully discussed in Chapter 41.

CHAPTER 43

1.

BUDGETED CASH FLOW FORECAST FOR THE YEAR
TO 31.12.19–6

Receipts		Quarter 1	Quarter 2	Quarter 3	Quarter 4
Cash b/f		500	166	(166⅔)	833⅓
Debtors		8,333⅓	10,666⅔	12,000	13,333⅓
	a	8,833⅓	10,833⅓	11,833⅓	14,166⅔
Payments					
Creditors		5,667	8,000	8,000	8,000
Expenses		3,000	3,000	3,000	3,000
	b	8,667	11,000	11,000	11,000
Cash c/f	(a-b)	166	(166⅔)	833⅓	3,166⅔

FORECAST PROFIT AND LOSS STATEMENT
FOR THE YEAR ENDED 31.12.19–6

	£	£
Sales		50,000
Less Cost of Sales		
Opening Stock	7,000	
Purchases	32,000	
Closing Stock	4,000	
		(35,000)
Gross Profit		15,000
Less Expenses		
Expenses	12,000	
Depreciation	8,000	
		(20,000)
Net profit/(loss)		(5,000)

BALANCE SHEET AS AT 31.12.–6

Fixed assets	£	£	£
Land and buildings	25,000	5,000	20,000
Motor vehicles	12,000	3,000	9,000
	37,000	8,000	29,000
Current assets			
Stock	4,000		
Debtors	10,666		
Cash	3,166		
		17,833	17,833
			46,833
Less Current Liabilities			
Creditors	5,333		
		(5,333)	
Net Current Assets			12,500
Capital Employed			41,500
Financed by			
Capital	40,000		
Profit/(Loss)	(7,500)		
	32,500		
Loan	9,000		
			41,500

PROFITABILITY RATIOS

		19–5	19–6
1.	$\dfrac{\text{Gross Profit}}{\text{Sales}} \times \dfrac{100}{1}$ =	30%	30%
2.	$\dfrac{\text{Net Profit}}{\text{Sales}} \times \dfrac{100}{1}$ =	–19%	–10%
3.	$\dfrac{\text{Expenses}}{\text{Sales}} \times \dfrac{100}{1}$ =	49%	40%

LIQUIDITY RATIOS

		19–5	19–6
1.	$\dfrac{\text{Debtors}}{\text{Sales}} \times 365$ =	36.5 days	77.8 days
2.	$\dfrac{\text{Stock}}{\text{Cost of sales}} \times 365$ =	73 days	42 days
3.	$\dfrac{\text{Creditors}}{\text{Purchases}} \times 365$ =	34 days	61 days
4.	$\dfrac{\text{Current assets}}{\text{Current liabilities}}$ =	1 : 4	1 : 3
5.	$\dfrac{\text{Current assets} - \text{Stock}}{\text{Current liabilities}}$ =	1 : 1	1 : 2½

Working Capital Ratio in Days

		No. of Days	No. of Days
6.	Stock	73	42
	+ Debtors	36.5	77.8
	– Creditors	(34)	(61)
		75.5	58.8

CHAPTER 45

2.
(i) Sales Revenue oe, (ii) Fixed Costs ag, (iii) Break Even £ Sales ob, (iv) Margin of Safety dh, (v) Budgeted Sales Revenue ok, (vi) Variable Cost o1 – oa, (vii) Budgeted Profit ok – o1.

3.
(a) FC/C = £180,000/£4 = 45,000 units or FC/C/s = 180,000/0.4 = £450,000.

(b) Profit Period   1 £82,000   2 (£5,000)   3 £40,000

	Period 1	2	3
(c) Reconciliation	20,000	60,000	(20,000)
Contribution Total	60,000	(60,000)	60,000
Absorbed Overhead	2,000	(5,000)	–
Overhead Exp. Variance			
Profit	82,000	(5,000)	40,000

4.

(a) Required total contribution, Profit 3 million, FC 11.4 million = 14.4 million less contributions from existing markets – Asia 2m, N. America 3.6m, W. Europe 7m, Africa 0.8m, total 13.4m. Contribution required from new markets, 1m, surplus production 0.5m (3m – 2.5m). Required contribution per unit

$$\frac{1m}{0.5m} = \$2$$

Add variable cost $6 = new selling price $8.

(b) MC is used for short term decision making. In the long term all costs must be recovered for a firm to continue and a required profit level to be achieved. It's horses for courses. Also when settling prices, the most important determinant is the market. Costs are fact, prices are policy taking account of fact.

CHAPTER 46

1.

Year 1	Marginal Cost (MC)		Absorption Cost (AC)	
		£		£
Sales: (8000 x 20)		160,000		160,000
Less Variable Cost				
Direct Labour (9000 x £5)	45,000		45,000	
Direct Material (9000 x £3)	27,000		27,000	
Variable Overhead				
(9000 x £4)	36,000		36,000	
	108,000			
Less Closing Stock (MC)				
$\frac{1000}{9000}$ x 108,000	12,000			
	96,000			
Fixed Factory Overhead	15,000	111,000	15,000	
TOTAL PRODUCTION COST			123,000	
Less Closing Stock (AC)				
$\frac{1000}{9000}$ x 123,000			13,666	
				109,334
GROSS PROFIT		49,000		50,666

Year 2	Marginal Cost		Absorption Cost	
		£		£
Sales: (9000 x 20)		180,000		180,000
Less Variable Cost				
Direct Labour (11000 x £5)	55,000		55,000	
Direct Material (11000 x £3)	33,000		33,000	
Variable Overhead				
(11000 x £4)	44,000		44,000	
	132,000		132,000	
Add Opening Stock (MC)	12,000			
	144,000			
Less Closing Stock (MC)				
$\frac{3000}{11000}$ x 132,000	36,000			
	108,000			
Fixed Factory Overhead	15,000	123,000	15,000	

	Marginal Cost		Absorption Cost
TOTAL PRODUCTION COST			147,000
Add Opening Stock (AC)			13,666
			160,666
Less Closing Stock (AC)			
$\frac{3000}{11000}$ x 147,000			40,090
			120,576
GROSS PROFIT		59,000	59,424

Year 3	Marginal Cost		Absorption Cost	
	£		£	
Sales: (14000 x £20)		280,000		280,000
Less Variable Costs				
Direct Labour (15000 x £5)	75,000		75,000	
Direct Material (15000 x £3)	45,000		45,000	
Variable Overhead				
(15000 x £4)	60,000		60,000	
	180,000		180,000	
Add Opening Stock (MC)	36,000			
	216,000			
Less Closing Stock (MC)				
$\frac{4000}{15000}$ x 180,000	48,000			
	168,000			
Fixed Factory Overhead	15,000	183,000	15,000	
TOTAL PRODUCTION COST			195,000	
Add Opening Stock (AC)			40,090	
			235,090	
Less Closing Stock (AC)				
$\frac{4000}{15000}$ x 195,000			52,000	
				183,090
GROSS PROFIT		97,000		96,910

To find the Net Profit

	Year 1	Year 2	Year 3
Marginal Cost			
Gross Profit	49,000	59,000	97,000
Less Expenses	15,000	18,000	21,000
Net Profit	34,000	41,000	76,000
Absorption Cost			
Gross Profit	50,666	59,424	96,910
Less Expenses	15,000	18,000	21,000
Net Profit	35,666	41,424	75,910

2.

(a) (i)   MC requires only VC to be allocated to products or departments whereas AC tries to allocate FC and VC.

(ii)   Different stock valuations. AC absorbs overheads into stock and does not charge them as a period cost until the stock is consumed. Thus matching costs with revenues.

(b) (i)   Absorption rate $B = \dfrac{£200,000}{400,000} = 50p$ per unit

Actual production for quarter = 110,000 units.
Fixed production overhead absorbed = 110,000 × 50p
= £55,000   Answer 4

(ii)
Absorbed fixed production overhead	£55,000
less Budgeted fixed production overhead	£50,000
Overabsorption	5,000

Answer 2

(iii)   Net Profit 2   £50,000
(iv)   Net Profit 1   £35,000

3.

(a)   1 Additional revenue £16 p.u. Marginal Costs:- RM 8, DL 4, VP Overhead 3.20, total 15.20. Additional profit 0.80 p.u. × 2,000 units = £1,600. Answer: accept the order.
2 Marginal Cost of buying £20 p.u. Marginal Costs:- RM 4, DL 8, Variable Pdn Overhead 6.40, total 18.40. Extra cost to buy 1.60 per unit. Answer: it costs more to buy ∴ continue to make.

(b)   MC assumes FC will not change. AC is misleading for make or buy decisions because unit costs do not remain constant but fall as output rises.

CHAPTER 48

1.

BUSINESS A

1. Rate Per Unit = $\dfrac{400000}{100000}$ = £4.00

2. Rate Per Direct Labour Hour = $\dfrac{400000}{500000}$ = £0.80

3. Rate Per Machine Hour = $\dfrac{400000}{300000}$ = £1.33

4. % of Direct Material = $\dfrac{400000}{2000000}$ = 20%

5. % of Direct Wages = $\dfrac{400000}{950000}$ = 42.1%

6. % Prime Cost = $\dfrac{400000}{2950000}$ = 13.56%

BUSINESS B

1. Rate Per Unit = $\dfrac{750000}{300000}$ = £2.50

2. Rate Per Direct Labour Hour = $\dfrac{750000}{1600000}$ = £0.4688

3. Rate Per Machine Hour = $\dfrac{750000}{800000}$ = £0.9375

4. % of Direct Material = $\dfrac{750000}{7000000}$ = 10.7%

5. % of Direct Wages = $\dfrac{750000}{3080000}$ = 24.4%

6. % Prime Cost = $\dfrac{750000}{10080000}$ = 7.4%

CHAPTER 49

2.

(a) Job Cost Estimates at different levels of output

Quantities	2000	5000	10000	20000
Variable Costs				
Paper	36	90	180	360
Other Material	3	7.50	15	30
Labour	4.80	12	24	48
Fixed Costs				
Selling	60	60	60	60
Artwork	20	20	20	20
Overheads	10	10	10	10
Total Cost	133.80	199.50	309.00	528.00
Profit mark up	44.60	66.50	103.00	176.00
Total Est. Selling Price	178.40	266.00	412.00	704.00
(i) Price per 1000	£89.20	£53.20	£41.20	£35.20
(ii) Cost of each leaflet	6.69p	3.99p	3.09p	2.64p

(b) Points to make:- able to compare actual costs with estimates, give reasons if variances occur and take corrective action, e.g. maintain cost and efficiency, change supplier, use different materials, change selling prices as appropriate to maintain profitability etc. Estimate profitability of the printing department.

CHAPTER 50

1.

(a) Problems – allocating profits or losses on the contracts to relevant periods of time. Taking account of interim payments and retention money. Valuing stocks and work in progress at the balance sheet date. Profit should only be taken on a contract when the outcome may reasonably be foreseen. The cost of work to completion together with any rectification costs which may ensue need to be considered. Prudence concept – only that part of profit which has been earned at the accounting date. Often referred to as the 'percentage complete'. W.I.P. calculated on a cost plus attributable profit less losses foreseen. Any progress payments received and receivable are deducted from this figure so that the net figure is placed in the Balance Sheet.

(b) Contract Account – Dr's WIP b/f 447,850, Plant b/f 83,465, Materials 46,412, Labour 31,283, Overhead 12,513, Plant purchased 21,478, Profit P/L 11,052, Total 654,053. Cr's WIP c/f 566,833, Plant c/f 87,220, Total 654,053, Balances b/f Dr WIP 566,833, Plant 87,220, Contractee Account – Dr Cash 480,000, Estimated Profit on Contract:- Price 620,000 *less* Costs to 1.7.-3 421,370, Material 46,412, Labour 31,283, Overhead 12,513,

Depreciation 17,723, Costs to completion: Material and Labour 25,000, Depreciation 17,220, Total costs 571,521, Profit 48,479.

$$\frac{\text{Cash received}}{\text{Work certified}} \times \frac{\text{Work Certified}}{\text{Price}} \times \text{Estimated Profit}$$

$$= \frac{480}{570} \times \frac{570}{620} \times 48,479 = 37,532 - 26,480 \text{ est. profit to date.}$$

$$= 11,052 \text{ this year}$$

WIP:- Costs 529,301 – Profit taken 37,532 = 566,833. Balance Sheet at 30.6.4. Plant Net 87,220. CA Stock and WIP 566,833 less Cash received on account 480,000, net 86,833.

2.

Contract Account (000's). Dr – Plant on site 100, Direct Materials site 460, Direct wages 350, Direct expenses 45, Hire of tower crane 40, Indirect labour 70, Salaries – supervisors 42, Surveyor's fees 8, Service cost 18, Hire of scaffolding 20, Overheads – site 60, Head Office expenses (portion of), 70, Accrued wages c/f 30, Accrued service costs c/f 2. Total 1,315. Cr – Value of plant on site c/f 950, Total 1,315. Dr – Cost of work certified b/f 950, Profit on contract to date 160, Profit in suspense 140, Total 1,250. Cr – Value of work certified 1,250. Dr – Value of plant on site b/f 75, Materials unused b/f 40, WIP b/f 250. Cr – Accrued wages 30, Accrued service costs 2, Profit in suspense 140.

Profit taken on contract to 31.3.-2
Value of work certified   1,250
Less Cost of work certified   950

Notional Profit   300
⅔ x 300 = 200
Reduced by Retentions = Cash Received
                             Total Value of Work Cert.

$$= \frac{1000}{1250} = 80\% \times 200 = \underline{\underline{£160}}$$

BALANCE SHEET Assets:- (Cost of Work done 1,200. Add profit taken 160, less cash received 1,000) = Contract WIP 360; Materials on site 40, Plant value on site 75. Liabilities:- Accruals:- wages 30, services costs 2.

CHAPTER 51

3.

(a) Terms fully explained in chapter 51.

(b) Basis of allocation:- Sales value of production

	Sales Value £		%			Allocation £
A	60,000/300,000	=	20	x 200,000	=	40,000
B	40,000/300,000	=	13.33	x 200,000	=	26,666
C	200,000/300,000	=	66.67	x 200,000	=	133,334
	300,000		100.00			200,000

(c) If further processed the position is:-

		A		B		C
Extra Revenue	(20-10)	10	(8-4)	4	(16-10)	6
Extra Costs		14		2		6
Gain/Loss		(4)		2		–
Recommendation	Not process		process		indifferent	

4.

(i) Process 1 – Dr Direct Materials, Units 2000 £4,000, Direct Wages 360, Production overhead 4,800, Production Overhead (400% wages) 1,440, Total 10,600. Dr Normal loss, 400 units £120, Abnormal loss, 200 units £1,310, transfer to Process 2, 1400 units £9,170, Total 10,600.

$$\text{Cost Per Unit} = \frac{10,600 - 120}{2,000 - 400} = \underline{£6.55}$$

(ii) Process 2 – Dr transfer in Process 1, 1,400 units £9,170, Direct Materials 3,100 units £18,600, Direct Wages £240, Production overhead 3,052, Production overhead (400% wages) 960, Abnormal gain 150 units £1,161, Total 4,650 units £33,183. Cr Normal loss 450 units £675, Finished Goods 4,200 units, £32,508, Total 4,650 units £33,183.

$$\text{Cost Per Unit} = \frac{32,022 - 675}{4,500 - 450} = \underline{£7.74}$$

(iii) Abnormal Loss Account – Dr Process units 200 £1,310. Cr Scrap units 200 units £60, Profit and Loss 1,250, Totals 200 units £1,310. Abnormal Gain Account – Dr Scrap 150 units £225, Profit and Loss £936, Totals 150 units £1,161. Cr Process 2, 150 units £1,161, Totals 150 units, £1,161.

(iv) Abnormal loss £1,250; Abnormal gain £(936).

(v) Finished Goods – Process 2 £32,508.

(b) See chapter on Valuation WIP and Concept Equivalent Units.

5.

(a) See chapter regarding normal and abnormal losses.

(b) Process 1 – workings to calculate abnormal gain/loss. Input 5,000 units, less 20% normal loss – 1,000 units = Normal output 4,000, less Actual output 3,800 = 200 units abnormal loss.
Normal Cost per unit 5,000kg = £4,900 – (1,000 units at 30p) = 300 = £4,600 ∴ $\frac{4,600}{4,000}$ = £1.15.
Process 1 Account – Dr Material 5000kg £2,500, Labour £800, Production overhead £1,600. Cr Process 2, 3800kg at £1.15 = £4,370, Normal loss 1,000kg at £0.30 = £300, Abnormal loss 200kg at £1.15 = £230, Totals 5,000kg £4,900.

Process 2 – workings to calculate abnormal gain/loss – Input 7,800 units, Normal cost £11,076; 10% normal loss, 780 units at £0.70 = £546. Normal output is therefore (7,800 – 780) = 7,020 valued at (11,076 – 546) = £10,530, CPU = £10,530/7,020 units = £1.50 p.u. Abnormal gain = (7,020 – 7,270) = +250, i.e. Normal output – Actual output.

Process 2 Account – Dr Process 1, 3,800kg at £1.15 = £4,370, Material 4,000 units at £0.80 = £3,200, Labour £1,753, Production overhead £1,753, Abnormal gain 250kg at £1.50 = 375. Cr Finished goods 7,270kg at £1.50 = £10,905, Normal loss 780kg at £0.70 = £546, Totals 8,050kg, Value £11,451.
Finished Goods Account – Dr Process 2, 7,270kg at £1.50 = £10,905.
Abnormal Loss Account – Dr Process 1: Normal loss 1,000kg at £0.30 = 300, Abnormal loss 200kg at £1.15 = 230. Cr Cash 1,200kg at £0.30 = 360, Balance to Profit and Loss Account £170, Totals 1,200kg £530.
Abnormal Gain Account – Dr Process 2: Normal loss 780kg £0.70 = £546, Balance to Profit and Loss account £200. Cr Process 2: Abnormal gain 250kg at £1.50 = £375, Cash 530kg at £0.70 = 371, Totals 780kg £746.

CHAPTER 52

1.

(a) (i) Sales variances are based on turnover.
(ii) Sales margin variances are based on profit or contribution. Differences are between budgeted and actual figures.
Both variances may be split into volume and price variances. In a multi-product business, the volume variance may be divided further into quantity and mix.
Sales margin variances are of more concern and usefulness to top management who wish to know why targets are or are not achieved in terms of operating profit. Sales variances related to turnover would be more useful to Sales and Marketing management.

(b) Idle time is associated with a standard costing system. It exists when factory operatives are paid but no production is taking place; machines are idle. The amount of idle time which is planned for will vary from business to business; hence what is standard depends on the type of business. The treatment of idle time variances would also depend on the nature of the business. Some businesses would treat a processing plant out of action for a shift due to unforeseen circumstances as idle time, e.g. fire or strikes by power workers (electricity etc). If the costs to which the idle time is applied can be regarded as a fixed overhead cost, then it is logical to treat the variance as a fixed overhead variance. If, on the other hand, it relates to a direct cost (variable cost), then it should be budgeted for and included in the direct hourly rate, e.g. direct labour rate.

2.

(a) Variances: Sales Price 400F, Material Price 1,000A, Material Usage 80A, Labour rate 200A, Labour efficiency 180F, Total Net Variances 700A.

See reasons why variances can occur in the Chapter.

(b) Forecasts and budgets are closely related but the distinction might be made finely within the following definitions:-

Forecast – is an estimate of revenues, costs or capital for a future period of time based on certain defined assumptions.

Budget – The ICMA define as:- "a plan quantified in money terms, prepared and approved prior to a defined period of time, usually showing planned income to be generated and/or expenditure to be incurred during that period and the capital to be employed to attain a given objective."

3.

(i) Standard Cost Summary: Materials – Alloy 15kob, 5kleg, Composite 8kob, 32kleg. Labour – Grade 1, 2kob, 1kleg; Grade 2, 2kob, 4kleg; Overheads 4kob, 5kleg. Total 31kob, 47klg.

(ii) Material Usage Variance: Alloy 570A, Composite 48F; Material Price Variance: Alloy 703A, Composite 825F. Labour Efficiency – Grade 1 = Nil; Grade 2 = 24F; Wage rate: Grade 1 = Nil; Grade 2 = 40F; Total Overhead Variance 4A.

(iii) Finished Stock Valuation: kob = Opening stock 16, add production 208, less sales 224 leaves closing stock 14 units at standard cost p.u. £31 = £434. Kleg = Opening stock 9, add production 152, less sales 135 leaves stock at close 26 units at standard cost p.u. £47 = £1,222; Total closing stock = £1,656.

4.
(a)   (i) SC = DEHG; (ii) AC = ACJG; (iii) MPV = ACFD; (iv) MUV = EFJH;
      (v) MCV = (ACFD + EFJH).

(b)   (i) Same answer as 41(b).
      (ii) The role of the budget committee is fully discussed in the chapter.

CHAPTER 53

1.

(a)(i)
	A	B
Total Profits (4 years)	50,000	60,000
Average Annual Profit	50,000/4	60,000/4
	= 12,500	15,000
Average Capital	40,000/2	40,000/2
Average Rate of Return	A 12,500/20,000	B 15,000/20,000
	= 62½%	= 75%

(ii)   Payback period assuming even cash flows: A — 1½ years, B — 2⁵⁄₁₂ years.
       If cash flows occurred at the year end, 2 and 3 years respectively.

(iii) NPV: A — £32,200; B — £34,142 assuming cash flows at year end.

A — Initial outlay — 50,000

End of Year	1	2	3	4
	+35,000	+30,000	+25,000	+10,000
Discount factor	.909	.826	.751	.683
	31,815	24,780	18,775	6,830

B — Initial outlay — 50,000

End of Year	1	2	3	4
	+20,000	+20,000	+24,000	+46,000
Discount factor	.909	.826	.751	.683
	18,180	16,520	18,024	31,418

Note: 10,000 depreciation has been added to profits in Year 4 to establish cash flow.

(b) and (c) are explained fully in the chapter.

2.
(a)(i) NPV is the sum of discounted future receipts and payments (cash flows) compared with the capital outlay at the start.
   (ii) One way to compute the cost of capital is to take the weighted average cost of the constituent parts of capital employed in the company.

(b)   Summarised cash flows £000's

Year	1	2	3	4	5
Sales	1,000	1,640	5,125	3,360	1,050
Less Costs:					
Labour, Material and Overheads }	825	1,328	4,175	2,880	995
Net Cash Flow	175	312	950	480	55
Discount factor	.893	.797	.712	.635	.567
NPV	156	249	676	305	31

ΣNPV stream 1,417 less initial investment 1,400, NPV + 17, therefore accept.

CHAPTER 55

1.

Journal Entries 19–0 — Dr Royalties payable 10,000, Short workings account 5,000. Cr Bank 15,000. 19–1: Dr Royalties payable 14,000, Short workings account 1,000. Cr Bank 15,000. Dr P&L 5,000. Cr Short workings account 5,000. Dr Bank 6,000. Cr Royalties receivable 4,000, Short workings receivable 2,000. 19–2: Dr Royalties payable 15,700. Cr Short workings account 700, Bank 15,000. Dr P&L 300. Cr Short workings account 300. Dr Bank 6,000. Cr Royalties receivable 4,500, Short workings receivable 1,500. Dr Short workings receivable 2,000. Cr P&L 2,000. 19–3: Dr Royalties payable 18,000. Cr Bank 1,800. Dr Bank 6,000, Short workings receivable 900. Cr Royalties receivable 6,900. Dr Short workings receivable 600. Cr Profit and Loss account 600.

WORKINGS: ROYALTIES PAYABLE

	BDL pdn.	CHA pdn.	Combined	Royalties at £2 p.u.	Short Workings £
19–0	5,000 units	—	5,000	£10,000	5,000
19–1	6,000 units	1,000	7,000	£14,000	1,000
19–2	7,000 units	850	7,850	£15,700	—
19–3	7,520 units	1,480	9,000	£18,000	—

ROYALTIES RECEIVABLE

	Sales Units	Royalties £5 p.u.	Short Workings
19–1	800	4,000	2,000
19–2	900	4,500	1,500
19–3	1,380	6,900	—

INDEX